Fundamentals of Game Design

ERNEST ADAMS

ANDREW ROLLINGS

PEARSON

Prentice Hall

Upper Saddle River, New Jersey 07458

Library of Congress Cataloging-in-Publication Data

Adams, Ernest.
 Fundamentals of game design/Ernest Adams and Andrew Rollings.
  p. cm.
 ISBN 0-13-168747-6 (alk. paper)
 1. Computer games—Design. 2. Computer games—Programming. 3. Video games—Design.
I. Rollings, Andrew, 1972- II. Title.
 QA76.76.C672A322 2006
 794.8'1536—dc22

2006023805

Vice President and Publisher: Natalie E. Anderson
Associate VP/Executive Acquisitions Editor, Print:
 Stephanie Wall
Executive Acquisitions Editor, Media: Richard Keaveny
Executive Acquisitions Editor: Chris Katsaropoulos
Product Development Manager: Eileen Bien Calabro
Editorial Supervisor: Brian Hoehl
Editorial Assistants: Rebecca Knauer, Kaitlin O'Shaughnessy
Executive Producer: Lisa Strite
Content Development Manager: Cathi Profitko
Senior Media Project Manager: Steve Gagliostro
Project Manager, Media: Alana Meyers
Director of Marketing: Margaret Waples
Senior Marketing Manager: Jason Sakos

Marketing Assistant: Ann Baranov
Senior Sales Associate: Joseph Pascale
Managing Editor: Lynda J. Castillo
Production Project Manager: Lynne Breitfeller
Manufacturing Buyer: Chip Poakeart
Production/Editorial Assistant: Sandra K. Bernales
Design Manager: Maria Lange
Art Director/Interior Design/Cover Design:
 Blair Brown
Cover Illustration/Photo: Northern Electrics
Composition: Integra
Project Management: BookMasters, Inc.
Cover Printer: RR Donnelley/Harrisonburg
Printer/Binder: RR Donnelley/Harrisonburg

Credits and acknowledgments borrowed from other sources and reproduced, with permission, in this textbook appear on appropriate page within text.

Pearson Education LTD.
Pearson Education Singapore, Pte. Ltd
Pearson Education, Canada, Ltd
Pearson Education–Japan

Pearson Education Australia PTY, Limited
Pearson Education North Asia Ltd
Pearson Educación de Mexico, S.A. de C.V.
Pearson Education Malaysia, Pte. Ltd

10 9 8 7 6 5 4 3 2
ISBN 0-13-168747-6

To Mary Ellen Foley, for love and wisdom.
Omnia vincit amor.
—Ernest Adams

For Romeo, 1999–2005
—Andrew Rollings

Contents in Brief

Contents

Game Design and Development Series Walk-Through

The Prentice Hall Game Design and Development Series provides you with all the resources you need to set up your own game curriculum, combining theory and practical applications to help prepare students for careers in the game industry. All of the books in this series are filled with real-world examples to help you apply what you learn in the workplace. This walk-through highlights the key elements you'll find in this book created to help you along the way.

Chapter Objectives. These short-term, attainable goals outline what will be covered in the chapter text.

Chapter Introduction. Each chapter begins with an explanation of why these topics are important and how the chapter fits into the overall organization of the book.

In the Trenches. Takes concepts from the book and shows how they are applied in the workplace.

IN THE TRENCHES: Game Idea Versus Design Decision

Here's a game idea: "Dragons should protect their eggs."

Here's a design decision: "Whenever they have eggs in their nests, female dragons will not move beyond visual range from the nest. If an enemy approaches within 50 meters of the nest, the dragon will abandon any other activity and return to the nest to defend the eggs. She will not leave the nest until no enemy has been within the 50 meter radius for at least 30 seconds. She will defend the eggs to her death."

See the difference? This is what creating design documents is about.

FYI. Additional information on topics that go beyond the scope of the book.

Key Point. Critical, not-to-be-forgotten information that is directly relevant to the surrounding text.

Commandment. Explicit prohibitions against bad design practices.

COMMANDMENT: Do Not Taunt the Player

A few designers think it's funny to taunt or insult the player for losing. This is mean-spirited and violates a central principle of player-centric game design—the duty to empathize. The player will feel bad about losing anyway. Don't make it worse.

Chapter Objectives

After reading this chapter and completing the exercises, you will be able to do the following:

- Know the essential elements of a game—rules, goals, play, and pretending—and what they do in the context of playing games.
- Know the formal definition of a game.
- Understand the nature of challenges and actions, as well as the formal definition of gameplay.
- Become familiar with the concepts of symmetry and asymmetry, fairness, and competition and cooperation.
- Learn the various benefits that computers bring to games.
- Become familiar with the ways in which video games entertain people.

Introduction

Before discussing game design, we must establish what games are and how they work. You might think that everybody knows what a game is, but the huge variety of games in the world means that it's best not to make assumptions based on personal experience alone. We begin by identifying the essential elements that a game must have, and then we define what a game is based on those elements. Then we go on to discuss what computers bring to gaming and how video games are different from conventional games. Finally, we look at the specific ways in which video games entertain people as well as enjoyable features of video games that you must learn how to design.

FYI   A Note on Terminology

Unfortunately, the game industry has not yet adopted standard names for its design elements, processes, and documents. We have tried to use terms that other professional developers would generally recognize, but we warn you that you cannot expect any given company to use these terms exactly the way we do. If you get confused, please see the Glossary for our definitions of terms.

KEY POINT

A good character is the most financially valuable part of any video game's intellectual property.

games take their name directly from *Sonic the Hedgehog, Crash Bandicoot,* what the marketing people call *mindsh* or brand. You can use the character in sell clothes and toys based on a characte other products. It's more difficult to do its gameplay.

The goal of character design, then, *appealing* (even if the character is a vill *believe in,* and that the player can *identif* characters). If possible, the character sh be distinctive enough, to be highly mem

Test Your Skills

Each chapter ends with exercises designed to reinforce the chapter objectives. Three types of evaluation are included. Exercises appear in Part One of the book, and Case Studies appear in Part Two.

Multiple Choice Questions. Test the reader's understanding of the text.

Exercises. Guided projects designed around individual concepts found in the chapter.

Case Study. An in-depth project covering the game genre introduced in the chapter.

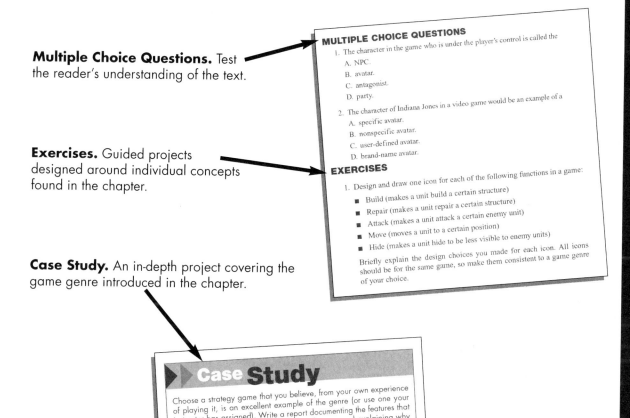

MULTIPLE CHOICE QUESTIONS

1. The character in the game who is under the player's control is called the
   A. NPC.
   B. avatar.
   C. antagonist.
   D. party.

2. The character of Indiana Jones in a video game would be an example of a
   A. specific avatar.
   B. nonspecific avatar.
   C. user-defined avatar.
   D. brand-name avatar.

EXERCISES

1. Design and draw one icon for each of the following functions in a game:
   - Build (makes a unit build a certain structure)
   - Repair (makes a unit repair a certain structure)
   - Attack (makes a unit attack a certain enemy unit)
   - Move (moves a unit to a certain position)
   - Hide (makes a unit hide to be less visible to enemy units)

   Briefly explain the design choices you made for each icon. All icons should be for the same game, so make them consistent to a game genre of your choice.

Case Study

Choose a strategy game that you believe, from your own experience of playing it, is an excellent example of the genre (or use one your instructor has assigned). Write a report documenting the features that place it in this genre as opposed to another one and explaining why you believe it is superior to others of its kind. Be sure to cover at least the following areas:

- Describe unit types and their attributes, including any special abilities. If you feel that the different forces in the game are well balanced or unbalanced, explain this with reference to the units and their attributes.

This icon appears in the margin wherever additional information or links to downloads can be found at the series' Companion Website, **www.prenhall.com/gamedev.**

Introduction

This book has its roots in an earlier work, *Andrew Rollings and Ernest Adams on Game Design,* and readers who already own that book will recognize its general structure. But make no mistake: *Fundamentals of Game Design* is not a new edition, but rather a new book. Much of our thinking has changed in the three years since *Rollings and Adams* was published. We have revised and formalized some of our definitions and introduced a number of important ideas that we did not have space for in the older work. We have also added four new chapters on the subjects of creative play, core mechanics, level design, and the design process itself.

One thing has not changed: Our approach remains strongly practical. Although we recognize and value the work of theoreticians, we seldom address it unless it has something of immediate benefit to the student of game design. Our perspective, based on our experience, is also unashamedly commercial; we expect our readers will want to make video games for sale, and a certain amount of our discussion relates to questions of markets and target audiences.

Fundamentals of Game Design is not a book on programming, nor on art, animation, music, audio engineering, or writing. Nor is it about project management, budgeting, scheduling, or producing. A budding game designer should learn something about all of those subjects, and we encourage you to consult other works in this series to broaden your education as much as you can. This book is entirely about game design—as much of the subject as we could put in. In fact, the book is so much longer than the earlier one that we have had to move two chapters and an appendix to the Companion Website at **www.prenhall.com/gamedev**. There you will find Chapter 21, "Online Games," and Chapter 22, "The Future of Gaming," as well as the Appendix, "Designing to Appeal to Particular Groups." All our design document templates are also available on the Companion Website, and you can copy them and use them in your own design work.

Why So Many Tabletop Games and Old Video Games?

As you read, you will notice that we frequently refer to tabletop games—card games such as poker, board games such as *Monopoly,* and so on. We do this for three reasons. First, those games are likely to be familiar to the largest number of people. Not all of our readers will have played computer games such as *Planescape: Torment*, and some will be too young to remember *Adventure*, but everyone has heard of chess. Second, simpler, noncomputerized games tend to be designed around a single principle, so they serve to illustrate that principle well. Finally, we believe that the essence of game design has little to do with the game's delivery medium. The principles common to all good games are independent of the means by which they are presented.

We also refer again and again to certain video games even though they may not be recent releases. Our book is filled with references to *Super Mario Bros. Tomb*

Raider, Half-Life, StarCraft, Planescape: Torment, Civilization, SimCity, The Secret of Monkey Island, Tetris, and even *Space Invaders.* Old or not, these are outstanding examples of their genres—among the greatest games of all time. And many are actually series rather than individual games; you can buy the latest edition and play it for yourself. They all reward study.

Who Is This Book For?

This book is aimed at anyone who is interested in designing video and computer games but doesn't know how to begin. More specifically, it is intended for university students and junior professionals in the game industry. Although it is a general, introductory text, more experienced professionals may find it a useful reference as well.

Our only explicit prerequisite for reading the book is some knowledge of video games, especially the more famous ones. It would be impossible to write a book on game design for someone who has never played a game; we have to assume basic familiarity with video games and game hardware. For a thorough and deeply insightful history of video games, we recommend Steven Poole's *Trigger Happy: Videogames and the Entertainment Revolution* (Poole, 2004).

We do expect that you will be able to write succinctly and unambiguously; it is an absolute requirement for a game designer, and many of our exercises are writing assignments. We also expect familiarity with basic high school algebra and probability, especially in the chapters on core mechanics, game balancing, and strategy games.

In this book, we assume that you are designing an entire game by yourself. We have two reasons for doing this. First, to become a skilled game designer, you should be familiar with all aspects of design, so we intend to cover the subject as if you will do it all. Second, even if you do have a team of designers, we cannot tell you how to structure or manage your team beyond a few generalities. The way you divide up their responsibilities will depend a great deal on the design culture of your group and the skills of the individuals on the team. From the standpoint of teaching the material, it is simplest for us to pretend that one person will do all the work.

How Is This Book Organized?

Fundamentals of Game Design is divided into two parts. The first twelve chapters are about designing games in general: what a game is, how it works, and what kinds of decisions you have to make to create one. The next ten chapters are about different genres of games and the design considerations peculiar to each genre.

Part One: The Elements of Game Design

Chapter 1 introduces games in general and video games in particular, including a formal definition of a game and *gameplay*. It also discusses what computers bring to games and lists the important ways that video games entertain.

Chapter 2 introduces the key components of a video game, the *core mechanics, user interface,* and *storytelling engine.* It also presents the concept of a *gameplay mode* and the structure of a video game. The last half of the chapter is devoted to the practice of game design, including our recommended approach, *player-centric* design.

Chapter 3 is about *game concepts*: where the idea for a game comes from and how to refine the idea. The audience and the target hardware (the machine the game will run on) both have a strong influence on the direction the game will take.

Chapter 4 speaks to the *game's setting and world*: the place where the gameplay happens and the way things work there. As the designer, you're the god of your world, and it's up to you to define its concepts of time and space, mechanics, and natural laws, as well as many other things: its logic, emotions, culture, and values.

Chapter 5 addresses *creative and expressive play*, listing different ways that your game can support creativity and self-expression from the players.

Chapter 6 addresses *character design*: inventing the people or beings that populate your game world—especially the character who will represent the player there (his *avatar*), if there is one. Every successful entertainer from Homer onward has understood the importance of having an appealing protagonist.

Chapter 7 delves into the problems of *storytelling and narrative*, introducing the issues of linear, branching, and foldback story structures. It also discusses a number of related issues such as scripted conversations and episodic story structures.

Chapter 8 is about *user interface design*: the way that the player experiences and interacts with the game world. A bad user interface can kill an otherwise brilliant game, so you must get this right.

Chapter 9 discusses *gameplay*, the heart of the player's mental experience of a game: the challenges he faces and the actions he takes to overcome them. It also analyzes the nature of *difficulty* in gameplay.

Chapter 10 looks at the *core mechanics* of a game, especially its *internal economy*, and the flow of resources (money, points, ammunition, or whatever) throughout the game.

Chapter 11 considers the issue of *game balancing,* the process of making multiplayer games fair to all players and controlling the difficulty of single-player games.

Chapter 12 introduces the general principles of *level design,* both universal principles and genre-specific ones. It also considers a variety of level layouts and proposes a process for level design.

Part Two: The Genres of Games

Chapter 13 is about the earliest, and still most popular, genre of interactive entertainment: *action games.*

Chapter 14 discusses another genre that has been part of gaming since the beginning: *strategy games*, both real-time and turn-based.

Chapter 15 is about *role-playing games*, a natural outgrowth of pencil and paper games such as *Dungeons & Dragons.*

Chapter 16 looks at *sports games*, which have a number of peculiar design challenges. The actual contest itself is designed by others; the trick is to map human athletic activities onto a screen and control devices.

Chapter 17 addresses *vehicle simulations*: cars, planes, boats, and other, more exotic modes of transportation such as tanks and mechs.

Chapter 18 is about *construction and management simulations*, in which the player tries to build and maintain something—a city, a theme park, a planet—within the limitations of an economic system.

Chapter 19 explores *adventure games*, an old and unique genre of gaming recently given new life by the creation of a hybrid type, the *action-adventure.*

Chapter 20 examines two other genres of games: *artificial life* and *puzzle games.*

Chapter 21 (available on the Companion Website) is devoted to *online games*, which is not a genre but a technology. Online games enable people to play with, or against, each other in numbers from two up to hundreds of thousands. Playing against real people that you cannot see has enormous consequences for the game's design. The second half of the chapter addresses the particular problems of *persistent worlds* like *EverQuest.*

Chapter 22 (available on the Companion Website) contains our thoughts on the future of video games and is not so much pedagogical as speculative.

Appendix A (available on the Companion Website) discusses designing to appeal to particular *target audiences*: hardcore players and casual players; men and women; children in general and girls in particular. It also includes a section on *accessibility issues* for players with impairments of various kinds.

What Will I Take Away from This Book?

This book teaches you of the principles of video game design and the fundamental issues that every designer faces in creating interactive entertainment. The first half of the book will give you the necessary groundwork in creating worlds, characters, stories, gameplay, core mechanics, and a user interface. It also shows you a process by which to approach the task. If you read it all, you should be able to design a video game regardless of genre. If you apply your imagination, you could even invent a new genre.

The second half of the book applies the principles of the first half to the most common game genres on the market today. You may not need to read every chapter; you should use them as reference materials for the genres that you're interested in. By combining your reading of the genre chapters with your own research, you'll see that the principles are not just abstract concepts but the basis for practical game designs.

The purpose of game design is to construct a coherent and unambiguous template from which you and other people on your team can build an entertainment product. This book will give you the tools to do that, from the initial idea to the final tuning stages.

Conventions Used in This Book

To help you get the most from the text, we've used a few conventions throughout the book.

Snippets and blocks of code are boxed and numbered, and can be downloaded from the Companion Website (**www.prenhall.com/gamedev**).

New key terms appear in ***bold italics***.

This icon appears in the margin wherever more information can be found at the series Companion Website, **www.prenhall.com/gamedev.**

IN THE TRENCHES: About In The Trenches

These show readers how to take concepts from the book and apply them in the workplace.

FYI *About FYIs*

These boxes offer additional information on topics that go beyond the scope of the book.

KEY POINT

Important information on game theory and mechanics summarized from nearby text.

COMMANDMENTS: About Commandments

Recommended design practices that should be implemented in your game design.

Instructor and Student Resources

Instructor's Resource Center

The Instructor's Resource Center is distributed to instructors only via our Companion Website and is an interactive library of assets and links. It includes:

- Instructor's Manual. Provides instructional tips, an introduction to each chapter, teaching objectives, teaching suggestions, and answers to end-of-chapter questions and problems.

- PowerPoint Slide Presentations. Provides a chapter-by-chapter review of the book content for use in the classroom.

- Test Bank. This TestGen-compatible test bank file can be used with Prentice Hall's TestGen software (available as a free download at **www.prenhall.com/testgen**). TestGen is a test generator that lets you view and easily edit test bank questions, transfer them to tests, and print in a variety of formats suitable to your teaching situation. The program also offers many options for organizing and displaying test banks and tests. A built-in random number and text generator makes it ideal for creating multiple versions of tests that involve calculations and provides more possible test items than test bank questions. Powerful search and sort functions let you easily locate questions and arrange them in the order you prefer.

Companion Website

The Companion Website (**www.prenhall.com/gamedev**) is a Pearson learning tool that provides students and instructors with online support. Here you will find:

- Interactive Study Guide, a Web-based interactive quiz designed to provide students with a convenient online mechanism for self-testing their comprehension of the book material.

- Additional Web projects and resources to put the concepts taught in each chapter into practice.

About the Authors

Ernest Adams is an American game design consultant currently working in England with the International Hobo game design group. In addition to his consulting work, he gives game design workshops and is a popular speaker at conferences and on college campuses. Mr. Adams has worked in the interactive entertainment industry since 1989 and founded the International Game Developers' Association in 1994. He was most recently employed as a lead designer at Bullfrog Productions, and for several years before that he was the audio/video producer on the *Madden NFL Football* product line at Electronic Arts. In his early career, he was a software engineer, and he has developed online, computer, and console games for everything from the IBM 360 mainframe to the Sony Playstation 2. Mr. Adams is the author of two other books and the *Designer's Notebook* series of columns on the *Gamasutra* developers' webzine. His professional Web site is at **www.designersnotebook.com**.

Andrew Rollings (co-author of the highly successful books *Game Architecture and Design* and *Andrew Rollings and Ernest Adams on Game Design*) has a B.S. in Physics from Imperial College, London, and Bristol University and has worked as a technical consultant spanning the games industry and the financial industry since 1995. You can find him at **www.hiive.com**.

Acknowledgments

Our first and greatest debt is to Mary Ellen Foley, The Word Boffin (**www.wordboffin.com**), a freelance editor of great skill and insight whose tireless labors have made this book far better than it might have been. Her contribution, invisible but essential, appears on every page.

It would be a rare developer indeed who had worked on every genre and style of game addressed in this book, and certainly neither of us can make that claim. When it came time to speak of subjects of which we had little direct experience, we relied heavily on the advice and wisdom of our professional colleagues. Nine people in particular have given us permission to quote extensively from their writing, which has enriched the book enormously. We owe a special debt of gratitude to:

Jessyca Durchin
Joseph Ganetakos
Scott Kim
Rick Knowles
Raph Koster
Steve Meretzky
Brian Moriarty
Chris Taylor
Carolyn Handler Miller

We hasten to add that any errors in the book should be laid at our door, not theirs.

We are also especially indebted to MobyGames (**www.mobygames.com**) whose vast database of PC and console games we consulted daily, and sometimes hourly, in our research.

Our thanks also go to Monty Clark for his assistance with the level design chapter. Our technical reviewers, Phillip Tavel, Philip Wallack, Todd Bailey, and Dep-Wah Davis, gave us invaluable advice and feedback on many of the chapters. Jen Sward provided both technical review and assistance with the exercises.

A number of our colleagues offered valuable suggestions about different parts of the manuscript; we are particularly grateful to Chris Bateman, Ben Cousins, Melissa Federoff, Lucy Joyner, and Chris Weaver for their advice.

Three students from the University of Skövde in Sweden volunteered to help create some of the exercises and sample answers for them. We were very pleased to have the assistance of Marcus Toftedahl, Douglas Furén, and Dan Thronström, and wish them the best in their game development careers.

Several people and institutions generously gave us permission to reproduce images:

MobyGames (**www.mobygames.com**)
Björn Hurri (**www.bjornhurri.com**)
Cecropia, Inc. (**www.cecropia.com**)
Pseudo Interactive (**www.psuedointeractive.com**)
Chronic Logic (**www.chroniclogic.com**) and Auran (**www.auran.com**)

Finally, no list of acknowledgements would be complete without recognizing the help of our editors at Prentice-Hall. Cat Skintik worked hard with us all through the final push to get the book done, wielding her blue pencil with wit and style as well as helping to create some of the exercises. Ginny Monroe and Dave Fender assisted through the early days. Emilie Herman and Stephanie Wall got the book off the ground, and Chris Katsaropulos kept the faith and rounded up additional help when it looked like the book might not be finished in time. We're also grateful for the assistance of Margot Hutchison, our agent at Waterside Productions, in helping to finalize the contract.

Part One

The Elements of Game Design

In Part One of *Fundamentals of Game Design,* we examine the essential principles of designing video games. The first chapter is an overview of our philosophy of what video games are and how they entertain. Chapter 2 explains several important design concepts and introduces the player-centric approach to the process of game design itself. It also describes several aspects of design in the commercial environment, including documents used and job roles. In Chapter 3, we explain how to get from the initial "great idea" stage to a formal game concept that is detailed enough to elaborate into a complete design.

The remaining chapters of Part One are devoted to specific aspects of video games that you will encounter when designing them. They are organized by subject matter: game worlds, creative play, character design, storytelling, user interface design, gameplay, core mechanics and game balancing, and level design. These chapters are presented in an order that runs approximately from the most aesthetically creative activities to the most practical and functional.

- **Chapter 1:** Games and Video Games
- **Chapter 2:** Design Components and Processes
- **Chapter 3:** Game Concepts
- **Chapter 4:** Game Worlds
- **Chapter 5:** Creative and Expressive Play
- **Chapter 6:** Character Development
- **Chapter 7:** Storytelling and Narrative
- **Chapter 8:** Creating the User Experience
- **Chapter 9:** Gameplay
- **Chapter 10:** Core Mechanics
- **Chapter 11:** Game Balancing
- **Chapter 12:** General Principles of Level Design

Chapter | 1

Games and Video Games

Chapter Objectives

After reading this chapter and completing the exercises, you will be able to do the following:

- Know the essential elements of a game—rules, goals, play, and pretending—and what they do in the context of playing games.
- Know the formal definition of a game.
- Understand the nature of challenges and actions, as well as the formal definition of gameplay.
- Become familiar with the concepts of symmetry and asymmetry, fairness, and competition and cooperation.
- Learn the various benefits that computers bring to games.
- Become familiar with the ways in which video games entertain people.

Introduction

Before discussing game design, we must establish what games are and how they work. You might think that everybody knows what a game is, but the huge variety of games in the world means that it's best not to make assumptions based on personal experience alone. We begin by identifying the essential elements that a game must have, and then we define what a game is based on those elements. Then we go on to discuss what computers bring to gaming and how video games are different from conventional games. Finally, we look at the specific ways in which video games entertain people as well as enjoyable features of video games that you must learn how to design.

What Is a Game?

Work consists of whatever a body is obliged to do, and . . . Play consists of whatever a body is not obliged to do.

—Mark Twain, *The Adventures of Tom Sawyer*

Games are related both to the human desire for play and to our capacity to pretend. *Play* is a wide category of nonessential, and usually recreational, human activities that are often socially significant as well. *Pretending* is the mental ability to establish a notional reality that the pretender knows is different from the real world, and that the pretender can create, abandon, or change at will. Playing and pretending are essential elements of playing games. Both have been studied extensively as cultural and psychological phenomena.

Toys, Puzzles, and Games

In English, we use the same word, *play,* to describe how we entertain ourselves with toys, puzzles, and games—although with puzzles, we more frequently say that we *solve* them. However, even though we use the same word, we do not play with them all in the same way. What differentiates these types of play is the presence, or absence, of rules and goals.

Rules are instructions that dictate how to play. A *toy* does not come with any rules about the right way to play with it, nor with a particular goal that you as a player should try to achieve. You may play with a ball or a stick any way you like. In fact, you may pretend that it is something else entirely. Toys that model other objects (e.g., a baby doll that resembles a real baby) might *suggest* an appropriate way to play, but the suggestion is not a rule. In fact, young children get special enjoyment by playing with toys in a way that subverts their intended purpose; treating a doll as a car, for example.

If you add a distinct goal to playing—a particular objective that you are trying to achieve—then the article being played with is not a toy but a *puzzle*. Puzzles have one rule that defines the goal, but they seldom have rules that dictate how you must get to it. Some approaches might be fruitless, but none are actually prohibited.

A *game* includes both rules and a goal. Playing a game requires pretending and is a more structured activity than playing with toys or puzzles. As such, it requires more maturity. As children develop longer attention spans, they start to play with puzzles and then to play games. Multiplayer games also require social cooperation, another thing that children learn to do as they mature.

> **KEY POINT**
>
> The essential elements of a game are rules, goals, play, and pretending.

The Definition of a Game

Defining any term that refers to a broad class of human behaviors is a tricky business, because if anyone can find a single counterexample, the definition is inaccurate. As a result, efforts to find unassailable definitions of such terms usually produce results so general as to be useless for practical purposes. The alternative is to acknowledge that a definition is not rigorous but serves as a convenient description to cover the majority of cases. With this in mind, we present our nonrigorous definition of a ***game:***

> *A game is a type of play activity, conducted in the context of a pretended reality, in which the participant(s) try to achieve at least one arbitrary, nontrivial goal by acting in accordance with rules.*

We recognize that there might be exceptions, activities somewhere that we would instantly recognize as a game, but don't conform to some part of our definition. So be it. Our purpose is to be practical rather than complete.

FYI | *Other Views*

There have been many efforts to define the word *game* over the years, made by people in fields as diverse as anthropology, philosophy, history, and, of course, game design. In *Rules of Play*, Salen and Zimmerman examine several of these definitions (Salen and Zimmerman, 2003, pp. 73–80). Most, but not all, make some reference to rules, goals, play, and pretending. Some include other elements such as decision-making or the quality of being a system. We don't try to refute or rebut any of these; we simply present our own definition to stand beside the others. It should be noted that some commentators such as Raph Koster, in *A Theory of Fun for Game Design,* disparage the distinctions between toys, puzzles, and games as irrelevant (Koster, 2004, p. 36). However, we feel that it is important to address them in this introductory text.

The Essential Elements of a Game

The essential elements of a game are play, a goal, rules, and pretending. Our definition refers to each of these elements and includes some additional conditions as well. In the next few sections, we look at each of these elements, and their significance in the definition, more closely.

Play   Play is a participatory form of entertainment, whereas books, films, and theater are presentational forms. When you read a book, the author entertains you; when you play, you entertain yourself. A book doesn't change, no matter how often you read it, but when you play, you make choices that affect the course of events. Theoreticians of literature and drama often argue that reading or watching is a conscious, active process and that the audience *is* an active participant in those forms of entertainment. Although we acknowledge the point, our concern here is with the actual content and not the interpretation of the content. With the rare exception of some experimental works, the audience does not actually create or change the content presented, even if their comprehension or interpretation does change over time. We would not go so far as to say that reading is *passive,* but it is not *interactive* in the sense of modifying the text.

In contrast, each time you play a game, you can make different choices and have a different experience. Play ultimately includes the freedom to act and the freedom to choose *how* you act. This freedom is not unlimited, however. Your choices are constrained by the rules, and this requires you to be clever, imaginative, or skillful in your play.

FYI   *Play in Other Languages*

English uses the same word, *play,* to describe both playing to achieve a goal and playing without one, but in Swedish, these activities are described by two different terms. Game-play is called *spela,* while goal-less play is called *lek.* These linguistic variations offer useful insights into the ways that humans think about play. For an extensive discussion of how play is described in many different languages, see Huizinga, Chapter 2 (Huizinga, 1971).

KEY POINT

Games are interactive. They require active players whose participation changes the course of events.

We will continue to use the term *play* despite the fact that you can play games for a serious purpose such as learning or research.

Pretending

> David: Is this a game, or is it real?
> Joshua: What's the difference?
>
>   —Exchange from the movie *WarGames*

Pretending is the act of creating a notional reality in the mind, which is one element of our definition. Another name for the reality created by pretending is the ***magic circle.*** This is an idea that Dutch historian Johan Huizinga originally identified in his book *Homo Ludens* (Huizinga, 1971) and expanded upon at some length in later theories of play. The magic circle is related to the concept of imaginary worlds in fiction and drama, and Huizinga also felt that it was connected to ceremonial, spiritual, legal, and other activities. For our purposes, however, the magic circle simply refers to the boundary that divides ideas and activities that are meaningful in the game from those that are meaningful in the real world. In other words, the boundary between reality and make-believe.

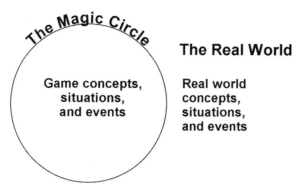

FIGURE 1.1 The magic circle, separating the real world from the pretended reality.

Players can even pretend things in the magic circle that are impossible in the real world (for example, "Let's pretend that I'm moving at the speed of light"). Figure 1.1 illustrates the magic circle.

FYI   *The Magic Circle*

Huizinga did not use the term *magic circle* as a generic name for the concept. His text actually refers to the *play-ground,* or a *physical* space for play, of which he considers the tennis court, the court of law, the stage, the magic circle (a sacred outdoor space for worship in "primitive" religions), the temple, and many others to be examples. However, theoreticians of play have since adopted the term *magic circle* to refer to the *mental* universe established when a player pretends. That is the sense in which we use the word.

We used the term *pretended reality* rather than *magic circle* in our definition because the former is self-explanatory and the latter is not. However, from now on we will refer to the magic circle because it is the more widely accepted term.

In single-player games, the magic circle is simply established by choosing to play. In multiplayer games, it is established by a convention agreed upon by the players. In other words, they all pretend together, and more important, they all agree to pretend the same things; that is, to accept the same rules. Although the pretended reality can seem very real to a deeply immersed player, it is still only a convention and can be renounced by refusing to play.

At first glance, you might not think there's much pretending involved in a physical game like soccer. After all, you aren't pretending to be someone else, and your actions are real-world actions. Even so, you are assigning artificial

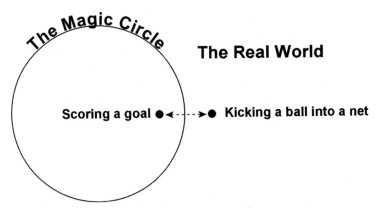

FIGURE 1.2 We pretend that real-world events have special meanings inside the magic circle.

KEY POINT

Within the magic circle, the players agree to attach a temporary, artificial significance to situations and events in the game. The magic circle comes into existence when the players join the game, in effect, when they agree to abide by the rules. It disappears again when they abandon the game or the game ends.

significance to the situations and events in the game, and this is an act of pretending. This idea is illustrated in Figure 1.2. In the real world, kicking a ball into a net is meaningless, but for the duration of a soccer game, the players (and spectators) pretend that kicking the ball into the net is a good thing to do and benefits the team that achieved it. Accepting and abiding by the rules is part of the pretending we do when we play a game.

FYI   *What Is Real?*

Some philosophers claim that all the world exists in a magic circle and there is no absolute reality or *real world* because human senses are not capable of detecting it with certainty. The merits of this perspective are debatable, but insofar as games are concerned, it is irrelevant. The point about the magic circle is that it is constructed at will and can be abandoned at will—something that is not true of the real world, however indefinable or inaccessible it may be. Moreover, the *contents* of the magic circle are indubitably established by the game designer and the players.

The distinction between the real world and the pretended reality is not always clear. If the events in the game are also meaningful in the real world, the magic circle becomes blurred. For example, various Mesoamerican Indian peoples used to participate in the *ball-court game,* a public activity that was superficially similar to basketball. From carvings that depict the game, it appears that the losers may have been ritually sacrificed to the gods. If so, the game was literally a matter of life and death—a matter of great importance in the real world. In spite of this, the ball-court game was not just a raw struggle for survival; it was played according to rules.

Gambling, too, blurs the magic circle because when you gamble, you bet real money on the outcome of a game. The process of gambling may or may not be an intrinsic part of the game itself. On the one hand, you can choose to play dominoes for money, but you can also play for matchsticks, or nothing at all. On the other hand, betting money in craps *is* an intrinsic part of the game; if you don't place a bet, you're not participating.

A Goal   A game must have a goal (or **object;** we use these terms inter-changeably throughout the book), and it can have more than one. As we observed previously, goalless play is not the same as game play. Even cre-ative, noncompetitive play still has a goal: creation. Others take this require-ment for a goal even further. For example, Salen and Zimmerman, in *Rules of Play* (Salen and Zimmerman, 2003, p. 80), require that a game have a "quantifiable outcome." We feel this definition is too restrictive. Consider an activity in which the participants collaborate to make a drawing of a scene in a limited time, with each one holding a crayon of a different color. This activity is clearly a game—it includes rules, a goal, play, and pretending, and the results will vary depending on the decisions of the players—but its outcome is not quantifiable. Similarly, the object of *SimCity* is to build and manage a city without going bankrupt, and as long as one does not go bank-rupt, the game continues indefinitely without any outcome. In fact, the object of a game need not even be achievable, so long as the players *try* to achieve it. Most early arcade games, such as *Space Invaders* and *Breakout,* gave the players an unachievable goal.

The goal of the game is defined by the rules and is *arbitrary* because the game designer can define it any way she likes. The goal of the children's card game Go Fish is to obtain *books*—collections of four cards of the same suit—but the definition of what is to be collected could be changed by changing the rules. A book has no intrinsic real-world importance; it's just a particular collection of cards. But within the context of a game of Go Fish, a book has a symbolic importance because the rules state that assembling it is a goal on the way to victory. The goal must be *nontrivial* because a game must include some element of **challenge.** Even in a game of pure chance such as craps or roulette, the players must learn to understand the odds and place bets that will most likely benefit them. Similarly, in a creative game, creation itself challenges the players. To do well requires skill. If the object can be achieved in a single moment, without either physical or mental effort, then the activity is not really a game. For example, children sometimes do a rudimentary form of gambling called Odds and Evens. Each flips a coin of identical value. If the results are odd (don't match), one child takes both coins; if they are even (do match), the other does. The odds are exactly 50 percent and there is no way to improve them; in fact, there is no decision-making at all. We do not classify this as a game because it does not include a challenge. The object is trivial and the process momentary. It is a form of betting, but not a game.

The rules of a game frequently characterize the game's goal as a *victory condition*—an unambiguous situation within the game at which point one or more of the players are declared the winners. For example, the victory condition for chess states that the first player to checkmate his opponent's king (an unambiguous situation) is the winner. In timed sports such as basketball, the victory condition states that when time runs out (the unambiguous situation), whichever team has the most points wins the game and the other team loses. A game designer can also establish additional rules about ties and tie-breaking mechanisms if he thinks it is important to have a clear winner.

The rule that determines when the game is over is called the *termination condition.* In two-player games, the termination condition is usually taken for granted: The game ends when one player achieves victory. Note that the victory condition does not necessarily end the game, however. In a game with more than two players, play can continue to determine who comes in second, third, and so on. A foot race (which is a game under our definition) does not end when the first runner crosses the finish line; it continues until the last runner does.

A strange game. The only winning move is not to play.

—Joshua, in the movie *WarGames*

Not all games include a victory condition. Some establish only a *loss condition,* a situation that indicates the end of the game by specifying which player has lost. Such a game can never be won but can only be abandoned. *Theme Park* is a good example: You can lose the game by running out of money and having your theme park collapse, but you cannot *win* it.

The rules and the goal of a game are entirely contained within the magic circle, but the concept of winning and losing transcends it to affect the real world as well. Winning is perceived as a meritorious achievement, and after the game is over, players take pride in having won. Winning can also earn real world benefits such as material rewards. But you don't have to include the ideas of victory and defeat in a game. They're optional elements that make the game more exciting and meaningful to the players.

The Rules   *Rules* are definitions and instructions that the players agree to accept for the duration of the game. Every game has rules, even if these rules are unwritten or taken for granted.

Rules serve several functions. They establish the object of the game and the meanings of the different activities and events that take place within the magic circle. They also create a contextual framework that enables the players to know which courses of action are permitted and to evaluate which course of action will best help them achieve their goal. Among the things that the rules define are the following:

- **The semiotics of the game**—This means the meanings and relationships of the various symbols that the game employs. Some symbols, such as innings and outs in baseball, are purely abstract. Others, such as armies in *Risk,* have a parallel in the real world that helps us to understand them. We do not discuss the theory of game semiotics in detail. It is a complex issue and the subject of ongoing research but beyond the scope of this book.

- **The gameplay**—This is defined later in this chapter in terms of challenges and actions.

- **The sequence of play**—This is the progression of activities that make up the game.

- **The goal(s) of the game**—This was described in the previous section.

- **The termination condition**—As described in the previous section, this is the condition that ends the game (if it has one).

- **Metarules**—The rules about the rules. These might indicate under what circumstances the rules can be changed or when exceptions to them may be allowed.

As a designer, the main thing that you need to know is that rules are definitions and instructions that have meaning within the magic circle and that you are free to invent abstract symbols and concepts as necessary to create a game. You must, however, make them comprehensible to the players!

> *The only permanent rule in Calvinball is that you can't play it the same way twice!*
>
> —Calvin, in "Calvin and Hobbes" by Bill Watterson

The rules need not be especially orderly; they are, after all, arbitrary. However, they should be unambiguous to avoid arguments over interpretation, and they should be coherent with no conflicts among them. If it is possible for conflicts to arise, the rules should include a metarule for determining which rule prevails. Ambiguous or conflicting rules are a sign of bad game design.

Things That a Game Is Not

Note that our definition of a game does not mention *competition* or *conflict*. Formal game theory requires that there be a conflict of interest among the players: that is, that one or more of them is trying to oppose the activities of one or more of the others as they try to achieve their goal while preventing the others from achieving theirs. For example, Salen and Zimmerman (Salen and Zimmerman, 2003, p. 80) describe a game as an "artificial conflict." Although this concept is essential to game theory, we believe that it is too restrictive a definition for our purposes because it excludes creative games and purely cooperative games. We discuss competition and cooperation in the *Competition and Cooperation* section later in this chapter; for now, understand that our definition of games is concerned with achievement but not necessarily the opposition of forces.

We take a broader view of games. We define a game as an *activity* rather than as a system of rules, as some theorists do. Although all games require rules, rules alone do not make a game. For a game to exist, it must be played; otherwise it is simply a theoretical abstraction. We prefer that you think of a game as an activity because that focuses your attention on the player—the person for whom the game is made—rather than on the rules.

Note also that our definition does not refer to entertainment or recreation. People most often play games for entertainment, but they sometimes play games for study, practice, or training in a serious subject. In this context, the definition of play becomes a bit vague because your boss can require that you "play" a game as part of your "work" (and if you're being paid to design games, you certainly should). In any case, we do not wish to claim that people play games *only* for entertainment.

Finally, our definition doesn't say anything about *fun*. Good games are fun and bad games are not, generally speaking, but fun is an emotional response to playing a game, not intrinsic to the game itself. Just because a game is no fun doesn't mean that it's not a game. In any case, as we discuss later in this chapter, we believe that fun is too narrow a concept to encompass all that games can do for the player.

Gameplay

There have been many efforts over the years to define what **gameplay** is. Game designer Sid Meier's famous definition is "a series of interesting choices" (Rollings and Morris, 2003, p. 61). Another designer, Dino Dini, defines it as "interaction that entertains" (Dini, 2004, p. 31). Although neither of these is obviously wrong, they're too general for practical use and not much help as you learn how to design a game. We again prefer a nonrigorous definition that might not cover all possible cases but provides a basis for thinking about game design. Our definition hinges on challenges and actions, so we look at them first.

Challenges   A *challenge* is any task set for the player that is nontrivial to accomplish. Overcoming a challenge must require either mental or physical effort. Challenges can be as simple as getting a ball through a hoop or as complex as making a business profitable. Challenges can be unique, recurring, or continuing. In action video games, the player frequently faces a recurring challenge to defeat a number of identical enemies, and then having done so, must overcome a unique challenge to defeat a particular *boss* enemy. In a combat flight simulator, shooting down enemy planes is a recurring challenge, whereas avoiding being hit by them is a continuing challenge. The player must do both at once to be successful.

You can also define a challenge in terms of other, smaller challenges. For example, you can give your player an overall challenge of completing an obstacle course and set up the obstacle course in terms of smaller challenges such as climbing over a fence, crawling under a barrier, jumping across a gap, and so on. The largest challenge of all in a game is to achieve its goal, but unless the game is extremely simple (such as tic-tac-toe), the players will always have to surmount other challenges along the way.

Most challenges in a game are direct obstacles to achieving the goal, although games might include optional challenges as well. You can include optional challenges to help the player practice or simply to provide more things for the player to do. In sports games, a team needs only to score more goals than its opponent(s) to win the game, but they may consider an optional challenge to prevent the opposing team from ever scoring at all.

The challenges in a game are established by the rules, although the rules don't always specify them precisely. In some cases, the players must figure out what the challenges are by thinking logically about the rules or by playing the game a few times. For example, the rules of *Othello* (Reversi) state only how pieces are converted from one color to another and that the object of the game is to have the most pieces of your own color when the board is filled. As you play the game, however, you discover that the corner spaces on the board are extremely valuable because they can never be converted to your opponent's color. Gaining control of a corner space is one of the major challenges of the game, but it's not spelled out explicitly in the rules.

Note that we say a challenge must be nontrivial but not that it must be difficult. Young children and inexperienced players often prefer to play games with easy challenges.

Actions   The rules specify what *actions* the players may take to overcome the challenges and achieve the goal of the game. The rules define not only what actions are allowed but also which ones are prohibited and which ones are required and under what circumstances. Games also permit optional actions that are not required to surmount a challenge but add to the player's enjoyment in other ways. For example, in the *Grand Theft Auto* games, you can listen to the radio in the car.

Many conventional games allow any action that is not prohibited by the rules. For example, in paintball, you may run, jump, crouch, crawl, climb, or make any other movement that you can think of to take enemy ground. Because video games are implemented by computer software, however, they can allow only actions that are built into the game. A video game offers a player a fixed suite of actions to choose from, which limits the number of ways in which a player can attack a challenge.

The Definition of Gameplay   Combining these two concepts produces the following definition:

> ***Gameplay*** consists of:
>
> - The challenges that a player must face to arrive at the object of the game, *and*
> - The actions that the player is permitted to take to address those challenges.

This definition lies at the heart of game design. Gameplay consists of challenges and actions, and we use this idea continually throughout the rest of the book. As a designer, you must create them both together. It's not enough to invent interesting challenges without the actions that will surmount them, nor to think of exciting actions without the challenges that they are intended to address. Games do sometimes permit additional actions that are not intended to solve a challenge, but the *essence* of gameplay is the challenge/action relationship.

Fantasy and imagination play an important role in entertaining the player, and some designers consider them to be elements of gameplay; in other words, the act of pretending that you are a pilot or a princess is an explicit part of the gameplay. We choose not to include these elements because they unnecessarily complicate the definition. A challenge might *imply* a fantasy-role (if you're trying to fly a plane, you must be a pilot), but we believe that you should define the player's fantasy independently of the gameplay for reasons we explain in the next chapter.

Fairness

Generally speaking, players expect that the rules will guarantee that the game is *fair.* Different societies, and indeed individual players, have varying notions of what is and is not fair. Fairness is not an essential element of a game but a culturally constructed notion that lies outside the magic circle. It is, in fact, a social metarule that can be used to pass judgment on the rules themselves. Players sometimes spontaneously decide to change the rules of a game during play if they perceive that the rules are unfair or that the rules are permitting unfair behavior. For all the players to enjoy a game, they must all be in general agreement about what constitutes fair play.

FYI   *Changing the Rules*

Whether the rules can be changed during play is usually determined by an often unwritten social convention, but in some cases, the procedure for changing the rules is described by the rules themselves. Games in which rules can be changed usually define two types of rules: the **mutable** (changeable) and the **immutable.** The immutable rules include instructions about when and how the mutable rules may be changed. *Nomic*, created by philosopher Peter Suber, is such a game.

It is particularly important that the players perceive a video game to be fair because, unlike conventional games, video games seldom give the players any way to change the rules if the players don't like them. One widely accepted definition of fairness is that all the players in a multiplayer game must have an equal chance of winning at the beginning of the game. The simplest way to achieve this is to make the game symmetric as described in the next section. In single-player video games, fairness is a complex issue that has to do with balance and with meeting players' expectations. This is discussed at much greater length in Chapter 11, "Game Balancing."

Symmetry and Asymmetry

In a *symmetric* game, all the players play by the same rules and try to achieve the same victory condition. Basketball is a symmetric game. The initial conditions, the actions allowed, and the victory condition are identical for both teams. Many traditional games such as chess and backgammon are symmetric in every respect except for the fact that one player must move first.

FYI *Who Goes First?*

In turn-based games, the fact that one player moves first can confer an advantage to one side or the other. For example, in tic-tac-toe among experienced players, *only* the person who goes first can win. However, if a game is designed in such a way that the advantage of going first is slight or nonexistent, this asymmetry can be ignored. In chess, only the weakest pieces on the board, pawns or knights, can move on the first turn, and they cannot move very far or establish a dominant position. The asymmetry of going first is considered irrelevant, so for practical purposes chess is a symmetric game.

People usually feel that if all players start in the same state, they all have an equal chance of winning. This assumes that the definition of fairness ignores differential skill on the part of the players. Occasionally, people agree that a highly skilled player must take a *handicap*—that is, they will impose a disadvantage on a skilled player in order to give the less-skilled players a better chance of winning. Amateur golf is the best-known example: Poor players are allotted a certain number of strokes per match that do not count against their score. On the other hand, professional golf, in which prize money is at stake, does not use this system and is purely symmetric.

In an *asymmetric* game, different players may play by different rules and try to achieve different victory conditions. Many games that represent real-world situations (for example, war games based on historical events) are asymmetric. If you play a war game about World War II, one side will be the Axis

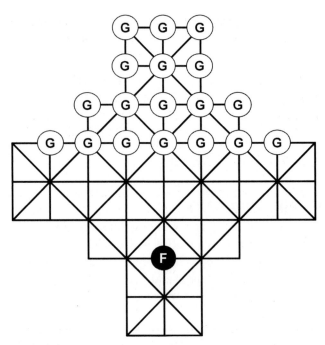

FIGURE 1.3 Fox and Geese: an asymmetric medieval board game.

and one the Allied powers. The two sides will necessarily begin at different locations on the map, with different numbers of troops and different kinds of weapons. As a result, it is often necessary for the two sides to have different objectives as well.

In asymmetric games, it is much more difficult to determine in advance whether players of equal skill have an equal chance of winning. As a result, people often adjust the rules of asymmetric games to suit their own notions of fairness. Figure 1.3 shows an asymmetric medieval board game called Fox and Geese. Several variants of this game exist because people have adjusted the rules to align it closer to their sense of fairness.

Competition and Cooperation

Competition occurs when players have conflicting interests; that is, when the players try to accomplish mutually exclusive goals. *Cooperation* occurs when the players try to achieve the same or related goals by working together. Players who are trying to achieve different, *unrelated* goals that are not mutually exclusive are neither competing nor cooperating—they are not really playing the same game. *Competition modes* are ways to build cooperation and competition into games:

- **Two-player competitive ("you versus me")**—The best-known mode, this is found in the most ancient games such as chess and backgammon.

- **Multiplayer competitive ("everyone for himself")**—Also familiar from games such as *Monopoly,* poker, and of course, many individual sports such as track and field athletics.

- **Multiplayer cooperative ("all of us together")**—All the players cooperate to accomplish the same goal. Conventional cooperative games are somewhat rare, but they are more common in video games. *Gauntlet* was a wonderful four-player cooperative arcade video game. *Sonic the Hedgehog 2* is a two-player cooperative game, and *Counter-Strike* has a cooperative mode.

- **Team-based ("us versus them")**—The members of a team cooperate, and the team collectively competes against one or more other teams. Familiar from soccer and many other team sports as well as partner games such as bridge.

- **Single-player ("me versus the situation")**—Familiar from solitaire card games as well as the vast majority of arcade and other video games such as the *Mario* series from Nintendo.

- **Hybrid competition modes**—Many games, such as *Monopoly,* prohibit players from cooperating with each other because such cooperation gives them an unfair advantage against another player. Others, however, specifically permit cooperation at times, even if the overall context of the game is competitive. *Diplomacy* is one such game; players may coordinate their strategies, but they also may renege on their agreements to their own advantage if they wish.

Many video games offer several different competition modes through a selection at the beginning of the game: single-player, team-based, or multi-player competitive (also called ***deathmatch***). A choice of competition modes broadens the market for these games but adds considerably to the work of designing them. In several cases, the designers clearly found one mode more interesting than another, adding the others as an afterthought. For example, *Dungeon Keeper* was a brilliant single-player game but was not well-designed for multiplayer play.

Conventional Games Versus Video Games

A game designer should be able to design all kinds of games, not just video games. A game designer must have a thorough understanding of the essential elements—play, rules, goals, and so on—and should be able to design an enjoyable game with nothing but paper and pencil. That's part of the reason we included so much material on games in general at the beginning of this chapter.

However, the purpose of this book is to teach you to design video games, and from now on we will concentrate on that. If you'd like to learn more about *general* game design, we recommend that you look at *Rules of Play* by Salen and Zimmerman (Salen and Zimmerman, 2003).

We defined a game in formal terms, but from this point forward, the word is frequently used in an informal sense to refer to the game *software.* When we say that "the game is smart" or "the game offers the player certain options," we are referring to the software, not to the play-activity itself. Likewise, when we refer to *game design,* we will be talking specifically about video games, not card, board, or other kinds of games. However, we will still sometimes refer to conventional games such as *Monopoly* when we feel that they illustrate a point particularly well.

Video games are a subset of the universe of all games. A ***video game*** is a game mediated by a computer, whether the computer is installed in a tiny keychain device such as a Tamagotchi or in a huge electronic play environment at a theme park. The computer enables video games to borrow entertainment techniques from other media such as books, film, karaoke, and so on. In this section, we look at what the computer brings to gaming.

Hiding the Rules

Unlike conventional games, video games do not require written rules. The game still *has* rules, but the machine implements and enforces them for the players. The players do not need to even know exactly what the rules are, although they do need instruction about how to play. In most video games, the computer sets the boundary of the magic circle because player actions are meaningful in the game only if the machine can detect them with its input devices. The computer also determines when the player reaches the goal. It adjudicates victory and defeat if those concepts are programmed into the game.

This means players no longer have to think about the game *as a game.* A player contemplating an action can simply try it, without having to read the rules to see whether the game permits it. This allows players to become much more deeply immersed in the game, to see it not as a temporary artificial environment with arbitrary rules, but as an alternate universe of which the player is a part.

Hiding the rules has one big disadvantage. If the players don't know the rules, they don't know how to optimize their choices. They can learn the rules only by playing the game. This is a reasonable design technique provided that the game includes hints about how to play it and what to expect. However, some video games force the player to learn by trial and error, which can make the game extremely frustrating. Many people deeply dislike having to learn by trial and error, and requiring a player to do so limits the market for that game to those players who are able to tolerate the frustration.

COMMANDMENT: Avoid Trial and Error

Provide adequate clues to enable players to deduce the correct resolution to a problem. Avoid creating challenges that can be surmounted only by trial and error. (Challenges that require physical skill and may be overcome with practice are an exception.)

Setting the Pace

In conventional games that don't use a timer, either the players or an independent referee sets the *pace* of the game—the rate at which the events required by the rules take place. In effect, it is up to the players to make the game *go*. The computer sets the pace of a video game and makes the game go. Unless specifically waiting for the player's input, the computer keeps the game moving forward at whatever pace the designer has set. This allows us to design fast and furious games that constantly throw enemies or other challenges at the player or slow and deliberative games in which the player can stop to think for as long as he wants. We can also modulate the pace, giving players a rest between periods of intense activity.

Presenting a Game World

Because a game world is fictional—a fantasy world—the game designer can include imaginary people, places, and situations. The players can think of themselves as make-believe characters in a make-believe place. With conventional games, this takes place primarily in the player's imagination, although it can be helped by printed boards, cards, and so on.

Video games can go much farther. Using a screen and speakers, video games present a fictional world the players can sense directly. Until recently, the poor state of computer graphics meant that the players had to use a lot of imagination, and of course, text-based computer games still intentionally rely on the player's imagination. However, it has always been a goal of game developers to present game worlds that seem as real as the fictional worlds in television or film. Although there remains a great deal of work to do, this goal is in sight. Modern video games are full of pictures, animation, movies, music, dialog, sound effects, and so on that conventional games cannot possibly provide. In fact, video games have become so photorealistic in recent years that some designers now experiment with a wider range of visual styles such as cel-shading, Impressionism, and so on.

At the fringes of the video game industry, some people are also making games of *augmented reality,* or *mixed reality,* in which computers are used in conjunction with real-world activities to play a game. Such games often make use of cellular telephones, video cameras, or global positioning systems as well as Web servers and a browser-based interface for some of the players. We do not discuss the design of such games here, but we encourage you to use the resources in the references if you are interested in learning more.

KEY POINT

Video games can present a designer's fictional game worlds to the player more directly than board games can, just as films can present a film director's imaginary worlds more directly than books can. This enables video games to entertain players in a wider variety of ways than conventional games do.

Artificial Intelligence

In 1959, IBM scientist Arthur Samuels devised a program that played checkers (Samuels, 1959). The program could also learn from its mistakes and eventually became good enough to beat expert human players. Much of the earliest research on artificial intelligence and games was of this sort as computer scientists tried to create artificial opponents that could play traditional games as competently as humans could. *Artificial intelligence* (AI) lets us play multiplayer games even when we don't have other people to play with.

However, AI brings considerably more to video gaming than artificial opponents for traditional games. Game developers use AI techniques for the following:

- **Strategy**—This means determining the optimal action to take by considering the possible consequences of a variety of available actions. Samuels' checker-playing program did this, but checkers is a game of *perfect information*, which means there is no hidden information and no element of chance. Modern video games usually have both hidden information and a large element of chance, so strategy is more difficult to compute.

- **Pathfinding**—This means finding the most advantageous routes through a simulated landscape filled with obstacles.

- **Natural language parsing**—Despite decades of research, computers still cannot understand ordinary written or spoken language well, but researchers are still very interested in using it for games. When this problem is solved, players will be able to give commands using natural sentences.

- **Natural language generation**—Video games currently produce language by playing combinations of previously recorded phrases or sentences. At the moment, they cannot generate language on their own. In time perhaps they will, which will make simulated people seem far more realistic. In the meantime, games use AI to select a sentence from their library of pre-recorded material that is most appropriate for the current game situation.

- **Pattern recognition**—This valuable technique has numerous applications including voice recognition, face recognition, detecting patterns of change in ongoing processes, and detecting patterns in player behavior. Human poker players use pattern recognition to establish a correlation between their opponent's behavior and their opponent's cards, which players can use to advantage later. Eventually, a computer might be programmed to do the same thing.

- **Simulated people and creatures**—Many games use simple AI techniques to create a behavioral model for simulated people or creatures. The simulated character seems to respond intelligently to the human player's

1

actions, at least within certain limits. The models are seldom complex, and a player can usually tell the difference between a simulated person and a real one within a few minutes. Simulating human beings is the most difficult and also the most important problem in game AI research.

Most current video games do not, in fact, contain much real AI. The point of video games is to entertain, not to simulate intelligence in depth, so they usually contain just enough AI to make the player feel as if the software is reasonably smart. The players—who are already immersed in the make-believe world anyway—are often happy to give the game credit for intelligence that it doesn't really possess. However, we can't afford to rely on this. Sometimes the AI fails, and the game breaks the players' immersion by doing something startlingly unintelligent. We need to continue to improve our AI so this doesn't happen, and the future looks promising. Technological advances in both hardware and software are allowing designers to create increasingly sophisticated artificial opponents and simulated characters. Artificial intelligence is one of the most important areas of research in game development.

How Video Games Entertain

At its most elementary level, game design consists of inventing and documenting the elements of a game. However, games don't exist in a vacuum; people create them to serve a purpose. That purpose might be training or study, but most often games are meant to entertain. You cannot become a successful game designer simply by creating games in the abstract. To make games for entertainment, you must learn to be an entertainer. In this section, we look at how games entertain people.

Different people enjoy different things, so we have both grand opera and motorcycle races as well as long, slow adventure games and short, frenetic arcade games. As a well-rounded game designer, you should be able to create games that entertain in a variety of ways.

COMMANDMENT: You Can't Please Everyone

It is not possible to design an ideal game that will please everyone because everyone does not enjoy the same thing. Do not try.

Gameplay

Games provide gameplay, that is, challenges and actions that entertain. People enjoy a challenge, as long as they have a reasonable expectation of being able to accomplish it. People will also try a challenge that they have almost no expectation of meeting if the risk is low and the reward is high. Challenge creates tension and drama. At the simplest level, presenting the player with a challenge amounts to asking the question, "Can you do it?" She'll enjoy trying to prove that she can.

People also enjoy executing the actions that the game offers. It's fun to fly a plane, shoot a rifle, design clothing, build a castle, or sing and dance. Video games let us do a lot of things that are expensive or impossible to do in real life, which is an important part of their appeal. The actions don't all have to be tied to a specific challenge; some things are fun to do even if they don't affect the outcome of the game. Many children's video games include toy-like elements to play with that ring, light up, change color, and so on.

COMMANDMENT: Gameplay Comes First

Gameplay is the primary source of entertainment in all video games. When designing a game, it is the *first* thing to consider.

Table 1.1 lists a large number of types of challenges that video games offer, along with classic examples from individual games or game series.

Aesthetics

Video games are an art form, so aesthetics are a part of their design. This doesn't mean a game has to be beautiful, any more than a film or a painting has to be beautiful. Rather, it must be designed with a sense of style and created with artistic skill. A game with clumsy animation, a muddy soundtrack, trite dialog, or sloppy artwork will disappoint players even if its gameplay is good.

Aesthetic considerations go beyond the game world, though. The interface graphics—buttons, numbers, type fonts, and so on—must complement the game world to create a consistent experience. Even the way the game responds to the player's button presses can be judged aesthetically. Animations should move smoothly and naturally; a slow, jerky, or unpredictable response will feel awkward. The physics of moving objects should look natural—or at least credible. Speed, accuracy, and grace are all part of a game's aesthetic appeal.

COMMANDMENT: Aesthetics Are Important Too

An ugly or awkward video game is a bad one, no matter how innovative its design or impressive its technology. Part of your job is to give your players aesthetic pleasure.

1

TABLE 1.1 Video game challenges.

Challenge Type	Classic Example
Physical Coordination Challenges	
Speed and reaction time	*Tetris*
Accuracy or precision (steering, shooting)	*Need for Speed*
Timing and rhythm	*Dance Dance Revolution*
Learning combination moves	*Street Fighter*
Formal Logic Challenges	
Deduction and decoding	*Mastermind*
Pattern Recognition Challenges	
Static patterns	*Heaven and Earth,* choosing an optimal layout for cards
Patterns of movement and change	*Sonic the Hedgehog,* behavior patterns of enemies
Time Pressure	
Beating the clock	*Frogger*
Achieving something before someone else	Indycar *Racing*
Memory and Knowledge Challenges	
Trivia	*You Don't Know Jack*
Recollection of objects or patterns	*Concentration*
Exploration Challenges	
Identifying spatial relationships	*Descent,* navigating in three dimensions
Finding keys (unlocking any space)	*Ultima*
Finding hidden passages	*Doom*
Mazes and illogical spaces	*Zork*
Conflict	
Strategy, tactics, and logistics	*Warcraft,* commanding armies
Survival	*Pac-Man,* avoiding being caught
Reduction of enemy forces	*Half-Life,* killing aliens
Defending vulnerable items or units	*ICO,* looking after a little girl who can't fight
Stealth	*Thief: The Dark Project,* avoiding being seen

▶▶ CONTINUED ON NEXT PAGE

Challenge Type	Classic Example
Economic Challenges	
Accumulating resources or points (growth)	*Civilization*
Establishing efficient production systems	*The Settlers*
Achieving balance or stability in a system	*SimEarth*
Caring for living things	*Creatures*
Conceptual Reasoning Challenges	
Sifting clues from red herrings	*Law and Order*, solving crimes
Detecting hidden meanings	*Planescape: Torment*, understanding characters' motivations from vague hints
Understanding social relationships	*Façade*, reconciling a quarreling couple
Lateral thinking	*The Incredible Machine*, building a machine from limited parts
Creation/ Construction Challenges	
Aesthetic success (beauty or elegance)	*The Sims*, assembling a photo album
Construction with a functional goal	*Mind Rover*, designing a fighting robot

The Graphics Versus Gameplay Debate In the early days of video games, the weakness of its display hardware seriously limited a game's graphics. Most of the game's appeal came from gameplay. With the growth of modern display technology, the graphics have taken on much greater importance, and creating them now consumes the majority of a game's development budget. Some designers and programmers, especially those who have been around since the early days, have become rather annoyed at the new dominance of graphics. They insist that graphics must be subordinate to gameplay in game design, and as proof, they point to examples of games with great graphics but very little gameplay, which offer poor value for the money.

This emphasis on graphics caused a serious problem in the early 1990s, when Hollywood studios thought they could take over the game industry because they could create better visuals than game publishers could. However, they failed. Hollywood didn't understand software engineering, didn't understand interactivity, and most important, didn't understand gameplay. The public refused to accept games with bad gameplay, no matter how spectacular the graphics. After a few false starts, Hollywood learned to work with game publishers rather than trying to become game publishers themselves as they realized that the two groups bring complementary skills to creating games.

We believe the graphics versus gameplay debate is no longer a meaningful one. The truth is that graphics and gameplay must work together to produce the total play experience. The graphics create the setting, which both sells the game and involves the player in the game's fantasy. The gameplay provides the challenge and things for the player to do. Both are essential to the player's enjoyment of the game.

The Importance of Harmony   Good games and game worlds possess *harmony,* which is the feeling that all parts of the game belong to a single, coherent whole. This quality was first identified by game designer Brian Moriarty. In his lecture, "Listen: The Potential of Shared Hallucinations," Moriarty (Moriarty, 1997) explains the concept of harmony so well that, with his permission, we use his own words to describe it:

> *Harmony isn't something you can fake. You don't need anyone to tell you if it's there or not. Nobody can sell it to you, it's not an intellectual exercise. It's a sensual, intuitive experience. It's something you feel. How do you achieve that feeling that everything works together? Where do you get this harmony stuff?*
>
> *Well, I'm here to tell you that it doesn't come from design committees. It doesn't come from focus groups or market surveys. It doesn't come from cool technology or expensive marketing. And it never happens by accident or by luck. Games with harmony emerge from a fundamental note of clear intention. From design decisions based on an ineffable sense of proportion and rightness. Its presence produces an emotional resonance with its audience. A sense of inner unity that has nothing to do with what or how you did something, it has something to do with **why.** Myst and Gemstone both have harmony. They have it because their makers had a vision of the experience they were trying to achieve and the confidence to attain it. They laid down a solid, ambient groove that players and their respective markets can relate to emotionally. They resisted the urge to overbuild. They didn't pile on a lot of gratuitous features just so they could boast about them. And they resisted the temptation to employ inappropriate emotional effects. Effects like shock violence, bad language, inside humor.*

> *You know, the suspension of disbelief is fragile. It's hard to achieve it and hard to maintain. One bit of unnecessary gore, one hip colloquialism, one reference to anything outside the imaginary world you've created is enough to destroy that world. These cheap effects are the most common indicators of a lack of vision or confidence. People who put this stuff into their games are not working hard enough.*

Harmony is an essential quality of a game's aesthetic appeal. With every design decision you make, you should ask yourself whether the result is in harmony with your overall vision. Too many games have elements that seem bolted on, last-minute ideas that somebody thought would be cool to include. Although every game design requires compromises, an important part of your job as a designer is to minimize the false notes or off-key elements that compromises tend to create.

COMMANDMENT: Strive for Harmony

A good game is a harmonious game. Try to find a way to make every aspect of your game fit together into a coherent, integrated whole.

Storytelling

Many games incorporate some kind of story as part of the entertainment they present. In conventional games, players can find it difficult to become immersed in a story because the players must also implement the rules. Stopping to implement the rules interrupts the players' sense of being in another place or being actors in a plot. Video games can mix storylike entertainment and gamelike entertainment almost seamlessly. To some extent, they can make a player feel as if he is *inside* a story, affecting its flow of events. This has enormous implications for game design and is one of the reasons that video games are more than simply a new kind of game; they are a completely new medium. Many video games—even those that involve the most frenetic action—now include elements of storytelling. We discuss this concept in detail in Chapter 7, "Storytelling and Narrative."

In fact, storytelling is *so* powerful as an entertainment device that one genre of video game—the adventure game—is starting to move away from the formal concept of a game entirely. Although we still call them *games,* adventure games are in fact a new hybrid form of interactive entertainment—the **interactive story.** We discuss this and other aspects of adventure games in more detail in Chapter 19, "Adventure Games." As time goes on, we can expect to see more new kinds of game/story/play experiences emerge that defy conventional descriptions. Video games aren't just games any more.

KEY POINT

Storytelling enables video games to entertain the player in ways that conventional games cannot and permits the creation of a new, hybrid form of entertainment: the interactive story.

Risks and Rewards

Risks and rewards as sources of entertainment are most familiar to us from gambling. You risk money by placing a bet, and you are rewarded with more money if you win the bet. However, risk and reward are key parts of *any* kind of competitive gameplay, even if no money is at stake. Whenever you play a competitive game, you risk losing in the hope that you will get the reward of winning. Risk and reward also occur on a smaller scale within the game. In a war game, when you choose a place to begin an attack, you risk the attack's being detected and repulsed, but if you are successful, you are rewarded by controlling new territory or depleting the enemy's resources. In *Monopoly*, you risk money by purchasing a property in the hope that you will be rewarded with income from rents later on.

Risk is produced by uncertainty. If a player knows exactly what the consequences of an action will be, then there is no risk. In gambling, the uncertainty is often produced by chance (which way will the dice fall?), but there are other ways to produce uncertainty as well. A game might have hidden information (where are the enemy's troops hiding?) revealed only after you take the risk. Even in a game such as chess, which has no hidden information and no element of chance, not knowing what your opponent will do produces uncertainty.

The risk/reward mechanism makes gameplay more exciting. Gameplay is entertaining all by itself because it lets the player attempt the challenges and perform the actions, but adding risks and rewards raises the level of tension and makes success or failure more meaningful to the player.

A game should always reward achievement, whether it was risky or not. The more difficult the achievement, the bigger the reward should be. Rewards can take various forms. Usually they advance the player's interests somehow, either by giving him something tangible that helps him play (such as money or a key to a locked area) or something intangible but still valuable, such as a strategic advantage. However, rewards don't have to affect the gameplay. Games that include a story reward the player's achievements by advancing the plot of the story by presenting a little more of it, often in a noninteractive video sequence. Games for children often reward achievements with flashing lights and ringing sounds.

Players' attitudes toward risk-taking vary. Some take an aggressive, inherently risky approach, whereas others prefer a defensive approach in which they try to minimize risk. You can design your game to suit one style or the other or try to balance the game so that neither really has an advantage.

> **KEY POINT**
>
> Playing a game is intrinsically entertaining, but adding risks and rewards to a game makes it more exciting.

COMMANDMENT: Risks Need Rewards

A risk must *always* be accompanied by a reward. Otherwise the player has no incentive to take the risk.

Novelty

People enjoy novelty: new things to see, to hear, and to do. Early video games were extremely repetitive and developed an unfortunate reputation for being monotonous. Nowadays, however, video games can offer more variety and content than any traditional game, no matter how complex. Not only can video games give the player new worlds to play in, but they can easily change the gameplay as the game progresses. So, for example, *Battlefield 1942* not only lets the player play as a foot soldier (one of several types, in fact), but also allows him to hop in a tank, an airplane, or a ship and play from those perspectives.

Novelty can even be an end in itself. In the *WarioWare* series from Nintendo, the player must play dozens of strange *microgames,* each of which lasts only a few seconds. Their constantly changing goals and graphical styles make *WarioWare* quite challenging, if rather disorienting. There aren't many games like it on the market, however. Novelty alone is not enough to sustain player interest. Most games rely more on theme-and-variations approaches, introducing a new element and giving the player the chance to explore it for a while before introducing the next one.

Learning

By learning, we don't mean "edutainment" or educational software. Learning is an aspect of playing a game, even just for entertainment, and people enjoy the learning process. This is the central thesis of Raph Koster's book, *A Theory of Fun for Game Design* (Koster, 2004). Although we don't agree with everything Koster says, the book is well worth reading. In the case of conventional games, the players have to learn the rules and then learn how to optimize their chances of winning. In video games, the players don't have a guide to the rules, so they have to learn how the game works by playing it. If you're playing a classic arcade game, over time you'll learn the movement and attack patterns of your enemies and figure out when they're vulnerable to a counterattack. Then you'll come across a new enemy and have to learn a new pattern. So long as a game keeps offering you new things to learn, it will remain enjoyable—assuming it was enjoyable to begin with! After you have learned everything about a game and have complete mastery over it, you might start to think that the game is boring. Koster asserts that this is inevitable, which is why people eventually abandon a game and pick up a new one. (This is more true of single-player games than it is of multiplayer games, because in multiplayer games the unpredictability of human opponents keeps them fresh.)

Learning isn't always easy and it isn't guaranteed to be fun, as we all remember from our days in school. People enjoy learning when at least one of two conditions is met: (1) it takes place in an enjoyable context, and (2) it provides useful mastery. A game should *always* provide an enjoyable context for learning; if it doesn't, there's something wrong with the game. A game should also offer useful mastery; the things that players learn should help them play the game more successfully. For further discussion of this issue, we recommend that you look at James Paul Gee's books, *What Video Games Have to Teach Us About Learning and Literacy* (Gee, 2004) and *Why Video Games Are Good for Your Soul* (Gee, 2005).

Creative and Expressive Play

People love to design and create things, whether clothing, creatures, buildings, cities, or planets. They also love to customize a basic template of some kind to reflect their own choices. This activity can have a direct influence on the gameplay (as when a player chooses a model of car to drive in a racing game) or can be purely cosmetic (as when a player chooses a color for the car). If a personal choice affects the gameplay, players won't always select the option the designer might consider the best option, even if they're told which one it is. They'll often choose one that they like regardless of the consequences. That's how strong the appeal of self-expression is.

As video game machines become more powerful and games begin to reach a wider audience, creative and self-expressive play become increasingly important. Research shows that girls and women, in particular, are often more motivated by a desire to express themselves through play than by a desire to defeat others in competition. We devote Chapter 5, "Creative and Expressive Play," entirely to the design issues of creative and expressive play.

Immersion

> . . . it was agreed, that my endeavours should be directed to persons and characters supernatural, or at least romantic, yet so as to transfer from our inward nature a human interest and a semblance of truth sufficient to procure for these shadows of imagination that willing suspension of disbelief for the moment, which constitutes poetic faith.
>
> — Samuel Taylor Coleridge, *Biographia Litteraria*, Chapter XIV

Coleridge was originally referring not to immersion but to an absence of skepticism. He wanted people who read his poems to accept the poems' romantic, imaginary people ("shadows of imagination") on "poetic faith," without asking questions. However, the term **suspension of disbelief,** as used by the game industry, has come to mean **immersion:** losing track of the outside world. Immersion is the feeling of being submerged in a form of entertainment, or rather, being unaware that you are experiencing an artificial world. When you are immersed in a book, movie, or game, you devote all your attention to it and it seems real. You have lost track of the boundaries of the magic circle. The pretended reality in which you are immersed seems as real as, or at least as meaningful as, the real world.

This feeling of immersion is deeply and satisfyingly entertaining to some players; others prefer not to become immersed and to remember that it's only a game while they play. People who take the game seriously find interruptions that break their sense of immersion jarring and disappointing. This is part of the reason that we place such emphasis on harmony.

Players become immersed in games in several ways:

- **Tactical immersion** is the sense of being "in the groove" in high-speed action games. It's sometimes called the Tetris *trance*. When playing such a game, the action is so fast that your brain has no time for anything else. You don't have time to think about strategy or a story line; the game is mostly about survival. To encourage tactical immersion, you must offer the player dozens of small challenges that can each be met in a fraction of a second. These small challenges must be fairly similar to one another—such as in an arcade shooter. Abrupt changes in the gameplay will destroy tactical immersion.

- **Strategic immersion** is the immersion of the chess master: observing, calculating, and planning. When deeply involved in trying to win a game, you are strategically immersed. You don't think about a story, characters, or the game world but focus strictly on optimizing your choices. To experience strategic immersion, the player must understand the rules of the game clearly so that she can plan her actions to her maximum advantage. Strategic immersion breaks down if a game confronts a player with a situation he has never seen before or if the game contains too many unpredictable elements. Unexpected or erratic behavior makes it impossible to plan.

- **Narrative immersion** is the feeling of being inside in a story, completely involved and accepting the world and events of the story as real. It is the same immersion as that produced by a good book or movie, but in video games, the player is also an actor within the story. Good storytelling—interesting characters, exciting plots, dramatic situations—produces narrative immersion. Bad storytelling—two-dimensional characters, implausible plots, or trite situations—destroys narrative immersion. So does gameplay that is inappropriate in the context of the story. If a player is immersed in a story about being a dancer, the gameplay should be about dancing, not about flying a plane or commanding an army.

You cannot create immersion purely by design. The game must also be attractive and well-constructed, or its flaws will break the player's sense of immersion. Also, you cannot design a game that pleases everyone, and players will not become immersed in a game they don't like. If you want to create an immersive game, you first must have a clear understanding of how your player likes to be entertained, then deliver the best entertainment experience to her that you can. We discuss the question of understanding your hypothetical player in more detail in Chapter 3, "Game Concepts."

Socializing

Most traditional games are multiplayer games, so since the earliest times, gaming has been a social activity. People love to play video games together too, and technology gives them lots of ways to do it:

- *Multiplayer local* gaming means two or more people playing together in one place. It's classic home console play for more than one person. Each player has his own controller, but they all look at the same screen. In some games the screen is split, and each player looks at her own part of it; in others, the players all see the same game world together.

- *Networked play,* also called *multiplayer distributed* gaming, refers to people playing against other people over a network at distributed locations. This is the way people play games over the Internet. To communicate with each other, they have to have a voice connection or type messages as they play.

- *LAN parties* are events in which a group of people all get together in one room, but each has his own computer hooked to the others by a local area network. This way they can talk to each other, but they can't see each other's screens.

- *Group play* occurs when a group of people get together in one room to play a *single*-player game. The player using the controller at any given time is said to be in the "hot seat," and the other players watch and offer advice. Players usually hand off the controller from one to the next as the gameplay changes, so as to have the person most skilled at the current challenges play during that part of the game. This style of play is particularly popular with children.

When designing a multiplayer game, it's important to think about the social aspect of entertaining people. By offering them chat mechanisms, bulletin boards, and other community-building facilities, you can extend the game's entertainment far beyond the gameplay alone. For more information about designing online games, see the Companion Website.

Companion Website

Summary

In this chapter you have learned that rules, goals, play, and pretending are the essential elements of a game, and how they work together to create the experience of playing one. You have been taught to think of gameplay in terms of challenges and actions, and you have looked at such important issues as winning and losing, fairness, competition, and cooperation. You should now be aware of some of the special benefits that computers bring to playing games and the manifold ways that video games entertain people. With this as a foundation, you're ready to proceed to the next chapter. There, you'll learn how games are structured, an approach to designing them, and what it takes to be a game designer.

Test Your Skills

MULTIPLE CHOICE QUESTIONS

1. Which of the following distinguishes games from toys?
   A. Toys have a pretended reality and games do not.
   B. Games have rules and toys do not.
   C. Games are more fun than toys.
   D. Playing with toys involves real-world activities, but playing games does not.

2. What are the essential elements in the formal definition of a game?
   A. Fun, pretending, and goals.
   B. Goals, play, competition, and players.
   C. Winning, losing, and rules.
   D. Play, pretending, rules, and goals.

3. Which of the following makes books and movies different from games?
   A. Books and movies tell stories and games do not.
   B. Games must always be fun, but books and movies don't have to be.
   C. Books and movies are presentational forms of entertainment, while games are interactive.
   D. Games always require more attention to appreciate them properly.

4. Which of these lies outside the magic circle?
   A. The buttons you press to play the game.
   B. The pretended reality of the game.
   C. The rules of the game.
   D. The story of the game.

5. Which of the following is *not* a function of the rules?
   A. Establishing a victory condition.
   B. Specifying the gameplay.
   C. Defining the sequence of play.
   D. Telling the story of the game.

6. Which two elements make up the gameplay of a game?

   A. Challenges and actions.

   B. Rules and play.

   C. Story and characters.

   D. Pretending and creating.

7. What is the simplest way to make a multiplayer game fair?

   A. Limit it to two players.

   B. Make it symmetric.

   C. Make it asymmetric.

   D. Handicap the strongest player.

8. Competition occurs when:

   A. Two teams are working together to achieve a goal.

   B. All the players are working on unrelated goals.

   C. The players are trying to accomplish mutually exclusive goals.

   D. A game has no victory condition.

9. Which is *not* a benefit unique to computerized gaming?

   A. Hiding the rules.

   B. Software that presents a game world.

   C. Artificial intelligence.

   D. Letting players change the rules.

10. What is the primary source of entertainment in all video games?

    A. Gameplay.

    B. Storytelling.

    C. Graphics.

    D. Harmony.

11. According to Brian Moriarty, which of the following produces a harmonious game?

    A. Design committees working together.

    B. Excellent technology.

    C. Design decisions based on proportion and rightness.

    D. Marketing and market surveys.

12. Why is it essential to offer the player a reward for taking an optional risk?
    A. It makes the game more fair.
    B. Without a reward the player has no incentive to take the risk.
    C. Players are only entertained by rewards.
    D. Risks and rewards are an essential part of every game.

13. Which of the following is not an entertaining quality of video games?
    A. Novelty.
    B. Learning.
    C. Gameplay.
    D. Algorithms.

EXERCISES

1. Create a competitive game for two players and a ball that does *not* involve throwing it or kicking it. Prove that it is a game by showing how it contains all the essential elements.

2. Using a chessboard and the types of pieces and moves available in chess, devise a cooperative game of some kind for two people, in which they must work together to achieve a victory condition. (You do not need to use the starting conditions of chess, nor all the pieces.) Document the rules and the victory condition.

3. Define a competitive game with a single winner, for an unlimited number of players, in which only creative actions are available. Be sure to document the termination and victory conditions.

4. Describe the elements of the gameplay in each of the following games: backgammon, poker, bowling, and Botticelli. (Use the Internet to look up the rules if you do not know them.)

5. List examples not already mentioned in this book of video games designed for single-player, multiplayer local, and multiplayer distributed play. Explain how the games' design supports these different modes.

DISCUSSION QUESTIONS

1. As a potential designer, do you see yourself as an artist, an engineer, a craftsman, or something else? Why do you see yourself that way?

2. Do you agree or disagree with our definition of a game? If you disagree, what would you add, remove, or change?

3. We have defined gameplay strictly in terms of challenges and actions, leaving out the game world or the story. Do you feel that this is appropriate? Why or why not?

4. Why is it fair if one athlete trains to become better but not fair if he takes drugs to become better? What does this say about our notions of fairness?

5. We've listed only the most important things that computers bring to gaming. What other things can you think of?

6. Our list of ways that video games entertain people is only a beginning. What else would you add?

Chapter 2

Design Components and Processes

Chapter Objectives

After reading this chapter and completing the exercises, you will be able to do the following:

- Understand the player-centric approach to game design and apply its principles to your own design practice.

- Know how the core mechanics and the user interface work together to create gameplay for the player.

- Explain how gameplay modes and shell menus make up the structure of a game.

- Recognize the three stages of game design (concept, elaboration, and tuning) and know what kinds of design work take place in each stage.

- Know the kinds of jobs required on a design team.

- Know the kinds of documents that a game designer is likely to need to make and what they are for.

- Know the qualities required of a good game designer.

Introduction

Game design is the process of:

- Imagining a game

- Defining the way it works

- Describing the elements that make up the game (conceptual, functional, artistic, and others)

- Transmitting that information to the team that will build the game

A game designer's job includes all of these tasks. In this chapter, we begin by discussing our approach to the task, called player-centric game design. We then introduce the central components of any video game, the core mechanics and the user interface. We show how these components are used in the design process. Finally, we examine the various job roles on a design team and some of the qualities that it takes to be a game designer.

In the video game industry, all but the smallest games are designed by teams of anywhere from three to 20 people. We cannot know what role you will play on such a team, and therefore we write as if you are the lead designer, responsible for overseeing everything. (If your team is small, or if you are designing alone, you may perform some or all of the roles yourself.) Our text is written as if you are designing for a home console machine or personal computer, although much of the material here is applicable to any game device.

Approaching the Task

Before we can discuss the process of game design itself, we must discuss how to approach it—that is, what you are actually trying to accomplish and how to think about it. Over the years, people have tried many approaches to game design, and some of them are better than others. A few tend to result in catastrophic failures. This book teaches you an approach that seems best to us.

Art, Engineering, or Craft?

Some people like to think of game design as an art, a process of imagination that draws on a mysterious wellspring of creativity. They think of game designers as artists, and they suppose that game designers spend their time indulging in flights of imagination. Other people, often more mathematically or technologically oriented, see game design as a type of engineering. They concentrate on the methodology for determining and balancing the rules of play. Game design to these people is a set of techniques. Aesthetics are a minor consideration.

Each of these views is incomplete. Game design is not purely an art because it is not primarily a means of aesthetic expression. Nor is game design an act of pure engineering. It's not bound by rigorous standards or formal methods. The goal of a game is to entertain through play, and designing a game requires both creativity and careful planning.

Interactive entertainment is an art form, but like film and television it is a collaborative art form. In fact, it is far more collaborative than either of those media, and the designer is seldom granted the level of creative control that a film director enjoys. Consequently, no single person is entitled to call himself the artist. Designing games is a *craft,* like cinematography or costume design. A game includes both artistic and functional elements: It must be aesthetically

> **KEY POINT**
>
> Game design is a craft, combining both aesthetic and functional elements. Craftsmanship of a high quality produces elegance.

pleasing, but it also must work well and be enjoyable to play. The greatest games—the ones whose reputations spread like wildfire and that continue to be played and discussed long after their contemporaries are forgotten—combine their artistic and functional elements brilliantly, achieving a quality for which the best word is *elegance*. Elegance is the sign of craftsmanship of the highest order.

The Player-Centric Approach

we favor an approach called ***player-centric game design.*** We believe this approach is the one most likely to produce an enjoyable game, which, in turn, will help it to be a commercially successful one. Many other factors affect the commercial success of a game as well: marketing, distribution, and the experience of the development team. Many of these are beyond the control of the game designer, so no design or development methodology can guarantee a hit. However, a well-designed game undoubtedly has a better chance of being a hit than a poorly designed one.

We define player-centric game design as follows:

> *Player-centric game design is a philosophy of design in which the designer envisions a representative player of a game the designer wants to create, then accepts two key obligations to that player:*

> - *The duty to entertain: A game's primary function is to entertain the player, and it is the designer's obligation to create a game that does so. Other motivations are secondary.*
> - *The duty to empathize: To design a game that entertains the player, the designer must imagine that he is the player and must build the game to meet the player's desires and preferences for entertainment.*

The first obligation, the duty to entertain, can be adapted somewhat if the game is intended for education, research, advertising, political, or other purposes, but for recreational video games it is imperative. If a player is going to spend time and money on your game, your first concern *must* be to see that he enjoys himself. This means that entertaining the player takes priority over your own desire to express yourself creatively. You must have a creative vision for your game, but if some aspect of your vision is incompatible with entertaining the player, you should modify or eliminate it.

The second obligation, the duty to empathize, requires you to place yourself in the position of a representative player and imagine what it will be like to play your game. You must mentally become the player and stand in his shoes. For every design decision that you make—and there will be thousands—you must ask yourself how it meets the player's desires and preferences about interactive entertainment. Note our emphasis on a *representative player.* It is up to you to decide what that means, but this hypothetical being must bear some resemblance to the customers that you want to actually buy the game. You cannot insist that your typical player be a highly skilled gamer unless you want to restrict your customer base to nothing but highly skilled gamers.

Player-centric game design means thinking about how the player will react to everything in your game: its artwork, its user interface, its gameplay, and so on. But that is only the surface. At a deeper level, you must understand what the player *wants* from the entire experience you are offering—what motivates her to play your game at all. To design a game around the player, you must have a clear answer to the following questions: Who *is* your player, anyway? What does she like and dislike? Why did she buy your game? The answer will also be influenced by the game concept that you choose for your game, which is why we discuss both player-centric design and game concepts together in Chapter 3.

This process of empathizing with your player is one of the things that differentiates games from presentational forms of entertainment. With books, paintings, music, and movies, it is considered artistically virtuous to create your work without worrying about how it will be received, and it's thought to be rather mercenary to modify the content based on sales considerations. But with a video game—whether you think of it as a work of art or not—you *must* think about the player's feelings about the game, because the player participates in the game with both thought and action.

In our opinion, player-centric game design produces the most entertaining, enjoyable games. However, there are two common misconceptions about player-centric design that you must avoid.

Misconception 1: I Am My Own Typical Player   For years, designers built video games, in effect, for themselves. They assumed that whatever they liked, their customers would also like. Because most designers were young males, they took it for granted that their customer base was also made up of young males. That was indeed true for a long time, but now it is a dangerous fallacy. As the market for games expands beyond the traditional gamer, you must be able to design games for other kinds of players. In the player-centric approach, this means learning to think like your intended players, whoever they may be: little girls, old men, busy mothers, and so on. You cannot assume that players will like what you like. Rather, you must learn to design for what *they* like. (You may also find that you grow to like a game that you didn't think you would as you work to design it!)

One of the most common mistakes that male designers make is to assume that male and female players are alike, when in fact they often have different priorities and preferences. For an excellent discussion of how to reach female players without alienating male ones, read *Gender Inclusive Game Design,* by Sheri Graner Ray (Ray, 2003). With every design decision, ask yourself, "What if the player is female?" Does your decision apply equally to her?

A few game developers argue that they don't want to work on any game that they personally wouldn't want to play—that if a game doesn't appeal to them, they won't have any "passion" for it and won't do a good job. Taken to its logical conclusion, that means we would never have games for young children, because young children can't build games for themselves. Insisting that you must have passion for your game or you can't do a good job on it is a very self-centered approach—the opposite of player-centric design. Instead of passion, we prefer professionalism, the willingness to work hard to do a good job because that's what you're paid for, regardless of whether you personally would choose to play your game for entertainment. If you are a true professional, you *can* create a brilliant game for an audience other than yourself. The design team on the game *Bratz: Rock Angelz* consisted entirely of adult men, yet the game was a big success because the designers learned how to think like a 10-year-old girl, its intended player. They talked to girls and women, studied other products that girls like, and took seriously their duty to empathize (Elling, 2006).

COMMANDMENT: You Are Not Your Player

Do not assume that you epitomize your typical player. Player-centric game design requires you to imagine what it is like to be your player, even if that person is someone very different from you.

Misconception 2: The Player Is My Opponent   Because arcade (coin-op) games have been around a long time, some of the techniques of arcade game design have crept into other genres where they are not appropriate. Arcade games make money by getting the player to put in more coins. Consequently, they are designed to be hard to play for more than a few minutes and to continually threaten the player with losing the game. This places considerable constraints on the designer's freedom to tell a story or to modulate the difficulty of the gameplay. The famous Japanese designer Shigeru Miyamoto, who invented the arcade game *Donkey Kong* (and with it the entire *Mario* franchise) eventually abandoned arcade game design because he found it too limiting.

The arcade model encourages the game designer to think of her player as an opponent. It suggests that the designer's job is to create obstacles for the player, to make it hard for the player to win the game. This is a profoundly wrongheaded approach to game design. It takes no account of the player's interests or motivations for playing. It tends to equate "hard" with "fun." And it ignores the potential of creative games, which may not include obstacles at all. Game design is about much more than creating challenges.

If you are working on multiplayer competitive games, in which the players provide the challenge for each other, you're less likely to make this mistake. But it's an easy trap to fall into when designing single-player games because it's up to you to provide the challenges. Never lose sight of the fact that your design goal is to *entertain* the player by a variety of means, not simply to oppose her forward progress through the game.

COMMANDMENT: The Player Is Not Your Opponent

Do not think of the player as your opponent. Game design is about *entertaining* the player, not opposing the player. There are many ways to entertain a player.

2

Other Motivations That Influence Design

In the commercial game industry, video games are always built for entertainment, but even so, several factors can influence the way a game is designed. In this section, we will examine some of them.

When a company chooses to build a game specifically for a particular market and to include certain elements in its design specifically to increase sales within that market, that game is said to be *market-driven*. You might think that any game made for sale should be market-driven. Experience shows, however, that most market-driven games aren't very good. You can't make a brilliant game simply by throwing in all the most popular kinds of gameplay. If you try, you get a game that doesn't feel as if it's about anything in particular. The best games are expressions of the designer's vision, which makes them stand out from other games.

The opposite of a market-driven game is a *designer-driven* game. In designer-driven games, the designer retains all creative control and takes a personal role in every creative decision, no matter how small. Usually he does this because he's convinced that his own creative instincts are superior to anyone else's. This approach ignores the benefits of play-testing or other people's collective wisdom, and the result is usually a botched game. *Daikatana* is an often-cited example.

Many publishers commission games to exploit a *license:* a particular intellectual property such as a book (*The Lord of the Rings*), movie (*Die Hard*), or sports trademark (*NHL Hockey*). These can be enormously lucrative. As a designer, you will work creatively with characters and a world that already exists, and you'll be making a contribution to the canon of materials about that world. One downside of designing licensed games is that you don't have as much creative freedom as you do designing a game entirely from your own imagination. The owners of the license will insist on the right to approve your game before it ships, as well as the right to demand that you change things they don't like. In addition, there is always a risk of complacency. A great license alone is not enough to guarantee success. The game must be just as good as if it didn't have a license.

A *technology-driven* game is designed to show off a particular technological achievement, most often something to do with graphics or a piece of hardware. Nintendo's original *Starfox* was specifically designed to exploit their FX graphics chip, for example. Console manufacturers often write technology-driven games when they release a new platform to show everyone the features of their machine. The main risk in designing a technology-driven game is that you'll spend too much time concentrating on the technology and not enough on making sure your game is really enjoyable. As with a hot license, a hot technology alone is not enough to guarantee success.

Art-driven games are comparatively rare. An art-driven game exists to show off someone's artwork and aesthetic sensibilities. Although such games are visually innovative, they're seldom very good because the designer has spent more time thinking about ways to present his material than about the player's experience of the game. A game must have enjoyable gameplay as well as great visuals. *Myst* is a game that got this right; it is an art-driven game with strong gameplay.

Integrating for Entertainment

When one particular motivation drives the development of a game, the result is often a substandard product. A good designer seeks not to maximize one characteristic at the expense of others but to integrate them all in support of a higher goal: entertaining the player.

- A game must present an imaginative, coherent experience, so the designer must have a vision.

- A game must sell well, so the designer must consider the audience's preferences.

- A game with a license must pay back the license's cost, so the designer must understand what benefits it brings and exploit them to the game's best advantage.

- A game must offer an intelligent challenge and a smooth, seamless experience, so the designer must understand the technology.

- A game must be attractive, so the designer must think about its aesthetic style.

Player-centric game design means testing every element and every feature against the standard: Does this contribute to the player's enjoyment? Does it entertain her? If so, it stays; if not, you should consider eliminating it. There's no easy formula for deciding this; the main thing is to make the effort. As we have already quoted designer Brian Moriarty, too many designers "pile on gratuitous features just so that they can boast about them," which means they're not designing player-centrically.

There are sometimes reasons for including features that don't directly entertain: They might be necessary to make other parts of the game work, or they might be required by the licensor. But you should regard them with great suspicion and do your best to minimize their impact on the player.

The Key Components of Video Games

In the last chapter, we discussed what a game is and what gameplay is. But where does gameplay come from, and how does the player interact with it? In order to create gameplay and offer it to the player, a video game is composed of two key components. These are not technical components but conceptual ones. They are the *core mechanics* and the *user interface.* Some games also use a third important component called the *storytelling engine,* but we will deal with it in Chapter 7, "Storytelling and Narrative." In this section, we introduce the core mechanics and the user interface and show how they work together to produce entertainment. Each of these components has a complete chapter devoted to it later in the book, so our discussion here is limited to defining their functions, not explaining how to design them.

Core Mechanics

One of a game designer's tasks is to turn the general rules of the game into a symbolic and mathematical model that can be implemented algorithmically. This model is called the **core mechanics** of the game. The model is more specific than the rules. For example, the general rules might say, "Caterpillars move faster than snails," but the core mechanics state exactly how fast each moves in centimeters per minute. The programmers then turn the core mechanics into algorithms and write the software that implements the algorithms. This book doesn't address technical design or programming but concentrates on the first part of the process, creating the core mechanics. That process is addressed at length in Chapter 10, "Core Mechanics."

The core mechanics are at the heart of any game, because they generate the gameplay. They define the challenges that the game can offer and the actions that the player can take to meet those challenges. The core mechanics also determine the effect of the player's actions upon the game world. The mechanics state the conditions for achieving the goals of the game and what consequences follow from succeeding or failing to achieve them. In a conventional game, the players are aware of the core mechanics because the players must implement the rules. In a video game, the core mechanics are hidden from the players. The players experience them only through play. If the players play the game over and over, they will eventually become aware of the game's mechanistic nature and learn to optimize their play to beat the game.

One quality of the core mechanics is their degree of **realism,** which we define below. A **simulation,** in the formal sense, is a mathematical or symbolic model of a real-world situation, created for the purpose of studying real-world problems. If it is to have any validity, the simulation must represent some part of the real world as closely as possible (though aspects of it may need to be simplified). A game, on the other hand, is created for the purpose of entertainment.

Even if it represents the real world to some degree, it will always include compromises to make it more playable and more fun. For example, a real army requires a large general staff to make sure the army has all the ammunition and supplies it needs. In a game, a single player has to manage everything, so to avoid overwhelming him, the designer abstracts these logistical considerations out of the model—that is to say, out of the core mechanics. The player simply pretends that soldiers never need food or sleep, and they never run out of ammunition.

All games fall along a continuum between the **abstract** and the **representational.** *Pac-Man* is a purely abstract game; it's not a simulation of anything real. Its location is imaginary, and its rules are arbitrary. *Grand Prix Legends* is a highly representational game: It accurately simulates the extraordinary danger of driving racing cars before the spoiler was invented. Although no game is completely realistic, we refer to this variable quality of games as their degree of realism. For the most part, however, we use the terms *abstract* and *representational* to characterize games at opposite ends of the realism scale.

You decide what degree of realism your game will have when you decide upon its concept. The decision you make determines how complex the core mechanics are.

User Interface

The concept of a ***user interface*** should be familiar to you from computer software generally, but in a game the user interface has a more complex role. Most computer programs are tools of some kind: word-processing tools, Web-browsing tools, painting tools, and so on. They are designed to be as efficient as possible and to present the user's work clearly. Games are different because the player's actions are *not* supposed to be as efficient as possible; they are obstructed by the challenges of the game. Most games also hide information from the player, revealing it only as the player advances. A game's user interface is supposed to entertain as well as to facilitate.

The user interface mediates between the core mechanics of the game and the player (see Figure 2.1). It takes the challenges that are generated by the core mechanics (driving a racing car, for example) and turns them into graphics on the screen and sound from the speakers. It also turns the player's button-presses and joystick movements on the keyboard or controller into actions within the context of the game. If it does this smoothly and naturally, the player comes to associate the button-press with the action. She no longer has to think, "I must press button A to apply the brakes." Instead she thinks, "Brakes!" and presses button A automatically. The user interface interprets the button-press as the braking action and informs the core mechanics; the core mechanics determine the effect of the braking and send an instruction back to the user interface telling it to show the result. The user interface adjusts the animation to show the car slowing down and presents it to the player. All this happens in a fraction of a second.

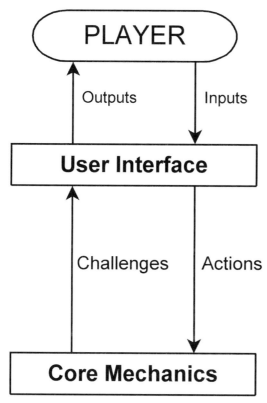

FIGURE 2.1 The relationships among core mechanics, user interface, and player.

Because the user interface lies between the player and the core mechanics, it is sometimes referred to as the ***presentation layer.***

The user interface does more than display the outputs and receive the inputs. It also presents the story of the game, if there is any, and creates the sensory embodiment of the game world—all the images and sounds of the world and, if the game machine has a vibrating controller, the vibrations of the world too. All the artwork and all the audio of the game are part of its user interface, its presentation layer. Two essential features of the user interface of a game are its *perspective* and its *interaction model,* as shown in Figure 2.2.

Interaction Models   As we described, the user interface turns the player's button-presses into actions within the game world. The relationship between the player's button-presses and the resulting actions is dictated by the game's ***interaction model.*** The model determines how the player projects her will, her choices and commands, into the game. In particular, it defines what she may and may not act upon at any given moment. Video games use a number of

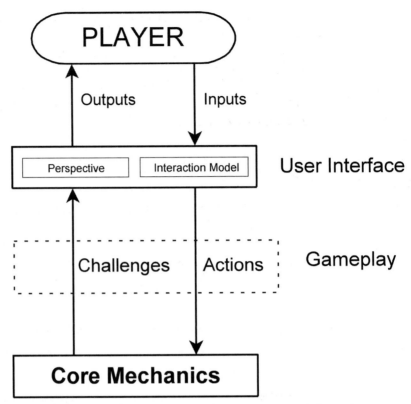

FIGURE 2.2 Perspective and interaction model are features of the user interface.

standard interaction models, including multipresence, avatar-based models, contestant models, and so on. In a multipresent model, for example, the player can act on different parts of the game world whenever she wants to, reaching "into" it from the "outside." In an avatar-based model, the player is represented by a character who already *is* inside the game world, and the player acts on the world through that character. Just as the visible parts of a game's user interface change during play, a game can have more than one interaction model depending on what is happening at the time. Interaction models are discussed at greater length in Chapter 8, "Creating the User Experience."

Perspectives   If a game includes a simulated physical space, or *game world,* then it will almost certainly use graphics to display that space to the player. The user interface must display the space from a visual *perspective:* a particular camera angle or point of view. Even if a game doesn't have a game world, it still may have a collection of data that it displays to the player in tables, charts, or some other form, and a given view of that data may be thought of as a sort of "conceptual perspective," a perspective formed upon the information provided.

We use the term *perspective* in this somewhat broader sense to include both visual and conceptual perspectives.

The most commonly used perspectives are first person and third person for presenting 3D game worlds and top-down, side-scrolling, and isometric for presenting 2D worlds. We discuss the question of game world dimensionality in Chapter 4, "Game Worlds," and address the merits of the different perspectives in Chapter 8, "Creating the User Experience."

FYI | *Games Without Graphics*

Many of the early computer games were text-based, designed to be played on a printing terminal attached to a mainframe computer. Text-only games still exist in the form of quizzes or trivia games, especially for small devices such as cell phones. **Interactive fiction**—text-only adventure games—has long since ceased to be a commercial genre, but it is still popular with a small group of hobbyists. Blind players can play text-only games using text-to-speech synthesizers. There is also a very small number of experimental audio-only games intended for the blind.

The Structure of a Video Game

You now know how the core mechanics of a game work with the user interface to create gameplay for the player. A game seldom presents all its challenges at one time, however, nor does it permit the player to take all actions at all times. Instead, most video games present a subset of their complete gameplay, often with a particular user interface to support it. Both the gameplay available and the user interface change from time to time as the player is required to meet new challenges or to view the game world from a different perspective. These changes sometimes occur in response to something the player has done, and at other times they occur automatically when the core mechanics have determined that they should. How and why the changes occur are determined by the game's **structure.** The structure is made up of *gameplay modes,* a vitally important concept in our approach to game design, and *shell menus.* In this section, we define what gameplay modes and shell menus are and discuss how they interact to form the structure.

Gameplay Modes

If a game is to be coherent, the challenges and actions available to the player at any given time should be conceptually related to one another. In hand-to-hand combat, for example, the player should be able to move around, wield his weapons, quaff a healing potion (though that may entail some risk), and perhaps run away or surrender. He should not be able to pull out a map or sit down to inventory his assets, even if those are actions he may take at other times in the game. Likewise, a race car driver should not be able to adjust the suspension of the car while driving it or drive the car while it's in the shop.

In short, unless a game is very simple, not all the challenges and actions that it offers will be available to the player at any one time. The player will only experience a subset of all the gameplay, usually derived from the real-world activity (fighting, driving, constructing, and so on) that the game is simulating at that moment. The user interface, too, must be designed to facilitate whatever activity is taking place. The graphics displayed for driving a racing car are necessarily different from those used for tuning it up in the shop. The perspective and interaction models will be different as well. When driving, the vehicle is the player's avatar on the racetrack, and the player usually sees the world from the cockpit; when tuning up the car, the player has omnipresent control over all of its parts, but the rest of the game world (the racetrack) is not accessible.

This combination of related items—available gameplay and supporting user interface at a given point in the game—collectively describe something that we call a *gameplay mode.* See Figure 2.3 for an illustration. In a given gameplay mode, the features of the game combine to give the player a certain experience that feels different from other parts of the game; that is, other gameplay modes. Because the game offers only a subset of all its challenges and actions in a given gameplay mode, the player is focused on a limited number of goals.

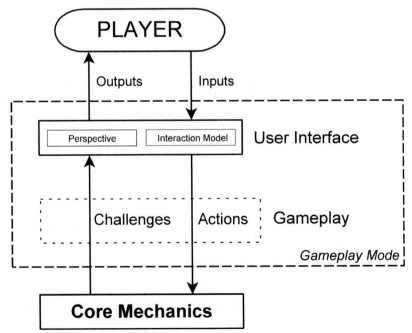

FIGURE 2.3 The large dashed box represents the gameplay mode.

Gameplay modes are central to our process for designing video games. We therefore provide the following formal definition:

> *A gameplay mode consists of the particular subset of a game's total gameplay that is available at any one time in the game, plus the user interface that presents that subset of the gameplay to the player.*

A game can be in only one gameplay mode at a time. When the gameplay available to the player *or* the user interface changes significantly, the game has left one mode and entered another. We include a change to the user interface as a change of mode because such changes redirect the player's focus of attention and cause him to start thinking about different challenges. Also, if the mapping between the buttons on the input device and the actions in the game changes sharply, the player will probably think of it as a new mode.

IN THE TRENCHES: Gameplay Modes in American Football

Video games about American football have many rapid and complex mode switches, especially when playing the team on offense; that is, the team that has the ball. The mapping between the buttons on the controller and the actions they produce in the game changes on a second-by-second basis. Here is the sequence necessary to select and execute a pass play in *Madden NFL Football:*

1. Choose the offensive formation to be used on the next play from a menu.
2. Choose the play to be called from another menu.
3. Take control of the quarterback. Call signals at the line of scrimmage. During this period only one man, who is *not* the quarterback, may move under the player's control. Snap the ball to the quarterback.
4. Drop back from the line of scrimmage and look for an open receiver. Choose one and press the appropriate button to pass the ball to him.
5. Take control of the chosen receiver and run to the place where the ball will come down. Press the appropriate button to try to catch the ball.
6. Run toward the goal line. At this point the ball may not be thrown again.

This process requires six different gameplay modes in the space of about 45 seconds.

Many of the earliest arcade games had only one gameplay mode. In *Asteroids,* for example, you flew a spaceship around a field of asteroids, trying to avoid being hit by one and shooting at them to break them up and disintegrate them. The perspective and the interaction model never changed, nor did the function of the controls. When you had destroyed an entire screenful of asteroids, you got a new screenful that moved somewhat faster, but that was all. From time to time an enemy spaceship appeared and shot at you, presenting new challenges (to avoid being shot, and to shoot the enemy), but because nothing else changed, it wasn't really a new gameplay mode. On the other hand, in *Pac-Man* you were chased by dangerous ghosts until you ate a large dot on the playfield. For a short period after that, the ghosts were vulnerable and would run away from you. Because this represents a significant change to the gameplay (and was a key part of the game's strategy), it can be considered a new gameplay mode even though the user interface does not change. As the designer, it's up to you to decide when the gameplay or the user interface has changed enough to be a new gameplay mode.

Figures 2.4 and 2.5 are screen shots from *Dungeon Keeper 2* illustrating two very different modes. The first, a management mode, shows an aerial perspective of an underground dungeon. It is used for building the dungeon, looking after the creatures who live there, and other strategic activities. The second, called possession mode in the game, is a first-person mode from the

FIGURE 2.4 Management mode in *Dungeon Keeper 2*.

The Structure of a Video Game

FIGURE 2.5 Possession mode in *Dungeon Keeper 2*.

point of view of one of the creatures. You cannot manage the dungeon from this mode; you can only fight enemies such as the ones visible in the picture. Possession mode is essentially tactical.

Not all gameplay modes offer challenges that the player must meet immediately. A strategy menu in a sports game is a gameplay mode because the player must choose the best strategy to help her win the game even though play is temporarily suspended while the player uses the menu. A character creation screen in a role-playing game or an inventory management screen in an adventure game both qualify as gameplay modes. A player's actions there have an influence on the challenges she will face when she returns to regular play.

Shell Menus and Screens

Whenever the player is taking actions that influence the game world, that is, actually playing the game, then the game is in a gameplay mode. However, most games also have several other modes in which the player *cannot* affect the game world, but can make other changes. These modes are collectively called **shell menus** because they are usually experienced before and after playing the game itself (they are a "shell" around the game, outside the magic circle). Examples of the kinds of activities available in a shell menu include loading and saving the game, setting the audio volume and screen resolution, and reconfiguring the

KEY POINT

If a player can take an action that influences the core mechanics—even if that influence is deferred—the game is in a gameplay mode. If he cannot, the game is in a shell menu or shell screen.

input devices for the player's convenience. A pause menu in a game is also a shell menu unless it lets the player take some action that affects the game world (such as making strategic adjustments in a sports game), in which case it is a gameplay mode. Noninteractive sequences such as cut-scenes and title screens are called shell screens.

Forming the Structure

The gameplay modes and shell menus of the game collectively make up the structure of the game. To document the structure, you can begin by making a list of all the modes and menus in the game. You must also include a description of *when* and *why* the game switches from one mode or menu to another: what event, or menu selection, causes it to change. Each mode or menu description should include a list of other modes and menus it can switch to and, for each possible switch, a notation about what causes it.

You can document the relationships among all the modes and menus by simply listing them all in a text editor. However, the result isn't easy to follow. We recommend that you document the structure of a game with a *flowboard,* a type of diagram described in the section *Flowboard,* later in this chapter.

Normally, a game moves among its shell menus in response to player actions and nothing else, although arcade games often display an ***attract loop*** that repeatedly shows a title screen, a short noninteractive video of a game in progress, and a high score table. During actual play, a game changes from one gameplay mode to another in response to player actions, or automatically as the circumstances of the game require. For example, in a soccer game, certain violations of the rules result in a penalty kick, in which a single athlete on one team tries to kick the ball past the opposing team's goalie and into the goal and the other athletes on both teams play no role. This is clearly a gameplay mode different from normal play. It is entered not by a specific player choice but by the occurrence of a rule violation.

Stages of the Design Process

Now that you have learned about the player-centric approach to game design and the key components and structure of a video game, you are ready to start thinking about how to go about designing one. Unfortunately, there are so many kinds of video games in the world that it is impossible to define a simple step-by-step process that will produce a single design document all ready for people to turn into content and code. Furthermore, unless a game is very small, it is not possible to create a complete design and then code it up afterwards. That is how

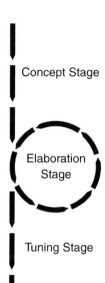

FIGURE 2.6 Three stages of the design process.

the game industry built games in the 1980s, but experience has shown that large games must be designed and constructed in an iterative process, with repeated playtesting and tuning, and occasional modifications to the design, throughout development. However, not all parts of the design process can be revisited. Some, such as the choice of concept, audience, and genre, should be decided once at the beginning and not changed thereafter. The process is therefore divided into three major parts:

- The ***concept stage,*** which you perform first and whose results do not change

- The ***elaboration stage,*** in which you add most of the design details and refine your decisions through prototyping and playtesting

- The ***tuning stage,*** at which point no new features may be added, but you can make small adjustments to polish the game

We have chosen to use the term *elaboration stage* rather than *development stage* because the latter runs the risk of being confused with *game development.* Figure 2.6 shows the three stages of the design process.

Each of these stages includes a number of design tasks. In the sections that follow, we will look at each stage and the different tasks that you will perform.

Chris Bateman and Richard Boon discuss the relative merits of various design processes in Chapter 1 of their book *21st Century Game Design* (Bateman, and Boon, 2006), and we encourage you to look at it for further discussion on the subject.

The Concept Stage

Client 2:   *Do I take it that you are proposing to slaughter our tenants?*
Mr. Wiggin: *Does that not fit in with your plans?*
Client 1:   *Not really. We asked for a simple block of flats.*
Mr. Wiggin: *Oh. I hadn't fully divined your attitude towards the tenants. You see I mainly design slaughterhouses.*

—*Monty Python's Flying Circus*, "The Architect Sketch"

In the concept stage of game design, you make decisions that you will live with for the life of the project. This stage establishes things about the game that are so fundamental, changing them later would wreak havoc on the development process because a great deal of the work done to implement the game would have to be thrown away. It's like constructing a building: You can revise the color scheme and the lighting design while it's still under construction, but you can't decide that you really wanted an airport instead of a hotel once the foundations are poured.

FYI *Concept Versus Preproduction*

Be sure that you don't confuse the concept stage of *design* with the preproduction stage of game *development*. Preproduction is a process borrowed from filmmaking. It's a planning stage of game development during which a developer is deciding what sort of game to make, testing some of those ideas, and figuring out the budget, schedule, and staff requirements. Preproduction ends when the funding agency, usually a publisher, gives the game the green light to proceed to full production. By that time, the concept stage of design is already over and the elaboration stage has begun. In fact, quite a lot of design work gets done during preproduction because that's how the team decides what the game will be. The concept stage of design usually requires only a few weeks; the preproduction stage of development can go on for several months.

Getting a Concept   All game designs must begin with a game concept; that is, a general idea of how you intend to entertain someone through gameplay and, at a deeper level, *why* you believe it will be a compelling experience. Many different considerations will influence your plans for the game concept. Part of creating a game concept includes deciding what genre your game will fit into, if any. Defining and refining a game concept is described in detail in Chapter 3, "Game Concepts."

Defining an Audience   Once you know what kind of experience you want to present, you have to think about who would enjoy that experience. In a commercial environment, publishers sometimes define their audience—a "target market"—and *then* think of a concept for a game to sell to them. In any case, the choices you make here will have important consequences for your game because, in player-centric design, you test every design decision against your hypothetical representative player to be sure that the decision helps to entertain your target audience.

Determining the Player's Role   In an abstract video game, the player doesn't get immersed in a fictional game world and so doesn't have much of a role. He is simply a player playing the game for its own sake. But in a representational game, the player does a lot more pretending. He pretends to believe in the game world, the avatar, and the situations the game puts him in. In such games, the player plays a role, and as a designer it is up to you to define what that role is. It could be an athlete, a general, a dancer, an explorer, a business tycoon, or any of a million other things that people fantasize about doing. Sometimes the roles in a game are multifaceted: In a sports game, the player often changes roles from an athlete on the field; to the coach planning strategy; to the general manager hiring and trading players. You must be able to explain the player's role clearly, because the role a game offers is part of how publishers decide to whether to fund that game, as well as how players decide whether to buy it.

Fulfilling the Dream   Abstract video games have arbitrary rules, so the player seldom has any preconceptions about what the game will, or won't, allow her to do. Representational video games, however, take place in a world that is at least somewhat familiar, and the player will come to the game with certain expectations and hopes. Representational games are about *fulfilling dreams*—dreams of achievement, of power, of creation, or simply of doing certain things and having certain experiences.

Once you have a game concept, a role, and an audience in mind, it's time to begin thinking about how you will fulfill your player's dream. What is the essence of the experience that you are going to offer? What kinds of challenges will the player expect to face, and what kinds of actions will she expect to perform? Deciding what it means to fulfill the dream is the first step on the road to defining the gameplay itself.

COMMANDMENT: Concept Elements Are Permanent

You must not make changes to the concept elements of your game—the game concept, audience, player's role, and dream that it fulfills—once you have started into the elaboration stage of design.

The Elaboration Stage

Once you have made the fundamental decisions about your game in the concept stage, it's time to move into the elaboration stage of design. At this point, your design work will begin to move from the general to the specific; from the theoretical to the concrete. In the elaboration stage, you normally begin working with a small development team to construct a prototype of the game. If you are planning to incorporate radically new ideas or new technology, your team may also build a testbed or technical demonstration to try them out. From this point on, you may take your design ideas and have the development team implement them in the prototype to see how they work in practice. Based on what you learn, you can then go back and refine them.

At some point during the elaboration stage, your game will (you hope!) get the green light from a funding agency and proceed to full production.

FYI | *The Danger of Irresolution*

The transition from the concept to the elaboration stage of design is a critical time. At this point, the most important decisions are "set in stone," so to speak; the foundations are poured. Some designers are reluctant to make this transition; they say they're "keeping their options open." They're afraid that they might have made a bad decision or that they might have overlooked something. The consequences of this irresolution are usually disastrous. If the most critical details are still shifting as the game goes into full production, the development team is never entirely sure what it's trying to build. The designer keeps coming around and asking for changes that require huge revisions to the code and content. Production becomes slow and inefficient. It's a sure sign of a lack of vision and confidence. Projects that get into this quagmire are usually cancelled rather than completed.

When you begin the elaboration stage, if you have a team of several people, it becomes possible to begin working on the design tasks in parallel. Once you are all agreed upon the fundamentals of the game, each designer can start work on his own particular area of responsibility.

This process of iterative refinement is not an excuse for introducing major changes into the game late in its development, nor for tweaking it endlessly without ever declaring it finished. Your goal is to build and ship a completed product.

Defining the Primary Gameplay Mode   The first task after you have locked down your concept is to define the primary gameplay mode of the game, the mode in which the player will spend the majority of his time. Most games have one clearly obvious gameplay mode. In a car racing game, it's driving the car. Tuning the car up in the shop is a secondary mode. In war games, the primary gameplay mode is usually tactical—fighting battles. War games often have a strategic mode as well, in which the player plans battles or chooses areas to conquer on a map, but he generally spends much less time doing that than he does fighting.

At this point it's not necessary to define every detail. The main things to work on are the components that make up the mode: the perspective in which the player will view the game world, the interaction model in which he will influence the game world, the challenges the world will present to him in that mode, and the actions available to him to overcome those challenges. Get those decisions down on paper, and then you can move on to the details of exactly how this is to happen.

Designing the Protagonist   If your game is to have a single main character who is the protagonist (whether or not the interaction model is avatar-based), it is essential that you design this character early on. You want the player to like and to identify with the protagonist, to care about what happens to her. If the perspective you chose for the primary gameplay mode was anything other than first person, the player is going to spend a lot of time looking at this character, so it's important that she be fun to watch. You must think about how she looks and also about how she behaves: what actions she is capable of, what emotions her face and body language can register, and what kind of language and vocabulary she uses. These issues are discussed in depth in Chapter 6, "Character Development."

Defining the Game World   The game world is where your game takes place, and defining it can be an enormous task. If the game world is based on the real world (as in a flight simulator, for example), then you can use photographs and maps of real places in order to create its appearance. But if it's a fantasy or science fiction world, you will have to rely on your imagination. And look and feel are only part of the task. There are many dimensions to a game world: physical, temporal, environmental, emotional, and ethical. All these qualities exist to serve and support the gameplay of your game, but they also entertain in their own right. We discuss defining the game world in Chapter 4, "Game Worlds."

Designing the Core Mechanics   Once you have a sense of the kinds of challenges and actions that you want to include in the primary gameplay mode, you can begin thinking about how the core mechanics will create those challenges and implement the actions. For example, if you plan to challenge the player to accumulate money, you have to define where the money comes from and what the player has to do to get hold of it. If you challenge the player to play a sport, you must think about all the athletic characteristics—speed, strength, acceleration, accuracy, and so on—that may be required by the sport. If your challenges involve symbolic rather than numeric relationships, as in a puzzle game, you will have to think about what those symbols are and how they are manipulated. Core mechanics are discussed in Chapter 10, "Core Mechanics."

Creating Additional Modes   As you were deciding upon your game concept, you may have realized that you would need more than one gameplay mode—for example, if you wanted to include separate strategic and tactical modes in a war game, or managing income and expenditures in a business simulation. Or you may have discovered that you will need additional modes while you were defining the primary gameplay mode and core mechanics. Now that you're in the elaboration stage, design the additional modes: their perspective, interaction model, and gameplay. You must also document what causes your game to move from mode to mode—the structure of your game, as described earlier in this chapter.

Do not create additional modes unnecessarily. Every extra mode requires more design work, more artwork, more programming, and more testing. It also complicates your game. Each mode should add to the player's entertainment and serve an important purpose that the game genuinely needs.

Level Design   Level design is the process of constructing the experience that will be offered directly to the player, using the components provided by the game design: the characters, challenges, actions, game world, core mechanics, and storyline if there is one. These components don't have to be completely finished in order for level design to begin, but there must be enough in place for a level designer to have something to work with. In the early part of the elaboration stage, the level designers will be working to create a typical *first playable* level. This level should not be the first one that the *player* will encounter because the first level in the game will be atypical as the player is still learning to play the game. Rather, it's called *first playable* because it's the first one the level designers create.

Creating a working first playable level is an important milestone in the development of a game because it means that testers can begin testing it. We discuss level design in Chapter 12, "General Principles of Level Design."

Writing the Story   Small video games seldom bother with a story, but large ones usually include a story of some kind. Stories help to keep the player interested and involved. They give her a reason to go on to the next level, to see what happens next. A story may be integrated with the gameplay in a number of different ways. Your story may occur within the levels as the player plays or it may simply be a transition mechanism between the levels—a reward for completing a level. The story may be embedded, with prewritten narrative chunks, or emergent, arising out of the core mechanics. It may be linear and independent of the player's actions, or it may go in different directions based on the player's choices. We address all these issues in detail in Chapter 7, "Storytelling and Narrative." However you choose to do it, you will be defining the story during the elaboration stage, usually in close conjunction with level design.

Build, Test, and Iterate   The great game designer Mark Cerny (*Spyro the Dragon, Jak and Daxter*) asserts that during the preproduction process of development, you should build, test, and then throw away no less than four different prototypes of your game. This may be extreme, but the underlying principle is correct. Video games must be prototyped before they can be built for real, and they must be tested at every step along the way. Each new idea must be constructed and tried out, preferably in a quick-and-dirty fashion first, before it is incorporated into the completed product. Cerny also argues that none of the materials you create for prototyping should ever find their way into the final product— or at least, that you should never count on it. By having a firm rule to this effect, you free your programmers and artists to work quickly to build the testbed, secure in the knowledge that they won't have to debug it later. If they're thinking about building maintainable code or final-quality artwork during the preproduction stage of development, the testing process will take far longer than it should.

Once development shifts from preproduction to production, the team is working on material that *will* go out to the customer, and it has to be built with special care. However, you still can't simply design something, hand your design off to the programmers, and forget it. Everything you design must be built, tested, and refined as you go. This is why in modern game development testers are brought in right from the beginning of a project rather than at the end as they used to be.

This is a book about game design, not game development and production, so we won't be discussing the details of managing production here. We recommend that you read *Game Architecture and Design* (Rollings and Morris, 2003) to learn about those processes.

The Tuning Stage

When you went from the concept stage to the elaboration stage, you locked down the game concept—the foundations of the game. During the elaboration stage, you fleshed out the concept and added new features as necessary. At some point, however, there will come a time at which the *entire* design must be locked—that is, no more features may be added to the game—and you enter the tuning stage. There's no good way to know exactly when this is. It's usually dictated by the schedule. If it would take all the remaining time left to complete and debug the game as the design stands, then clearly you can't add anything more to the design without making the project late! However, this is more of a reactive than a proactive approach to the issue. The design should really be locked at the point at which the designers feel that it is complete and harmonious, even if there is time for more design work.

Once the design has been locked, there's still work for the designers to do. Design work enters the tuning stage, during which you can make small adjustments to the levels and core mechanics of the game as long as you don't introduce any new features. This stage, more than any other, is what makes the difference between a merely good game and a truly great one. Tune and polish your game until it's perfect. Polishing is a subtractive process, not an additive one. You're not putting on new bells and whistles but removing imperfections and making the game shine.

Game Design Teams

A large video game is almost always designed by a team. Unlike Hollywood, in which guilds and unions define the job roles, the game industry's job titles and responsibilities are not standardized from one company to another. Companies tend to give people titles and tasks in accordance with their abilities and, more important, the needs of a project. However, over the years a few roles have evolved whose responsibilities are largely similar regardless of what game or project they are part of.

- **Lead Designer.** This person oversees the overall design of the game and is responsible for making sure that it is complete and coherent. She is the "keeper of the vision" at the highest and most abstract level. She also evangelizes the game to others both inside and outside the company and is often called upon to serve as a spokesperson for the project. Not all the lead designer's work is creative. As the head of a team, she trades away creativity for authority, and her primary role is to make sure that the design work is getting done and the other team members are doing their jobs properly. A project will have only one lead designer.

- **Game Designer.** The game designer defines and documents how the game actually works: its gameplay and its internal economy. Game designers also conduct background research and assemble data that the game may need. On a large project, these jobs may be split up among several game designers, all reporting to the lead designer.

- **Level Designer.** Level designers take the essential components of the game provided by the game designers—the user interface, core mechanics, and gameplay—and use those components to design and construct the individual levels that the player will play through in the course of a game. Level design used to be considered an inferior position to game designer, but modern level designers frequently need to be able to build 3D models and program in scripting languages. As a result, level design is now a specialized skill, or set of skills, and is considered just as important as game design. A project usually has several level designers reporting either to a lead level designer or to the lead designer.

- **User Interface Designer.** If a project includes this as a separate role, the role may be filled by one or more people responsible for designing the layout of the screen in the various gameplay modes of the game and the function of the input devices. In large, complex games, this can easily be a full-time task. An otherwise brilliant game can be ruined by a bad user interface, so it is a good idea to have a specialist on board. Large developers are increasingly turning to usability experts from other software industries to help them test and refine their interfaces.

- **Writer.** Writers are responsible for creating the instructional or fictional content of the game: introductory material, backstory, dialog, cut-scenes, and so on. (Writers do not, generally speaking, do technical writing—that is the responsibility of the game designers.) Few games require a full-time writer; the work is often subcontracted to a freelancer or done by one of the other designers.

Two other positions have a large amount of creative influence on a game, although they do not normally report to the lead designer. Rather, they are people with whom a game designer can expect to have a lot of interaction over the course of a project.

- **Art Director.** The art director, who may also be called the lead artist, manages production of all the visual assets in the game: models, textures, sprites, animations, user interface elements, and so on. The art director also plays a major role in creating and enforcing the visual style of the game. Within the team hierarchy, the art director is usually at the same level as the lead designer, so it is imperative that the two of them have a good working relationship and similar goals for the project.

- **Audio Director.** Like the art director, the audio director of a game oversees production of all the audible assets in the game: music, ambient sounds, effects, and dialog or narration. Typically there is not as much of this material as there is of artwork, so the audio director may be working on several projects at once. Audio is critical to creating a mood for the game, and the lead designer and audio director work together to establish what kinds of sounds are needed to produce it.

COMMANDMENT: Don't Design by Committee

Do not treat the design work as a democratic process in which each person's opinion has equal value ("design by committee"). One person must have the authority to make final decisions, and the others must acknowledge this person's authority.

Documenting the Design

As part of their job, game designers produce a series of documents to tell others about their game design. Exactly what documents they produce and what the documents are for vary from designer to designer and project to project—but they usually follow a common thread.

Why Do We Need Documents?

Beginning programmers, especially those who want to get into the game industry, often make the mistake of thinking up a game and then diving in and starting to program it right away. In modern commercial game development, however, this kind of ad hoc approach is disastrous. Different projects require different degrees of formality, but all serious game companies now insist on having some kind of written documentation as design work progresses.

As we said before, a key part of game design is transmitting the design to other members of the team. In practice, a lot of that communication takes place not through the documents themselves but during team meetings and conversations over lunch. That doesn't mean that there's no point in writing design documents, however. The documents record decisions made and agreed upon orally; they create a paper trail. More important, the process of writing a document turns a vague idea into an explicit plan. Even if no one reads it at all, an idea written down is a decision made, a conclusion reached. If a feature of a game is not described in writing, there's a good chance that it has been overlooked and that someone will have to make it up on the fly—or, worse, that each part of the team will have a different idea of what they intended to do. It's far easier and cheaper to correct a design error before any code is written or artwork is created. Depending on the size of the game, wise developers will allot anywhere from one to six months for pure design work before starting on development, usually in combination with some throwaway prototype for testing gameplay ideas.

IN THE TRENCHES: Game Idea Versus Design Decision

Here's a game idea: "Dragons should protect their eggs."

Here's a design decision: "Whenever they have eggs in their nests, female dragons will not move beyond visual range from the nest. If an enemy approaches within 50 meters of the nest, the dragon will abandon any other activity and return to the nest to defend the eggs. She will not leave the nest until no enemy has been within the 50 meter radius for at least 30 seconds. She will defend the eggs to her death."

See the difference? This is what creating design documents is about.

Types of Design Documents

This section is a short introduction to the various types of documents a game designer might be asked to create. This isn't an exhaustive list, nor will every project need all of the items on the list. Rather, these are some of the most commonly used ones.

The high concept and game treatment documents are sales tools, designed to help communicate the game concept to a funding agency such as a publisher. They are usually written in a word processor such as Microsoft Word and distributed in paper form. The other documents used to be written on paper as well, but it is increasingly common in the game industry to create them as pages on a Web site. As long as you can keep the Web site secure, it's a good way of documenting a game design so that all the members of the team can access it, and you can update it easily. You'll need a good site construction tool such as NetObjects Fusion. Another, even easier, alternative is to create a wiki, a tool for letting anybody read and edit hypertext documents. Once the wiki software is installed on the company server, the whole team can edit the content using only a browser. It's important to make sure you have revision control and backups so that you can revert to a previous edition if someone deletes a page by accident.

Companion Website

You can find samples (or pointers to samples) of design documents on the Companion Website.

High Concept Document   The high concept document is not a document from which to build the game. Just as the purpose of a résumé is to get you a job interview, the purpose of a high concept document is to get you a hearing from someone, a producer or publishing executive. It puts your key ideas down on paper in a bite-size chunk that he can read in a few minutes. Like a résumé, it should be short—not more than two to four pages long.

It's also worthwhile to write high concept documents for yourself, to record ideas that you might want to work on in the future.

Game Treatment Document   A game treatment presents the game in a broad outline to someone who's already interested in it and wants to hear more about it. Like a high concept document, it's primarily a sales tool. The treatment is designed both to satisfy initial curiosity and to stimulate real enthusiasm for the game. When you give a presentation about your game to a publisher, you should hand him the game treatment at the end so he'll have something to take away and look at, something that will float around his office and remind him of your game. Your goal at this point is to get funding of some sort, either to create a more thorough design or a prototype or (preferably!) to develop the entire game.

The initial treatment is still a simple document—almost a brochure that sums up the basic ideas in the game. A good way of picturing what to write in a treatment is to imagine that you are making a Web site to help sell your game; then throw in some business and development details for good measure.

Character Design Document   A character design document is specifically intended to record the design of one character who will appear in your game, most often an avatar. Its primary purpose is to show the character's appearance and above all her *moveset*—a list of animations that documents how she moves, both voluntarily and involuntarily. It should include plenty of concept art of the character in different poses and with different facial expressions. In addition, it should include background information about the character that will help to inform future decisions: her history, values, likes and dislikes, strengths and weaknesses, and so on. Character design is discussed in Chapter 6, "Character Development."

World Design Document   The world design document is the basis for building all the art and audio that portray your game world. It's not a precise list of everything in the game but, rather, background information about the kinds of things the world will contain. If you have a large landscape or cityscape, for example, the world design document should include a map. You need not supply every detail, just a general overview. This information will be used by the level designers and artists to create the actual content. Be sure also to note the sources of ambient sounds in the world so the audio designers can build them in at the appropriate locations.

 The world design document should also document the "feel" of the world, its aesthetic style and emotional tone. If you want to arouse particular emotions through images and music, indicate how you will do so here.

Flowboard   A flowboard is, as the name suggests, a cross between a flowchart and a storyboard. Storyboards are linear documents used by filmmakers to plan a series of shots; flowcharts are used by programmers (though rarely nowadays) to document an algorithm. A flowboard combines these two ideas to document the structure of a game.

 Although you can create a flowboard in an editor such as Visio, it's actually quicker and easier to make one on several sheets of paper and stick them on a large blank wall. Each sheet of paper is used to document one gameplay mode or shell menu. On each page, write the name of the mode clearly at the top. Then, in the center of the page, draw a quick sketch of the screen as it will appear in the mode, showing the perspective (if appropriate) and user interface items that will appear on it. Leave plenty of space around the edges. Off to the sides of the sketch, document the menu items and inputs available to the player and what they do. You can also list the challenges that will arise in that mode, although that's less important—the key thing is to indicate the player actions that will be available. Then draw arrows leading to the other gameplay modes or shell menus and indicate under what circumstances the game makes a transition from the current mode to the next one. By creating one mode per page and putting them up on the wall, you allow everyone in the office to see the structure of the game. You can also easily make revisions by adding new sheets and marking up the existing ones.

Story and Level Progression Document   This document records the large-scale story of your game, if it has one, and the way the levels will progress from one to the next. If you're making a small game with only one level (such as a board game in computerized form) or a game with no story, you need not create this document. However, if the game will have more than one level, or the player will experience a distinct sense of progress throughout the game, then you will need such a document. You're not trying to record everything that can happen in the game, but rather a general outline of the player's experience from beginning to end. If the game's story will branch based upon the player's actions, this is the place to document it and indicate what decisions will cause the game to take one path rather than another. Here also you indicate *how* the player will experience the story: whether it's told via cut-scenes, mission briefings, dialog, or other narrative elements.

Bear in mind that the story or level progression is not the same as the game's structure. An entire story can take place in only one gameplay mode; likewise, a game can have many different gameplay modes but no story at all. Although the game changes from mode to mode over time, and the story also progresses over time, the two are not necessarily related.

The Game Script Document   Back when games were smaller, it was common to incorporate all of the preceding documents except for the high concept and treatment into a single massive tome, the game script (or "bible"). As games have gotten larger, the industry has tended to break out the character, world, and story documentation into individual documents to make them more manageable. The game script is still used, however, to document a key area not covered by the others: the rules and core mechanics of the game.

As a good rule of thumb, the game script should enable you to play the game. That is, it should specify the rules of play in enough detail that you could, in theory, play the game without the use of computer—maybe as a (complicated) board game or table-top role-playing game. This doesn't mean you should actually sit down and play it as such, but it should theoretically be possible to do so, based solely on the game script document. Sitting down and playing paper versions of game ideas is a very inexpensive way of getting valuable feedback on your game design. For designers without huge teams and equally huge budgets, we heartily encourage paper-play testing.

The game script does not include the technical design, though it may include the target machine and minimum technical specifications required. However, it does not address how the game is built or implemented in software. The technical design document, if there is one, is usually based on the game script and is written by the lead programmer or technical director for the game. Technical design is beyond the scope of this book. If you want to know more about technical design, read *Game Architecture and Design* (Rollings and Morris, 2003).

Anatomy of a Game Designer

Like all crafts, game design requires both talent and skill. Talent is innate, but skill is learned. Effective game designers require a wide base of skills. The following sections discuss some of the skills that are most useful for the professional game designer. Don't be discouraged if you don't possess all of them. It's a wish list—the characteristics we would like to see in a hypothetical "ideal designer."

Imagination

A game exists in an artificial universe, a make-believe place governed by make-believe rules. Imagination is essential to creating this place. It comes in various forms:

- Visual and auditory imagination enables you to think of new buildings, trees, animals, creatures, clothing, and people—how they look and sound.

- Dramatic imagination is required for the development of good characters, plots, scenes, motivations, emotions, climaxes, and conclusions.

- Conceptual imagination is about relationships between ideas, their interactions and dependencies.

- Lateral thinking is the process of looking for alternative answers, taking an unexpected route to solve a problem.

- Deduction is the process of reasoning from a creative decision you've made to its possible consequences. Deduction isn't ordinarily thought of as imagination, but the conclusions you arrive at will produce new material for your game.

FYI *Imagination Includes Adaptation*

Imagination does not consist only of the ability to invent new things. It's also valuable to be able to look at an old idea and breathe new life into it with a fresh approach. J.K. Rowling does this brilliantly in her *Harry Potter* novels. She still has witches flying on broomsticks, but she invented the sport of Quidditch, which is played while flying on them.

Technical Awareness

Technical awareness is a general understanding of how computer programs, particularly games, actually work. You don't have to be a software engineer, but it is extremely valuable to have had a little programming experience. Level designers, in particular, often need to be able to program in simple scripting languages. Get to know the technical capabilities of your target platform. You must also be aware of what your machine cannot do (for example, understand ordinary speech) so that you won't create unworkable designs.

Analytical Competence

Analytical competence is the ability to study and dissect something: an idea, a problem, or an entire game design. No design is perfect from the start; game design is a process of iterative refinement. Consequently, you must be able to recognize the good and bad parts of a design for what they are.

One example of an analytical task is detecting dominant (that is, unbeatable or nearly unbeatable) strategies at the design phase and weeding them out before they get into the code, as in the infamous *Red Alert* "tank rush." In *Command & Conquer: Red Alert,* tanks on the Soviet side were so much more effective than any other unit that an experienced player could dedicate all production to cranking out a few tanks and then immediately storm the opposition base before the enemy had a chance to get a production line set up.

Mathematical Competence

Designers must have basic math skills, including trigonometry and the simpler principles of probability. Balancing games that feature complex internal economies, such as business simulations or real-time strategy games, can require you to spend a lot of time looking at numbers. You don't need a PhD in mathematics, but you should be comfortable with the subject. You may be able to handle most of the requirements with a spreadsheet program such as Microsoft Excel.

Aesthetic Competence

Although you need not be an artist, you should have a general aesthetic competence and some sense of style. Far too many games are visual clones of one another, depending on stereotypes and clichés rather than real imagination. It's up to you (along with your lead artist) to set the visual tone of the game and to create a consistent, harmonious look.

We encourage you to expand your aesthetic horizons as much as you can. Learn a little about the fundamentals of art: the principles of composition, and which colors coordinate and which clash. Find out about famous art movements—Art Nouveau, Surrealism, Impressionism—and how they changed the way we see things. Watch movies that are famous for their visual style, such as *Metropolis*. Then move on to the more practical arts: architecture, interior decoration, industrial design. The more aesthetic experience you have, the more likely you are to produce an artistically innovative product.

General Knowledge and the Ability to Research

The most imaginative game designers are those who have been broadly educated and are interested in a wide variety of things. It helps to be well versed in such topics as history, literature, art, science, and political affairs. More important, you must know how to research the subject of your game. It's tempting just to use a search engine on the Internet, but that's not very efficient because the information it presents will be haphazard and disorganized and might not be reliable. The encyclopedia is a better place to start for any given subject. From there, you can increase your knowledge of a particular area by moving on to more specialized books or TV documentaries.

Writing Skills

A professional game designer actually spends most of his time writing, so a designer *must* have good writing skills. This means being clear, concise, accurate, and unambiguous. Apart from having to write several detailed documents for each design, you might be expected to produce the story narrative or dialog—especially if the budget won't stretch to a scriptwriter.

Design writing comes in several forms:

- Technical writing is the process of documenting the design in preparation for development. The essential mechanisms of the game have to be answered unambiguously and precisely.

- Fiction writing (narrative) creates the story of the game as a whole—a critical part of the design process if the game has a strong storyline. Some of this material may appear in the finished product as text or voiceover narration. The game's manual, if there is one, often includes fictional material as well.

- Dialog writing (drama) is needed for audio voiceovers and cinematic material. Dialog conveys character, and it also can form part of the plot. A class in playwriting or screenwriting will teach you a lot about writing dialog.

A designer must be able to convey the details of the design to the rest of the team, create the textual and spoken material that will appear in the game, and help sell the idea to a publisher. Good writing skills are essential to accomplish these things successfully.

2

Drawing Skills

Some skill at basic drawing and sketching is highly valuable, although not absolutely required for a designer if you have a concept artist to work with. The vast majority of computer games rely heavily on visual content, and drawings are essential when pitching a product to a third party. Game-publishing executives will be interested in a hot concept, a hot market, or a hot license, but only pictures really excite them. The images will remain in their memories long after they forget the details.

The Ability to Compromise

A professional game designer must be able to compromise on details and integrate a variety of opinions while preserving a consistent, holistic vision of the game. Different people on the development team and at the publishing company will have concerns about their own areas of expertise (programming, art, music, and so on), and their opinions will pull and push the design in different directions. As the designer, you may be tempted to seek sole ownership of the vision and insist that things must be exactly as you imagined them. You must resist the temptation to do that, for two reasons:

- First, you must allow your team some ownership of the vision as well, or its members won't have any motivation or enthusiasm for the project. No one builds computer games solely for the money; we're all here so that we can contribute creatively.

- Second, a designer who can't deliver in a team environment, no matter how visionary she may be, doesn't stay employed for long. You must be able to work successfully with other people.

Compromise means more than just negotiating with other people, however; it also means working within the prevailing circumstances. In many cases, you'll be given a task that limits you to designing a genre clone or a heavily restricted licensed property. On a commercial project, you will almost certainly be told, rather than get to choose, the target hardware upon which your game will run. Your project will always have a desired budget and schedule that it is expected to meet. A professional designer must be able to work within these constraints and to make the compromises necessary to do so.

Summary

This chapter puts forward the view that game design is not an arcane art but rather a craft, just like any other, that can be learned with application.

Video games are not created by a mysterious, hit-or-miss process. Instead, they are recreational experiences that the designer provides to the players through rules and a presentation layer. A game is designed by creating a concept and iden-tifying an audience in the concept stage, fleshing out the details and turning abstract ideas into concrete plans in the elaboration stage, and adjusting the fine points in the tuning stage. All video games have a structure, made up of gameplay modes and shell menus, that you must document so your teams know what they are building and how it fits together. In the course of this process, you will use a wide variety of skills to create a wide variety of documents for your team. And at all times, you should seek to create an integrated, coherent experience for your player that meets your most important obligation: to entertain her.

Test Your Skills

MULTIPLE CHOICE QUESTIONS

1. Which of the following is *not* an essential skill for a game designer?

   A. Technical writing.

   B. Research.

   C. Programming.

   D. Fiction writing.

2. Game design is which of the following?

   A. An art.

   B. A form of engineering.

   C. A science.

   D. A craft.

3. Which are the two duties of a designer using the player-centric approach?

   A. To empathize and to entertain.

   B. To impress and to make money.

   C. To be imaginative and to be efficient.

   D. To be accurate and under budget.

4. A gameplay mode is

   A. any kind of menu that appears in a game.

   B. the subset of a game's gameplay that is available at one time, plus the user interface that presents it.

   C. the state of the core mechanics at any given point in the game.

   D. a document for defining the gameplay.

5. A flowboard is a means of documenting a game's
   A. programming.
   B. artwork.
   C. story.
   D. structure.

2

6. Which of the following is *not* an interaction model?
   A. Avatar-based.
   B. Multipresence.
   C. Third-person.
   D. Contestant.

7. Which of the following design tasks belongs in the concept stage?
   A. Level design.
   B. Designing the core mechanics.
   C. Designing the game world.
   D. Identifying an audience.

8. Which of the following must you *not* do after leaving the concept stage?
   A. Redefine the game concept.
   B. Modify the core mechanics.
   C. Change the game's story.
   D. Add any additional gameplay modes.

9. In the tuning stage, the designer's function is restricted to
   A. testing the game.
   B. refining details without adding features.
   C. adding only minor gameplay modes.
   D. writing and recording dialog.

10. On a large design team, the lead designer's job is primarily to
    A. work with the marketing team to devise the best way to sell the game.
    B. create and document the core mechanics.
    C. oversee the work of the other designers.
    D. negotiate with the publisher.

11. Which of the following design documents is primarily a sales tool rather than a design tool?

    A. The game script.

    B. The flowboard.

    C. The game treatment.

    D. The world design.

12. Which document is one that a game designer does not create?

    A. The high concept.

    B. The technical design.

    C. The story and level progression.

    D. The flowboard.

EXERCISES

Companion
Website

In these exercises, you will document existing games for practice. Your instructor may require that you do so with certain particular games that he is familiar with and will set the expected scope of the work—the amount of material he wants to see. Use a document template from the Companion Website or one supplied by your instructor.

1. Document the primary gameplay mode of a reasonably simple game that you like. Be sure to include a sketch of the screen, including perspective and user interface; a list of all the buttons and menu items available in that mode; and a list of the other modes that this mode can switch to. Describe the challenges and actions that make up the mode.

2. Take a classic, well-known arcade game with a small number of gameplay modes and shell menus, and create a flowboard for it. (As you cannot hand in an entire wall of pages, create a miniature version with two or three gameplay modes per sheet.)

3. Document the level progression of a well-known game that you have played all the way through, such as *StarCraft* or *Doom 3*. (If the game does not have explicit levels, as in *Half-Life,* document major areas or sections of the game.) Describe the game world in each level and the types of challenges that it presents. If the levels are integrated into a story, explain how each level supports or relates to the story.

4. Research one of the following art or design styles from history and write a short paper to explain how it might help to establish an emotional tone in a video game: Impressionism, Constructivism, Symbolism, Pop Art, Art Deco, Art Nouveau. Back up your argument with examples from famous paintings or other works in that style.

DISCUSSION QUESTIONS

1. What are the strengths and weaknesses of player-centric game design? In what ways might it conflict with other requirements imposed on the game or the desires of the game designer?

2. Do you feel that our list of qualities in an ideal game designer is complete? What other qualities might you add? Are there any that you would remove?

3. Our list of members of a design team does not include a lead programmer. Should it? Suggest some arguments for and against.

Chapter | **3**

Game Concepts

Chapter Objectives

After reading this chapter and completing the exercises, you will be able to do the following:

- Take a game idea and add the necessary material to make it into a design concept.
- Define the player's role or roles in the game.
- Know the different genres of games and think about which one your game may belong to.
- Know how to choose a target audience for your game and understand some of the special considerations associated with designing for specialized markets such as children, the disabled, and foreign consumers.
- Plan the progress of your game.
- Understand the differences among the various kinds of game machines and how those differences affect the way people play on them.

Introduction

Designing a video game begins with an idea. This chapter discusses how to turn that idea into a *game concept,* a more fleshed-out version of the idea that can be used as the basis for further discussion and development. Creating a game concept is what you do in the concept stage of game design. Your goal at this point should be to write the high concept document that we described in Chapter 2, "Design Components and Processes." To do this, you don't have to have all the details worked out yet, but you do need a clear understanding of what your game is about, and you must be able to answer certain essential questions about the game itself, the player's role in it, and the target audience. Here, we discuss how to make those decisions.

Getting an Idea

You can find game ideas almost anywhere but only if you're looking for them. Creativity is an active, not a passive, process. Look everywhere; some of the most mundane things could be hiding a game idea. *BurgerTime,* for instance, was a silly but highly successful arcade game about assembling hamburgers.

One idea isn't enough. It's a common misconception that a brilliant game idea will make you a fortune. In fact, this occurs extremely rarely. Even if you think you have the game idea of the century, you should always be on the lookout for more. Make a note of each one and go on. If one seems especially promising, then you can start to expand and refine it, but don't let that prevent you from thinking about other games as well. When coming up with game ideas, more is always better.

Dreaming the Dream

A lot of computer games are light entertainment, designed to while away a few minutes with a puzzle or a simple challenge. But larger, richer games begin with a dream. If you've ever thought to yourself, "I wish I could . . . " or "Imagine what it would be like to . . . ," then you've taken an important step on the road to creating a computer game. Computers can create almost any sort of visual experience you can imagine, even experiences that are physically impossible in the real world. The design of a computer game begins with the question, "What dream am I going to fulfill?"

Perhaps it's a dream of exploring a dungeon infested with monsters. Perhaps it's a dream of coaching a football team. Perhaps it's a dream of being a fashion designer. But before you do anything else, you must dream the dream. Understand it. Feel it. Know who else dreams it and why.

Game Ideas from Other Media

Books, movies, television, and other entertainment media can be great sources of inspiration for game ideas, so long as the ideas include plenty of activity. Cop shows from the 1970s inspired the game *Interstate '76* (see Figure 3.1). Movies such as the James Bond series often inspire games. Any story containing exciting action with something important at stake can form the kernel of a game. Think over the books you've read and the movies you've seen and ask yourself whether any of the activities in them could serve as the basis for a game.

You can't, of course, steal other people's intellectual property. Even if the *Pirates of the Caribbean* ride at Disneyland seems like the basis for a great game, you can't make it without Disney's approval. But you can certainly make a light-hearted game about pirates—as LucasArts did with its *Monkey Island* series.

FIGURE 3.1 *Interstate '76* was a great game inspired by another medium.

You should also look beyond the usual science fiction and fantasy genres and beyond the usual sources like novels and movies. How about poetry? Beowulf's epic battle with the monster Grendel and then his even more terrible battle with Grendel's mother in a cave at the bottom of a lake sound like the basis for a game. "The Charge of the Light Brigade" might make you wonder about cavalry tactics. Would a game based on cavalry warfare be interesting to anyone? It's worth thinking about.

Game ideas can crop up in all sorts of unlikely places. The smash-hit game *The Sims* was partly inspired by a nonfiction book called *A Pattern Language,* which is about the way people's lives are affected by the design of their houses. Just as great scientists look at even the most common things in the world— light, air, gravity—and ask how they work, great game designers are always looking at the world and wondering what parts of it can be made into a game. The trick to finding original ideas, beyond the elf-and-wizard combinations that have been done so often, is to develop a game designer's instincts, to look for the fun and challenge even in things that don't sound like games at all.

Game Ideas from Other Games

A great many people who play computer games want to design them as well. When you play a lot of games, you develop a sense of how they work and what their good and bad points are. Playing games is a valuable experience for a game designer. It gives insight and lets you compare and contrast the features of different games.

Sometimes new game ideas are motivated by a desire to improve an existing game. We think, "If I had designed this game, I would have. . . " To learn from other games, you have to pay attention as you play. Don't just play them for fun; look at them seriously and think about how they work. Take notes especially of things that you like or don't like and of features that seem to work particularly well or not well at all. How do resources flow into the game? How do they flow out? How much of your success comes from luck? How much from skill?

As creative people, our instinct is to devise totally new kinds of games that have never been seen before. Unfortunately, publishers want games that they are sure they can sell, and that usually means variations of existing games, perhaps with a new twist that can be used in marketing. This explains why we keep seeing sequels and thinly disguised copies of earlier games. As designers, we have to learn to balance the tension between our own desire to innovate and the publisher's need for the comfortably familiar. Leonardo da Vinci warned against persistent imitation, however, in his *Treatise on Painting:*

> *The painter will produce pictures of little merit if he takes the work of others as his standard; but if he will apply himself to learn from the objects of nature he will produce good results. This we see was the case with the painters who came after the Romans, for they continually imitated each other, and from age to age their art steadily declined. . . . It is safer to go directly to the works of nature than to those which have been imitated from her originals, with great deterioration and thereby to acquire a bad method, for he who has access to the fountain does not go to the water pot.*

Deriving game ideas from other games tends to produce games that look or work alike. Studying other games is an excellent way to learn how they function, but if pursued exclusively, imitation produces similarity and, ultimately, mediocrity. The greatest games break new ground. They're unlike anything seen on the store shelves before.

Communicating Your Dream to Others

A dream is a fantasy that you have by yourself; a computer game is something that you make for someone else. You and your development team are entertainers. If your game is in a well-known genre and setting (for example, a World War II flight simulator), you can be pretty certain that a number of people already share your dream. But if your game is in a new setting (a futuristic city of your imagination, for example)—and especially if you are opening up a new genre—you have to be very careful and thorough in communicating your dream to others. Some of the first questions a publishing executive is going to ask you are, "Why would anyone want to play this game?" and "What's going to make someone buy this game instead of another?"

So what does it mean to entertain someone? Many people think entertainment is synonymous with having fun, but even that isn't completely straightforward. People have fun in all kinds of ways. Some of those ways involve hard work, such as gardening or building a new deck. Some of them involve frustration, such as solving a puzzle. Some, such as athletic competitions, even involve pain. One person's entertainment is another person's insufferable boredom. To build a game that entertains, you must know *who* it will entertain and *how*. In Chapter 1, "Games and Video Games," we discussed a variety of ways in which video games entertain people. Keep them in mind as your work takes you from dream to game.

From Idea to Game Concept

In Chapter 2 we described a game concept as "a general idea of how you intend to entertain someone through gameplay." That description was accurate enough for an overview, but in order to discuss game concepts in detail, we need a more complete explanation.

A game concept is a description of a game detailed enough to begin discussing it as a potential commercial product—a piece of software that the public might want to buy. It should include, as a minimum, the following key points:

- The **high concept statement:** a two- or three-sentence description of what the game is about. Here's a high concept statement for a game about street football: *The game at its grittiest. No pads, no helmets, no refs, no field. Just you and the guys, a ball, and a lot of concrete.*

- The player's role(s) in the game, if the game is representational enough to have roles. If the player will have an avatar, describe the avatar character briefly.

- A proposed primary gameplay mode, including perspective, interaction model, and general types of challenges the player(s) will experience in that mode

- The genre of the game or an explanation of why its gameplay does not fit into any existing genre

- A description of the target audience for the game

- The name of the machine on which the game will run, and details of any special equipment the game will require (for example, a camera or dance mat)

- The licenses that the game will exploit, if any

- The competition modes that the game will support: single-, dual-, or multiplayer; competitive or cooperative

- A general summary of how the game will progress from beginning to end, including a few ideas for levels or missions and a synopsis of the storyline, if the game has one

- A short description of the game world

You should put all these items into a high concept document. This chapter discusses how to think about these issues, except for a few that are self-explanatory or were addressed in earlier chapters. You can see a sample high concept document on the Companion Website.

In a commercial environment, a publisher will want to see several additional details: the game's potential competition, the ***unique selling points*** (often abbreviated USPs) that will make your game stand out in the marketplace, and possible marketing strategies and related merchandising opportunities.

As you can see, a game concept is much more than an idea. It is an idea that you have thought about and begun to develop. A game concept contains enough detail to begin discussing how it will feel to play the game and what further design work will be needed to create the game.

The Player's Role

To understand your own game and to explain it to others, you must know what the player will do, and in a sense, what the player will *be* in the game world—what her role is. These are the first questions you face in creating your game concept.

What Is the Player Going to Do?

It's sometimes tempting to start thinking about a game in terms of its setting or its characters. For example, "Wouldn't it be fun to play a game set in ancient Rome?" or "Wouldn't it be fun to play a game as Indiana Jones?" These are reasonable ideas, and of course many games have been made from both of them. However, you cannot make a game from a setting or character alone. The first step toward turning the idea into a game concept is to answer the question, "What is the player going to do?"

This is *the* single most important question you can ask yourself at the concept stage. You don't have to answer it in precise terms yet ("the X button kicks and the O button punches"), but you do have to know the general answer. For games in some genres, the answer is simple and obvious: drive a tank or play hockey. For games in other genres, such as role-playing games, the question may have many answers: explore, fight, cast spells, collect objects, buy and sell, talk to dragons.

Video games allow someone to play—that is, to *act*. She has purchased the game in order to *do* something, not just to see, hear, or read something. Interactivity is the *raison d'être* of all gaming; it is what sets gaming apart from presentational forms of entertainment such as books and movies. The correct answer to the question, "Wouldn't it be fun to play a game set in ancient Rome?" is another question: "Yes, it would. What kinds of things could a player do in ancient Rome?"

> **COMMANDMENT:** Think About Player Actions First
>
> Do not start designing the story, avatar, game world, artwork, or anything else until you have answered the question, "What is the player going to do?"

Defining the Role

Playing a game, especially board games and computer games, often involves playing a *role* of some sort. In *Monopoly,* the role is real estate tycoon. In *From Russia with Love,* the role is James Bond. Defining the player's role in the game world is a key part of defining your game's concept. If the player's role is difficult to describe, that role might be difficult for the player to grasp as well, and that may indicate conceptual problems with the game. This doesn't mean that the role always has to be simple or that the player sticks to just one role per game. In many sports games, for example, the player can be an athlete, a coach, or the general manager. In team games, the player often switches from one athlete to another as play progresses.

Shifting roles work well in a sports game because the game's audience understands them, but if a game takes place in a less familiar world with less familiar objectives, the roles must be made especially clear. If the player's role changes from time to time—especially involuntarily—the player must know why it changed and how to adapt to the new circumstances.

If you explain the player's role clearly, it helps him to understand what he's trying to achieve and what rules govern the game. In Sierra Online's *Police Quest* series, for instance, the player takes on the role of a real-world police officer. Real police officers can't just shoot anything that moves; they have to obey strict rules about when and how to use their guns. Tactical combat simulations such as *Tom Clancy's Rainbow Six* and *Counter-Strike* also implement real-world rules, placing the player in the shoes of a real Special Forces soldier. By telling the player that the role is based on reality rather than fantasy, the game designer ensures that the player knows his actions will have to be more cautious than in the usual frenetic shooter.

In defining the player's role, you will face the question of how realistic you want your game to be. At the concept stage, you need not—and should not—start defining the details of the core mechanics and the presentation layer, but you should have a general idea of whether you want your game to be abstract or representational. That decision may be influenced by other considerations such as the target audience, discussed in the section *Defining Your Target Audience* later in this chapter.

> **KEY POINT**
>
> The easier it is to explain the player's role, the easier it will be for the publisher, the retailer, and the customer to understand it . . . and to decide to spend money on it.

Choosing a Genre

In describing movies or books, the term *genre* refers to the content of the work. Historical fiction, romance fiction, spy fiction, and so on are genres of popular fiction. With video games, however, *genre* refers to the types of challenges that a game offers. In games, the genres are independent of the content. Action games are one genre; they can be set in the Old West, in a fantasy world, or in outer space, and they will still be action games. The designer and commentator Greg Costikyan prefers the term *game style* rather than *game genre* to avoid this difference in meaning among the different media (Costikyan, 2005), but we will continue to use *genre* because it is more widely recognized.

3

> *A genre is a category of games characterized by a particular set of challenges, regardless of setting or game-world content.*

The Classic Game Genres

As you flesh out your concept, you should consider whether or not it falls into one of the classic video game genres described below. In later chapters, we'll look at these genres in detail, examining each to see how it differs from the others and what special design considerations apply to it. For now, here's a brief introduction to the genres.

- **Action games** include physical challenges. They may also incorporate puzzles, races, and a variety of conflict challenges, typically among a small number of characters. Action games often contain simple economic challenges as well, usually involving collecting objects. They seldom include strategic or conceptual challenges.

- **Strategy games** include strategic (naturally), tactical, and sometimes logistical challenges. They may also offer economic and exploration challenges to lengthen the game and give it more variety. Once in a while, they also have a physical challenge thrown in for spice, but this often annoys strategically minded players.

- Most **role-playing games** involve tactical, logistical, and exploration challenges. They also include economic challenges because the games usually involve collecting loot and trading it in for better weapons. They sometimes include puzzles and conceptual challenges, but rarely physical ones.

- Real-world simulations include **sports games** and **vehicle simulations,** including military vehicles. They involve mostly physical and tactical challenges but not exploration, economic, or conceptual ones.

- **Construction and management games** such as *RollerCoaster Tycoon* primarily offer economic and conceptual challenges. Only rarely do they involve conflict or exploration, and they almost never include physical challenges.

- **Adventure games** chiefly provide exploration and puzzle-solving. They sometimes contain conceptual challenges as well. Adventure games may include a physical challenge also, but only rarely.

- **Puzzle games** offer logic challenges and conceptual challenges almost exclusively, although occasionally there's time pressure or an action element.

You will probably find that it's much easier to design a game that fits within one well-known genre than it is to design one outside of any existing genre. If you choose to design in an existing genre, you can study the many games that already belong to it for inspiration. You will also know which challenges to concentrate on and which to leave out.

Hybrid Games

Some games cross genres, combining features not typically found together. This occasionally happens when two people on the design team want the game to belong to different genres, and they compromise by including challenges from both. Crossing genres is also sometimes an effort to appeal to a larger audience by including elements that audiences for both genres will like. By far the most successful hybrid is the action-adventure, as seen in the more recent *Legend of Zelda* games. (The earlier 2D *Zelda* games were almost entirely action games.) Action-adventures are still mostly action, but they include a story and puzzles that give them some of the qualities of adventure games.

Although it can add flavor and interest to a game, crossing genres is a risky move. Rather than appealing to two groups, you might end up appealing to neither. Many players (and game reviewers) prefer particular genres and don't want to be confronted by challenges of a kind that they normally avoid. Retailers who plan to purchase a certain number of games from each genre for their stores might not know on which shelf to put the game, and so will shy away from it entirely.

However, you should not allow these genre descriptions to circumscribe your creativity—especially at the concept stage. If you have a wholly new, never-before-seen type of game in mind, design it as you envision it; don't try to shoehorn it into a genre to which it doesn't belong. A game needs to be true to itself, so a truly hybrid game may need to mix challenges that aren't typically presented together. But don't mix characteristics of different genres without good reason; a game should cross genres only if it genuinely needs to as part of the gameplay. A flight simulator with a logic puzzle inserted in the middle of the game just to make the game different from other flight simulators will only annoy flight sim fans.

Defining Your Target Audience

A common misconception among game designers is that all players enjoy the same things that the designer enjoys, so the designer has only to examine his own experience to know how to make a game entertaining. This is dangerous hubris. The reason for making a computer game is to entertain an audience. You must think about who those people are and what they like.

Unless you have been commissioned by a single individual, you design a game for a class of people, not for one person. At this early stage, you must think about your audience broadly, as a group of people that you hope will enjoy your game. One of the first questions a publisher will ask you is, "Who will buy this game?" Think carefully about the answer. What characteristics are your players likely to have in common? What things set them apart from other gamers? What challenges do they enjoy? More important, what challenges do they *not* enjoy? What interests them, bores them, frustrates them, excites them, frightens them, and offends them? Answer these questions, and keep the answers close at hand as you design your game.

A game concept is not complete without a statement describing its intended audience.

 FYI *The Player-Centric Philosophy and the Target Audience*

As we explained in Chapter 2, the player-centric philosophy of game design requires that you think about how your design decisions affect a representative player's experience of the game. This approach ensures that your decisions serve the player's interests first, especially in the later stages of development when you will often be tempted to make decisions based on cost or convenience.

Defining a target audience is not the same as player-centric design. You can apply the player-centric approach only *after* you have defined the target audience. You must begin by asking yourself the question, "Who am I trying to entertain?" Once you have that answer, you can use it to apply the player-centric approach to other design issues, asking yourself, "Does this feature entertain a representative player from my target audience?"

The Dangers of Binary Thinking

You can't make a game for everyone, so your target audience will necessarily be a subset of all possible players, a subset determined by your answers to the questions "Who will enjoy this game?" and "What kinds of challenges do they like?" As you answer these questions, you may be tempted to assume that the people in one category (adult men, for example) are a special audience that has nothing in common with people in other categories (adult women, children, teenagers, and so on). This is *binary thinking:* assuming that if group A likes a thing, everyone outside that group *won't* like it. It's unsound reasoning and will actually cause you to lose part of your potential customer base, as the following sections demonstrate.

Reasoning Statistically about Player Groups Suppose you ask a group of players to rate their level of interest in a particular game on a scale of 0 to 10, with 0 representing no interest at all and 10 being fanatical enthusiasm. Like many phenomena, the overall population's level of interest will resemble a bell-shaped curve, with small numbers of people at the extremes and the majority somewhere in the middle. If you graph the responses of men and women separately, you may find for a given game that the two groups have different arithmetic means; that is, the centers of their bell-shaped curves fall at different places on the graph.

Figure 3.2 shows this phenomenon. For the hypothetical game in question, men's mean level of interest is at about 5.5, while women's mean level of interest is at 4.5.

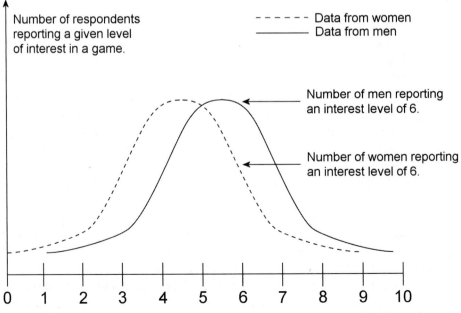

FIGURE 3.2 Reported level of interest in a game on a 0–10 scale.

Note that while the graph does support the statement, "Men have a higher level of interest in this game women do," in fact, there is a large area of overlap indicating that a significant portion of the women surveyed are interested in the game as well. Furthermore, the number of women reporting an interest level of 6 is about two-thirds that of the number of men reporting the same interest level. In other words, two-fifths of the people reporting an interest level of 6 are women—far too many to simply ignore.

This is only a hypothetical example. With some games, the level of overlap may be small, and there is no point in trying to reach out to an audience that simply isn't there. A game for five-year-olds won't appeal to many fifteen-year-olds. Our point, however, is that for most ordinary games there will be *some* overlap among different populations. It would be foolish to ignore, or worse yet, offend a minority audience simply because it is in the minority, without knowing how many people fall into that category. If you ignore or repel a significant minority, you're throwing money away, something your publisher won't thank you for.

Strive for Inclusiveness, not Universality   You cannot make a game that appeals to everyone by throwing in a hodgepodge of features because group A likes some of them and group B likes others. If you do, you will produce a game that has too many features and no harmony. For instance, you can't make a game that appeals to action fans, to strategy fans, and to fans of management simulations by combining kung fu, chess, and *Monopoly*—the result would be a mess that appeals to none of them. On the other hand, you can include a storyline in a kung fu game so long as the storyline doesn't interfere with the gameplay. The storyline adds depth to the game without driving away its key market of fighting-game enthusiasts, and it might attract the interest of people who otherwise wouldn't pay any attention to a fighting game.

Certain groups are turned off by particular content or features. For example, women don't much care for material that portrays them as brainless sex objects; parents won't buy games for their kids if the games are nothing but blood and gore; members of minority races (and many in the majority too) are naturally offended by racist content. These are the most obvious examples, but there are more subtle ones as well. Women are generally more sensitive to the aesthetics of a game than men are, and they are less likely to buy a game with ugly artwork. Some players have no interest in narrative material and will be put off if they are forced to watch it in a genre that doesn't normally include narratives. (This is why we said the storyline in the kung fu game, above, mustn't interfere with the gameplay.) These examples illustrate the effects of *exclusionary material*—content or features that serve to drive players away from a game that they otherwise might like. Your goal should be to make the best game that you can about your chosen subject, while avoiding exclusionary material that will reduce the size of your audience.

> **COMMANDMENT:** Keep Exclusionary
> Material Out of Your Game
>
> To reach a large audience while still creating a harmonious, coherent
> game, don't try to attract everyone by adding unrelated features. Instead,
> work to avoid repelling people who might otherwise be attracted.

Core Versus Casual

The most significant distinction among player types is not between console-
game players and computer-game players, nor between men and women, nor
even between children and adults. The most significant distinction is between
hardcore (usually just abbreviated as "core") gamers and casual gamers.

Core gamers play a lot of games. Games are more than light entertainment
to them; games are a hobby that demands time and money. Core gamers
subscribe to game magazines, chat on game bulletin boards, and build fan Web
sites about their favorite games. Above all, core gamers play for the exhilaration
of defeating the game. They tolerate frustration well because of the charge they
get out of finally winning. The greater the obstacle, the greater the sense of
achievement. Core gamers thrive on competition. They don't like games that are
easy; they like games that are challenging.

By comparison, casual gamers play for the sheer enjoyment of the experience. If the game stops being enjoyable or becomes frustrating, the casual
gamer will stop playing. For the casual gamer, playing a game must be entertaining, whether it's competitive or not. A casual gamer is simply not willing to
spend hours learning complex controls or getting killed again and again until he
finds the one weak point in an otherwise invincible enemy; he feels that he has
better things to do with his time. To design a game for casual gamers, you have
to give them a sense of rapid progress and achievement.

In reality, of course, there are as many types of gamer as there are games;
everyone has her own reason for playing computer games. But the casual/core
distinction is a very powerful one. If you design a game specifically for one
group, you almost certainly won't have a lot of sales to the other group. A few
very well-designed games manage to appeal to both: *Goldeneye,* for example,
could be played happily by both core and casual gamers. Core gamers could set
the game at the highest difficulty level and drive themselves crazy trying to cut
15 seconds off the last time it took to play a mission. Casual gamers could
set the game at the easiest level and blast away, enjoying the game's smooth
controls and visual detail.

Other Distinctions

Several other groups exhibit particular trends in their game-playing preferences, and we'll mention them briefly here. Note that this section is about

choosing a target audience, not about actually designing a game for one. If you want to make your game particularly appealing to a special group, see "Designing to Appeal to Particular Groups" on the Companion Website for more information.

- **Men and women.** Men and women are not nearly as different as various works of pop psychology would like us to believe. A large number of games are made with only male players in mind, but it doesn't take much to make them more appealing to women as well. See Sheri Graner Ray's *Gender Inclusive Game Design* for a thorough discussion of the subject.

- **Children and adults.** Children's gaming preferences and abilities differ much more sharply from those of adults than men's differ from women's. Children have different motor and cognitive skills, different attention spans, and different linguistic abilities, and all of these change dramatically as children grow up. Most important, however, games designed for children must be appealing and acceptable to their parents as well. There is a vast amount of research on creating entertainment for children. If you're interested in targeting this market specifically, we suggest that you start with Chapter 9 of the book *Digital Storytelling: A Creator's Guide to Interactive Entertainment* by Carolyn Handler Miller.

- **Boys and girls.** For years, the male-dominated game industry had a preconceived notion that girls didn't play video games, so the designers didn't bother to think about girls. This idea was wrong, however. Girls *were* playing video games, in spite of the industry's neglect. Still, boys' and girls' interests differ more widely than men's and women's do, and making games that appeal to girls requires knowledge that few designers have. "Designing to Appeal to Particular Groups" contains a discussion about games for girls, quoting extensively from Jesyca Durchin's brilliant 2000 Game Developers' Conference lecture.

- **Players with disabilities.** A number of developers are working to improve the accessibility of video games to players with disabilities. Although few games are made specifically for people with special needs, it is easy and inexpensive to make games more accessible. You can make your game available to the deaf by including subtitles for spoken dialog and providing visual as well as auditory cues for particular events; you can allow players with visual impairments to adjust the contrast of the screen and the font size of any text in the game.

- **Players of other cultures.** The process of adapting a game for sale in a country other than the one for which it was made is called *localization*. The process involves more than just translating the text to a different language and rerecording the audio; for the game to be a hit, numerous cultural factors must be taken into account. It will be far easier to make a game enjoyable to people in other countries if you have planned it that way and considered them a part of your target audience from the beginning. Designing for localization is outside the scope of this book, but if you want a worldwide market, we suggest that you research the subject.

Progression Considerations

As we said in Chapter 2, if your game will be a long one, the player will need a sense of progress through it. At this stage of game design, you must decide what will provide that sense of progress: levels, a story, or both. Will your game be so large that it should be divided into levels? Will your levels be unrelated, and all available to the player at any time, or will they be organized into a sequential or branching configuration, in which completing a level makes the next one available? What types of conditions will determine when a player has completed a level? The genre that you have chosen will help you to determine your answers.

The other question is whether you want a story. Stories give games a context and a goal. Some genres, such as sports and puzzle games, don't usually include stories because their context is self-explanatory. In other genres, such as role-playing and adventure games, the story is a large part of the game's entertainment. Representational games frequently have a story; abstract games generally don't, although *Ms. Pac-Man* was an exception in a small way. Stories about abstract characters are seldom very involving.

If you do choose to have a story in your game, you don't have to know exactly what narrative content you want to include at the concept-formation stage. All you need to know is whether you want a story and, if so, what its overall direction will be. You should be able to summarize it in a sentence or two; for example: "Jack Jones, leader of a secret DEA task force, will conduct a series of raids against the drug barons, ending in an apocalyptic battle in the cocaine fields of Colombia. Along the way, some of the people he encounters will not be quite what they seem." Errors in the storyline are much easier to correct than errors in the gameplay, and gamers will forgive story errors more quickly as well. Make sure you understand your game first; then build your story into it.

COMMANDMENT: The Story Comes Later

Do not spend a lot of time devising a story at the concept stage. This is a cardinal error, frequently made by people who are more used to presentational media such as books and film. You *must* concentrate most of your efforts on the gameplay at this point.

Types of Game Machines

When you first start fleshing out your game concept, you should concentrate on the dream, the player's role, and the target audience. However, a game concept is not complete without a statement about which machine (or machines) the game will run on. Some genres of games are better suited to one kind of machine than another, and all machines have features and performance characteristics—input and output devices, processor speed, storage space—that will define the scope of the game. You need to know the strengths and weaknesses of the different types of machines and how they are used by their owners.

Home Game Consoles

A home game console is usually set up in the living room or a bedroom. The player sits holding a dedicated controller in both hands, 3 to 6 feet away from a relatively low-resolution display, the television. This means that games designed for the home console machine cannot be as intricate as the typical personal computer game. The graphics have to be simpler and bolder, and the control method and user interface must be manageable with the controller provided. The kind of precision pointing that's possible with a mouse is much more difficult with most controllers, even with analog joysticks. Still, you are guaranteed that every machine will ship with a standardized controller; you don't have to cope with the huge variety of controllers and joysticks available for the personal computer.

Because the television is designed to be seen by several people at once, and because the console usually allows for at least two controllers, console machines are excellent for multiplayer games in which all the players look at the same screen. This means that every player can see what every other player is doing on the screen, which is a consideration in the design of some games. On the other hand, until recently, home consoles had no hard disk drives, so there was little space in which to store data between games. Games designed for consoles aren't as customizable as personal computer games, for the same reason.

Home consoles tend to have graphics display hardware of comparable power to the graphics hardware in personal computers but slower central processing units and less RAM than personal computers. Because consoles sell for $200–$400 once they have been available for a year or so the manufacturer has to cut the hardware design to the bone to keep the cost down. This means that, as computing devices, consoles are less powerful than personal computers and more difficult to program. On the other hand, their low price means that there are far more of them around, which creates a larger market for their games.

Services such as Xbox Live have begun to network console machines, although this is not yet the standard way that people play. The single-player or multiplayer local experience is still the most common one.

Personal Computers

A personal computer (PC) is usually set up away from the communal living space, on a computer desk. In this case, the player has a keyboard, a mouse, possibly a joystick, and (more rarely) a dedicated game controller such as those on console machines. The player sits 12 to 18 inches away from a relatively small (compared to the television) high-resolution display. The high resolution means that the game can have subtle, detailed graphics. The mouse allows precision pointing and a more complex user interface. The keyboard enables the player to enter text conveniently and send messages to other players over a network, something that is nearly impossible with console machines.

The personal computer is quite awkward for more than one person to use. The controls of a PC are all designed for one individual, and even the furniture it usually sits on—a desk—is intended for a solitary use. PC games are rarely designed for more than one person to play on a single machine. On the other hand, a PC is very likely to be connected to the Internet, whereas consoles are just now beginning to get this capability. The PC is still the machine of choice for multiplayer networked games.

The great boon of PC development is that anyone can program one; you don't have to get a license from the manufacturer or buy an expensive development station. Consequently, personal computers are at the cutting edge of innovation in computer gaming. They're the platform of choice for small-scale, low-demand projects; interactive art; and other experimental forms of interactive entertainment.

The great bane of PC development is that no two machines are alike. Because they're customizable, there are millions of possible configurations. In the early days of the game industry, this was a real nightmare for programmers. Fortunately, the Windows and Macintosh operating systems have solved many of these problems by isolating the programs from the hardware. Still, games tend to require more from the machine than other applications do, and configuration conflicts still occur.

Handheld Game Machines

Handheld game machines are a hugely popular and very inexpensive form of entertainment, used in the West mainly by children. (In Japan, significant numbers of adults use them too.) Handhelds support few add-on features; the input and output devices are usually fixed. These machines have a smaller number of buttons than a console controller does and only a small LCD screen. Their CPUs are slower than their console counterparts but still have enough CPU speed to run sophisticated games. The Sony PSP represented a huge jump in the power and display quality of handheld game machines.

The cheapest handheld machines offer a fixed set of built-in games, but the more versatile handhelds accept games stored on ROM cartridges and the PSP now supports a small optical disk. Cartridges store much less data than the CD-ROMs or DVD discs that home consoles and computers use. Designing for a cartridge machine places severe limits on the amount of video, audio, graphics, and animation that you can include in the game. Because they're solid-state electronics, though, the data on a cartridge is available instantly. There's no delay in loading data, as there is with optical media devices.

The handheld game market is very lucrative, but creating a game for one will test your skills as a designer. With less storage space, you have to rely on gameplay rather than content to provide the entertainment.

Mobile Phones and Wireless Devices

Mobile phones recently arrived on the gaming scene, and while there is a great deal of interest in them, it has proven difficult to find a reliably profitable business model. Phones provide less processing power and less memory than dedicated handhelds; the games are therefore smaller, and the public is reluctant to pay much money for them. Skins and ring tones, not games, account for most of the money being made in mobile phone content at the moment. But the worst thing about developing for mobile phones is the utter lack of standardization. The screens are all different sizes and color depths; the processors are different; the operating systems are different. Even the layout of the buttons is nonstandard, making it difficult to be certain what user interface design will be convenient across a range of phones.

However, mobile phones and other wireless devices such as the Nintendo DS do have one distinct advantage over traditional game handhelds: Wireless devices permit portable networked play. Players can compete against other people while riding on trains or waiting for an appointment. Setting up a networked game on mobile phones usually requires making a deal with a cellular service provider. Also, unlike dedicated game machines, phones do not require a license from the hardware manufacturer. Anyone can write a program for a mobile phone.

Other Devices

Games show up on all sorts of other devices these days. The more specialized the device is, the more important it is to have a clear understanding of its technical limitations and its audience.

Airlines are starting to build video games into their seats; these games tend to be aimed at children. Personal digital assistants (PDAs) provide a great new platform for small, simple games for adults. Video gambling machines, too, enjoy growing popularity. Because they are so heavily regulated and not sold to consumers, they really constitute an industry unto themselves, but video gambling games require programmers and artists just like any other computer game. And, of course, arcade machines, although not as popular as they once were, still provide employment to game developers.

Because these devices occupy niche markets and often have peculiar design restrictions, we won't be addressing them in detail. This is a book about game design in general, so we concentrate on games for all-purpose game machines: home consoles and personal computers.

Summary

In this chapter, you've learned what a game concept is and what decisions you have to make to create a high concept document. You should now understand the importance of defining the player's role. You have also learned the distinctions among game genres and how to think about choosing a target audience—particularly with respect to its degree of dedication to gaming. And you should have an idea of how your choice of machine affects the way people will play your game.

Creating a game concept is like designing the framework of a building: It gives you the general outlines but not the details. The remainder of this part of the book is dedicated to creating those details.

Test Your Skills

MULTIPLE CHOICE QUESTIONS

1. Which of the following should be part of a game concept?
   A. Your resume, showing that you're qualified to design a game.
   B. The back story that explains how the main character acquired his superpowers.
   C. A detailed explanation of how the overtime rules will settle ties.
   D. A brief description of the character's avatar.

2. Which question must you answer first?
   A. What does the player's avatar look like?
   B. What special input devices will the player need?
   C. What is the player going to do?
   D. What is the story of how the player's avatar entered the game world?

3. If the game you're working on doesn't fit into an existing game genre, you should
   A. make sure you don't mention any known genres that would confuse anyone reading the high concept document.
   B. hide the fact that you aren't working within a genre by wowing them with your artwork, animation, or music.
   C. include an explanation of why the gameplay doesn't fit into any known genre.
   D. go back to the drawing board; games must fit into known genres.

4. What sets any game apart from presentational forms of entertainment is
   A. interactivity.
   B. computer technology.
   C. creation of imaginary worlds.
   D. suspension of disbelief.

5. When looking around for game ideas, it's best to
   A. stick with a winner; always take your characters and actions from the latest movie releases.
   B. not spread yourself too thin; stick to one idea until you've polished it to perfection.
   C. be alert; look at any situation you find yourself in, and see if it lends itself to gameplay.
   D. flatter your game design idols by making sequels to their hit games.

6. Deriving game ideas exclusively from other games
   A. guarantees success equal to that of the previous game.
   B. tends to produce games that look or work alike and lead ultimately to mediocre games.
   C. ensures innovation because you will need to work to make your game a bit different.
   D. saves money on design and on marketing, making it possible to spend more on innovative graphics and audio.

7. The primary challenges in a construction and management game are likely to be
   A. economic and conceptual.
   B. exploration and conquest.
   C. almost exclusively logical.
   D. physical and under time pressure.

8. You want to make your first commercial game a hybrid that crosses two genres, but you know this is risky because
   A. instead of doubling your audience, it might be that nobody likes the game.
   B. retailers may not know how to shelve it and thus might be reluctant to sell it.
   C. you will need to be proficient at designing in two different genres.
   D. all of the other answers are correct.

9. Player-centric design means
   A. defining your game's target audience.
   B. keeping in mind how your design decisions affect the experience of a representative player.
   C. working closely with marketing to test your game on focus groups of gamers.
   D. making sure everyone on the team is a gamer, with extensive experience playing games in your game's genre.

10. Exclusionary material is
    A. proprietary content for which you negotiate exclusive rights.
    B. content or features that serve to drive players away from a game that they otherwise might like.
    C. undocumented features, outside the main gameplay, that will draw in a bigger audience, such as puzzles that make use of your action game world.
    D. content or features included in the game idea, which you discard when sharpening up your concept document.

11. The most significant distinction among player types is
    A. male or female.
    B. kids and adults.
    C. console or PC.
    D. core or casual.

12. *Localization* refers to
    A. disk protection so that game materials only work on computers sold in the same region.
    B. the game data pertaining to local conditions and status that is displayed on a screen at one time.
    C. the process of adapting a game for sale in a country or culture other than the one for which it was designed.
    D. developing a game in house, as opposed to outsourcing development.

13. Which of these is true of a game's story?
    A. Stories can supply the game with a context and goal.
    B. To be successful, a game must have a storyline.
    C. If a game has a storyline, then it can't be an action game.
    D. None of the other answers are true.

14. Games designed for home game consoles probably

    A. are meant to be played by children.

    B. will present design problems because you can't assume all players will have the same kind of controller.

    C. will offer a chat feature for interacting with other players.

    D. cannot use small graphics because the display screen is a TV.

15. Your guerrilla development team is ready to set the game world on fire with an experimental, massively multiplayer interactive art project. The platform of choice is then

    A. immaterial; at the game concept stage, it's too early to choose a platform.

    B. a new handheld device you'll patent to give your team total control.

    C. a home console because of the number of them already out there in homes.

    D. the PC, because development won't require a special license or development station.

EXERCISES

1. Create a high concept document for one of your favorite games or one that your instructor assigns.

2. Write a short paper contrasting the player's roles in a *Tomb Raider* game and a *Civilization* game.

3. Certain genres are more often found on one kind of machine than on another. Write an essay explaining which machine each genre works best on and why. How do the machine's features and the way that it is used in the home facilitate or hinder the gameplay in each genre?

DESIGN QUESTIONS

Once you have a game idea in mind, these are the questions you must ask yourself in order to turn it into a fully fledged game concept. You don't have to be precise or detailed, but you should have a general answer for all of them.

1. Write a high concept statement: a few sentences that give a general flavor of the game. You can make references to other games, movies, books, or any other media if your game contains similar characters, actions, or ideas.

2. What is the player's role? Is the player pretending to be someone or something, and if so, what? Is there more than one? How does the player's role help to define the gameplay?

3. Does the game have an avatar or other key character? Describe him/her/it.

4. What is the nature of the gameplay, in general terms? What kinds of challenges will the player face? What kinds of actions will the player take to overcome them?

5. What is the player's interaction model? Omnipresent? Through an avatar? Something else? Some combination?

6. What is the game's primary perspective? How will the player view the game's world on the screen? Will there be more than one perspective?

7. Does the game fall into an existing genre? If so, which one?

8. Is the game competitive, cooperative, team-based, or single-player? If multiple players are allowed, are they using the same machine with separate controls or different machines over a network?

9. Why would anyone want to play this game? Who is the game's target audience? What characteristics distinguish them from the mass of players in general?

10. What machine or machines is the game intended to run on? Can it make use of, or will it require, any particular hardware such as dance mats or a camera?

11. What is the game's setting? Where does it take place?

12. Will the game be broken into levels? What might be the victory condition for a typical level?

13. Does the game have a narrative or story as it goes along? Summarize the plot in a sentence or two.

Chapter 4

Game Worlds

Chapter Objectives

After reading this chapter and completing the exercises, you will be able to do the following:

- Know the various dimensions of a game world and understand how they affect the player's experience of the game.

- Define an appropriate physical model for your game world, including its dimensionality, scale, and what happens at the boundaries.

- Explain the relationship between game time and real time and decide how time will behave in your game.

- Create the culture and environment of a game world, set the level of detail that it will offer, and define a visual and auditory style for it.

- Know some of the techniques for influencing the player's emotions.

- Be aware of how the ethics of a game world can differ from the ethics of the real world and the implications that has for public acceptance of your game.

- Understand the multidimensional nature of *realism* as it applies to games and how it affects the player's expectations about the experience the game will give her.

Introduction

Games entertain through gameplay, but many also entertain by taking the player away to an imaginary place—a **game world.** (We also use the terms *world, setting,* and *game setting* interchangeably with *game world.*) In fact, the gameplay in most single-player video games appears to the player as interactions between himself and the game world. This chapter defines a game world and introduces the various dimensions that describe a game world: the physical, temporal, environmental, emotional, and ethical dimensions, as well as a quality called *realism.*

What Is a Game World?

A game world is an artificial universe, an imaginary place in which the events of the game occur. When the player enters the magic circle and pretends to be somewhere else, the game world is the place she pretends to be.

Not all games have a game world. A football game takes place in a real location, not an imaginary one. Playing football still requires pretending because the players assign an artificial importance to otherwise trivial actions, but the pretending doesn't create a game world. Many abstract games, such as tic-tac-toe, have a board but not a world—there is no imaginary element in playing the game. Chess has only a hint of a world; although the board and the moves are abstract, the names of the pieces suggest a medieval court with its king and queen, knights and bishops. *Stratego* has a slightly more elaborate world: The board is printed to look like a landscape, and the pieces are illustrated with little pictures, encouraging us to pretend that they are colonels and sergeants and scouts in an army. *Stratego* could be played entirely abstractly, using only numbers and a bare grid for a board, but the setting makes it more interesting.

The game world in a video game is traditionally presented by means of pictures and sound: art, animation, music, and audio effects. Not all game worlds have a visible or audible component, however. In a text adventure, the player creates the images and sounds of the world in his imagination when he reads the text on the screen. Designing such a world is a matter of using your literary skills to describe it in words.

Game worlds are much more than the sum of the pictures and sounds that portray them. A game world can have a culture, an aesthetic, a set of moral values, and other dimensions that we explain in this chapter. The game world also has a relationship to reality, whether it is highly abstract, with little connection to the world of everyday things, or highly representational, attempting to be as similar to the real world as possible.

> **KEY POINT**
>
> In defining your game world, it will be tempting to start drawing pictures right away, especially if you're artistically inclined anyway. That's good in the early stages of design; you will need concept art to pitch your game. But don't make the mistake of thinking that nice drawings are enough. Your game world must support and work with the core mechanics and gameplay of your game. To make the world serve the game well, you must design it carefully. Otherwise you may forget to address an important issue until late in the development process, when it's expensive to make changes.

The Purposes of a Game World

Games entertain by several means: gameplay, novelty, social interaction (if it is a multiplayer game), and so on. In a game such as chess, almost all the entertainment value is in the gameplay; few people think of it as a game about medieval warfare. In an adventure game such as *Escape from Monkey Island*, the world is essential to the fantasy. Without the world, *Escape from Monkey Island* would not exist, and if it had a different world, it would be a different game. One of the purposes of a game world is simply to entertain in its own right: to offer the player a place to explore and an environment to interact with.

As a general rule, the more that a player understands a game's core mechanics, the less the game world matters. Mastering the core mechanics requires a kind of abstract thought, and fantasy can be a distraction. Serious chess players don't think of the pieces as representing actual kings and queens and knights. When players become highly skilled at a game such as *Counter-Strike*, they no longer think about the fact that they're pretending to be soldiers or terrorists; they think only about hiding, moving, shooting, ambushing, obtaining ammunition, and so on. However, this kind of abstract play, ignoring a game's world, usually occurs only among experienced players. To someone who's playing a game for the first time, the world is vital to creating and sustaining her interest.

The other purpose of a game's world is to sell the game in the first place. It's not the game's mechanics that make a customer pick up a box in a store but the fantasy it offers: who she'll be, where she'll be, and what she'll be doing there if she plays that game.

4

The Dimensions of a Game World

A game's world is defined by many different properties. Some, such as the size of the world, are quantitative and can be given numerical values. Others, such as the world's mood, are qualitative and can only be described with words. Certain properties are related to one another, and we have characterized these related sets of properties as **dimensions** of the game world. To fully define your world and its setting, you need to consider each of these dimensions and answer certain questions about them.

The Physical Dimension

Video game worlds are almost always implemented as some sort of simulated physical space. The player moves his avatar in and around this space or manipulates other pieces or characters in it. The physical properties of this space determine a great deal about the gameplay.

Even text adventures include a physical dimension. The player moves from one abstract location, usually called a *room* even if it's described as outdoors, to another. Back when more people played text adventures, the boxes the games came in used to carry proud boasts about the number of rooms in the game. Gamers could take this as a very rough measure of the size of the world they could explore in the game and, therefore, the amount of gameplay that the game offered.

The physical dimension of a game is itself characterized by several different properties: spatial dimensionality, scale, and boundaries.

Spatial Dimensionality   One of the first questions to ask yourself is how many spatial dimensions your physical space will have. It is essential to understand that the dimensionality of the game's physical space is not the same as how the game will *display* that space (the perspective) or how it will implement the space in the software. How to implement and display the space are separate but related questions. The former has to do with technical design, and the latter has to do with user interface design. Ultimately, all spaces must be displayed on the two-dimensional surface of the monitor screen.

These are the typical dimensionalities found in video games:

■   **2D.** A few years ago, the vast majority of games had only two dimensions. This was especially noticeable in 2D side-scrolling games such as *Super Mario Bros.* (see Figure 4.1). Mario could run left and right and jump up and down, but he could not move toward the player (out of the screen) or away from him (into the screen). Two-dimensional worlds have one huge advantage when you're thinking about how to display them: The two dimensions of the world directly correspond to the two dimensions of the monitor screen, so you don't have to worry about conveying a sense of depth to the player. On the other hand, a number of games with 2D game worlds still use 3D hardware accelerators for display so that objects appear three-dimensional even

FIGURE 4.1 *Super Mario Bros.*, the classic 2D side-scrolling game.

though the gameplay does not make use of the third dimension. The more recent *SimCity* games are a good example. Two-dimensional worlds may seem rather old-fashioned nowadays, but there are still many uses for them, especially in smaller devices such as mobile phones.

■ **2.5D,** typically pronounced "two-and-a-half D." This is found in game worlds that appear to be a three-dimensional space but in reality consist of a series of 2D layers, one above the other. *StarCraft*, a war game, shows plateaus and lowlands, as well as aircraft that pass over obstacles and ground units. Objects can be placed and moved horizontally within a layer with a fine degree of precision, but vertically an object must be in one plane or another; there is no in between. Flying objects can't move up and down in the air; they're simply in the air layer. See Figure 4.2.

■ **3D.** Three true dimensions. Thanks to 3D hardware accelerators and modeling tools, 3D spaces are now easier to implement. They give the player a much greater sense of being inside a space (building, cave, spacecraft, or whatever) than 2D spaces ever could. With a 2D world, the player feels as if he is looking *at* it; with a 3D world, he feels as if he is *in* it. 3D worlds are great for avatar-based games with exploration

FIGURE 4.2 *StarCraft*, with plateaus and lowlands visible.

FIGURE 4.3 *Tomb Raider: The Angel of Darkness,* a fully 3D environment.

challenges, such as the *Tomb Raider* series (see Figure 4.3). Most large games for personal computers and consoles now use three dimensions, but many small casual games still need only two.

- **4D.** If you want to include a fourth dimension for some reason (not counting time), we suggest that you implement it as an alternate version of the 3D game world rather than an actual four-dimensional space. In other words, create two (or more) three-dimensional spaces that look similar but offer different experiences as the avatar moves among them. For example, the game *Legacy of Kain: Soul Reaver* contained two versions of the same 3D world, the spectral realm and the material realm, with different gameplay modes for each. The landscape was the same in both, but the material realm was lit by white light while the spectral realm was lit by blue light, and the architecture was distorted in the spiritual realm (see Figure 4.4). The actions available to the player were different in each realm. The realms looked similar but were functionally different places governed by different laws. In the movie version of *The Lord of the Rings,* the world that Frodo inhabits while he is wearing the Ring can be thought of as an alternate plane of reality as well, overlapping the real world but appearing and behaving differently.

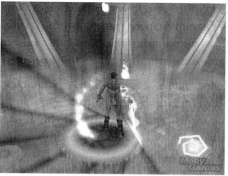

FIGURE 4.4 *Legacy of Kain: Soul Reaver*'s material (left) and spiritual (right) realms. Notice how the walls are slightly twisted in the spiritual realm and the overlay indicator is different.

When first thinking about the dimensionality of your game space, don't immediately assume that you want it to be three-dimensional because 3D seems more real or makes the best use of your machine's hardware. As with everything else you design, the dimensionality of your physical space must serve the entertainment value of the game. Make sure all the dimensions will contribute meaningfully. Many games that work extremely well in two dimensions don't work well in three. *Lemmings* was a hit 2D game, but *Lemmings 3D* was nowhere near as successful because it was much more difficult to play. The addition of a third dimension detracted from the player's enjoyment rather than adding to it.

Scale   By *scale,* we mean both the *absolute* size of the physical space represented, as measured in units meaningful in the game world (meters, miles, or light-years, for instance) and the *relative* sizes of objects in the game. If a game is purely abstract and doesn't correspond to anything in the real world, the sizes of objects in its game world don't really matter. You can adjust them to suit the game's needs any way you like. But if you are designing a game that represents (if only partially) the real world, you'll have to address the question of how big everything should be to both look real and play well. Some distortion is often necessary for the sake of gameplay, especially in war games; the trick is to distort without harming the player's suspension of disbelief too much.

In a sports game, a driving game, a flight simulator, or any other kind of game in which the player will expect a high degree of verisimilitude, you have little choice but to scale things to their actual sizes. In old 2D sports games, it was not uncommon for the athletes to be depicted as 12 feet tall to make them more visible, but nowadays players wouldn't tolerate a game taking such liberties with reality. Serious simulations need an accurate representation of the physical world.

Similarly, you should scale most of the objects in first-person games accurately. Fortunately, almost all first-person games are set indoors or within limited areas, seldom larger than a few hundred feet in any dimension, so this doesn't create implementation problems. Because the player's perspective is that of a person walking through the space, objects need to look right for their surrounding area. You might want to slightly exaggerate the size of critical objects such as keys, weapons, or ammunition to make them more visible, but most things, such as doors and furniture, should be scaled normally.

If you're designing a game with an aerial or isometric perspective, you might need to distort the scale of things somewhat. The real world is so much larger and more detailed than a game world that it's impossible to represent objects in their true scale in such a perspective. For example, in modern mechanized warfare, ground battles can easily take place over a 20-mile front, with weapons that can fire that far or farther. If you were to map an area this size onto a computer screen, an individual soldier or even a tank would be smaller than a single pixel, completely invisible. Although the display will normally be zoomed in on one small area of the whole map, the scale of objects will have to be somewhat exaggerated so that they're clearly identifiable on the screen.

Games frequently distort the relative heights of people and the buildings or hills in their environment. The buildings are often only a little taller than the people who walk past them. (See Figure 4.5 for an example.) To be able to see the roofs of all the buildings or the tops of all the hills, the camera must be positioned above the highest point in the world. But if the camera is too high, the people would hardly be visible at all. To solve this problem, the game simply does not

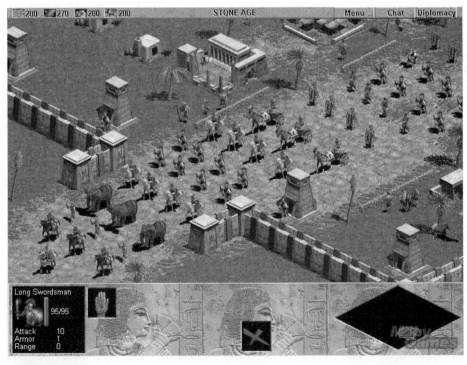

FIGURE 4.5 In *Age of Empires*, the buildings are only a little taller than the people.

include tall buildings or hills and exaggerates the height of the people. Because the vertical dimension is seldom critical to the gameplay in products such as war games and role-playing games, it doesn't matter if heights are not accurate, as long as they're not so inaccurate as to interfere with suspension of disbelief.

Designers often make another scale distortion between indoor and outdoor locations. When a character walks through a town, simply going from one place to another, the player will want the character to get there reasonably quickly. The scale of the town should be small enough that the character takes only a few minutes to get from one end to another unless the point of the game is to explore a richly detailed urban environment. When the character steps inside a building, however, and needs to negotiate doors and furniture, you should expand the scale to show these additional details. If you use the same animation for a character walking indoors and outdoors, this will give the impression that the character walks much faster outdoors than indoors. However, this seldom bothers players—they'd much rather have the game proceed quickly than have their avatar take hours to get anywhere, even if that would be more accurate.

This brings up one final distortion, which is also affected by the game's notion of time (see *The Temporal Dimension,* later in this chapter), and that is the relative speeds of moving objects. In the real world, a supersonic jet fighter can fly more than a hundred times faster than an infantry soldier can walk on the ground. If you're designing a game that includes both infantry soldiers and jet fighters, you're going to have a problem. If the scale of the battlefield is suitable for jets, it will take infantry weeks to walk across; if it's suitable for infantry, a jet could pass over it in the blink of an eye. One solution to this is to do what the real military does and implement transport vehicles for ground troops. Another is simply to accept a certain amount of distortion and create jets that fly only four or five times as fast as people walk (this trick was used in *StarCraft*). As long as the jet is the fastest thing in the game, it doesn't really matter how much faster it is; the strike-and-retreat tactic that jets are good at will still work. Setting these values is all part of balancing the game, as discussed in more detail in Chapter 9, "Gameplay."

Boundaries   In board games, the edge of the board constitutes the edge of the game world. Because computers don't have infinite memories, the physical dimension of a computer game world must have an "edge" as well. However, computer games are usually more immersive than board games, and they often try to disguise or explain away the fact that the world is limited to maintain the player's immersion.

In some cases, the boundaries of a game world arise naturally, and we don't have to disguise or explain them. Sports games take place only in a stadium or an arena, and no one expects or wants them to include the larger world. In most driving games, the car is restricted to a track or a road, and this, too, is reasonable enough.

Setting a game underground or indoors helps to create natural boundaries for the game world. Everyone expects indoor regions to be of a limited size, with walls defining the edges. The problem occurs when games move outdoors, where players expect large, open spaces without sharply defined edges. A common solution in this case is to set the game on an island surrounded by water or by some other kind of impassable terrain: mountains, swamps, or deserts. These establish both a credible and a visually distinctive "edge of the world."

In flight simulators, setting the boundaries of the world creates even more problems. Most flight simulators restrict the player to a particular area of the real world. Because there are no walls in the air, there's nothing to stop the plane from flying up to the edge of the game world, and the player can clearly see when he has arrived there that there's nothing beyond. In some games, the plane just stops there, hovering in midair, and won't go any farther. In *Battlefield 1942,* the game tells the player that he has left the scene of the action and forcibly returns him to the runway.

A common solution to the edge-of-the-world problem is to allow the flat world to "wrap" at the top, bottom, and sides. Although the world is implemented as a rectangular space in the software, objects that cross one edge appear at the opposite edge—they wrap around the world. If the object remains centered on the screen and the world appears to move beneath it, you can create the impression that the world is spherical. This was used to excellent effect in Bullfrog Productions' game *Magic Carpet.* Another Bullfrog game, *Populous: The Beginning,* actually displayed the world as a sphere on the screen, not just a wrapping rectangle (see Figure 4.6).

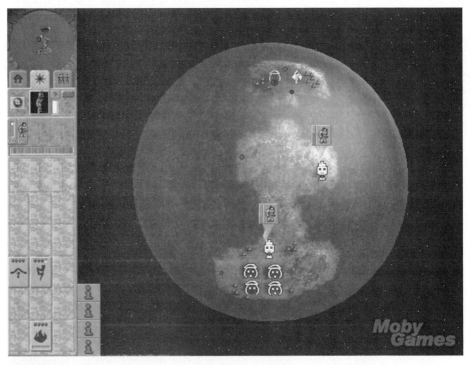

FIGURE 4.6 *Populous: The Beginning* was set on a genuinely spherical world.

The Temporal Dimension

The *temporal dimension* of a game world defines the way that time is treated in that world and the ways in which it differs from time in the real world.

In many turn-based and action games, the world doesn't include a concept of time passing: days and nights or seasons and years. Everything in the world idles or runs in a continuous loop until the player interacts with the game in some way. Occasionally, the player is put under pressure by being given a limited amount of real-world time to accomplish something, but this usually applies to only a single challenge and is not part of a larger notion of time in the game.

In some games, time is implemented as part of the game world but not part of the gameplay. The passage of time creates atmosphere and gives the game visual variety, but it doesn't change the game's challenges and actions. This usually feels rather artificial. If the player can do exactly the same things at night that she can during the daytime and no one ever seems to sleep, then there's little point in making the distinction. For time to really support the fantasy, time must affect the experience in ways besides the purely visual.

Baldur's Gate, a large role-playing game, is a good example of a game in which time is meaningful. At night, shops close and the characters in the game run an increased risk of being attacked by wandering monsters. It's also darker and hard to see. Taverns are open all day and all night, which is reasonable enough, but the customers don't ever seem to leave and the bartender never goes off shift. In this way, the game's use of time is a little inconsistent, but the discrepancy serves the gameplay well because you can always trade with the bartender and pick up gossip no matter what time it is. The characters do need rest if they've been on the march for a long while, and this makes them vulnerable while they're sleeping. In the underground portions of the game, day and night have less meaning, as you would expect.

Variable Time   In games that do implement time as a significant element of the gameplay, time in the game world usually runs much faster than in reality. Time in games also jumps (as it does in books and movies), skipping periods when nothing interesting is happening. Most war games, for example, don't bother to implement nighttime or require that soldiers get any rest. In reality, soldier fatigue is a critical consideration in warfare, but because sleeping soldiers don't make exciting viewing and certainly aren't very interactive, most games just skip sleep periods. Allowing soldiers to fight continuously without a pause permits the player to play continuously without a pause also.

The Sims, a game about managing a household, handles this problem a different way. The simulated characters require rest and sleep for their health, so *The Sims* depicts day and night accurately. However, when all the characters go to sleep, the game speeds up considerably, letting hours go by in a few seconds. As soon as anyone wakes up, time slows down again.

The Sims is a rather unusual game in that it's chiefly about time management. The player is under constant pressure to have his characters accomplish all their chores and get time for sleep, relaxation, and personal development as well. The game runs something like 48 times as fast as real life, so it takes about 20 minutes of real time to play through the 16 hours of game-world daytime. However, the characters don't move 48 times as fast. Their actions look pretty normal, about as they would in real time. As a result, it takes them 15 minutes according to the game's clock just to go out and pick up the newspaper. This contributes to the sense of time pressure. Because the characters do everything slowly (in game terms), they often don't get a chance to water their flowers, which consequently die.

Anomalous Time   In *The Settlers III,* a complex economic simulation, a tree can grow from a sapling to full size in about the same length of time that it takes for an iron foundry to smelt four or five bars of iron. This is a good example of *anomalous time*: time that seems to move at different speeds in different parts of the game. Blue Byte, the developer of *The Settlers,* tuned the length of time it takes to do each of the many tasks in the game to make sure that the game as a whole would run smoothly. As a result, *The Settlers* is very well balanced at some cost to realism. However, it doesn't disrupt the fantasy because *The Settlers* doesn't actually give the player a clock in the game world. There's no way to compare game time to real time, so in effect, the game world has no obvious time scale (see Figure 4.7).

Another example of anomalous time appears in *Age of Empires,* in which tasks that should take less than a day in real time (gathering berries from a bush, for example) seem to take years in game time according to the game clock. *Age of Empires* does have a time scale, visible on the game clock, but not everything in the world makes sense on that time scale. The players simply have to accept these actions as symbolic rather than real. As designers, we have to make them work in the context of the game world without disrupting the fantasy. As long as the symbolic actions (gathering berries or growing trees) don't have to be coordinated with real-time actions (warfare) but remain essentially independent processes, it doesn't matter if they operate on an anomalous time scale.

Letting the Player Adjust Time   In sports games and vehicle simulations, game time usually runs at the same speed as real time. An American football game is, by definition, an hour long, but because the clock stops all the time, the actual elapsed time of a football game is closer to three hours. All serious computerized football games simulate this accurately. Verisimilitude is a key requirement of most sports games; if a game does not accurately simulate the real sport, it might not be approved by the league, and its competitors

FIGURE 4.7 Activities in *The Settlers III* take anomalous lengths of time, but the game does not include a clock.

are bound to point out the flaw. However, most such games also allow the players to shorten the game by playing 5- or 10-minute quarters instead of 15-minute quarters because most people don't want to devote a full three hours to playing a simulated football game. This is also a useful feature in testing; it would take far too long to test the product if you had to play a full-length game every time.

Flight simulators also usually run in real time, but there are often long periods of flying straight and level during which nothing of interest is going on; the plane is simply traveling from one place to another. To shorten these periods, many games offer a way to speed up time in the game world by two, four, or eight times—in effect, making everything in the game world go faster than real time. When the plane approaches its destination, the player can return the game to normal speed and play in real time.

The Environmental Dimension

The environmental dimension describes the world's appearance and its atmosphere. We've seen that the physical dimension defines the properties of the game's space; the environmental dimension is about what's in that space. The environmental characteristics of the game world form the basis for creating its art and audio. We'll look at two particular properties: the cultural context of the world and the physical surroundings.

Cultural Context   When we speak of the *cultural context* of a game, we're talking about culture in the anthropological sense: the beliefs, attitudes, and values that the people in the game world hold, as well as their political and religious institutions, social organization, and so on—in short, the way those people live. These characteristics are reflected in the manufactured items that appear in the game: clothing, furniture, architecture, landscaping, and every other manmade object in the world. The culture influences not only what appears and what doesn't appear (a game set in a realistic ancient Egypt obviously shouldn't include firearms), but also how everything looks—including the user interface. *Cleopatra: Queen of the Nile* is an excellent example of a game's culture harmonizing with its user interface; see Figure 4.8. The appearance of objects is affected not only by their function in the world, but also by the aesthetic sensibilities of the people who constructed them; for example, a Maori shield will look entirely different from King Arthur's shield.

The cultural context also includes the game's backstory. The backstory of a game is the imaginary history, either large-scale (nations, wars, natural disasters)

FIGURE 4.8 The cultural context of *Cleopatra: Queen of the Nile* influences everything on the screen, including the icons and text.

or small-scale (personal events and interactions), that preceded the time when the game takes place. This prior history helps to establish why the culture is the way it is. A warlike people should have a history of warfare; a mercantile people should have a history of trading. In designing the backstory, don't go into too much depth too early, however. As we warned in Chapter 3, "Game Concepts," the story must serve the game, not the other way around.

For most game worlds, it's not necessary to define the culture or cultures in great detail. A game set in your own culture can simply use the things that you see around you. The *SimCity* series, for example, is clearly set in present-day America (European cities are rarely so rectilinear), and it looks like it. But when your game begins to deviate from your own culture, you need to start thinking about how it deviates and what consequences that deviation has.

Physical Surroundings   The physical surroundings define what the game actually looks like. This is a part of game design in which it's most helpful to be an artist or to work closely with one. In the early stages of design, you don't need to make drawings of every single thing that can appear in the game world (although sooner or later someone is going to have to do just that). For the time being, it's important to create concept sketches: pencil or pen-and-ink drawings of key visual elements in the game. Depending on what your game is about, this can include buildings, vehicles, clothing, weaponry, furniture, decorations, works of art, jewelry, religious or magical items, logos or emblems, and on and on. See *Grim Fandango* (Figure 4.9) for a particularly distinctive example. Constructed artifacts in particular are influenced by the game's culture. A powerful and highly religious people are likely to have large symbols of their spirituality: stone temples or cathedrals. A warlike nomadic people will have animals or vehicles to carry their gear and weapons suitable for use on the move. (Note that these might be future nomads, driving robo-camels.)

Nor should you neglect the natural world. Games set in urban or indoor environments consisting entirely of manufactured objects feel sterile. Think about birds and animals, plants and trees, earth, rocks, hills, and even the sky. Consider the climate: Is it hot or cold, wet or dry? Is the land fertile or barren, flat or mountainous? These qualities, all parts of a real place, are opportunities to create a visually rich and distinctive environment.

If your world is chiefly indoors, of course, you don't have to think about nature much unless your character passes a window, but there are many other issues to think about instead. Where does the light come from? What are the walls, floors, and ceilings made of, and how are they decorated? Why is this building here? Do the rooms have a specific purpose, and if so, what? How can you tell the purpose of a room from its contents? Does the building have multiple stories? How does the player get from one floor to another?

Physical surroundings include sounds as well as sights: music; ambient environmental sounds; the particular noises made by people, animals, machinery,

FIGURE 4.9 *Grim Fandango* combines Aztec, Art Deco, and Mexican Day of the Dead themes.

and vehicles. Thinking about the sounds things make at the same time that you think about how they look helps create a coherent world. Suppose you're inventing a six-legged reptilian saddle animal with clawed feet rather than hooves. How does that creature sound as it moves? Its scales might rattle a bit. Its feet are not going to make the characteristic clop-clop sound of a shod horse. With six legs, it will probably have some rather odd gaits, and those should be reflected in the sound it makes.

The physical surroundings are primarily responsible for setting the tone and mood of the game as it is played, whether it's the lighthearted cheerfulness of *Mario* or the dimly lit suspense of the *Thief* series (see Figure 4.10). The sound, and especially the music, will contribute greatly to this. Think hard about the kind of music you want, and consider what genres will be appropriate. Stanley Kubrick listened to hundreds of records to select the music for *2001: A Space Odyssey,* and he astonished the world with his choice of "The Blue Danube" for the shuttle docking sequence. You have a similar opportunity in designing your game.

Detail   Every designer must decide how much detail the game world needs— that is to say, how richly textured the world will be and how accurately modeled its characteristics will be. To some extent, your answer will be determined by the level of realism that you want, but technical limitations and time constraints

FIGURE 4.10 Hiding in the shadows in *Thief II: The Metal Age*.

will necessarily restrict your ambitions. No football game goes to the extent of modeling each fan in the stadium, and few flight simulators model all the physical characteristics of their aircraft. Detail helps to support the fantasy, but it always costs, in development time and in memory or disk space on the player's machine. In an adventure game, it should, in principle, be possible to pick up everything in the world; in practice, this just isn't practical. In consequence, the player knows that if an object *can* be picked up, it must be important for some reason; if it can't be picked up, it isn't important. Similarly, in god games, it's common for all the people to look alike; they're often male adults. Bullfrog Productions once designed a god game with both male and female adults, but there wasn't enough time for the artists to model children as well. People simply had to be born into the world full grown. Lionhead's *Black and White,* on the other hand, managed to include men, women, and children.

Here's a good rule of thumb for determining the level of detail your game will contain: Include as much detail as you can to help the game's immersiveness, *up to* the point at which it begins to harm the gameplay. If the player must struggle to look after everything you've given him, the game probably has too much detail. (This is one of the reasons war games tend to have hundreds rather than hundreds of thousands of units. The player in a war game can't delegate tasks to intelligent subordinates, so the numbers have to be kept down to a size that he can reasonably manage.) A spectacularly detailed game that's no fun to play won't sell many copies.

Defining a Style   In describing how your world is going to look, you are defining a visual style for your game that will influence a great many other things as well: the character design, the user interface, perhaps the manual, and even the design of the box and the advertising. You actually have two tasks to take on here: defining the style of things *in* your world (that is, its intrinsic style), and also defining the style of the artwork that will *depict* your world. They aren't the same. For example, you can describe a world whose architectural style is inspired by Buddhist temples but draw it to look like a *film noir* movie. Or you could have medieval towns with half-timbered houses but depicted in a slightly fuzzy, Impressionistic style. You must choose both your content and the way in which you will present that content.

Both decisions will significantly influence the player's experience of the game, jointly creating a distinct atmosphere. In general, the style of depiction tends to superimpose its mood on the style of the object depicted. For example, a Greek temple might be architecturally elegant, but if its style of drawing suggests a Looney Tunes cartoon, players will expect something wacky and outrageous to take place there. The drawing style imposes its own atmosphere over the temple, no matter how majestic it is. For one example, take a look at *XIII* (see Figure 4.11). All the locations in *XIII* were rendered in a flat-shaded style reminiscent of the comic book that inspired the game.

FIGURE 4.11 *XIII* overlays the Anasazi cliff dwellings of the American Southwest, and many other places, with a comic book style.

Unless you're the lead artist for your game as well as its designer, you probably shouldn't—or won't be allowed to—do this alone. Your art team will have ideas of its own, and you should listen to those suggestions. The marketing department might insist on having a say as well. It's important, however, that you try to keep the style harmonious and consistent throughout your game. Too many games have been published in which different sections had wildly differing art styles because no one held and enforced a single overall vision.

Overused Settings   All too often, games borrow settings from one another or from common settings found in the movies, books, or television. A huge number of games are set in science fiction and fantasy worlds, especially the quasi-medieval, sword-and-sorcery fantasy inspired by J. R. R. Tolkien and *Dungeons & Dragons*, popular with the young people who used to be the primary—indeed, almost the only—market for computer games. But a more diverse audience plays games nowadays, and they want new worlds to play in. You should look beyond these hoary old staples of gaming. As we mentioned in Chapter 3, *Interstate '76* was inspired by 1970s TV shows. It included cars, clothing, music, and language from that era, all highly distinctive and evocative of a particular culture. *Interstate '76* had great gameplay, but what really set it apart from its competitors was that it looked and sounded like nothing else on the market.

Especially if you are going to do science fiction or fantasy, try to make your game's setting distinctively different. At present, real spacecraft built by the United States or Russia look extremely functional, just as the first cars did in the 1880s, and the spacecraft in computer games tend to look that way also. But as cars became more common, they began exhibiting stylistic variation to appeal to different kinds of people, and now there is a whole school of aesthetics for automotive design. As spacecraft become more common, and especially as we start to see personal spacecraft, we should expect them to exhibit stylistic variation as well. This is an area in which you have tremendous freedom to innovate.

The same goes for fantasy. Forget the same old elves, dwarves, wizards, and dragons (Figure 4.12). Look to other cultures for your heroes and villains. Right now about the only non-Western culture portrayed with any frequency in games is Japanese (feudal, present-day, and future) because the Japanese make a lot of games and their style has found some acceptance in the West as well. But there are many more sources of inspiration around the world, most untapped. Around AD 1200, while the rulers of Europe were still holed up in cramped, drafty castles, Islamic culture reached a pinnacle of grace and elegance, building magnificent palaces filled with the riches of the Orient and majestic mosques of inlaid stone. Yet this proud and beautiful civilization seldom appears in computer games because Western game designers haven't bothered to learn about it or don't even know it existed. Set your fantasy in Valhalla, in Russia under Peter the Great, in the arctic tundra, at Angkor Wat, at Easter Island, or at Machu Picchu.

FIGURE 4.12 Yet another quasi-medieval setting: *Armies of Exigo*.

Sources of Inspiration   Art and architecture, history and anthropology, literature and religion, clothing fashions, and product design are all great sources of cultural material. Artistic and architectural movements, in particular, offer tremendous riches: Art Nouveau, Art Deco, Palladian, Brutalism. If you haven't heard of one of these, go look it up now. Browse the Web or the art, architecture, and design sections of the bookstore or the public library for pictures of interesting objects, buildings, and clothing. Carry a digital camera around and take pictures of things that attract your eye, then post the pictures around your workspace to inspire yourself and your coworkers. Collect graphic scrap from anywhere that you find it. Try old copies of *National Geographic*. Visit museums of art, design, and natural history if you can get to them; one of the greatest resources of all is travel if you can afford it. A good game designer is always on the lookout for new ideas, even when he's ostensibly on vacation.

It's tempting to borrow from our closest visual neighbor, the movies, because the moviemakers have already done the visual design work for us. *Blade Runner* introduced the decaying urban future; *Alien* gave us disgustingly biological aliens rather than little green men. The problem with these looks is that they've already been borrowed many, many times. You can use them as a quick-and-dirty backdrop if you don't want to put much effort into developing your world, and players will instantly recognize the world and know what the game is about. But to stand out from the crowd, consider other genres. *Film noir,* the Marx Brothers, John Wayne westerns, war movies from the World War II era, costume dramas of all periods—from the silliness of *One Million Years B.C.* to the Regency elegance of *Pride and Prejudice,* they're all grist for the mill.

Television goes through its own distinct phases, and because it's even more fashion-driven than the movies, it is ripe for parody. The comedies of the 1950s and 1960s and the nighttime soaps of the 1970s and 1980s all had characteristic looks that seem laughable today but that are immediately familiar to most adult Americans. This is not without risk; if you make explicit references to American popular culture, non-Americans and children might not get the reference. If your gameplay is good enough, though, it shouldn't matter.

The Emotional Dimension

The emotional dimension of a game world defines not only the emotions of the people in the world but, more important, the emotions that you, as a designer, hope to arouse in the player. Multiplayer games evoke the widest variety of emotions, because the players are socializing with real people and making friends (and, alas, enemies) as they play. Single-player games have to influence players' emotions with storytelling and gameplay. Action and strategy games are usually limited to a narrow emotional dimension, but other games that rely more heavily on story and characters can offer rich emotional content that deeply affects the player.

The idea of manipulating the player's emotions might seem a little strange. For much of their history, games have been seen only as light entertainment, a means to while away a few hours in a fantasy world. But just because that's all they have been doesn't mean that's all they *can* be. In terms of the richness of their emotional content, games are now just about where the movies were when they moved from the nickelodeon to the screen. Greater emotional variety will enable us to reach new players who value it.

Influencing the Player's Feelings   Games are intrinsically good at evoking feelings related to the player's efforts to achieve something. They can create "the thrill of victory and the agony of defeat," as the old *ABC's Wide World of Sports* introduction used to say. Use the elements of risk and reward—a price for failure and a prize for success—to further heighten these emotions. Games can also produce frustration as a by-product of their challenges, but this isn't a good thing; some players tolerate frustration poorly and will stop playing if it gets too high. To reduce frustration, build games with player-settable difficulty levels and make sure the easy level is genuinely easy. Excitement and anticipation, too, play large roles in many games. If you can devise a close contest or a series of stimulating challenges, you will generate these kinds of emotions.

Construction and management simulations, whose challenges are usually financial, arouse the player's feelings of ambition, greed, and desire for power or control. They also offer the emotional rewards of creative play. Give the player a way to amass a fortune, then let him spend it to build things of his own design. The *SimCity* and various Tycoon games (*RollerCoaster Tycoon, Railroad Tycoon,* and so on), do this well. Artificial life games and god games such as *Black and White* or *The Sims* let the player control the lives of autonomous people and creatures for better or worse, satisfying a desire to be omnipotent over a world of beings subject to the player's will. (This may not be a very admirable fantasy, but it's one that a lot of people enjoy having fulfilled.)

To create suspense, surprise, and fear, use the time-honored techniques of horror films: darkness, sudden noises, disgusting imagery, and things that jump out at the player unexpectedly. Don't overdo it, however. A gore-fest becomes tedious after a while, and Alfred Hitchcock demonstrated that the shock is all the greater when it occurs infrequently. For suspense to work well, the player needs to feel vulnerable and unprepared. Don't arm him too heavily; the world's a lot less scary when you're carrying a rocket launcher around. **Survival horror** is a popular subgenre of action game, as seen in the *Silent Hill* and *Resident Evil* series, that uses these approaches.

Another class of emotions is produced by interactions between characters and the player's identification with one of them. Love, grief, shame, jealousy, and outrage are all emotions that can result from such interactions. (See Figure 4.13 for a famous example.) To evoke them, you'll have to use storytelling techniques, creating characters that the player cares about and believes in and credible relationships between them. Once you get the player to identify with someone, threaten that character or place obstacles in his path in a way that holds the player's interest. This is the essence of dramatic tension, whether we're watching Greek tragedy or reading *Harry Potter*. Something important must be at stake. The problem need not necessarily be physical danger; it can also be a social, emotional, or economic risk. The young women in Jane Austen's novels were not in imminent peril of death or starvation, but it was essential to their family's social standing and financial future for them to make good marriages. The conflict between their personal desires and their family obligations provides the tension in the novels.

A good many games set the danger at hyperbolic levels with extreme claims such as "The fate of the universe rests in your hands!" This kind of hyperbole appeals to young people, who often feel powerless and have fantasies about being powerful. To adults, it just sounds a bit silly. At the end of *Casablanca,* Rick said, "The problems of three little people don't amount to a

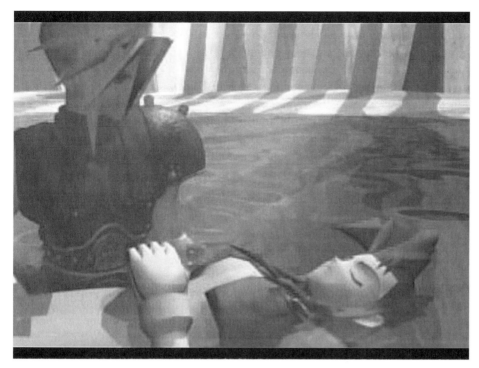

FIGURE 4.13 The death of Aeris, from *Final Fantasy VII*.

hill of beans in this crazy world," but he was wrong. The whole movie, a movie still popular over a half century after its first release, is about the problems of those three little people. For the duration of the film, these problems hold us entranced. It isn't necessary that the fate of the world be at stake; it is the fates of Rick, Ilsa, and Victor that tug at our hearts.

> ## COMMANDMENT: Avoid Implausible Extremes
>
> Don't make your game about the fate of the world if you are serious about producing emotional resonance with your audience; the fate of the world is too big to grasp. Make your game about the fate of people instead.

The Limitations of Fun   Most people think that the purpose of playing games is to have fun, but *fun* is a rather limiting term. It tends to suggest excitement and pleasure, either a physical pleasure such as riding a roller coaster, a social pleasure such as joking around with friends, or an intellectual pleasure such as playing cards or a board game. The problem with striving for fun is that it tends to limit the emotional range of games. Suspense, excitement, exhilaration, surprise, and various forms of pleasure fall within the definition of fun, but not pity, jealousy, anger, sorrow, guilt, outrage, or despair.

You might think that nobody in their right mind would want to explore these emotions, but other forms of entertainment—books, movies, television—do it all the time. And, in fact, that's the key: Those media don't provide only fun; they provide entertainment. People can be entertained in all sorts of ways. Movies with sad endings aren't fun in the conventional sense, but they're still entertaining. Although we say that we make games, what we in fact make is interactive entertainment. The potential of our medium to explore emotions and the human condition is much greater than the term *fun game* allows for.

All that said, however, bear in mind that most publishers and players want fun. Too many inexperienced designers are actually more interested in showing how clever they are than in making sure the player has a good time; they place their own creative agenda before the player's enjoyment. As a designer, you must master the ability to create fun—light enjoyment—before you move on to more complex emotional issues. Addressing unpleasant or painful emotions successfully is a greater aesthetic challenge and is commercially risky besides.

You Can't Paint Emotion by Numbers The idea that games should include more emotional content and should inspire more emotions in players has been gaining ground in the game industry for several years. Unfortunately, this has produced a tendency to look for quick and easy ways to do it, mostly by relying on clichés. The young man whose family is killed and who is obsessed by his desire for revenge or the beautiful princess who needs to be rescued both belong more to fairy tales than to modern fiction. That may be all right if your game aspires to nothing more, but it won't do if you're trying to create an experience with any subtlety. Beware of books or articles that offer simple formulas for emotional manipulation: "If you want to make the player feel X, just do Y to the protagonist." An imaginative and novel approach to influencing the players' feelings requires the talents of a skilled storyteller. Paint-by-numbers emotional content has all the sensitivity and nuance of paint-by-numbers art.

The Ethical Dimension

The ethical dimension of a game world defines what right and wrong mean within the context of that world. At first glance, this might seem kind of silly—it's only a game, so there's no need to talk about ethics. But most games that have a setting, a fantasy component, also have an ethical system that defines how the player is supposed to behave. As designers, we are the gods of the game's world, and we establish its morality. When we tell a player that he must perform certain actions to win the game, we are defining those actions as good or desirable. Likewise, when we say that the player must avoid certain actions, we are defining them as bad or undesirable. The players who come into the world must adopt our standards or they will lose the game.

In some respects, the morality of a game world is part of its culture and history, which we earlier classed with the environmental dimension, but we've broken it out for separate discussion because it poses special design problems. The ethics of most game worlds deviate somewhat from those of the real world—sometimes they're entirely reversed. Games allow, even require, you to do things that you can't do in the real world. The range of actions that the game world permits is typically narrower than in the real world (you can fly your F-15 fighter jet all you want, but you can't get out of the plane), but often the permitted actions are quite extreme: killing people, stealing things, and so on.

Moral Decision-Making   On the whole, most games have simple ethics: clobber the bad guys, protect the good guys. It's not subtle but it's perfectly functional; that's how you play checkers. Not many games explore the ethical dimension in any depth. A few include explicit moral choices, but unfortunately, these tend to be namby-pamby, consistently rewarding good behavior and punishing bad behavior. Such preachy material turns off even children, not to mention adults. But you can build a richer, more involving game by giving the player tough moral choices to make. Ethical ambiguity and difficult decisions are at the heart of many great stories and, indeed, much of life. Should you send a platoon of soldiers to certain death to save a battalion of others? How would you feel if you were in the platoon?

FYI   *The Peculiar Morality of America's Army*

America's Army, a team-based multiplayer first-person shooter (FPS) game distributed free by the U.S. Army, is intended to serve as an education and recruiting tool, teaching players how real soldiers are supposed to fight (Figure 4.14). It differs from most FPS games in two significant ways. First, it requires that the player act in conformance with the actual disciplinary requirements of the Army, so it detects and punishes dishonorable behavior. The Army is anxious to make the point that soldiering comes with serious moral responsibilities. Second, and rather strangely, all sides in a firefight see themselves as U.S. soldiers, and they see the enemy as rather generic terrorists. The Army did not want to give any player the chance to shoot at American soldiers, even though they are obviously shooting at one another. So a player sees himself and his teammates as U.S. soldiers carrying M-16 rifles, but his opponents see him and his teammates as terrorists carrying AK-47s. In other words, everyone perceives himself as a

▶▶ CONTINUED ON NEXT PAGE

FIGURE 4.14 Our guys get the drop on somebody who also thinks he's one of our guys.

good guy and his opponents as a bad guy, and the game's graphics literally present two different versions of reality to each team. By avoiding a politically unacceptable design (letting players shoot at American soldiers in a game made by the U.S. Army), they created a moral equivalence: The question of who is in the right is purely a matter of perspective.

America's Army's trick of displaying different versions of the game world to different players may be unique among video games. We would be interested to see some other uses for it.

In many role-playing games, you can choose to play as an evil character who steals and kills indiscriminately, but other characters will refuse to cooperate with you and might even attack you on sight. It's easier to get money by robbing others than by working for it, but you may pay a price for that behavior in other ways. Rather than impose a rule that says, "Immoral behavior is forbidden," the game implements a rule that says, "You are free to make your own moral choices, but be prepared to live with the consequences." The player can play however he sees fit, but there are advantages and disadvantages either way. This is a more adult approach to the issue than simply punishing bad behavior.

All that said, we strongly discourage creating games that reward or even allow the player to do truly hateful things. One of the most repugnant games ever created was a cartridge for the Atari 2600 console called *Custer's Revenge*, in which the player's avatar, a cowboy, was supposed to try to rape a Native American woman who was tied to a pole. (The cartridge was independently published and was not supported or endorsed by Atari.) This kind of thing is beyond bad taste; it's pathological. Games that expect a player to participate in sexual assault, torture, or child abuse serve only to gratify their designers' sick fantasies while tarnishing the reputation of game industry as a whole. Although no one would condemn all cinema on the basis of one offensive movie, interactive entertainment is still a young enough medium that we all get tarred with the same brush . Like it or not, one game can affect the entire industry. The best way to avoid censorship is to exercise some judgment in the first place.

You must be sure to explain the ethical dimension of your game clearly in the manual, in introductory material, or in mission briefings. For example, some games that have hostage-rescue scenarios make the death of a hostage a loss condition: If a hostage dies, the player loses. This means that the player has to be extra careful not to kill any hostages, even at the risk of his own avatar's life. In other games, the only loss condition is the avatar's death. In this case, many players will shoot with complete abandon, killing hostages and their captors indiscriminately. In real life, of course, the truth is somewhere in between. Police officers who accidentally shoot a hostage are seldom prosecuted unless they've been grossly negligent, but it doesn't do their careers any good. You can emulate this by penalizing the player somehow. To be fair to the player, however, you need to make this clear at the outset.

The ethical dimensions of multiplayer games, whether online or local, are an enormous and separate problem. We discuss this at length in Chapter 21, "Online Games," which is available on the Companion Website.

Companion Website

A Word about Game Violence   It's not part of our mission in this book to debate, much less offer an answer for, the problem of whether violent video games cause violent behavior in children or adults. This is a psychological question that will be resolved only after prolonged and careful study. Unfortunately, a good many people on both sides of the issue seem to have made up their minds already, and arguments continue to rage in the halls of Congress and elsewhere, supported for the most part by very few facts.

For you, as a designer, however, we do have a few suggestions. The essence of many games is conflict, and conflict is often represented as violence in varying degrees of realism. Chess is a war game in which pieces are killed—removed from the board—but nobody objects to the violence of chess; it's entirely abstract. American football is a violent contact sport in which real people get injured all the time, but there are no serious efforts to ban football, either.

The only way to remove violence from gameplay would be to prohibit most of the games in the world because most contain violence in some more-or-less abstract form. The issue is not violence, per se, but how violence is portrayed and the circumstances under which violence is acceptable.

Games get into political trouble when they have a close visual similarity to the real world but an ethical dimension that is strongly divergent from the real world. The game *Kingpin* encouraged the player to beat prostitutes to death with a crowbar, with bloodily realistic graphics. Not surprisingly, it earned a lot of criticism. On the other hand, *Space Invaders* involved shooting hundreds of aliens, but it was so visually abstract that nobody minded. In other words, the more a game resembles reality visually, the more its ethical dimension should resemble reality as well, or it's likely to make people upset. If you want to make a game in which the player is encouraged to shoot anything that moves, you're most likely to stay out of trouble if those targets are nonhuman and just quietly disappear rather than break apart into bloody chunks. Tie your ethical realism to your visual realism.

Computer games are about bringing fantasies to life, enabling people to do things in make-believe that they couldn't possibly do in the real world. But make-believe is a dangerous game when played by people for whom the line between fantasy and reality is not clear. Young children (those under about age eight) don't know much about the real world; they don't know what is possible and what isn't, what is fantasy and what is reality. An important part of raising children is teaching them this difference. But until they've learned it, it's best to make sure that any violence in young children's games is suitably proportionate to their age. The problem with showing violence to children is not the violence, per se, but the notion that there's no price to pay for it. For a detailed and insightful discussion of how children come to terms with violence, read *Killing Monsters: Why Children Need Fantasy, Super Heroes, and Make-Believe Violence* by Gerard Jones (Jones, 2002)

Ultimately, the violence in a game should serve the gameplay. If it doesn't, then it's gratuitous and you should consider doing without it. A few designers, mostly young and male, seem to think that deliberately including gratuitous violence in their games is a gesture of rebellion against the antiviolence crusaders. We encourage these gentlemen to grow up and to remember who the game is for. Our customers don't buy games to see rebellious gestures; they buy them to be entertained.

Realism

In Chapter 2, "Design Components and Processes," we introduced the concept of *realism* in the context of a discussion about core mechanics. All games, no matter how realistic, require some abstraction and simplification of the real world. Even the multimillion-dollar flight simulators used for training commercial pilots are incapable of turning the cockpit completely upside down. This event is so rare (we hope) in passenger aircraft that it's not worth the extra money it would take to simulate it.

The degree of realism of any aspect of a game will be found on a continuum of possibilities from highly representational at one end to highly abstract at the other. Players and game reviewers often talk about realism as a quality of an entire game, but in fact, the level of realism differs in individual components of the game. Many games have highly realistic graphics but unrealistic physics. A good many first-person shooters accurately model the performance characteristics of a variety of weapons—their rate of fire, size of ammunition clips, accuracy, and so on—but allow the player to carry about ten of them at once with no reduction in speed or mobility. Therefore, realism is not a single dimension of a game world, but a multivariate quality that applies to all parts of the game and everything in it. (If you're mathematically inclined, think of realism as a vector over every aspect of the game, with values ranging from 0, entirely abstract, to 1, entirely realistic. However, no value will ever equal 1 because nothing about a game is ever entirely realistic—if it were, it would be life, not a game.)

The representational/abstract dichotomy is mostly useful as a starting point when thinking about what kind of a game you want to create. On the one hand, if you're designing a cartoony action game such as *Banjo-Kazooie,* you know that it's going to be mostly abstract. As you design elements of the game, you'll need to ask yourself how much realism you want to include. Can your avatar be hurt when he falls long distances? Is there a limit to how much he can carry at once? Do Newtonian physics apply to him, or can he change directions in midair?

On the other hand, if you're designing a game that people will expect to be representational—a vehicle or sports simulation, for example—then you have to think about it from the other direction. What aspects of the real world are you going to remove? Most modern fighter aircraft have literally hundreds of controls; that's why only a special group of people can be fighter pilots. To make a fighter simulation accessible to the general public, you'll have to simplify a lot of those controls. Similarly, a fighter jet's engine is so powerful that certain maneuvers can knock the pilot unconscious or even rip the plane apart. Are you going to simulate these limitations accurately, or make the game a little more abstract by not requiring the player to think about them?

As we have said, every design decision you make must serve the entertainment value of the game. In addition, every design decision must serve your goals for the game's overall degree of realism. Some genres demand more realism than others. It's up to you to establish how much realism you want and in what areas. During the design process, you must continually monitor your decisions to see if they are meeting your goals.

Summary

At this point, you should know when and where your game takes place. You will have answered a huge number of questions about what your world looks like, what it sounds like, who lives there, and how they behave. If you've done it thoroughly, your game world will be one in which a player can immerse himself, a consistent fantasy that he can believe in and enjoy being part of. The next step is to figure out what's going to happen there.

Test Your Skills

MULTIPLE CHOICE QUESTIONS

1. A game world is
   A. an essential element of every game.
   B. the mental state of a player playing a game.
   C. the fictional setting of a game, if it has one.
   D. a "presentation layer" that is unrelated to the game's rules or gameplay.

2. In defining the physical dimension of a game world, it is important to consider its
   A. length, width, depth, and duration.
   B. dimensionality, scale, and boundaries.
   C. aesthetic and musical styles.
   D. relationship to the player's own surroundings.

3. Having an unexplained boundary in a representational game world
   A. is a good way to create a sense of surrealism.
   B. appears to the player as a violation of the laws of physics.
   C. is unavoidable due to the limitations of 3D hardware.
   D. may harm the player's immersion in the world.

4. In game worlds that are simulations of some kind, time usually moves at a rate
   A. faster than that of the real world.
   B. slower than that of the real world.
   C. the same as that of the real world.
   D. that can always be adjusted by the player.

5. What is anomalous time?

   A. Time whose rate can be adjusted by the player.

   B. Time in which different things appear to change at inconsistent rates.

   C. Time that flows backward.

   D. Time whose rate is different from real-world time.

6. In a fictional game world, the cultural characteristics of the imaginary inhabitants

   A. define everything about the game world.

   B. are abstractions that won't affect the final product.

   C. have a direct bearing on the rate of time in the game world.

   D. influence the appearance and function of all the manmade objects in the game world.

4

7. Which of the following is *not* a reason for limiting the amount of detail in a game?

   A. Development costs and time.

   B. Player ability to manage the game.

   C. Limitations of the target hardware.

   D. The size of the publisher's marketing budget.

8. Defining the aesthetic style of a game includes deciding the style of the content of the game world itself and which other decision?

   A. The programming language that the developers should use.

   B. The dimensionality of the physical dimension.

   C. The size of the audio budget.

   D. The style of the art with which you present the world.

9. Which is a disadvantage of borrowing a commonly used fictional setting?

   A. The players will be unfamiliar with the world and uncertain of its rules.

   B. It is more difficult to design a consistent, harmonious look for the world.

   C. It may be difficult to differentiate your game from similar ones on the market.

   D. Testing and balancing the game are harder to do.

10. Which are reasonable sources to study for inspiration in designing a fictional world?

    A. Botany, zoology, and geography.

    B. Myths, fables, and stories.

    C. History, biography, and architecture.

    D. All of the above.

11. Traditional gameplay mechanics are good at producing which group of emotions?

    A. Jealousy, hatred, and fear.

    B. Envy, love, and bitterness.

    C. Triumph, dejection, and frustration.

    D. All of the above.

12. Which kinds of games are likely to evoke the greatest variety of emotions?

    A. Card games.

    B. Handheld games.

    C. Multiplayer games.

    D. Role-playing games.

13. Why are video games more ethically problematic than noninteractive forms of entertainment?

    A. Video games can require the player to act unethically if he wants to get to the end of the game.

    B. The characters in video games are more well rounded than in other media.

    C. Video games are necessarily more violent than other forms of entertainment.

    D. All of the above.

14. When is it important to make the ethical system of a game world clear to the player?

    A. Only when the players are likely to be children.

    B. Whenever it is possible for the player's avatar to die in the game.

    C. When the game contains religious themes.

    D. When the game's ethical system deviates significantly from that of the real world.

EXERCISES

1. Imagine that you could use any content you liked in a game without regard for copyright. Choose one of the following game genres and then select a famous painter, photographer, or filmmaker, and a famous composer or musician, whose work you would like to use to create the appropriate emotional tone for your game. Create a short

presentation (PowerPoint or similar) that shows how the images and music work together for your purpose. The genres are action (survival horror subgenre), real-time strategy (modern warfare), or children's nonviolent adventure game.

2. Write an essay discussing two contrasting systems of morality in games you have played or in two games assigned by your instructor. What actions does each game reward, and what actions does it punish? Address the relationship between right behavior in the two game worlds and right behavior in the real world.

DESIGN QUESTIONS

Questions to Ask Yourself about the Physical Dimension

1. Does my game require a physical dimension? What is it used for? Is it an essential part of gameplay or merely cosmetic?

2. Leaving aside issues of implementation or display, how many imaginary spatial dimensions does my game require? If there are three or more, can objects move continuously through the third and higher dimensions, or are these dimensions partitioned into discrete "layers" or zones?

3. How big is my game world, in light-years or inches? Is accuracy of scale critical, as in a football game, or not, as in a cartoon-like action game?

4. Will my game need more than one scale, for indoor versus outdoor areas, for example? How many will it actually require?

5. How am I going to handle the relative sizes of objects and people? What about their relative speeds of movement?

6. How is my world bounded? Am I going to make an effort to disguise the "edge of the world," and if so, with what? What happens if the player tries to go beyond it?

Questions to Ask Yourself about the Temporal Dimension

1. Is time a meaningful element of my game? Does the passage of time change anything in the game world even if the player does nothing, or does the world simply sit still and wait for the player to do something?

2. If time does change the world, what effects does it have? Does food decay, and do light bulbs burn out?

3. How does time affect the player's avatar? Does he get hungry or tired?

4. What is the actual purpose of including time in my game? Is it only a part of the atmosphere, or is it an essential part of the gameplay?

5. Is there a time scale for my game? Do I need to have measurable quantities of time, such as hours, days, and years, or can I just let time go by without bothering to measure it? Does the player need a clock to keep track of time?

6. Are there periods of time that I'm going to skip or do without? Is this going to be visible to the player, or will it happen seamlessly?

7. Do I need to implement day and night? If I do, what will make night different from day? Will it merely look different, or will it have other effects as well? What about seasons?

8. Will any of the time in my game need to be anomalous? If so, why? Will that bother the player? Do I need to explain it away, and if so, how?

9. Should the player be allowed to adjust time in any way? Why, how, and when?

Questions to Ask Yourself about the Environmental Dimension

1. Is my game world set in a particular historical period or geographic location? When and where? Is it an alternate reality, and if so, what makes it different from ours?

2. Are there any people in my game world? What are they like? Do they have a complex, highly organized society or a simple, tribal one? How do they govern themselves? How is this social structure reflected in their physical surroundings? Are there different classes of people, guilds, or specialized occupations?

3. What do my people value? Trade, martial prowess, imperialism, peace? What kinds of lives do they lead in pursuit of these ends? Are they hunters, nomadic, agrarian, industrialized, even postindustrial? How does this affect their buildings and clothing?

4. Are my people superstitious or religious? Do they have institutions or religious practices that will be visible in the game? Are there religious buildings? Do the people carry charms or display spiritual emblems?

5. What are my people's aesthetics like? Are they flamboyant or reserved, chaotic or orderly, bright or subtle? What colors do they like? Do they prefer straight lines or curves?

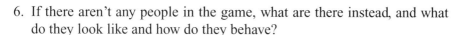

6. If there aren't any people in the game, what are there instead, and what do they look like and how do they behave?

7. Does my game take place indoors or outdoors, or both? If indoors, what are the furnishings and interior decor like? If outdoors, what is the geography and architecture like?

8. What are the style and mood of my game? How am I going to create them with art, sound, and music?

9. How much detail can I afford in my game? Will it be rich and varied or sparse and uncluttered? How does this affect the way the game is played?

Questions to Ask Yourself about the Emotional Dimension

1. Does my game have a significant emotional dimension? What emotions will my game world include?

2. How does emotion serve the entertainment value of my game? Is it a key element of the plot? Does it motivate characters in the game or the player himself?

3. What emotions will I try to inspire in the player? How will I do this? What will be at stake?

Questions to Ask Yourself about the Ethical Dimension

1. What constitutes right and wrong in my game? What player actions do I reward and what do I punish?

2. How will I explain the ethical dimensions of the world to the player? What tells him how to behave and what is expected of him?

3. If my game world includes conflict or competition, is it represented as violence or as something else (racing to a finish, winning an economic competition, outmaneuvering the other side)?

4. What range of choices am I offering my player? Are there both violent and nonviolent ways to accomplish something? Is the player rewarded in any way for minimizing casualties, or is he punished for ignoring them?

5. In many games, the end—winning the game—justifies any means that the game allows. Do I want to define the victory conditions in such a way that not all means are acceptable?

6. Are any other ethical questions present in my game world? Can my player lie, cheat, steal, break promises, or double-cross anyone? Can she

abuse, torture, or enslave anyone? Are there positive or negative consequences for these actions?

7. Does my world contain any ethical ambiguities or moral dilemmas? How does making one choice over another affect the player, the plot, and the gameplay?

8. How realistic is my portrayal of violence? Does the realism appropriately serve the entertainment value of the game?

Chapter | 5

Creative and Expressive Play

Chapter Objectives

After reading this chapter and completing the exercises, you will be able to do the following:

- Describe self-defining play as a way a player can project his personality into the game world through his selection of an avatar and the avatar's attributes.

- Explain creative play as a way to allow players to design or construct as part of the gameplay.

- Understand the difference between constrained creative play and freeform creative play.

- Know how games can provide storytelling play by allowing players to create their own stories.

- List ways in which you can provide a player additional creative freedom by allowing her to modify a game.

Introduction

Playing any game involves an element of self-expression because the decisions a player makes reflect his play style: cautious or reckless, aggressive or defensive, and so on. Video games can let players express themselves in the ways traditional games always have and in a variety of other ways as well. In this chapter, we examine several types of creative play that you can build into a game: self-defining play, in which players modify the avatar that represents them in the game; constrained creative play, in which players may exercise their creativity but only within certain limits; freeform, or unconstrained, creative play; and storytelling, in which players present other players with a drama of their own invention. We end with a brief discussion of some features you may wish to include to allow players to modify your game for their own entertainment: level editors, mods, and bots.

Self-Defining Play

When a player selects a token to represent herself in *Monopoly*, she chooses an avatar and so engages in an act of self-definition. Many games allow the player to choose an avatar from a number of different ones available and to customize the avatar in various ways. Because the avatar represents the player in the game world, we call these activities *self-defining play*. Players greatly enjoy defining themselves, choosing an avatar that either resembles themselves physically (if it's a human character) or that is a fantasy figure with whom they identify. Female players in particular like to choose or design avatars that resemble themselves and dislike having to play with avatars that they find unappealing. Boys and men are more willing to play with a default avatar supplied by the game.

Self-defining play gives the player an opportunity to project his personality into the game world by means other than gameplay choices. It takes several forms:

- **Avatar selection** allows the player to choose from a number of predefined avatars, usually at the beginning of the game. These avatars are most often humanoid characters, but in driving and flying games, they're vehicles. Many driving games start the player with a small selection of cars, motorcycles, or whatever vehicles are involved and make new choices available as the player's performance improves. You can let the player purchase a new car with winnings earned in previous races, for example. The right to choose a new and more powerful avatar serves as a powerful reward to some players.

- **Avatar customization** allows the player to modify the appearance or abilities of her avatar by selecting interchangeable features. In role-playing games, this often takes the form of giving the avatar new skills, clothing, weapons, and armor. In driving games, the customizable features may include the paint color of the car and its engine, transmission, tires, and brakes. Customization can occur both at the beginning of the game and through upgrades awarded or purchased as the game goes on. In this way, a player creates a unique character of his own design.

- **Avatar construction** gives the player the greatest freedom of all; he can construct his avatar from the ground up, choosing every detail from a set of available options. Usually offered in role-playing games, avatar construction allows the player to choose such features as the sex, body type, skin color, and clothing of the avatar, as well as the avatar's strength, intelligence, dexterity, and other functional attributes. The online RPG *Star Wars Galaxies* offers a particularly extensive avatar construction feature, as does the single-player RPG *The Elder Scrolls: Oblivion* for the PC.

The attributes that a player may modify can be divided into those that affect the gameplay, which we call *functional attributes,* and those that don't affect the gameplay, which we call *cosmetic attributes.* (Some designers prefer the term *aesthetic attributes,* but the meaning is the same.) We examine them more closely in the next two sections.

Functional Attributes

When the core mechanics of the game incorporate avatar attributes in their calculations, those attributes have an influence on the gameplay, so we call them **functional attributes.** Functional attributes can be further divided into **characterization attributes,** which define fundamental aspects of a character and change slowly or not at all, and **status attributes,** which give the current status of the character and may change frequently. For the purposes of creative play, we're interested in the characterization attributes.

You have probably heard of the six characterization attributes used in *Dungeons & Dragons*: strength, dexterity, intelligence, wisdom, charisma, and constitution. Each of these attributes affects a character's ability to perform certain actions in the game: fight, cast magic spells, charm others, withstand poisons, and many other tasks. When *Dungeons & Dragons* players create a character, they receive a certain number of points (usually obtained by rolling dice) to distribute among these attributes. How they distribute them—giving more to dexterity and less to intelligence, for instance—establishes the character's strengths and weaknesses. These strengths and weaknesses, in turn, determine how the player must play with the character to be successful in the game: taking advantage of the strengths and avoiding situations in which the weaknesses render the player vulnerable.

When players assign values to the functional attributes of their characters, they define themselves in a creative way. Hardcore players, whose main interest is in winning, tend to look for the setting that will give them the greatest advantage in the game—that is, to optimize the attributes' influence on the core mechanics. Casual players either don't worry about the assignments much, or they select settings that will allow for interesting role-playing. A character who is highly charismatic but physically weak, for example, will have to be played quite differently from a conventional warrior.

If you allow players to assign any legitimate value to their functional attributes, some players will set up their attributes in the best possible configuration, and the game will be very easy for them. Many designers don't like this, because they see the players as their opponents. We believe this is the wrong reason for disallowing it; your goal is to entertain the player, not to oppose him. However, you can legitimately prevent it if it might introduce bugs into your game or make the game difficult to test. We recommend the following:

- Give players a fixed or random number of points to assign among all their attributes, as in *Dungeons & Dragons*. This allows them to make interesting choices and create an avatar who reflects their own personality or fantasies without unbalancing the game. If you generate a random number of points for the player, we suggest you use a nonuniform distribution as *Dungeons & Dragons* does in order to avoid producing unusually strong or weak characters. See *Random Numbers and the Gaussian Curve* in Chapter 10, "Core Mechanics."

- Include a set of default, or recommended, settings so players who want to get started quickly can do so without spending a lot of time setting attributes. This is especially valuable for players who don't understand how the attributes affect the gameplay anyway. They will find it frustrating to be required to set attributes when they don't know how the attributes affect the game and all they want to do is get into the game and start playing. They will appreciate being given a reasonable default.

- Allow players to *earn* the right to set their character's functional attributes any way they like by completing the game with constrained attributes first. You can also offer this right explicitly as a cheat feature of the game, so players will know they're getting an unusual advantage.

We have explained functional attributes with reference to *Dungeons & Dragons* simply because it provides one of the most familiar examples, but many, many games use functional attributes. First-person shooters typically give the player a choice of weapons, and when a player chooses a sniper rifle over a submachine gun, she is choosing something important about her character and the way she will play the game.

Cosmetic Attributes

Cosmetic attributes don't have any effect on the player's ability to perform actions or overcome challenges; that is, they're not part of the core mechanics of the game. Cosmetic attributes exist to let the player define himself in the game world, to bring his own personal style to the avatar. The paint color of a racing car has no effect on the car's performance characteristics, but the player will enjoy the game more if he can choose a color that he likes. One cosmetic attribute—shape—differentiates the tokens in *Monopoly*.

In multiplayer video games, cosmetic attributes can play a more important role because other players rely on visual appearances to make decisions. A few years ago, some bright player in a first-person shooter game got the idea to design an avatar that looked exactly like a crate. The other players assumed that they were looking at an actual crate and so ignored it, then were surprised when they were shot by someone in a room that apparently contained only a crate. In online role-playing games, players also use cosmetic attributes to identify themselves as members of a particular clan or group.

Cosmetic attributes make a game more fun at a low implementation cost. Because they don't affect the gameplay, they don't have to be tested and balanced as thoroughly as a functional attribute. Just be sure that your cosmetic attributes really *are* cosmetic. Avatar body size may sound like a cosmetic attribute, but if you later decide to take it into account when performing combat calculations (bigger people make bigger targets, for instance), then size becomes a functional attribute after all.

Typical cosmetic attributes for human characters include headgear, clothing, shoes, jewelry, hair color, eye color, skin color, and body type or size. Players typically customize paint color and decals or insignia of vehicles.

IN THE TRENCHES: Should Gender Be a Functional or Cosmetic Attribute?

Should the sex of an avatar have an effect on gameplay? Because men generally have more upper-body strength than women do and women are generally more dexterous than men are, you may be tempted to build these qualities directly into your core mechanics: to restrict the strength of female avatars and to restrict the dexterity of male ones.

However, unless you're making an extremely realistic simulation game, we recommend against associating bonuses or penalties with one sex or the other. First, although men as a group are *generally* stronger than women, it is not true that all men are stronger than all women. Women who exercise are often stronger than men who don't, and men who play the piano are usually more dexterous than women who don't. There are always exceptions and overlaps. Second, video games provide a form of escapism. Players like to imagine themselves doing things that they can't do in the real world. If you impose real-world rules on what is meant to be their fantasy experience, you take some of the fun out of it.

We think it's better to allow the players to construct their avatars to suit their own styles of play rather than establishing an arbitrary standard connected to gender. Leave gender as a cosmetic attribute and let the players adjust their functional attributes, such as strength and dexterity, independently.

Creative Play

Many games offer the player the chance to design or build something. In *SimCity*, it's a city; in *Barbie Fashion Designer*, it's clothing. People enjoy designing and building things, and this kind of play is the main point of construction and management simulations.

If you offer creative play, you should allow players to save their creations at any time and reload them to continue working on them. You should also let players print their creations out, take screenshots, copy them to other players' machines, and upload them to Web sites. Sharing creations contributes to the fun.

Computerized creative play falls into two categories, *constrained creative play* and *freeform creative play.* No computer can create absolutely unconstrained play; software can offer the player only the actions that the designer chooses to implement, and the program will always be limited by the amount of memory available. A computerized game necessarily restricts creative play to whatever domain the game supports—painting, composing music, animation, and so on. When we speak of freeform creative play, we mean that few or no rules limit what the player can do within the confines of the game world, although play remains constrained by the domain and the machine's physical limitations.

Constrained Creative Play

If the player may only create within artificial constraints imposed by the rules, we describe the activity as **constrained creative play.** Constraining creativity may sound undesirable, but it really just provides a structure for the player's creativity. This type of gameplay grows out of some familiar ideas: the expressive power offered by creativity tools; the growth in the number of actions available to a player as games progress; and the fact that players must overcome challenges in order to succeed. These may be combined in various ways, as we discuss next.

Play Limited by an Economy   In *SimCity,* the player can't build a whole city immediately; it costs money to zone each empty plot of land, and he can use only the money he has available. As his city prospers, he earns more money and so can establish new neighborhoods. Once he gets enough money, new features such as stadiums and airports, which were too expensive at the early stages of the game, become available to him. So long as the player continues to produce economic growth, he can make his city ever larger and add more and more facilities.

Construction and management simulations routinely implement this system of structuring the player's creativity. He must successfully manage an economy in order to construct larger creations and also to get additional creative power. This is a system closely related to that found in role-playing games, in which players must gain experience in order to learn new magic spells, and to that found in strategy games, in which players must harvest resources in order to perform the research necessary to get better weapons. In those genres, the economy of the game limits the player's ability to have adventures and fight wars; in creativity games, the economy limits the player's ability to create. The primary challenge in such games is successful economic management, with creative power serving as the reward for success.

This system rewards skill, granting players more exciting and powerful tools once they master the tools they already have. Educational software also makes use of this mechanism.

Creating to Physical Standards   Another approach to constrained creative play gives players all the tools and resources they would like but requires them to construct an object that meets certain requirements, usually having to do with making the object perform a function. For example, *Mind Rover* from CogniToy lets players design and build virtual robots that then do battle with other robots supplied by the game. The player gets a set of standard parts including driving and steering devices, sensors, and weapons, and can also program her robot using a simple programming mechanism. Once the player constructs a robot, she sets it in operation to attack a predesigned robot built from similar parts. The player takes no action at this point; the artificial intelligence she constructed for the robot handles the fighting. By watching its behavior, she can refine her design until her robot finally wins the battle.

Another game, *Bridge Construction Set,* requires the player to construct bridges over a river. The bridge must not only stand up but also support the weight of a train traveling across. The game contains a sophisticated physics simulation to calculate the stresses on each part of the bridge. *Bridge Construction Set* combines the challenge of meeting physical standards with an economic challenge: Each element of the bridge costs money, and the player must stay within a budget. Later challenges in the game require the player to build larger bridges, but the game gives her more money to build them with.

Whenever you require the player to build to a standard and test his construction, when he fails he needs to know why—otherwise he can't learn the principles upon which you based the standards. *Bridge Construction Set* includes a feature to show the players which parts of the bridge experience the greatest stress.

Creating to Aesthetic Standards   With an adequate physics simulation, any game can test a player's creativity against a physical standard. An architecture game can test a building both for structural integrity and also for usability—rooms with no way to get into them are useless.

Aesthetics present a much larger problem, because they don't consist of a set of universal laws in the way that Newtonian physics does. To test the aesthetic quality of a player's creations, you have to set some standards of your own. Consider some of the following options:

- **Test against a fixed set of rules that you establish.** A game about clothing design could include well-known rules about color combinations, not mixing stripes with polka dots, and using fabric textures that harmonize and complement each other. This system rewards players who know the rules and conform to them. It's good for teaching the basics, but it doesn't encourage brilliant but unconventional combinations.

- **Create a system of trends that the player can research.** If you want to make a game in which creative challenges change over time, the way fashion trends change from year to year, design a system in which the standard against which you measure the player's work fluctuates. Each attribute of the player's product could be tested against a trend with its own rate of variation, so—using the clothing example again—hemlines might move up and down over a 10-year period, and preferred fabrics might change from synthetics to natural fibers over a 20-year period. The periodicity should never be completely regular or predictable, however. The trend information should be hidden from the player but partially accessible via a research process. When Ernest Adams ran a series of game design workshops on this theme, participants suggested several options for doing this research. The player, in the role of a fashion designer, could attend parties within the game and listen to computer-generated gossip, some of which would include clues about current trends; he could read automatically created fashion magazines and newspapers for clues; or he could even break into other fashion designers' workshops to find out about their works in progress.

- **Allow the public to vote online.** You can let the players upload their creations to a Web site and let the community vote on them. This system relieves the computer of the responsibility for determining the aesthetic quality of the player's creations, but it significantly lengthens the time scale of the game—the player may have to wait hours or days until the votes come in unless the game has a large player base. You will also have to build a secure system that rewards players for voting and prevents vote-rigging.

Freeform Creative Play and Sandbox Mode

If a game lets the player use all the facilities that it offers without any restrictions on the amount of time or resources available (other than those imposed by technological limitations), then we can say that it supports *freeform creative play.* Many games that normally offer constrained creative play also include a special mode that removes ordinary constraints. This mode is traditionally called *sandbox mode.* Sandbox mode lets the player do whatever he wants but usually doesn't offer the same rewards as the constrained mode—and may not offer any rewards at all. In this mode, the game resembles a tool more than a conventional video game.

Two particularly interesting, though very early, forms of freeform creative play appeared in *Pinball Construction Set* and *Adventure Construction Set.* These games allowed the player to construct games that he or someone else could play. Much of the fun came from trying out the resulting game to see how it played and making refinements—in effect, they permitted game development (within quite restricted domains) without all the work of full-scale development.

In a more recent example of freeform play, Will Wright's game *Spore* is designed to let players design creatures with different numbers of heads, limbs, eyes, and other features and see how they interact and evolve.

Storytelling Play

5

Some players enjoy creating stories of their own, using features provided by a game, which they can then distribute online for others to read. *The Movies,* by Lionhead Software, stands as the most ambitious project of this kind to date. The purpose of the game is to let people make their own movies and share them online. *Stunt Island,* from LucasArts, also enabled people to film their own movies, but it concentrated on stunts involving vehicles rather than actors. More important, *The Movies*, unlike *Stunt Island*, allows players to export movies so they can edit their films using external tools such as Adobe Premiere. The movies in *Stunt Island* could be viewed only within the game itself and could not be exported because the game did not actually capture the images but simply recreated the scene using the game engine for each viewing.

The Movies offers more expressive power than any other storytelling game yet made, but it does require a lot of effort from the players. If you want to make a game with similar features, you will have to work with the programmers to design a system that allows players to set up cameras in the game world, record the images and sounds generated by the game engine, and edit them.

However, you don't have to go that far. *The Sims* proved to be a huge success with a much simpler storytelling mechanism: Players can create characters and construct houses for them to live in and then initiate events by giving commands to the characters. *The Sims* also lets players capture screen shots from the game, put captions under them, organize them into storyboards, and upload them to a Web site for others to see. Telling stories this way requires much less complex software than *The Movies* uses, and the players don't have to know how to edit video.

An even easier solution involves generating a log of the player's activities in text form. She can then edit this log any way she likes, turning her raw game actions and dialog into narrative form.

Game Modifications

To give your players the utmost creative freedom with your game, you can permit them to modify the game itself—to redesign it themselves. Game modifications, or *mods,* are extremely popular with the hardcore gamer community and almost an obligatory feature of any large multiplayer networked game (apart from server-based games such as *Everquest*).

Providing the player with mod-building tools also makes good business sense. Your game's original content can keep people interested for only a certain amount of time, but if people can build mods that make use of your game engine (as they can with the *Unreal* and *Half-Life 2* engines), people will continue to buy your game just to be able to play the mods.

Allowing for mods is more of a programmer's problem than a designer's problem, so we don't discuss them in much detail.

Level Editors

A level editor allows players to construct their own levels for a game. Some level editors permit players only to define a new landscape; others allow them to define new characters as well; and a few go so far as to permit rebuilding the entire game. Generally, however, a good level editor lets the player construct a completely new landscape, place challenges in it, and write scripts that the game engine can operate. If you work on a large game for commercial sale, your team will almost certainly include tools programmers who will build a level editor for the level designers to use. To make the level editor available to the players, rather than useful only as an in-house tool, it must be as robust and well-designed as the game software itself. Two superb level editors that you should study are the 2D *StarCraft* Campaign Editor, which is included with *StarCraft,* and the *Hammer* 3D editor that comes with *Half-Life 2.* For further reading about level editors and other design tools, see Richard Rouse's article, "Designing Design Tools" in the *Gamasutra* developers' webzine (Rouse, 2000).

Bots

A *bot* is an artificially intelligent opponent that the player can program for himself. (*Bot* also has a secondary meaning: a program that help players cheat at multiplayer networked games. We're talking about the other kind.) By building bots, players can create tougher and smarter opponents than those that normally ship with the game (usually a first-person shooter). Some players use bots as sparring partners for practice before playing against real people in online tournaments. *Quake III Arena* contains a great deal of support for bots, and a number of third-party tools, such as *BotStudio,* have been built to help players create them.

Dangers of Allowing Mods

Mods bring with them certain risks. When you allow players to modify your game, you risk the possibility that they will create a mod that includes material you would never use yourself: pornographic or racist content, for example. You might find people distributing a highly offensive variant of your game but one that still displays your company's name and logo when it starts up. The public might be sophisticated enough to realize that a game designer shouldn't be held responsible for the contents of homemade mods, but then again it might not be. The general public doesn't know much about video game development, and the politicians who seek to regulate video games know even less.

Summary

Players love to express themselves and to build things. In this chapter, we looked at options for self-expression through avatar selection, customization, and creation. We also examined both freeform and constrained creative play and discussed some of the different kinds of constraints that you may impose on a player's creativity to produce challenges. We noted some options for permitting storytelling play and ended with a brief discussion about allowing players to modify your game. With these tools in hand, you should be able to add support for creative play to your game.

5

Test Your Skills

MULTIPLE CHOICE QUESTIONS

1. Which is *not* an example of self-defining play?

   A. Choosing the color of the car your character drives.

   B. Choosing to play a character with high charisma and low strength.

   C. Choosing to play a character using the recommended attribute settings.

   D. Choosing to play the levels out of order and tackle the harder challenges first.

2. Which of these statements is generally true?

   A. Female players tend to be happy to play with a default avatar.

   B. Boys tend to dislike playing with avatars they find unappealing.

   C. Female players tend to like to design avatars that look like themselves.

   D. Men tend to prefer to play with attractive, well-dressed avatars.

3. If you allow a player to select between an ax or a bow for his avatar, you are allowing
   A. cosmetic challenges.
   B. avatar customization.
   C. game modification.
   D. freeform creative play.

4. Which ways of setting an avatar's functional attributes should you never implement?
   A. Letting players set all attributes to optimal values to make the game easy.
   B. Making players earn the right to set their character's functional attributes to optimal values.
   C. Letting players choose preset default values.
   D. None; all of the above are legitimate design choices.

5. How can you best improve the playing experience for a player who does not understand how an avatar's attributes may affect gameplay?
   A. Allow the player to assign any value to functional attributes.
   B. Allow the player to play through the entire game in a tutorial mode to learn how attributes affect gameplay.
   C. Leak some cheats via gamer Web sites
   D. Include good default settings a player can use to get started quickly without worrying about setting attributes.

6. Cosmetic attributes play their most important role in multiplayer games because
   A. other players rely on visual appearances to make decisions.
   B. in multiplayer games all characters must belong to readily identifiable clans.
   C. cosmetic attributes form part of the core mechanics.
   D. these attributes are especially inexpensive to implement in multiplayer games.

7. One feature you must be sure to design if you want to foster creative play is
   A. a way to export a design to another software package such as Photoshop.
   B. a way to share a player's creations by printing or uploading to a Web site.
   C. multiple templates that a player can use as the basis for her own creations.
   D. links to real-world design studios a player can use to find inspiration.

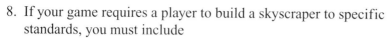

8. If your game requires a player to build a skyscraper to specific standards, you must include

    A. a wide variety of building materials.

    B. a construction foreman NPC.

    C. a method of measuring the economic impact of the building in the surrounding neighborhood.

    D. a method of explaining what happened if the building falls over.

9. Which of the following would *not* be a way to test the aesthetic quality of a player's creation?

    A. Test the creation against a fixed set of established rules.

    B. Test the creation against a system of aesthetic trends that the player researches.

    C. Test the creation to see that it stands up to physical forces.

    D. Set up a Web site that allows players to vote on each other's creations.

10. Players really use a game more like a tool than an entertainment form when you give them a(n)

    A. avatar customization feature.

    B. sandbox mode.

    C. constrained mode.

    D. cosmetic attribute generator.

11. How could you allow a player to experience storytelling play from an action or adventure game?

    A. Log the player's actions and dialog to create a text narrative.

    B. Give points for aesthetics in addition to performance.

    C. Add more side quests that involve narrative.

    D. Allow players to modify their avatar's functional attributes.

12. Which of the following is a reason for adding mod-building tools to a game?

    A. You cannot build a game today without including them.

    B. They keep players interested in a game longer.

    C. They require very little programming to implement.

    D. They make games longer and therefore more attractive to hardcore gamers.

5

13. When using a level editor, a player can do all of the following *except*

    A. construct a completely new landscape.

    B. place challenges in a new landscape.

    C. write scripts for the game engine to operate.

    D. change the algorithms compiled into the original game software.

14. How can you allow a player to create more challenging opponents in a game?

    A. Ramp up the AI.

    B. Have the NPCs get harder to beat as the player gets better at the game.

    B. Allow the player to build bots.

    D. Add an expert mode to the game.

15. One good reason to disallow modifications in a game is because

    A. the player is your opponent and you shouldn't let him beat you.

    B. players may create offensive content that could harm your game's reputation.

    C. casual players will never use the modification options.

    D. modifying a game damages immersion.

EXERCISES

1. Using a game that you are familiar with and that permits avatar customization or construction (or one that your instructor assigns), identify and document those functional and cosmetic attributes of the avatar that the player may modify. In the case of the functional attributes, indicate how they affect the gameplay.

2. Think of an idea for a game that permits the player to construct something you have not seen in commercial games (no cities, buildings, or vehicles). Assume that you will constrain the player's abilities via an economy but allow him to earn new tools and features for his construction over time. Design a set of elementary parts from which the item may be constructed, and specify a price for each part. Include a number of upgrades—more expensive parts that replace cheaper versions. Write a short paper explaining the domain in which the player will be creating, and supply your list of parts, giving them in the order in which the player will earn the ability to buy them (cheapest to most expensive). Also indicate in a general way how the item that the player constructs can be used to earn money. Your instructor will inform you of the scope of the exercise.

3. Choose a domain in which the player must construct something to meet an aesthetic standard for which a known set of aesthetic rules exists in the real world, such as architecture, clothing design, music, interior decoration, landscaping, or a domain that your instructor assigns. Research your chosen domain to learn its aesthetic rules. (Because many such rules change over time, you may choose a period from history if you can find adequate documentation.) Be careful not to confuse rules about usability with those about aesthetics. Write a short paper explaining your domain, including the range of choices that the player may make in constructing something, and document the aesthetic rules. Provide references to your sources.

DESIGN QUESTIONS

As you design your game, ask yourself the following questions about creative and expressive play:

1. What features do you want to include in order to allow the player to define herself in the game: avatar selection, customization, or creation from the ground up? What attributes can she change, if any?

2. How will you make clear to the player the possible consequences of his avatar customization decisions, so that he can make informed choices? Where will you provide this information?

3. If you offer creative play, what will its domain be? What limitations will the machine impose?

4. Do you plan to offer constrained creative play? If so, what will be the constraining factor or factors—economics, physics, or aesthetics? Will the game provide a growth path to gradually free the player of constraints? In the case of aesthetics, how will you implement an aesthetic judgment mechanism, and how will the results of that judgment become clear to the player? Will aesthetically appealing creations earn more money, win prizes, produce points, or gain some other reward?

5. Will you offer freeform creative play? If so, will it be part of ordinary play, or will it be a separate sandbox mode? If you do offer freeform creative play, can the player's creations affect the gameplay?

6. Does your game include features for storytelling play? What will they be? How can you seamlessly integrate such features into the rest of the game?

7. Do you plan to allow mods? What will you let players modify? Can they create new levels, bots, or narrative material? What tools will you want to ship to support these activities?

8. How will you create a sense of community between the players and allow them to share their creations with others?

Chapter 6

Character Development

Chapter Objectives

After reading this chapter and completing the exercises, you will be able to do the following:

- Know the basic goals of character design in games.
- Recognize the difference between a player-defined avatar and a specific or nonspecific avatar.
- Know the issues involved in making non-gender-specific characters.
- Know the visual and behavioral attributes used to help create characters in games.
- Use the attributes of either art-driven or story-driven character design to create your own game characters.

Introduction

> It is our choices, Harry, that show what we truly are, far more than our abilities.
>
> —J. K. Rowling, *Harry Potter and the Chamber of Secrets*

Character design is an important aspect of telling stories and evoking an emotional response in both stories and games. Whether it's based on the visual look of the character or the emotional depth of the backstory, the character we play and those we interact with help make the game world believable to us. Heroes, villains, innocents-in-distress, and bystanders: Without these characters to carry us forward, the game would be an empty shell.

In this chapter, we discuss how to design compelling and believable characters. We start by defining the characteristics of the avatar character, both player-designed and built-in. A discussion of the issues inherent with gender

specific character design follows, with attention paid to the common game stereotypes to be avoided. We also discuss the attributes associated with characters and how you can use them to design your own characters: visual, behavioral, and audible. Art-driven character design and story-driven character design are discussed. A final section on the impact of audio design on your characters concludes the chapter.

The Goals of Character Design

Games in many genres structure gameplay around characters. Action games (especially the fighting and platform subgenres), adventure games, action-adventure hybrids, and role-playing games all use characters extensively to entertain. Players need well-designed characters to identify with and care about—heroes to cheer and villains to boo. The best games also include complex characters who aren't heroes or villains but fall somewhere in between, characters designed to intrigue the player or make the player think. If characters aren't interesting or appealing, the game will be less enjoyable.

Many factors combine to determine the degree to which a character appeals to people. He need not be attractive in the conventional sense of being pleasant to look at, but he must be competently constructed—well-drawn or well-described. His various attributes should work together harmoniously; his body, clothing, voice, animations, facial expressions, and other characteristics should all join to express him and his role clearly to the player. (Disharmonious elements can be introduced for humor's sake, however, as with the cute but foul-mouthed squirrel in the *Conker* series.) Characters should be distinctive rather than derivative. Even a stereotypical character should have something that sets him apart from others of the same type.

A good character should also be credible. Players come to know a character through her appearance and actions, and if that character then does something at odds with her familiar persona, players won't believe it. An evil demon from the underworld can't be seen worrying about orphans. For that matter, neither can James Bond. Simple characters must be consistent. Richer characters, with more human frailties, may be more inconsistent, but even so, players must feel that the character holds certain core values that she will not violate.

Avatar characters have an extra burden: The player must want to step into their shoes, to identify with them, and to play as them. We discuss this in more detail in the next section.

Important business considerations enter into character design as well. Customers identify many games by their key characters; that's why so many games take their name directly from their characters: *Super Mario Bros., Sonic the Hedgehog, Crash Bandicoot, Duke Nukem.* Good characters occupy what the marketing people call *mindshare,* consumer awareness of a product or brand. You can use the character in a book, movie, or TV series; you can sell clothes and toys based on a character; you can use a character to advertise other products. It's more difficult to do these things with the game's world or its gameplay.

The goal of character design, then, is to create characters that people *find appealing* (even if the character is a villain, like Darth Vader), that people can *believe in,* and that the player can *identify with* (particularly in the case of avatar characters). If possible, the character should do these things well enough, and be distinctive enough, to be highly memorable to the players.

The Relationship Between Player and Avatar

Lara Croft is attractive because of, not despite of, her glossy blankness—that hyper-perfect, shiny, computer look. She is an abstraction, an animated conglomeration of sexual and attitudinal signs—breasts, hotpants, shades, thigh holsters—whose very blankness encourages the viewer's psychological projection. Beyond the bare facts of her biography, her perfect vacuity means we can make Lara Croft into whoever we want her to be.

—Steven Poole, "Lara's Story"

We use the term *avatar* to refer to a character in a game who serves as a protagonist under the player's control. (The original term is Sanskrit and in the Hindu religion refers to a bodily incarnation of a god.) Most action and action-adventure games provide exactly one such character. Many role-playing games allow the player to manage a party of characters and switch control from one to another, but if winning a role-playing game is contingent upon the survival of a particular member of the party, then that character is effectively the player's avatar (though some games require that more than one character survive). The player usually sees the avatar on screen more than any other character, if the game is presented in the third person. Displaying the avatar requires the largest number of animations, which must also be the smoothest animations, or you risk annoying the player. The avatar's movements must be attractive, not clumsy, unless clumsiness is part of the avatar's character.

The nature of the player's relationship with the avatar varies considerably from game to game. Whether the player designed the avatar herself, whether the game displays the avatar as a visible and audible presence, how the player controls the avatar's movements, and many other factors influence that relationship.

Player-Designed Avatar Characters

While most games have an established character as the player's avatar, role-playing games, especially multiplayer online ones, almost always give players considerable freedom to design an avatar to their own specifications. They can choose the avatar's race, sex, body type, hair, clothing, and other physical attributes, as well as a large number of other details, such as strength and dexterity, that have a direct effect on the way the avatar will perform in challenging situations. (For more information on these attributes, see Chapter 15, "Role-Playing Games.") Figure 6.1 shows an example character creation screen from *Star Wars Galaxies*. In such games, the avatar is a sort of mask the player wears, a persona she adopts for the purposes of the game. Because the player herself designs the avatar, the avatar has no personality other than what the player chooses to create. In such games, then, your task as a game designer is not to create avatars for the players but to provide the necessary tools to allow players to create avatars for themselves. The more opportunities for personal expression you can offer, the more the players will enjoy exercising their creativity.

FIGURE 6.1 *Star Wars Galaxies* gives the player many options for designing her own avatar.

Specific and Nonspecific Avatars

In games in which the player does *not* get to design or choose an avatar but must use one supplied by the game, the relationship between the player and the avatar varies depending on how completely you, the designer, specified the avatar's appearance and other qualities.

The earliest adventure games, which were text-based, were written as if the player *himself* inhabited the game world. The avatar wasn't a character with its own personal history; the game was written as if the avatar *was* the player. However, because the game didn't know anything about the player, it couldn't depict him or say much about him. Such avatars were *nonspecific*—that is, the designer didn't specify anything about them. A number of later text adventures asked for the player's name and sex when the game started and used that information within the story, but the avatar remained essentially a nonspecific character. A nonspecific avatar is simply a means for the player to interact with the world, and the player may identify with it completely.

The nonspecific avatar does not belong entirely to the past, however. Gordon Freeman, the hero of *Half-Life,* does not speak and is never even seen in the game (although he does appear on the box). The designers did this deliberately; *Half-Life*, a first-person shooter in a world with no mirrors, offers Gordon as an empty shell for the player to inhabit.

However, game designers soon began to find this model too limiting. They wanted to develop games in which the avatar had a personality of his own, someone who belonged in the game world rather than being a visitor there. It's awkward to write a story around a character whose personality the designer knows nothing about. Besides, designers working on the early graphical games had often shown the player *some* kind of an avatar, even if it was only a simple white shape like the anonymous cowboy in Midway's *Gun Fight* (see Figure 6.2). As soon as you depict a person visually, he begins to exhibit some individuality. When graphics became standard for all commercial games, designers needed to create avatars that people could see, and that meant making them more specific.

Modern games with strong storylines use detailed characters who have histories and personalities of their own. The Nameless One from *Planescape: Torment* (who, despite not knowing his name, definitely comes equipped with a past and a number of personal relationships that affect his life) and Nancy Drew from the many *Nancy Drew* games (and of course all the books that preceded them) make good examples. These are *specific* avatars, and the player's relationship with them is more complex than it is with a nonspecific avatar. The player is not the avatar—clearly the player is not Nancy Drew—yet the player controls the avatar, so in what sense is the avatar still Nancy Drew? With a specific avatar, the player's relationship to her is more like that of the reader's relationship to the hero of a novel. The reader is not the hero, but the reader does identify with her: The reader wants to know what will happen to the hero, hopes that things will turn out well for her, and so on. The difference is that in a game,

FIGURE 6.2 *Gun Fight* (1975) was an early game with a simple but distinctive avatar.

the player can help and guide the hero rather than just read about her. But—at least in some games—the specific avatar is also free to reject the player's guidance. If the player asks April Ryan (from *The Longest Journey*) to do something dangerous, she refuses with comments such as, "That doesn't seem like a good idea." Specific avatars sometimes have minds of their own.

Between the two extremes of nonspecific and specific avatars lies a middle ground in which the avatar is only partially characterized—specified to a certain degree but not fully detailed. For many games, especially those *without* strong stories, it's better to create the avatar as a sort of cartoonish figure (even if he's depicted photorealistically). Many avatars in action games fit this description. Mario isn't a real plumber, he's a cartoon plumber in the same way that Bugs Bunny is a cartoon rabbit rather than a real one. Lara Croft, too, has more looks than personality; she's a stand-in for the player, not a three-dimensional human being.

The Effects of Different Control Mechanisms

The way a player feels about an avatar depends somewhat on how the player controls the avatar in the game. In the case of Nancy Drew and the avatars in all other point-and-click adventure and computer role-playing games, the player's control is *indirect;* he doesn't steer the avatar around but points to where he wants the avatar to go, and the avatar walks there of her own accord. The player feels more like a disembodied guide and friend than a personal inhabitant of the game world.

Lara Croft and Mario, in contrast, are under *direct* control: The player steers their bodies through the game world, running, swimming, jumping, and fighting as necessary. The player becomes them and revels in the abilities that they have that he does not. But he doesn't worry too much about their feelings. That's partly because Lara and Mario are only partially specified, but it's also because exercising so much control makes them more puppets than persons.

Male and Female Players and Characters

Early in the history of video games, the possibility that male players (who used to make up the majority of the market) would be unwilling to play female avatars concerned some designers: Men might find identifying with a female character somehow threatening. Lara Croft (Figure 6.3) demonstrated that this is not a problem, at least as long as the character is acting in a role that men are comfortable with. Lara engages in traditionally masculine activities, so men are happy to enter the game as Lara. They might be less comfortable with an avatar who engaged in more traditionally feminine activities.

FIGURE 6.3 Lara Croft (here seen in *Tomb Raider III*, 1998) is adventurous but hypersexualized.

exhibit a complex personality and she doesn't change much during the course of the game—either behaviorally or visually—then this is often the best way to do it. Such an approach is called *art-driven character design.* It works well for games with fairly simple, cartoonlike characters. Art-driven design also makes a lot of sense if you hope to exploit the character in a number of other media besides video games: comic books and toys, for example.

Story-driven character design, an alternative to art-driven, is defined in the section that follows this. Both visual and behavioral design techniques are used in creating your character, but every designer works well with one design development pattern as a primary approach.

Character Physical Types

We begin with the basic body types of game characters, and some of the ways that they may be depicted.

Humanoids, Nonhumanoids, and Hybrids   Characters in video games fall into three general categories: human or humanoid; nonhumanoid; and hybrids. (A small number of characters appear as disembodied voices or animate objects, but we don't include them here because we're talking specifically about visual design.) Humanoid characters have two arms, two legs, and one head, and their bodies and faces are organized like a human's. The more you deviate from this arrangement, the less human a character seems. Truly human characters can have either realistic human proportions or exaggerated ones in a cartoon style, but if you use cartoon proportions, you had better use a cartoon drawing style as well. A photorealistic human with exaggerated proportions will read as disturbingly deformed.

Nonhumanoid characters include those shaped like vehicles or machines (often indicated by the presence of metal and wheels), animals, or monsters. In the *Star Wars* universe, R2-D2 is clearly a machine, albeit one with endearing qualities. R2 has three legs with wheels on the bottom, a variety of mechanical appendages, and a head, but no real face. The Daleks of *Doctor Who* are also machines, at least as seen from the outside, for similar reasons. Animals, even imaginary ones, look organic; the presence of more than two legs and/or the presence of wings distinguishes them from humanoids. Skin covered with fur, scales, or feathers further sets them apart. Many video game characters, such as Crash Bandicoot, have animal-like heads but humanoid bodies; we would classify them as humanoids rather than animals. Designers often modify the faces of animal-like humanoids, shortening the muzzle and bringing the eyes to the front, to make them more like humans as well.

Monsters are distinguished by such characteristics as significantly asymmetric bodies, a different facial arrangement (eyes below the nose or jaws that move sideways, for example), and extreme proportions. Many of their qualities are borrowed from orders of animals that humans in some societies find frightening or repulsive: reptiles, insects, and the more bizarre sea creatures.

Claws, fangs, oozing slime, and an armorlike exoskeleton all add to a monster's appearance of alienness and danger.

Hybrids include beings such as mermaids or human/machine combinations. Davros, the creator of the Daleks, had a humanoid torso and head but a mechanical bottom half. The Borg from *Star Trek* and C-3PO from *Star Wars* read as humanoids rather than true hybrids, however, as they still follow the rules for humans: two arms, two legs, and one head in the appropriate configuration. Cylons, from the popular *Battlestar Galactica* series, are hybrid machines/humans. In the latest incarnation of this show, they push the boundaries of how visuals can deceive the viewer as to what is human and what is not.

Cartoonlike Qualities   Relatively few art-driven characters are drawn with ordinary proportions or with photorealistic features. Rather, they are exaggerated in various ways that should be familiar to you from comic books and cartoons. These exaggerations serve as convenient symbols to indicate a character stereotype. Four of the most common are *cool, tough, cute,* and *goofy.* A character isn't always limited to one of these qualities, however; he can sometimes shift from one to another as circumstances require.

- **Cool** characters never get too upset about anything. The essence of cool is detachment. If something irritates them, it's only for a moment. A rebellious attitude toward authority often accompanies cool. Cool characters often wear sunglasses and their body language is languid; when not doing anything else, they slouch. Frequently clever or wisecracking, cool characters may, depending on the situation, use their wits rather than brute force to overcome an obstacle. Ratchet, from the *Ratchet and Clank* series, exemplifies the cool character. Though cool characters are often drawn as insouciant when standing still, their game actions (jumping, running) are usually fast and focused.

- **Tough** characters exemplify physical aggression. Often male—although Lara Croft would be classed as a tough character—they are often drawn with exaggerated height and bulk. They use large, expansive gestures and tend to talk with their fists. Tough characters are frequently *hypersexualized* as well (see the next section). Duke Nukem is a tough character. Yosemite Sam is a tough character whose small stature leavens his toughness with a comic quality. Animations for tough characters are usually big and abrupt, fast moving and aggressive. Postures that lean forward, implying motion and action even where there is none, are common.

- **Cute** characters are drawn with the proportions of human babies or baby animals: large eyes and oversized heads. They have rounded rather than angular bodies, dress in light colors, and have a general demeanor of cheerfulness, although they may exhibit moments of irritation or determination. Mario is the ultimate cute video game character. Animations of cute characters usually allow characters to achieve things that they physically could not accomplish in the real world: jumping wide gaps, climbing long ropes, firing weapons larger than themselves. They usually look innocent and detached.

- **Goofy** characters have slightly odd proportions and funny-looking, inefficient walks and other movements. Their behavior is largely comedic. Like cool characters, they are seldom upset by anything for long, but their physical awkwardness means that they are definitely not cool. The Disney character named Goofy is a perfect example; among video games, Crash Bandicoot is a goofy character. Animations for a goofy character in a game sometimes include the goofiness, as long as it doesn't affect the player's experience of the play. Tripping while running can be humorous, but if the character dies because of the visual joke, he won't appreciate it. Instead, the humor is saved for cut-scenes or idle moments where there is no game impact.

These are of course far from all the cartoonlike character types possible; consider the mock-heroism of Dudley Do-Right and George of the Jungle, the twisted evil of the witch in *Snow White,* and so on. Figure 6.5 shows a variety of cartoonlike characters.

6

FIGURE 6.5 Several cartoon characters from video games and other media.

Note that for the most part these are Western classifications. Art styles vary wildly among different cultures, particularly for characters. Japanese animation often uses large eyes and tiny mouths for characters, but the mouths sometimes swell to huge sizes when they shout, which looks grotesque to Americans. The animé style also sometimes gives cute childlike faces to sexually provocative women, producing—to Western eyes at least—somewhat disturbing results. European cartoon characters often seem ugly and strange to Americans, too. Asterix and Tintin, two exceptions, enjoy huge worldwide success. If you want your game to sell in a number of different countries, study those countries' native cartoon and comic styles closely to make sure you don't violate local expectations.

FYI *Cool Without Attitude*

Kids hate goody-two-shoes characters just as much as parents dislike characters with foul attitudes—but just because a character doesn't cop an attitude with authority figures doesn't make him a goody-two-shoes. The *Scooby Doo* kids provide a pretty good example of characters who retain their appeal with kids despite not being rebellious. Kids like to identify with the characters' intelligence, bravery, and resourcefulness. Scooby is funny, too, because despite his large size, he is a coward. But because he's a dog and not a child, Scooby doesn't get picked on or treated with contempt for being scared. This is actually a very clever piece of character design: Children know that no matter how scary the situation is, Scooby is even more scared than they are, so they can feel virtuous for being braver than he is.

The design of art-driven characters depends considerably on the target audience. For example, the adjectives *cute* and *scary* will mean different things to a 5-year-old and a 25-year-old. *Doom*-style monsters certainly won't go down well in a Mario-esque adventure.

Conker's Bad Fur Day presented an interesting twist on this rule. Rare, the developers, transplanted their cute children's characters into a game for adults (or rather, adolescent boys), full of bad language and vulgar jokes. But it's a one-way transformation; you wouldn't want to insert the jokes into a game genuinely intended for children.

Hypersexualized Characters Hypersexualization refers to the practice of exaggerating the sexual attributes of men and women in order to make them more sexually appealing, at least to teenagers. Male characters get extra-broad chests and shoulders, huge muscles, prominent jaws, and oversized hands and feet. Female characters get enormous breasts, extremely narrow waists, and wide hips. Skimpy clothing makes sure they display their physical attributes as much as possible, and sexually suggestive poses further drive the point home (as if there were any doubt). Both sexes boast unrealistic height, with heads that seem disproportionately small and with extra-long legs. High heels often further exaggerate women's height.

Duke Nukem typifies the hypersexualized male character, but most of the male characters in fighting games fit the bill. Lara Croft is the best-known example of a hypersexualized female character among the hundreds populating any number of video games. Comic book superheroes (male and female) are also traditionally hypersexualized, a quality that got comic books into trouble with the U.S. Congress in the 1950s.

Such characters obviously sell well to young men and teenaged boys, but by now these images are clichéd. So many stereotypical he-men and babes have been created over the years that it's difficult to tell them apart, and any new game that relies on such images runs the risk of being lumped in with all the others. This may actually obscure any technological or game design advances you have made. Finally, hypersexualized characters really appeal only to a puerile audience. They actively discourage older players, who've seen it all before, and female players. Strip clubs are male preserves; a character that looks as if she just stepped out of one sends clear signals that female players are not wanted or welcome. (To give her her due, Lara Croft's hiking boots, backpack, and khaki clothing do set her apart from the common run of women clad in chain mail bikinis or skintight leather.)

In short, we discourage hypersexualizing characters just for their titillation value. It limits your market and seldom adds much. You might get away with it if it's intentionally done for laughs; putting Cate Archer into a 1960s retro catsuit worked out well for the designers of *No One Lives Forever* because of the game's humorous context. But *No One Lives Forever* was also an excellent game in its own right. Big breasts won't sell a poor game, as the developers of *Space Bunnies Must Die!* discovered.

Clothing, Weapons, Symbolic Objects, and Names

When designing ordinary human beings, body shape is only the beginning. In the real world, we have only a limited ability to change our bodies, so instead we express our personal style through things that we hang on the outsides of our bodies: clothing and accessories. In a video game, the player can more easily see who is who—especially important in situations requiring snap decisions, like a shooter game—if characters' clothing and props uniquely identify them. Indiana Jones wears a certain hat and khaki clothes, and he carries a bullwhip. Darth Vader's flowing black cape, forbidding helmet, and even the sound of his breathing instantly set him apart from everyone else in the *Star Wars* universe. Crucial for avatars, this rule applies to a lesser extent to minor characters.

A character's choice of weapons tells a lot about him, too. On the one hand, a meat cleaver or an axe is a tool repurposed for use as a weapon, so it suggests crude, and bloody, violence. On the other hand, a rapier's thin elegance suggests a dueling aristocrat. Indiana Jones can use his bullwhip to get himself out of all kinds of scrapes; it's a symbol of his resourcefulness. That he generally prefers the nonlethal bullwhip and carries a pistol only as a backup (in the movies, anyway) sends the message that he'd rather not kill if he doesn't have to.

Hairstyles and jewelry tend to remain the same in games even when clothing changes. Both function as good identifiers if you make them visible and distinctive enough. Jewelry, in particular, doesn't wear out, isn't easily modified, and has a long history of magic, meaning, or mysticism: consider engagement rings, wedding rings, medals, the crucifixes of Christianity and the steel bracelets of the Sikhs. If you want a magical power or status transferred to another character, you can easily do it by transferring a crown, ring or chain of gold, or gems. You don't necessarily have to give jewelry a meaning; as long as it's visually distinctive, it will help to identify the character and define his style.

IN THE TRENCHES: Concept Art and Model Sheets

Concept art consists of drawings made early in the design process to give people an idea of what something in the game will look like—most often, a character. Many people involved in the game design, development, and production process will need such pictures. This includes everyone from the programmers (who might need to see a vehicle before they can correctly model its performance characteristics in software) to the marketing department (who will want to know what images they can use to help sell the game). By creating a number of different versions of a character, you can compare their different qualities and choose the one you like the best to be implemented by the game's modeling and animation teams.

Concept art shouldn't take too long to draw—minutes, not hours. The object isn't to produce final artwork; the concept drawings shouldn't end up in the final product at all. Rather, its purpose is to explain and inspire.

Figure 6.6 shows a character drawn by artist Björn Hurri. Told only to draw an imaginary Mongol horsewoman as the hero of an action-adventure game, and without any reference materials, he made a number of key decisions about her age, features, clothing, and weapons, all of which are visible in the picture. Her emotional temperament comes through in the image as well—this is not a woman to be trifled with. Good concept art like

▶▶ CONTINUED ON NEXT PAGE

▶▶ CONTINUED

FIGURE 6.6 Concept art of a fantasy Mongol horsewoman.
Courtesy of Björn Hurri.

this definitely bears out the old adage that a picture is worth a thousand words.

Another visualization tool that you should consider using is the **model sheet,** a traditional animator's device. A model sheet shows a number of different poses for a single character all on one page, representing different emotions and attitudes through his or her facial expression and body language. This lets you compare one with another and gives you more of an overall feel for the character than a single image can do. Figure 6.7 is a model

▶▶ CONTINUED ON NEXT PAGE

sheet from *The Act,* a coin-op game by Cecropia Inc. that uses hand-drawn animation.

NOTE: only seldom use this "wild" hair look for attitude. Most of time keep normal hair

Seq. 12
Page 4

Edgar
Clean-Up Model

Copyright © 2005 Cecropia, Inc.
All rights reserved.

FIGURE 6.7 A model sheet of the Edgar character from *The Act.*
Copyright © 2005 by Cecropia Inc., All rights reserved.

You can also give your characters distinctive names and ethnicities if appropriate. Consider how the men of Sergeant Rock's Easy Company in the old DC Comics World War II series reflected the ethnic diversity of America with names such as Dino Manelli, Izzy Cohen, and "Reb" Farmer—not to mention our square-jawed American hero, Sgt. Frank Rock.

There is a flip side to using such obvious names. Naming your characters in such a fashion lends them a cartoonlike style. This may be exactly what you need for some games, but for others it is not necessarily such a good fit. If realism is your aim, for instance, then such an unrealistic collection of names, each obviously chosen to represent an ethnicity or a stereotypical group, cheapens the final result. Notice that we, the authors of this book, are not called Ernest O'Scribe or Andrew Penn-Wielder.

Names do not have to spell out explicitly the character's persona. The name of Sylvester Boots, the hero of *Anachronox*, says little or nothing about his personality, though his nickname, *Sly*, is altogether more revealing. Lara Croft's name, although it does not immediately seem to indicate anything about the character, does (to English sensibilities, at least) imply a degree of upper-class Englishness.

Color Palette

As you work on your character's appearance, also think about creating a color palette for him—specifically, his clothing. People in games seldom change clothes, which saves money on art development and helps to keep them visually distinctive. In the early *Tomb Raider* games, Lara Croft wore a teal-colored shirt unique to her; no other object or character used that color. If you spotted teal, you'd found Lara. Comic-book superheroes furnish another particularly strong example. Superman wears a lot of red in his cape, boots and shorts; blue in his suit; and a small amount of yellow in his belt and *S* logo. Batman wears dark blue, black, and again a small amount of yellow as the background to his logo. Characters can share a palette if the proportions of the colors vary from individual to individual.

Choose your color palette to reflect your character's attitudes and emotional temperament. As upholder of "truth, justice, and the American way," Superman's colors are bright and cheery; the red and blue of his uniform recall the American flag. Batman, the Dark Knight of Gotham City—a much grittier, more run-down place than Superman's Metropolis—dresses in more somber colors.

Sidekicks

Hero characters are sometimes accompanied by sidekicks. A tough hero may travel with a cute sidekick (or vice versa) to provide some variety and comic relief. The cheerful look of Miles "Tails" Prower, the two-tailed fox who accompanies Sonic the Hedgehog, complements Sonic's expression of determination and mischief. Sidekicks appear in many action games now that increases in computing power allow for them: *Jak and Daxter, Ratchet and Clank,* Link and his fairy from the *Zelda* series. Banjo and Kazooie were, in the first game, really only one avatar; they could only work together (Kazooie rode around inside Banjo's backpack). Later in the series, they began to operate independently some of the time.

Sidekicks offer several benefits. They allow you to give the player additional moves and other actions that would not be believable in a single character; they extend the emotional range of the game by showing the player a character with a different personality from the hero; and they can be used to give the player information she wouldn't necessarily get any other way. Link's fairy, for example, doesn't do very much, but she offers valuable advice at key points in the game.

Creating Character Depth

The visual appearance of a character makes the most immediate impact on the player, and you can convey a lot of things about the character through his appearance, but you can't convey everything. Nor does his appearance necessarily determine what role he will play in a story, how he will behave in different situations, or how he will interact with the game's core mechanics. To address those issues, you have to give your attention to deeper questions about who the character is and how he behaves.

If you begin your character design with the character's role, personality, and behavior rather than his appearance, you are doing *story-driven character design*. In story-driven design, you decide these things first and only then let the artists begin to develop a physical appearance for the character. Artists often like to work from a detailed description; it helps them to understand and visualize the character.

Even games that you would not expect to have fully developed characters can gain much by including them. Consider the multiformat title *SSX Tricky*, shown in Figure 6.8. This is an extreme sports snowboarding game that pays attention to character development. The player can make friends, foster rivalries, and enhance her character throughout the game. The addition of these storylike elements makes it more than a simple sports game. The player chooses a character and begins to identify with her. This creates a greater sense of immersion in the game, and best of all, it's not prescripted. The player chooses her own friends—or enemies—from the other characters at will, and her choices do affect the gameplay. You can be sure that the people you antagonize will try their hardest to sabotage your run, and there will be a few sharp words exchanged at the finish line.

FIGURE 6.8 *SSX Tricky* is a sports game that includes real character development.

Admittedly, it's not complex interpersonal interaction and it could be taken further, but it's refreshing to see real character development attempted in the sort of games for which it has never before been considered. Interaction between characters is one of the most interesting aspects of stories—sometimes more so than the actual plot. Although a plot details the path of a story (we cover this in the next chapter), the characters' interactions add the flavor and subtlety that differentiate a well-crafted story from a fifth-grade English composition assignment.

Role, Attitudes, and Values

Every character in a story plays a role, just as every character in a movie plays a role even if only as an extra. The moment a character appears for any reason, the audience needs to know something about him. For minor characters, appearance and voice may convey all the information the audience needs—we don't need a detailed biography of the coffee-shop waitress who only appears for thirty seconds.

Major characters need richer personalities, however, and to design them you will have to envision the character in your head and then answer a large number of questions about them. In his 2001 article "Building Character: An Analysis of Character Creation," designer Steve Meretzky recommends that you create a character background paper, or ***backgrounder,*** for each one. You don't necessarily have to write it in narrative form; lists of qualities will do. The main thing is to get the information down on paper so that it's documented somewhere. Meretzky suggests that you consider the following:

Where was the character born?

What was his or her family life like as a kid?

What was his education?

Where does he live now?

Describe his job.

Describe his finances.

Describe his taste in clothes, books, movies, etc.

What are his favorite foods?

What are his favorite activities?

What are his hobbies?

Describe any particular personality traits and how they manifest.

Is he shy or outgoing? Greedy or giving?

Does he have quirks?

Does he have superstitions?

Does he have phobias?

What were the traumatic moments in his life?

What were his biggest triumphs?

Describe his important past romances.

Describe his current romantic involvement or involvements.

How does he treat friends? Lovers? Bosses? Servants?

Describe his political beliefs, past and present.

Describe his religious beliefs, past and present.

What are his interesting or important possessions?

Does he have any pets?

Does he have unusual talents?

What's the best thing that could happen to him?

The worst thing?

Does he drink tea or coffee?

Obviously this list is intended primarily for documenting ordinary humans, not sentient robo-camels or creatures of the underworld; if you set your game in the realm of fantasy, you'll have to adjust the list above as necessary. But in all cases, your goal is to become the world expert on this character, to know everything worth knowing about him. Try to imagine how he will behave in a variety of situations.

Once you know the answers to these questions, you can begin to think about how they will manifest themselves in your game's story. If your character is slightly dishonest, say—a small-time crook but not a villain—how will you make this clear to the player? One of the cardinal rules of fiction writing is that you should show—rather than tell—things about the characters to the reader. This goes double for video games, in which players expect to be interacting most of the time and show little tolerance for expository material. How, then, will you show your characters' personalities? Consider these three factors: *appearance, language*, and *behavior*. Appearance we deal with in the section *Visual Appearances* above; language we address in the section *Audio Design*, below. Appearance and language quickly and directly establish character but may produce stereotypes if you're not careful. The third, behavior, is the most subtle way of conveying character to the audience. Appearances can be deceiving, and deeds matter more than words. But establishing character through behavior takes longer; you must give the player the opportunity to observe a character's actions. What will your character do, what events might he get caught up in that will cause him to display his true nature?

Attributes

By attributes we mean the data values that describe a character's location, state of health, property, emotional condition, relationships with others, and so on—symbolic or numerical variables that can change as the player plays the game.

Attributes form part of the game's core mechanics, but deciding on appropriate values is also a part of character design.

Attributes can be divided roughly into those that change frequently and by large amounts, and those that change infrequently and by only small amounts or not at all. The former we call **status attributes** because they give the current status of the character, which can change frequently. The latter we call **characterization attributes** because they define the bedrock details of a character's personality which—unless the character is mentally ill—shouldn't change much. These are not industry standard terms (the industry has not yet settled on a standard), but we find them useful. In the *Dungeons & Dragons* universe, *hit points* (or health) is a status attribute; it changes moment by moment during a fight. *Constitution* is a characterization attribute referring to the character's overall degree of hardiness and resistance to injury or poison; it changes rarely or not at all.

In the past, most video games limited characters' attributes to physical details such as their health and inventory. In recent years, more games have made an effort to model social relationships and emotional states. The standout example of the latter is *The Sims,* a game simulating the behavior of people living in a suburban neighborhood. A set of characterization attributes for each character (called a sim) determines, in part, its affinity for other sims; those with conflicting qualities won't get along well if forced to interact. The original version of the game called those attributes neat, outgoing, active, playful, and nice. Status attributes named hunger, comfort, hygiene, bladder, energy, fun, social, and room represented sims' personal needs, which could be met by directing them to perform appropriate activities (such as visiting a neighbor or taking a shower) or by improving their surroundings. An overall happiness value went up or down depending on whether the sim's needs were being met. Few games had ever bothered to measure their characters' happiness before!

The Sims's model was simple but more sophisticated than anything that had yet been tried. As games get more complex and their stories get richer, there will undoubtedly be much more detailed models of human emotional states and relationships.

Defining your characters' attributes is part of character design, but the attributes that a character needs depend entirely upon the genre and the nature of the gameplay, and so we won't try to give any more examples or information here. Instead, we'll discuss attributes in each of the chapters devoted to genres in which characters play a significant role: action games, role-playing games, strategy games, and adventure games.

Character Dimensionality

In everyday language, people often speak disparagingly of characters in books and movies as two-dimensional. By this they mean that the character isn't very interesting, doesn't grow or change, doesn't feel fully human, or adheres to a stereotype without any nuances. This criticism usually applies to heroes and villains; it's not realistic to expect everyone who appears in a story to be a fully rounded character with his own quirks and foibles. (Books and movies about small groups of people sometimes manage to achieve a thorough realization of virtually the entire cast of characters; see Thornton Wilder's *The Bridge of San Luis Rey* or Gabriel García Márquez's *One Hundred Years of Solitude* for examples.)

We propose a slightly more formal use of the idea of character dimensionality, which may help you in defining characters for computer games. We classify characters into four groups: zero-, one-, two-, and three-dimensional. A character's degree of emotional sophistication and the ways in which his behavior changes in response to emotional changes determines his degree of dimensionality. We'll describe each group by referring to the kinds of characters found in *The Lord of the Rings*, simply because that story is so well known.

- **Zero-dimensional** characters may display only discrete emotional states. A zero-dimensional character may exhibit any number of such states, but there is no continuum of states; that is, the character's emotional state will never move smoothly from one state into another or show evidence of being in two states at the same time; there is no such thing as "mixed feelings." The nameless orcs in *The Lord of the Rings* feel only two emotions: hate and fear. The orcs hate the heroes and attack whenever they feel they outnumber their enemies, and they fear the heroes and run away whenever they feel vulnerable or outnumbered. This minimal level of emotional variability is typical of the enemies in a simple shooter game (see Figure 6.9).

  The emotional simplicity of zero-dimensional characters can make them comic. The characters in classic Warner Brothers cartoons—Bugs Bunny, Sylvester the cat, et al.—change almost instantaneously from one extreme emotion to another.

- **One-dimensional** characters have only a single variable to characterize a changing feeling or attitude; in other respects their character is largely fixed. In *The Lord of the Rings,* the dwarf Gimli is hostile and suspicious toward elves at first, but over time his respect for the elf Legolas grows until they are boon companions. His other attitudes don't change

● **HATE**   ● **FEAR**

FIGURE 6.9 Zero-dimensional characters have binary emotional states with no mixed feelings. They may have more than two.

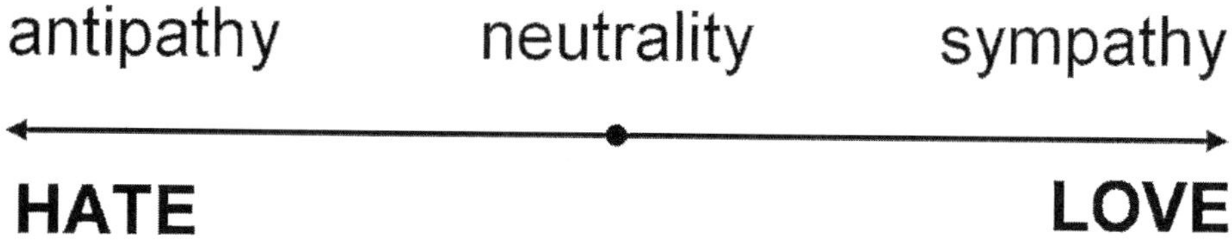

antipathy   neutrality   sympathy

HATE   LOVE

FIGURE 6.10 One-dimensional characters have a single variable that describes an emotion that changes over time.

much. The movies make him a more one-dimensional character than the book does (see Figure 6.10).

■ **Two-dimensional** characters are described by multiple variables that express their impulses, but those impulses don't conflict. Such variables are called *orthogonal*; that is, they describe completely different domains, which permits no emotional ambiguity. In *The Lord of the Rings*, Denethor is a two-dimensional character. He has a variety of strong emotions—pride, contempt, despair—but he never faces a moral dilemma. His senses of duty and tradition trump all other considerations, even when they are wildly inappropriate (see Figure 6.11).

■ **Three-dimensional** characters have multiple emotional states that *can* produce conflicting impulses. This state of affairs distresses and confuses them, sometimes causing them to behave in inconsistent ways. Most of the major characters in *The Lord of the Rings* are three-dimensional, especially those who are tempted by the Ring. Frodo and above all Gollum are three-dimensional; Gollum's conflicting desires have driven him mad (see Figure 6.12).

If you plan to allow conflicting emotional states to exist in a character, then you must decide how this conflict manifests itself so that the player perceives it. At any given time, one state will dominate, but if the character really is of two minds about something, his behavior may become erratic as one

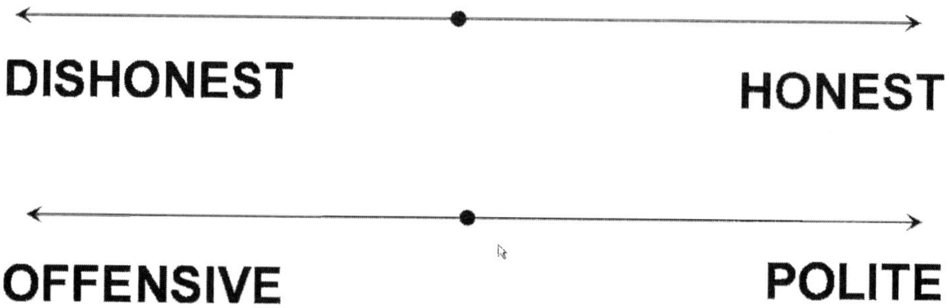

DISHONEST   HONEST

OFFENSIVE   POLITE

FIGURE 6.11 Two-dimensional characters have multiple, nonconflicting impulses.

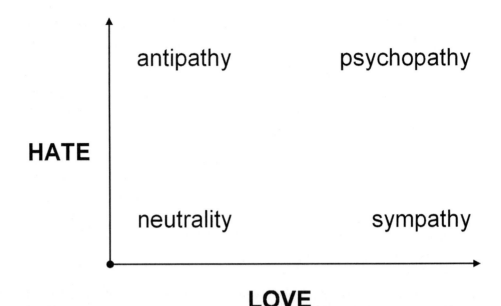

FIGURE 6.12 Three-dimensional characters can have conflicting impulses that produce inconsistent behavior.

emotion dominates and then another. For example, a person doing something he really doesn't want to do may be visibly reluctant, change his mind in the middle, or even subconsciously take some action that sabotages his own efforts. We don't have time to discuss this issue in depth here, but you will have to think long and hard about how to portray your characters' mixed feelings, and you should also discuss the problem with both your programmers (who will have to implement the necessary algorithms) and your artists (who will have to create animations showing, for example, reluctance or uncertainty).

We encourage the development of more games with three-dimensional characters. April Ryan in *The Longest Journey* and the Nameless One in *Planescape: Torment* both faced a number of moral dilemmas and questions about what it meant to be who they were. This kind of writing helps to improve the public perception of our medium as an art form worthy of serious consideration.

Character Growth

If a game aspires to be more than a simple adventure, if it seeks to have a meaningful story and not just a series of exciting episodes, then it must include character growth of some kind.

The way in which character growth takes place varies by genre. Action games typically restrict growth to new moves and new powerups; the character's mental states do not change. Adventure games, which depend on strong characters and plots, allow for a more literary type of change: personal and emotional growth, unrelated to gameplay. Role-playing games focus on character growth as one of the game's top-level challenges. Role-playing games offer several dimensions for growth: personal, if the story is rich enough; skills, such as the ability to use magic or weapons; and strength, intelligence, or any number of such character attributes.

To build character growth into your game, you'll have to decide *which* characters will grow (most often the hero, if there is one) and *how* they will grow. Physically? Intellectually? Morally? Emotionally? Games use physical growth, in abilities and powers, more than any other kind of growth because it is easy to implement and show to the player.

Then ask yourself how you will implement this growth within the game—through changes in numeric or symbolic attributes, or through changes in the plot of the story, or some other means? How will growth affect the gameplay, if at all? Finally, how will it be represented to the player? Some of your options include displaying numbers on the screen to show the growth (the crudest method), changing the character's appearance, changing the actions available to the player if the character is an avatar, and showing that the character has matured by changing his language and behavior (a more subtle method).

Character Archetypes

Many stories that follow the Hero's Journey pattern identified by Joseph Campbell include archetypal characters—that is, characters of types that have been fundamental to storytelling since the days of myth, that are found in the stories of virtually all cultures, and that may even be fundamental to the human psyche. (The psychologist Carl Jung originated the concept of character archetypes, and while his work is increasingly out of fashion in psychological circles, students of the humanities and literature still find it useful.) These characters assist or impede the hero in various ways on his journey. In *Banjo-Kazooie,* for example, Bottles the mole teaches the protagonists (and thereby the player) a number of things they need to know to fulfill their quest, so he fits neatly into the archetype of the *mentor* character. Christopher Vogler's book *The Writer's Journey* gives a condensed treatment of Joseph Campbell's work for screenwriters and discusses these archetypes in depth. For how to make best use of characters who represent these archetypes in your own games, we suggest you refer to Vogler's book.

We don't believe that you should implement character archetypes slavishly, or that a game must have all or even any of them. Video games do not necessarily have to be heroic journeys, and good characters don't have to fit into neat little boxes.

Audio Design

Audio design, both sound effects and language, is also a part of character design. You will need to work with your team's audio director—and sometimes defer to her experience—to find the right effects and voice for your character.

Sound Effects

The sounds a character makes tell us something about her personality, even if she doesn't speak. Sounds—anything from a gunshot, to a shouted "Hi-yah!" accompanying a karate chop, to a verbal "Aye, aye, sir"—confirm acceptance of the player's command. Sounds also signal injury, damage, or death. The sound of a punch that we're all familiar with from the movies is in fact quite unrealistic, but we're used to it and we know what that *THWAP!* means when we hear it. Likewise, drowning people don't really go "glug glug glug," but that's what we expect. Much of sound design involves meeting psychological expectations. Deep sounds suggest slow and strong characters; high sounds suggest light and fast ones. The tone of the sound a thing makes should confirm and harmonize with its visual texture: metallic objects make metallic sounds. As usual, however, incongruity can be funny, so you can mismatch sounds and visuals on purpose for comedic effect. As you define your character's movements and behaviors, think about what sounds should be associated with her.

Voice and Language

The way a character speaks conveys an enormous amount of information. We've broken this down into various elements:

- **Vocabulary** indicates the age, social class, and level of education of the character. People who don't read much seldom employ big vocabularies. Teenagers always use a slang vocabulary of their own in order to exclude adults. Beware, however: If you use too much current slang, your game will sound dated six months after publication. Conversely, period slang can help set a game in a different time—calling a gun a *roscoe* promptly suggests the hardboiled detective fiction of the 1930s and 1940s. In all cases, a light touch is best unless you're deliberately trying to be funny.

- **Grammar and sentence construction** also convey information about education and class; bad grammar reveals bad schooling. Although it's not really valid, we associate articulacy and long, complex sentences with intelligence.

- **Accent** initially tells us something about a person's place of origin and social class. City people and country people speak differently the world over. Accent is also, unfortunately, thought of as an indicator of intelligence. (This can backfire; smart lawyers from the American South occasionally play up their southern accents to fool their northern opponents into thinking they're not as bright as they really are.) We encourage you not to resort to the "dumb redneck" stereotype; it is as offensive in its way as the "dumb Negro" stereotypes of 1930s radio plays were.

- **Delivery** refers to the speed and tone of the person's speech. Slow speech is—again, mistakenly—often associated with a lack of intelligence, unless the speaker is an Eastern mystic, in which case slow speech can be mistaken for wisdom. Try to steer clear of stereotypes. Speed and tone can still work for you, indicating your characters' excitement, boredom, anxiety, or suspicion. The speaker's tone conveys an attitude or emotional state: friendly, hostile, cynical, guarded, and so on.

- **Vocal quirks** include things like a stutter (Porky Pig), lisp (Sylvester the cat), and catchphrases that identify a character ("Eh . . . what's up, doc?" from Bugs Bunny).

Consider how *The Simpsons* defines its characters' education, intelligence, and interests through language. Homer's limited vocabulary and simple sentences show that he's not well educated; the kinds of things he says indicate that his interests are chiefly food and beer. Marge's middle-sized vocabulary goes with her middle-class outlook on life; from her statements we see that she's concerned with work, friends, and her children. Lisa is the scholar of the family, interested in reading, writing, and music; she has an unusually rich vocabulary for her age and speaks in long, complex sentences. Bart's use of language varies considerably based on his situation, from moronically crude when he's playing a practical joke to quite sophisticated when he's making an ironic observation. Bart is a carefree hedonist but self-aware enough to know it and even comment on it. He's a postmodern sort of character.

StarCraft, which drew on a variety of American accents to create several different types of characters, exhibited some of the most interesting uses of language in games in recent years. Although designers did include the regrettable redneck Southerner stereotype, they also included the southern aristocrat and western sheriff speech patterns for Arcturus Mengsk and Jim Raynor, respectively; the laconic, monosyllabic diction of airline pilots for the Wraith pilots; a cheerful, competent midwestern waitress for the pilots of the troop transports; and a sort of anarchic, gonzo biker for the Vulture riders. This gave the game a great deal of character and flavor that it would have otherwise lacked if it had used bland, undifferentiated voices.

Summary

Character creation is an important part of computer game design. We've come far since we created the rudimentary characters of the early days, and character design continues to become increasingly sophisticated. For many games, simple, iconic characters will do. However, as our medium continues to mature, more games will need rich and deep characters as well. Whether a player defines the avatar she uses in the game or a designer creates a complete character for her to use, the designer has to make characters belong in the game world they inhabit, making them complete, compelling, and believable.

Test Your Skills

MULTIPLE CHOICE QUESTIONS

1. The character in the game who is under the player's control is called the
   A. NPC.
   B. avatar.
   C. antagonist.
   D. party.

2. The character of Indiana Jones in a video game would be an example of a
   A. specific avatar.
   B. nonspecific avatar.
   C. user-defined avatar.
   D. brand-name avatar.

3. If you can't see or hear the avatar, it's most likely a
   A. specific avatar.
   B. nonspecific avatar.
   C. user-defined avatar.
   D. robo-camel.

4. A first-person shooter employs what type of control?
   A. Indirect.
   B. Direct.
   C. Over-the shoulder.
   D. First-person view.

5. C-3PO is best described as belonging to what physical type?
   A. Humanoid.
   B. Hybrid.
   C. Nonhuman.
   D. Machine.

6. What would you consider including in the visual design of a cartoon character who needs to be fast?
   A. Make him tall.
   B. Give him big muscles like a body builder.
   C. Give him long legs.
   D. Give him legs like a kangaroo.

7. Which cartoonlike quality best describes Mario?

    A. Cute.

    B. Wise guy.

    C. Goofy.

    D. Cool.

8. The color palette you choose for a character is a good way of showing

    A. her level of intelligence.

    B. her level of strength.

    C. her temperament.

    D. none of the above.

9. Sidekick characters are useful because they

    A. let you give the player extra things to do.

    B. show a character with a different personality from the hero.

    C. give you a way to give advice to the player.

    D. all of the above.

10. In creating character depth, you should concentrate on which three factors?

    A. Appearance, jump distance, target market.

    B. Physical attributes, gender, target market.

    C. Appearance, language, behavior.

    D. Gender, age, attributes.

11. Status attributes are those that change

    A. frequently, but incrementally.

    B. incrementally, and rarely.

    C. often, and by a large degree.

    D. rarely, and by a large degree.

12. Characterization attributes consist of

    A. personality attributes that change a lot.

    B. personality that is formed before the age of five.

    C. personality attributes that change rarely and only by a small amount.

    D. attributes that describe physical appearance only.

6

13. Which of the following characters would you classify as zero-dimensional?

    A. James Bond.

    B. A nameless bad guy in a James Bond film.

    C. One of James Bond's girlfriends.

    D. Homer Simpson.

14. What is one of the methods used in computer role-playing games to show character growth?

    A. Armor and clothing.

    B. Increased challenges.

    C. Increased inventory capacity.

    D. Increased strength.

15. A large vocabulary usually indicates

    A. a good student.

    B. intelligence.

    C. memorization skills.

    D. educational background.

EXERCISES

1. Design a human, two-dimensional character for a computer game in three different versions: child, teenager, and adult. The design must include several distinct attributes (visual or personal) that signify the character's age and level of maturity at each stage. Make the character's emotional temperament different at each stage and suggest some events that might have happened to the character that would account for the change. Your instructor will give you the scope of the assignment; we recommend 2–5 pages.

2. Choose a game that you've never played whose box displays a cartoon-like avatar character. What does the character's general appearance tell you? What attributes does the character possess that make players want to play? What kind of player is the character designed to appeal to? Is there anything you'd like to add, and in that case, why? Is there anything you want to remove? Why?

3. Think of someone you know, a friend, family member, or even yourself. Think about the qualities that are the most dominant characteristics of this person's personality—his key attributes, if he were a game

character—and write those down. Then imagine the person in one of the following scenarios:

- The person is wrongfully accused of a serious crime—murder or armed robbery, for example.

- Earth is invaded by an enormous alien armada, whose objective is to blast everyone to bits.

- The person wakes up from sleep to find herself in another body in another place, but with the same personality.

Write a short essay addressing the following questions. What would your chosen person do in these situations? Situations like these are extremely unusual, but what if they happened? Would an ordinary person like the one you've chosen be a compelling and appealing character? (As an example, think about Tom Cruise's character in the movie *War of the Worlds*. Was he believable? Why or why not?)

4. Try designing two characters whose strengths and weaknesses complement each other, so that while they seem very unalike, they actually work together quite well. (Consider Banjo and Kazooie as an example.) Choose a game genre and design characters and attributes suitable for that genre. Show how their qualities complement each other when the characters are together but leave each character vulnerable to the game's dangers when they are apart.

DESIGN QUESTIONS

As you begin the task of developing characters for a game, consider the following questions:

1. Are the game's characters primarily art-based or story-based?

2. What style is your art-based character drawn in: cartoon, comic-book superhero, realistic, gothic? Will your character be exaggerated in some way: cute, supersensual, or otherwise?

3. Do your art-based characters depend upon visual stereotypes for instant identification, or are they more subtle than that? If they are more subtle, how does their appearance support their role in the game?

4. Can the player tell by looking at a character how that character is likely to act? Are there reasons in the story or gameplay for wanting a character's behavior to be predictable from his appearance, or is there a reason to make the character ambiguous?

5. If the game offers an avatar, does the avatar come with a sidekick? What does the sidekick offer the player—information, advice, physical assistance?

How will the sidekick complement the avatar? How will the player be able to visually distinguish between the two of them at a glance?

6. With a story-based character, how will you convey the character's personality and attitudes to the player? Through narration, dialog, gameplay, backstory, or other means?

7. What about the avatar will intrigue and interest the player?

8. What about the avatar will encourage the player to like him?

9. How will the avatar change and grow throughout the game?

10. Do the characters correspond to any of Campbell's mythic archetypes? Or do they have less archetypal, more complex roles to play, and if so, what are they?

11. How do the character's grammar, vocabulary, tone of voice, and speech patterns contribute to the player's understanding of the character?

Chapter 7

Storytelling and Narrative

Chapter Objectives

After reading this chapter and completing the exercises, you will be able to do the following:

- Discuss why stories are important to video games and know the definitions of story and narrative in games.
- Know the differences in player actions, in-game events, and narrative. Understand how to use story, character, and narrative to engage the player more deeply into your game.
- Describe the difference between linear and nonlinear storytelling.
- Design a foldback, nonlinear story with multiple endings.
- Understand how you can use episodic storytelling to encourage players to subscribe to additional versions of your franchise.

Introduction

Storytelling is a feature of daily experience. We do it without thinking about it when we recount some experience we have had, whether it is the commonplace story of how we were cut off while driving to the store, or how the golf match went with our friends, or a fiction made up for story time with our children. Stories are a part of our lives, though we often don't recognize them as such. We also consume stories constantly—fictional ones through novels, movies, plays, and television; nonfictional ones through books, documentaries, and the news media.

Video games often include fictional stories that go beyond the events of the games themselves. Game designers add stories to enhance a game's entertainment value, to keep the player interested in a long game, and to help sell the game to prospective customers.

In this chapter, we look at how stories and games relate to one another. We focus mostly on games that rely heavily on stories, though the chapter covers stories within all genres. We address what makes a good story and how to keep the stories from overwhelming the gameplay of a video game. Our definitions of *interactive story* and *narrative* are followed by a discussion of linear and nonlinear storytelling and mechanisms for advancing the plot. We then address *scripted conversations*, which allow the player to participate in dialog with nonplayer characters (NPCs). We conclude this chapter with the topic of episodic storytelling, a device made more possible than ever before with the Internet.

Why Put Stories in Games?

Debate on the subject of stories in games has simmered for many years, boiling up and cooling down as game designers, game theorists, and players dispute issues such as whether stories belong in games and, if so, what these stories should be like and how they should work (see the FYI, *The Great Debate,* on page 183). Many players want a story along with their gameplay, and some game genres—role-playing games, action-adventures, and above all adventure games—definitely require one. Whether a story will improve a game depends on the genre and how rich a story you want to tell. Although a story won't help in all cases, we offer four good reasons for including a story in your game:

- **Stories can add significantly to the entertainment that a game offers.** Without a story, a game reduces to a contest: exciting, but artificial. A story gives the contest a context. A story creates a more vivid fantasy world in which to set the activities of the game; it facilitates the essential act of *pretending* that all games require. A story provides greater emotional satisfaction by providing a sense of progress toward a dramatically meaningful, rather than an artificial, goal.

- **Stories attract a wider audience.** The added entertainment value of a story will, in turn, attract more people to a game. Many players need a story to motivate them to play; if the game offers only challenges and no story, they won't buy it. While adding a story makes development of the game more expensive, it also makes the game appeal to more people. On the other hand, players who *don't* need a story are free to ignore the story.

- **Stories help keep players interested in long games.** Simple, quick games such as *Bejeweled* don't need a story and would probably feel a bit odd if one were tacked on; that would be like adding a story onto a game of checkers or tic-tac-toe. In a short game, getting a high score provides all the reward the player needs. But in a long game—one that lasts for many hours or even days—simply racking up points isn't enough reason for most players to carry on. Furthermore, stories offer novelty. A long game needs variety, or it will begin to feel repetitive and boring; a compelling story provides that variety.

- **Stories help to sell the game.** It's difficult to show gameplay via printed posters, magazine ads, and the box the game comes in. Gameplay, as an active process, isn't always easy to explain in words or static pictures. But your publisher's marketing department can depict characters and situations from your game's story and even print part of the story itself in their advertising materials.

We can't teach you the fundamentals of good storytelling here; you can choose from many hundreds of books and classes on creative writing for that. Instead, we show how stories may be incorporated into video games and how interactive stories differ from traditional ones. Designing characters, an important part of any kind of storytelling, is covered in depth in Chapter 6, "Character Development."

There isn't one right way to include a story in a game; how you do it depends on what kind of entertainment experience you want to deliver and what kind of player you want to serve. We address those issues later in this chapter.

7

FYI   *The Great Debate*

Among theoreticians, interactive storytelling is the single most hotly debated issue in all of game design. What does *interactive storytelling* actually mean? Is such a thing possible? Should we do it? *How* should we do it? What are we trying to achieve by doing it? How can we determine if we're doing it well? And the problem gets worse: The game industry doesn't even know what to *call* it. *Interactive storytelling, interactive narrative, interactive drama, interactive fiction,* and *storyplaying* have all been proposed. In the 1990s, the academic community began to consider the issue and drew its own battle lines. The narratologists (people who study narrative) conducted fierce and often impenetrable arguments with the ludologists (people who study games and play) in the learned pages of scholarly journals. Search the Internet for "interactive narrative" and you will be overwhelmed by a confusing tide of conflicting verbiage.

These interesting and sometimes important arguments may eventually change the industry, but in the meantime you need to build a game. We suggest that you be guided by our preferred approach to any such game design problem: player-centric design. Don't worry about the theoretical arguments. Build a story into your game if you believe it will help to entertain the player, and don't build one in if it won't.

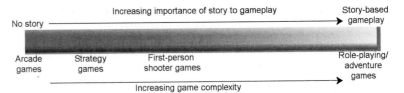

FIGURE 7.1 The story spectrum.

The type of game you choose to build will determine whether it needs a story and, if so, how long and how rich that story should be. A simple game such as *Space Invaders* requires only a one-line backstory and nothing else: "Aliens are invading Earth, and *only you* can stop them." Indeed, such a game should *not* include any more story than that; a story would only distract the player from the frenetic gameplay. At the other end of the spectrum, adventure games such as *Dreamfall* and *Discworld Noir* offer stories as involved as any novel. These games could not exist without their stories; storytelling offers up to half the entertainment in the game. See Figure 7.1 for an illustration of the story spectrum.

A few games have allowed the storytelling to overshadow the gameplay and gave the player little to do. This was a common mistake in the early days of making video games based on movie or book franchises. Critics and players uniformly considered them poor games because they violated the commandment that *Gameplay Comes First.* A designer must always keep that commandment in mind, no matter where the original franchise idea came from.

The following factors affect how much of a story a game should include, and you should take them into account when making your decision:

- **Length.** As we said in the previous section, the longer a game, the more it benefits from a story. A story can tie the disparate events of a longer game into a single continuous experience and keep the player's interest.

- **Characters.** If the game focuses on individual people (or at least, characters the player can identify with, whether human or not) then it can benefit from a story. If the game revolves around large numbers of fairly anonymous people—such as the visitors in *Theme Park*—then adding a story won't be easy.

- **Degree of realism.** Abstract games generally don't lend themselves to adding much of a story; representational ones often do. You may find it difficult to write a compelling story about a purely artificial set of relationships and problems, while a realistic game can often benefit from a story. This rule does not hold in all cases: Highly realistic vehicle simulators and sports games usually don't include stories because the premise of the game doesn't require one; on the other hand, *Ms. Pac-Man,* an abstract game, did tell a cute little story because the game included characters.

- **Emotional richness.** Ordinary single-player gameplay seldom inspires any but a few emotions: pleasure in success; frustration at failure; determination, perhaps; and occasionally an *aha!* moment when the player figures out a puzzle. Deeper emotions can come only when the player identifies with characters and their problems, which happens within a well-written story. If you want to inspire a greater variety of emotions, you'll need to write a story to do it.

You may also want to include a story to set your game apart from games using similar gameplay mechanics. The gameplay of *Half-Life* is virtually identical to that of any other first-person shooter, but the story sets it apart.

Key Concepts

Before we discuss the design processes required to put a story into your game, we introduce a number of key concepts that you'll need to understand, because they come up again and again throughout our discussion.

Story

In the loosest definition, a story is an account of a series of events, either historical or fictitious. On that basis, a few people would say that every game contains a story; even *Tetris* includes a story because the action of the game can be recounted afterward—that is, described by someone who saw the match to someone who didn't see it. Although theoretically correct, this position isn't very useful to a game designer. The description of a *Tetris* game would be a supremely uninteresting story because of the game's endless repetition and its lack of emotional content apart from that produced by the player's own success or failure. It is so bad a story as to be not worth telling. If we're going to incorporate stories into games, they should be *good* stories.

Requirements of Good Stories For the purpose of putting good stories into games, we need to expand the original definition. A minimally acceptable *story,* then, must be *credible, coherent,* and *dramatically meaningful.*

Credible simply means that people can believe the story, although in the case of fiction, they may have to suspend some disbelief to make belief possible. Many fantasy and science fiction stories, incredible in real-world terms, become perfectly believable once the reader accepts their premises. Even fantasy and science fiction stories, however, must offer characters that the audience can sympathize with, identify with, or recognize as convincing. If a character isn't believable, the story is flawed.

Humorous stories don't have to be as credible as serious ones. Different audiences also tolerate varying levels of credibility, so you should test your story on several people to see if they find it believable.

Coherent means that the events must not be irrelevant or arbitrary but must harmonize to create a pleasing whole. Even if some events are not related by cause and effect or some events just add color, all events still have to belong in the story. A story about the Apollo space program that included events from the first-century Roman invasion of Judea would be incoherent because the Roman invasion of Judea had no connection at all with the Apollo program. On the other hand, if the story of the Apollo program included a scene of Galileo building his telescope, that could be harmonious because his use of the telescope to study the heavens represents an important milestone in astronomy that ultimately led to the moon landings.

To be *dramatically meaningful*, the story's events have to involve something, or preferably someone, the listener cares about. The story must be constructed in such a way as to encourage the listener to identify with one or more of the story's characters. When a game tells a story, the dramatically meaningful events may be explicitly planned by the writer, or they may arise naturally out of the process of playing. Either way, all events must contribute to the player's involvement in the story through identification with characters and interest in what happens to those characters. See *Dramatic Tension* and *Gameplay Tension* later in this chapter.

> **KEY POINT**
>
> A good story must, at minimum, be a credible and coherent account of dramatically meaningful events.

Interactive Stories To define an interactive story, we must revisit the definition of a good story given in the Key Point. *Account* implies that the events happened in the past, which is why stories—even those set in the future—are normally written using the past tense. An interactive story, on the other hand, takes place now, with the player in the middle of the series of events, moving forward through those events. Furthermore, the player's actions form part of the story itself, which makes an interactive story very different from a story presented to a passive audience. In fact, an interactive story includes three kinds of events:

- *Player events,* actions performed directly by the player. In addition to giving the player actions to perform as part of gameplay—actions intended to overcome challenges—you can also give the player actions to perform as part of the story. Role-playing by talking to other characters, for example, might serve the needs of the story even if overcoming challenges does not require that action. If the player's actions can affect the plot of the story and change its future, we call them *dramatic actions.* Some player actions are not dramatic, however: Some player events aimed at overcoming challenges may not affect the plot.

- *In-game events,* that is, those events initiated by the core mechanics of the game. These events may be responses to the player's actions (such as a trap that snaps when the player steps on a particular stone) or independent of the player's actions (such as a simulated guard character checking to see that the castle doors are locked). The player might be able to intentionally cause these events to occur, to change the way they occur, or to prevent them entirely—which is part of what makes the story interactive.

■ *Narrative events,* whose content the player *cannot* change, although he may be able to change whether they occur or not. A narrative event *narrates* some action *to* the player; he does not interact with it. Narrative events are described in the *Narrative* section following this one.

With this in mind, we offer the following formal definition of an *interactive story.*

> An **interactive story** is a story that the player interacts with by contributing actions to it. A story may be interactive even if the player's actions cannot change the direction of the plot.

This definition of interactive story differs from those of many of our colleagues, who often assert that if the player's actions do not change the direction of the plot (that is, the plot is *linear*) the story is not interactive. We disagree. A player will still feel as if he is interacting with a story even if his actions do not change future events. The player contributes to the sequence of events, and that is what matters. We discuss the distinction between stories that cannot be changed and those that can in the sections *Linear Stories* and *Nonlinear Stories* later in this chapter.

Notice that our definition does not say anything about quality. Remember that to be a *good* story, a story's events must be credible, coherent, and dramatically meaningful. The player's actions constitute events in the story, so the more that those actions are credible, coherent, and dramatically meaningful events, the better the story will be. (Even an action that is not a *dramatic action*—one that changes the plot, as explained earlier—can still be *dramatically meaningful*; that is, it can be about something the player cares about.) When designing an interactive story, you shouldn't give the player things to do that don't credibly belong in the story; the result will be incoherent.

In most games with an interactive story, the player's actions move the plot along. When the player overcomes a challenge, the game responds with the next event in the story. If the player doesn't overcome a challenge, either the story comes to a premature end (as it would when, say, the avatar dies in the attempt) or the story simply fails to advance—the player doesn't see future story events until he manages to get past the specific obstacle. However, there are exceptions to this arrangement; in some games the story progresses whether or not the player meets the game's challenges. We address this issue in detail later in the section *Mechanisms for Advancing the Plot.*

Narrative

The definition of *narrative* itself is open to debate, but we use a definition that conforms pretty closely to that used by theorists of storytelling. Narrative consists of the *text* or the *discourse* produced by the act of narration. In an interactive story, narrative is the part of the story that you, the designer, narrate to your player—as opposed to those actions that the player performs, or those events that the core mechanics create.

> **Narrative** *refers to story events that are narrated—that is, told or shown—by the game to the player. Narrative consists of the noninteractive, presentational part of the story.*

The Role of Narrative   The primary function of narrative in a video game is to present events over which the player has no control. Typically these events consist of things that happen to the avatar that the player cannot prevent and events that happen when the avatar is not present, but we still want the player to see or to know about them.

Narrative also allows you to show the player a prolog to the game if you want to. It not only introduces the player to the situation in the game—the game's main challenge—but also to the game world itself. Although the sights and sounds of your game, the graphics and audio, create the immediate physical embodiment of your game's world (*how* the world looks), they can't explain its history and culture (*why* it looks that way). If you don't design that culture and history, the game world will feel like a theme park: all false fronts and a thin veneer over the game's mechanics. To establish a feeling of richness and depth, you must create a background, and some of that background can be revealed through narration.

Commonly Used Narrative Blocks   Many video games use blocks of narrative material—brief episodes of noninteractive content—to tell parts of the story. Designers commonly use a narrative block as an opening sequence, to introduce the story at the beginning of the game; as an ending sequence, to wrap up the story when the player completes the game; as an interlevel sequence, which often takes the form of a briefing about what the player will encounter in the next level (or chapter or mission); or in the form of **cut-scenes,** that is, short noninteractive sequences presented during play that interrupt it momentarily.

The game *Half-Life*, for example, begins with a movie in which Gordon Freeman, the player's avatar, takes a tram ride through the Black Mesa research complex while a voice explains why he is there. This opening sequence introduces the game world and sets the stage for the experience to follow.

Narrative blocks presented between levels tend to last from 30 seconds to four or five minutes. Those at the beginning and end of the game are sometimes longer still, as they provide important narrative bookends to the entire experience. In *Halo 2*, the introduction scene is more than five minutes long.

Cut-scenes during play, on the other hand, should be shorter because they interrupt the flow and rhythm of the player's actions. Players who like fast-moving genres such as real-time strategy games or action-adventures will be annoyed if you keep them listening or watching for too long without giving them something to do. Players of slower-moving games such as adventure games or role-playing games tolerate long cut-scenes better.

> **COMMANDMENT:** Noninteractive Sequences Must Be Interruptible
>
> All narrative material *must* be interruptible by the player. Provide a button that allows players to skip the sequence and go on to whatever follows, even if the sequence contains important information that players need to know to win the game. A player who isn't playing the game for the first time already knows what the narrative contains.

Forms of Narrative   Narrative in a video game can take many forms. A pre-rendered movie, a cut-scene displayed by the graphics engine, scrolling text that introduces a mission, voiceover commentary that explains the backstory of the game, or even a long monolog by a character can all be considered narrative elements of the game.

We make one exception to this definition. A single, prerecorded line of dialog spoken by a game character might be considered to be narrative because the player can't change it as it is being played back. However, dialog in games usually occurs in an interactive context, with the player choosing a line for her character to say, and the game choosing, based on what the player's avatar said, an appropriate line in response. Therefore, we do not consider *individual* lines of dialog to be narrative. A long, *noninteractive* dialog between NPCs, on the other hand, qualifies as narrative.

Balancing Narrative and Gameplay   Because playing games is an active process and watching a narrative is a passive one, the player notices the difference between them. A simple arcade game such as *Tempest* presents no narrative—it is entirely gameplay. A novel or a movie offers no gameplay—it is entirely narrative. The more narrative you include, the more the player sits doing nothing, simply observing your story.

But players don't play games in order to watch movies; they play in order to act. Any game that includes narrative elements must find an appropriate balance between the player's desire to act and the designer's need to narrate. If you offer too much narrative and too little gameplay, players will feel that your game gives bad value for the money they paid. Players pay for the opportunity to act out a fantasy. If most of your game's content is noninteractive, they'll feel cheated—they won't get the experience that they paid for.

Too much narrative also tends to make the game feel as if it's on rails, the player's actions serving only to move the game toward a predestined conclusion. Unless you've written a game with multiple endings, the conclusion *is* predestined, but you want to make the player feel as if he actively participates in the story. When the designer takes over too much of the telling, the player feels as if he's being led by the nose. He doesn't have the freedom to play the game in his own way, to create his own experience for himself.

The *raison d'être* of all computer gaming is *interactivity*: giving the player something to do. The trick, then, is to provide enough narrative to enrich the game world and motivate the player but not so much as to inhibit his freedom to meet the game's challenges in whatever way he chooses. Consider this paraphrase of the words of the wizard Gandalf in *The Lord of the Rings*: "We cannot choose the times in which we live. All we can decide is what to do with the time that is given us." The player cannot decide the world in which he plays; that is for you to determine. But he must have the freedom to act within that world, or there is no point in playing.

When you create your game's narrative segments, try to avoid seizing control of the player's avatar. In too many games, the narrative suddenly takes over and makes the avatar do something that the player might not choose to do. It is fair to change the world around the avatar in response to the player's actions; it is less fair to take control of the avatar away from the player.

Dramatic Tension and Gameplay Tension

Many designers are led astray by a false analogy between two superficially similar concepts, *dramatic tension* and *gameplay tension*. Here we define these terms, discuss their role in entertaining the player, and explain why you shouldn't confuse them.

Dramatic Tension When a reader reads (or a viewer watches) a story, she feels **dramatic tension**, the sense that something important is at stake coupled with a desire to know what happens next. (Screenwriters call this *conflict,* but as we use that term to refer to the opposition of hostile forces in a game, we prefer dramatic tension, which is more accurate in any case.) Dramatic tension is the essence of storytelling, whatever the medium. *Cliffhangers*—exciting situations at the ends of book chapters or TV shows that remain unresolved until the next chapter or episode—increase the audience's sense of dramatic tension and ensure they'll stick around to see the situation resolve. At the climactic event of a story, the action turns, so that instead of the tension mounting, the tension begins to fall.

Gameplay Tension When a player plays a game, he feels **gameplay tension**, also a sense that something important is at stake and a desire to know what happens next. But gameplay tension arises from a different source than dramatic tension does; it comes from the player's desire to overcome a challenge and uncertainty about whether he will succeed or fail. In multiplayer games, the player's uncertainty about what his opponents will do next also creates gameplay tension.

The False Analogy Game designers have tended to perceive an analogy between dramatic tension and gameplay tension, as if the two terms simply denoted the same feeling. However, the analogy is a false one. Dramatic tension depends on the reader's identification with a character (or several of them) and curiosity about what will happen to that character. Gameplay tension does not require any characters. A darts player feels gameplay tension in wondering whether he can hit the bull's-eye, but that situation provides dramatic tension only if the outcome matters to a character in the context of a story.

A key difference between dramatic tension and gameplay tension lies in the differing abilities of these feelings to persist in the face of *randomness* and *repetition*. By *randomness* we mean unpredictable and arbitrary changes in the course of events. *Repetition* refers to identical (or extremely similar) events occurring at different times in the progress of the story or game.

Dramatic tension, and reader interest in the dramatic subject, fades in the presence of both randomness and repetition. If the events in a story seem random—accidental and unrelated to one another—the reader will wonder why he is bothering to read it. Likewise, no story should include identical events that repeat themselves more than once or twice. If a police officer knocks on a potential witness's door and there's nobody home, he shouldn't have to do it more than once or twice before he gets an answer. Having this happen again and again in a story would be boring. (In some circumstances repetition can be played for laughs, if not overdone—in *The Secret of Monkey Island,* every time the hero escaped from a hut in which he was confined, the natives put a bigger lock on the door until the door looked like a bank vault. But even this was not completely repetitive, because each lock the natives added looked different.)

Gameplay tension, on the other hand, easily tolerates both randomness and repetition for much longer. Poker and *Tetris* include a lot of randomness and repetition yet retain their gameplay tension.

Consider the following dialog from the British television science fiction comedy *Red Dwarf.* Arnold Rimmer, sitting around one evening with his room-mate, Dave Lister, recounts every detail of a game of *Risk,* die-roll by die-roll, that he played ten years earlier. Lister asks him repeatedly to shut up, and Rimmer can't understand why.

RIMMER: *But I thought that was because I hadn't got to the really interesting bit.*

LISTER: *What really interesting bit?*

RIMMER: *Ah well, that was about two hours later, after he'd thrown a three and a two and I'd thrown a four and a one. I picked up the dice . . .*

LISTER: *Hang on Rimmer, hang on . . . the really interesting bit is exactly the same as the dull bit.*

RIMMER: *You don't know what I did with the dice though, do you? For all you know, I could have jammed them up his nostrils, head-butted him on the nose and they could have blasted out of his ears. That would've been quite interesting.*

> LISTER: *OK, Rimmer. What did you do with the dice?*
>
> RIMMER: *I threw a five and a two.*
>
> LISTER: *And that's the really interesting bit?*
>
> RIMMER: *Well, it was interesting to me, it got me into Irkutsk.*
>
> —*Red Dwarf* series 4, episode 6, "Meltdown"

Two lines in this exchange illustrate the point quite clearly. Lister says, "The really interesting bit is exactly the same as the dull bit," and later Rimmer says, "Well, it was interesting to me, it got me into Irkutsk." Like *Tetris*, *Risk* is full of repetition and randomness. Rimmer believes that it's interesting because he confuses the gameplay tension that he felt—will I conquer Irkutsk?—with dramatic tension.

COMMANDMENT: Randomness and Repetition Destroy Dramatic Tension

The narrative events in a game's story must not occur randomly or arbitrarily, nor should the narrative repeat itself, even if the play itself is repetitive.

The Storytelling Engine

To design a game that includes a story, you must interweave the gameplay—the actions taken to overcome the game's challenges—with the narrative events of the story. Narrative events must be interspersed among the gameplay events in such a way that all events feel related to each other and part of a single sequence that entertains the player. If the gameplay concerns exactly the same subject matter as the narrative—and it should, in order to present a coherent and harmonious whole—then the entire experience, play and narrative together, will feel like one continuous story.

The storytelling engine does the weaving. We introduced the storytelling engine briefly in Chapter 2, "Design Components and Processes," as the third major component of a video game along with the core mechanics and the user interface. Unlike the other two, the storytelling engine is optional; if the game doesn't tell a story, it doesn't have a storytelling engine.

Just as the core mechanics generate the gameplay, the storytelling engine manages the interweaving of narrative events into the game. The core mechanics oversee the player's progress through the game's challenges; the storytelling engine oversees the player's progress through the game's story. The storytelling

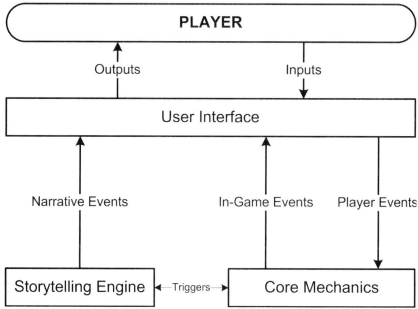

FIGURE 7.2 The relationship between storytelling engine, core mechanics, and user interface.

7

engine and core mechanics must work together to create a single, seamless experience.

Figure 7.2 illustrates the relationship between the storytelling engine, core mechanics, user interface, and player. You will notice that Figure 7.2 resembles Figure 2.1 from Chapter 2. Figure 2.1 showed how the core mechanics produce and manage gameplay. Figure 7.2 shows how both the core mechanics and storytelling engine together produce the experience of interacting with a story.

As we said in *Interactive Stories* earlier, an interactive story contains three types of events: player events, in-game events, and narrative events. The core mechanics manage the player events and in-game events, as the figure shows. The storytelling engine manages the narrative events. However, the storytelling engine does more than just play movies or cut-scenes; it also keeps track of the progress of the story and determines what part of the plot should come next.

Notice that a double-headed arrow labeled Triggers connects the storytelling engine to the core mechanics in Figure 7.2. At times, the core mechanics may determine that the interaction should stop and the storytelling engine should present some narrative—for instance, when a player completes a level. The core mechanics send a message to the storytelling engine saying that the player finished the level and the storytelling engine should now display any interlevel narrative events. Likewise, the storytelling engine can send a trigger back to the core mechanics when a narrative event finishes (or when the player interrupts a narrative event), telling the core mechanics to resume play.

The storytelling engine doesn't sit idle during play, however. As the player progresses, the mechanics continually send triggers to the storytelling engine—that way, the storytelling engine can keep up with what's going on. If, for example, the player makes a key decision that will affect the story later on, the core mechanics inform the storytelling engine of the decision.

Similarly, during play the storytelling engine can determine that the story has reached a critical plot point and trigger the core mechanics to cause changes to the internal economy of the game. Suppose the story says, "When the avatar reaches the bridge, he will be attacked by a highwayman in a cut-scene and robbed of all his property." The core mechanics, tracking the player's progress through the game world, send a message to the storytelling engine, "The avatar has reached the bridge." The storytelling engine detects that this is a key point, halts play, and displays a cut-scene showing the robbery. Then it transmits a message back to the core mechanics saying, "Transfer the avatar's inventory to the highwayman and resume play."

Normally, the level designers do the work that actually implements these events in the game. Among the level designer's tools for level-building will be a mechanism for detecting the avatar's position and for triggering both the cut-scene and the transfer of the avatar's property. At the moment, a development company cannot license a storytelling engine from a middleware company the way it can license a graphics engine or a physics engine, but that may change. Still, at a conceptual level it will help you to design the story and its interaction with the gameplay if you think of these events in terms of triggers sent between the two separate components, the core mechanics and the storytelling engine.

As you can see, the storytelling engine plays a critical role in weaving the gameplay and narrative together to create the whole experience. We refer to the storytelling engine frequently throughout the rest of this chapter.

Linear Stories

Up to this point, we haven't addressed a key issue: Can the player change the progress of the story? From the earliest days of computer gaming, designers have been intrigued by the possibility of creating stories in which the player can influence the plot and change the outcome. We refer to stories that the player cannot change as *linear stories* and those that the player can change as *nonlinear stories*. We address nonlinear stories in the next section.

A linear story in a video game looks similar to a linear story in any other medium, in that the player cannot change the plot or the ending of the story. In a game, however, the player still faces challenges as he goes through the story, and in fact the challenges form part of the story itself. Thus, a linear story in a game is still an interactive story, but the player's interactions are limited to contributing actions. Still, many games use this format. Consider *Half-Life* and

StarCraft: Both told linear stories, the outcome of which the player could not change, but the player performed many actions as part of the story along the way.

Creating linear stories offers many advantages, which explains why, after a flurry of experimentation with nonlinear ones in the 1990s, the game industry largely returned to this practice. Use of linear stories within games comes with disadvantages as well. Here are some of the pros and cons to consider when designing your own story.

- **Linear stories require less content than nonlinear ones.** If a player can only ever experience one fixed sequence of events, you only need to create material for those events. Developing the game using a linear story requires less time and money.

- **The storytelling engine is simpler.** The storytelling engine managing a linear story has to keep track of only a single sequence of plot events. Because the player cannot change the course of events, the storytelling engine doesn't need to record critical decisions that the player makes: There aren't any. The storytelling engine will be easier to implement in software if you use a linear story.

- **Linear stories are less prone to bugs and absurdities.** If the sequence of events remains the same regardless of players' actions, you can guarantee that the story makes sense. Allowing the sequence of events to vary introduces the risk of error, so the storytelling engine must guarantee that the events make sense. If the player wrecks a car during play in a game with a nonlinear story, the storytelling engine must ensure that the game does not present any subsequent gameplay or narrative material that shows the car undamaged. If you're not careful, you can introduce what the film industry calls *continuity errors*: things that look different from the way they should look, given the events of preceding scenes, because narrative material can't change to keep up with game events. Linear stories don't incur this risk. If a car is wrecked as part of the story, it stays wrecked; if it mustn't be wrecked, then you must not give the player any way *to* wreck it.

- **Linear stories deny the player dramatic freedom.** The player may have freedom to do a lot of things in the game, but none of it is **dramatic freedom**; that is, her actions don't influence the story apart from causing it to progress. As we mentioned in the previous paragraph, if the story requires a functional car throughout, then the gameplay *cannot* allow the player to wreck the car. We discuss this issue in more depth in the section *Endings* later.

- **Linear stories are capable of greater emotional power.** We explain this point in more detail in a later section in this chapter, *Emotional Limits of Nonlinear Stories*.

Note that if you want to tell a strictly linear story, that decision will have consequences for any story you plan to treat as a journey (as many are). See the section *The Story as a Journey* later in this chapter.

Nonlinear Stories

If you allow the player to influence future events and change the direction of the story, then the story is nonlinear. We examine two of the most common structures for nonlinear stories—*branching stories* and *foldback stories*—in detail in the next two sections. A third approach, *emergent narrative,* is more of a research problem than a standard industry technique, and we introduce it briefly. Finally, we look at an important question for any teller of nonlinear stories: How many endings should the story have?

Branching Stories

A **branching story** allows the player to have a different experience each time he plays the game. The story offers not one plot line but many that split off from each other at different points. As the designer, you decide on the different possible plot lines and how they relate to each other. During play, the storytelling engine keeps track of which plot line the player is following at any given time. When the story reaches a *branch point*—a place where the current plot line subdivides—the core mechanics must send a trigger to the storytelling engine to tell it which of the possible branches of the story the player will follow next.

Game events—either player events or in-game events generated by the core mechanics (such as an action taken by an AI-driven NPC)—determine which branch the story will take. Player events that influence the direction of the story fall into two categories: efforts to overcome a challenge or decisions that the story asks the player to make. Branch points connected with player decisions will have one branch for each option that you offer to the player. Typically, branch points associated with challenges have only two branches leading on from the branch point, one for success and one for failure, though you can also create different numbers of branches for different degrees of success if you want to. We address the emotional consequences of branches based on challenges versus those based on choices in the section *Endings* later in the chapter.

Immediate, Deferred, and Cumulative Influence   If the events that control which way the plot will branch occur right before the branch itself, those events have *immediate* influence on the story. However, the events could have happened earlier. The player can make a decision early in the game that influences a branch point much later, in which case that decision has *deferred* influence, or he can make a whole series of decisions throughout the game that cumulatively affect a branch point, such that his actions and decisions, taken together, have *cumulative* influence.

If you use deferred or cumulative influence, you must make it clear to the player what the possible consequences of his decisions will be. Giving him a choice early in the game without warning that this choice will have long-term repercussions, then directing the player down a different branch of the story tree hours or days later, will feel unfair. Furthermore, if he wants to change his mind, he has to go all the way back to where he first made the choice, choose differently, and then play all the way through the game again. And he can only do this at all if he realizes how his decisions affected the current branch, which may not be obvious.

For example, if you allow a player to choose right at the beginning of a role-playing game whether he will play as a healer character or a fighter character, you should tell him that such an important choice will have significant deferred consequences throughout the game.

Trivial decisions—which color hat will I wear?—should have only trivial consequences. If a trivial decision has a profound consequence, the player will feel cheated: He didn't know that the decision mattered and had no reason to expect it to matter. Attaching important consequences to trivial decisions violates the requirement that stories be credible and dramatically meaningful. *The Hitchhiker's Guide to the Galaxy*, a text adventure, did this for comedic and ironic purposes, but most players and critics judged it to be an unreasonably difficult game for exactly this reason: The player couldn't predict what the consequences of his actions would be.

7

COMMANDMENT: Be Clear About Consequences

Give players a reasonable amount of information about the possible consequences of their decisions, especially if the decision's consequences are deferred, so that they can make informed choices. Don't tie important consequences to what seem to be trivial decisions.

The Branching Story Structure   A diagram of a branching story looks somewhat like a tree, although by convention the root—the beginning of the story—appears at the top, so that the tree branches out as it goes down the page and the story goes forward in time. Figure 7.3 shows a small part of the structure of a branching story.

Each of the circles in Figure 7.3 represents a branch point, and each arrow represents a branch, that is, the player's movement along a plot line to the next branch point. The storytelling engine keeps track of the player's position in the story at any given moment.

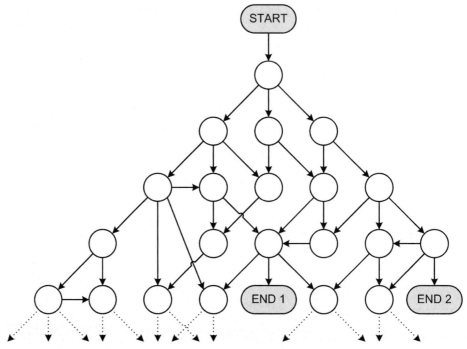

FIGURE 7.3 Part of the structure of a branching story.

As you look at Figure 7.3, be sure to note the following:

■ The branch points don't always have the same number of branches leading away from them. A story can branch in any number of directions at any given point.

■ The branches go down or sideways, but they never go back up again. The diagram depicts the possible progress of a story, and stories always move forward in time, never backward. In the course of playing a single game, the plot will never follow the same branch or pass through the same branch point twice. This enforces the rule that stories must not contain identical repeating events and helps avoid the risk of continuity errors, as discussed earlier.

■ Unlike branches on a real tree, different branches can merge; that is, different plot lines can converge. Many branch points can be reached by more than one path.

■ The diagram depicts two possible endings that may be reached by different paths. The complete diagram would show additional endings farther down.

■ The diagram shows only one start point, but in fact a story could have several start points if the player made a key decision before the story actually began. The player might select one of several different characters to be his avatar, and that choice could determine where the story begins. Or the storytelling engine could choose from among several designated start points at random just to make the beginning different each time the player plays the game.

The branching story mechanism is the classic method for creating interactive stories that give players lots of dramatic freedom. Branching plot lines let you tell a story in which the player's actions strongly affect the plot, and he can see the effect of his actions if he plays the game more than once and makes different decisions the second time through.

Disadvantages of the Branching Story   Be aware of the following three serious disadvantages of the branching story mechanism before you decide to use that structure for your game's story.

- **Branching stories are extremely expensive to implement** because each branch and each branch point require their own content. In Figure 7.3, a player can experience at most six branch points in playing from the top to the bottom of the figure—not very many. That represents six player choices or challenges. After six choices—for example, to take the left fork of the road, to enter the building, to go upstairs instead of down, to talk to the old woman, to accept a letter she offers, to leave the room—the player has barely started the game. Yet even this simplified example involves 21 branch points and 35 different branches, each of which requires its own story content: gameplay and narrative material. If none of the branches merged again, there would be even more. This rapid growth in the number of branches is called the ***combinatorial explosion.*** (Combinatorics is the field of mathematics that studies the number of possible combinations of a set of things—in this case, a set of branch points in a branching story.)

  As a result, most modern games don't actually include much branching, and they often include long periods during which the player plays but doesn't change the story. *Wing Commander*, a space combat simulator, contained a branching story, but it branched only between missions, not during them. Eventually, the *Wing Commander* series abandoned branching storylines entirely because they proved to be too expensive.

- **Every critical event** (those that affect the entire remainder of the plot) **has to branch into its own unique section of the tree.** Suppose a character can live or die at a particular branch point. If he dies, he must never be seen again, which means none of the plot lines from his death onward can include him. His death requires an entirely separate part of the tree that can never merge back into the rest—otherwise, he might reappear after the player knows that he's dead. If this happens with two characters, the game requires *four* separate versions of the story: a version in which both live; a version in which both die; a version in which A lives and B dies; and a version in which B lives and A dies. Again, the number of possible combinations explodes.

■ **The player must play the game repeatedly if he wants to see all the content.** If the storyline branches based on how well the player meets the game's challenges and he's very successful, then the next time he plays he will have to deliberately play badly in order to learn the dramatic consequences of his failure! A lot of players would consider this to be absurd. They've paid a great deal of money for the content in the game, and the only way to see it all is to play badly part of the time. This factor further contributed to the industry's abandoning stories that branch frequently.

If you want to make a branching story, you will have to plan out the structure in the concept stage of design. You should not actually write the story at that point in the design process, but you won't be able to plan a budget or schedule for your game unless you know how much content it will require, and a branching story's resource requirements expand very rapidly.

If you find that these drawbacks discourage you from using a branching structure, you can choose the compromise that the game industry most often uses when it creates nonlinear stories today: the foldback story.

Foldback Stories

Foldback stories represent a compromise between branching stories and linear ones. In a foldback story, the plot branches a number of times but eventually *folds back* to a single, inevitable event before branching again and folding back again to another inevitable event. This may happen several times before the end of the story. See Figure 7.4 for a simplified example. Notice that the dark gray points in the diagram aren't true branch points: They either offer branches that actually end up at the same place (although the player takes a different path to get there), or they merge some plot lines together but only offer one onward path. Because the branching storylines must eventually converge somehow, there will always be at least one of these prior to each inevitable event. *Monkey Island* follows this format, as do many of the traditional graphic adventure games.

Most foldback stories have one ending, as shown in the figure, but this isn't a requirement. You can construct a foldback story that branches outward to multiple different endings from its last inevitable event.

Foldback stories offer players dramatic freedom but in more limited amounts. The player believes that her decisions control the course of events, and they do at times, but she cannot avoid certain events no matter what she does. She may not notice this the first time that she plays and may think that the story reflects her own choices at all times. If she plays the game more than once,

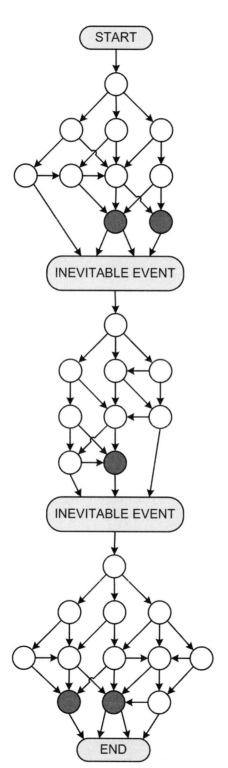

FIGURE 7.4 Simplified structure of a foldback story.

7

however, she will suspect that some events are inevitable and that the apparent control she enjoyed on the first play-through was an illusion. This is not necessarily a bad thing and can be useful to you as a storyteller. There's no reason why an interactive story must offer the player a way to avoid *any* event that she doesn't want to experience. After all, stories have always included the occasional event that the protagonist can do nothing about. If Scarlett O'Hara could have prevented Atlanta from being burned in *Gone with the Wind*, the story would have had a very different outcome and lost much of its emotional power. We think it's reasonable to use inevitable events to establish plot-critical situations that the player cannot reasonably expect to prevent or change.

The foldback story is the standard structure used by modern games to allow the player some dramatic freedom without the cost and complexity of a branching story. Developers routinely construct the interactive stories in adventure games and role-playing games as foldback stories. Of all forms of nonlinear interactive storytelling, it is the easiest to devise and the most commercially successful.

If you want to create a foldback story, you should choose critical turning points in the plot to be the inevitable events. They need not always be large-scale events like the burning of Atlanta. They simply should be events that change things forever and from which there is no turning back. The hero facing his final challenge, for instance, or the death of an important character, both work well as inevitable events.

Emergent Narrative

Emergent narrative, a term devised by Marc LeBlanc, refers to storytelling produced entirely by player actions and in-game events and without any narrative blocks (which he calls *embedded narrative*) created by a writer (LeBlanc, 2000). The story *emerges* from the act of playing. There is no separate storytelling engine and no preplanned story structure, either linear or branching; in principle, anything can happen at any time so long as the core mechanics permit it.

Playing *The Sims* can create emergent narratives because the game simulates the activities of a group of characters and contains no prewritten narrative blocks. However, *The Sims* is not really a device for telling stories to the player because it gives the player so much control that he doesn't feel as if he's *interacting* with a story but rather that he's *creating* a story. The game is more of an authoring tool. (See Chapter 5, "Creative and Expressive Play," for further discussion of player storytelling as a form of creative play.)

The chief benefit of emergent narrative is that the sequence of events is not fixed by a linear or branching structure, so the player enjoys more dramatic freedom. He can bring about any situation that the core mechanics will let him create. However, the player can control the story's events only to the extent that he can control the core mechanics through his play. If the designer set up the core mechanics in such a way as to force a particular situation on the player, his experience can be just as restricted as in a foldback story.

LeBlanc himself points out that emergent narrative is not without its problems. For one thing, it requires that the core mechanics be able to automatically generate credible, coherent, and dramatically meaningful stories—an extremely tall order. Core mechanics are defined in terms of mathematical relationships rather than human ones; how can they produce reasonable human behavior? How can we make them generate emotionally satisfying stories algorithmically? At the moment, with the field in its infancy, nobody knows. Furthermore, the core mechanics must limit repetition and randomness, and at the moment, the core mechanics of most games produce a lot of both. To all those problems we would add that emergent narrative seems to offer nothing for conventionally trained writers to do, and it might not be wise to give up on ordinary writers just yet, given the millennia of storytelling experience they represent.

We don't know of any commercial games that make use of purely emergent narrative without any embedded—that is, prewritten—material. The industry does not yet have any software that generates stories good enough for commercial entertainment products. At the moment, emergent narrative remains an experimental technique, part of an AI research field known as *automated storytelling*, which offers great potential for the future.

Endings

Readers find the ending of a story one of its most critical emotional moments. Storytellers craft their endings to evoke specific feelings in the audience— sometimes even in the very last sentence. But an interactive story can have multiple endings. How many endings should your story have?

FYI *Premature Endings Don't Count!*

By *ending* we mean a true conclusion to the story, not a premature ending caused by the player failing to meet a challenge. While dying in the middle of a long role-playing game does amount to losing the game, it's not really the end of the story, simply an interruption in the player's experience of that story. The player will undoubtedly restart the game and continue if she finds playing the game a compelling experience. Premature endings should be quick because they're only temporary, so don't squander resources creating a lot of narrative material to accompany premature avatar death. Nor should you make the player wait a long time to get started again. Many modern games don't even require the player to reload the game after a premature ending; they reload automatically for her, restarting near where she left off. Other games simply don't let the avatar die at all, to avoid the whole issue.

Include multiple endings if you want to give the player an outcome that reflects the dramatic actions he took throughout the story—those actions that actually matter to the story, as opposed to actions irrelevant to the drama, such as reorganizing his inventory or buying nicer clothing. However, the player's desire for an outcome that reflects his actions varies somewhat depending on what those actions were. Players' dramatic actions in a game may be divided into those taken to surmount a *challenge* and those in which the player makes a *choice*.

Challenges and Choices Ordinary competitive games, those without stories at all, still offer more than one ending: The player wins or she loses, depending on how well she played. So if the player meets your game's challenges well, you might want the story to end well, and if she meets them badly, you might let the story end badly. Just as the final score of an ordinary competitive game reflects the player's skill in a numeric way, so the outcome of the story can reflect the player's skill in a dramatic way. In general, players expect that if they meet all the game's challenges and make it to the end, the story will end in some reasonably positive way, reflecting the skill that got the player successfully to the end. If bad play produces a *premature* ending, as we described above, you're under no obligation to create a fully fledged conclusion for it. When a game's dramatic actions consist mostly of those taken to overcome challenges, players usually tolerate stories that offer only one ending.

If, on the other hand, the different possible endings reflect the player's *dramatic choices*—critical decisions the player made in the course of the interactive story—rather than his ability to overcome challenges, then the player will definitely expect her choices to affect the outcome of the story. For the game to tell her that a choice is important, and then to find out that it really isn't, is distinctly disappointing. You may wish to create a number of endings to show the consequences of the player's dramatic choices. Games that include a lot of decision-making—especially moral choices, which feel dramatically important—should be nonlinear and offer multiple endings.

When to Use Multiple Endings Devise multiple endings for your story if—and only if—each one will wrap up the story in a way both dramatically meaningful and emotionally consistent with the player's choices and play. If you didn't give the player a lot of dramatic freedom, then there's no point in giving her different endings. On the other hand, if you have told the player that her actions and especially her choices are crucial to the ending, then you should live up to that promise and give her whatever ending her actions earn. You may have to create several endings, depending on how many critical choices you gave the player.

For a more detailed discussion, see the Designer's Notebook column, "How Many Endings Does a Game Need?" (Adams, 2004).

Granularity

Granularity, in the context of games that tell a story, refers to the frequency with which the game presents elements of the narrative to the player. Consider *StarCraft,* which tells a long story that runs throughout all thirty missions available in the game but generally presents narrative (in the form of conversations among the major characters of the story) only between the missions. Because the missions take anywhere from 20 minutes to over an hour to complete, the game presents narrative blocks rather infrequently, so we can say that the storytelling in *StarCraft* exhibits *large granularity.* The *Wing Commander* series of games also told a story between missions and so also illustrates large granularity.

LucasArts's famous adventure games—the *Monkey Island* and *Indiana Jones* series—offered the player a small amount of narrative every time she solved a puzzle. This could happen as frequently as every four or five minutes, so the storytelling in these games shows *small granularity.* LucasArts games also used shorter narrative blocks, generally in the form of cut-scenes or spoken exposition.

There's no fixed standard for what constitutes small or large granularity; you will find the term mostly useful for comparing the relative granularity of one game to another.

In theory, the storytelling in a game may have *infinitesimal granularity*—that is, an interweaving of story and gameplay with such fine granularity that the player, unaware of narrative events as separate from the rest of the game, sees the game as one seamless interactive experience. Game developers have long attempted to achieve this quality for interactive storytelling with varying degrees of success. Generally, games come closest to reaching this goal if all story events pertain to the avatar and his actions (as in *Half-Life,* for instance) rather than if the story includes other events that the player must simply sit and watch.

Note that different authors use *granularity* to refer to a variety of different game design concepts: how frequently the player may take action; the degree to which the game reflects the player's achievements through point-scoring; and so on. Because of this ambiguity, we avoid all use of the term except with respect to interactive storytelling.

7

Mechanisms for Advancing the Plot

In presentational media, the plot of a story advances at the rate at which the reader reads or the display mechanism displays. In a video game, the story-telling engine causes the plot to advance but not at a fixed rate and not always triggered by the same mechanisms each time it advances. Different games use different triggers to tell the storytelling engine to move forward. In some games, succeeding or failing at a challenge triggers plot advancement. In others, the avatar's journey through the game world makes the story advance; in such games, entering a room or area may act as the trigger. In a very few games, the passage of time alone makes the plot advance, rather than anything the player does. In the next three sections, we look at these mechanisms more closely. Each approach brings with it strengths and weaknesses, and you will have to choose the one that works best for the story that you want to present.

The Story as a Series of Challenges or Choices

In a good many games, the plot advances as the player meets challenges or makes decisions. In a war game or a vehicle simulator, completing a mission or level might advance the plot. *StarCraft* advanced the plot only when the player successfully completed a level, while *Wing Commander* advanced its plot whether the player succeeded or failed at a mission, but the story proceeded in different directions depending on how the mission ended. In both of these large-grained stories, neither time nor progress through space affected the plot, only the fact that the level had come to an end.

This system works well for games that involve no travel at all or those in which travel itself doesn't affect the plot. In a combat flight simulator, the player can fly all over the sky, but none of that travel influences the story. What affects the story is shooting down enemy planes or being shot down by them.

Suspended, a text-based puzzle game from Infocom, also used this mechanism. All game and story events took place in a restricted area, a small group of rooms. Solving puzzles in the different rooms caused the plot to advance.

Sometimes the trigger for advancing the story isn't surmounting a challenge but making a choice or decision. Role-playing games often give the player important decisions to make, such as whether or not to join a particular guild, the consequences of which significantly affect the story. Once the player makes a decision—and decisions are often irreversible—the plot advances.

If you require the player to succeed at challenges in order to advance the plot, the storytelling will proceed in fits and starts. The player will sense that the story stalls every time he's stymied by a challenge, then starts up again when he meets the challenge. That doesn't matter much in large-grained stories—the player only expects storytelling at long intervals anyway—but in small-grained ones it feels rather mechanical.

Adventure games and role-playing games use this approach, but they combine it with avatar travel as a means of triggering plot advances, somewhat reducing the mechanistic feel of the plot advancement. They treat the story as a journey, which is the topic we take up next.

The Story as a Journey

If your game involves an avatar on a journey, that is, a game in which much of the activity involves moving the avatar from place to place in the game world, you may choose to have the avatar's movements trigger the storytelling engine to advance the plot. Games that use this approach almost always set up obstacles to travel, so the avatar cannot move through the game world freely but must overcome the obstacles to reach new areas. In effect, then, the story as a journey consists of a series of challenges and sometimes choices—as we've discussed—but adds a travel element: The plot advancement can also be triggered by the player's mere arrival in an area rather than by a specific challenge.

Presenting a story as a journey offers the following benefits:

- **It automatically provides novelty.** Because the player continually sees new things as he moves through the world, the experience remains fresh and interesting. The game gets the novelty that it needs to keep the player's interest from the visual appearance of the world, so you don't have to write as much novel dramatic material.

- **It allows the player to control the pace.** Most games allow the player freedom to decide when to move and when to stand still. Unless the gameplay imposes a time limit, the player remains free to control the pace of the story—to stop and think about the characters and the game world and to explore without time pressure. The story progresses only when the player triggers that progress by moving.

Many games use not merely a journey but specifically the Hero's Journey story structure identified by folklorist Joseph Campbell. Some designers find the Hero's Journey's mix of challenges and travel particularly well suited to single-player, avatar-based game designs. For more information on the Hero's Journey we suggest you read Campbell's *The Hero with a Thousand Faces* (Campbell, 1972) and Christopher Vogler's discussion specifically for writers, *The Writer's Journey* (Vogler, 1998).

If you treat the story as a journey and you make it a linear story, although the player might be able to move her avatar backward through the game world, no more dramatic events can occur in areas she's already visited. For this reason, many adventure games periodically require the player to pass through *one-way doors*—travel mechanisms that cannot be reversed, though they may take the form of something other than actual doors. In *The Secret of Monkey Island*, the hero got off a ship and onto an island by shooting himself out of a cannon. Once off the ship, there was no way back. The mechanism guaranteed that the plot moved forward, along with the avatar.

Computer role-playing games routinely treat stories as journeys but use highly nonlinear stories. The party can explore a large area, generally choosing any direction at will (though the game will include mechanisms for keeping them out of regions the party isn't yet strong enough to tackle).

The Story as a Drama

A small number of games treat the story as a drama that progresses at its own pace, advancing with the passage of time itself. In this case, the core mechanics don't send triggers to the storytelling engine to advance the plot; rather, the story-telling engine advances the plot on its own and sends triggers to the core mechanics to indicate when it's time to offer some gameplay.

The game *Night Trap* operated as a drama. The story unfolded in real time, whether or not the player took any action. Set at a party in a suburban house, the game assigned the player the goal of protecting partying teenagers from a group of invading monsters. The house was conveniently fitted with a security system consisting of closed-circuit cameras and various traps that, when the player set them off, would catch and contain any monster nearby. The player watched the different rooms on the security cameras and set off the traps if a monster appeared and tried to harm one of the teenagers who, in typical horror-movie fashion, were extraordinarily oblivious to it all. *Night Trap* required the player to switch his view from camera to camera, following the various events of the party and looking out for the monsters. If the player did nothing and a monster dragged one of the kids away, the player lost points.

Night Trap consisted almost entirely of storytelling; the players didn't act except to switch from one camera to another or to trigger a trap. Because the story progressed whether or not the player did anything, each game always took the same amount of time to play.

The more recent, noncommercial game *Façade* also presents a story as a drama. In *Façade,* the player visits a couple of old friends and quickly realizes that their marriage is in trouble. The player can help them work through their problems—or not—by engaging in dialog with them. The entire game takes place in the couple's apartment, and like *Night Trap,* the story progresses even if the player does nothing. But the player's actions during the game profoundly affect both the direction that the story takes and its ending.

Emotional Limits of Interactive Stories

Video games that don't include a story, that is, games that primarily entertain via the challenge and achievement of gameplay, don't try to arouse complex emotions in their audiences. They limit themselves to the thrill of victory and the agony of defeat, or perhaps to the frustration of repeated failure. But with a story, you can create other kinds of feelings as well. By crafting characters that the audience cares about and subtle relationships among those characters, you have a chance to make your audience feel (in sympathy with the characters) betrayal by a lover, satisfaction at justice done, or a protective instinct for a child.

However, the nature of the interactive medium imposes some limits on what you can do. In this section, we look at the emotional limitations of nonlinear stories and of avatar-based interaction models.

Emotional Limits of Nonlinear Stories

When you tell a nonlinear story, you give the player the freedom to make choices that significantly affect the relationships among the characters, which may include decisions that feel emotionally wrong—or at least that don't conform to what you, as a storyteller, would like the player to do. Suppose that you tell a story based on *Hamlet*, but you give the player controlling Hamlet a number of options. He could simply flee the situation and never return to Denmark; ignore his father's ghost and forgive his mother and uncle; try to assassinate his uncle and assume the throne himself; or just kill himself. None of these outcomes is quite as interesting as what Shakespeare actually wrote; in fact, some of them would bring the story to a bland and unsatisfactory conclusion.

By offering the player the power to change the course of the story—or at least to change the ending—you agree to accept the player's decisions, even decisions that are not ideal in ordinary storytelling terms. You cannot guarantee that the player will experience the most emotionally powerful resolution you feel that your story offers unless you confine the player to a single resolution (and even then, the player may prefer a different ending because individual taste varies).

Designers often restrict otherwise nonlinear stories to a single ending simply to guarantee that the players experience the emotionally meaningful outcome the designer planned. That means that the player's dramatic freedom before reaching the ending was merely an illusion. Players tolerate that in exchange for a satisfying ending, so long as you didn't promise them that their choices would change an ending which, in fact, was fixed from the start.

Emotional Limits of Avatar-Based Games

An avatar-based game is analogous to a story written in the first person. Because we presume the narrator of a first-person story to be alive, the audience knows that regardless of what happens in the story, the narrator must have survived to write the story afterwards. This isn't absolutely always the case—the narrator in the novel *Allan Quatermain*, for instance, dies near the end and another character finishes telling the story—but it does mean that whatever peril the narrator got into earlier in the book, we knew he would get out of it. As a result, first-person stories can't create quite as much concern for the life of the narrator as third-person stories can. A first-person story can have a depressing ending, but the narrating character cannot die prematurely.

A similar limitation applies to avatar-based games. Players know that an avatar should survive to the end of the game. Over the years, the avatar's premature death signified the player's failure to meet a challenge rather than being an actual element of the story, so the death of the avatar carries almost no emotional impact. The player simply reloads the game and tries again.

If you really want to affect the player's feelings with the death of a character, your game should kill not the avatar but one of the avatar's friends. Two famous examples occurred in the games *Planetfall* and *Final Fantasy VII*. In *Planetfall,* the player's sidekick, a wisecracking robot, sacrificed himself at a critical moment in order to allow the player to go on. Players often cite this as the first really emotionally meaningful moment in a computer game. In *Final Fantasy VII*, the villain kills Aeris Gainsborough, the player's ally. Nothing the player does can prevent this, and players often mention this death, too, as a particularly emotional moment in a game.

Party-based interaction models offer you more freedom to kill off members of the cast than avatar-based ones because the other members of the party remain to carry the story along. Two different television shows serve as good examples. *The Fugitive* could not have tolerated the death of Dr. Kimble, the hero of the show—equivalent to the avatar in an avatar-based game. On the other hand, the long-running *Law and Order* series about New York detectives and prosecutors has an ensemble cast with no single hero. Over the many years that it has aired, the entire cast has changed as one character or another has come and gone. The show continues to run because its central premise doesn't depend on any single individual.

KEY POINT

Many of the traditional rules for writing good stories in noninteractive media don't apply to interactive media. A new medium requires new rules. Be wary of slavishly applying principles from other forms (such as Aristotle's principles for drama or Robert McKee's observations about screenwriting) to interactive stories. If it doesn't work for you, throw it out!

Scripted Conversations and Dialog Trees

Natural language refers to ordinary language as spoken or written by human beings. Computer scientists devised the term to contrast ordinary human language with *computer* (or *programming*) *languages*. The extremely difficult problem of making computers understand and react appropriately to natural language—whether the language occurs as conversation or instruction—has puzzled artificial intelligence researchers for decades.

As game designers, we would like to be able to include natural language in our games without trying to solve a decades-old research problem. We want the player to be able to engage in conversations with nonplayer characters, especially in storytelling games. A **scripted conversation** allows us to approximate this. (Note that level design makes use of a technique often called "scripting" or "scripted events," which is a different, unrelated phenomenon.)

When entering a scripted conversation, either because the player chooses to speak to an NPC or an NPC chooses to speak to the player, the game enters a new gameplay mode created for the purpose. All other actions normally become

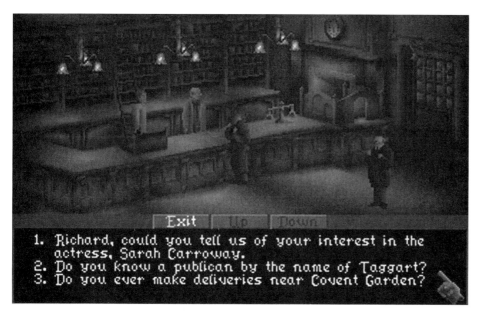

FIGURE 7.5 The conversation menu in *The Lost Files of Sherlock Holmes*.

unavailable. The player can't speak or type his dialog but instead chooses a prewritten line of dialog from a menu (see Figure 7.5). When the player chooses a line of dialog, the game plays or prints an appropriate response from the NPC, after which the system gives the player a new menu of lines to choose from. This process goes back and forth until either the NPC refuses to speak to the player any longer or the player chooses to end the conversation.

As the NPC says phrases the player hasn't heard before, the player may ask for elaboration, end the conversation, or switch the subject to a different topic. Offering the useful option, "Tell me again about . . . ," enables the player to return to an earlier point in the conversation and go through the NPC's responses again if he didn't pay close enough attention the first time. To end the conversation, the player chooses a line clearly intended as a farewell message ("Thanks for your help. Maybe I'll talk to you again later."), or occasionally an NPC may cut off the conversation with a line such as "I don't have anything else to tell you" or "I won't talk to you if you're going to be rude."

Structure of a Dialog Tree

Scripted conversations may be designed using a *dialog tree,* a branching structure something like the branching story tree already considered but in which each branch represents a line of dialog the player may choose. Unlike a branching story, the arrows can go backward as well as forward because players sometimes want to repeat parts of their conversations. Each branch point (or *node*) in

FIGURE 7.6 A simplified diagram of part of a dialog tree.

the tree represents a different menu that can be displayed to the player. The menu contains both the selection of lines of dialog available to the player and the NPC's response to each possible line. From each menu item, an arrow indicates which node, that is, which new menu of dialog options, the player will see next. The conversation passes through menu after menu as the conversation progresses. See Figure 7.6 for a simple example.

Note that in Figure 7.6, the maximum number of exchanges the player can have, starting from the top, is three. As with branching stories, if the menus continue to branch without folding back, you will soon get a combinatorial explosion of menus. In practice, they frequently converge, or link back to previous menus.

Dialog trees would be easy to create, except that sometimes we want different factors, even several factors, to influence what choices the player has and how the NPCs respond. Dialog trees are seldom actually as simple as Figure 7.6 makes them look. An NPC's response won't necessarily be rigidly connected with a player's menu choice. Some other factor, such as the level of the avatar's *charisma* attribute, may influence the NPC's reply. Likewise, role-playing games that include a diplomacy skill or a negotiation skill may give players with high skill levels extra menu items, so that they can say things that unskilled characters cannot.

If such factors will affect your dialog, you should sit down with your programmers and devise a system of notation that will be easy for you to create and easy for them to understand; they have to understand all of the factors and when those factors come into play so they can write the software that actually implements the system.

Benefits of Scripted Conversations

Although scripted conversation forces the player to say only the lines available in the script, it produces a sequence of plausible remarks and replies. It also gives you a way to illustrate both the avatar's and the NPC's personalities through something other than their appearances. You can write their lines in such a way that you give them distinct personalities of their own. For instance, Guybrush Threepwood, the hero of the *Monkey Island* games, uses phrases that reveal him as a wise guy who seldom takes anything seriously. The character's vocabulary, grammar, dialect, and—if the game features recorded audio—tone of voice and accent provide important cues.

In addition to letting the player discuss a variety of topics with a given NPC, the menu system allows the player to choose from a variety of different attitudes in which she says essentially the same thing, enabling her to project herself into the game as, for example, aggressive, deferential, formal, or flippant. The NPC can then respond to each phrase differently, in whatever way his personality dictates. An easy-going character might find a flippant response amusing and may choose to reveal more information to the player, while a powerful character who brooks no nonsense might be offended by wisecracks and refuse to talk to the player any more. (If you take this approach and the NPC's information is vital to the plot, make sure that either the powerful NPC gets over his snit after a while or there's some other way for the player to obtain the information.)

The scripted conversation is not merely a mechanism for giving the player information, however. It's a real part of the story, and the player's choices can have a distinct effect on the progress of the game. If an NPC asks the player to entrust him with a valuable secret, then the player's decision, whether to tell or not to tell, could have far-reaching consequences. The player has to choose responses based on her assessment of the NPC's character—to which you, the designer, must provide clues.

For a more detailed discussion of different ways of designing scripted conversations, we encourage you to read Chapter 14, "Dialogue Engines," of the book *Game Writing: Narrative Skills for Videogames,* edited by Chris Bateman (Bateman, 2006).

When to Write the Story

It is one of our strict commandments, first discussed in Chapter 3, "Game Concepts," that you must not write the story during the concept stage of design but only later during the elaboration stage. During the concept stage, your job is to define the player's role and the kinds of gameplay that he will experience in that role. You may make a list of episodes or levels that you would like to include in the game during the concept stage, and you can think about what the player may do in each level, but you must not write the whole story yet. (As we said above, you will need to lay out the *structure* of a branching story before you try to compute the budget for the entire project, but you should not actually write the story itself.)

We want you to wait to write the story because, until you know what gameplay the game will offer, you do not know what kinds of challenges the player will face and what sorts of actions she will be permitted to take. Even more important, you don't yet know what sorts of actions she *won't* be able to take. It's easy to write a story that includes too many different kinds of actions—actions that the programmers may not have time to implement in software. If you've written a story that includes the player's avatar riding a horse as well as traveling on foot and only later decide not to implement horseback riding for technical reasons, you've wasted a lot of time.

The task of writing the story falls into the second major stage of game design, the elaboration stage. You should begin writing *after* you define the game's primary gameplay mode, and preferably after you define all the major gameplay modes you will offer, because the details of those modes will tell you what sorts of actions the player can take and under what circumstances. In reality, writing the story will be an iterative process that takes place in conjunction with level design because level design creates the moment-by-moment sequence of experiences that the player can go through. You can write a story with large granularity if it presents narrative only between levels, in pieces after completing the design of each level, or even after all the levels are designed. But if narrative events can occur within a level, then you must write the story as you design the levels.

Other Considerations

We wrap up the discussion of interactive stories by addressing the frustrated author syndrome and episodic and serial delivery, including a few thoughts about how the industry may tell stories in the future.

Avoid the Frustrated Author Syndrome

Game designers who would really rather be authors in noninteractive media—would-be movie directors, for example—often make a couple of key mistakes when writing interactive stories. First, they tend to write linear stories while pretending to themselves and to the players that the story offers more interactivity than it really does, promising a big role for the player and then actually giving him almost none at all. The game *Critical Path* illustrates this problem; its introduction suggested that the player would get to do all kinds of exciting things when in fact its story was so rigidly linear that the avatar died every time the player deviated from the storyline in any way. (Rumors say that developers named the game *Critical Path* as an effort to justify this weakness.)

Players see the second symptom of frustrated author syndrome as they sit through large quantities of narrative when they would really rather be playing.

Although an excellent game in other respects, *The Longest Journey* included one scene that consisted of 20 minutes of nonstop monolog by a nonplayer character. That would be a long soliloquy even for Shakespeare! The game's designer, Ragnar Tørnquist, who originally trained as a screenwriter, admitted afterward that this was an error. Never forget that players come to play—to *do* something. Almost any sophisticated story requires some narrative, but you must parcel out narrative in reasonably sized blocks. Players won't want to sit through much more than three or four minutes of narration at a time, and many will get frustrated long before the three-minute mark.

COMMANDMENT: Be a Game Designer, Not a Filmmaker

Don't design a game to show off your skills as a film director or an author. Design a game to entertain by giving the player things to do. Always give the player more gameplay than narration. The player, not the story, is the star of the show.

Episodic Delivery

Most of our discussion so far has concentrated on individual stories that come to a definite end. However, a publisher will hope to exploit the popularity of a hit game by producing one or more sequels, a situation now so commonplace that in this section we address designing for it intentionally. The game industry has expressed much interest in the business opportunities that episodic delivery might offer, selling players entertainment a few hours at a time instead of in a single large chunk, as games sold at retail do now.

There are three main formats for delivering multipart stories, as indicated in Figures 7.7, 7.8, and 7.9 and discussed in the following sections. The television

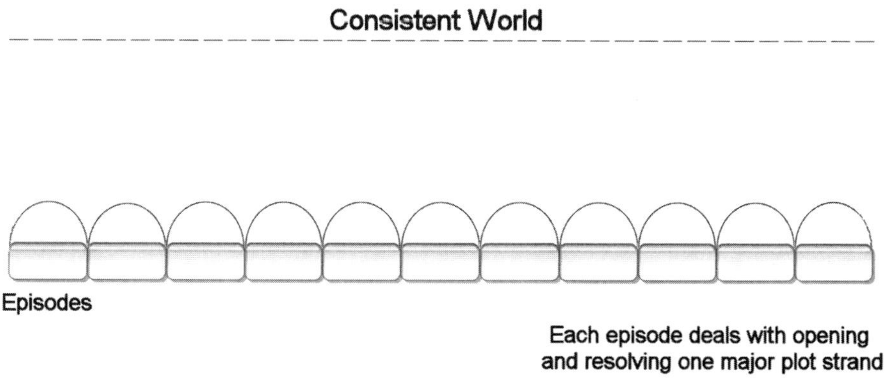

Consistent World

Episodes

Each episode deals with opening and resolving one major plot strand

FIGURE 7.7 An example of unlimited series structure.

Consistent World

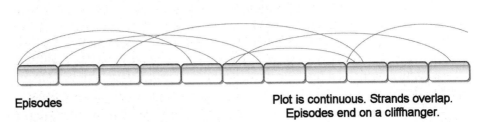

Episodes

Plot is continuous. Strands overlap.
Episodes end on a cliffhanger.

FIGURE 7.8 An example of serial structure.

industry has more experience at delivering multipart stories than the game industry does, so we will describe them in familiar TV terms.

Unlimited Series   An *unlimited series* comprises a set of episodes, each consisting of a self-contained story in which the plot is both introduced and resolved. A single theme or context runs through the entire series but not a single plot; in fact, the stories exist so independently of each other that episodes can be viewed in any order and still make sense. American evening TV dramas used this format almost exclusively up through the early 1980s: In each episode of *Columbo*, Columbo solves exactly one crime. Each episode can be viewed individually with little disadvantage. A consistent world and an overarching theme tie the series together. Because each episode offers a self-contained story, the producers can create as many episodes as they want (see Figure 7.7).

The majority of games and their sequels use the unlimited series format. Each game in the series contains a complete story set against the consistent world. Sometimes the publicity materials claim that sequels carry on the story from the previous game, but often the connection between them is flimsy; in any case the player gets a thorough introduction, so even if he didn't play the previous game, he can still enjoy the current one.

Consistent World

Overall Storyline

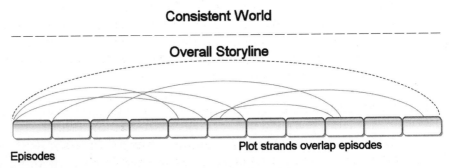

Episodes

Plot strands overlap episodes

FIGURE 7.9 An example of a limited series.

Serials   A *serial* consists of a (theoretically) infinite sequence of episodes. In a serial, plot lines extend over several episodes, developing simultaneously but at different rates so that only rarely does any plot begin and end within a single episode. Consequently, the episodes are not self-contained, and if you see an isolated episode without seeing what went before, you won't know what's going on. To maintain interest, each episode generally ends at a critical point in a major plot strand, creating a cliffhanger that the writers hope will create a strong desire to see the next episode. Soap operas depend on this format.

Serials rely on a large cast of characters who come together in smaller groups to play out each of several different (and often unrelated) plot lines, of which some, at any one time, may be beginning, coming to a climactic point, or ending. With no single overarching plot, events usually center on a group of people in a specific location or on a small group of families. Serials lack the grand sense of resolution that the hero's journey provides. Instead, they offer opportunities to observe different characters interacting under a variety of stresses. The cliffhanger at the end of each episode may involve some shocking revelation or event that leaves us wondering how a key character will react to the news or the change in situation.

It's a fair bet that we will see efforts to create interactive serials over the next few years, because the game industry would like to find a way to get players hooked on a story—and therefore paying to play it, episode after episode—in the same way that TV viewers seem hooked on serial dramas. Each episode of such an interactive serial can't be a multihour blockbuster of the sorts that the video game industry makes today; these games take too long to build. TV soap operas typically lower their production values and deliver short episodes frequently rather than long episodes infrequently, and we would expect interactive serials to work the same way. Figure 7.8 depicts the structure of a serial.

Limited Series   A *limited series* includes features of both the unlimited series and the serial. The limited series often combines single-episode plot lines, begun and resolved within one episode, with other plot lines that carry over from one episode to another. Unlike the unlimited series or the serial, however, a limited series also maintains one overarching plot line that runs throughout all episodes and eventually comes to a definite end, which is what makes the series limited. Recent examples of limited series include the TV shows *Babylon 5* and *24*.

Unlike the serial, the limited series format doesn't rely heavily on cliffhangers to create interest in the subsequent episodes. Instead, the overall plot line provides the driving interest, and the cliffhanger becomes only a secondary means of keeping the viewer's interest (see Figure 7.9).

Potential and Limits of Episodic Delivery   The industry already makes games in the unlimited series format, but we believe that it may start making games in the limited series format as well, to encourage players to buy the whole set. Developing games as limited series will require more money and planning but may prove to be worth it for a game that a publisher can be certain will be a hit. The *Harry Potter* series of games, based on the books and movies, will probably prove to be a limited series: When the overarching story ends, the series of games will end just as the author plans for the series of books to end. The speed of change of technology may prove a problem, in that the later games may not be able to rely on the earlier games' code without appearing dated. Rewriting the software in the middle of the series would cancel out the cost savings generated by planning the whole series at the beginning.

If the industry can find a way to make content quickly and cheaply on a continuing basis, we may eventually see interactive serials, with no fixed episode count and a constantly evolving story. Running such games in Web browsers over the Internet makes the most sense because the Web offers cheaper development and delivery compared to standalone games. If our prediction proves true and publishers develop limited serial games for the Web, then to be profitable, those games may need to use an advertising-based business model; few players will pay for Web-based games because there are so many free ones available.

Currently, most efforts to develop content on a continuing basis involve maintenance and expansion of ***persistent worlds***—massively multiplayer online games rather than episodically delivered serials. The MMOGs use a subscription business model, and once proprietors recoup the extremely high level of investment required to set up such a game, they can be extremely profitable.

If you're working on a PC or console game, we don't recommend that you intentionally leave its story unfinished. It's too much of a disappointment to play for hours only to find that you are required to buy another game to find out how the story ends; critics roasted the few games that took that approach. A long game should end with its major problem resolved, either for good or ill. If you want to leave room for a sequel, the sequel should be about a *different* problem that arose during the course of the first story. *Star Wars IV: A New Hope* serves as a perfect example: The story ended with the heroes destroying the Death Star (the movie's major problem), but with Darth Vader (a character introduced during the story) getting away to cause trouble later on. The story in *StarCraft* ended with the destruction of the Overmind (its major problem), but with Sarah Kerrigan, a key character, having apparently turned traitor and gone on to lead a renegade faction against the heroes of the first story. Unless your story is quite explicitly part of a multipart story and you can guarantee that all parts will eventually be told, players deserve some resolution at the end of a game—especially a long game.

Summary

Most video games will benefit from the addition of a good story, one that is credible, coherent, and dramatically meaningful. A designer should not attempt to write a movie or a novel when making the video game story, however; he should remember that interactivity is the reason people play games. Whether you decide to make a linear, nonlinear, or a foldback, multiple-ending story for your game will depend on the gameplay and genre you've designed in the concept phase. For more engaging gameplay, deeper emotional response from the player, and greater satisfaction upon completing the game, designers should work on a good story that maintains player interest, that shows character growth, that balances narrative elements with gameplay, and that, above all else, remains a fun game to play.

Test Your Skills

MULTIPLE CHOICE QUESTIONS

1. What must a good story consist of, at a minimum?
   A. Good character, good plot, good locations.
   B. Dramatic tension in the gameplay choices.
   C. A credible and coherent account of dramatically meaningful events.
   D. Dramatic actions.

2. An interactive story requires a player to
   A. contribute to changing the ending.
   B. change the direction of the plot.
   C. watch narrative scenes.
   D. contribute actions to the story.

3. A player event is defined as
   A. an event performed by the player that forms part of the story.
   B. an event that occurs in response to a player's action.
   C. an event that cannot be altered by changing the story.
   D. a cut-scene that involves the player avatar.

4. Activating a trip wire in a first-person shooter game could be considered
   A. a player event.
   B. a deferred event.
   C. an in-game event.
   D. an accident.

5. Watching as your avatar is taken hostage by aliens would be
   A. a narrative event.
   B. an in-game event.
   C. gameplay tension.
   D. a dramatic event.

7

6. If a player's actions cannot change the direction of the story, it is *not*
   A. an interactive story.
   B. a linear story.
   C. a nonlinear story.
   D. an episodic story.

7. Which is the best definition of *narrative* in the video game industry?
   A. A movie-like sequence.
   B. Voiceover material read by a narrator.
   C. The noninteractive parts of a story.
   D. Telling, not showing, the story by using text.

8. Which of the following is a commandment for video game story developers?
   A. Noninteractive sequences must be interruptible.
   B. Don't make noninteractive sequences more than 10 percent of the overall game.
   C. Keep branching storylines as broad as possible.
   D. Write the story before designing gameplay.

9. How does randomness affect dramatic tension?
   A. Good stories are made better when the story seems natural, almost random.
   B. Gameplay should be as random as possible, making the player more tense.
   C. Dramatic tension will suffer with too many random events.
   D. Narrative events should seem arbitrary to the player, to heighten gameplay tension.

10. Player events that will have a deferred influence on the story should be, at the time of the action,
    A. hidden from the player.
    B. obvious to the player.
    C. random.
    D. cumulative.

11. Changes to plot lines that happen right after an action are caused by
    A. nondramatic player actions.
    B. events with immediate influence.
    C. events with deferred influence.
    D. branching story structure.

12. Good design of dramatic actions requires that

    A. trivial decisions have only trivial consequences.

    B. important choices are made in perilous situations.

    C. deferred consequences are best kept secret.

    D. unimportant actions, such as inventory management, are well designed.

13. What is one reason why branching games are not often made?

    A. Players didn't like the replayability.

    B. Combinatorics make it too expensive to implement.

    C. Having only two choices was found to be dull.

    D. They take too long to play.

14. Devise multiple endings for your story to

    A. advance the plot.

    B. reduce replayability.

    C. add meaning to the player's choices and actions.

    D. add emotional depth.

15. What does a dialog tree do?

    A. Requires players to watch cut-scenes that tell the story.

    B. Triggers story events based on completing a quest.

    C. Defines an NPC's personality.

    D. Relates player dialog actions to future dialog choices.

7

EXERCISES

1. Game writers often find themselves asked to write content with very limited information, and they have to make it up as best they can. This is an exercise about writing dialog in such a situation. Assume the following scenario: An adventurer arrives at an old ruin. The main entry gate is guarded by a huge stone golem that has to be convinced to let the adventurer pass through. The player might take three different approaches to the conversation at hand: *intimidation, admiration,* or *subterfuge*. Write a scripted conversation for this situation in which, at each menu, the player has a choice of three options corresponding to each of the three approaches. Your conversation must include no fewer than four exchanges, counting introducing and parting dialog lines. If the player chooses a consistent approach throughout the conversation, the golem opens the gate; if the player does not, the golem refuses and the conversation ends.

2. This exercise is a case study. Choose a game that you have played through (or one that your instructor assigns) that contains a story. Analyze the story according to the principles introduced in this chapter and write an essay (your instructor will inform you of the required length) addressing the following questions. Is it a linear or a nonlinear story, and if nonlinear, what story structure does it use? Does it have more than one ending? What is its granularity? What kinds of narrative does the story use (cut-scenes, scrolling text, voiceover narration, etc.)? What proportion of the player's actions are dramatically meaningful versus dramatically irrelevant? Considering all the player actions, in-game events, and narrative events, do you feel it is a good story according to the requirements for credibility, coherency, and dramatic meaningfulness? Why or why not? Does the story evoke any emotions other than those associated with victory and defeat? If so, give an example.

3. Pick a linear story of your own choice from a book or a movie and write a half-page summary of the plot (don't start with *War and Peace*). Then make a nonlinear story out of it by introducing no fewer than three branch points into the story at what you consider to be key moments in the plot—points at which an event could have occurred differently or one of the characters could have taken a different action from the one portrayed by the original story. (Each branch point may have as few as two options, but you can include more if you like.) Draw a diagram of the result, and show the options at each branch you introduce. The diagram should include the original plot as well. Write a brief summary of the consequences of the alternate branches arising from taking a different path. If you want, you can fold back the story to a single ending, or leave it branching with multiple endings. If you include multiple endings, be sure they credibly follow as a result of the particular path taken through the branching storyline you created.

DESIGN QUESTIONS

1. How do the actions that you make available to the player work with the story in your game such that the story remains credible, coherent, and dramatically meaningful?

2. How will you design your gameplay to be sure that the player does not experience so much randomness or repetition that it harms the dramatic tension of your story?

3. Will the story in your game be linear or nonlinear?

4. If your story is nonlinear, will the story branch or fold back? What kinds of things will cause it to branch: challenges, choices, or both? Will you allow deferred or cumulative influences, or will all influences be immediate?

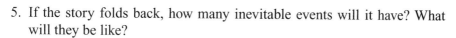

5. If the story folds back, how many inevitable events will it have? What will they be like?

6. How many endings will your story have? How does each ending reflect the player's play and/or choices throughout the game?

7. What will be the size of your game's granularity? How and when are narrative events interwoven with game events and player actions?

8. What mechanism will you use to advance the plot? Travel, events, time, or some combination?

9. Can the story begin at the beginning of the game, or would the game benefit from a prolog as well?

10. Will the game include narrative (that is, noninteractive) material? What role will it play—an introduction, mission briefing, transitional material, a conclusion, character definition? Is the narrative essential for the player to understand and play the game?

11. What form will the narrative material take? Pages in the manual? Scrolling text in the program? Movies? Cut-scenes? Voiceover narration? Monologs by characters?

12. What actions might the player take that are story actions but not efforts to overcome challenges? Conversations? Construction? Exploration?

13. Will the game include scripted conversations? Between the player and which characters? For what purpose?

14. Will the story be multipart? If so, how will the plot lines be handled: as an unlimited series, a limited series, or a serial?

7

Chapter 8

Creating the User Experience

Chapter Objectives

After reading this chapter and completing the exercises, you will be able to do the following:

- Explain how a game's user interface mediates between the player and the game's core mechanics to create the user experience.
- Discuss how principles of player-centric interface design can answer questions about what the player needs to know and wants to do.
- Know the basic steps required to design a game's user interface.
- List options that can help to control a game's complexity.
- Describe the five well-known interaction models.
- List the most commonly used game perspectives and discuss their advantages and disadvantages.
- Describe how visual elements such as the main view and feedback elements supply information a player needs to know to succeed in the game.
- Explain how audio elements such as sound effects and music affect the user experience.
- Know the types of one-dimensional and two-dimensional input devices and discuss how they affect the game experience.
- List the most commonly used navigation systems and explain how each system controls action in a game.

Introduction

The user interface brings the game to the player, taking the game from inside the computer and making it visible, audible, and playable. It creates the player's experience and, as such, has an enormous effect on whether she perceives the game as satisfying or disappointing, elegant or graceless, fun or frustrating.

In this chapter, we first discuss the general principles of user interface design and propose a process for designing your interface, along with some observations about how to manage its complexity. Then we define two key concepts related to game interfaces: *interaction models* and *perspectives.* We then delve into specifics, examining some of the most widely used visual and audio elements in video games and analyzing the functionality of various types of input devices. Because the overwhelming majority of video games include some notion of moving characters or vehicles around the game world, we turn next to consider a variety of navigation mechanisms as they are implemented in different perspectives and with different input devices. The chapter concludes with a few observations on how to make your game customizable.

What Is the User Experience?

> *What works is better than what looks good. The* looks good *can change, but what works, works.*
>
> —Ray Kaiser Eames, Designer and Architect

We've used the term *user experience* in the title of this chapter to emphasize the fact that a game's user interface (UI) actually presents the entertainment experience to the player. (For this reason, the user interface is often also called the *presentation layer.*) As we showed you in Figure 2.1, the user interface lies between the player and the internals of the game—that is, the core mechanics and the storytelling engine, which together contain all the data about the game's story, its rules, and its current state. The core mechanics and the storytelling engine should know nothing about the input and output devices of the machine—that way the internals of the game are independent of the hardware and can be more easily ported to another machine. The user interface's role is to take a portion of the internal data and present it to the player in visible and audible forms. The UI also takes the player's button-presses in the real world and interprets them as actions in the game world, passing on those actions to the core mechanics.

A game's user interface plays a more complex role than does the UI of most other kinds of programs. Most computer programs are tools, so their user interfaces allow the user to enter and create data, to control processes, and to clearly see the results. As part of a tool, the user interface must offer the user maximum control, information, and flexibility. A video game, on the other hand, exists to entertain, and while its user interface must be easy to learn and use, it doesn't tell the player everything that's happening inside the game, nor does it give the player maximum control over the game. It mediates between the internals and the player, creating an experience for the player that feels to him like gameplay and storytelling.

The user interface also implements two important mechanisms we introduced in Chapter 1, "Games and Video Games": the *interaction model,* which determines how the player interacts with the game world, and the *perspective,* which determines how the player sees the game world (that is, how the game's camera behaves).

In a more concrete sense, the user interface produces the game software's outputs on the machine's output devices and accepts the game software's inputs from the machine's input devices. The outputs traditionally consist of pictures and sound; the inputs, of button-presses and the movements of a joystick or mouse. In this chapter, we refer to the outputs as the *visual elements* and *audio elements* of the user interface and to the inputs as the *control elements.* When the game gives important information to the player about his activities, the state of the game world, or the state of his avatar (such as health or money remaining), we say that it gives *feedback* to the player—that is, it informs him of the effects of his actions. The visual and audio elements of the user interface that provide this information, we call *feedback elements.*

FYI *Terminology Issues*

The term *button* is unfortunately overloaded, as it sometimes refers to a physical button on an input device that the player can press and at other times refers to a visual element on the screen, drawn to look like a button, which the player can click with the mouse. In order to disambiguate the two, in this chapter we will always refer to physical buttons on an input device as *controller buttons* and those on the screen, triggered by the mouse, as *screen buttons. Keys* refers to keys on a computer keyboard. We use the term *key* interchangeably with *controller buttons* because they both transmit the same type of data.

Menus and screen buttons both appear on the screen as visual elements, but clicking on them with the mouse sends a message to the internals of the game, which makes them control elements as well. Furthermore, the appearance of a screen button may change in response to a click, making it a mechanism for giving information as well as for exercising control. We rely on your experience with computers to understand from context what we're talking about when we write of these things.

Any discussion of user interface design runs into a chicken-and-egg problem: We can't tell you how to design a good user interface without referring to common visual elements such as power bars and gauges, and we can't introduce the common visual elements without making references to how they're used. In order to address the most critical information first, we've chosen to start with the principles of interface design. If you encounter a reference to an interface element you've never heard of, see the section *Visual Elements* later in this chapter for an explanation.

Dozens, perhaps hundreds, of published books address user interface design, and we do not try to duplicate all that material here. We concentrate specifically on user interfaces for games, how they interact with the game's mechanics, and how they create the entertainment experience for the player. To read more about user interfaces in general, see *The Elements of User Experience* by Jesse James Garrett (Garrett, 2003).

Player-Centric Interface Design

The player-centric approach taught in this book applies to user interface design, as it does to all aspects of designing a game. Therefore, we keep discussion tightly focused on what the player needs to play the game well and how to create as smooth and enjoyable an experience as possible.

About Innovation

While we encourage innovation in almost all aspects of game design—theme, game worlds, storytelling, art, sound, and of course gameplay—we urge caution about innovation in user interface design. Although you will want your player to be impressed by the originality of your gameplay, the player will almost certainly prefer a familiar UI. Over the years, most genres have evolved a practical set of feedback elements and control mechanisms suited to their gameplay. We encourage you to research these systems by playing other games in your chosen genre and to adopt whichever of them you find appropriate for your game. If you force the player to learn an unfamiliar user interface when a perfectly good one already exists, you frustrate the player and reduce his enjoyment of the game.

If you do choose to offer a new user interface for a familiar problem, be sure to allow the player to customize it in case he doesn't like it. We address this further in *Allowing for Customization,* near the end of this chapter.

Some General Principles

The following general principles for user interface design apply to all games regardless of genre:

- **Be consistent.** This applies to both aesthetic and functional issues; your game should be stylistically as well as operationally consistent. If you offer the same action in several different gameplay modes, assign that action to the same controller button or menu item in each mode. The names for things that appear in indicators, menus, and the main view should be identical in each location. Your use of color, capitalization, type-face, and layout should be consistent throughout related areas of the game.

- **Give good feedback.** When the player interacts with the game, he will expect the game to react—at least with an acknowledgment—immediately. When the player presses any screen button, the game should produce an audible response even if the button is inactive at the time. An active button's appearance should change either momentarily or permanently to acknowledge the player's click.

- **Remember that the player is the one in control.** Players want to feel in charge of the game—at least in regard to control of their avatars. Don't seize control of the avatar and make him do something the player may not want. The player can accept random, uncontrollable events that you may want to create in the game world or as part of the behavior of nonplayer characters, but don't make the avatar do random things the user didn't ask him to do.

- **Limit the number of steps required to take an action.** Set a maximum of three controller-button presses to initiate any special move unless you need combo moves for a fighting game (see Chapter 13, "Action Games"). The casual gamer's twitch ability tops out at about three presses. Similarly, don't require the player to go through menu after menu to find a commonly used command. (See *Depth versus Breadth* later in the chapter for further discussion.)

- **Permit easy reversal of actions.** If a player makes a mistake, allow him to undo the action unless that would affect the game balance adversely. Puzzle games that involve manipulating items such as cards or tiles should keep an undo/redo list and let the player go backward and forward through it, though you can set a limit on how many moves backward and forward the game permits.

- **Minimize physical stress.** Video games famously cause tired thumbs, and unfortunately, repetitive stress injuries from overused hands can seriously debilitate players. Assign common and rapid actions to the most easily accessible controller buttons. Not only do you reduce the chance of injuring your player, but you allow him to play longer and to enjoy it more.

- **Don't strain the player's short-term memory.** Don't require the player to remember too many things at once; provide a way for him to look up information that he needs. Display information that he needs constantly in a permanent feedback element on the screen.

- **Group related screen-based controls and feedback mechanisms on the screen.** That way, the player can take in the information he needs in a single glance rather than having to look all over the screen to gather the information to make a decision.

■ **Provide shortcuts for experienced players.** Once players become experienced with your game, they won't want to go through multiple layers of menus to find the command they need. Provide shortcut keys to perform the most commonly used actions from the game's menus, and include a key reassignment feature. See the section *Allowing for Customization* at the end of the chapter.

What the Player Needs to Know

Players naturally need to know what's happening in the game world, but they also need to know what they should do next, and most critically, they need information about whether their efforts are succeeding or failing, taking them closer to victory or closer to defeat. In this section, we look at the information that the game must present *to* the player to enable her to play the game. Notice that in keeping with a player-centric view of game design, we discuss this mostly in terms of questions the player would ask.

Where am I? Provide the player with a view of the game world. We call this visual element the *main view.* If she can't see the whole world at one time (as she usually can't), also give her a map or a mini-map that enables her to orient herself with respect to parts of the world that she can't currently see. You should also provide audio feedback from the world: ambient sounds that tell her something about her environment.

What am I actually doing right now? To tell the player what she's doing, show her her avatar, party, units, or whatever she's controlling in the game world, so she can see it (or them) moving, fighting, resting, and so on. If the game uses a first-person perspective, you can't show the player's avatar, so show her something from which she can infer what her avatar is doing: If her avatar climbs a ladder, the player sees the ladder moving downward as she goes up. Here again, give audio feedback: Riding a horse should produce a clop-clop sound; walking or running should produce footsteps at an appropriate pace. Less concrete activities, such as designating an area in which a building will be constructed, should also produce visible and audible effects: Display a glow on the ground and play a definitive *clunk* or similar sound.

What challenges am I facing? Challenges such as puzzles, combat, or steering a vehicle can be shown directly in the main view of the game world; display the corridor of the maze, the onrushing barbarians, the road ahead, and so on. Some challenges make noise: Monsters roar and boxers grunt. To show conceptual or economic challenges, you may need text to explain the challenge; for example, "You must assemble all the clues and solve the mystery by midnight."

Did my action succeed or fail? Show animations and indicators that display the consequences of actions: The player punches the bad guy and the bad guy falls down; the player sells a building and the money appears in her inventory. Accompany these consequences with suitable audio feedback for both success and failure: a whack sound if the player's punch lands and a whiff sound if the player's punch misses; a ka-ching! when the money comes in.

Do I have what I need to play successfully? The player must know what resources she can control and expend. Display indicators for each: ammunition, money, mana, and so on.

Am I in danger of losing the game? Show indicators for health points, power, time remaining before a timed challenge ends, or any other resource that must not be allowed to reach zero. Use audio signals—alarms or vocal warnings— to alert the player when one of these commodities nears a critical level.

Am I making progress? Show indicators for the score, the percentage of a task completed, or the fact that a player passed a checkpoint.

What should I do next? Unless your game provides only a sandbox-type game world in which the player can run around and do anything she likes in any order, players need guidance about what to do. You don't need to hold their hands every step of the way, but you do need to make sure they always have an idea of what the next action could or should be. Adventure games sometimes maintain a list of people for the avatar to talk to or subjects to ask NPCs about. Race courses over unfamiliar territory often include signs warning of curves ahead.

How did I do? Give the player emotional rewards for success and (to a lesser extent) disincentives for failure through text messages, animations, and sounds. Tell her clearly when she's doing well or badly and when she has won or lost. When she completes a level, give her a debriefing: a score screen, a summary of her activities, or some narrative.

COMMANDMENT: Do Not Taunt the Player

A few designers think it's funny to taunt or insult the player for losing. This is mean-spirited and violates a central principle of player-centric game design—the duty to empathize. The player will feel bad about losing anyway. Don't make it worse.

What the Player Wants to Do

Just as the player needs to know things, the player wants to do things. You can offer him many things to do depending upon the game's genre and the current state of the game, but some actions crop up so commonly as to seem almost universal. We list some extremely common actions here.

Move. The vast majority of video games include travel through the game world as a basic player action. How you implement movement depends on your chosen interaction model and perspective. You have so many different options that we devote a section, *Navigation Mechanisms,* to movement later in this chapter.

Look around. In most games, the player cannot see the whole game world at one time. In addition to moving through the world, he needs a way of adjusting his view of the world. In avatar-based games, he can do this through the navigation mechanism (see *Navigation Mechanisms*). In games using multipresent and other interaction models that provide aerial perspectives, give him a set of controls that allow him to move the virtual camera to see different parts of the world.

Interact physically with nonplayer characters. In games involving combat, this usually means attacking nonplayer characters, but interaction can also mean giving them items from the inventory, carrying or healing them, and many other kinds of interactions.

Pick portable objects up and put them down. If your game includes portable objects, implement a mechanism for picking them up and putting them down. This can mean anything from picking up a chess piece and putting it down elsewhere on the board to a full-blown inventory system in a role-playing game in which the player can pick up objects in the environment, add them to the inventory, give them to other characters, buy them, sell them, or discard them again. Be sure to include checks to prevent items from being put down in inappropriate places (such as making an illegal move in chess). Some games do not permit players to put objects down, in order to prevent the players from leaving critical objects behind.

Manipulate fixed objects. Many objects in the environment can be manipulated in place but not picked up, such as light switches and doors. For an avatar-based game, design a mechanism that works whenever the avatar is close enough to the object to press it, turn it, or whatever might be necessary. In other interaction models, let the player interact more directly with fixed objects by clicking on them. You can simplify this process by giving fixed objects a limited number of states through which they may be rotated: a light switch is on or off; curtains are fully open, halfway open, or closed.

Construct and demolish objects. Any game that allows the player to build things needs suitable control mechanisms for choosing something to build or materials to build with, selecting a place to build, and demolishing or disassembling already-built objects. It also requires feedback mechanisms to indicate where the player may and may not build, what materials he has available, and if appropriate, what it will cost. You should also include controls for allowing him to see the structure in progress from a variety of angles. For further discussion of construction mechanisms, see Chapter 18, "Construction and Management Simulations."

Give orders to units or characters. Players need to give orders to units or characters in many types of games. Typically this requires a two- or three-step process: designating the unit to receive the order, giving the order, and optionally giving the object of the order, or *target*. Orders take the form of verbs, such as *attack, hug, open,* or *unload,* and targets take the form of direct objects for the verbs, such as *thug, dog, crate,* or *truck,* indicating what the unit should attack, hug, open, or unload.

Conduct conversations with nonplayer characters. Video games almost always implement dialog with NPCs as *scripted conversations* conducted through a series of menus on the screen. See *Scripted Conversations and Dialog Trees* in Chapter 7, "Storytelling and Narrative."

Customize a character or vehicle. If your game permits the player to customize his character or vehicle, you will have to provide a suitable gameplay mode or shell menu for it. The player may want to customize visible attributes of avatar characters, such as hair, clothing, and body type, as well as invisible ones, such as dexterity. Players like to specify the color of the vehicles they drive, and they need a means of adjusting a racing car's mechanical attributes because this directly affects its performance.

Talk to friends in networked multiplayer games. Multiplayer online games must give players opportunities to socialize. Build these mechanisms though chat systems and online bulletin boards or forums.

Pause the game. With the exception of arcade games, any single-player game must allow the player to pause the action temporarily.

Set game options. Outside the game world, the player may want to set the game's difficulty level, customize the control assignments (see *Allowing for Customization* later in this chapter), or adjust other features such as the behavior of the camera. Build shell menus to allow the player to do this.

Save the game. All but the shortest games must give the player a way of stopping the game and continuing from the same point when the player next starts up the game software. See *Saving the Game* in Chapter 9, "Gameplay."

End the game. Don't forget to include a way to quit!

The Design Process

You will recall that in Chapter 2, "Design Components and Processes," we divided the game design process into three stages: concept, elaboration, and tuning. Designing the user interface takes place early during the elaboration stage. There's no point in designing it any earlier; if you do so before the end of the concept phase, the overall design may change dramatically and your early UI work will be wasted.

In this section, we give the steps of the UI design process. Remember that definitions for many of the components you will use to design your game's UI can be found later in this chapter.

Define the Gameplay Modes First

A gameplay mode consists of a camera perspective, an interaction model, and the gameplay (challenges and actions) available. A lead designer generally defines the gameplay modes and, in a commercial development team, would then hand them off to a UI designer. Still, because the UI designer must implement the lead designer's ideas for camera perspectives and interaction models, the task of gameplay mode definition cannot be entirely separated from that of UI design.

In any case, the first job in the elaboration stage will be to design the *primary* gameplay mode, the one in which the player spends the majority of her time. We discuss gameplay in Chapter 9, "Gameplay." See *Interaction Models* and *Perspectives* later in this chapter for details about each of them. Once you have chosen (or been given) the perspective, interaction model, and gameplay for the primary gameplay mode, you can begin to create the details of the user interface for that mode.

When you have designed the primary gameplay mode, move on to the others that you think your game will need. Plan the structure of the game using a flowboard, as described in Chapter 2, "Design Components and Processes." In addition to gameplay activities, don't forget story-related activities. Design modes for delivering narrative content and engaging in dialog if your game supports it. Be sure to include a means to interrupt narrative and get back to gameplay.

If your game provides a small number of gameplay modes (say, five or fewer), you can start work on the user interfaces as soon as you decide what purpose each mode serves and what the player will do there. However, if the game provides a large number of modes, then you should wait until *after* you have planned the structure of the game and you understand how the game moves from mode to mode. Gameplay modes do not typically use completely different user interfaces but share a number of UI features, so it's best to define all of the modes before beginning UI work.

Once you have the list of gameplay modes, start to think about what visual elements and controls will be needed in each. Using graph paper or a diagramming tool such as Microsoft Visio, make a flowchart of the progression of menus, dialog boxes, and other user interface elements that you intend to use in each mode. Also document what the input devices will do in each.

You will usually need to define a different user interface for each gameplay mode your game offers. Occasionally gameplay modes can share a single UI when the modes differ only in the challenges they offer. If you want to allow the player to control the change from one mode to another, your user interface must offer commands to accomplish these mode changes.

Steps in designing a game's user interface include, for each mode, designing a screen layout, selecting the visual elements that will tell the player what she needs to know, and defining the inputs to make the game do what she wants to do. We'll take up these topics in turn. Throughout the remainder of this discussion, we'll assume that you're working on the user interface for the most important mode—the primary gameplay mode—although our advice applies equally to any mode.

IN THE TRENCHES: Build a Prototype UI

Experienced designers always build and test a prototype of their user interfaces before designing the final specifications for the real thing. When you have the names and functions of your UI elements for a mode worked out, you can begin to build a prototype using placeholder artwork and sounds so that you can see how your design functions. Don't spend a lot of time creating artwork or audio on the assumption that you'll use it in the final product; you may have to throw it away if your plans change. Plenty of good tools allow interface prototyping including graphics and sound with minimal programming required. You can make very simple prototypes in Microsoft PowerPoint using the hyperlink feature to switch between slides. Macromedia Flash offers more power, and if you can do a little programming, other game-making tools such as Blitz Basic (**www.blitzbasic.com**) will let you construct a prototype interface.

Your prototype won't be a playable game but will only display menus and screen buttons and react to signals from input devices. It should respond to these as accurately as possible given that no actual game software supports it. If a menu item should cause a switch to a new gameplay mode, build that in. If a controller button should shoot a laser, build the prototype so that at least it makes a *zap* noise to acknowledge the button press.

As you work and add additional gameplay modes to the proto-type, keep testing to see if it does what you want. Don't try to build it all at once; build a little at a time, test, tune, and add some more. The finished prototype will be invaluable to the programming and art teams that will build the real interface.

Choosing a Screen Layout

Once you have a clear understanding of what the player does in the primary (or any) mode and you've chosen an interaction model and a perspective, you must then choose the general screen layout and the visual elements that it will include.

All on-screen UI features will be oriented on and around the main view of the game world. The main view will be the largest visual element on the screen, but you must decide whether it will occupy a subset of the screen—a window—or whether it will occupy the entire screen and be partially obscured by overlays. See *Main View,* later in the chapter, for more information about your options.

During our research for this chapter, we examined more than 2,000 screen captures taken from games produced over the past 25 years. Nine designs occurred especially frequently (counting all symmetric variations as one design).

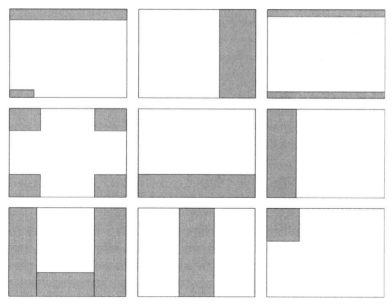

FIGURE 8.1 Common screen layouts.

Figure 8.1 shows how they look. White areas indicate the main view of the game world, and gray areas indicate feedback elements and onscreen controls. Any one of these would make a good start for the layout of your user interface.

You will need to find a balance between the amount of screen space that you devote to the main view and the amount that you devote to feedback elements and onscreen controls. Fortunately this seldom presents a problem in personal computer and console games, which use high-resolution screens. It remains a serious challenge for handheld devices and a very serious one indeed for mobile phones, which do not yet have standardized screen sizes and shapes.

Telling the Player What He Needs to Know

What, apart from the current view of the game world, does the player need to see or to know about? What critical resources does he need to be aware of at all times, and what's the best way to make that information available to him? Select the data from your core mechanics that you want to show, and choose the feedback elements most suited to display those kinds of data using the list in *Feedback Elements,* later in this chapter, as a guide. Also ask yourself what warnings the player may need and then decide how to give both visual and audible cues. Use the general list we gave you in *What the Player Needs to Know* earlier in this chapter, but remember that the gameplay you offer might dictate a slightly different list and that your game may include unique elements that have never been used before.

Once you have defined the critical information, move on to the optional information. What additional data might the player request? A map? A different viewpoint on the game world? Think about what feedback elements would best help him obtain these things and how to organize access to such features.

Throughout this process, keep the general principles of good user interface design in mind; test your design against the general principles listed in *Some General Principles* earlier in this chapter.

Letting the Player Do What She Wants to Do

Now you can begin devising an appropriate control mechanism to initiate every action the player can take that affects the game (whether within the game world or outside of it, such as saving the game). Refer to the list provided earlier in *What the Player Wants to Do* to get started.

What key actions will the player take to overcome challenges? Refer to the genre chapters in this book, as these mention special UI concerns for each genre. What other actions unrelated to challenges might she need: moving the camera, participating in the story, expressing herself, or talking to other players online? Create visual and audible feedback for the actions to let the player know if these succeeded or failed.

You'll need to map the input devices to the player's actions in the game based on the interaction model you have chosen (see *Interaction Models* later in this chapter). Games vary too much for us to tell you exactly how to achieve a good mapping; study other games in the same genre to see how they use onscreen buttons and menus or the physical buttons, joysticks, and other gadgets on control devices. Use the latter for player actions for which you want to give the player the feeling that she's acting directly in the game without mediation by menus. Whenever possible, borrow tried-and-true techniques to keep it all as familiar as possible.

Work one gameplay mode at a time, and every time you move to a new gameplay mode, be sure to note the actions it has in common with other modes and keep the control mechanisms consistent.

Shell Menus

Shell menus allow the player to start, configure, and otherwise manage the operation of the game before and after play. The screens and menus of the shell interface should allow the player to configure the video and audio settings and the game controls (see *Allowing for Customization* later in the chapter), to join in multiplayer games over a network, to save and load games, and to shut down the game software.

The player should not have to spend much time in the shell menus. Provide a means to let players get right into the action by one or two clicks of a button.

A surprising number of games include awkward and ugly shell menus because designers assumed that creating these screens could wait until the last minute. Remember, the shell interface is the first thing your player will see when he starts up the game. You don't want to make a bad impression before the player even gets into the game world.

Managing Complexity

As game machines become more powerful, games themselves become increasingly complex with correspondingly complex user interfaces. Without a scheme for managing this complexity, you can end up with a game that players find extremely difficult to play—either because no one can remember all the options (as with some flight simulators) or because so many icons and controls crammed onto the screen (as in some badly designed strategy games) leave little room for the main view of the game world. Here we discuss some options for managing your game's complexity.

Simplify the Game

This option should be your first resort. If your game is too complex, make it simpler. You may do this in two ways: *abstraction* and *automation*.

Abstraction   When you *abstract* some aspect of a complicated system, you remove a more accurate and detailed version of that aspect or function and replace it with a less accurate and detailed version or no version at all. This makes the game less realistic but easier to play. If the abstracted feature required UI control or feedback mechanisms, you may save yourself the trouble of designing them.

Many driving games don't simulate fuel consumption; the developers abstracted this idea out of the game. They don't pretend that the car runs by magic—the player can still hear the engine—but they just don't address the question. Consequently, the user interface needs no fuel gauge and no means of putting fuel in the car. The player doesn't have to think about these things, which makes the game easier to play.

Automation   When you *automate* a process, you remove it from the player's control and let the computer handle it for her. When the game requires a choice of action, the computer chooses, thus simplifying the game. Note that this isn't the same as abstraction because the underlying process remains part of the core mechanics; you just don't bother the player about it. The computer can take over the process entirely, in which case, again, you can save the time you would have spent on designing UI, or you can build the manual controls into the game but keep them hidden unless the player chooses (usually through an option in a shell menu) to take over manual control.

If you let the player choose between an automated or manual control over a game feature, you can refer to the two options as *beginner's mode* and *expert mode* in the menu where she makes the choice. You might want to reward the player for choosing the more complex task, such as choosing to shift the gears of a racing car manually, by making the manual task slightly more efficient than the automated one once the player has learned to do it well. If the automated task is perfectly efficient, the player has no incentive to learn the manual task.

Depth Versus Breadth

The more options you offer the player at one time, the more you risk scaring off a player who finds complex user interfaces intimidating. A UI that provides a large number of options simultaneously is said to be a *broad* interface. If you offer only a few options at once and require the player to make several selections in a row to get to the one he wants, the user interface is said to be *deep*.

Broad interfaces permit the player to search the whole interface by looking for what he wants, but finding the one item of current interest in that broad array takes time. Once the player learns where to find the buttons or dials, he can usually find them again quickly. Players who invest the (sometimes considerable) training time find using a broad interface to be efficient; they can quickly issue the commands they want. The cockpit of a commercial passenger aircraft qualifies as an enormously broad interface; with such a huge array of instruments, the pilot can place his hand on any button he needs almost instantly, which makes flying safer. On the other hand, pilots must train for years to learn them all.

Deep interfaces normally offer all their choices through a hierarchical series of menus or dialog boxes. The user can quickly see what each menu offers. He can't know in advance what sequence of menu choices he must make to find the option he wants, so the menus must be named and organized coherently to guide him. Even once he learns to find a particular option, he still has to go through the sequence of menus to get to it each time. On the other hand, using a well-designed deep interface takes almost no training.

It's a good idea to offer both a deep and a broad interface at the same time; deep for the new players, broad for the experienced ones. You can do this on the PC by assigning shortcut keys to frequently used functions. The large number of keys on a PC keyboard enables you to construct a broad interface easily. Console machines, with fewer controller buttons available and no mouse for pointing to screen elements, offer fewer options for creating broad interfaces.

If you can only offer one interface, we recommend that you make the breadth and depth of your interface roughly equal; but try not to make anything more than three or four levels deep if you can help it. When deciding how to structure menus, categorize the options by frequency of access. The most frequently accessed elements should be one or two steps away from the player at most. The least frequently accessed elements can be farther down the hierarchy.

Context-Sensitive Interfaces

A context-sensitive interface reduces complexity by showing the player only the options that she may actually use at the moment. Menu options that make no sense in the current context simply do not display. Microsoft Windows takes a middle path, continuing to show unavailable menu options in gray, while active menu items display in black. This reduces the user's confusion somewhat because she doesn't wonder why an option that she saw a few minutes ago has disappeared.

Graphic adventures, role-playing games, and other mouse-controlled games often use a context-sensitive pointer. The pointer changes form when pointed at an object with which it can interact. When pointing to a tree, for instance, it may change to the shape of an axe to indicate that pressing the mouse button will cause the tree to be cut down. The player learns the various things the mouse can do by pointing it at different objects in the game world and seeing how it changes.

Avoiding Obscurity

A user interface can function correctly and be pretty to look at, but when the player can't actually tell what the buttons and menus do, it is *obscure*. Several factors in the UI design process tend to produce obscurity, and you should be on the lookout for them:

- **Artistic overenthusiasm.** Artists naturally want to make a user interface as pleasing and harmonious as they can. Unfortunately, they sometimes produce UI elements that, while attractive, convey no meaning.

- **The pressure to reduce UI screen usage.** Using an icon instead of a text label on a screen button saves space, and so does using a small icon instead of a large one. But icons can't convey complicated messages as well as text can, and small simple icons are necessarily less visually distinctive than large complex ones. When you reduce the amount of space required by your UI, be sure you don't do so to the point of making its functions obscure.

- **Developer familiarity with the material.** *You* know what your icons mean and how they work—you created them. That means you're not the best judge of how clear they will be to others. Always test your UI on someone unfamiliar with your game. See whether your test subjects can figure out for themselves how things work. If it requires a lot of experimentation, your UI is too obscure.

Interaction Models

In Chapter 2, "Design Components and Processes," we defined the *interaction model* as the relationship between the player's inputs via the input devices and the resulting actions in the game world. You create the game's interaction model by deciding how the player's controller-button presses and other real-world actions will be interpreted as game world activities by the core mechanics. The functional capabilities of the various input devices available will influence your decisions, and we discuss input devices at length in *Input Devices* later in the chapter. We do not have room here to discuss button assignments in detail, so you should play other games in your genre to find examples that work well.

In practice, interaction models fall into several well-known types:

- *Avatar-based,* in which the player's actions consist mostly of controlling a single character—his avatar—in the game world. The player acts upon the world *through* the avatar and, more important, generally can influence only the region of the game world that the avatar currently inhabits. An avatar is analogous to the body of a human being: To do something in our world, we have to physically take our bodies to the place where we want to do it. That doesn't mean an avatar must be human or even humanoid; a vehicle can be an avatar. To implement this mode, therefore, many of your button-assignment decisions will center on navigation, which we discuss in *Navigation Mechanisms* later in the chapter.

- *Multipresent* (or *omnipresent*), in which the player can act upon several different parts of the game world at a time. In order to do so, you must give him a perspective that permits him to see the various areas that he can change; typically, an aerial perspective. Chess uses a multipresent interaction model; the player may ordinarily move any of his pieces (which can legally move) on any turn. Your decisions to implement this mode will concentrate on providing ways for the player to select and pick up, or give orders to, objects or units in the environment.

- The *party-based* interaction model, in which small groups of characters generally remain together as a group. This model is most commonly found in role-playing games. In this model, you will probably want to use point-and-click navigation and an aerial perspective.

- The *contestant* model, in which the player answers questions and makes decisions, as if a contestant in a TV game show. Navigation will not be necessary; you will simply have to assign different decision options to different buttons.

- The *desktop* model mimics a computer (or a real) desktop and is ordinarily found only in games that represent some kind of office activity, such as business simulations.

A coherent design that follows common industry practice will probably fit into one of these familiar models. You can create others if your game really requires them, but if you do so, you may need to design more detailed tutorial levels to teach your player the controls.

Perspectives

Old video games, especially those for personal computers, used to treat the game screen as if it were a game board in a tabletop game. Today we use a cinematic analogy and talk about the main view on the screen as if it displayed the output of a movie camera looking at the game world. In our discussion of perspectives, we make numerous references to the game's *virtual camera.*

Like the interaction model, the game's *perspective* grows out of a cluster of design decisions about how you want the player to view the game world, what the camera focuses on, and how the camera behaves. Certain perspectives work best with particular interaction models, so as we introduce the most common game perspectives, we will discuss the appropriate interaction models for them at the same time.

A note on terminology: We use terms adopted from filmmaking to describe certain kinds of camera movements. When a camera moves forward or back through the environment, it is said to *dolly,* as in *the camera dollies to follow the avatar.* When it moves laterally, as it would to keep the avatar in view in a side-scrolling game, it *trucks.* When it moves vertically, it *cranes.* When a camera swivels about its vertical axis but does not move, it *pans.* When it swivels to look up or down, it *tilts.* When it rotates around an imaginary axis running lengthwise through the lens, it is said to *roll.* Games almost never roll their cameras except in flight simulators; as in movies, the player normally expects the horizon to be level.

8

The 3D Versus 2D Question

Before we discuss perspectives in detail, we address the question of when games should use a 3D graphics display engine and when they should stick to 2D graphics technology. If a game uses 2D graphics, the first-person and third-person perspectives will not be available; those perspectives require a 3D engine.

Virtually all large standalone games running on powerful game hardware such as a personal computer or home game console employ 3D. (Small games and those played within a Web browser often still use 2D graphics.) With modern hardware now standard, you should use 3D graphics *provided* that you have the tools, the skills, and the time to do it well. If you do *not* have the more complex tools and the specialized skills to get good results, you should not try it. Good-looking 2D graphics are always preferable to bad-looking 3D graphics.

This question becomes a critical issue on mobile phones and personal digital assistants. With no 3D graphics acceleration hardware, if these devices display 3D graphics, they must do it with software rendering—a complex task and one that taxes the slow processors that run these gadgets. Think twice before committing yourself (and your programming team) to providing 3D graphics on such platforms.

While it may take the player a while to detect weak AI or bad writing in a game, bad graphics show up from the first moment he starts to play. Here, above all, heed the principle that if you cannot do it well, don't do it at all.

First-Person Perspective

In the *first-person perspective,* used only in avatar-based gameplay modes, the camera takes the position of the avatar's own eyes. Therefore, the player doesn't usually see the avatar's body, though the game may display handheld weapons, if any, and occasionally the avatar's hands. The first-person perspective also works well to display the point of view of the driver of a vehicle; it shows the terrain ahead as well as the vehicle's instrument panel but not the driver herself. It conveys an impression of speed and helps immerse the player in the game world. First-person perspective also removes any need for the player to adjust the camera and, therefore, any need for you to design UI for camera adjustment. To look around, the player simply moves the avatar.

Advantages of the First-Person Perspective   Note the following benefits of the first-person perspective compared with the third-person perspective:

- Your game doesn't display the avatar routinely, so the artists don't have to develop a large number of animations, or possibly any image at all, of the avatar. This can cut development costs significantly because you need animations only for those rare situations in which the player can see the avatar: cut-scenes, or if the avatar steps in front of a mirror.

- You won't need to design AI to control the camera. The camera looks exactly where the player tells it to look.

- The players find it easier to aim ranged weapons at approaching enemies in the first-person perspective for two reasons. First, the avatar's body does not block the player's view; second, the player's viewpoint corresponds exactly with the avatar's, and therefore, the player does not have to correct for differences between his own perspective and the avatar's.

- The players may find interacting with the environment easier. Many games require the player to maneuver the avatar precisely before allowing him to climb stairs, pick up objects, go through doorways, and so forth. The first-person perspective makes it easy for the player to position the avatar accurately with respect to objects.

Disadvantages of the First-Person Perspective   Some of the disadvantages of the first-person perspective (as compared with third-person) include:

- Because the player cannot see the avatar, the player doesn't have the pleasure of watching her or customizing her clothing or gear, both of which form a large part of the entertainment in many games. Players enjoy discovering a new animation as the avatar performs an action for the first time.

- Being unable to see the avatar's body language and facial expressions (puzzlement, fear, caution, aggression, and so on) reduces the player's sense of her as a distinct character with a personality and a current mood. The avatar's personality must be expressed in other ways, through scripted interactions with other characters, hints to the player, or talking to herself.

- The first-person perspective denies the designer the opportunity to use cinematic camera angles for dramatic effect. Camera angles create visual interest for the player, and some games rely on them heavily: *Resident Evil,* for example, and *Grim Fandango.*

- The first-person perspective makes certain types of gymnastic moves more difficult. A player trying to jump across a chasm by running up to its edge and pressing the jump button at the last instant finds it much easier to judge the timing if the avatar is visible on screen. In the first person, the edge of the chasm disappears off the bottom of the screen during the approach, making it difficult to know exactly when the player should press the button.

- Rapid movements, especially turning or rhythmic rising and falling motions, can create motion sickness in viewers. A few games tried to simulate the motion of walking by swaying the camera as the avatar moves; this also tends to induce motion sickness.

Third-Person Perspective

Games with avatar-based interaction models can also use the ***third-person perspective.*** The most common perspective in modern 3D action and action-adventure games with strongly characterized avatars, it has the great advantage of letting the player see the avatar. The camera normally follows the avatar at a fixed distance, remaining behind and slightly above her as she runs around in the world so as to allow the player to see some way beyond the avatar into the distance.

The standard third-person perspective depends on an assumption that threats to the avatar will come from in front of her. Some games now include fighting in the style of martial-arts movies, in which the avatar can be surrounded by enemies; consider recent games in the *Prince of Persia* series. To permit the player to see both the avatar and the enemies, the camera must crane up and tilt down to show the fight from a raised perspective.

Designing the camera behavior for the third-person perspective poses a number of challenges, as we discuss next.

Camera Behavior When the Avatar Turns   So long as the avatar moves forward, away from the camera, the camera dollies to follow; you should find this behavior easy to implement. When the avatar turns, however, you have several options:

- The camera keeps itself continuously oriented behind the avatar, as in the *chase* view in flight simulators (see Chapter 17, "Vehicle Simulations," for further discussion). Using this option, the camera always points in the direction in which the avatar looks. This arrangement allows the player to always see where the avatar is going, which is useful in high-speed or high-threat environments. Unfortunately, the player never sees the avatar's side or front, only her back, which takes some of the fun out of watching the avatar. Also, a human avatar can change directions rapidly (unlike a vehicle), and the camera must sweep around quickly in order to always remain behind her, which can produce motion sickness in the player.

- The camera reorients itself behind the avatar somewhat more slowly, beginning a few seconds after the avatar makes her turn. This option enables the player to see the avatar's side for a few seconds until the camera reorients itself. Because the camera moves more slowly in this maneuver, fewer players will find the images dizzying.

- The camera reorients itself behind the avatar only after she stops moving. The least-intrusive way to reorient the camera, this does mean that if the player instructs the moving avatar to turn and run back the way she came, she runs directly toward the camera, which does not reorient itself; instead it simply dollies away from her to keep her in view. The player cannot see any obstacles or enemies in the avatar's way because they appear to be behind the camera (until the instant before she runs into them). *Toy Story 2: Buzz Lightyear to the Rescue!* used this option; the effect, while somewhat peculiar, worked well in the game's largely nonthreatening environment.

If you plan for the camera to automatically reorient itself, you can give the player control over how quickly the reorientation occurs, a switch known as *active camera mode* or *passive camera mode*. This adjustment determines the length of time before the camera reorients itself so as to take up a position behind the avatar's back. In active mode, the camera either remains oriented behind the avatar at all times or reorients itself quickly; in passive mode, it either orients itself slowly or only when the avatar stops moving. This setting helps players affected by vertigo.

Intruding Landscape Objects   What happens when the player maneuvers the avatar to stand with her back to a wall? The camera cannot retain its normal distance from the avatar; if it did, it would take up a position on the other side of the wall. Many kinds of objects in the landscape can intrude between the avatar and the camera, blocking the player's view of her and everything else.

If you choose a third-person perspective, consider one of the following solutions:

- Place the camera as normal but render the wall (and any other object in the landscape that may come between the camera and the avatar) semitransparent. This allows the player to see the world from his usual position but makes him aware of the presence of the intruding object.

- Place the camera immediately behind the avatar, between her and the wall, but crane it upward somewhat and tilt it down, so the player sees the area immediately in front of the avatar from a raised point of view.

- Orient the camera immediately behind the avatar's head and render her head semitransparent until she moves so as to permit a normal camera position. The player remains aware of her position but can still see what is in front of her.

When the player moves the avatar such that an object no longer intrudes, return the camera smoothly to its normal orientation and make the object suitably opaque again, as appropriate.

Player Adjustments to the Camera   In third-person games, players occasionally need to adjust the position of the camera manually to get a better look at the game world without moving the avatar. If you want to implement this, assign two buttons, usually on the left and right sides of the controller, to control manual camera movement. The buttons should circle the camera around the avatar to the left or right, keeping her in focus in the middle of the screen. This enables the player to see the environment around the avatar and also to see the avatar herself from different angles.

Toy Story 2: Buzz Lightyear to the Rescue! used a different adjustment: The left and right buttons caused the avatar to pivot in position while the camera swept around to remain behind his back. This changed the direction the avatar faced as well as moving the camera and proved to be helpful for lining the avatar up for jumps.

Allowing the player to adjust the camera can help with the problem of intruding landscape items, but only as a stopgap, not a real solution.

Aerial Perspectives

Games with party-based or multipresent interaction models use an aerial perspective to allow the player to see a large part of the game world and several different characters or units at once. These perspectives give priority to the game world in general rather than to one particular character.

In games with multipresent interaction models, provide a means for the player to scroll the main game view around to see any part of the world that he wants (although parts of it may be hidden by the *fog of war;* see Chapter 14, "Strategy Games," for a discussion of the fog of war). With party-based interaction models, you may reasonably restrict the player's ability to move the camera to the region of the game world where the party is.

Top-Down Perspective Designers now usually reserve the top-down perspective, once standard for the main game view, to show maps in computer and console games. Easily implemented using 2D graphics, the top-down perspective remains in common use on smaller devices.

The *top-down perspective* shows the game world from directly overhead with the camera pointing straight down. In this respect, it resembles a map, so players find the display familiar. Its easy implementation using 2D graphics keeps it in common use on smaller devices, but its many disadvantages have led designers to use other methods on more powerful machines.

For one thing, the top-down point of view enables the player to see only the roofs of buildings and the tops of people's heads. To give a slightly better sense of what a building looks like, artists often draw them *cheated*—that is, at a slight angle even though that is not how a building should appear from directly above. (See Figure 18.1 for a top-down view with cheated buildings.)

The top-down perspective also distances the player from the events below. He feels remote from the action and less attached to its outcomes. It makes a game world feel like a simulation rather than a place that could be real.

Isometric Perspective The isometric perspective solves some of the problems presented by the top-down perspective, and because draftsmen developed isometric projection for two-dimensional display of 3D objects well before the computer age, it works well on systems without 3D graphics. An isometric projection shows the game world from an angle such that all three dimensions can be seen at once. If the game world is rectilinear (as they almost always are in the isometric perspective) and oriented on the cardinal compass points with north at the top of the map, then the isometric perspective shows the world from the southwest, looking toward the northeast, with north at the upper-left corner of the screen. This perspective requires an elevated camera position but not the extreme elevation of a top-down projection. See Figure 4.5 for a typical example of an isometric perspective.

An isometric projection distorts reality in that faraway objects don't get smaller as they recede into the distance. That's not the way we normally see the world, but because the camera does not display much of the landscape at one time, players don't mind the slight distortion. Because the isometric perspective is normally drawn by the 2D display engine using interchangeable tiles of a fixed size, the player can truck or dolly the camera above the landscape but cannot pan, tilt, or roll it. Some versions allow the player to shift the camera orientation from facing northeast to one of the other ordinal points of the compass in order to see other sides of objects in the game world. Doing this requires the artists to draw four sets of tiles, one for each possible camera orientation. Some also include multiple sets of tiles drawn at different scales, to let the player choose an altitude from which to view the world.

The isometric perspective brings the player closer to the action than the top-down perspective and allows him to see the sides of buildings as well as the roofs, so the player feels more involved with the world. It also enables him to see the bodies of people more clearly. Real-time strategy games and construction and management simulations, both of which normally use multipresent interaction models, routinely display either the isometric perspective or its modern 3D equivalent, the free-roaming camera. Some role-playing games that use a party-based interaction model still employ isometric perspective (see Figure 15.4).

Free-Roaming Camera   For aerial perspectives today, designers favor the *free-roaming camera,* a 3D perspective that evolved from the isometric perspective and is made possible by modern 3D graphics engines. It allows the player considerably more control over the camera; she can crane it to choose a wide or a close-in view; she can tilt and pan in any direction at any angle, unlike the fixed camera angle of the isometric perspective. The free-roaming camera also displays the world in true perspective: Objects farther away seem smaller. The biggest disadvantage of the free-roaming camera is that you have to implement all the controls for moving the camera and teach the player how to use them.

Context-Sensitive Perspectives   Context-sensitive perspectives require 3D graphics and are normally used with avatar-based or party-based interaction models. In a *context-sensitive perspective,* the camera moves intelligently to follow the action, displaying it from whatever angle best suits the action at any time. You must define the behavior of the camera for each location in the game world and for each possible situation in which the avatar or party may find themselves.

ICO, an action-adventure game, implemented context-sensitive perspective, using different camera positions in different regions of the world to show off the landscape and the action to the best advantage. This made *ICO* an unusually beautiful game (see Figure 13.12). Context-sensitive perspectives allow the designer to act as a cinematographer to create a rich visual experience for the player. Seeing game events this way feels a bit like watching a movie because the designer intentionally composed the view for each location.

This approach brings with it two disadvantages. First, composing a view for each location requires a great deal more effort on the part of designer and programmers than implementation of other perspectives. Second, a camera that moves of its own accord can be disorienting in high-speed action situations. When the player tries to control events at speed, he needs a predictable viewpoint from which to do so. The context-sensitive perspective suits slower-moving games quite well, and frenetic ones less well. Some games, such as those in the survival horror series *Silent Hill,* use a context-sensitive perspective when the avatar explores but switch to a third-person or other more fixed perspective when she gets into fights.

Other 2D Display Options

For the sake of completeness, we briefly mention a number of approaches to 2D displays now seldom used in large commercial games on PCs and consoles but still widely found in Web-based games and on smaller devices. Modern games that intentionally opt for a retro feel, such as *Alien Hominid* and *Strange Adventures in Infinite Space,* also use 2D approaches.

- **Single-screen.** The display shows the entire world on one screen, normally from a top-down perspective with cheated objects. The camera never moves. *Robotron: 2084* provides a classic example. (See the left side of Figure 13.1.)

- **Side-scrolling.** The world of a side-scroller—familiar from an entire generation of games—consists of a long 2D strip in which the avatar moves forward and backward, with a limited ability to move up and down. The player sees the game world from the side as the camera tracks the avatar.

- **Top-scrolling.** In this variant of the top-down perspective, the landscape scrolls beneath the avatar (often a flying vehicle), sometimes at a fixed rate that the player cannot change. This forces the player to continually face new challenges as they appear at the top of the screen.

- **Painted backgrounds.** Older graphical adventure games displayed the game world in a series of 2D painted backgrounds rather like a stage set. The avatar and other characters appeared in front of the backgrounds. The artists could paint these backgrounds from a variety of viewpoints, making such games more visually interesting than side-scrolling and top-scrolling games, constrained only by the fact that the same avatar graphics and animations had to look right in all of them. (See Figure 19.9 for an example.)

Visual Elements

Having introduced the major interaction models and perspectives you may wish to offer in your game, we now turn to the visual elements that you can use to supply information that the player needs to know.

Main View

The player's main view of the game world, from whatever perspective you choose, should be the largest element on the screen. You must decide whether the main view will appear in a window within the screen with other user interface elements around it, or whether the view will occupy the whole screen and the other user interface elements will appear on top of it. We address these options next. (See also *Choosing a Screen Layout,* earlier in the chapter.)

Windowed Views   In a windowed view, the oldest and easiest design choice, the main view takes up only part of the screen, with the rest of the screen showing panels displaying feedback and control mechanisms. You'll find this view most frequently used by games with complicated user interfaces such as construction and management simulations, role-playing games, and strategy games, because they require so many on-screen controls (see Figure 15.4 for a typical example). Using a windowed view does not mean that feedback elements *never* obscure the main view, only that they need to do so less often because most of them are around the edges.

The windowed view really does make the player feel as if she's observing the game world through a window, so it harms immersion somewhat. It looks rather like a computer desktop user interface, and you see this approach more often in PC games than in console games. The loss of immersion, undesirable for high-speed games in which the majority of the player's actions take place in the window itself, matters less when the game requires a great deal of control over a complex internal economy and the player needs access to all those controls at all times.

8

Opaque Overlays   If you want to create a greater sense of immersion than the windowed view offers, you can have the main view fill all or almost all of the screen and superimpose graphical elements on it in *overlays,* small windows that appear and disappear in response to player commands. The most common type, the *opaque overlay,* entirely obscures everything behind it (see Figure 18.5 for an example). Opaque overlays carve a chunk out of the main view, but when they're gone the player can see more of the game world than in a windowed view, and she doesn't feel as if she's looking through a window.

Action games that don't need a lot of UI elements on the screen often use *borderless* opaque overlays—overlays that don't appear in a box. Compare the rather old-fashioned windowed view on the left side of Figure 13.2 with the borderless opaque overlays on the right side. The overlays obscure only a small part of the main view, which otherwise runs edge-to-edge.

Semitransparent Overlays   Semitransparent overlays let the player see partially through them. See Figure 16.3 for an example. Semitransparent overlays feel less intrusive than opaque ones and work well for things such as instruments in the *cockpit-removed view* in a flight simulator, described in Chapter 17,

"Vehicle Simulations." However, the bleed-through of graphic material from behind these overlays can confuse the information that the overlay presents. You can barely read the semitransparent overlay in the upper left corner of Figure 17.5 because it consists of light colors with a light sky behind.

We suggest that you use semitransparent overlays only for graphical information such as the baseball diamond mini-map in Figure 16.3, not for text. Players find it irritating to read text with graphics underneath it, especially moving graphics.

Feedback Elements

Feedback elements communicate details about the game's inner states—its core mechanics—to the player. They tell the player what is going on, how she is doing, what options she has selected, and what activities she has set in motion.

Indicators   *Indicators* inform the player about the status of a resource, graphically and at a glance. We will use common examples from everyday life as illustrations. The meaning of an indicator's readout comes from labels or from context; the indicator itself provides a value for anything you like. Still, some indicators suit certain types of data better than others, and where appropriate, we will mention this. Choose indicators that fit the theme of your game and ones that don't introduce anachronisms; a digital readout or an analog clock face would both be shockingly out of place in a medieval fantasy.

Indicators fall into three categories: general numeric, for large numbers or numbers with fractional values; small-integer numeric, for integers from 0 to 5; and symbolic, for binary, tristate, and other symbolic values. Here are some of the most common kinds of indicators, with their types.

- **Digits.** General numeric. (A car's odometer.) Unambiguous and space-efficient, a digital readout can display large numbers in a small screen area. Digits can't be read easily at a glance, however; *171* can look a lot like *111* if you have only a tenth of a second to check the display during an attack. Worse, many types of data the player needs—health, mana, and armor strength—can't be appropriately communicated to the player by a number; no one actually thinks, "I feel exactly 37 points strong at the moment." Use digits to display the player's score and amounts of things for which you would normally use digits in the real world: money, ammunition, volumes of supplies, and so on. Don't use digits for quantities that should feel imprecise, such as popularity.

- **Needle gauge.** General numeric. (A car's speedometer.) Vehicle simulations use duplicates of the real thing—speedometers, tachometers, oil pressure levels, and so on—but few other games require needle gauges. Generally easy to read at a glance, they take up a large amount of screen space to deliver a small amount of information. You can put two needles on the same gauge if you make them different colors or different lengths and they both reflect data of the same kind; an analog clock is a two-needle gauge (or a three-needle gauge if another hand indicates seconds). Use needle gauges in mechanical contexts.

- **Power bar.** General numeric. (On an analog thermometer, the column of colored fluid indicating temperature.) A power bar is a long, narrow colored rectangle that becomes shorter or longer as the value that it represents changes, usually to indicate the health of a character or time remaining in a timed task. (The name is conventional; power bars are not limited to displaying power). When the value reaches zero, the bar disappears (though a framework around the bar may remain). If shown horizontally, by convention zero is at the left and the maximum at the right; if shown vertically, zero is at the bottom and maximum is at the top. The chief benefit of power bars is that the player can read the approximate level of the value at a glance. Unlike a thermometer, they rarely carry gradations. You can superimpose a second semitransparent bar of a different color on top of the first one if you need to show two numbers in the same space. Many power bars are drawn in green when full and change color to yellow and red as the value indicated reaches critically low levels to help warn the player. Power bars are moderately space efficient and, being thematically neutral, appear in all sorts of contexts. You can make themed power bars; a medieval fantasy game might measure time with a graduated candle or an hourglass.

- **Small multiples.** Small-integer numeric. (On a mobile phone, the bars indicating signal strength.) A small picture, repeated multiple times, can indicate the number of something available or remaining. *Small multiples* have long been used for lives remaining in action games, which often employed an image or silhouette of the avatar. Nowadays designers use them for things the avatar can carry, such as grenades or healing potions, although you should limit the maximum number to about 5; beyond that the player can't take in the number of objects at a glance and must stop to count the pictures. To make this method thematically appropriate for your game, simply choose an appropriate small picture.

- **Colored lights.** Symbolic. (In a car, various lights on the instrument panel.) Lights are highly space efficient, taking up just a few pixels, but can't display much data, normally indicating binary (on/off) values with two colors, or tristate values with three (off/low/high). Above three values, players tend to forget what the individual colors mean, and bright colors are not thematically appropriate in some contexts. Use a suitable palette of colors.

- **Icons.** Symbolic. (In a car, the symbols indicating the heating and air conditioning status.) Icons convey information in a small space, but you must make them obvious and unambiguous. Don't use them for numerical quantities but for symbolic data that record a small number of possible options. For example, you can indicate the current season with a snowflake, a flower, the sun, and a dried leaf. This will be clear to people living in the temperate parts of the world where these symbols are well known, but it would work less well in cultures where snow is never seen. The player can quickly identify icons once she learns what they mean, and you can help her learn by using a *tooltip,* a small balloon of text that appears momentarily when the mouse pointer touches an icon for a few seconds without clicking it. Don't use icons if you need large numbers of them (players forget what they mean) or if they refer to abstract ideas not easily represented by pictures. In those cases, use them with text alongside, or use text instead. Make your icons thematically appropriate by drawing pictures that look as if they belong in your game world. The icons in *Populous: The Beginning,* set in a Stone Age fantasy world, were excellent (see Figure 4.6).

■ **Text indicators.** Symbolic. Text represents abstract ideas well, an advantage over other kinds of indicators. In *Civilization III,* for example, an advisor character can offer the suggestion, "I recommend researching Nationalism." Finding an icon to represent nationalism or feudalism or communism, also options in the game, poses a problem. On the other hand, some people find text boring, and two words can look alike if they're both rendered in the same color on the same color background. The worst problem with text, however, is that it must be localized for each language that you want to support. (See *Text* later in this chapter.)

We strongly encourage you to read the books of Dr. Edward Tufte for more information on conveying data to the player efficiently and readably, particularly *The Visual Display of Quantitative Information* (Tufte, 2001).

Mini-Maps   A *mini-map,* also sometimes called a *radar screen,* displays a miniature version of the game world, or a portion of it, from a top-down perspective. The mini-map shows an area larger than that shown by the main view, so the player can orient himself with respect to the rest of the world. To help him do this, designers generally use one of two display conventions: *world-oriented* or *character-oriented* mini-maps.

■ The world-oriented map displays the entire game world with north at the top, just like a paper map, regardless of the main view's current orientation. An indicator within the mini-map marks that part of the game world currently visible in the main view (see Figure 4.2). In a multipresent game, you can use the world-oriented map as a camera control device: If the player clicks on the map, the camera jumps to the location clicked.

- The character-oriented map displays the game world around the avatar, placing him at the center of the map facing the top of the screen. If the player turns the avatar to face in a new direction in the game world, the landscape, rather than the avatar, rotates in the map. These mini-maps don't show the whole game world, only a limited area around the avatar, and as the avatar moves, they change accordingly. They're often round and for this reason are sometimes called radar screens. Because the landscape rotates in the map, character-oriented mini-maps sometimes include an indicator pointing north, making the map double as a compass.

Because the mini-map must be small (usually 5 to 10 percent of the screen area), it shows only major geographic features and minimal non–mission-critical data. Key characters or buildings typically appear as colored dots. Areas of the game world hidden by the fog of war appear hidden in the mini-map also.

A mini-map helps the player orient himself and warns him of challenges not visible in the main view, such as nearby enemies in a strategy or action game or a problem developing in a construction and management simulation. Mini-maps typically show up in a corner of the screen. You can find them in virtually any game that uses aerial perspectives and many others as well. Figures 4.2, 4.5, 4.6, and 4.8 all contain mini-maps.

Use of Color   You can always double the amount of data shown in a numeric indicator by having the color of the indicator itself represent a second value. You might, for example, represent the speed of an engine with a needle gauge, and the temperature of that engine by changing the color of the needle from black to red as it gets hotter. Colors work best to display information that falls into broad categories and doesn't require precision within those categories. Consider the green/yellow/red spectrum used for safety/caution/danger: It doesn't display a precise level of safety but conveys the general level at a glance. (Note our warnings about color-blind players in Appendix A, "Designing to Appeal to Particular Groups," on the Companion Website.)

Colors are also very useful for differentiating groups of opponents, however, and you can apply them to uniforms and other insignia. This is especially handy if the shapes or images of the actual units are identical regardless of which side they're on . . . as any chess player knows!

You can also use color as a feedback element by placing a transparent color filter over the entire screen. Some first-person shooters turn the whole screen reddish for a few frames to indicate that the avatar has been hit.

Character Portraits

A character portrait, normally appearing in a small window, displays the face of someone in the game world—either the avatar, a member of the player's party in a party-based game, or a character the player speaks to. If the main view uses an aerial perspective, it's hard for the player to see the faces of characters in the game, so a character portrait gives the player a better idea of the person he's dealing with. Use character portraits to build identification between your player and his avatar or party members and to convey more about the personalities of nonplayer characters. An animated portrait can also function as a feedback element to give the player information; *Doom* famously used a portrait of the avatar as a feedback element, signaling declining health by appearing bloodier and bloodier. This portrait also allowed the player to see his avatar even though playing a first-person shooter.

Screen Buttons and Menus

Screen buttons and menus enable the player to control processes too complex to be managed with controller buttons alone. They work best with the mouse as a pointing device but can also be used with a D-pad or joystick. Because a console doesn't have a mouse, console games make less use of screen buttons and menus than do PC games, one of several reasons console games tend to be less complex than PC games.

Screen buttons and menus should be so familiar to you from personal computers that we do not discuss them in detail here, though we do note a couple of key issues to keep in mind. First, an overabundance of buttons and menus on the screen confuses players and makes your game less accessible to casual players (see *Managing Complexity,* earlier in the chapter). Second, unless you use the desktop perspective, try to avoid making your buttons and menus look too much like an ordinary personal computer interface. The more your game looks like any other Windows or Macintosh application, the more it harms the player's immersion in the game. Make your screen-based controls fit your overall visual theme.

Text   Most games contain a fair amount of text, even action games in which the player doesn't normally expect to do much reading. Text appears as a feedback element in its own right, or as a label for menu items, screen buttons, and to indicate the meaning of other kinds of feedback elements (a needle gauge might be labeled *Voltage,* for example). You may also use text for narration, dialog (including subtitles), a journal kept by the avatar, detailed information about items such as weapons and vehicles, shell menus, and as part of the game world itself, on posters and billboards.

Localization   *Localization* refers to the process of preparing a game for sale in a country other than the one for which you originally designed the game. Localization often requires a great many changes to the software and content of the game, including translating all the text in the game into the target market's preferred language. In order to make the game easily localizable, you should store all the game's text in text files and never embed text in a picture. Editing a text file is trivial; editing a picture is not.

> ## COMMANDMENT: Keep Text Separate from Other Content
>
> *Never* have the programmers build text into the program code. *Never* build text that the player is expected to read into an image such as a texture or a shell screen background. Store all text in one or more text files.

The only exception to this rule applies to text used purely as decoration when you don't expect the player to read it or understand what it says. A billboard seen in a game set in New York should be in English and remain in English even after localization *if* the billboard text doesn't constitute a crucial clue.

Note that a word and its translation may differ in length in different languages, so that a very short menu item in English can turn into a very long menu item in, say, German. When you design your user interface, don't crowd the text elements too close together; the translations may require the extra space.

Typefaces and Formatting   Make your text easily readable. The minimum size for text displayed on a screen should be about 12 pixels; if you make the characters any smaller, they became less legible. If the game will be localized to display non-Roman text such as Japanese, 12 pixels is the bare minimum, and 16 pixels is distinctly preferable.

If you're going to display a lot of text, learn the rules of good typesetting. Use mixed uppercase and lowercase letters for any block of text more than three or four words long. Players find text set entirely in uppercase letters difficult to read; besides, it looks like SHOUTING, creating an inappropriate sense of urgency you might not want. (On the other hand, in situations that *do* require urgency, such as a warning message reading *DANGER,* uppercase letters work well.)

Choose your typefaces (fonts) with care so that they harmonize both with the theme of your game and with each other. Avoid using too many different typefaces, which looks amateurish. Be aware of the difference between *display fonts* (intended for headlines) and ordinary *serif* and *sans serif* fonts (intended for blocks of text) such as Times or Arial, respectively.

Avoid *monospaced* or *fixed width* fonts such as Courier, in favor of proportional fonts, such as Times, unless you need to display a table in which letters must line up in columns. For other uses, fixed width fonts waste space and look old-fashioned and unattractive.

8

Audio Elements

We have already spoken a little about sound in our discussion of player feedback. Here we address sound in more detail, looking at several different areas: sound effects, ambient sounds, music, and dialog and voiceover narration.

Always include a facility that allows the player to adjust the volume levels of the music and of all the other effects independently—including turning one or the other off completely. Many players tire of hearing the music but still want to hear the sound effects and ambient sounds. Bear in mind that not all your players will have perfect hearing, and the more control you can give them, the better. See *Accessibility Issues* in Appendix A, "Designing to Appeal to Particular Groups."

Sound Effects

The most common use of sound in a game is for sound effects. These sounds correspond to the actions and events of the game world—for example, a burst of gunfire or the tight squealing of tires as a car slides around a corner. In the real world, sound often presents the first warning of approaching danger, so use sound as an indicator that something needs the player's attention. Suspense movies do this well, and you can borrow techniques from them: Play the sound of footsteps or the sound of a gun being cocked before the player can see it. You can also use sound to provide feedback about aspects of the game under the player's control, such as judging when to change gears in a racing game by listening to the pitch of the engine.

You should also include sound effects as audible feedback in your user interface, not just in the game world. At the very minimum, screen buttons should make an audible *click* when pressed, but try to find interface effects that harmonize with the theme of your game world (as long as they're not corny). Be sure to support audio feedback from the UI with visual feedback too, so that when players hear a click or beep or buzz, the visual feedback directs them to the issue that generated the audible signal. We interpret events that we can see more easily than by audio alone.

Ambient Sounds

Just as the main view gives the player visual feedback about where she is, ambient sounds give her aural feedback. Traffic sounds tell her that she's in an urban street; cries of monkeys and exotic birds suggest a jungle. Anything that ordinarily makes distinctive sounds in the real world, such as a fountain or a jackhammer, should make the same sound in your game.

A first- or third-person game should definitely use *positional audio* if the platform's audio devices support it. Positional audio refers to a system in which different speakers present sounds at different volume levels, allowing you to position the point sources of sound in the three-dimensional space of the world. Some personal computers support as many as seven speakers, but even two-speaker stereo can help a player detect where a sound is coming from. Correctly positioning sound sources in the 3D space helps the player to orient himself and to find things that he may be searching for, such as a river, an animal, or another member of the party.

Don't overuse ambient sounds, especially in games that mostly feature mental challenges. A cacophonous environment isn't conducive to thought. Your ambient sounds must also work with the music you choose, which we address next. You may also be limited by the capabilities of your audio hardware, because some machines support only a small number of channels for simultaneous playback; when playing all the sound effects, you may not have channels left to use for ambient sounds.

Music

Music helps to set the tone and establish the pace of your game. Think about what kind of music will harmonize with the world and the gameplay that you're planning. Music sends strong cultural messages, and those too must fit thematically with the rest of the game. A pentatonic scale composition for the shamisen (a traditional Japanese lute) might work well in a medieval Japanese adventure game but would certainly sound out of place in a futuristic hi-tech game. You will probably collaborate with the audio director to choose or compose music for the game. Many larger commercial games now use licensed music from famous bands.

The music doesn't have to support the game world at every moment; you can choose music to create a contrasting effect at times. The introductory movie for *StarCraft* used classical opera as its theme, set against scenes in which admirals calmly discussed the war situation as they prepared to abandon the men on the planet below to their fate. The choice of music accentuated the contrast between the opulence and calm of the admiral's bridge and the hell of war on the surface. In a simpler example, the tempo of the music featured in certain levels of *Sonic the Hedgehog* was out of sync with the pace of the level, which, in a subtle way, made the game harder to play. We encourage you not to overuse these techniques, however; the rarer they are, the more effective they are.

In the real world, few pieces of music last as long as an hour, but players may hear the same music for several hours at a stretch in a game. Whatever you choose, be sure it can tolerate repetition. Avoid background music with a wide dynamic range; the louder parts will become intrusive and remind the player that the music repeats itself.

For some years, the game industry has experimented with the difficult problem of writing music that changes dynamically in response to current game situations, a technique called *adaptive music*. Developers would like to provide music that correctly anticipates the player's actions and upcoming game events so that the music further enhances the mood of the game, as movie music does. Movies are not interactive, however, so the composer knows what will be happening at every moment. Adaptive music must follow and even anticipate unpredictable situations. Creating adaptive music remains an experimental technique for the moment.

On the other hand, game musicians have become extraordinarily skilled at *layering*—writing separate but harmonizing pieces of music that the audio engine delivers simultaneously by mixing them together at different levels of volume. The engine determines which piece should be most clearly heard depending on what happens in the game.

If you would like to know more, we suggest you read *Audio for Games: Planning, Process, and Production,* by Alexander Brandon (Brandon, 2004) and *The Fat Man on Game Audio: Tasty Morsels of Sonic Goodness* by George "The Fat Man" Sanger (Sanger, 2003).

Dialog and Voiceover Narration

Many games with strong storylines, particularly adventure and role-playing games, make great use of recorded dialog and voiceover narration. Sports games use recorded audio to produce play-by-play and color commentary. Other kinds of games play back smaller bits of dialog to build atmosphere and provide feedback. Real-time strategy games often use spoken words as feedback to indicate that units received their orders or completed a task and need new orders. Finally, just about any kind of game can use spoken material to provide information, from mission briefings to the care and feeding of your virtual pet.

From a user interface standpoint, you should be aware of two key things that set spoken words apart from other forms of audio feedback. First, the human brain rapidly tires of hearing the same words played back repeatedly, and the longer the sentence, the worse the problem. If you plan to play voice material in response to in-game events or player actions that occur repeatedly, you *must* record multiple variants and mix them up at random when you play them back. You may frequently repeat short clips such as "Aye aye, sir" and "Strike three!" (though we still recommend you record several variants), but if you want to deliver a warning using a longer sentence, such as, "Sire, your peasants are revolting!" you must either have a large number of variants available or, better yet, play the sentence only once when the problem first occurs and then use visual feedback for as long as the problem continues. If the kingdom suffers a *second* peasant revolt later, you can play the sentence again.

Second, we cannot emphasize enough that *writing and acting must be good.* The quality of writing in the vast majority of games ranges from terrible to barely passable, and the voice acting is frequently worse than the writing. Players tolerate a sound effect that's not quite right, but an actor who can't act instantly destroys immersion. Don't use actors whose voices don't work thematically with the material, either. You wouldn't use the voice of an eighteenth-century English

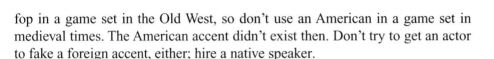

fop in a game set in the Old West, so don't use an American in a game set in medieval times. The American accent didn't exist then. Don't try to get an actor to fake a foreign accent, either; hire a native speaker.

For more information on writing for games, we suggest you read *Game Writing: Narrative Skills for Videogames,* edited by Chris Bateman (Bateman, 2006).

Input Devices

In this book, we have placed little emphasis on the game machine's hardware, because the variety of processors, display screens, data storage, and audio devices makes it impossible to address them comprehensively. We have expected you to design with your machine's processing facilities and output devices in mind. In the case of input devices, however, certain standards have evolved that we can address. We also feel that it is critically important that you understand the capabilities, strengths, and weaknesses of the various devices because they constitute the means by which your player will actually project his intentions and desires into the game. Designing for them well makes the difference between a seamless experience and a frustrating one.

We concentrate on the most common types of input devices for handheld, PC, and console games, the sorts normally shipped with the machine and to which you can expect any player to have access. The new motion-sensitive controllers from Nintendo and Sony show promise for the future, but as yet no standards for using them have evolved.

We don't address extra-cost items such as flight control yokes, steering wheels, rudder pedals, dance mats, fishing rods, bongo drums, cameras, and microphones. If you build a game that cannot be played without these items, you limit the size of your market to a specialist audience, and we cannot address such issues in a work on general game design. We encourage you to design for the default control devices shipped with a machine if at all possible. Only support extra-cost devices if using them significantly enhances the player's experience, or if you are intentionally designing a technology-driven game to exploit the device.

For most of their history, input devices for personal computers differed greatly from those of game consoles, so the two were best discussed separately. Console games never used analog joysticks; PC games never used D-pads. Now, both machines can use either, so we discuss the various input devices independently of the platforms.

Terminology

The discussion below uses the game industry's standard terminology for the kinds of data that control devices send to the processor as the result of player inputs. You may find some familiar terms that nevertheless require explanation, because the game industry uses those terms in ways that may differ from what you're used to.

Most input devices—the mouse being a notable exception—default to a *neutral position*. To send a signal to the game, the user must push, pull, grasp, or press the physical device to deflect it from this neutral position, and a spring-loaded mechanism returns it to the neutral position when the player releases the device. Joysticks and D-pads return to center; buttons and keys return to the off state.

A device that can return only two specific signals and no other we call a binary device, the signals generally being interpreted as off and on. The other common kind of input device transmits a value from a range of many possible values and the industry, for historical reasons, calls these analog devices. Any game control device can be classed as either analog or binary, though all of the technology is digital.

Don't confuse the type of data (binary or analog) with the *dimensionality* of the device. A one-dimensional device transmits one datum, and a two-dimensional device transmits two data, regardless of whether they transmit binary or analog data.

A device that returns data about its current position as measured from the neutral position provides *absolute* values. Such a device—a joystick, for example—can travel only a limited distance in any direction and so transmits values in a range from zero to its maximum.

Other devices offer virtually unlimited travel and have no neutral position. These return *relative* values, that is, the relative distance that the device has traveled from its previous position. Mouse wheels and track balls are examples; the player may rotate them indefinitely.

Two-Dimensional Input Devices

Two-dimensional input devices allow the player to send two data to the game at one time from a single device.

Directional Pads (D-Pads)   We begin our discussion with directional pads (D-pads), the most familiar form of directional control mechanism on game machines, still offered by many smaller handheld machines as the only two-dimensional input device. Console and PC controllers often supply a D-pad in addition to a joystick to provide backward compatibility with older software.

A D-pad is a circular or cross-shaped input device on a game controller constructed with binary switches at the top, bottom, left, and right edges. The D-pad rocks slightly about its central point and, when pressed at any edge, turns on either one switch or, if the player presses between two adjacent switches, two. It can, therefore, send directional information to the game in eight possible directions: up, down, left, and right with each of the individual sensors, and

FIGURE 8.2 The original Atari 8-way joystick and the Nintendo GameCube controller.

upper-left, upper-right, lower-left, and lower-right when the player triggers two sensors together. (See Figure 8.2; the cross-shaped device at the lower left of the controller on the right is a D-pad.)

The D-pad gives the player a crude level of control over a vehicle or avatar; she is able to make the vehicle move in any of the eight major directions but not in any other. You should use D-pads for directional control only if you have no better device available. D-pads do remain useful alongside a joystick; you can assign to the D-pad functions requiring less subtle control, such as scrolling the main view window in one of the eight directions, leaving the joystick free for such tasks as avatar navigation control.

Joysticks   Joysticks developed from an early aircraft flight control device (still used in fighter planes but replaced by the control yoke in modern civilian aircraft). It is a single vertical stick anchored at the bottom that can be tilted a limited amount in any direction. When the game software checks the position of the joystick, it returns two absolute, analog data: an X-value indicating tilt to the left or right, and a Y-value indicating the tilt forward or back.

A joystick offers a finer degree of control than a D-pad does. The Nintendo GameCube controller on the right in Figure 8.2 features two small joysticks, one to the upper left of the D-pad and one marked with C at the lower center. (Early video game machines shipped with an 8-way joystick: a device that looked like an analog joystick but actually functioned as a D-pad. The joystick on the left in Figure 8.2 is an 8-way joystick.)

Modern joysticks built for use with combat flight simulators may include a large number of other controller buttons as well: one or more fire buttons, used to fire weapons; a *hat switch* on the top of the stick, functionally equivalent to a D-pad; a slider that can be used as a throttle; and switches triggered by twisting the stick to the left or right. All of these ultimately amount either to controller buttons or sliders. Here we concern ourselves only with the tilting action of the basic device.

Joysticks make ideal steering controls for vehicles. To return to a default—flying straight and level, for instance—the player only has to allow the joystick to return to the neutral position. Since joysticks may travel only a limited amount in any direction, they allow the player to set a direction and a *rate* of movement. The UI interprets the degree of tilt as indicating the rate. For instance, moving a joystick to the left causes an airplane to roll to the left; moving it farther left causes the airplane to roll faster.

Joysticks don't work well for precise pointing; when the player lets go, the joystick returns to center, which naturally causes it to point somewhere else. To allow the player to point a cursor at an object *and leave it there* while she does something else, use a mouse. Efforts to port mouse-based games to console machines, substituting a joystick for the mouse, have an extremely poor success rate.

The Mouse (or Trackball)   We're all familiar with mice from personal computers. A mouse returns two data that consist of X and Y values, but these are *relative* data, indicating how far the player moved the mouse relative to its previous location. A mouse offers more precise positioning than a joystick and unlimited travel in any direction on the two-dimensional plane in which it operates. This unlimited relative movement makes a mouse ideal for controlling things that can rotate indefinitely in place, so first-person PC games virtually always use mice to control the direction in which the avatar looks. Because it stays where it is put, a mouse is invaluable for interfaces in which the player needs to let go of the pointing device from time to time to do something else.

Note that when a mouse is used specifically to control a cursor on the screen, the driver software converts the mouse's native relative data into absolute data for the cursor position. This choice of either absolute or relative modes lends the mouse great flexibility.

A mouse wheel constitutes a separate knob with unlimited movement that also functions as a controller button when pressed. Not all mice come with mouse wheels, however, and you cannot count on them. If you support the mouse wheel, supply alternative controls.

The mouse's lack of a neutral position makes it weak as a steering mechanism for vehicles that need a default behavior—driving straight or flying straight and level. The player must find the vehicle's straight or level position herself rather than allowing the device to snap back into neutral. You may want to designate an extra controller button that returns the vehicle to its default state if the mouse will be your primary control option.

Designers find mice generally more flexible input devices than joysticks, but players find them more tiring to use for long periods.

Touch-Sensitive Devices   Personal digital assistants (PDAs) and the Nintendo DS machine offer the player a touch-sensitive screen, and laptop personal computers usually come with a touch pad below the keyboard. These devices return absolute analog X and Y positions indicating where they are touched, as a mouse cursor does. Unlike a mouse, you can make a touch-sensitive device's cursor return to a neutral position whenever you detect that the player has stopped touching the device. Touch-sensitive screens may be manipulated by the fingers or a stylus; touch pads usually cannot detect a stylus, and must be touched with the fingers, which tends to make fingers sore after long use.

One-Dimensional Input Devices

One-dimensional input devices send a single value to the game. Ordinary controller buttons and keys send binary values; knobs, sliders, and pressure-sensitive buttons send analog values.

Controller Buttons and Keys   A controller button or a keyboard key sends a single binary value at a time: on when pressed and off when released. Despite this simplicity, buttons and keys may be used in a variety of ways:

- **One-shot actions.** Treat the on signal as a trigger, a message to the game to perform some action immediately (ignoring the off signal). The action occurs only once, when the player presses the button; to perform it twice, he must press the button again. You might use this to let players fire a handgun, firing once each time they hit the button.

- **Repeating actions.** The on signal tells the game to begin some action and to repeat it until it receives the off signal from the same button, at a repetition rate determined by the software. You could let the players fire a machine gun continuously from button press to button release.

- **Continuous actions.** The button's on signal initiates a continuous action, and its off signal ends it. Golf games use this to give a player control over how hard the golfer swings the club; the player presses the button to start the golfer's backswing and releases it to begin the swing itself; the longer the backswing, the harder the golfer will hit the ball. Some football games allow the player to tap the button quickly to throw a short pass or to hold it down for a moment before release to throw a long pass, with the length of time between button's on and off signals determining the distance thrown.

Console game controllers feature anywhere from one to about ten buttons. Buttons on the top face of the controller, to be pressed with the thumbs, are known as *face buttons*. Others, known as *shoulder buttons,* appear on the part of the controller facing away from the player, under the index fingers. Faced with large numbers of buttons, the player can find it quite difficult to remember what

8

they all do. Here, as elsewhere, be sure to maintain consistency from one game-play mode to another, and if an industry standard has evolved for your game's genre, do not depart from it without good reason.

Personal computer keyboards have 110 keys, allowing for very broad user interfaces indeed. Players can assign keys to functions that might otherwise require selecting options on the screen with the mouse, provided that you allow for it. Be sure to assign actions to keys in such a way that the letter printed on the key becomes a mnemonic for the action, for example, F for flaps, B for brakes, or other similarities.

Knobs, Sliders, and Pressure-Sensitive Buttons You rarely find knobs (also sometimes called *Pong paddles* for historical reasons) nowadays, although the mouse wheel functions as a knob. Limited-travel knobs can move only so far, like a volume knob on a stereo, and return an absolute value. Unlimited-travel knobs, including the mouse wheel, may be spun continuously and return relative data. Knobs are generally not self-centering; they stay where the user puts them. Knobs, especially large ones, offer fine unidimensional control.

Converting a game designed for a knob to a joystick seldom produces good results, for the same reason that a mouse-based game does not convert well to a joystick: The joystick's combination of limited travel and self-centering contradicts the game's original design. (Also, while the game ignores the second value from the 2D joystick, the additional freedom of movement confuses the player somewhat.) The arcade game *Tempest* used a large, heavy knob that could be spun continuously; when ported to a console machine with a joystick, players enjoyed the game less despite the improved graphics.

A slider is a small handle that moves along a slot in the controller, which constrains its travel. It returns an absolute position and stays where the player puts it. You find sliders usually used as adjuncts to joysticks for flight simulators; the slider controls the throttle for the engine, letting the player set his speed and leave it there.

A few controllers, such as the Nintendo GameCube controller on the right in Figure 8.2, include analog pressure-sensitive buttons that, instead of transmitting a binary on or off value, send a number that indicates how hard the player presses. This gives the player a finer degree of control than an ordinary binary controller button.

Navigation Mechanisms

Navigation mechanisms allow the player to tell an avatar, vehicle, or other mobile unit how to move. When a player gives movement commands, the avatar must respond in a consistent and predictable way.

We will use the term *avatar* to refer to the general case of a character or object that can be made to move under player control. Designers usually find creating vehicle navigation systems easier than creating ones for characters because input devices more closely resemble a vehicle's controls than they do an avatar's body.

Terminology

When the player uses a joystick, a D-pad, or a mouse and keyboard to control an avatar that walks over a landscape, we refer to the action as *steering*. We assume that players steer using a joystick except where otherwise indicated; for most purposes, you may consider a joystick interchangeable with a D-pad but offering finer control. We don't address steering wheels for cars or control yokes for aircraft here as they should be self-explanatory.

If a vehicle or character can move freely in three dimensions, such as an aircraft or spacecraft, it *flies*.

If the player designates a point in the landscape and the character or vehicle moves to that target without further player control, the game uses *point-and-click navigation*.

Screen-Oriented Steering

In screen-oriented steering, when the player moves the joystick toward the top of the screen, the avatar moves toward the top of the screen. Implementation details vary somewhat depending on the perspective; we briefly document several major variants.

Top-Down and Isometric Perspectives   In a top-down or isometric perspective in which the player sees the avatar from above, moving the joystick in the direction of one edge of the screen causes the avatar to instantly turn and face that edge of the screen, then move in that direction. Classic arcade games that used a top-down perspective, such as *Gauntlet,* used this simplest of all steering methods.

2D Side-Scrolling Games   In traditional side-scrollers, the joystick controls left and right movement as it does for the top-down perspective. The player controls the avatar's vertical jumps to platforms using a separate controller button. Moving the joystick up can augment the effect of the jump button; moving the joystick down may be left undefined; and because the game world is 2D, the avatar cannot move away from or toward the player.

3D Games   Three-dimensional games usually use avatar-oriented rather than screen-oriented steering to provide a consistent set of controls regardless of camera angle, but rare exceptions do exist. *Crash Bandicoot* provides the best-known example. When the player pushes the joystick up, the avatar moves toward the top of the screen, which is also forward into the 3D environment, away from the player. Moving the joystick down makes the avatar turn to face the player and move toward him through the 3D environment. Pushing the joystick left or right makes the avatar turn to face and then move in that direction.

Unlike avatar-oriented steering, in this model left and right cause the avatar to *move* in those directions with the camera continuing to face forward and to show the avatar from the side. In this respect, *Crash Bandicoot* feels rather like a side-scroller with an additional dimension. In avatar-oriented steering, addressed next, left and right cause the avatar to *turn and face* in those directions *but not to move* while the camera swings around to remain behind him.

Avatar-Oriented Steering

In avatar-oriented steering, the only suitable model for first-person games, pushing the joystick up causes the avatar to move forward in whatever direction she currently faces, regardless of her orientation to the screen. However, implementation of avatar-oriented steering varies somewhat from one device to another, so we discuss devices individually in the following sections.

Avatar-oriented steering remains consistent regardless of the perspective. It presents a slight disadvantage in games using aerial perspectives: Avatar-oriented steering can be rather disorienting when the avatar faces the bottom of the screen, yet the player must push the joystick up to make it walk down to the bottom of the screen.

Joystick and D-Pad Controls   As stated above, pushing the joystick up makes the avatar move forward in whatever direction she faces. Pushing the joystick down makes the avatar move backward away from the direction she faces, while continuing to face the original direction; that is, she walks backward. In some vehicle simulators, *down* applies the brakes rather than reversing the direction of movement, and the player must press a separate controller button to put the vehicle in reverse. Pushing the joystick to the left or right makes the avatar turn to face toward the left or right or turns the wheels of a vehicle. The avatar does not move in the environment if the joystick moves directly to left or right; the player must push the joystick diagonally to get forward (or backward) motion in addition to a change of direction. This feels more natural with vehicles than it does with characters.

Mouse-Based Control   With mouse-based navigation, now standard for first-person PC games, the mouse only controls the direction in which the avatar faces, and the player uses the keyboard to make the avatar move. Moving the mouse left or right causes the avatar to turn in place, to the left or the right, and to a degree in proportion to the distance the mouse moves. Up and down mouse movements tilt the camera up or down, which becomes important if the player wants the avatar to climb or descend, but these commands do not move the avatar. Considerably more flexible than a joystick-based system, mouse-based navigation allows the player to look around without moving the character.

Keys on the PC's keyboard control movement. The standard arrangement for players who use their right hands for the mouse and left hands for the keyboard uses W to produce forward movement in the direction the avatar currently faces; movement continues as long as the player holds the key down. S works similarly for moving backward (or applying the brakes). A and D produce movement at right angles to the direction the avatar faces, left or right respectively, thus producing the feeling of sliding sideways while facing forwards. This sideways movement is often called *strafing.*

Flying

Flying presents a further complication because it involves moving through three dimensions while a two-dimensional input device such as a joystick offers control in only two. Control over movement in the third dimension must be handled by a separate mechanism, either extra controller buttons or an additional joystick. How you implement this depends on the nature of the aircraft itself, generally taking as your model the mechanisms in real aircraft. Navigational controls in modern flying games are almost always intended for use in the first-person perspective from inside the cockpit. (See Chapter 17, "Vehicle Simulations," for further details.)

Fixed-Wing Aircraft   The player maneuvers the aircraft using the joystick to *pitch* (the equivalent of a camera's tilt) or roll, and the engine pulls the plane in the direction the nose faces. A throttle control, generally a slider or keys that increase and decrease the engine speed by fixed increments, sets the rate of forward movement. When flying straight and level, forward on the joystick pushes the nose down, producing descent, and back pulls the nose up, causing it to climb. Left on the joystick causes the plane to roll to the left while remaining on the same course; right rolls it to the right in the same manner. To turn in the horizontal plane, the pilot rolls the aircraft in the desired direction and pulls back at the same time, so the nose follows the direction of the roll, producing a banked turn. When the joystick returns to center, the plane should fly straight and level at a speed determined by the throttle.

Helicopters   Game user interfaces typically simplify helicopter navigation, which is more complicated than flying fixed-wing aircraft. The joystick controls turning and forward or backward movement, and a slider control or keys cause the helicopter to ascend or descend. Left on the joystick causes the helicopter to turn counterclockwise about its vertical axis but not to actually go in that direction unless also moving forward. Right causes the equivalent rotation to the right. Forward propels the helicopter forward, and back the reverse.

(Real helicopters can also slide sideways while facing forward; to implement this would require extra controls, which few games do.) When the joystick returns to center, the helicopter should gradually slow down through air friction until it remains hovering above a fixed point in the landscape. A separate key set or slider controls vertical movement.

Spacecraft   Most designers treat spacecraft as they would fixed-wing aircraft, although in one variant left or right on the joystick causes the vehicle to *yaw* (the equivalent of panning a camera), turning about its vertical axis to face in a different direction, rather than rolling.

Point-and-Click Navigation

Aerial or context-sensitive perspectives in which the player can clearly see his avatar, party, or units as well as a good deal of the surrounding environment can use point-and-click navigation. In a game with a multipresent or party-based model, the player first chooses which unit or units should move (unnecessary in an avatar-based model), then in all cases the player selects a destination in the environment, and the unit or avatar moves to that location automatically using a *pathfinding* algorithm (an artificial intelligence technique to avoid obstacles). Typically the player can select one of two speeds: If he holds down a special key while selecting the location, the vehicle moves more quickly (a humanoid character runs rather than walks).

This technique is most often used in real-time strategy and party-based role-playing games in which many units may need to be given their own paths and the player does not have time to control them all precisely. If a unit cannot get to the location the player designated, that unit either goes as far as it can and then stops or, upon receipt of the command, warns the player that it cannot proceed to an inaccessible destination. Point-and-click also used to be common for adventure games but has begun to be replaced by avatar-oriented navigation.

Using point-and-click navigation, the player can indicate precisely where he wants the unit to end up without concerning himself about avoiding obstacles, a convenience in cluttered environments where the player may not clearly see which objects actually block the path. It is also helpful in context-sensitive perspectives because the player cannot always see clearly how the avatar should get from one place to another and often has no freedom to move the camera.

At times, it can be a disadvantage that the player cannot control the path that the unit takes, so point-and-click navigation frequently needs to include a *waypoint* mechanism. This system allows the player to designate intermediate points, called waypoints, that the unit must pass through one by one on its way to the final destination. Waypoints enable the player to plot a route for the unit and so exercise some control over how the units get to where they are going.

Allowing for Customization

One of the most useful, and at the same time easiest to design, features you can offer your player is to allow him to customize his input devices to suit himself. Normally you handle this via a shell menu, although a few PC games store the information in a text file that the player can edit. Two of the most commonly needed customizations are:

- **Swap left and right mouse buttons.** If the mouse has more than one button, left-handed and right-handed players will need different layouts. Providing a mirror image of your standard layout takes little trouble, so don't make players go through a function-reassignment process just for this; give them a feature that allows them to simply swap the current assignments.

- **Swap the up and down directions of the mouse or joystick in first-person 3D games.** Some players like to push the mouse or joystick up to make their avatar look up (an idea borrowed from screen-oriented steering in 2D games); others like to pull it down to look up (an idea borrowed from airplane joysticks). Either works just as well, and you might as well let the player play as she prefers—so let the players reorient these signals if they want.

The term *degree of freedom* refers to the number of possible dimensions that an input device can move through. An ordinary key or button has one degree of freedom: It can only move up and down. A joystick or mouse has two degrees of freedom: It can move up and down, left and right. If two devices, both binary or both analog, (see our discussion in *Input Devices* earlier) have the same degree of freedom, you can generally let the player interchange them, although there will be practical difficulties if one device is self-centering and the other is not or if one allows unlimited travel and the other does not. When exchanging assignments between two devices not identical in every way, some functionality or convenience is almost always lost.

Almost all games assign some of their player actions to particular keys or buttons. Your game should include a *key reassignment* shell menu that allows players to assign actions to the keys they prefer. If your game includes menus, also allow the player to assign menu items to keys so he can select them quickly without using the mouse. You may need to enforce some requirements: If the game requires that a particular action must be assigned to a key (for example, the fire-weapon action in a shooter game), don't let the player exit the shell menu if the action remains unassigned.

When implementing a shell menu for key reassignment, be sure to show *all* the current assignments, *all* the game features not currently assigned to keys, and *all* the currently unassigned keys on the same screen. Many games don't do this, so when the player wants to assign a feature to a key, he can't tell which keys already carry actions and which do not.

Be sure to save the player's customizations between games, so he doesn't have to set them up every time he plays. If you want to be especially helpful, let players save different setups in separate, named profiles so that each player can have his own set of customizations. Include a *Restore Defaults* option so the player can return his customizations to the original factory settings.

Summary

When game reviewers praise a game highly, they cite its user interface more often than any other aspect of the game as the feature that makes the game great. The gameplay may be innovative, the artwork breathtaking, and the story moving, but a smooth and intuitive user interface improves the player's perception of the game like nothing else.

In this chapter, we have introduced you to interaction models and perspectives, two concepts central to game user interfaces. We looked at ways to manage the complexity of an interface and a number of visual and audio elements that games use, and we examined input devices and navigation mechanisms in detail.

If you tune and polish your interface to the peak of perfection, your players will notice it immediately. Give it that effort, and your work will be well justified.

Test Your Skills

MULTIPLE CHOICE QUESTIONS

1. Which of the following questions reflects information that a player needs to know to be able to play a game?

   A. Am I making progress?

   B. How do I turn off the sound effects?

   C. Can my actions be easily reversed?

   D. Can I customize my character?

2. Steps in designing a game's user interface include all of the following *except*

   A. designing a screen layout.

   B. selecting visual elements that tell a player what she needs to know.

   C. creating narrative material.

   D. defining the inputs for the game.

3. An example of how you could use abstraction to simplify a pioneer adventure game would be to

   A. let the computer handle the feeding of your oxen.

   B. build in an expert mode option for advanced players.

   C. create both broad and deep interfaces.

   D. not model how much sleep your characters need.

4. A broad interface would most likely be used in a game that requires

   A. research through a series of menus and dialog boxes.

   B. easy access to a wide variety of controls.

   C. first-person perspective.

   D. two-dimensional input devices.

5. What interaction model requires you to provide ways for players to give orders to units in the game environment?

   A. Contestant model.

   B. Avatar-based model.

   C. Multipresent model.

   D. Desktop model.

6. When the game's virtual camera moves vertically, it is said to

   A. dolly.

   B. truck.

   C. pan.

   D. crane.

7. When a game uses first-person perspective, the player sees her avatar

   A. if she looks in a pool of water.

   B. from a side view.

   C. straight on from the front.

   D. from a point over the avatar's left shoulder.

8. When using a top-down perspective, artists can improve the look of the environment by

   A. making the tops of the buildings transparent.

   B. making the people as big as the buildings.

   C. cheating the depiction of the buildings.

   D. craning the virtual camera.

9. You are creating a game that gives the player the experience of riding a bicycle in the Tour de France. You would most likely choose to put the game's controls

    A. on the input device only.

    B. around the edges of a windowed view.

    C. on semitransparent overlays.

    D. on context-sensitive overlays.

10. To allow the player to keep track of his progress around France in the Tour de France game, include a

    A. needle gauge showing current health.

    B. small multiple indicator of the days spent riding.

    C. colored overlay of areas that are especially challenging.

    D. mini-map showing the route.

11. If a game's chosen platform supports it, you can inform a player of the location of noisy objects by using

    A. quad audio.

    B. positional audio.

    C. surround audio.

    D. ambient audio.

12. Which of the following is *not* a two-dimensional input device?

    A. D-pad.

    B. Joystick.

    C. Slider.

    D. Mouse.

13. In screen-oriented steering, when the player moves the joystick toward the top of the screen, the avatar

    A. moves to the bottom of the screen.

    B. will not move until a button is pressed.

    C. moves to the next waypoint.

    D. moves to the top of the screen.

14. In avatar-oriented steering for a game that uses mouse control,

    A. the mouse controls the direction the avatar faces, and the keyboard makes the avatar move.

    B. the keyboard controls the direction the avatar faces, and clicking a mouse button makes the avatar move.

    C. the mouse controls both the direction the avatar faces and the speed that the avatar moves.

    D. the mouse controls the direction the avatar faces, and the mouse wheel controls avatar turns.

15. As a general rule, you can allow a player to make all of the following customizations *except*

    A. swapping left and right mouse buttons.

    B. swapping up and down directions of the mouse or joystick.

    C. exchanging key input for mouse input.

    D. changing the default key assigned to a specific action to another key.

EXERCISES

1. Design and draw one icon for each of the following functions in a game:

    - Build (makes a unit build a certain structure)
    - Repair (makes a unit repair a certain structure)
    - Attack (makes a unit attack a certain enemy unit)
    - Move (moves a unit to a certain position)
    - Hide (makes a unit hide to be less visible to enemy units)

    Briefly explain the design choices you made for each icon. All icons should be for the same game, so make them consistent to a game genre of your choice.

2. In this exercise, you will practice designing user interfaces for two different gameplay modes, each of which has different indicators. Using the descriptions of the modes below, decide how best to display the functions to the player and sketch a small screen mock-up showing how these indicators can be positioned on the screen. Briefly explain your design decisions.

    In the primary gameplay mode, the avatar can move around in the game world and do different things such as attacking, talking to NPCs, and so on. The mode is avatar-based in the third-person perspective.

8

Functions/indicators:

- Character's health
- Character's position in the game world
- Currently chosen weapon
- Waypoint to the next mission
- Character visibility to enemies (indicate that, if the character stands in shadows or in darkness, he is less visible to enemies)

In the secondary gameplay mode, the player will enter vehicle races that include shooting at other vehicles driven by nonplayer characters. The perspective is first person.

Functions/indicators:

- Vehicle health
- Vehicle speed
- Primary weapon ammo left
- Type of secondary weapon mounted, if present (if not present, so indicate)
- Position in race
- Laps remaining of race

3. In this exercise, you will design the same UI, once for breadth and once for depth. Make the broad UI no more than two levels deep at any point. Make the deep UI at least three levels deep at one point, offering no more than three options at the top level. Present the UIs by making flowcharts showing the different levels of interaction or how you group different functions. Include all the following functions. Briefly explain your design decisions.

Attack	Defend	Guard	Patrol	Move
Set waypoint	Choose weapon	Research	Build barracks	Build headquarters
Build hospital	Destroy	Repair	Harvest	Save current game
Load game	Quit game	Change video settings	Change sound settings	Change control settings

4. A game intended for a console needs to have its functions mapped to a game pad with a limited number of buttons. Make a button layout that supports all the actions in the primary gameplay mode (described below). Discuss the pros and cons of your button layout.

The game pad has the following button layout:

- A D-pad
- One analog joystick
- Four face buttons
- Two shoulder buttons

(Note: This is the button layout of the Sony PSP, excluding the start and select buttons.)

The main gameplay mode has the following actions:

Normal attack	Hard attack	High attack (attack upward)	Low attack (attack downward)	Block
Jump	Crouch	Move forward	Move backward	Strafe left
Strafe right	Rotate left	Rotate right	Choose weapon	Use health pack

DESIGN QUESTIONS

As you design the user interface for each mode in your game, consider the following questions:

1. Does the gameplay require a pointing or steering device? Should these be analog, or will a D-pad suffice? What do they actually do in the context of the game?

2. Does the function of one or more buttons on the controller change within a single gameplay mode? If so, what visual cues let the player know this is taking place?

3. If the player has an avatar (whether a person, creature, or vehicle), how do the movements and other behaviors of the avatar map to the machine's input devices? Define the steering mechanism.

4. How will the major elements of your screen be laid out? Will the game use a windowed view, opaque overlays, semitransparent overlays, or a combination?

5. What perspective will the main view use? What interaction model does the gameplay mode use? Is it one of the common ones or something new? How does the perspective support the interaction model?

6. Does the game's genre, if it has one, help to determine the user interface? What standards already exist that the player may be expecting the game to follow? Do you intend to break these expectations, and if so, how will you inform the player of that?

8

7. Does the game include menus? What is the menu structure? Is it broad and shallow (quick to use, but hard to learn) or narrow and deep (easy to learn, but slow to use)?

8. Does the game include text on the screen? If so, does it need provisions for localization?

9. What icons does the game use? Are they visually distinct from one another and quickly identifiable? Are they culturally universal?

10. Does the player need to know numeric values (score, speed, health)? Can these be presented through nonnumeric means (power bars, needle gauges, small multiples), or should they be shown as digits? If shown as digits, how can they be presented in such a way that they don't harm suspension of disbelief? Will you label the value and if so, how?

11. What symbolic values does the player need to know (safe/danger, locked/unlocked/open)? By what means will you convey both the value and its label?

12. Will it be possible for the player to control the game's perspective? Will it be necessary for the player to do so in order to play the game? What camera controls will be available? Will they be available at all times or from a separate menu or other mechanism?

13. What is the aesthetic style of the game? How do the interface elements blend in and support that style?

14. How will audio be used to support the player's interaction with the game? What audio cues will accompany player actions? Will the game include audio advice or dialog?

15. How does music support the user interface and the game generally? Does it create an emotional tone or set a pace? Can it adapt to changing circumstances?

Chapter | 9

Gameplay

Chapter Objectives

After reading this chapter and completing the exercises, you will be able to do the following:

- Understand the basic principles that a designer should follow to make games fun.

- Explain how the hierarchy of challenges requires players to complete atomic challenges, sub-missions, and missions to accomplish the ultimate goal of winning the game.

- Define intrinsic skill and stress and discuss how these factors contribute to the difficulty of the game.

- List challenges commonly used in games, including physical coordination challenges, exploration challenges, conflict challenges, and economic challenges, among others.

- Define actions in the context of the game world and describe how actions are selected to allow a player to meet specific challenges or serve other functions in the game.

- Discuss the arguments in favor of and opposed to supplying a saving mechanism and explain the most widely used methods for saving a game.

Introduction

In Chapter 1, "Games and Video Games," we define *gameplay* as consisting of the challenges and actions that a game offers: challenges for the player to overcome and actions that let her overcome them. Games also include actions unrelated to gameplay, but the essence of gameplay remains the relationship between the challenges and the actions available to surmount them.

We begin this chapter with a discussion of how we make games fun, setting out some things to be aware of and principles to observe. We then introduce some important ideas related to gameplay: the hierarchy of challenges and the concepts of skill, stress, and difficulty. The bulk of the chapter consists of a long list of types of challenges that video games offer, with some observations about how to present them, mistakes to avoid, and how to adjust their difficulty. We turn next to actions, listing a number of common types found in games. Finally, we address the questions of if, when, and how to save the game.

Making Games Fun

As we asserted in Chapter 1, the game designer's primary goal is to provide entertainment, and gameplay is the primary means by which games entertain; without gameplay, an activity may be fun, but it is not a game. Entertainment is a richer and more manifold idea than fun is. Nevertheless, most games concentrate on delivering fun rather than offering moving, thought-provoking, or enlightening entertainment. How, then, do we provide fun?

Execution Matters More Than Innovation

Genius is one per cent inspiration, ninety-nine per cent perspiration.

—Thomas Edison (attributed)

We adjust Edison's number slightly but keep the same idea. Ninety-five percent of what makes a game fun has nothing to do with imagination or creativity. The vast majority of things that make a game *not* fun—boring or frustrating or irritating or simply ugly and awkward—result from bad execution rather than a bad idea. The number one reason a game fails to be fun is that it contains elementary errors. A surprising amount of the job of making a game fun, therefore, simply consists of avoiding those things that reduce fun. Our breakdown of the different aspects of game development that contribute to fun follows:

- **50 percent** of making a game fun consists of avoiding errors. Bad programming, bad music and sound, bad art, bad user interfaces, and bad game design all ruin the player's fun. Basic competence will get you up to average.

- **35 percent** of making a game fun comes from tuning and polishing. Not bug fixing—that's in the first 50 percent—but attention to detail, getting everything perfect. Long and dedicated tuning sets a good game apart from a mediocre one.

- **10 percent** of making a game fun comes from imaginative variations on the game's premise, taking the elements of the game and constructing an enjoyable experience out of them. Of this, level designers contribute 9 percent and the game designer contributes 1 percent.

- **4 percent** of making a game fun results from true design innovation: the game's original idea and subsequent creative decisions that you make.

- **1 percent** of making a game fun emerges from an unpredictable, unanalyzable, unnamable quality—call it luck, magic, or stardust. You can't make it happen, so you might as well not worry about it. But when you can feel it's there, be careful about making changes to your design from that point on. Whatever it is, it's fragile.

So innovation by the game designer contributes no more than 5 percent to the fun of the game: 4 percent from the original idea and the 1 percent that you add to the level design process (assuming you don't design the levels yourself). That may make it sound as if there's not a lot of point in game design. But to build a game, someone must design it and design it well. Most game design decisions give little room for innovation, but they're still necessary. A brilliant architect may design a wonderful new building, but it still needs heat and light and plumbing, and in fact the majority of the work required to design that building goes into creating those mundane but essential details. The same is true of game design.

Finding the Fun Factor

There's no formula for making your game fun, nothing that anyone can set out as a reliable pattern and tell you that, if you just slot in a really cool monster here and a fabulously imaginative weapon there, the resulting game is guaranteed to be fun every time. What we can provide is a set of principles to keep in mind as you design and build your game; without them, you risk producing a game that's no fun.

- **Gameplay comes first.** Before all other considerations, create your game to give people fun things to do. A good many games aren't fun because the designers spent more time thinking about their graphics or their story than they did thinking about creating gameplay.

- **Get a feature right or leave it out.** It is far worse to ship a game with a broken feature than to ship a game with a missing feature. Shipping without a feature looks to players like a design decision; a debatable decision, possibly, but at least a deliberate choice. Shipping with a broken feature tells players for certain that your team is incompetent. Broken features destroy fun.

- **Design around the player.** We base everything in this book on player-centric game design, as we explained in detail in Chapter 2, "Design Components and Processes." You must examine *every* decision from the player's point of view. Games that lose sight of the player lose sight of the fun.

- **Know your target audience.** Different groups of players want different things. You don't necessarily have to aim for the mass market, and in fact it's much harder to make a game that appeals broadly than it is to make a game that appeals to a niche market you know well. But whatever group you choose, *know* what they want and what they think is fun, and then provide it.

- **Abstract or automate parts of the simulation that *aren't* fun.** If you model your game on the real world, leave out the parts that aren't fun. But remember your audience: To somebody who just wants a chance to drive a fast car, changing the tires isn't fun, but to a hardcore racing fan, changing the tires *is* fun and a critical part of the experience. If—and only if—you have the time and resources, you may include two modes. Otherwise, choose one market and optimize the fun for the members of that market.

- **Be true to your vision.** If you envision the perfect sailing simulation, don't add powerboat racing as well because you feel that adding features might attract a larger market. (Marketing people are notorious for asking game designers to do this.) Instead, adding powerboats will distract you from your original goal and cut in half the resources you were planning to use to perfect the sailing simulation. Both halves will be inferior to what the whole could have been. You will lose the fun, and without it you won't get the bigger market anyway.

- **Strive for harmony, elegance, and beauty.** A lack of aesthetic perfection doesn't take *all* the fun out of a game, but the absence of these qualities appreciably diminishes it. And a game that is already fun is even *more* fun if it's beautiful to look at, to listen to, and to play with.

The Hierarchy of Challenges

When you're up to your ___ in alligators, it's hard to remember that your original objective was to drain the swamp.

—Unattributed

In all but the smallest games, the player faces several challenges at a time, organized in a **hierarchy of challenges.** Ultimately, he wants to complete the game. To accomplish that, he must complete the current mission. Completing the mission requires completing a *sub-mission,* of which the current mission probably has several. At the lowest level, he wants to deal with the challenge that immediately faces him: the enemies threatening him at the moment, perhaps, or the locked door for which he needs the right spell. These last we call ***atomic*** *challenges* (*atomic* in the sense of *indivisible*). Atomic challenges make up sub-missions; sub-missions make up missions; and missions make up the ultimate goal: completing the game.

Figure 9.1 illustrates this idea. It displays the hierarchy of challenges for a (very) small action-adventure game. The entire game consists of three missions or game levels; each level consists of three sub-missions, the last of which pits the player against a level boss. Each sub-mission consists of three atomic challenges, of which the final one (marked in boldface) completes the sub-mission. The gray boxes indicate the challenges the player faces simultaneously at one particular moment in the middle of level 2. At the atomic level, we find him trying to solve a puzzle; doing so will help him to—or allow him to proceed to—destroy the critical object, all of which contributes to succeeding in the Destroy Object sub-mission, which itself makes up a part of winning level 2. Ultimately, he hopes to win the entire game.

Game designer Ben Cousins proposed this notion of a hierarchy but in a slightly different form. For more information on Cousins' original scheme, see *In the Trenches: Cousins' Hierarchy* later in this chapter.

To design your game, you create this hierarchy and decide what challenges the player will face. During play, the player focuses most of her attention on the atomic challenges immediately facing her, but the other, higher-level challenges will always be in the back of her mind. Her awareness of the higher-level challenges creates anticipation that plays an important role both in entertaining her and in guiding her to victory. In the remainder of this section, we discuss how the hierarchy affects the player's experience and what that means for game design.

Informing the Player about Challenges

Video games normally tell the player directly about some challenges, which we call **explicit challenges,** and leave him to discover others on his own, which we call **implicit challenges.** In general, games give the player explicit instructions about the topmost and bottommost levels of the hierarchy but leave it to him to figure out how to approach the intermediate levels. The topmost level includes the victory condition for the entire game, and games tend to present their overall victory condition explicitly. They may also state an explicit victory condition for each level. Normally, the game's *tutorial levels* teach the player explicitly how to meet the atomic challenges. (For more on tutorial levels, see the discussion on that topic in Chapter 12, "General Principles of Level Design.") Unless you provide completely self-explanatory gameplay *and controls*, you should always include one or more tutorial levels in your game or an explanation of the controls and how to use them to meet atomic challenges.

You should always tell the player about the victory condition or she won't know what she's trying to accomplish. You don't have to tell the complete truth, however. In storytelling games, you'll usually want to keep the outcome a surprise. Many stories start by telling the player one thing, but plot

KEY POINT
Make the victory condition and the atomic challenges explicit. Be sure the player always has some overarching goal in mind toward which she works. Never leave her without a reason for continuing to play.

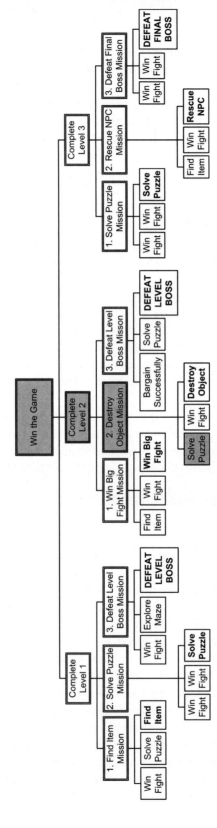

FIGURE 9.1 A hierarchy of challenges for a small action-adventure.

twists along the way deepen and complicate matters. She may change or meet a goal only to find it replaced by another, more important goal. Detective stories, in particular, are famous for this. (Don't do it more than three or four times in any one story, though, or the player will start to be irritated about being repeatedly lied to. Detectives are also famous for getting irritated about being lied to.) Be sure that the player gets whatever information she needs to *think* she clearly knows the victory condition so she's never left without any motivation.

The Intermediate Challenges

Most designs leave intermediate-level challenges implicit. If you give the player nothing to do except follow explicit instructions, it doesn't feel like a game; it feels like a test. Part of the player's fun lies in figuring out—whether through exploration, through events in the story, or by observing the game's internal economy—what he's supposed to do. Armed with the knowledge of both the victory condition at the top and the right way to meet the atomic challenges at the bottom, he has the tools to figure out the intermediate challenges—if you have constructed them coherently. (See *Avoid Conceptual Non Sequiturs* in Chapter 12, "General Principles of Level Design," for an example of how *not* to construct an intermediate-level challenge.)

For a good many games, overcoming the intermediate-level challenges requires only that the player meet all the lowest-level ones in sequence. That's how most action games work, and what Figure 9.1 illustrates. If the player beats all the enemies and gets past all the obstacles, he finishes the level. If he finishes all the levels, he wins the game.

In more complex games, the player may have a choice of ways to approach an intermediate-level challenge. Suppose the explicit top-level challenge—the victory condition—in a war game consists of defeating all the enemy units, and the atomic challenge consists of destroying one enemy unit. The simple and obvious strategy would apparently be to destroy all the enemy units one by one, but the player isn't likely to get that chance. Most war games include a production system for generating new units, so even if the player can kill off enemy units one by one, his opponent can probably produce new ones faster than he can destroy them. Disrupting the enemy's production system is often an effective strategy, while protecting his own production system ensures that he can eventually overwhelm the enemy with superior numbers. Neither the specification of the victory condition nor of the atomic challenges explicitly includes the intermediate-level challenge of *disrupt the enemy's production system,* and protecting his own production system doesn't destroy enemy units at all. The player must figure out what he should do by observation and deduction and, by planning and experimentation, find ways to accomplish his goals. The observation, deduction, planning, and experimentation all add to the fun.

9

You construct these implicit, intermediate challenges for the player to figure out. The conventions of the genre you've chosen will guide you, but keep in mind a couple of points:

- **The most interesting games offer multiple ways to win.** To give your player a richer experience, design your game so that he can win in a variety of ways—that is, so that meeting *different* intermediate challenges will still get him to victory. Different strategies may be better or worse, but if you only permit one right way to win, you don't reward the player's lateral thinking skills. The game becomes an exercise in reading the designer's mind.

- **Recognize and reward victory no matter how the player achieves it.** Players will think of things to try that you might not have anticipated; even if you've given them multiple ways to win, they may find another way entirely. If the player achieves the victory condition, even in a completely unexpected way, he deserves credit for it. Don't test to see if he got there in one of the ways that you intended; just test to see if he got there.

Figure 9.2 illustrates the idea of offering multiple ways to win a war game. The victory condition is to capture the flag. The hierarchy is organized as before, except that the dotted lines indicate a *choice of possible approaches* rather than a *sequence of required sub-missions* as in Figure 9.1. As before, the gray boxes indicate the challenges in the player's mind at one particular moment—in this case, assuming that he chose to use a stealth approach and sent units out to scout.

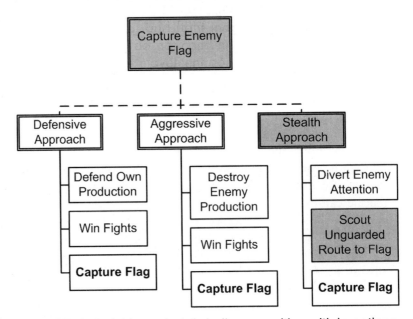

FIGURE 9.2 A hierarchy of challenges with multiple options.

Simultaneous Atomic Challenges

Although the player simultaneously faces several challenges in the hierarchy the farther up the hierarchy a challenge lies, the less of her attention that challenge demands on a moment-by-moment basis. But games can also present several atomic challenges at once. These divide the player's attention. If she can deal with them one at a time at her own pace (as in a turn-based game), then they're not really different from sequential challenges, but if she has to surmount them all in a limited amount of time, then adding simultaneous challenges makes the game more stressful. (We discuss stress in *Skill, Stress, and Absolute Difficulty* later in the chapter.)

An early and still common way of creating simultaneous atomic challenges, typical of side-scrolling shooter games, consisted of bombarding the player with enemies. Each represents a significant risk, and the player must defeat each one while fending off the others. A player who works quickly can generally defeat these added enemies one at a time while keeping the others at bay.

Other games present more complex and interrelated simultaneous challenges. In its default mode, *SimCity* imposes no victory condition; its highest-level challenge is to achieve economic growth so the player can expand his city. (Expanding the city itself isn't a challenge, just a series of choices available so long as the player brings in enough money to keep going.) The player won't attain economic growth unless he can provide a balanced supply of services to the city. The city needs police protection *and* power *and* hospitals *and* water and so on, all at the same time; each represents an atomic challenge, and all must be met simultaneously. The complex juggling of competing needs requires regular attention and frequent action. Furthermore, unlike fighting enemies, the player can never finish balancing the services; the juggling act never stops.

It's part of your job to design the hierarchy of challenges and decide how many of them the player will face at once: both vertically up the hierarchy and at the bottom of the hierarchy. The more simultaneous atomic challenges he faces under time pressure, the more stressful the game will be. The more different levels of challenge he has to think about at once—especially if he can't simply achieve the higher ones by addressing the lower ones in sequence—the more complex and mentally challenging the game will be.

9

IN THE TRENCHES: Cousins' Hierarchy

Ben Cousins, in an article for *Develop* magazine, suggested thinking of gameplay as a hierarchy (Cousins, 2004). We have adopted his idea for this book but modified it somewhat and used different terminology. Cousins referred, for example, to *atoms of interaction* rather than *atomic challenges*.

▶▶ CONTINUED ON NEXT PAGE

▶▶ CONTINUED

Cousins studied the game *Super Mario Sunshine* by making a video recording of the screen while he played, then examining the results in a video editor, which enabled him to identify the atoms of interaction in the game. By thinking about what he was trying to accomplish at each moment as he played, he found that he could organize the gameplay into a five-level hierarchy with "Complete the whole game" as the topmost interaction, "Complete the current game level" as the second level of the hierarchy, and so on down to individual atoms of interaction at the bottom level.

Cousins studied an action game; action games typically require players to use specific low-level actions to meet low-level challenges (to get across the chasm, jump). In other genres, however, there isn't a one-to-one mapping between challenges and actions even at the atomic level. Some challenges may be overcome by several different kinds of actions; overcoming others requires complex sequences of actions. Accordingly, we have not included actions in our hierarchy, making ours a hierarchy of challenges only.

We recommend Cousins' technique of analyzing the way that games organize their gameplay by examining them second-by-second in a video editor.

Skill, Stress, and Absolute Difficulty

Most of our discussion about gameplay difficulty we reserve for Chapter 11, "Game Balancing," but we introduce some important distinctions here because the terms involved will come up in our discussion of different types of gameplay later in this chapter. While these are not industry standard terms, we find them useful.

In this chapter, we are concerned with controlling the absolute difficulty of the challenges that you will present to the player. Two different factors determine the absolute difficulty of a challenge. We define these as *intrinsic skill required* and *stress*. In Chapter 11, we will address additional factors that affect the player's perceptions about how easy or hard the game is.

Intrinsic Skill

We define the ***intrinsic skill required*** by a challenge as the level of skill needed to surmount the challenge *if you give the player an unlimited amount of time in* *which to do it.* The intrinsic skill required for a challenge may be computed from the conditions of the challenge but leaving out any element of time pressure. How you measure the skill level of a challenge varies with the type of challenge and can involve physical tasks, mental tasks, or both. Consider three examples:

- An archer aiming at a target requires a certain level of skill to hit the target. It takes more skill to hit the target if you move the target farther away or make it smaller. The archer gets an unlimited amount of time to aim. Even if he takes more time, it does not change the skill required.

- Sudoku puzzles printed in the newspaper often include a rating that indicates whether they are easy or hard to solve. The player may take as long as he wants to solve the puzzle, so the rating reflects an intrinsic quality of the puzzle—how many clues the player gets—rather than the effect of a time limit.

- A trivia game requires the player to know certain factual knowledge. Some questions are about familiar facts and some are about obscure facts. The skill level required by a question doesn't change if you give the player more time to answer.

Some challenges *must* include time pressure by the way they are defined—a test of the player's reaction time, for example. A test of pure reaction time (hit the button when the light comes on) requires no intrinsic skill at all. The carnival game *Whack-a-Mole* is a real-world example.

Stress

If a challenge includes time pressure, a new factor comes into play, *stress.* **Stress** measures how a player perceives the effect of time pressure on his ability to meet a challenge requiring a given level of intrinsic skill. The shorter the time limit, the more stressful the situation. Succeeding in a stressful game requires both quick reflexes and a quick mind. The challenges of *Tetris* do not require a great deal of intrinsic skill—if the player had plenty of time to think about the task, it would be easy to keep the blocks from piling up—but we class *Tetris* as stressful because the player must complete the task under time pressure. Golf, on the other hand, demands skill without being stressful—at least, in the sense in which we use the term. It would be considerably more stressful if the rules imposed more time pressure.

Games often create physical stress on the player's body. Time pressure requires players to use their eyes and hands more quickly; it makes them stiffen their muscles, and it raises their heart rates and adrenaline levels. Many people love this sensation, but you should modulate the pacing of your game to give them time to rest. We discuss this at length in *Vary the Pacing* in Chapter 12, "General Principles of Level Design."

Absolute Difficulty

KEY POINT

The *absolute difficulty* of a challenge consists of a combination of the *intrinsic skill required* to meet the challenge without time pressure and the *stress* added by time pressure.

Absolute difficulty refers to intrinsic skill required and stressfulness put together. When a game offers multiple difficulty levels, the easy mode both demands less skill and exerts less stress than the hard mode. Some players like a challenge that demands a lot of skill but can't tolerate much stress. If they know they have plenty of time to prepare for a challenge, they're perfectly happy for the challenge to require great skill. Others thrive on stress but don't have much skill. Simple, high-speed games like *Tetris* and *Collapse!* suit them best. See Figure 9.3 for a graph showing the relationship of intrinsic skill and stress in various games or tasks. The higher the task ranks on both scales, the greater its difficulty.

When you're deciding how difficult you want your game to be, think about both skill levels and stress, and keep your target audience in mind. Teenagers and young adults handle stress better than either children or older adults because teenagers and young adults have the best vision and motor skills. When you allow the player to set a difficulty level for the game, try to preserve an inverse relationship between skill level and stress at that particular level of difficulty. If a challenge requires more skill, give the player longer to perform it, and vice versa.

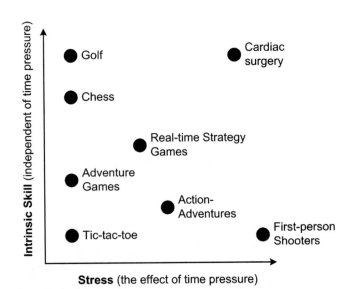

FIGURE 9.3 Intrinsic skill required versus stress in different tasks.

Commonly Used Challenges

This section presents commonly used challenges you should understand. Because games can set a top-of-the-hierarchy challenge of just about anything—take on the role of Jason and win the golden fleece, use your zombie army to drive the werewolves out of your ancestral home, capture a giant squid from the ocean deeps, win a rodeo competition—we can't discuss all the possible top-of-the-hierarchy goals. This discussion focuses on lower-level challenges, many of which could be classified as atomic challenges.

This list may help you to think about the kinds of traditional challenges you'd like to include in your game, but you're free to design any type of challenge you can imagine if you can make it workable. Players always appreciate innovative challenges; a beautiful setting or interesting overall concept only gets you so far. Gameplay is in the challenges.

Throughout this section, we will include observations from time to time about ways to make a particular type of challenge easier or harder. Most of these comments concentrate on making them easier because novice game developers frequently make their games too hard without realizing it.

Physical Coordination Challenges

Physical coordination challenges test a player's physical abilities, most commonly hand-eye coordination. One of the earliest coin-op video games, *Pong,* required only this one skill to win. Physical coordination challenges remain a basic component of arcade gaming and a significant part of most video games to this day. They fall into several subcategories, which we discuss in the following sections.

The absolute difficulty of a physical coordination challenge most frequently relates to the amount of time pressure the player is under; to make such a challenge easier, simply give the player more time. We will address exceptions, where they occur, with each subcategory.

Speed and Reaction Time   Speed challenges test the player's ability to make rapid inputs on the controls, and reaction time challenges test his ability to react quickly to events. Both of these usually appear in combination with other types of challenges, most often other coordination challenges. You can expect to find speed and reaction time challenges in platform games, shooters, and fast puzzle games such as *Tetris*. From the frenetic button-banging of Konami's 1983 arcade game *Track & Field* (two buttons controlled an athlete's legs; the player pressed them alternately to make the athlete run) to the modern-day frenzy of *Quake 4*, speed and reaction-time challenges perennially please those who have the reflexes for them.

Accuracy and Precision   Steering and shooting comprise the majority of tests of accuracy or precision, though you can devise many more. Steering includes navigating characters as well as vehicles. Usually found in action and action-adventure games, sports games, and vehicle simulations, accuracy and precision challenges increasingly feature in role-playing games, such as *Fable,* which include a combat element.

Accuracy challenges need not take place within time limits; in a sport such as archery, athletes may take as long as they want to line up a shot but still face a considerable challenge. To make an accuracy challenge easier or harder, adjust the degree to which the physics engine in the game forgives errors in the inputs. For example, the player of an archery game ordinarily needs to position the joystick or mouse within a particular range of values to hit the bull's-eye; you can make the game easier by widening that range.

Intuitive Understanding of Physics   Vehicle simulations require more than just an ability to steer a vehicle; they also require an intuitive understanding of the physics of the game world. Players must learn, usually through experience, a car's braking distance, acceleration rate, at what rate it may take a turn without sliding off the road, and so on. Learning and internalizing these features of the game world and the vehicle constitute another challenge. Games such as pool and darts also require the player to develop an intuitive understanding of physics. We include these under physical coordination challenges because the player tends to develop a visceral rather than an intellectual understanding of these aspects of the game world (darts players don't need to know calculus), which finds its expression in successful physical coordination.

You can help the player develop an intuitive understanding of the game's physics. First, make sure the physics remains consistent. The physics engine must be reliable and produce predictable results. Programmers handle the physics engine, but you should also keep this in mind. Second, the simpler the physical model of the world, the easier it will be for the player to develop that intuitive understanding. Sports games often simplify their physics to help the player. For example, many sports games don't implement the physical property of inertia for an athlete running under the player's control because the player wants to be able to turn his player instantaneously and will find it harder to get used to the game if he cannot. Flight simulators, too, model the physics of flight with greater and lesser degrees of accuracy depending on how easy the designer wants to make it for the player to understand how the airplane behaves.

Timing and Rhythm   Side-scrolling action games rely heavily on timing challenges, in which the player learns to dodge swinging blades and attack predictable enemies. Rhythm challenges, tests of the player's ability to press the right button at the right time, feature in dance games such as *Dance Dance Revolution* and other music-based games such as *Donkey Konga* and *Guitar Hero*.

The popularity of rhythm-based games resulted in a significant aftermarket in specialty input devices such as dance mats and electronic conga drums.

Combination Moves   Many fighting games require complex sequences of joystick moves and controller-button presses that, once mastered, allow the player's avatar to perform some especially powerful feat. (See *Fighting Games* in Chapter 13, "Action Games.") Executing a combo move requires speed, timing, and a good memory, too: The player has to remember the button sequence and produce it perfectly at just the right time. You can make combination moves easier by shortening them, requiring fewer presses.

Logic and Mathematical Challenges

Logical and mathematical reasoning has been part of gameplay since the dawn of human history. Logic provides the basis for strategic thinking in any turn-based game of perfect information and many other games in which the player can make precise deductions from reliable data. In this section, we confine ourselves to logic *puzzles,* and we deal with strategic thinking in *Strategy,* later in the chapter.

Mathematics underlies all games in which chance plays a role or the player does *not* have reliable data and so must reason from probabilities. Such games present explicit mathematical challenges to the player: If he doesn't compute the odds when playing poker, or at least know the odds and reason correctly given what he knows, he's much more likely to lose.

In the broadest sense, any game that includes numeric relationships offers a mathematical challenge, because the player must learn how those relationships work. Much of the time, games present mathematical challenges implicitly, couching numeric relationships in other terms: physics, strategy, or economics. (For an example from strategy, see our discussion of Lanchester's laws in Chapter 14, "Strategy Games.") We deal with implicit mathematical challenges in other sections of this chapter.

Formal Logic Puzzles   A puzzle is a mental challenge with at least one specific solution. *Formal logic* means classic deductive logic in which the definition of the puzzle contains, or explains, everything the player needs to know to solve the puzzle. A formal logic puzzle can be solved by reasoning power alone. It shouldn't require any outside knowledge. Many other types of puzzles require logic too, but they also expect the player to supply some additional information.

A logic puzzle typically presents the player with a collection of objects related in ways that are consistent but not directly obvious. To solve the puzzle, the player must put the objects into a specified configuration. The player manipulates the objects and receives feedback about their relationships, which he eventually comes to understand by observation and deduction. Rubik's Cube, a classic logic puzzle with a simple mechanism, consists of so many cubes which move in ways so intricately interrelated that it is quite difficult to solve.

Adventure games often present logic puzzles as combination locks or other machinery that the player must learn to manipulate because those devices make sense in the fantasy world that the game presents. Other puzzle-based games don't try to be realistic but concentrate on offering an interesting variety of challenges.

To adjust the difficulty of a logic challenge, raise or lower the number of objects to be manipulated and the number of possible ways in which the player can manipulate them. A Rubik's Cube with four faces per side (a $2 \times 2 \times 2$ cube) instead of nine ($3 \times 3 \times 3$) would be far easier to solve.

Players normally get all the time they need to solve puzzles. Because different people bring differing amounts of brainpower to the task, requiring players to solve a puzzle within a time limit might make the game impossible for some. Exceptions to this rule can sometimes succeed; *ChuChu Rocket* offers both a time-limited multiplayer mode and an untimed mode.

A few games do not make the correct solution clear at the outset of the puzzle. The player not only has to understand how the puzzle works but also guess at the solution she must try to achieve. We consider this bad game design: It forces the player to solve the puzzle by trial and error alone because there's no way to tell when she's on the right track. In order to open the stone sarcophagus at the end of *Infidel,* the player had to find the one correct combination of objects out of 24 possible combinations. The game gave no hints about which combination opened the box; the player simply had to try them all.

COMMANDMENT: Avoid Trial-and-Error Solutions

Solving most logic puzzles requires a certain amount of experimentation, but the player must be able to make deductions from his experiments. Do not make puzzles that can *only* be solved by trial and error.

Mathematical Challenges Games don't usually test the player's mathematical abilities explicitly but often do require the player to reason about probabilities. Many games include an element of chance or require the player to make educated guesses about situations of which he has only an imperfect knowledge. Consider *Microsoft Hearts* (see Figure 9.4) as an example of a game giving imperfect information. Initially, the player does not know what cards the other players hold, but a skilled player can work out to a reasonable degree of certainty what those cards must be by using the information revealed as cards are passed and played during the game.

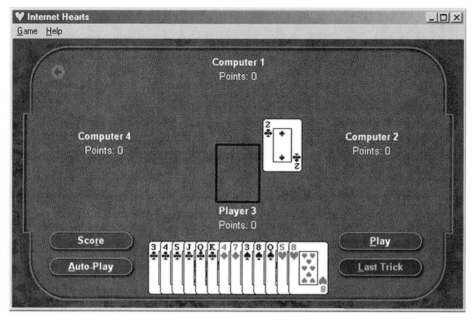

FIGURE 9.4 *Microsoft Hearts.*

Races and Time Pressure

In a *race,* the player attempts to accomplish something before someone else does, whether that involves a physical race through space or a race to create a structure, to accumulate something, or to do practically anything as long as the game can distinguish which player finishes first. Normally we think of races as peaceful, involving competition without conflict, but races can be combined with fighting and many other kinds of challenges.

Time pressure discourages careful strategic thought and instead encourages direct, brute-force solutions. With only 15 seconds to get through a host of enemies and disarm a bomb, the player won't stop to pick off enemy units one by one with sniping shots; he's going to mow them down and charge through the gap, even if that means taking a lot of damage.

Time pressure increases the stress on a player and changes the feeling of the gameplay considerably, sometimes for better and sometimes for worse. In something like a car racing game, time pressure is an essential part of the experience, but we urge caution in adding time pressure to challenges that aren't ordinarily based on time constraints. You will deter some players entirely and make the challenge more difficult in any case. To keep the absolute difficulty level constant, whenever you increase the time pressure on a player, you should also reduce the amount of intrinsic skill required.

Factual Knowledge Challenges

Direct tests of the player's knowledge of factual information generally occur only in trivia and quiz games. In any other type of game, you must either present all the factual knowledge required to win the game somewhere *in* the game (or the manual) or make it clear in the game's marketing materials that players will need some factual knowledge. It's not fair to require the player to come up with some obscure fact from the real world in order to make progress through the game; doing so also detracts from full immersion.

Note the difference between factual knowledge challenges and conceptual reasoning challenges (discussed in *Conceptual Reasoning and Lateral Thinking Puzzles,* later in the chapter). If an adventure game features a puzzle the player can't solve without knowing that helium balloons rise or that metal objects conduct electricity, we would characterize such a puzzle as a conceptual reasoning challenge, not a factual knowledge challenge.

Trivial Pursuit, the popular board game that tests players' factual knowledge in several different domains, also runs as a video game on a variety of platforms.

> **COMMANDMENT:** Make It Clear When Factual Knowledge Is Required
>
> If your game requires factual knowledge from outside the game world to win, you must make this clear to the player in advance.

Memory Challenges

Memory challenges test the player's ability to recall things that she has seen or heard in the game. Adventure games and role-playing games often make use of memory challenges. Players can defeat memory challenges by taking notes, so you may want to impose a limit on the length of time you give them to memorize material they must recall. To make a memory challenge easier, give them longer to memorize it and ask that they recall it soon after memorizing it rather than much later.

Memory challenges often form one component of exploration challenges. In Raven's *Star Trek Voyager: Elite Force,* for example, the player must remember the layout of complex tunnels onboard the Borg cube.

Pattern Recognition Challenges

Pattern recognition challenges test the player's ability to spot visible or audible patterns or patterns of change and behavior. One of the most common instances of a pattern recognition challenge crops up in action games when a large number of identical enemies, each of which behaves in a predictable way, confronts the player. The player can try alternative strategies until he finds one effective against that enemy, then use that strategy to vanquish any number of enemies that attack using the same pattern. To make things harder and more interesting, the boss enemy at the end of a level usually has a different and more complex pattern of behavior from the smaller enemies that preceded it.

Visual clues often figure in pattern recognition challenges. In *Doom,* secret doorways could be found by searching for areas of wall that looked slightly different from the norm. *Dungeon Master* required the player to use pattern recognition skills to decipher the complex systems of runes governing spells and spell casting.

To make pattern recognition challenges easier, make the patterns shorter, simpler, and more obvious. To make them harder, make the patterns longer, more intricate, and more subtle.

Exploration Challenges

Exploration is often its own reward. Players enjoy moving into new areas and seeing new things, but exploration cannot be free of challenge or it becomes merely sightseeing. Design obstacles that make the players earn their freedom to explore.

Spatial Awareness Challenges   The most basic form of exploration challenge simply requires the player to learn her way around an unfamiliar and complicated space. In the old text adventure games, this was particularly difficult because the games lacked visual cues, but even modern 3D environments can be made so tangled that they're hard to navigate. Unfamiliar architecture also challenges the player; navigation is easier when things look the way she expects them to look. *Descent* required the player to move around a warren of similar corridors inside an asteroid and complicated matters further by setting the environment in zero gravity, so the player perceived no obvious *up* or *down* to help orientation.

To make spatial awareness challenges easier, give the player a map that always shows his location precisely within the game world. If you want to give the player a map but make it slightly more difficult, give him a map of the game world that doesn't include his location, so he has to work it out from landmarks.

Locked Doors   We use *locked door* as a generic term for any obstacle that prevents the player from proceeding through the game until he learns the trick for disabling it. A sheet of ice covering a cave entrance that melts if you build a fire constitutes a locked door for game design purposes. Assuming, for discussion only, you want an actual door, you can require that the player find a key elsewhere and bring it back, find and manipulate a hidden control that opens the door, solve a puzzle built into the door, discover a magic word that opens the door, defeat the doorkeeper in a test of skill, or perform some other task—just make sure you offer an interesting and fresh challenge.

Avoid using an unmarked switch far from the door. *Doom* featured these, and they weren't much fun. Arriving at a locked door and seeing no means of opening it or any clue, the player had to search the entire world pressing unmarked switches at random, returning to see whether one of the switches had opened the door. Worse yet, in a few cases the switch *did* open the door, but only for a little while. If the player didn't get back to the door in time, he found it locked again and assumed that switch must not have been the right one.

Traps A *trap* is a device that harms the player's avatar when triggered—possibly killing her or causing damage—and, in any case, discouraging her from going that way or using that move again. Similar to a locked door with higher stakes, a trap poses an actual threat. Traps can take a variety of forms:

- Some fire once and then are harmless.
- Others fire and require a certain rearming time before they can fire again.
- Still others respond to particular conditions but not to others, like a metal detector at an airport, and the player must learn what triggers the trap and how to avoid triggering it.

A player may simply withstand some traps that don't do too much damage; he may disarm or circumvent other traps. A trap the player can find only by falling into it is really just the designer's way of slowing the player down; if you make these, don't make many of them because the player can only find them by trial and error and they become frustrating after a while. For players, the real fun comes in outwitting traps: finding and disabling them without getting caught. This gives players a pleasurable feeling of having outfoxed you.

Mazes and Illogical Spaces A maze is an area in which every place looks alike, or mostly alike; to get out, the player must discover how the rooms or passages relate to each other, usually by wandering around. Good designers implement mazes as logic or pattern-recognition puzzles, in which the player can deduce the organization of the mazes from clues found in the rooms. Poor mazes offer no clues and make the player find the way out by trial and error. Mazes are now considered rather old-fashioned and difficult to justify in the context of a story, but they can still be fun to solve if you make them truly clever and attractive.

In illogical spaces, areas do not relate to each other in a way that the player might reasonably expect. In text adventures, a player often found that going north from area A took you to area B, but going south from area B did not take you back to area A. Illogical spaces require the player to keep a map, because he can't rely on his common sense to learn his way around. Now also considered outdated, and more difficult to implement with today's 3D engines, illogical space challenges still crop up from time to time. If you use them, do so sparingly, and only if you can explain their presence: "Beware! There is a rip in the fabric of space-time!"

Teleporters   Teleporters superseded illogical spaces in the game designer's toolkit. A *teleporter* is any mechanism that suddenly transports the player from where she is to someplace else, often without warning if the designer created no visual representation for the teleporter device. Several hidden teleporters in an area can make exploration difficult. Teleporters can further complicate matters by not always working the same way, teleporting the player to one place the first time they are used but to some other place the second time, and so on. You can also use one-way teleporters if you want to leave the player with no way to get back.

   To make the exploration challenge created by teleporters easier, make the teleporter predictable and reversible, so the player can return at will to where she came from. (A good many games include teleporters not as a challenge but as a visible and optional feature to let the player jump across large distances that she has already explored.)

Conflict

We define a ***conflict challenge*** as one requiring the direct opposition of forces, some of which are under player control. If one player must beat the others by opposing or impeding them directly, the challenge qualifies as conflict, even without combat or violence. Checkers has no bloodshed but still presents conflict challenges. Classic activities to overcome conflict challenges include taking away another player's resources and impeding another player's ability to act.

FYI | *Conflict Challenges Versus Conflict of Interest*

Formal **game theory** is a field of mathematics that studies situations that contain a **conflict of interest.** By that definition, any game in which players are rivals for victory contains conflict. However, in pole-vaulting, darts, and many other games, that opposition applies only at the top of the challenge hierarchy. At lower levels, the players do not (and sometimes are forbidden to) impede each other directly. Even in *Monopoly*, the rules provide no means by which players may choose to target each other for hostile action. Such games may contain a conflict of interest but no conflict challenges. The players must achieve their top-level goal not through the direct opposition of forces but through vaulting over the higher bar, throwing darts more accurately, or whatever other atomic challenges the game specifies.

The asymmetric board game Fox and Geese (introduced in Chapter 1, "Games and Video Games") gives the two players different conflict challenges. The fox tries to eat the geese by jumping over them on the board (taking away the other player's resources). The geese try to trap the fox while moving in configurations that prevent the fox from jumping over them (preventing the enemy from acting).

Create interesting conflict challenges by varying such factors as:

- The scale of the action (from individuals to whole armies)

- The speed at which the conflict takes place (from turn-based, allowing the players all the time they want, to frenetic activity as in action games)

- The complexity of the victory conditions (from simple survival to complex missions with goals and subgoals)

Many action games focus on the immediate, exciting, visceral excitement of personal conflict. The player generally controls an avatar that battles directly against one or more opponents, often at high speeds.

Conflict challenges can be broken down into strategy, tactics, logistics, and other components we discuss here in turn.

Strategy   *Strategy* means planning, including taking advantage of your situation and resources, anticipating your opponent's moves, and knowing and minimizing your weaknesses. A strategic challenge requires the player to carefully consider the game (a process called situational analysis) and devise a plan of action. In a turn-based game of *perfect information* (one that contains no element of chance or hidden information), players may use *pure strategy* to choose their moves by analyzing possible future states of the game. Chess is a classic game of perfect information. (Note that in formal game theory, pure strategy has a special meaning, but we use the term *pure strategy* in an informal sense to distinguish it from applied strategy.)

Succeeding in a game of pure strategy requires a talent for systematic reasoning that relatively few people possess in a high degree. Computer game developers usually aim to attract a broad audience, so few of them offer these kinds of challenges. Instead, they hide information from the player and include elements of chance, making situational analysis to some extent a matter of guesswork and of weighing probabilities rather than a matter of logic. Such games call for applied strategy. Real-time strategy (RTS) games normally require applied strategy and offer economic and exploration challenges as well, making RTS games accessible to players with less skill at logic and providing other ways to win besides strategy alone.

Tactics   *Tactics* involve putting a plan into execution, accomplishing the goals that strategy calls for. Tactics also require responding to unexpected events or conditions: new information or bad luck. Even chess involves tactics—responding to opponent's moves requires tactical skill.

You can design a purely tactical game with no strategy. A small-squad combat game in which the soldiers continually move into unknown territory contains no opportunities for strategy—a player can't plan if she doesn't know where she's going or what she's up against—but contains many opportunities for tactics, such as keeping soldiers covered, taking advantage of their particular skills, and so on.

Logistics The business of supporting troops in the field and bringing fresh troops to the front lines is called logistics. Most war games don't bother with logistical challenges such as transporting food and fuel to where the troops can use them; players tend to find combat entertaining but find logistics a boring distraction from the combat.

Modern RTS games routinely include one important logistical challenge: weapons production. Unlike war board games, in which the player often starts with a fixed number of troops, RTSs require the player to produce weapons and to research new types of weapons using a limited amount of raw material. The production facilities themselves must be constructed and then defended. Adding this new logistical challenge to what was formerly a purely combat-oriented genre changed the face of war gaming. (See Chapter 14, "Strategy Games.")

In role-playing games, the limited size of the characters' inventories presents another logistical challenge, requiring players to decide what to carry and what to leave behind. Equipping and balancing a party of heterogeneous characters with all that they need to face a dangerous adventure occupies a significant amount of the player's time.

Survival and Reduction of Enemy Forces The fundamental challenge in any game based on conflict is survival. The player must preserve the effective playing time—the lives—of his units, or he cannot achieve the victory condition. In a few games, survival itself constitutes the victory condition regardless of other achievements, but in most, survival is necessary, but not sufficient, to win.

The converse of the survival challenge is the challenge to reduce enemy forces. To design such a challenge, you must create rules that determine how a unit may be removed from the game. Chess and checkers provide examples of such rules: *capture by replacement* and *capture by jumping,* respectively. War games implement simulated combat using complex mathematical models and track the health of each unit, which may be reduced by repeated attacks until reduction to zero destroys the unit.

Defending Vulnerable Items or Units The player may be called upon to defend other units or items, especially items that cannot defend themselves. In chess, all units protect the king. To meet such a challenge requires that the player know not only the capabilities and vulnerabilities of her units but also those of the entity she must protect. She must be prepared to sacrifice some units to protect the vital one.

Stealth The ability to move undetected, an extremely valuable capacity in almost any kind of conflict, especially if the player takes the side of the underdog, can form a challenge in its own right. Games occasionally pose challenges in which the victory condition cannot be achieved through combat but must be achieved through stealth. *Thief: The Dark Project* was designed entirely around this premise. It required players to achieve their missions by stealth as much as possible and to avoid discovery or combat if they could.

Stealth poses a considerable problem in the design of artificial opponents for war games. In a game with no stealth, the AI-driven opponent has access to the complete state of the game world; to include stealth, you must restrict the opponent's knowledge, limit its attention, leave it ignorant of whole regions of the game world. You decide what the AI opponent does and doesn't know and define what steps it takes, if any, to gain further information.

Economic Challenges

An *economy* is a system in which resources move either physically from place to place or conceptually from owner to owner. This doesn't necessarily mean money; any quantifiable substance that can be created, moved, stored, earned, exchanged, or destroyed can form the basis of an economy. Most games contain an economy of some sort. Even a first-person shooter boasts a simple economy in which the player obtains ammunition by finding it or taking it from dead opponents and consumes it by firing his weapons. Health points are also part of the economy, being consumed by hits and restored by medical kits. You can make the game easier or harder by adjusting the amount of ammunition and number of medical kits, so that a player running short of fire power or health must carefully manage his resources.

The behavior of resources, as defined by the core mechanics of the game, creates economic challenges. Some games, such as *SimCity,* consist almost entirely of economic challenges. Such games tend to have flattened challenge hierarchies in which the atomic challenges appear similar to the overall goal of the game. Other games, such as first-person shooters, combine economic challenges with others such as conflict and exploration. We address the internal economies of games at length in Chapter 10, "Core Mechanics."

Accumulating Resources Many games challenge the player to accumulate something: wealth, points, or anything else deemed valuable. Acquisition of this kind underlies *Monopoly* and many other games in which the top-level challenge is to accumulate more money, plutonium, or widgets than other players. The game challenges the player to understand the mechanisms of wealth creation and to use them to his own advantage. In the case of *Monopoly,* the player learns to mortgage low-rent properties and use the cash to purchase high-rent ones because high-rent properties produce more in the long run.

Achieving Balance   Requiring your players to achieve balance in an economy gives them a more interesting challenge than simply accumulating points, especially if you give them many different kinds of resources to manage. Players in *The Settlers* games juggle quantities of raw materials and goods that obey complex rules of interaction: Wheat goes to the mill to become flour, which goes to the bakery to become bread; bread feeds miners who dig coal and iron ore, which goes to the smelter to become iron bars, which then go to the blacksmith to become weapons; and so on. Produce too little of a vital item and the whole economy grinds to a halt; produce too much and it piles up, taking up space and wasting time and resources that could be better used elsewhere.

Caring for Living Things   A peculiar sort of economic challenge involves looking after a person or creature, or a small number of them, as in *The Sims* and *Creatures*. Unlike a large-scale simulation such as *Caesar*, in which the player must build and manage an entire town by meeting all of the economic and other challenges such a problem presents, these smaller-scale simulations focus on individuals. The game challenges the player to meet the needs of each individual and possibly improve its development. Because the game measures and tracks these needs via numeric terms, these qualify as economic challenges.

Conceptual Reasoning and Lateral Thinking Puzzles

We group *conceptual reasoning puzzles* and *lateral thinking puzzles* together because they both require *extrinsic knowledge,* that is, knowledge from outside the domain of the challenge itself. This sets them apart from formal logic puzzles in which all the knowledge required to solve the puzzle must be contained within its definition. Lateral thinking puzzles and conceptual reasoning puzzles may still require the use of logical thinking, however.

Conceptual Reasoning   *Conceptual reasoning puzzles* require the player to use his reasoning power and knowledge of the puzzle's subject matter to arrive at a solution to a problem. In one round of the online multiplayer game *Strike a Match,* a number of words or phrases appear, and as they do, the player must find conceptually related pairs: if *Kong* appears, should the player watch out for a match with *King* (a movie) or *Hong* (a place) or *Donkey* (a video game)?

Another sort of conceptual challenge occurs in mystery or detective games, in which the player must examine the evidence and deduce which of a number of suspects committed the crime and how. In the game *Law and Order,* based on the television series of the same name, players follow clues, ignore red herrings, and arrive at a theory of the crime, assembling the relevant evidence to demonstrate proof. In order to succeed, however, the players must have some familiarity with police forensic techniques as well as an understanding of human motivations for committing crimes. These details are extrinsic knowledge, not spelled out as part of the definition of the puzzle.

You may find designing conceptual reasoning challenges a lot of fun because they offer a lot of scope to the designer, but you'll work harder when creating these than putting together simpler trials such as physical or exploration challenges.

Lateral Thinking   Lateral thinking puzzles are related to conceptual reasoning puzzles, but they add a twist: The terms of the puzzle make it clear to the player that what seems to be the obvious or most probable solution is incorrect (or the necessary elements to achieve the obvious solution are unavailable). The player must think of alternatives instead. A classic test of lateral thinking—and one used to demonstrate that chimpanzees possess this faculty—requires the subject to get an item down from a high place without using a ladder. Deprived of the obvious solution, he must find some other approach, such as putting a chair on top of a table, climbing up on the table, and then up on the chair. Because chairs do not ordinarily belong on tables, and neither chairs nor tables are intended for climbing, the test requires the subject to transcend her everyday understanding of the functions of objects.

Lateral thinking puzzles often require the player to use extrinsic knowledge gained in real life, but to use it in unexpected ways. In *Escape from Monkey Island,* the player has to put a deflated inner tube onto a strange-looking cactus to make a giant slingshot (or catapult), which requires knowing that inner tubes are stretchy. Adventure games frequently include lateral thinking puzzles. You must be careful not to make the solution too obscure or to rely on information that goes beyond common knowledge; you can expect the average adult player to know that wood floats, but you cannot expect the player to know that cork comes from the bark of certain species of Mediterranean oak tree (that challenge belongs in a trivia game). Provide hints or clues to help a player who gets stuck. In general, the more realistic the game, the more it may rely on extrinsic knowledge because players know that they can count on their real-world experience being meaningful in the game world. In a highly abstract or highly surreal game, the player won't expect common-sense experience to be of any use. Such games may still include lateral thinking puzzles, but the knowledge required to solve them must be available within the game.

Actions

As we explained in Chapter 8, "Creating the User Experience," the user interface links the input devices in the real world to actions that take place in the game world. *Actions*, as we use the term, refers to events in the game world directly caused by the user interface's interpreting a player input. If the player presses a button on a game controller and the user interface maps that button to striking a cue ball in a game of pool, striking the cue ball constitutes an action. If the cue ball knocks another ball into a pocket, that is an event, but not an action; the movement of the other ball is a *consequence* of the player's action.

FYI | *No Hierarchy of Actions*

We explained challenges in terms of a hierarchy because that hierarchy remains in the player's mind throughout the game, a collection of goals that she works to achieve. You might think, then, that there should be an equivalent hierarchy of actions—that if the game presents the high-level challenge "try to defeat the boss monster," there should be a high-level action called "defeat the boss monster."

We don't describe actions in terms of a hierarchy because a hierarchy of actions doesn't benefit either you or the player. Making up an artificial high-level action (defeat the boss monster) to go with a high-level challenge isn't terribly useful. If you tell the player, "To defeat the boss monster, perform the defeat the boss monster action," he hasn't learned anything. There's no such button on the controller, so what good does it do him?

Instead, we define actions in low-level terms, as events resulting directly from the player's use of the control devices. In fact, a game's tutorial levels often teach players how to defeat monsters not in terms of game actions but in terms of real-world button-presses. Tutorials say, "Attack monsters using your punch, kick, and throw shuriken buttons." It's up to the player to figure out how to combine these to defeat the boss monster.

9

Actions for Gameplay

Most of the actions that a player takes in a game will be intended to meet the challenges that she faces. We cannot possibly provide a list of all the kinds of gameplay-related actions that players can perform in game worlds; they vary from the simple and concrete, such as *fire weapon,* to those as complex and abstract as *send covert operatives to arouse antigovernment sentiment in a hostile nation*—which the player could do in *Balance of Power* by choosing a single item on a menu. We encourage you to study other games in the genre you have chosen to see what actions they support.

The interaction model that you have chosen for a particular gameplay mode determines a lot about the kinds of actions available in that mode. If you use an avatar-based interaction model, then the actions available to the player will, for the most part, consist of influencing the game world through the avatar.

In games using a multipresent model, the player acts indirectly by issuing commands to units, which themselves act within the game world (as in real-time strategy games) or acts directly on features of the world itself (as in construction and management simulations and god games).

Don't expect a one-to-one mapping between actions and challenges; many games include a large number of types of challenges but only a small number of actions, leaving the player to figure out how to use the actions in various combinations to surmount each challenge. Puzzles frequently do this. Faced with a scrambled Rubik's Cube, the player can take only one action: She can rotate one face of the cube 90 degrees. The solution to the puzzle consists entirely of making similar rotations.

Games offer many challenges but limited numbers of actions for two reasons. First, if you give the player a large number of actions to choose from, you must also provide a large user interface, which can be confusing to the player and increase the difficulty of learning the game. (If you implement a context-sensitive interface that chooses the correct action for the user based on context, you don't give the player the freedom to try interesting combinations.) Second, a large number of actions usually requires a large number of animations to display them all. This makes the game expensive to develop.

Many great games implement only a small number of actions but still let the player use them to overcome a wide variety of challenges. If you are imaginative enough, the challenges will be so interesting that the player will never notice.

Defining Your Actions

To define the actions that you'll implement, begin by thinking about the player's role in the game. At the concept stage of your project, you asked, "What is the player going to do?" and should have written down some general answers to that question. Now it's time to go into detail for each gameplay mode. Begin with the primary mode. If you wrote, "In the primary gameplay mode, the player will drive a car," think about exactly what actions driving entails. Pressing the accelerator, turning the steering wheel, and braking, of course, but what else? Shifting the gears? Turning on the lights? Using the handbrake? Some of the actions you decide on may have to do with challenges; others will simply be another part of the role.

Next, look at the challenges you designed for the primary gameplay mode. Begin with the atomic challenges you plan to offer; for each atomic challenge, write down how you expect the player to overcome it. Your answers will probably consist of individual actions or small combinations of actions. Ben Cousins has argued that game designers should spend most of their effort defining and refining the way that actions overcome atomic challenges because the player spends most of his time performing those actions (Cousins, 2004); this is excellent advice.

After you define the actions that will meet the atomic challenges, consider the intermediate and higher-level challenges in the gameplay mode. Can they all be met with the actions you've defined, or will they require additional ones? Add those to the list.

Finally, consider actions unrelated to gameplay that you may want to make available to the player. You may already have some that come with the player's role, but you may want to include others for other reasons. See the list in the next section for some ideas.

Once you have been through this process for the primary gameplay mode, do it all again for each of the other modes. When you believe you have comprehensive lists of all the actions that you want to include in each mode, you're ready to start defining the user interfaces for the different modes: assigning actions to control mechanisms. (See Chapter 8, "Creating the User Experience.")

Actions That Serve Other Functions

Games include many actions that allow the player to interact with the game world but not engage in gameplay. Games also offer actions that aren't specifically play activities but give the player control over various aspects of the game. The following list describes a number of types of non–challenge-related actions.

- **Unstructured play.** You will almost certainly want to include some fun-to-perform actions that don't address any challenge. Players often move their avatars around the game world for the sheer fun of movement or to see a new area even if it offers no challenges, referred to as sightseeing. You may want to include actions just because they're part of the role. In most driving games, honking the horn accomplishes nothing, but if you couldn't honk the horn, the game would feel incomplete.

- **Actions for creation and self-expression.** See Chapter 5, "Creative and Expressive Play," for a discussion of actions allowing players to create and customize things, including avatars. Much of the activity in construction and management simulations consists of creative play rather than gameplay, although the player's actions are often constrained by limitations imposed by the game's internal economy.

- **Actions for socialization.** Players in multiplayer games, especially online games, need ways to talk to each other, to form groups, to compare scores, and to take part in other community activities. See Chapter 21, "Online Games" available on the Companion Website.

- **Actions to participate in the story.** Participating in interactive dialog, interacting with NPCs, or making decisions that affect the plot all constitute actions that allow the player to participate in a story even if those actions don't directly address a challenge. The more of them you offer, the more your player feels she is taking part in a story.

- **Actions to control the game software.** The player takes many actions to control the game software, such as adjusting the virtual camera, pausing and saving the game, choosing a difficulty level, and setting the audio volume. Some such actions may affect the game's challenges (setting the difficulty level certainly does), but the player doesn't take them specifically to *address* a challenge.

Saving the Game

Saving a game takes a snapshot of a game world and all its particulars at a given instant and stores them away so that the player can later load the same data, return to that instant, and play the game from that point. Saving and restoring a game is technologically easy, and it's essential for testing and debugging, so it's often slapped in as a feature without much thought about its effect on gameplay. As designers, though, it's our job to think about anything that affects gameplay or the player's experience of the game.

Saving a game stores not only the player's location in the game but also any customizations she might have made along the way. In *Michelle Kwan's Figure Skating Championship,* for example, the player could customize the body type, skin tone, hair color and style, and costume of the skater. The player could even load in a picture of her own face. The more freedom you give the player to customize the game or the avatar, the more data must be saved. Until recently, this limited the richness of games for console machines, but now console machines routinely come with enough storage to save a lot of customization data.

Reasons for Saving a Game

Reasons for saving a player's game or allowing him to save it include:

- **Allowing the player to leave the game and return to it later.** This is the most important reason for saving the game. In a large game, it's an essential feature. It's not realistic and not fair to the player to expect him to dedicate the computer or console machine to a 40-hour game from start to finish with no break.

- **Letting the player recover from disastrous mistakes.** In practice, this usually means the death of the avatar. Arcade games, which offer no save-game feature, traditionally give the player a number of lives and chances to earn more along the way. Until recently, console action games have tended to follow the same scheme. Richer games, such as role-playing or adventure games, usually give the player only one life but allow him to reload a saved game if his avatar dies or he realizes that he cannot possibly win the game.

■ **Encouraging the player to explore alternate strategies.** In turn-based strategic games, saving the game allows the player to learn the game by trying alternative approaches. If one doesn't seem to work, he can go back to the point at which he committed himself and try another approach.

Consequences for Immersion and Storytelling

Saving a game is not always beneficial to the player's experience. The act of saving a game takes place outside the game world and, as a consequence, saving harms the player's immersion. If a game tries to create the illusion that the player inhabits a fantasy world, the act of saving destroys the illusion. One of the most significant characteristics of real life is that you cannot return to the past to correct your errors; the moment you allow a player to repeat the past, you acknowledge the unreality of the game world.

The essence of a story is dramatic tension, and dramatic tension requires that something be at stake. Reloading a game with a branching storyline affects the player's experience of the story because if he can alter the future by returning to the past and making a different decision, nothing really hangs in the balance. Real-world decisions bring permanent consequences; some can be modified in the future, but the original decision itself cannot be unmade. But when a player follows first one branch of a branching storyline and then goes back in time and follows another branch, he experiences the story in an unnatural way. The consequences of his actions lose their meaning, and his sense of dramatic tension is either reduced or destroyed completely. What is a benefit to strategic games—the chance to try alternate strategies—presents problems for storytelling.

Nevertheless, we feel that the arguments for saving outweigh these disadvantages. If the player destroys his immersion by repeatedly reloading the game, that is his choice and not the fault of the game designer or the story. As we pointed out in Chapter 7, "Storytelling and Narrative," a weakness of branching storylines is that they require the player to play the game again if he wants to see plot lines that he missed on his first play-through. Allowing the player to save and reload makes that easier for him. He may always choose not to reload if he doesn't want to.

Ways of Saving a Game

Over the years, designers have devised a variety of different ways of saving a game, each with its own pros and cons for immersion and gameplay.

Passwords   If your game runs on a device with no storage at all (a rarity nowadays), you can't save the game in the middle of a level, but you can let the player restart the last level attempted. Each time the player completes a level, give her a unique password that unlocks the next level. At start-up, ask if she wants to enter a password, and if she does so correctly, load the level unlocked by that password. She can go directly to that level without having to replay all the earlier ones. This method also allows her to go back and replay any completed level if she wants to.

Save to a File or Save Slot   The player may interrupt play and save the current state of the game either to a file on the hard drive or, more usually, to one of a series of named "save slots" managed by the game program. When the player wants to begin the saved game, he tells the program to load it from the directory of files or slots. This allows the player to keep several different copies, saved at different points, and to name them so that he can remember which one is which.

Unfortunately, while this is the most common way of saving, it's also the method most harmful to the game's immersiveness. The user interface for managing the files or save slots necessarily looks like an operating system's file-management tool, not like a part of the fantasy world that the game depicts. You can harmonize this procedure better with appropriate graphics, but saving almost always takes the player out of the game world. Some games salvage the immersion to some degree by calling the file system the player's *journal* and making it look as if the saved games are kept in a book.

Quick-Save   Fast-moving games in which the player's avatar stays in more or less constant danger (such as first-person shooters) frequently offer a quick-save feature. The player presses a single button to save the game instantly at any time, without ever leaving the game world. The screen displays the words *Quick saved* for a moment, but otherwise the player's immersion in the world remains unperturbed. The player can reload the game just as swiftly by pressing a quick-load button. The game returns immediately to its state at the last quick-save, without going out of the game world to a file-management screen.

Disadvantages of quick-save arise because saving so quickly usually means the player doesn't want to take the time, and isn't offered the chance, to designate a file or slot. Most such games offer only one slot, although some let players designate a numbered slot by entering a digit after they press the quick-save button. Players remember which slot is which when quick-loading. Quick-save sacrifices flexibility to retain immersion and speed.

Automatic Save and Checkpoints   A few games automatically save the state of the game when the player exits, so players can leave and return at any time without explicitly saving. This harms the player's immersion least of all, but if the player has recently experienced a disaster, he has no way to recover from it. More often, games save whenever the player passes a checkpoint, which may or may not be visible to him. Checkpoint saving is less disruptive than quick-saving because the player never has to do anything. The player *can* go back and undo a disaster, provided that the disaster happened after the most recent checkpoint. But it means that the player can't choose to save whenever he wants or choose to restart at some earlier point. If the checkpoints occur infrequently, he might lose a great deal of progress in the event of a disaster. Although it's better for immersion from the player-centric standpoint, automatic checkpoint saving is inferior to quick-saving. With quicksave, the player always has the option *not* to save if for some reason he enjoys the risk of having to go back a long way. With automatic checkpoints, he has no choice.

A few games offer optional checkpoint saving, in which the player may choose to save or not every time he reaches a checkpoint. This gives him a little more control but still doesn't allow him to save at will, which we regard as preferable.

To Save or Not to Save

A few designers don't allow players to save their games within certain regions of the game or even to save at all. If the player can save and reload where he wants and without limit, he can solve puzzles or overcome other obstacles by trial and error rather than by skill, or he can use the saving system to avoid undesirable random events; if something bad happens by chance, the player can reload the game repeatedly until the undesirable event doesn't occur. This reduces the game's difficulty, and some designers argue against allowing players to save on that basis.

We disagree. Preventing the player from saving in order to make the game more difficult is lazy game design, adding difficulty without adding fun. If you really want to make the game harder, devise harder challenges. Forcing the player to replay an entire level because he made a mistake near the end wastes his time and condemns him to frustration and boredom.

You may not like it if a player repeatedly reloads a game to avoid a random event or to solve some problem by trial and error rather than skill, but the player doesn't play (or buy) the game to make you feel good. He might need to save the game for perfectly legitimate reasons. The notion that saving makes a game too easy assumes that the player is your opponent, a violation of the player-centric principle. Most games now recognize that players want—and sometimes need—to cheat by offering cheat codes anyway.

It's the player's machine; it's not fair to penalize him just because he has to go to the bathroom or because it's now his little brother's turn to play. Choose which mechanism works best for your game, weighing the advantages and disadvantages of each, but do let the player save the game, and preferably, whenever and wherever he wants to. It does no harm to your game to give the player the freedom to choose when he wants to save—or whether he wants to save at all. We strongly believe in players' fundamental right to be able to stop playing without losing what they have accomplished.

> **COMMANDMENT:** Allow the Player to Save and Reload the Game
>
> Unless your game is extremely short or your device has no data storage, allow the player to save and reload the game. His right to exit the game without losing the benefit of his achievements supersedes all other considerations.

Summary

Gameplay is the heart of a game's entertainment, the reason players buy and play games. We began the chapter with some principles to keep in mind in order to make gameplay fun. Next we examined the *hierarchy of challenges,* the fact that a player experiences several challenges at once, and defined the concept of atomic challenges. We noted the difference between the *intrinsic skill* required by a challenge and the *stress* that time pressure puts on a player and how these two elements combine to create *difficulty.*

Gameplay itself took up most of the chapter, with definitions and discussions of the many types of challenges that video games employ and various ways of adjusting their difficulty level. From challenges, we turned to the actions that you can offer the player, which include actions not directly related to gameplay. Finally we discussed the pros and cons of different ways of saving the game, an important feature for any game more than a few minutes long.

Armed with this information and with a little research, you should be able to analyze the gameplay of most of the video games currently for sale and to design others using similar kinds of challenges and actions.

Test Your Skills

MULTIPLE CHOICE QUESTIONS

1. The main reason a game fails to be fun is that it
   A. has too many levels.
   B. contains stereotyped characters.
   C. contains elementary errors.
   D. has challenges that are too easy.

2. Which of the following is *not* a principle that contributes to a fun game?
   A. Get a feature right or leave it out.
   B. Be true to your vision.
   C. Know your target audience.
   D. Design around the marketing campaign.

3. A player who needs a tool right now to cut down the thorn trees preventing him from getting into the castle is facing a(n)
   A. atomic challenge.
   B. intermediate challenge.
   C. logical challenge.
   D. economic challenge.

4. Games generally give the player explicit instructions about
   A. intermediate challenges.
   B. the victory condition for the entire game.
   C. simultaneous challenges.
   D. pattern recognition challenges.

5. A player needs intrinsic skill to
   A. press a button repeatedly to make a gun shoot.
   B. direct an avatar in exploring a game world.
   C. solve a mathematical code in a puzzle.
   D. communicate with nonplayer characters.

6. In an archery game, which victory condition includes both factors that contribute to absolute difficulty?
   A. The player who places the most arrows in the center ring in two minutes wins.
   B. The player who places the most arrows in the center ring wins.
   C. The player who hits the target the most times wins.
   D. The value of arrows that miss the target are subtracted from those that hit the center ring.

7. Examples of physical coordination challenges include
   A. putting objects in a specific order and understanding probabilities.
   B. recalling information and detecting traps.
   C. accumulating resources and understanding strategy.
   D. shooting rapidly and learning a vehicle's acceleration rate through experience.

9

312 CHAPTER 9 | Gameplay

8. When you design a challenge that will involve increasing time pressure, what should you do to keep the same level of absolute difficulty?

    A. Increase the intrinsic skill required at the same rate.

    B. Reduce the intrinsic skill required as the time pressure increases.

    C. Add simultaneous challenges as time pressure increases.

    D. Give players a way to reduce time pressure.

9. An example of a pattern recognition challenge might be

    A. snares set in wooded areas that can catch the player unawares.

    B. learning that a golden orb can always defeat a bloodbeast.

    C. testing all the doors to see if they lead to secret passages.

    D. learning to manage resources so that just enough manufactured items are produced.

10. The logistical challenge routinely included in real-time strategy games is

    A. weapons production.

    B. accumulating construction materials.

    C. solving logistical puzzles.

    D. racing to complete a factory.

11. If you require a player to figure out a way to get across a narrow, deep chasm in a forest when her only tool is an ax, you are asking her to demonstrate

    A. logistical thinking.

    B. strategic planning.

    C. lateral thinking.

    D. tactical planning.

12. Why do games offer many challenges but limited actions?

    A. Challenges are easier to create than actions.

    B. Actions are less important than challenges in gameplay terms.

    C. A player-centric approach requires the designer to concentrate on challenges.

    D. Offering many actions would require a large interface and many animations.

13. Which of the following is an action that does *not* contribute to gameplay?

    A. Steering a car.

    B. Picking up a weapon.

    C. Turning off sound effects.

    D. Opening a door.

14. One of the best reasons to allow a player to save a game is to

    A. recover from a disaster.

    B. eliminate the possibility that he will cheat.

    C. prevent him from using trial and error to solve challenges.

    D. avoid having to deal with the avatar death issue.

15. To avoid harming a player's immersion when saving,

    A. give the player a button to click that will take her to a Save dialog box.

    B. save the game automatically when the player exits or passes a checkpoint.

    C. have the player press a key combination and then type a password to save the file.

    D. allow the player to save only during cut-scenes.

EXERCISES

1. Write the rules for a simple, single-player, PC-based puzzle game like *Bejeweled* but make up your own mechanics for earning points. Document all the challenges and actions of the game. You must create at least ten different *kinds* of atomic challenges. Indicate what action the player should use to surmount each challenge and what reward the player gets for doing so. You must also create and document at least four actions that are not intended to meet challenges but serve some other purpose. You do not have to design a user interface in detail but may find it helpful to make and submit a quick sketch of the screen and the layout of the controls.

2. Choose an action or action-adventure game you are familiar with (or your instructor will assign one). Document the challenge hierarchy of the first level in the game that is *not* a tutorial level, diagramming it out as in Figure 9.1. (If the level includes more than fifty sequential atomic challenges, you may stop after fifty, but be sure to include any level bosses or major challenges that occur at the end of the level.) If you have the necessary software, play partway through the level, take a screen shot, and indicate on your diagram what challenges you were facing at that moment, similar to the gray boxes in Figure 9.1. If you faced simultaneous challenges, indicate that also. Submit the screen shot along with your diagram.

3. Think of a game you are familiar with that permits the player to achieve victory by different strategies, similar to Figure 9.2. Write a short essay documenting each approach and how the hierarchy of challenges (including the intermediate challenges) differs in each one. If one strategy seems more likely to achieve victory than another, say so and indicate why. Your instructor will give you the scope of the assignment.

4. Choose a single- or multiplayer role-playing game that you are familiar with (or your instructor will assign one). Identify all the actions it affords. (You may find the manual helpful.) Divide the actions into those intended to meet challenges, those that participate in the story, those that facilitate socializing with other players (if any), housekeeping operations such as inventory management, and those that control the software itself. If another category suggests itself, document it. Also note any actions that fall into more than one category and indicate why. The size of the game that you or your instructor selects will determine the scope of the assignment.

5. Choose ten different types of challenges from among the ones listed in *Commonly Used Challenges* in this chapter. For each type, devise one example challenge and *two* example actions that overcome it (this may rule out some types). Describe the challenge and the two actions in a paragraph, ten paragraphs in all.

DESIGN QUESTIONS

1. What types of challenges do you want to include in your game? Do you want to challenge the player's physical abilities, his mental abilities, or both?

2. Game genres are defined in part by the nature of the challenges they offer. What does your choice of genre imply for the gameplay? Do you intend to include any cross-genre elements, challenges that are not normally found in your chosen genre?

3. What is your game's hierarchy of challenges? How many levels do you expect it to have? What challenges are typical of each level?

4. What are your game's atomic challenges? Do you plan to make the player face more than one atomic challenge at a time? Are they all independent, like battling enemies one at a time, or are they interrelated, like balancing an economy? If they are interrelated, how?

5. Does the player have a choice of approaches to victory? Can he decide on one strategy over another? Can he ignore some challenges, face others, and still achieve a higher-level goal? Or must he simply face all the game's challenges in sequence?

6. Does the game include implicit challenges (those that emerge from the design), as well as explicit challenges (those that you specify)?

7. Do you intend to offer settable difficulty levels for your game? What levels of intrinsic skill and stress will each challenge require?

8. What actions will you implement to meet your challenges? Can the player surmount a large number of challenges with a small number of actions? What is the mapping of actions to challenges?

9. What other actions will you implement for other purposes? What are those purposes—unstructured play, creativity and self-expression, socialization, story participation, or controlling the game software?

10. What save mechanism do you plan to implement?

9

Chapter | 10

Core Mechanics

Chapter Objectives

After reading this chapter and completing the exercises, you will be able to do the following:

- Explain the functions of the core mechanics in a game.
- Describe the key components—resources, entities, attributes, and mechanics—that define how a game works.
- Explain how a game's internal economy controls the way resources and entities are produced, consumed, and exchanged by means of sources, drains, converters, and traders.
- Discuss how the core mechanics implement both challenges and player actions to manage gameplay.
- Know how to design the core mechanics of a game by writing specifications to document the entities and the functioning of the mechanics.
- Understand how to use random numbers in a game.

Introduction

The core mechanics of a game determine how that game actually operates: what its rules are and how the player interacts with them. We begin this chapter by defining the core mechanics and explaining their role in creating the entertainment experience. We also discuss how they differ between real-time and turn-based games and how the core mechanics are related to level design. Next we address the key concepts of core mechanics: *resources, entities,* and *mechanics.* We explain these concepts and how they may be used to specify rules precisely.

From the general features of core mechanics, we turn to their specific implementation in the ***internal economy*** of games, a set of mechanics that governs the flow of quantities. We also look at how mechanics are used to create gameplay by implementing both challenges and actions. Having introduced all these aspects of core mechanics, we describe an approach for actually designing them, which involves reexamining early design work and rendering it specific and concrete. The chapter concludes with a brief discussion of the subject of random numbers and how to use them in games.

What Are the Core Mechanics?

Isn't the greatest rule of all the rules simply to please?

—Molière

In Chapter 2, "Design Components and Processes," we explain that the software of a video game implements the rules for the player so he doesn't have to implement them or even know them all. We also introduce the core mechanics, calling these the heart of the game, and we say that they determine what challenges the player faces and what actions he can take. In this chapter, we examine the core mechanics in further detail and offer a formal definition.

> *The core mechanics consist of the data and the algorithms that precisely define the game's rules.*

Turning Rules into Core Mechanics

In the early stages of design, you may have only a hazy idea of the details of your game's rules. Early on, you may say, "Players will be penalized for taking too long to get through the swamp" or "Players will have only a limited time to get through the swamp." But that description does not supply sufficient information to build a game. What is the penalty? How long does the player have? Designing the core mechanics defines the rules precisely and completely. That same rule in the core mechanics might read something like, "When the avatar enters the swamp, the black toadstools begin to emit a poison gas that the player can see filling the screen, starting at the bottom and rising at a rate of one game-world inch every three seconds; by the end of 3 minutes, the gas will reach the height of the avatar's face, and if by that time the avatar is still in the swamp, the avatar dies. If the avatar returns to the swamp later, the gas will be gone but the process will start over again from the beginning." In this example, the clauses beginning with *when* and *if* state algorithms, and *one game-world inch every three seconds* and *3 minutes* are examples of data that also forms a part of the rule.

10

The Rules and Core Mechanics of Monopoly

The rules of *Monopoly,* as Parker Brothers ships them with the game, take up less than three full pages. However, the rules printed on the paper are not sufficient to build a computer game: They don't include complete documentation of all the data necessary to play. To properly specify the core mechanics of *Monopoly,* you would have to include not only the printed rules but the prices of each of the properties on the board, the different amounts of rent that may be collected at each location (including special mechanics for the utilities and railroads), the layout of the board, and the effects of all the Chance and Community Chest cards. A full specification of the core mechanics of *Monopoly* is considerably more detailed than the general rules.

Where Are the Core Mechanics?

The core mechanics—the precise definition of the rules—remain the same whether you keep them in your head, write them on paper, or implement them in any programming language you like. Although the mechanics remain the same, their *implementation* varies as your project goes through the different stages of the design and development process. First you document the algorithms in ordinary language in a design document; at that point, if you want to change the mechanics, you edit the document. Later you may build a spreadsheet containing the algorithms and data and tweak them there. Or you might make a *paper prototype* that allows you to play the game, writing the values of the variables on pieces of paper and manipulating them yourself according to the algorithms you've worked out, to see if the algorithms produce the game experience you want to offer. Using what you learn, you may update the design documents or just let the spreadsheets become the official implementation. The core mechanics remain the rules of the game; only the implementation has changed.

Eventually the core mechanics, as complete as you can make them, should be so precisely stated that the programmers can write code using your core mechanics document or your spreadsheet as specifications. The algorithms of the core mechanics become the algorithms in their code, and the data required by the core mechanics reside in files so that the game software can read them in as necessary. At this point, if you want to change the mechanics, you ask the programmers to change the code or the data files. You should in principle also change the design documents; in practice, designers seldom do this because the code and files have become the authorized implementation of the core mechanics. In short, the core mechanics are wherever your team considers their *official* implementation to be: in the design documents, the spreadsheets, or in the code and data files.

The player does not experience the core mechanics directly. She can't point to something on the screen and say, "Those are the core mechanics." If you apply player-centric design principles, all of the core mechanics work together to provide a good game experience even though players don't know what core mechanics are and can only infer the functionality of the core mechanics from the way the game behaves.

FYI   *Core Mechanics as a Template for Software Design*

The **game engine** is the part of the software that implements the game's rules. While the core mechanics spell out the rules of the game in detail, so that in practice they specify what the game engine will do, the core mechanics do not dictate exactly *how* the game engine will do it. For example, you might specify the core mechanics in a turn-based role-playing game to require that, when a fight occurs, the character with the highest dexterity rating will land his blow ahead of the others, with blows from other fighters landing in order according to their dexterity ratings. That's as far as the core mechanics go to specify how the software should work. Don't worry about defining the precise algorithm for sorting the fighters by dexterity rating because the choice of algorithm doesn't change the result. All that matters is that the fighters end up hitting in the order of dexterity. You need not (and should not) concern yourself with which sorting algorithm is best. That decision is the programmer's to make. In short, if there is more than one way to achieve the same effect in the game, let the programmers decide which one to use.

You don't have to know how to program to design the core mechanics, but you must be generally familiar with algorithmic processes. We address this in more detail in *Mechanics* later in the chapter.

10

The Core Mechanics as Processes

If you get a job in the game industry, you will hear industry professionals talk about the core mechanics as if the mechanics actively take part in the game: The core mechanics "talk to the storytelling engine" or "signal the UI." But rules can't act. You would never say of *Monopoly* that the rules do anything beyond perhaps "allowing" the player to take a particular action or "specifying" a penalty. So what's going on?

With the core mechanics serving (in a nontechnical way) as the specification for the game engine and eventually existing as implemented in the code of the game engine, you can see that the relationship between the two is extremely close. So references to the core mechanics may sound like references to the engine itself. As long as you understand that the core mechanics consist of algorithms and data that precisely define the rules, it doesn't really matter if you imply that the core mechanics perform work actually carried out by the game engine; algorithms, after all, describe processes. When these algorithms exist only in the core mechanics document, they obviously can't do anything, but when the programmers turn them into code, they can.

Therefore, when we say, "The core mechanics send triggers to the story-telling engine," it's shorthand for a longer sentence that reads, "The game engine, using algorithms specified by the core mechanics, sends triggers to the storytelling engine." We choose to avoid that unnecessarily awkward construction and refer instead to the core mechanics as a collection of active processes that perform a number of activities during play. In reality, the game engine, not the core mechanics, accepts input signals from the user interface, sends signals to the storytelling engine, and so on.

Functions of the Core Mechanics in Operation

During play, the core mechanics (as implemented by the game engine) operate behind the scenes to create and manage gameplay for the player, keep track of everything that happens in the game world, and work with the story-telling engine to help tell the story. The following list details what core mechanics do:

- **Operate the internal economy of the game.** The core mechanics specify how the game or the player creates, distributes, and uses up the goods on which the game bases its economy. We address this, their most important role, in detail later in the chapter, in *The Internal Economy*.

- **Present active challenges** to the player via the user interface, as specified by the level design. Passive challenges, such as a chasm that the avatar must jump over, don't have mechanics of their own. We further discuss this distinction later in the chapter in *Challenges and the Core Mechanics*.

- **Accept player actions** from the user interface and implement their effects.

- **Operate the artificial intelligence** of nonplayer characters and artificial opponents.

- **Switch the game from mode to mode.** The core mechanics keep track of the current gameplay mode and, whenever a mode change occurs (either because the nature of the game requires it or the player requests it), the core mechanics switches modes and informs the user interface to update the UI accordingly.

- **Transmit triggers to the storytelling engine** when in-game events or dramatically significant player actions occur.

Real-Time Games Versus Turn-Based Games

Your specification of the core mechanics will read somewhat differently depending on whether your game is turn-based or takes place in real time.

Most video games operate in real time, so the core mechanics specify the parameters of a living world that operates on its own whether the player acts or not. Many of the mechanics you design will be *processes* that operate continuously or for extended periods. AI-driven characters go about their business, traps check to see if they should spring upon anyone, banks collect and pay interest, and so on. When you specify one-shot *events* rather than continuous processes, the events will often occur as a direct or indirect consequence of player actions or because some process detects a special condition, such as when a runner crosses the finish line in a race. (We discuss events and processes in greater detail in *Mechanics*, later in the chapter.)

In a turn-based game, the core mechanics don't do anything at all until a player takes his turn. Once he has done so, the core mechanics can compute the effects of his actions on the game world. Then the mechanics remain idle while the next player takes *her* turn, and so on. In some games, all the players enter their intended actions simultaneously while the mechanics remain idle; once the players finish for that turn, the core mechanics compute the effect of all players' actions.

In a turn-based game, then, your design for the mechanics will read like a specification for a sequence of events rather than a set of processes that operate all the time. You will state the effects of each possible action and what other computations take place as a consequence. While you may design processes for a turn-based game, you must realize that processes do not really operate continuously; they only run between player turns. Your design for a process in a turn-based game must include points at which the process may safely be interrupted for the next player's turn.

Core Mechanics and Level Design

Most video games for consoles and personal computers present gameplay in separate levels (also called chapters, missions, or scenarios, depending on the genre), each with its own set of initial conditions, challenges, and termination conditions. Level designers plan, construct, and test these levels, as discussed in Chapter 12, "General Principles of Level Design."

Ordinarily, the level design specifies the *type*, *timing*, and *sequence* of challenges that appear during play, whereas the core mechanics specify how different challenges actually work. When a level starts up, the core mechanics read the level design data from a file. The initial state of the game world for each level; the challenges, actions, and NPCs for each level; and the victory conditions for the levels reside as data in level design files (see Figure 10.1) unless the game consists of only one level or creates randomized levels. In the latter case, the core mechanics must include mechanics for setting up the level before the game first enters a gameplay mode.

10

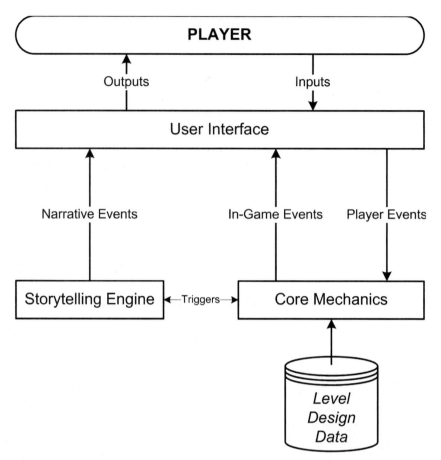

FIGURE 10.1 The core mechanics read the level design data from files.

Therefore, your design for the core mechanics should specify *how* challenges work in general but not exactly *which* challenges each level will contain. As you design the core mechanics, concentrate on those features of the game that will be needed in more than one level, and leave special-case features found only in a particular level to the level designer. It may be that the level designer can create code for those features using a *scripting language* and won't have to ask the game's programmers to do it.

This doesn't mean that you can push all of the work off onto the level designers, though. Think of the features you create in the core mechanics as being like LEGO blocks that the level designers will use to build their level. In a war game, the core mechanics, not the level designs, define how all the units in the game move and fight. Once you design all of the units, the level designers can use your information on how the units operate to construct exciting levels featuring those units.

Key Concepts

To design the core mechanics, you must document the different components that will define how your game works: *resources, entities, attributes,* and *mechanics.* In this section, we define these terms. Although you do not have to be a programmer to design a game, you wouldn't be a game designer if you didn't intend for your ideas to eventually turn into computer programs. You will need to have at least a nodding acquaintance with how programmers think about data and the relationships between different items of data, ideas that will crop up in this discussion.

Resources

The term **resource** refers to types of objects or materials the player can move or exchange, which the game handles as numeric quantities, performing arithmetic operations on the values. *Resource* does not refer to specific instances of these types of objects but the type itself in an abstract sense. Marbles constitute a resource in your game if your player can pick up marbles, trade them, and put them down again, but *resource* doesn't describe a specific marble in your player's pocket or even a specific collection of marbles; it describes marbles generally. *Marbles* are a resource, but *the 15 marbles in the player's pocket* are an *instance* of a resource: a particular collection of marbles.

The core mechanics define the processes by which the game uses or trades resources; that is, the rules by which specific instances of resources—one lump of gold, the marbles in the player's pocket, the ammo in her inventory, the water in her reservoir—can legally be moved from place to place or from owner to owner. They also define how specific instances of resources come into and go out of the game entirely.

Note that if you build a level full of flowers but the player can't do anything with them and nothing ever happens to them, the flowers set the stage and contribute aesthetically but do not constitute a resource, and the core mechanics will not need to take flowers into account. On the other hand, if the player can pick flowers and sell them, then flowers become a resource. Even if the player can do nothing with flowers except put them in a vase, flowers still form a resource: Some of them have changed location, and the vase probably has an attribute stating how many flowers it can hold, which the core mechanics can check to be sure the player doesn't overfill it.

A resource may be of a type that can be handled as individual items, such as marbles, or of a type that cannot be divided into individual items, such as water (although water may be measured in volumetric units).

Games often treat nonphysical concepts such as *popularity* or vague concepts such as *resistance to poison* as resources, even though we don't ordinarily think of these as quantities that can be measured and even bought and sold. Part of a game designer's job involves quantifying the unquantifiable—turning such abstract qualities as *charisma* or *pugnacity* into numbers that a program can manipulate.

Entities

An *entity* is a particular instance of a resource or the state of some element of the game world. (A light may be *on* or *off,* for instance.) A building, a character, or an animal can be an entity, but perhaps less obviously a pile of gold or a vessel of water can be an entity. The state of a traffic light that at any given time might be red, green, or yellow can also be an entity.

Be sure you understand the difference between resources and entities. Remember that a resource is only a type of thing, not the thing itself. A specific airplane is an entity, but if your game includes a factory that manufactures airplanes, such that management of the supply of airplanes makes up part of the gameplay, then airplanes, as a commodity, constitute a resource even though each individual airplane remains an entity. Earlier, we said that marbles can be a resource but a marble in the player's pocket is not; now we can say that each marble in his pocket is an entity. Points qualify as a resource, but the player's score is an entity, pertaining only to that player, recording a number of points scored.

Simple Entities   The player's score or the current state of a traffic light can be completely specified by a single datum; we call this a ***simple entity.*** The single value stored in this datum can be numeric, such as a score, or symbolic, such as the possible states of a traffic light: red, green, or yellow. We discuss the differences between numeric and symbolic values in *Numeric and Symbolic Relationships* later in the chapter.

Once you decide to add a symbolic entity, such as a traffic light, to the game world, you will need to define it in the core mechanics as a simple entity, specifying its initial state and providing a list of all its possible states. For a numeric entity, you'll need to define an initial quantity and the range of possible legal values. In the tuning stage of design, you will spend a great deal of time adjusting these values, so don't worry too much about getting them exactly right at first.

Compound Entities   It may take more than one data value to describe an entity. In a flying game, in which characterizing the wind requires stating both its speed and its direction, the wind is a ***compound entity.*** Each of these values is called an *attribute.*

An ***attribute*** is an entity that belongs to, and therefore helps to describe, another entity. To describe the wind, we need to know the values of its speed attribute and its direction attribute. We can specify the wind's speed with a numeric value and its direction with a symbolic value (one of the set that includes *northwesterly, westerly, southwesterly,* and so on). In this case, each attribute of our overall entity (the wind) is itself a simple entity, but this is not always, and not even usually, the case.

Attributes may themselves be compound entities. In a sports game, a team has attributes such as its name, home town, and statistics, as well as its collection of athletes, each of whom is an entity with his own attributes such as speed and agility. In a driving game, the car the player drives is a compound entity with attributes that describe its performance characteristics. In a business simulation, factories will be compound entities with attributes for rates of production, stock on hand, and so forth. Most of the entities you will define for any game, other than the most elementary of games, will be compound entities. See Figure 10.2 for an example of three types of entities, one simple, one compound containing only simple attributes, and one compound containing both simple attributes and another compound entity. Note that the gray boxes are only labels to aid understanding; their contents are not stored as data.

We discuss attributes at some length in both Chapter 5, "Creative and Expressive Play," and in Chapter 6, "Character Development," so we will not repeat that information here. Be aware, however, that you don't use attributes only for characters. *Any* entity in the game may have attributes that describe it: Vehicles have performance characteristics, factories have production rates, and so on.

As with any simple entity, you should choose an initial quantity or state for an attribute when you decide to include the attribute in your game.

A Simple Numeric Entity

Points Scored
1,755,245

A Compound Entity with Two Attributes

Wind	
Speed	35
Direction	Northwest

A Compound Entity Containing Another Compound Entity as an Attribute

Avatar	
Name	Voldarok
Money	25
Health	117
Race	Elf
Location	Feasting Hall
Inventory	
# Items	5
Item 1	Sword
Item 2	Shield
Item 3	Food
Item 4	Helmet
Item 5	Armor

FIGURE 10.2 Examples of three different entities.

If you are a programmer, you may have noticed that entities sound a lot like *objects* in object-oriented programming: They include variables for storing numeric and symbolic values and may be made up of other entities in the same way that programming objects may be made up of other objects. And like *classes* of objects in programming, entities have associated mechanics (though programmers would call them *functions* or *methods*) for manipulating these data.

For most practical purposes, you can treat entities and programming objects as identical, and if you happen to program as well as design your game, you will certainly implement entities as objects in your code. We have chosen to use the term *entity* rather than *object* because we normally use *object* in the everyday sense to refer to some physical item in the game world.

Unique Entities If your game contains only one entity of a particular type, then that is a ***unique entity.*** In most adventure games, the objects that the avatar can pick up are unique entities. The avatar itself in most games is a unique entity because there is usually only one avatar. In a football game, the football is a unique entity, because there may never be two footballs in play at any one time.

Note that the airplanes mentioned in the previous section are not unique entities even if each carries its own serial number and particular state of repair. They still may be treated collectively, bought and sold in groups, and considered to be a resource.

Defining Entities for Your Game As you specify your core mechanics, you will need to create entities for any character, object, or substance that the game needs to manipulate and for any value that the game needs to remember. In the case of items such as footballs, vehicles, money, and health, determining what attributes each entity requires will probably seem obvious—although defining their mechanics won't always be simple. You may also need to create entities that hold quantities or readings required by the user interface. Every indicator in the user interface needs an entity that reflects the indicator's state or appearance.

Suppose you want to warn the player when a valuable resource, such as fuel in a car's gas tank, reaches critically low levels. You would normally put a needle gauge in the user interface to show the fuel level, and you may like to add a warning light to draw the player's attention to the gauge. The light can be either on or off. To support the light, you would need to define an entity called *fuel warning* that can exist in two states. During play, the user interface checks the state of the fuel warning entity to display the appropriate image of the light. You would also need to create a mechanic (discussed in *Mechanics,* later in the chapter) to define precisely what conditions change the state of the fuel warning entity.

You may wonder why you should create an additional entity and mechanic for the state of the warning light rather than have the user interface software check the fuel level and decide for itself whether to turn on the warning light. Professionals keep the mechanics in one part of the design and the UI in another. That way, the UI designer won't have to worry about underlying mechanics; she can concentrate on screen layouts and usability considerations, and if you want to adjust the point at which the light comes on during the tuning stage of design, you can do so without interfering with the user interface itself.

Mechanics

Mechanics document how the game world and everything in it will behave. Mechanics state the relationships among entities, the events and processes that take place among the resources and entities of the game, and the conditions that trigger events and processes. The mechanics describe the overall rules of the game but also the behavior of particular entities, from something as simple as a light switch up to the AI of a very smart NPC.

A *global mechanic* is a mechanic that operates throughout the game. Other mechanics may apply only in particular gameplay modes and not in others. Any game with more than one gameplay mode will need at least one global mechanic governing the change from mode to mode.

Relationships Among Entities   If the value of one entity depends upon the value or state of another entity (or other entities), you need to specify the *relationship* between the entities involved. In the case of numeric entities, you express the relationship mathematically. Many role-playing games, for example, define character levels in terms of experience points earned; when a character earns a certain amount of experience, his level goes up. The formula may be given by a simple equation, such as *character level = experience points ÷ 1,000,* or a more complicated equation, or it may require looking the value up in a table. If the nature of this relationship remains constant throughout the game, you need not worry about specifying *when* it should actually be computed; let the programmers decide that. Just specify the relationship itself.

Events and Processes   When you describe an event or a process, you state that *something happens:* A change occurs among, or to, the entities specified in the mechanics.

An *event* is a specific change that happens once when triggered by a *condition* (defined in the next section) and doesn't happen again until triggered again. "When the player picks up a golden egg" specifies a trigger condition, and "he gets two points" defines an event.

A *process* refers to a sequence of activities that, once initiated, continues until stopped. A player action or other game action starts a process that runs until something stops it.

Both events and processes may consist of whole sequences of actions that the computer must take. When you document such a sequence, be clear about the order in which things should happen. Part of the sequence *getting dressed* might be, "First put on socks, then put on shoes." If you leave the language ambiguous and the programmer misinterprets your meaning, you will introduce a bug into the game.

Designing the core mechanics requires the greatest clarity and precision of language. Ambiguous mechanics turn into buggy code.

Conditions   Use conditions to define what causes an event to occur and what causes a process to start or stop. Conditional statements often take the form *if* (condition) *then* (execute an event, or start or stop a process); *whenever* (condition) *take action to* (execute an event, or start or stop a process); and *continue* (a process) *until* (condition). Mechanics defining victory and loss conditions conform to this style.

You can also define conditions in negative terms, such as *if* (condition) *then do not* (execute an event, or start or stop a process), although a condition in this form is incomplete. "If the mouse is wearing its cat disguise, the cat won't attack it," doesn't provide enough information because it doesn't tell the programmers when the cat *does* attack the mouse. Use this form of conditional mechanic for indicating exceptions to more general rules already specified: "When a cat sees a mouse, the cat will attack it. But if the mouse is wearing its cat disguise, the cat won't attack it."

Entities with Their Own Mechanics   Some mechanics define the behavior of only one type of entity and nothing else in the game, in which case you should figure out the details and document the entity and its associated exclusive mechanics together. This will make it easier for the programmers to build the game and for you to find the documentation if you need to change something.

Examples of entities with their own mechanics include symbolic entities that require special mechanics to indicate how they change state; numeric entities whose values are computed from other entities by a formula; nonplayer characters with AI-controlled behavior (the AI definition consists of mechanics); and entities that act autonomously even if their behavior doesn't really qualify as artificial intelligence, such as a trap that triggers whenever a character comes near. In the case of a triggered trap, you would define its various attributes, both functional and cosmetic, and a set of mechanics that indicate exactly what sets it off and what kind of damage it does to the character who triggers it.

IN THE TRENCHES: Analyzing a Mechanic

Let's go back to the sample mechanic we introduced in Chapter 2, "Design Components and Processes," and identify its various components. To specify the idea, "Dragons should protect their eggs," we designed a mechanic that reads as follows: "Whenever they have eggs in their nests, female dragons will not move out of visual range of the nest. If an enemy approaches within 50-meters of the nest, the dragon will abandon any other activity and return to the nest to defend the eggs. She will not leave the nest until no enemy has been within the 50-meter radius for at least 30 seconds. She will defend the eggs to her death."

This mechanic makes up one small part of the specification of a female dragon's artificial intelligence. It applies to all female dragons at any time, so it belongs in the core mechanics, not in the design of a level. (Although if dragons appeared in only one level, this mechanic could be part of that level's design, and if the dragon were a unique entity, mechanics relating to its behavior would be specified along with its definition and appear nowhere else.)

Here's how this mechanic looks with the components identified:

"*Whenever* they have *eggs* in their *nests* (a condition about a relationship between a resource, eggs, and an entity, the nest, such that *eggs in nest* > 0), *female dragons* (each one an entity) will not *move* (a process) *out of visual range of the nest* (a condition placed on the movement process). If an *enemy* (an entity) *comes within 50 meters of the nest* (a condition), the dragon will *abandon any other activity* (end her current process) and *return to the nest* (a process) to *defend the eggs* (a process). She will not *leave the nest* (initiate a process) until *no enemy has been within the 50 meter radius for at least 30 seconds* (a complicated condition that prevents her from initiating the process of leaving the nest). She will defend the eggs *to her death* (a condition indicating that the dragon will not initiate any other process while defending the eggs, such as running away)."

Even this, complex as it is, isn't complete. It doesn't say whether or not eggs can be destroyed or removed from the nest and, if so, what the dragon will do about it. It doesn't state how *visual range* should be computed, how the dragon goes about returning to her nest, or what defending the eggs actually consists of. It also includes a negative condition ("she will not leave the nest until . . . ") without a general rule stating when she *would* leave the nest in the first place. All that information must be included elsewhere in the definition of the dragon's AI and the definition of a nest and an egg. If you don't define these things specifically, the programmers will either come and ask you to, or they will make a guess for themselves.

10

Numeric and Symbolic Relationships

Here we discuss the differences between the numeric and symbolic relationships and how you may combine them to achieve your design goals for the core mechanics.

Numeric Relationships   By a *numeric relationship,* we mean a relationship between entities defined in terms of numbers and arithmetic operations. For example, the statement "A bakery can bake 50 loaves of bread from one sack of flour and four buckets of water" specifies a numeric relationship between water, flour, and bread. Another example could be "The probability of an injury occurring to an athlete in a collision with another athlete is proportional to the weight difference between the two athletes and their relative speeds at the time of the collision." Although this second example leaves the precise details up to the programmer to decide, it does specify a numeric relationship: *Weights* and *speeds*, both numeric attributes of the athletes, go into computing the *probability of an injury,* a numeric entity. (Remember that an attribute is just an entity that belongs to another entity.)

Defining numeric relationships precisely requires some familiarity with algebra and arithmetic. First, you must ensure that you use meaningful equations; if you write that the *speed the convoy will travel* is in part a function of the quantity defined by (*the weight of supplies*) ÷ (*number of pack horses – number of camp followers*), you may very well end up with a divide-by-zero error. Because the resulting value interacts with other parts of the mechanics, changes in the way you calculate that value will have a domino effect, ultimately influencing the gameplay itself, and you must be able to understand and predict these effects. Chris Crawford's *Balance of Power: International Politics as the Ultimate Global Game* (Crawford, 1986) remains one of the best books ever written on numeric relationships in the core mechanics. Although it is out of print, used copies are still available from online bookstores.

Numeric relationships lie at the heart of internal economies, and we discuss them further in *The Internal Economy,* later in the chapter.

Symbolic Relationships   The values of symbolic entities—*red, on, empty, found,* and the like—cannot be added together or otherwise manipulated mathematically. You must specify all the states that a symbolic entity may represent, and the relationships among them, without equations. For instance, the *red, yellow,* and *green* states of a traffic light are not related to each other numerically; they're simply different. To use a traffic light, you must document how it gets into each of its possible states and how the light being in each of those states affects the behavior of *other* entities. To define the behavior of an NPC driver who sees a traffic light, you would write three separate mechanics into his AI; one for each state of the light, to say how the driver reacts to seeing a red light, a yellow light, or a green light. When any entity in the game (such as a driver) interacts with a symbolic entity (such as a traffic light), you must state exactly what happens for each possible symbolic state of the entity. If you leave one state out, no interaction will occur.

A binary (two-state) entity is sometimes called a *flag.* You will often create flags in your game to document whether the avatar has entered locations, overcome specific obstacles, and so on.

We don't discuss symbolic relationships much further in this chapter because they are relatively easier to define and their results are easier to predict; numeric relationships provide more of a challenge. Although it is possible to create extremely complicated symbolic relationships (think about Rubik's Cube), most of the symbolic relationships in games tend to be rather simple.

> **KEY POINT**
>
> The values of numeric entities may change according to arithmetic processes, but you must create mechanics that explicitly change symbolic entities from state to state.

Integrating Symbolic and Numeric Relationships   Although you cannot perform arithmetic operations on symbolic values, you can define how symbolic entities change from state to state in terms of other numeric data. If the symbolic entity *fuel warning* can take the values *on* and *off,* you can define a mechanic for each of the states based on the quantity of fuel available: "When the amount of fuel goes below 2 gallons, the *fuel warning* value switches to *on.* When the amount of fuel rises to 2 gallons or more, the *fuel warning* value switches to *off.*"

You can also use symbolic entities to control mathematical operations on other numeric entities. In a vehicle simulation, the state of the transmission is symbolic; the transmission is either in one gear or another, and you can't add gears together. But the symbolic state of the transmission defines the mathematical ratio between the speed of the incoming driveshaft from the engine and the speed of the outgoing driveshaft to the rear axle. For each gear (symbolic state of the transmission), you must create a mechanic that states the input to output ratio that it produces, such as, "In first gear, the ratio is 3.83 to 1. In second gear, the ratio is 2.01 to 1. In third gear, the ratio is 1.46 to 1," and so on.

10

The Internal Economy

An *economy* is a system in which resources and entities are produced, consumed, and exchanged in quantifiable amounts. Most games have an internal economy, though the complexity and importance of the internal economy varies considerably from genre to genre. You can find further discussion of internal economies in Chapter 18, "Construction and Management Simulations."

A game designer spends part of her time designing and tuning her game's economy, and the more complex the economy, the more time she will need to spend. This section introduces aspects of an internal economy, which we explain by reference to both a simple action game (a shooter) and a complex game (a construction and management simulation).

IN THE TRENCHES: Mechanics Outside of the Internal Economy

The internal economy of a game includes those resources and mechanics that the player knows about and tries to manipulate. These include data that may be displayed by the user interface or that form part of the victory and loss conditions. Designers generally do not consider those mechanics over which the player exerts no control to be part of the internal economy. The mechanics that define the AI of nonplayer characters, for example, make up part of the core mechanics but not part of the internal economy of the game.

A mechanic governing avatar and vehicle movement may or may not be considered part of the internal economy, depending on whether movement produces or consumes any resource. A serious car racing simulation treats fuel as a resource that the engine converts to kinetic energy (another resource) as the engine drives the car forward. The brakes consume kinetic energy, slowing the car down, and this wears out the brakes. Only the most realistic racing games bother to simulate fuel consumption, kinetic energy, or brake wear, and in those games, such factors can legitimately be considered part of the internal economy. Less sophisticated vehicle simulations make the vehicle stop and go at the player's command without incorporating any concept of resource production or consumption. Similarly, in most games featuring a humanoid avatar, the avatar can walk, climb, jump, and fight indefinitely without ever needing food; these processes do not consume anything. For the most part, then, the mechanics of movement don't form part of a game's internal economy unless the physics simulation is sophisticated enough to justify its inclusion.

Sources

If a resource or entity can come into the game world, having not been there before, the mechanic by which it arrives is called a *source.*

In a simple shooter, the game begins with some resources, such as ammunition or enemies, already in the game world, but more resources may appear at *spawn points,* designated locations where the core mechanics insert new resources into the game world and therefore into the economy. Players commonly associate spawn points with the appearance of monsters, and indeed, monsters are part of the economy, being produced at spawn points and consumed by conflict with the avatar. Each spawn point is governed by a mechanic that specifies its location, what kind of resource it generates, and at what frequency. Industry professionals sometimes refer to locations at which new resources appear—a spawn point, the square marked *Go* on a *Monopoly* board, or the like—as *sources,* but this is shorthand; they mean to refer to the mechanic that governs the generation of resources at a particular location.

Sources often produce resources automatically (or, at least, produce resources automatically once the player starts them going, for example, by building a factory). You will need to define a *production rate,* either fixed or variable, and different sources may produce the same resource at different rates. *The Settlers III* features a character called a forester, who plants saplings in the landscape at a rate defined by the mechanics governing his behavior. The mechanic also causes him to stop working when the area gets too full of trees.

Sources can be global mechanics: A mechanism that pays the player interest at regular intervals on the money he owns but cannot interact with anything else would be one example. Sources can also make up part of the mechanics governing the behavior of entities. The forester character in *The Settlers III* is an entity, a character in his own right.

Sources can be *limited* or *unlimited.* In *Monopoly,* the Go square constitutes an unlimited source—according to the rules, it can never run out of money. (If the bank runs low, the banker may make more money by writing on paper.) But the collection of houses and hotels stored in the bank is a limited source: Once the banker sells all the houses and hotels, no more may come into the game. The forester character in *The Settlers III* is also an unlimited source of saplings; he never runs out of saplings.

Drains

A ***drain*** is a mechanic that determines the consumption of resources—that is, a rule specifying how resources permanently drop out of the game (not to be confused with a *converter*, which we'll discuss next). In a shooter game, the player firing his weapon drains ammunition—that's what makes ammunition, a resource, disappear. Being hit by an enemy shot drains health points. Enemies drain out of the game by dying when their health points reach zero. The most common drain in a CMS is *decay*—ongoing damage to the player's constructions that the player must spend resources to reverse or repair. (Decay is also sometimes called entropy, although technically *entropy* refers to increasing disorder rather than loss of resources.) Typical decay mechanics look something like this: "Each section of road includes a numeric attribute indicating its level of decay as a percentage, with zero indicating that the section is new and 100 indicating that the section is fully decayed and impassable. Sections of roads begin to decay 3 months after construction ceases, and 3 percent is added to their level of decay every year, plus an additional 1 percent for every 100,000 car trips over the section in the course of that year. When decay reaches or exceeds 100 percent, the road section becomes impassable and it must be replaced."

Because resources are valuable, the player wants to know why a resource disappears from the world and what benefit compensates for its loss. In *Monopoly,* players get money from the bank by passing Go—in effect, for no reason at all— but whenever a player has to give money back to the bank, the game provides a reason: The player owes income tax, incurs a fine, or something similar. Players don't mind getting money for free, but when they have to spend it, they want to know why. Explain your drains.

Converters

A *converter* is a mechanic—and usually an entity, too—that turns one or more resources into another type of resource. In designing a converter, you must specify its production rate and the input-to-output ratio that governs the relationship of resources consumed to resources produced. *The Settlers III* offers several examples. The windmill converts grain into flour at a rate of one to one, so one bag of grain produces one bag of flour. It takes 20 real-time seconds to turn one bag of grain into one bag of flour, so the rate of production of flour works out to three bags per minute. The iron smelter turns one load of ore into one iron bar, consuming one load of coal in the process. However, if fed charcoal instead of coal, the smelter requires three loads of charcoal for each iron bar because charcoal is less efficient than coal.

Traders

A *trader* mechanic governs trades of goods, generally between the player and the game. In a stock-trading game, the trader may be a faceless financial construct; in a role-playing game, the trader usually comes in the form of a blacksmith who trades in swords or something similar.

Traders cause no change in the game world other than reassignment of ownership. If you trade your old dirk and a gold coin for a new short sword, then in theory the game still contains that dirk, that coin, and that short sword, although all three articles have been assigned to new owners. The trader could, if your game permits it, sell the old dirk to the next player who comes along. (Note that this makes traders different from converters. A converter that produces new short swords from old dirks consumes the dirks in the process.)

You can also build a bargaining feature into the mechanics of a trader, such that it sells at a high price but can, via a user interface mechanism designed for the purpose, lower its price after a little haggling. Your scheme might make some traders more flexible than others, thereby encouraging players to shop around for the best deal.

FYI   *The Problem of Runaway Profits*

A player must never be able to repeatedly buy an item from a trader at a low price and sell it back at a higher price unless you set limits on the process. If players can buy from and sell to traders indefinitely and rapidly and they can sell something for more than they paid for it, they will exploit this ruthlessly, piling up huge fortunes by endlessly buying and reselling and ignoring the rest of the game.

You can use various schemes to prevent this. You can make it impossible to make a profit by requiring all subsequent sales to be for less than the original purchase price. If you want players to be able to make a reasonable profit, place limits on the amount of buying and selling they can do: Require that they wait a while before selling an item back again, or have the trader refuse to sell items to them more than a certain number of times or refuse to buy goods back. The trader itself can have limited funds and be unable to buy if funds run out. In a multiplayer game, you can let players buy and sell at a profit to one another but not to an automated or NPC trader. Transactions among the players don't change the total amount of money in the game; it's selling things back to a trader who has an unlimited supply of money that has the potential for abuse.

Production Mechanisms

Production mechanism describes a class of mechanics that make a resource conveniently available to a player. These include sources that bring the resource directly into the player's hands, but they can also include special buildings, characters, or other facilities that gather resources from the landscape and make them available to the player. Many real-time strategy games employ special characters to perform this function. For instance, in the *Command & Conquer* series, a harvester vehicle collects a resource called tiberium and carries it to a refinery where it is converted into money that the player can use to buy weapons. The harvester is a production mechanism; the refinery is a converter.

Tangible and Intangible Resources

If a resource possesses physical properties within the game world, such as requiring storage space or transportation, the resource is said to be *tangible*. On the other hand, if it occupies no physical space and does not have to be transported, it is *intangible*. In a shooter game, ammunition is tangible—it exists in physical form in the environment, and the avatar has to carry it around. Most construction and management simulations treat money as intangible: it exists as a meaningful resource in the game world but takes up no space and has no particular location.

A number of games treat resources in a mixed fashion, sometimes tangible and sometimes intangible. In *Age of Empires,* food and building materials had to be transported from their production points to a storage facility; during transport, these items could be stolen or destroyed by an enemy. Once stored, however, materials became intangible: They could not be seized or destroyed even if the enemy demolished the storage facility.

Similarly, most construction and management simulations and real-time strategy games don't require a resource to be physically transported before it can be spent or consumed; the commodity simply vanishes. When constructing a building in *Age of Empires,* the player doesn't transport the stone from the storage pit to the construction site. This takes an extra management burden off the player. We discuss the gameplay implications of intangible resources at greater length in the section *Logistics* in Chapter 14, "Strategy Games."

Feedback Loops, Mutual Dependencies, and Deadlocks

A production mechanism that requires some of the resource that the mechanism itself produces constitutes a ***feedback loop*** in the production process. (Note that this use of the term *feedback* is not related to the feedback elements we discussed in Chapter 8, "Creating the User Experience." In the context of a user interface, *feedback* refers to a means of giving the player information about the effects of his actions upon the game world. In the context of an internal economy, *feedback* refers to resources that are *fed back* into a production mechanism.)

So long as the mechanism has a supply of the resource to start with and the mechanism produces more than it requires, there's nothing wrong with this. But if for any reason the system runs out of the resource, the mechanism won't be able to produce any more. This condition, called a ***deadlock,*** locks up that part of the economy unless you provide some other supply of the resource—a way to *break the deadlock.*

The Settlers III contained a feedback loop. The player requires stone to build a stonecutter's hut, in order to house a stonecutter who produces more stone (see Figure 10.3). Ordinarily, the game starts with some stone already in storage, so if the player builds a stonecutter's hut right away, the stonecutter will produce the stone needed for other activities. However, if the player uses up all her stored stone constructing other buildings, she might not have enough to build a stonecutter's hut, and she will be in a deadlock—hut building can't proceed without stones; stones can't be produced without a hut. *The Settlers III* provides a way to break the deadlock: The player can demolish another building and get back enough raw stone to build a stonecutter's hut

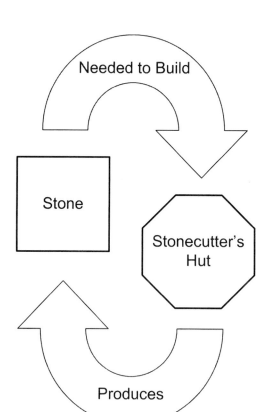

FIGURE 10.3 The feedback loop in
The Settlers III.

after all. Note that the stonecutter's hut doesn't actually need stone to
operate, but the player does need stone to build it in the first place. As long
as the player builds and retains one stonecutter's hut, she shouldn't get into a
deadlock.

Two production mechanisms that each require the other's output as their
input in order to work are ***mutually dependent.*** Again, there's a loop in the
process. If the resources produced by either one are diverted elsewhere and production stops for lack of input, this, too, can produce a deadlock.

In designing your game's internal economy, you need to watch out for
deadlocks, which can occur whenever there's a loop in the production process.
To avoid deadlocks, either avoid such loops or provide an alternative source for
one of the resources. This is the point of collecting $200 when you pass Go in
Monopoly. A player who owns no properties can't earn money by collecting
rent, but without rent, the player can't buy properties: a deadlock. *Monopoly*
solves this by giving the players money to start with and by giving them $200
every time they pass Go. As the game progresses, that $200 becomes less
significant, but it is enough to break a deadlock.

10

COMMANDMENT: Provide Means to Break Deadlocks

If your internal economy contains either feedback loops or mutual dependencies, be sure you include a means to break a deadlock if one occurs.

Static and Dynamic Equilibrium

It's possible to design a system in such a way that, left alone, it enters a state of equilibrium. Static equilibrium is a state in which the amounts of resources produced and consumed remains constantly the same: Resources flow steadily around without any significant change anywhere. Dynamic equilibrium occurs when the system fluctuates through a cycle. It's constantly changing, but it eventually returns to a starting point and begins again. (We use these terms as they are defined in economics, not in physics. In physics, static equilibrium means all forces on an object are equally balanced, so the object does not move. In economics, it means that supply and demand for goods are balanced, and although the goods themselves move, the amounts do not change.)

Here's an example of static equilibrium. Suppose you have a miller grinding wheat to make flour and a baker baking bread from the flour. If the bakery consumes the flour at exactly the same rate at which the mill produces it, then the amount of flour in the world at any one time will remain static. If we then upset the system by stopping the bakery for a while, the flour will build up. When the bakery restarts, the amount of flour available will be static at the new level. The system returns to static equilibrium because the key factors—the production and consumption rates of the mill and the bakery—have not changed (see Figure 10.4).

Now let's suppose that there is only one person to do both jobs. She mills enough to bake three loaves of bread; then she bakes the three loaves; then she mills again; and so on. This is an example of dynamic equilibrium: Conditions are changing all the time, but they always return to the same state after a while because the process is cyclic. If we tell the woman to stop baking and only mill for a while, and then resume baking later, again the flour builds up. When she resumes baking, the system settles into a new state of dynamic equilibrium (see Figure 10.5).

When a game such as a construction and management simulation settles into a static equilibrium, players can easily judge the effect of their actions on the system by making one small change and watching the results. This makes the game easy to learn and play. Dynamic equilibrium is more difficult for players to handle. With the system in constant flux, it's hard to tell whether the changes players see result from a natural process or from something they've done. We have a similar problem making ecological decisions about our planet. For many years, people

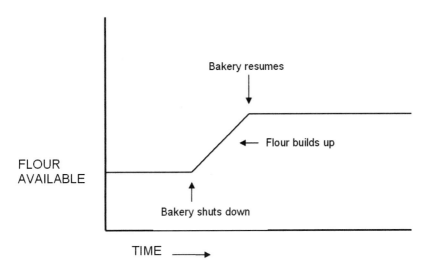

Static Equilibrium

FIGURE 10.4 An example of static equilibrium.

believed that the environment should be in a state of static equilibrium (in the economic sense)—that there should always be exactly enough plants for the herbivores and exactly enough herbivores for the carnivores, and any deviation from this was caused by environmental mismanagement. More recently, we've come to realize that sizes of animal populations fluctuate naturally and that big changes do not necessarily result from human actions; such changes can occur in the ordinary course of events. This makes environmental management all the more difficult.

Settling into a state of equilibrium, static or dynamic, takes the pressure off the player. She can simply watch the game run for a while and make adjustments

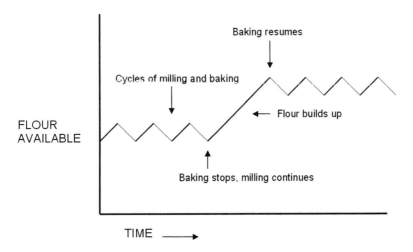

Dynamic Equilibrium

FIGURE 10.5 A new state of dynamic equilibrium.

10

when she feels like it. Some construction and management simulations do work that way, but most give the player more of a challenge. Rather than settling into equilibrium, the designers build in a factor that requires the player to take action to prevent the system from running out of some needed resource. To use our milling–baking metaphor, perhaps the player has to take action to keep the mill supplied with wheat. If the player doesn't keep an eye on the wheat supply, both milling and baking come to a halt. In *Age of Empires,* farms produce food automatically, but after a while they stop working and the player must intervene to rebuild them.

Whether your system settles into equilibrium or runs down without player action, one thing is certain: The player should always have to do something to obtain growth—he should have to press on the gas pedal of your game, as it were. If the system can grow constructively and profitably of its own accord, there's no reason for the player to interfere. This is the player's primary challenge: figuring out how to produce growth using the many (metaphorical) levers and knobs that you provide via the core mechanics. In effect, the player is himself an element of the economy, and growth should be dependent on his active participation.

Core Mechanics and Gameplay

Figure 10.1 shows that, during play, the core mechanics present challenges to the player and accept actions from the player, both mediated by the user interface. So far, our discussion has concentrated on the core mechanics as a description of a system, without addressing the role of the player. The core mechanics manage the gameplay of the game, implementing all player actions and many challenges; in this section, we discuss how that works.

Challenges and the Core Mechanics

The core mechanics implement the mechanisms by which most challenges operate and perform tests to see whether a challenge has been surmounted. The challenges that the core mechanics present may appear at any level of the challenge hierarchy, from atomic challenges to the victory condition for the entire game. Remember that the level design actually specifies the type and placement of individual challenges for each level, but the core mechanics implement challenges, if necessary, when the player encounters them.

Passive Challenges   Suppose the level designers want to set up a purely static obstacle as a challenge, such as a wall that the avatar must climb over in an action game. You would not need to create an entity to represent the wall or a mechanic to present the challenge itself; the wall would simply be an unchanging feature of the landscape. The mechanics play a role in implementing the action the player takes to meet the challenge (climbing) but play no role in presenting the challenge itself. We designate this type of challenge a *passive challenge*.

If the level designers need to detect that a player has conquered a passive challenge (in order to give a reward, perhaps), they will design a special event that occurs when the avatar arrives on the other side of the wall—that is, when the avatar's location attributes meet a condition that the level designers establish. Otherwise, the player's presence on the other side implies success, which doesn't require any special mechanics.

Active Challenges   Suppose that the level designers want to set up a more complex challenge for the player, such as a puzzle that the player manipulates to unlock a door. Your design for the core mechanics must supply the level designers with the necessary entities and mechanics to define the puzzle, allow the player to interact with it, display the consequences of her actions, and detect when the puzzle has reached its solution state. This type of challenge we call an *active challenge*.

An enemy character that the player must defeat in combat represents another active challenge. The core mechanics define the characteristics and the AI of the enemy character. The level designers will place that character at a location in the landscape by setting his location attributes and perhaps will also set some other attributes, such as health and ammunition. In effect, your design creates the tools and parts that the level designers will use to build levels, create puzzles, position enemies, and so on. In a long game, the level designers will probably reuse the same tools several times to create variants of the same challenge in different parts of the game. (This is one of the reasons why the same characters seem to appear over and over in a game: The level designers reuse the basic mechanics.)

Actions and the Core Mechanics

The challenges in a game vary from level to level in type, frequency, sequence, and other respects, but the actions available to the player normally do not change from level to level except that, in some games, more actions become available as the player progresses through the game. Consequently, the level designers play a smaller role in determining what actions will be available than they do in choosing challenges for a level, though they can choose challenges that tend to require the use of some actions more than others. (Sometimes level designers also specify that familiar actions should *not* be available. See *Make Atypical Levels Optional* in Chapter 12, "General Principles of Level Design.")

Player Actions Trigger Mechanics   When you design the core mechanics, you must specify a mechanic that implements each action in each gameplay mode, which will either initiate an event or start or stop a process. When the user interface detects data arriving from an input device, UI routines determine what action the player desires by checking the assignment of actions to buttons

> **KEY POINT**
> Passive challenges do not require mechanics to operate, though level designers may want to establish a condition to detect when the challenge has been surmounted.

> **KEY POINT**
> Active challenges require mechanics that implement their activity.

10

(or similar control devices) established by the gameplay mode's interaction model. The UI then triggers whatever mechanic you have specified for that action.

Let's look at a simple example from a first-person game. When a player presses a button assigned to the *crouch* action, the UI triggers a *crouch* mechanic that implements the action. You must define this mechanic to do two things. First, it changes a symbolic *posture* attribute of the avatar from the *walking upright* state to the *crouching* state. (This attribute may affect other mechanics—it could influence how big a target the crouching figure presents—but the *crouch* mechanic does not implement those effects itself.) Next, because all actions should be accompanied by feedback, your *crouch* mechanic lowers the value of a numeric attribute of the avatar that determines how far the avatar's head is above the ground. The graphics engine will detect this and show the first-person view from a crouching, rather than an upright, perspective.

Actions Accompanied by Data   More complicated actions may involve manipulation or storage of data that arrives from the user interface. In such cases, you must create both an event mechanic that implements the action and an entity that stores the data. The user interface will set the value of the entity for the mechanic to interpret.

Suppose that in our first-person game, the player uses a mouse to control which direction the avatar faces, and he moves the mouse to the right. This input translates into an action, causing the avatar to turn to the right. But a mouse is an analog device, not a binary one like a controller button, so in addition to the information that the mouse moved, the UI also sends data about how far it moved. This event requires a mechanic that must interpret the data and make the appropriate changes to the avatar's direction-facing attribute.

> **KEY POINT**
>
> Implement actions in the core mechanics by creating mechanics that the user interface can trigger and entities that the user interface can supply with data from the input devices.

Designing the Core Mechanics

Entia non sunt multiplicanda praeter necessitatem. (Do not create more entities than necessary.)

—Attributed to William of Occam

Designing the core mechanics consists of identifying the key entities and mechanics in the game and writing specifications to document the nature of the entities and the functioning of the mechanics. This is the very heart of the game designer's job, and the more complex the game, the longer it will take—sometimes weeks or months. Because there are so many kinds of games you can make, we can describe the process only in general terms. Use your knowledge of existing games and of your chosen genre to fill in the details.

Reading this chapter alone gives you the tools to document your core mechanics, but it doesn't contain the information necessary to create a balanced game. Don't start designing your mechanics until you have also read Chapter 11, "Game Balancing."

Goals of Core Mechanics Design

Before we start our discussion of how to go about designing the core mechanics, we want to remind you of what you are actually trying to achieve with your design. Never forget that your ultimate goal is to create entertainment for the player—that's the point of our quote from Molière at the beginning of the chapter. But in addition to this overarching objective, certain principles will help you to design an enjoyable game efficiently.

Strive for Simplicity and Elegance   The most elegant games operate from the smallest number of rules. Some of the greatest games are those whose mechanics are extremely simple yet still manage to offer interesting variety. As our quote from William of Occam suggests, try to avoid making your mechanics too complex. Simple games are easier for players to learn, and that gives simple games a broader appeal than complicated ones.

You can maintain players' interest with a variety of content that explains a small number of mechanics in a large number of ways. As we mentioned in *FYI: The Rules and Core Mechanics of* Monopoly, the general rules of *Monopoly* are simple, but the Chance and Community Chest cards create additional interest. The majority of these cards concern the transfer of money to or from the player who draws the card—a simple mechanic—but each card gives a different explanation for why the money is being transferred (such as "Income tax refund, collect $20"). The explanations are purely cosmetic, but they add variety. You can build similar features into your own game while still keeping the rules simple.

Look for Patterns, Then Generalize   Learn to recognize patterns in your ideas for your game and to convert them into generalized systems rather than trying to document dozens of individual cases. Here's an example. Suppose you decide that swamp leeches really belong in water and that a swamp leech should lose 10 points of health for every minute that it's out of the water. Later, you decide that a salamander (a mythical fire-loving creature) should lose 5 points of health for every minute that it's out of the fire. A pattern emerges: Certain creatures are dependent upon their native environment, and they lose health at a specified rate when they leave it. Instead of describing this mechanic over and over for each creature, explain the general case only once, for all environment-dependent creatures. Note that each creature in the game will need two attributes to support this mechanic: a symbolic attribute indicating what the creature's native environment is (include a special value if the creature is not dependent on any environment), and a numeric attribute stating the rate at which the creature loses health when out of its environment (the value should be zero if the creature is not environment-dependent). Then, as you design each creature in your game,

10

you can decide what values these attributes should have without having to document the whole mechanism again.

By designing general patterns rather than individual cases, you can more easily understand how your game really works, and you will also make it easier for the programmers to program it. The programmers can write general-case code that applies most of the time, rather than having to write separate subroutines for each creature. You can still create a few special cases for variety or when circumstances require it. In *Monopoly,* the rules for collecting rent on colored properties (the ones named after streets) are the general case, while the railroads and utilities are special cases that create additional interest. But try to avoid creating large numbers of special cases.

Don't Try to Get Everything Perfect on Paper   Unless you're designing a trivially simple game, you won't get everything perfectly right on paper, because you won't be able to compute the effects of all your mechanics in your head. Designing core mechanics (and just about everything else in a video game, too) requires iterative refinement. Create a first draft of your mechanics and then build a prototype that implements them, either in a spreadsheet program or in software. Test and adjust your mechanics using the prototype. If you try to get everything exactly right on paper, you won't ever get the project finished. Although this may sound odd, it is more important to be clear and precise in your documentation than it is to be accurate. You will find it much easier to correct a mechanic that doesn't work quite the way you expected than to try to resolve ambiguous language late in the development process.

A Note about Level of Detail   You can design core mechanics at any level of detail, but there are tradeoffs. If you document the core mechanics minutely, with no detail left unaddressed, the programmers can turn your mechanics directly into code very quickly. That seems like a good idea in principle, but in practice you will almost certainly be swamped with work. Designers who try to document every single thing about the core mechanics delay their projects—or cause them to be canceled.

The problem at the opposite end of the spectrum, leaving too much unclear, is almost as bad. Either the programmers will have to come and ask you for further details, or they will make their best guess for themselves. If you have clearly communicated your vision to them, and you see eye to eye about how the game should work in principle, then their guesses may be good ones. But in practice, the programmers will often make assumptions other than what you intended, and you'll notice the mistake in the tuning phase. It can be time-consuming to go back and correct bugs introduced by ambiguous design decisions.

To find a happy medium, make use of traditional gaming conventions where appropriate to avoid overloading yourself. If your game features some very ordinary scenarios and you are confident that the programmers will know what you mean, you can afford to use general language. You don't have to write, "When a car's *number of laps* attribute goes over 500, set the *eligible to win* flag to TRUE for that car. Continuously check all cars to see if the *location* attributes of the cars that are eligible to win show that they are on or beyond the finish line. Set the *winner* entity with the number of the first car whose *location* attribute meets that condition." It's okay just to say, "The first car that has completed all 500 laps and crosses the finish line is the winner" because this is a perfectly familiar situation.

The less familiar the mechanisms that you document, the more specific you need to be, especially if any of them run counter to convention. In the dart game 301, the player *starts* with a score and *reduces* that score by the amount that he hits on the dartboard. The object of the game is to be the first to achieve a score of exactly zero. As this runs counter to convention, it's the sort of thing you have to explain more precisely. Similarly, the mechanic that describes the behavior of female dragons in *In Practice: Analyzing a Mechanic* earlier in the chapter requires more detail because female dragons are entirely imaginary; nobody can count on his existing experience with dragons to know how they should behave.

If you know how to program even a little bit, you can write *pseudo-code* to document processes that you need to explain extremely carefully. Pseudo-code includes the *if* and *while* statements that indicate conditional or repeated operations but without exact variable names or the other syntactic features of a real programming language. Pseudo-code can be handy in circumstances that call for precise explanations, which is why we encourage potential designers to take at least one class in programming. It doesn't much matter what language you study, as long as it includes the concepts of conditional and repeated execution.

Revisit Your Earlier Design Work

To begin designing the core mechanics, go back to your earlier design work and reread it with an eye to identifying entities and mechanics. Make a list of the nouns and verbs that you encounter. Whenever you come across a noun in your design documents, that noun will be probably be implemented in the core mechanics as an entity, a resource, or both. Whenever you see a verb, that action will probably be implemented as a mechanic. Also watch for sentences that include the words *if, when,* and *whenever.* These designate conditions that will become part of the mechanics.

Look particularly closely at the following items:

- **Your answers to the question, "What is the player going to do?"** The answers to this question give the player's role and some information about the challenges he will face and the actions he will perform. They will include some of the most critical nouns and verbs of all. Even if the answer is simply "fly an airplane," it contains the key verb for the whole game, *fly,* and the key noun, *airplane.*

- **Your flowboard of the game's structure.** Each gameplay mode and shell menu represents a separate state of the mechanics, so the mechanics will require a symbolic entity to keep track of the current gameplay mode during play.

■ **Your list of gameplay modes and your plans for them.** Be sure to pay special attention to the challenges and actions you plan to offer the player in each mode and any user interface feedback and control mechanisms you have specified.

■ **The general outline of the story you want to tell,** if any. If it's a branching or foldback story, look at the structure that you made for it. Take note of the circumstances that cause it to branch. You will convert these into conditions.

■ **The names of any characters** you planned for your story. Unless these characters only appear in narrative events, they will certainly be entities in the core mechanics.

■ **Your general plans for each level in the game.** Unless the level designers are already at work, you won't have specific details, but you will know what kinds of things you wanted to include in each level.

■ **The progression of the levels** that you want to provide, if the levels progress in a sequence. Note whether any information carries over from level to level; you will create entities to store the data.

■ **Any victory or loss conditions** that you expect to use (or that you anticipate the level designers will want to establish).

■ **Any non-gameplay actions** that you may wish to include, such as moving the virtual camera, pausing or saving the game, and other forms of creative play.

Certain nouns and verbs in this material may not apply to the core mechanics. If a noun describes a passive landscape feature that acts as a challenge or something purely cosmetic, you can cross it off your list. If a verb describes an activity unrelated to gameplay, such as setting the volume level of the sound effects, you can cross that off, too.

List Your Entities and Resources

Once you have your list of nouns, decide whether each represents a resource, an independent entity, an attribute of another entity—or perhaps none of the above, in which case, you can cross those off the list. Now you have a list of resources and entities. For each item on your list, consider these questions:

■ Does the noun describe a resource—some item or substance that changes in a general way throughout the game? Or does it describe an entity, a particular value or quantity?

- If the noun describes an entity, is the entity simple or compound? If simple, is it symbolic or numeric? If symbolic, what states can it take? If numeric, what is the range of numbers? What will its initial symbolic or numeric value be? These initial data form a critical part of the core mechanics that you will tune throughout the development process. Write them down in your document or in a spreadsheet.

- If the noun describes a compound entity, what attributes describe it? (They might be elsewhere on the list, or you might have to invent some new ones.) Add any new attributes to your definition of the compound entity and go back to the previous question to determine their qualities.

Unless a game offers only one gameplay mode and no shell menus (which would be extremely rare), it will undoubtedly require an entity to record which gameplay mode or shell menu the game occupies at any given time.

This process will give you an initial list of all the resources and entities your game features. It won't be a complete list; you will undoubtedly add more as work goes on. If your early design stated generalities but not specifics, add the details now. Suppose you wrote, "Level 5 will consist mostly of formal logic puzzles." At this point, you must define the entities that the level designers will require to build the formal logic puzzles. Will the player drag tiles, flip switches, and click on colored marbles? Then add tiles, switches, and marbles to your list of entities. Now you've got some attributes to think about: The tiles have positions, the switches have states, and the marbles have colors. Write it all down.

Add the Mechanics

With your list of entities and list of verbs, you're ready to start defining the mechanics. Again reread your earlier design work. If any sentence includes or implies the word *somehow,* now is the time to define exactly how. "The player gets money" or "gets money somehow" must turn into a precise specification of when the player's money entity increases and by what amount.

As you read, remember that mechanics consist of *relationships, events, processes,* and *conditions.*

Think about Your Resources   Start with any resources that you identified in the previous step and think about how they flow through the game. What sources bring them into the game? What drains remove them? Can they be traded or converted automatically into another resource? Every source, every drain, and every conversion requires mechanics that determine how a conversion operates, when, and at what rate. Also ask yourself what happens when the resource runs out. If nothing much changes, you may not need the resource. Because a resource is a general concept rather than a specific quantity like an entity, you may be able to determine a lot about a resource's mechanics just by thinking through the resource flow in the economy.

Remember that games that don't deal in numeric quantities don't have resources. Such games contain only symbolic entities.

Study Your Entities   Once you have a good grasp of your resources' sources, drains, and conversions, move on to your entities. Go down your list of entities and ask the following questions about each one:

- Does this entity store an amount of a resource, and if so, have I already documented how it works in the previous step?

- What events, processes, and relationships affect the entity? What conditions apply to these events, processes, and relationships?

- What events, processes, and relationships does the entity contribute to? What conditions apply to them?

- What can the entity do by itself, if anything? Any entity that can do something by itself—whether the entity is as simple as a detector or as complicated as an NPC—requires mechanics to define what it does and how.

- What can the player do *to* the entity, if anything? If the player can manipulate the entity, he requires an action to do so, and actions require mechanics.

- Is this a symbolic entity? If so, it requires mechanics to control how the entity gets into each of its possible states.

Many of the verbs in your list of verbs will be associated with particular entities, so as you examine an entity, check to see which verbs apply to it and what mechanics they imply.

Analyze Challenges and Actions   Go over the list of challenges and actions that you intend to offer in each gameplay mode. All the active challenges and each action must have an associated mechanic and possibly some associated data. (If it requires data, you should already have an entity defined for it.) How does the action affect the world? How does the challenge affect the avatar or the other entities under the player's control? Use the answers to these questions to document your mechanics.

Look for Global Mechanics   Global mechanics operate all the time, regardless of what gameplay mode or level the game may be in. Global mechanics include those that implement actions such as pausing the game or, if the player can win or lose in more than one gameplay mode or level, detecting the victory or loss conditions. (In many games, the level designers specify a different victory condition for each level, but the loss conditions—such as running out of money or health—remain the same in every level.) Go down your list of verbs and see how many of them describe global mechanics, and then define how each of them works.

Random Numbers and the Gaussian Curve

So many games make use of random numbers that, although you may not know any programming, you should understand how to use random numbers in a computer game.

When a computer generates random numbers, by convention it always does so as a real number value greater than or equal to 0 but less than 1. In statistical calculations, probabilities are always expressed as a fractional value between 0 and 1, so an event with *a probability of 0.1* has 1 chance in 10, or 10 percent, of occurring. To see if an event with a given probability occurs, the computer generates a random number, then checks to see if the random number is less than the event's probability. If so, the event happens. The random number will always be less than 1, so if an event's probability is exactly 1, the event always happens. The random number will never be less than 0, so if an event's probability is 0, it will never happen.

In the *Numeric Attributes* section of Chapter 14, "Strategy Games," we discuss a number of ways to use random numbers when computing things such as whether a weapon hits the point at which it's aimed. A weapon with an accuracy rating of 0.8 hits its mark 80 percent of the time. To see whether a particular shot hits, generate a random number and compare the number to the weapon's accuracy rating. If the random number is less than the rating, the weapon hits.

Pseudo-Random Numbers

Random-number generation algorithms normally take an input value, called a *seed,* that determines the sequence of random numbers the algorithm produces. If the seed is identical each time the game is played, the sequence of random numbers that the algorithm generates will be identical each time, too. In other words, it's as if each time you played a board game, you got the exact same sequence of die rolls that you got the last time you played. Each roll is different from the previous roll, but the sequence of rolls is identical. Such numbers are called *pseudo-random*.

This feature is extremely useful when tuning the game's mechanics. When you make adjustments to the mechanics, it can be difficult to determine what the effect of your change was if the operation of chance keeps changing the game. By using the same seed each time you play, you always get the same random numbers, so the effects of chance don't change from one playing to the next. The mechanics become *deterministic* and predictable. This quality is also essential for bug-fixing. If a bug happens by chance, it might not happen the next time someone plays the game, so the programmer won't be able to find it and fix it. If the game uses pseudo-random numbers, the bug should be easier to reproduce.

Naturally, in the final version of the game that the customer buys, you won't want the effects of chance to be the same on each play through. Just before the game is ready to ship, the programmers will change the code to take

10

the seed from some random source, such as the system clock, so the player will get a different experience each time he plays.

Uniform Distribution

When a computer generates a random number, it ordinarily does so with a *uniform distribution*. That means the chance of getting any one number exactly equals the chance of getting any other number. It's like rolling a single die: There's an equal chance that a die will land on any one of its faces. That is exactly the behavior you will want whenever you ask the computer to choose among a certain number of equally probable options. For example, if you specify that four possible answers in a multiple-choice quiz game should be presented to the player in a random order, you'll want the possibilities to be mixed up so that each answer has an equal chance of being presented first, second, third, or fourth.

You can create a uniformly distributed die roll value by the following formula (and discarding any digits after the decimal point in the result):

Die Roll = (Random number × Number of faces on the die) + 1

Nonuniform Distribution

In other circumstances, you may not want the random values to be evenly distributed but may instead want some values to occur frequently and others to occur only rarely. Suppose you're doing a game about Olympic archery. The player will compete against an artificial opponent, and you want to use a random number to decide where the artificial opponent's arrow lands. At the Olympics, the chances that an archer will hit the bull's-eye are pretty high. The chances that he'll miss the target entirely are extremely low. In specifying where the arrow lands, you won't want it to be uniformly distributed across the target, but to have a better chance of landing in the middle than anywhere else.

One of the simplest ways to achieve this result is to generate more than one uniformly distributed random number (that is, roll several dice) and add the resulting numbers together to give you a value. This does not yield a uniform distribution of values; the values will tend to cluster around a central point, with few values at the extremes.

Here's an example. We all know that if you roll two six-sided dice and add them together, the chances of rolling a 7 are much higher than the chance of rolling a 2 or a 12. But how much higher? As you design the core mechanics of your game, this is something you'll need to know.

Rolling two six-sided dice and adding the results can produce any of 11 possible values, from 2 (two 1s) to 12 (two 6s). Of 36 possible combinations of two six-sided dice, only one combination yields a 2: throwing two 1s. On the other hand, there are six possible ways to get a 7: 1 + 6, 2 + 5, 3 + 4, 4 + 3, 5 + 2, and 6 + 1. So when you roll two six-sided dice, you're six times as likely to roll a 7 as you are to roll a 2.

The rules of *Dungeons & Dragons* specify that certain types of random numbers must be generated by rolling *three* six-sided dice and adding them together. With three dice, the chances are even higher that the result will be somewhere in the middle. There are 216 possible combinations, producing 12 possible values from 3 (1 + 1 + 1) to 18 (6 + 6 + 6). There are 27 ways to throw a 10 or an 11, but again, only one way to throw a 3 or an 18. In other words, you're 27 times as likely to roll a 10 as you are an 18.

The Gaussian Curve

When you add dice together like this, the probability of each possible result forms a bell-shaped, or *Gaussian,* curve, a phenomenon familiar to mathematicians. Figure 10.6 shows a graph of all the possible results when rolling three six-sided dice and adding the resulting numbers.

It's important that you realize what this means for your game. If you use this additive dice mechanism and you specify that a player must roll an 18 to succeed at a task, he has only one chance in 216 of actually rolling it. That's less than one-half of 1 percent. In other words, it will almost never happen. This system is *not the same* as rolling one die with 16 faces numbered from 3 to 18. With one such die, the chance of rolling an 18 is identical to the chance of rolling any other face, one in 16, or 6.25 percent. That's far more than one chance in 216.

These curves describe many phenomena in the universe, from the pattern of water droplets falling from a central point to the intelligence levels of animals

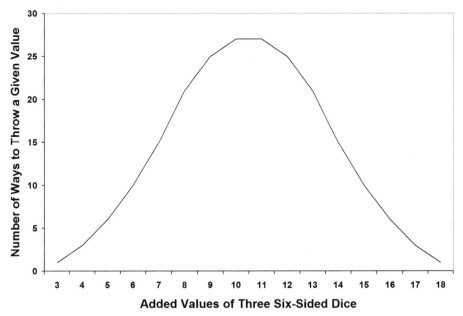

FIGURE 10.6 The Gaussian curve produced by rolling three six-sided dice and adding the resulting numbers.

(and humans). To put it succinctly, most things lie somewhere in the middle of the curve; rare things lie in the extremes. When that's the sort of effect you want in your game design, use a Gaussian distribution.

Summary

By now you should have a clear understanding of what core mechanics are and what they do in games. Mechanics consist of algorithms and data that govern the way the game is played, and we have shown you how to document them in the form of resources, simple and compound entities, and mechanics composed of events, processes, and conditions. We also explained the idea of an internal economy—a system whereby resources flow from place to place or from owner to owner, all governed by mechanics.

Be sure that you read Chapter 11, "Game Balancing," before starting to design your core mechanics.

Test Your Skills

MULTIPLE CHOICE QUESTIONS

1. Which of the following is *not* a way that you might work out core mechanics during the design and development process?

   A. Using ordinary language in a design document.

   B. Using a spreadsheet to organize algorithms and data.

   C. Using a paper prototype that allows you to play the game.

   D. None of the above.

2. During play, the core mechanics are responsible for

   A. customizing a player's avatar.

   B. controlling the relationship between input devices and game actions.

   C. controlling nonplayer characters and artificial opponents.

   D. all of the above.

3. Which of the following would be considered a resource rather than an entity?

   A. Ivory beads used as a medium of exchange.

   B. A forest of trees that an adventuring party passes through.

   C. A sword that confers increased strength to an avatar.

   D. A stream that marks a boundary between clan territories.

4. As you specified core mechanics for a biking simulation, you would have to create an entity for

A. the amount of water the avatar is carrying if the game allows the avatar to drink.

B. the bicycle.

C. the number of miles the avatar travels in a day.

D. all of the above.

5. A process is a(n)

A. specific change that happens once when triggered by a condition.

B. activity that, once initiated, continues until stopped.

C. sequence of conditions that the software must meet.

D. relationship between entities defined in terms of numbers.

6. A mechanic that determines the consumption of resources is a

A. source.

B. converter.

C. feedback loop.

D. drain.

7. A trader mechanic causes no change in the game world other than

A. turning one resource into another type of resource.

B. removing enemies from the game as they die.

C. reassignment of ownership.

D. generating resources at a specific location.

8. Which of the following situations constitutes a feedback loop?

A. You need a paved road on which to drive your trucks to the only plant that offers road-surfacing materials.

B. You need a fast-running stream to turn a mill wheel to grind wheat for bread.

C. As you lose troops in battle, you have to call up more troops from the reserves.

D. You can smelt more iron ore than your miners supply so you need to add another mining crew.

10

9. Which of the following represents an active challenge?

A. A ladder the avatar must climb.

B. A traffic light that can change from red to yellow to green.

C. A gate that the player must figure out how to unlock.

D. all of the above are active challenges.

10. In the case of a complicated action that involves manipulation or storage of data, you must create

    A. both the user interface and the level design.

    B. both an event mechanic for the action and an entity to store the data.

    C. both an event mechanic for the action and a drain to prevent deadlock.

    D. both an event to trigger the action and a resource to provide an entity.

11. Which of the following options is a way to document processes you need to explain carefully?

    A. Use a spreadsheet to record the attributes you're going to need.

    B. Hand your high concept document over to a programmer to be coded.

    C. Create a flowboard to track processes in the game.

    D. Use pseudo-code if you know it to detail conditional and repeated operations.

12. A noun in your design document can generally be implemented as a(n)

    A. mechanic.

    B. entity.

    C. drain.

    D. condition.

13. Which of the following is an example of a global mechanic?

    A. A mechanic that turns on a light when oil pressure is low in a racing car.

    B. A mechanic that lets an avatar flip a certain light switch in the game world.

    C. A mechanic that checks to see if time has run out in a football game.

    D. A mechanic that fires a weapon when the player presses a button.

14. To generate a random number with uniform distribution, you could use

    A. one six-sided die.

    B. one eight-sided die.

    C. two six-sided dice and add the displayed numbers.

    D. either A or B.

15. The significant feature of a Gaussian curve is that

    A. most values cluster in the center with few values at the extremes.

    B. most values display at the extremes with few values in the center.

    C. values are spread fairly evenly so the curve is relatively shallow.

    D. most values display in the negative portion of the curve.

EXERCISES

1. Devise and document the core mechanics for a traditional analog alarm clock. The alarm clock possesses the following indicators: an hour hand, a minute hand, a hand indicating the time at which the alarm should go off, and a buzzer. It also has the following input devices: a knob to set the time, a knob to set the time at which the alarm will go off, and a two-state switch that arms the alarm when the switch is in one position and cancels it in the other. (Assume that it is an electric clock and does not need to be wound.) Explain what entities are needed inside the clock, what processes operate within it, and what conditions and mechanics govern the functioning of the alarm. (You don't have to learn clock making; just explain the movement of the hands in terms of the passage of time.)

2. Research the history and rules of *Tetris* using the Internet, then perform the following exercises:

   a. Devise an entity that contains enough attributes to describe the tetromino (a *Tetris* block) that is currently under the player's control. Name each attribute in the entity; state whether it is symbolic or numeric; and if symbolic, list its possible values. Your entity should include one cosmetic attribute.

   b. Document the effect of each of the player actions allowed in *Tetris* on the attributes of the currently falling tetromino. Bear in mind that some actions have different effects depending on which tetromino is currently falling. Where this is the case, be sure to document the effects of the action on each different type of tetromino.

   c. Document one of the scoring systems for *Tetris* (there are several; you may choose one), indicating what condition of the play field causes the *score* numeric entity to change and by how much. Your mechanic for changing the score should include as a factor the current *game level* (another numeric entity). Also document what makes the current game-level entity change.

3. Using a real-time strategy game or construction and management simulation of your choice (or one that your instructor assigns), write a short paper describing its resources, sources, drains, converters, production mechanisms that are *not* sources (if any), and traders (if any). Note whether the game has any feedback loops or mutual dependencies; if so, indicate whether any mechanism exists to break a possible deadlock.

4. Define a mechanic for a trap that harms a character when it detects the character's presence and then must wait for a period before it can detect another character. Document the condition that triggers the trap (the nature of the sensing mechanism), the character attribute(s) that change when the trap is triggered, and the length of the reset wait period. Incorporate one or

10

more nonuniform random numbers to determine the amount of damage done and explain how they are computed. Indicate what states the trap may be in and what causes it to change from state to state. Most important, include a vulnerability or weakness in the sensing mechanism that could either (a) set off the trap without harming a character or (b) allow a character to move within range of the trap's sensor mechanism *without* setting it off. (For example, a pressure-sensor in the floor would not go off if the character weighed less than a certain amount.) Propose a means by which a clever player could exploit this weakness to avoid the trap.

DESIGN QUESTIONS

1. What entities and resources will be in the game? Which resources are made up of individual entities (such as a resource of airplanes consisting of individual planes that the computer can track separately) and which are described by mass nouns (such as water, which cannot be separated into discrete objects)?

2. What unique entities will be in the game?

3. Which entities will actually include other entities as part of their definition? (Remember that an avatar may have an inventory, and an inventory contains objects.)

4. What attributes describe each of the entities that you have identified? Which attributes are numeric and which are symbolic?

5. Which entities and resources will be tangible, and which will be intangible? Will any of them change from one state to another, like the resources in *Age of Empires*?

6. What mechanics govern the relationships among the entities? Remember that any symbolic entity requires mechanics that determine how it can get into each of its possible states and how other entities interact with each possible state. Which entities have their own mechanics connected only with themselves?

7. Are there any global mechanics in the game? What mechanic governs the way the game changes from mode to mode?

8. For each entity and resource, does it come into the game world at a source, or does it start off in a game world that does not provide a source for additional entities or resources? If it does come in at a source, what mechanics control the production rate of the source?

9. For each entity and resource, does it go out of the game world at a drain, or does it all remain in the game world and never leave? If it does go out at a drain, what conditions cause it to drain?

10. What conversion processes exist in your world? What trader processes exist? Do any feedback loops or mutual dependencies exist? What means have you provided to break or prevent deadlocks?

11. Can your game get into a state of equilibrium, static or dynamic? Does it include any form of decay or entropy that prevents states of equilibrium from forming?

12. How do mechanics create active challenges? Do you need to establish any mechanics to detect if a challenge has been surmounted?

13. How do mechanics implement actions? For each action that may arrive from the user interface, how do the core mechanics react?

14. For autonomous entities such as nonplayer characters, what mechanics control their behavior? What mechanics define their AI?

10

Chapter 11

Game Balancing

After reading this chapter and completing the exercises, you will be able to do the following:

- List qualities that characterize a balanced game.
- Define a dominant strategy and discuss ways to avoid dominant strategies in both player-versus-player and player-versus-environment games.
- Know how to use the element of chance in a game so that player skill still ultimately determines the outcome of the game.
- List strategies for making both symmetric and asymmetric player-versus-player games fair.
- List strategies for making player-versus-environment games fair.
- Understand types of difficulty and explain ways to manage difficulty to maximize the player's enjoyment of the game.
- Discuss the phenomenon of positive feedback and discuss ways to control positive feedback in the game.
- Recognize qualities of unbalanced games such as stagnation and triviality and explain how they can be avoided.
- List design methods that can make fine-tuning easier.

Introduction

To be enjoyable, a game must be balanced well—it must be neither too easy nor too hard, and it must feel as if it is fair, both to players competing against each other and to the individual player on his own. In this chapter, we introduce the various qualities that characterize a balanced game and what you must do to obtain them. We begin by addressing dominant strategies and how to avoid them, including means for setting up and balancing both transitive and intransitive relationships among player choices and ways of making them simultaneously interesting and well-balanced. We also discuss how to incorporate chance into games in such a way that the game still rewards the better player.

The bulk of the chapter examines two major issues of balance: fairness and difficulty. The meaning of *fairness* differs between player-versus-player and player-versus-environment games, and we address each separately. The question of difficulty applies primarily to player-versus-environment games, and we expand upon ideas introduced in Chapter 9, "Gameplay," explaining the various factors that affect the player's perception of difficulty and how to manage those factors.

Next we look at the role of positive feedback in games: how to use it and how to control it. Finally, we briefly discuss the problems of stagnation, trivialities, and how to design your game in order to make the tuning stage of the process easier.

What Is a Balanced Game?

So divinely is the world organized that every one of us, in our place and time, is in balance with everything else.

—Johann Wolfgang von Goethe

As with so many other game design concepts, the conventional notion of **balance** defies formalization. In the most general sense, a balanced game is fair to the player (or players), is neither too easy nor too hard, and makes the skill of the player the most important factor in determining his success. In practice, several different game features combine to produce these qualities, and game balancing refers to a collection of design and tuning processes that create those qualities in a game under development.

The concept of balance differs considerably depending upon whether we speak of games in which a player plays against one or more opponents (whether human players or artificial opponents implemented by software) or of games in which a player faces challenges posed by the game world, without an opponent. The first type of game, in which the player faces one or more opponents (even artificial ones), we call **player-versus-player (PvP)** games. We call the second type **player-versus-environment (PvE)** games. As we discuss issues of balance and techniques for balancing a game, we will note how they differ for PvP and PvE games.

A well-balanced game of either type, PvP or PvE, possesses the following characteristics:

- **The game provides meaningful choices.** If the game allows the player to choose from several possible strategies for approaching the game's challenges, no strategy should be so much more effective than the others that there is no point in ever using a different one. If such a **dominant strategy** exists, it indicates a poorly balanced game. When a game gives a player a choice of strategies, each strategy must have a reasonable chance of producing victory. We discuss dominant strategies in *Avoiding Dominant Strategies* later in the chapter.

- **The role of chance is not so great that player skill becomes irrelevant.** This does not mean that a player cannot have bad luck, but in the long run—over the course of a long game or over the course of many short games—a better player should be more successful than a poor one.

A well-balanced player-versus-player game also possesses the following qualities:

- **The players perceive the game to be fair.** As we explained in Chapter 1, "Games and Video Games," the exact meaning of fairness varies among different players. We address this further in *Making PvP Games Fair*.

- **Any player who falls behind early in the game gets a reasonable opportunity to catch up again before the game ends.** The definition of *early in the game* and *a reasonable opportunity* will vary depending on how long the designer expects a game to last. If a player falls behind in the first ten minutes of a two-hour game and the rules give him no chance of catching up, most players would perceive that game as unfair, and we would judge the game poorly balanced. Similarly, a game that the designer intends to last two hours but that someone invariably wins in fifteen minutes also gives other players no time to catch up or even to test their skill. These imbalances often indicate problems with positive feedback, a game feature that we discuss in *Understanding Positive Feedback* later in the chapter.

- **The game seldom or never results in a stalemate,** particularly among players of unequal ability. A stalemate disappoints players because their efforts produce no victor. If stalemates occur frequently among players of unequal ability, the game violates the principle that player skill should influence the outcome more than any other factor. Chess, though a well-balanced game, can still end in a stalemate, but this seldom happens between players of unequal ability. Other games, such as backgammon, make stalemates impossible. We address this in *Understanding Positive Feedback*.

In a well-balanced player-versus-environment game, these characteristics should be evident:

- **The player perceives the game to be fair.** In a PvE game, the player's perception of fairness involves a number of factors and is complicated by the absence of an opponent. We address these issues in *Making PvE Games Fair* later in the chapter.

- **The game's level of difficulty must be consistent.** The *perceived difficulty* of the game's challenges (described later) remains within a reasonable range so as not to surprise the player with abrupt jumps or drops. The perceived difficulty may be low or high but should not change suddenly, especially within a single game level. We discuss this in detail in *Managing Difficulty* later in the chapter.

Balancing a game consists of using the required design and tuning techniques to be certain the game exhibits these properties. We discuss these techniques in the remainder of the chapter.

Avoiding Dominant Strategies

A *strategy* is a plan for playing a game, usually according to a principle or approach that the player believes is likely to produce success. One player may favor an aggressive approach while another may depend on a defensive approach, for instance, but each thinks his strategy has the better chance of bringing victory. The term *dominant strategy,* which comes from formal game theory, refers to a strategy that reliably produces the best outcome a player may achieve, no matter what his opponent does. Dominant strategies are undesirable because once a player discovers one, he never has any reason to use any other strategy. It makes all other choices pointless and thus limits the fun the player can have with such a game. Still worse is a dominant strategy that one player may use but another player may not, which can occur in asymmetric games (discussed in *Balancing Asymmetric Games,* later in this chapter). When that occurs, the dominant strategy not only obviates other strategies, it makes the game unfair. Designing your game's mechanics to avoid a dominant strategy is, therefore, an essential part of game balancing.

Sometimes one single choice can be a dominant strategy, if that one choice gives the player enough of an advantage. In this section, we'll speak of player strategies, options, and choices interchangeably because any of these may be the cause of one strategy's dominating all others.

Strategies that avoid loss or prevent an opponent from scoring points can also qualify as dominant. Prior to 1955, a basketball team could use endless delaying tactics to kill time on the clock to preserve their lead—a dominant strategy because it prevented the other side from getting control of the ball and scoring. Leagues implemented the shot clock to force the team with possession in such situations to shoot the ball, thus creating more opportunities for their opponents to get it back.

Dominant Strategies in Video Games

Video games seldom permit players to use strategies so strongly dominant that they absolutely guarantee victory, although some, whether PvP or PvE games, allow powerful strategies that give the player little reason to use any other. By far the best-known dominant strategy in any PvP video game was the tank rush in Westwood's *Command & Conquer: Red Alert.* An experienced player playing as the Soviet side could devote all of her energies to producing a large force of tanks in the early part of the game, then use those tanks to attack the nascent enemy base en masse. Against an unprepared opponent, this almost always produced a victory; an experienced opponent could prepare for the onslaught, but the tank rush remained so effective that it took the fun out of the game. Many players added an additional rule to the game—no tank rushes allowed—just to balance this problem.

Several editions of *Madden NFL Football* included unstoppable offensive plays that guaranteed success against an AI-controlled opponent. Fighting games, too, are especially prone to dominant strategies. In both fighting games and football games, the large numbers of possible combinations of offensive and defensive actions makes it difficult to test them all. Badly designed characters can also result in dominant strategies; in *Super Street Fighter II Turbo,* the secret character Akuma's unbeatable attack, the air fireball, leaves the rest of the characters with no chance. Tournament matches ban the use of Akuma to ensure fair play.

In the next few sections, we discuss ways that dominant strategies can emerge in a video game and how to avoid them or remove them by use of balancing methods.

Handling Transitive Relationships among Player Options

The term *transitive* describes a relationship among three or more entities such that if A stands in a certain relationship to B and B stands in the same relationship to C, then A stands in the same relationship to C also. If you may correctly draw this conclusion, the relationship displays a property called *transitivity. Greater than* in arithmetic provides an example of a transitive relationship: If A is greater than B and B is greater than C, then A is greater than C.

If a transitive relationship exists among a player's strategic options, then option A is better than option B, and option B is better than option C. Why, then, would a player ever use option C? Selecting option A becomes a dominant strategy. To use a concrete example, if you design a game so that an aggressive strategy is always better than a defensive one and a defensive strategy is always better than a stealthy one, a smart player always chooses the aggressive strategy—it is superior to all the others.

To correct this imbalance, you may impose direct costs on using each strategy, costs that counteract the superiority of the stronger strategies and so give players a reason to consider the (formerly) weaker strategies as well. To draw an analogy, a lot of kids who would like to ride horses have to ride bikes instead because, even though horses are more fun to ride, they cost a lot of money.

Suppose you build a road-racing game in which players vie to earn the most prize money available over a series of races. You offer the player the chance to buy one of three cars made by three different manufacturers, such as

Ford, Dodge, and Chevrolet. To make this a meaningful choice, you decide to create some variety among the cars, such that the Ford is faster than the Dodge, and the Dodge is faster than the Chevrolet. If they all cost the same amount and their performance is identical in other ways, choosing the Ford constitutes a dominant strategy. However, if you price each car in proportion to its advantage, so that the Ford costs the most and the Chevrolet costs the least, the game regains balance. Because earning money, not merely winning races, secures victory, the financial disadvantage offsets the speed advantage of a fast car if you set the costs correctly.

Setting up direct costs that exactly counter the advantages of certain choices does balance the game, but such a clear and obvious balancing mechanism will produce a game that seems rather bland. The player can see that there's no real difference among the choices. To create a more interesting choice for the player, you can instead impose **shadow costs.** *Shadow cost,* a term from economic theory, refers to secondary, or hidden, costs that lie behind the apparent costs of goods or services. For our purposes, a shadow cost is one that the designer creates but doesn't warn the player about explicitly. It serves to balance the game without being blatant about the mechanisms. For instance, giving the Ford a smaller fuel tank that requires the car to stop to refuel more often in the road race could counter its speed advantage. The smaller fuel tank serves as a shadow cost that the player becomes aware of through repeated play.

You can hide a shadow cost completely by building it into the mechanics and not documenting it in the game's manual—for instance, not telling the players how big the fuel tanks in the cars are, so they have to find it out through trial and error. More often, a shadow cost is available to the player but not obvious so, continuing the same example, the player might be able to learn the sizes of the fuel tanks by comparing the numbers on the fuel gauges in each car, but the instructions for the game don't draw attention to it.

Players of PvE games often feel that entirely hidden shadow costs are unfair because the player cannot know what costs lurk behind the scenes or learn to compensate for them. For example, if a game reduces a character's accuracy at throwing a javelin in proportion to the weight of the character's backpack (on the theory that throwing a javelin while wearing a heavy backpack is bound to be rather uncertain) but never explains this to the player in the manual or anywhere else, the player can't learn to compensate for it. He finds that his accuracy worsens at times, but he can't understand why. If he does figure it out, he will probably cry foul and post a warning on an Internet gaming forum for the benefit of other players. A number of game publishers deliberately hide shadow costs from the players but reveal the costs in printed strategy guides that the player must pay extra for. We regard this as an abusive practice.

In practice, designers most often use transitive relationships to **upgrade** a player's powers during her progress through the game. The player begins with a single option, the weakest, and works her way up to better ones. In other words, she starts with the Chevrolet, then receives the Dodge as a reward for good

11

performance, and later still receives the Ford. This creates positive feedback, which we address in a later section. If you also make it possible for a player to *lose* her upgrade due to poor performance—going back to the Dodge after a bad performance in the Ford—you can create an interesting progression/regression dynamic that can lead to some taut and suspenseful gameplay. Take care to ensure that the player can reestablish her previous level once she does well again.

Intransitive Relationships (Rock-Paper-Scissors) If the relationship between strategies or other player options is *intransitive,* then just because A beats B and B beats C, you can't assume that A also beats C. Game professionals use *intransitive relationship* to mean not merely a lack of transitivity but an explicit loop in which option A beats option B, B beats C, and C beats A (see Figure 11.1). The game rock-paper-scissors (also called scissors-paper-stone and Rochambeau) works that way: Paper beats rock, rock beats scissors, scissors beat paper. This results in a balanced, three-way intransitive relationship (although intransitive relationships are not confined to systems of only three entities).

The rock-paper-scissors (or RPS) mechanism is a classic design technique for avoiding dominant strategies and forms the basis for balancing player strategies in many games. Designer David Sirlin has pointed out that *Virtua Fighter 3* includes RPS relationships among general types of moves available to the player: Attacking moves beat throwing moves, throwing moves beat blocking moves, and blocking moves beat attacking moves (Sirlin, 2000). *The Ancient Art of War,* an early example of a video game that included an RPS relationship,

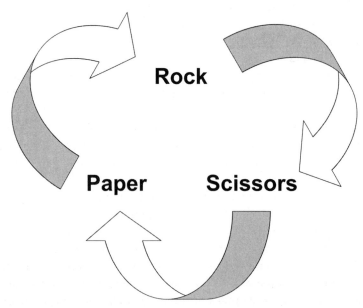

FIGURE 11.1 A three-way intransitive relationship, with arrows indicating which option beats another.

offered players three unit types: knights, archers, and barbarians. Knights had an advantage over barbarians, barbarians over archers, and archers over knights.

As we explain further in Chapter 14, "Strategy Games," a direct implementation of the RPS model without any modifications fails to meet the needs of modern war games due to its simplicity. It doesn't offer any interesting choices—there's no reason to choose any one unit or strategy over any of the others. However, as Sirlin points out, you can adjust the system to produce different benefits. If you give the player different amounts of money for winning with rock, paper, or scissors, players have to think not only about which object their opponent might choose but which choice earns the most money.

Now imagine a system in which instead of just allowing each choice to beat another in all circumstances, as in rock-paper-scissors, one choice is marginally better than others in some circumstances but not in others. You can make this adjustment in the core mechanics of your game, and it need not be a war game. For example, suppose you set up a race between a lizard, a frog, and a mouse. The lizard does best on rocky ground; the frog does best in swamps; and the mouse does best on grassy ground. If you design the mechanics such that these advantages remain slight rather than overwhelming, it will take a while for the players to learn about the system of advantages. Make the race course a complex mixture of rocks, grassland, and swamps, and give players partial but not total freedom over the routes they take. Add some shadow costs: The frog is generally slower than the others overall; the mouse has to stop for air every fifteen seconds while swimming; and the lizard slows down sharply at transitions between types of ground. If you set these values carefully, your game remains balanced, and players will have some interesting decisions to make about which creature they would rather play with.

Orthogonal Unit Differentiation   In his lecture at the 2003 Game Developers' Conference, "Orthogonal Unit Differentiation," game designer Harvey Smith argued that each type of unit a player can control in a game (a car, a soldier, an RPG character, or anything else the player can command) should be orthogonally different from all the others. By orthogonal, he meant that each kind of unit should be unlike the others in a different dimension, not simply more or less powerful when measuring in one dimension. Our example of the Ford, Dodge, and Chevy in the preceding section differentiates between them in the same dimension–speed–so they are not orthogonally different.

To make the player's choice of units more interesting and to offer her a larger variety of strategies, Smith suggested that units should not only differ in the magnitude of their power at performing one task, as our Fords and Dodges did, but also should display entirely different qualities. Ideally, every type of unit should possess capabilities that no other unit has, and this gives each type a distinct role to play in the game. Otherwise, there's little point in including a weaker unit in the game except as part of an upgrade path to a stronger one.

The more diverse the types of challenges in your game, the easier you will find it to create orthogonally differentiated unit types. In a realistic car racing game, all the cars face the same challenge and must be constructed to similar standards, which makes racing games a poor field for examples of orthogonal differentiation. Player success depends more on driving skill than on the attributes of their cars, which is appropriate for a racing game. In a war game, however, opportunities to create orthogonally differentiated units abound. Some units may fly or travel on water, whereas others may not; some may transport other units; some may possess ranged weapons and others only hand-to-hand weapons; and so on. You cannot directly compare the advantages of a unit that wields hand-to-hand weapons with the advantages of one that heals the wounded: These qualities make the player's choices more interesting, and success in the game consists of deploying the appropriate combination of units to defeat the enemy's forces.

Orthogonally differentiated units also help to prevent dominant strategies from arising if you define the victory condition in such a way that the player must use a variety of different units in order to win the game. Many inexperienced chess players rely on using the queen aggressively, wrongly believing this a dominant strategy because she is the most powerful piece on the board. In fact, however, each type of chess piece plays a role and they work cooperatively. Although the queen does possess exactly the same qualities as the rooks and bishops, she cannot control the board alone; she needs the help of the other pieces. The types of pieces exhibit enough diversity to keep games interesting and prevent dominant strategies.

Dominant Strategies in PvE Games

As we explained in Chapter 9, "Gameplay," most games offer a large number of different types of challenges but a somewhat smaller number of actions with which to overcome them. One action may overcome several different types of challenges. This encourages players to experiment to find the right action or combination of actions to surmount each type of challenge, whereas offering one unique action for each type of challenge would make for a dull game.

Implementing fewer actions does introduce a potential problem, however. By creating actions that can overcome several different kinds of challenges, you risk accidentally creating *exploits,* actions so powerful because of a weakness in the design that the player becomes unstoppable. This occasionally happens when players use an action in a way that you did not expect. For example, in an old side-scrolling space-shooter game on the Super Nintendo Entertainment System (which we will not name to prevent embarrassment on the part of the individuals responsible), the player could, after upgrading her weapons to a certain level, make her way through the rest of the game without ever losing a life by traveling as low on the screen as possible and keeping her finger on the fire button. Although clearly unintended, this position made her invulnerable to enemy attacks.

No one has yet invented a way to prevent these problems other than thorough play-testing, trying as many actions and as many combinations as possible on each challenge. The smaller the number of actions that you implement in your game, the less likely you are to introduce a dominant strategy by accident because you will be able to test them all rigorously. Be especially careful with powerups and special actions that give the player more power than usual; these require extra testing.

The Role of Chance

The role of chance varies enormously from game to game. Some games, such as checkers, make no use of chance at all; in others, such as craps, chance is all-important. We've said that skill, not chance, must be the primary factor in determining the player's success. If chance plays a role, how can we ensure that the more skillful player wins? We have several recommendations.

- **Use chance sparingly.** Design the game so that chance affects only a minority of the player actions that lead to victory and the majority of actions depend on skill. This is the simplest solution, but it's not suitable for all types of games.

If chance is to play a larger role in the game, balance its effects as follows:

- **Use chance in frequent challenges with small risks and rewards** rather than infrequent challenges with large risks and rewards. Poker provides a good example. Chance plays a large role in each hand, but smart players don't bet large amounts on a single hand; they count on the cumulative effect of good play over many hands. Player skill remains the major factor that determines winners if a game includes enough hands. This approach also appears in war games, in which chance plays a role in the mechanics governing combat between individual units (although not a large role) but plays no direct role in the victory and loss conditions of the mission. The influence of chance on victory and loss occurs frequently but only on a small scale, so good luck tends to cancel out bad luck over time, leaving skill to determine long-term results.

- **Allow the player to choose actions to use the odds to his advantage.** If the player knows the probabilities that significant events will occur, he can make decisions that he believes will be to his advantage. Even in a game in which chance plays an enormous role, such as craps, the player may choose to bet on different outcomes that he believes more or less probable. His skill in making decisions in his favor on the basis of the odds thus plays a role in determining his success. Video games seldom tell players the odds explicitly, but with experience players come to learn the odds and make good decisions. If a player has *no* possibility of acquiring knowledge of the odds and gets no opportunity to decide whether to take a risk, chance plays too large a role.

- **Allow the player to decide how much to risk.** Allow the player to choose how much he places at risk at frequent intervals. By offering the player this choice, you give him more control over his resources and so tend to reward skill. This again becomes critically important in gambling games, as in the poker example above. If you do not let the player choose how much to risk on any given challenge that involves chance, then the game should not risk too much on his behalf. In a war game, for example, chance typically affects the accuracy of each shot. By sending a unit into combat, the player risks a few health points on each shot and cannot choose how many points he risks. However, he almost always has the option to withdraw the unit from combat (retreat); the number of points at risk is seldom very large; and one shot typically affects only one unit.

Put simply, don't use chance to determine large issues unless the player explicitly chooses to take large risks (and has the option not to).

Making PvP Games Fair

As we explained, part of your job includes making sure that your game is fair and that players perceive it to be fair. Fairness means something different in PvP games than it does in PvE games, so we discuss them separately. Players generally consider a PvP game to be *fair* if they believe (1) the rules give each player an equal chance of winning when play begins and (2) the rules do not advantage or disadvantage players unequally during the game in ways that they cannot influence or prevent apart from the operation of chance (in moderation).

Balancing Games with Symmetry

In designing a PvP game, you must decide early on if you want the game to be symmetric or asymmetric. We introduce the concept of symmetry in Chapter 1, "Games and Video Games"; see the section *Symmetry and Asymmetry* for a refresher if you need one. The concept doesn't apply to PvE games; all PvE games are asymmetric because there is only one player.

You will find it easiest to create a PvP game that players perceive as fair if you make the game symmetric. Each player begins with the same resources, has the same options available to her, faces the same challenges, and tries to achieve the same victory condition. The vast majority of traditional games (chess, backgammon, *Othello,* and so on) follow this pattern. So, too, does *Monopoly,* in which each player begins with $1,500 and all launch their tokens from the Go square. One player gets to go first, but because a random roll of the dice controls who begins the game, players accept this as fair. (See *FYI: Who Goes First?* in Chapter 1, "Games and Video Games," for further discussion.)

So long as whatever you do for one player you do for all the others, your game will remain fair, and little else needs to be said. However, video game players generally consider symmetric games rather uninteresting. Symmetric games don't allow players to control different forces and study their relative strengths and weaknesses the way asymmetric games do. Symmetric games also feel rather contrived, because little in the real world is symmetric.

In PvP games, dominant strategies most often occur under asymmetric rules (we address those issues in the next section), but a dominant strategy can also occur in symmetric games. Because all players start with symmetric attributes and positions, they all may use this superior strategy, so it does not create an unfair advantage for one player. Nevertheless, such a strategy leaves the players with only one good option, so the game isn't as fun as it could be.

Balancing Asymmetric Games

Asymmetric PvP games run a greater risk of suffering from dominant strategies because the players effectively play by different rules. In Fox and Geese, which we introduced in Chapter 1, "Games and Video Games," one player controls a single fox on the game board while the other player controls 11 geese (see Figure 1.3 in Chapter 1). The fox may move in any direction and jump over the geese, while the geese may only move toward the fox. The victory condition for the fox is to jump over all the geese (removing them from the board), whereas the victory condition for the geese is to trap the fox so that it cannot move. Thus, the rules provide entirely different units, available actions, and victory conditions for each side. In designing an asymmetric game, you must test the mechanics for each type of competitor against every other possible type of competitor to make sure that none has a dominant strategy that confers an advantage over all his opponents. This lengthy and involved procedure makes it more likely that a mistake will get past the testers.

In addition to the risk of dominant strategies emerging, players often disagree on the fairness of an asymmetric game. It becomes much harder to judge whether a game really gives all players an equal chance of winning and doesn't disadvantage any player who plays by different rules or with different resources. These arguments often result in variants—alternate versions of the rules—which arise to rectify what players see as problems. Several variants of Fox and Geese have emerged: one that puts more geese on the board, one that includes two foxes instead of one, one that lets the geese move backward as well as forward, and so forth.

The Point Assignment System   You can balance a more complex asymmetric game than Fox and Geese by giving the players identical quantities of raw materials at the beginning of the game and then letting them choose what units to build using the raw materials. The Macintosh game *Spectre* allowed players to design a tank by assigning points to three attributes: speed, armor (defensive strength), and shot power (offensive strength). Each player got the same number of points, so none had a built-in advantage, but each could construct a tank that matched his own preferred style of play.

The point distribution system, while generally fair, doesn't absolutely guarantee that no dominant strategy will emerge. The risk always exists that one particular combination of features may be superior to any other combination. To help prevent this, the attributes to which the player can assign points should be orthogonally related. One attribute should not affect the domain of another attribute. Having two closely related attributes, such as health and armor, undermines the point system. The player should not be able to gain the same effect by pumping points into one attribute as she could by pumping the points into another.

Also, make sure that spending a point on one attribute magnifies the unit's power in that dimension to the same degree that it would magnify powers in other dimensions if the player spent that point on any other attributes. This means that, for example, if the player can spend 10 points on strength to double the unit's strength, spending 10 points on intelligence should not multiply the unit's intelligence by 1,000. If using a point on intelligence produces a significantly greater chance of winning than using it on strength, a dominant strategy will emerge: Players will always put all their points into intelligence.

The Example of *StarCraft* *StarCraft* offers the most well-balanced combination of asymmetric features in any war game available, which explains why, despite being several years old, it remains a favorite at gaming tournaments. The game offers players a choice of three races called the Terrans (or humans), the Protoss, and the Zerg. Each race produces flying attack units, construction units, small infantry units, and so on. Most important, building these units carries approximately equivalent costs, in terms of raw materials needed: A Zerg, a Protoss, and a Terran each must use similar amounts of resources to build units that provide equivalent fighting power. The capabilities of the units, however, vary from race to race; therefore, the game is asymmetric. The Terran construction unit can repair damaged units, so assigning additional construction units to a job can speed repairs. Damaged Zerg units may heal themselves without the need for a repair unit, but only at a fixed rate. Protoss units possess both health, which cannot be replaced by any means, and shields, which the Protoss may recharge at special locations. Because Protoss units possess both health and shields, they usually cost about twice as much as their counterparts in the other races.

We strongly encourage you to study *StarCraft* as an example of a well-balanced asymmetric game. Buy a strategy guide for the game and read about the attributes of the units. Notice how their costs tend to balance their abilities. The balance in *StarCraft* makes use of both direct costs (computed from the amount of raw material required to build a unit) and shadow costs—hidden weaknesses.

IN THE TRENCHES: Cheating AI and Secret Asymmetry

In a single-player PvP game, the player takes on an artificial opponent and tries to defeat it in exactly the same way she would a human player. Sometimes the single-player competition mode in a PvP game is just an added feature in an otherwise multiplayer PvP game. When a game is designed this way, the player naturally tends to assume that the artificial opponent plays by the same rules that a human player would play by in its place.

Unfortunately, the artificial intelligence in many games isn't good enough to beat a human opponent on equal terms. AI can beat most human players in games such as chess and checkers but has a harder time with Go and a very hard time with complex war games. To help the AI, designers occasionally let it cheat. Some classic cheats include allowing the AI to see units that should be hidden by the fog of war; making the AI-controlled units tougher than the player's units, while claiming that they are identical; or giving the artificial opponent a faster production rate for valuable resources than the player gets for the same resources. In effect, what the player thinks is a symmetric game is secretly asymmetric; the artificial opponent plays by different rules.

You should only use this approach as a last resort. Although it can produce a well-balanced single-player PvP game, players *hate* it when they discover that the AI is cheating against them (and with enough effort, they will always discover it eventually). A better solution is to be open about the artificial opponent's advantages and build them into a set of different difficulty levels for the player to choose from. This allows the player to decide for himself how tough an opponent he wants to face, and the game doesn't have to pretend to be symmetric.

11

Balance Issues for Persistent Worlds

We discuss persistent worlds in Chapter 21, "Online Games," on the Companion Website but address a couple of issues here in the context of balancing.

Companion Website

Persistent worlds are never symmetric and are always intrinsically unbalanced because long-time players accumulate significant resources and experience that put newcomers at a disadvantage. As a result, online games *must* provide protection and encouragement for beginning players. Most now allow players to avoid PvP combat unless they specifically want to engage in it (we address this at further length in "Online Games" on the Companion Website), but online games must also give new players a chance to earn resources, explore areas without finding them already crowded by others, take up interesting occupations, and so on. A persistent world cannot be a zero-sum game: New resources must constantly flow into it from outside for new players to find.

The designers of persistent worlds, unlike designers of standalone games, can rebalance on the fly, changing the rules after their customers begin play. Such rule changes, while sometimes necessary, tend to cause howls of outrage from players who have optimized their play according to the existing rules and enjoy the game as it stands. Most persistent world games have had to implement rule changes this way to rectify design errors and to correct imbalances.

In spite of such changes, the persistent world *Asheron's Call* remains fundamentally unbalanced in favor of magic users. Apparently that's what the magic users want, and obviously the publishers want to hold their audience. In this case, designers balance the game in such a way that the majority of players enjoy the game in the way they like to play it rather than in such a way as to make the game objectively fair. The aim of this balance involves ongoing sales and politics more than it involves equal distribution of resources or opportunities—but as a designer, you may be required to consider how market forces call for a different kind of balance.

Making PvE Games Fair

Because the challenges in PvE games come from the environment rather than from other players, making a fair game involves more than giving all players equal opportunities to succeed. In general, players expect a fair PvE game to exhibit qualities enumerated below. Some may not appear to have much to do with balance, but we mention them here because they constitute part of a player's notion of fairness.

- **The game should offer the player challenges at a consistent level of difficulty,** with no sudden peaks or valleys. Players regard sudden spikes in difficulty as unfair. We devote the next section, *Managing Difficulty,* to this important issue.

- **The player should not suddenly lose the game without warning and through no fault of his own.** So-called *learn-by-dying* designs, once commonplace, are now considered unfair. *The Immortal,* an old Electronic Arts game, notoriously required the player to learn by dying. Fortunately, it allowed players to restart the game indefinitely without having to start over at the beginning, but repeated character death still wasn't much fun. You can easily avoid this by providing the player with adequate warnings of dangers ahead.

- **A stalemate should not occur.** Stalemates can result from deadlock (see Chapter 10, "Core Mechanics") or from other combinations of circumstances that prevent the player from winning *or* losing. If a player fails to pick up a critical item in an adventure game and then passes through a one-way door that prevents him from retrieving the item, he's in a stalemate. He hasn't lost the game, but he can't win it either. Well-designed games won't let the player proceed without the item. Some don't let players put items down once they have picked them up, just to help avoid this problem. Study your mechanics carefully to see if the game can ever enter a state that completely precludes victory but does not meet a loss condition. If it can, you should either change that state to a loss condition or—preferably—redesign the mechanics to prevent the game from ever getting into that state.

- **The game doesn't ask the player to make critical decisions without adequate information.** The ZX Spectrum game *Monty on the Run* by Gremlin Graphics required the player to choose at the beginning of the game exactly five items to take with her as she tried to escape her pursuers. Unfortunately, it gave her no clues about which items would be needed; she could find out only by trial and error. Give players the information they need.

- **All the factual knowledge required to win the game should be contained within the game.** Players should not have to do research outside the game world to win a game, with the sole exception of trivia games. We discuss this at greater length in Chapter 9, "Gameplay."

- **The game should not require the player to meet challenges not normally presented in the game's genre** (such as a formal logic puzzle in a flight simulator). If the game belongs to a hybrid genre, you must make this clear before the player starts to play.

Managing Difficulty

Psychologist Mihaly Csikszentmihalyi observed that people performing tasks enter an enjoyable state of peak productivity, which he calls *flow,* when (among other things) their abilities balance the difficulty of the tasks they face. If the challenges are too difficult, people become anxious; if the challenges are too easy, people become bored (Csikszentmihalyi, 1991). Csikszentmihalyi's observations apply to games as well as to other tasks. Balancing a game, then, includes managing the difficulty of its challenges to try to keep the players within the flow state—the point at which their abilities just match the problems they face. This provides another example of the player-centric approach: Your goal is not simply to set a level of difficulty but to think about how to adjust that difficulty to maximize the player's enjoyment. See Figure 11.2 for an illustration.

In Chapter 9, "Gameplay," in the section *Skill, Stress, and Difficulty,* we introduced two factors, the intrinsic skill required (ISR) to overcome a challenge

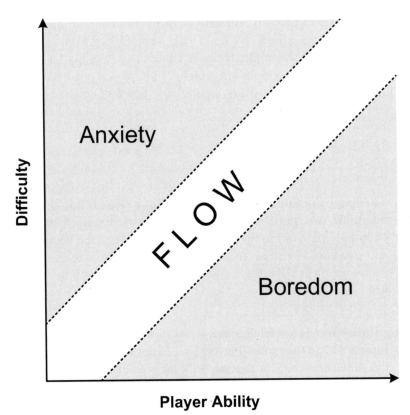

FIGURE 11.2 The balance between difficulty and ability, producing Csikszentmihalyi's idea of *flow*.

and the stress placed on the player by time pressure, that combine to form the *absolute difficulty* of the challenge. Here we extend our discussion of difficulty to take into account two additional factors, ultimately arriving at the idea of *perceived difficulty*—the type that matters to the player. As we explained in the preceding section, the perceived difficulty of a well-balanced game must remain within a certain range and not take sudden spikes or dips.

Because game challenges fall into many extremely different domains—physical coordination, factual knowledge, formal logic, pattern recognition, and so forth—no metric exists for comparing difficulty across these domains. Even within a given domain, such as factual knowledge challenges, it may be hard to decide when one challenge is more difficult than another; questions of fact that some audiences find hard are easy for other audiences. Most Americans would be unable to answer many factual knowledge questions about the history of Angola, and eight-year-olds would certainly struggle with complex logic puzzles. Consequently, our discussion of the subject makes no reference to any audience or unit of measure.

Factors Outside the Designer's Control

In managing the difficulty of a game, you command a number of factors that we introduce later in the chapter, but a few remain outside your knowledge or control. You cannot know how much time the player has already spent playing other games similar to yours—or, more accurately, facing challenges similar to those that you offer. We call this factor **previous experience.** (The experience the player gains while playing *your* game we call in-game experience, and we address it later in this chapter.)

You also cannot know how much **native talent** the player brings to the game: hand-eye coordination, reasoning faculties, and so on. Consequently, our discussion of perceived difficulty does not address either previous experience or native talent. We address these factors when we come to the question of difficulty modes in *Establishing Difficulty Modes* later in the chapter.

Finally, in multiplayer games, the skill of the player's opponents plays the greatest role in determining how hard it is to beat them, and you do not control that. Consequently, you don't have to put as much effort into managing difficulty throughout the game, so long as the game is fair. You still have to set the difficulty of individual challenges posed by the environment in a multiplayer game, however. The height of the basketball hoop and the size of the rim determine how hard it is to shoot a ball through the hoop in absolute terms, but how hard it is to win the game depends on the quality of the opposing team.

FYI   *Offering Cheats to the Player*

Many games try to account for differences in previous experience and native talent among the players by offering so-called cheats: hidden options that the player may use to gain an extra advantage. Cheats originally arose as a convenience feature for game testers, allowing them to jump ahead in the game, bypass certain challenges, and so on, so that they could go quickly to the part of the game they needed to test. Eventually designers realized that players could benefit from cheats too, and they began to leave the cheats as hidden features in the shipped version of the product. This practice is now so widespread as to be standard.

In spite of its ubiquity, however, we consider depending on the use of cheats to be a sign of poor game balancing. If a player cannot get through a game without using a cheat, the game is too hard. Instead of offering a hidden cheat that the player must search the Internet to discover, simply build the cheat in as a normal feature of the game's easiest difficulty mode and leave it out of the harder modes.

11

KEY POINT

The designer controls four key factors that create perceived difficulty: intrinsic skill required, stress, power provided by the game, and in-game experience. The major factors the designer cannot control are previous experience and native talent.

Types of Difficulty

Players care most about *perceived difficulty*; what matters is how hard the player finds surmounting a given challenge. To design a challenge at your target level of perceived difficulty, you must take into account four factors: intrinsic skill required and stress, both introduced in Chapter 9, "Gameplay," as well as power provided and in-game experience, defined in the following section. We also introduce absolute difficulty and relative difficulty, concepts that are helpful when trying to gauge in advance how difficult players will find the challenges you design for them and that allow us to develop an equation, of sorts, for establishing the perceived difficulty of a challenge.

Absolute Difficulty   To judge the *absolute difficulty* of a challenge, compare the amounts of intrinsic skill required to meet the challenges and the stress that the challenge imposes to that of a trivial challenge of the same type. For instance, in an action game, a trivial enemy would stand still, could not harm the avatar, and could be killed with one punch. If you design another enemy that takes more effort to kill (because it has more health points), that moves around (requiring more intrinsic skill to hit), and that hits the avatar back (thereby placing the player under time pressure—stress—to kill the enemy before the enemy kills the avatar), you can be confident you have designed an enemy more difficult to defeat, in absolute terms, than the trivial enemy that established the baseline. In effect, the absolute difficulty of a challenge equals the intrinsic skill required and the stress of the challenge *compared to the trivial case.*

You will find the concept of absolute difficulty useful when you need to compare the difficulty levels of different challenges. In general, if one enemy has twice as many health points as another, all other things being equal, it survives twice as long under assault, making it twice as hard to defeat.

Relative Difficulty and Power Provided   You cannot determine how the player perceives the difficulty of a challenge through absolute difficulty alone. You must also take into account two more factors. The first is the amount of power that the game gives to the player to meet the challenge. *Power provided* measures, by means appropriate to the situation, the player's strength: the health and powers of his avatar, the size and makeup of his army, the performance characteristics of his racing car, or whatever factors apply. In the simple example we described in the previous section, power provided would refer to the amount of damage the avatar can do when hitting the enemy and the avatar's resistance to damage: the number of health points that he has to lose before dying. Note that power provided is not related to native talent: It is a factor you control. In some games, the power provided may change owing to the action of positive feedback, which we discuss later in the chapter.

The *relative difficulty* is the difficulty of a challenge relative to the player's power to meet that challenge. For example, in an RPG, a player playing a level 1 knight will find it much harder, in absolute terms, to defeat a large enemy than a small one. But a player playing a level 5 knight won't find it nearly so hard to defeat that same large enemy because the game provides a level 5 knight with so much more power than it provides a level 1 knight.

If the power provided to the player doesn't change throughout the game, then you may ignore this distinction between absolute and relative difficulty. But most games include an upgrade progression whereby the player gains power as the game progresses because the new powers keep the player interested in the game and give her the feeling of accomplishing more. As a result, when level designers build challenges into the game world, they must also take into account the power provided to the player to meet those challenges. The level designers have to know, for example, that by the time the player reaches the fourth level, he will have earned three major weapon upgrades and a faster vehicle, so they set the difficulty of the fourth level's challenges relative to that level of power provided. To simplify managing the difficulty, many games don't allow the player to carry powers over from level to level; instead, the level designers themselves set the amount of power provided separately for each level and take it into account accordingly as they devise challenges. In persistent worlds, in which each individual player has his own amount of power provided, earned through his earlier play, the game must either warn players in advance against trying a mission that is too hard or flatly exclude them from such missions.

Perceived Difficulty and In-Game Experience   As they progress through a game, players learn to use the game's user interface more efficiently, and they learn at an intuitive level how the core mechanics of the game work. *In-game experience* at meeting any particular type of challenge may be measured by the amount of time the player has already spent meeting similar challenges within your game. (Remember that you cannot control for previous experience with other games.) The more in-game experience a player has, the easier he will perceive a given type of challenge to be. Thus, when the level designers build a challenge into a level, they must take into account the player's amount of in-game experience with the same type of challenge. If the player already has a lot of in-game experience with challenges of that type, the level designers should consider raising the challenge's absolute difficulty to compensate.

The *perceived difficulty* of a challenge the difficulty that the player actually senses, and the type we are most concerned with—consists of the relative difficulty minus the player's experience at meeting such challenges. Remembering that relative difficulty is absolute difficulty minus power provided, we can put all these factors together into a single equation such that

$$perceived\ difficulty = absolute\ difficulty - (power\ provided + in\text{-}game\ experience)$$

Note that we offer no units of measurement for these variables, so if you want to compute actual values for them, you will have to find a way of measuring their quantities based on the challenges that you plan to include in your game. The equation serves more as a useful principle for you to understand than as a value you can really compute.

Creating a Difficulty Progression

In a balanced game, the perceived difficulty of challenges presented to the player either should not change or should rise, so the player feels that later challenges present greater difficulty than those at the beginning. (If a game becomes easier to play, players will definitely feel that the game is unbalanced.) In order to achieve this, you have to take into account the player's increasing in-game experience and build in appropriate increases in absolute difficulty. If you wish to, you can also build in increases in the power provided by the game. Figure 11.3 shows this progression graphically. Notice the gap between the absolute and relative levels of difficulty. This gap represents power provided by the game to meet challenges, which widens steadily as the player gains power.

The gap between relative difficulty and perceived difficulty on the graph represents the player's increasing in-game experience as she plays. At the beginning of the game, the perceived difficulty exactly equals the relative difficulty because the player has no in-game experience at all. As time goes on, her perception changes as she gets more practice.

If the available power grows at exactly the same rate as the absolute difficulty goes up, the relative difficulty will be a flat line, as illustrated in Figure 11.4. In that case, a level 5 knight would find it exactly as hard to kill a level 5 troll in the middle of the game as a level 1 knight would find it to kill a level 1 troll at the beginning

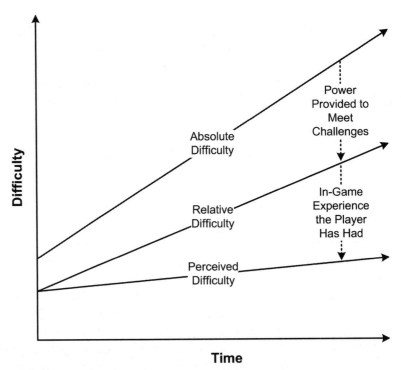

FIGURE 11.3 Absolute, relative, and perceived levels of difficulty.

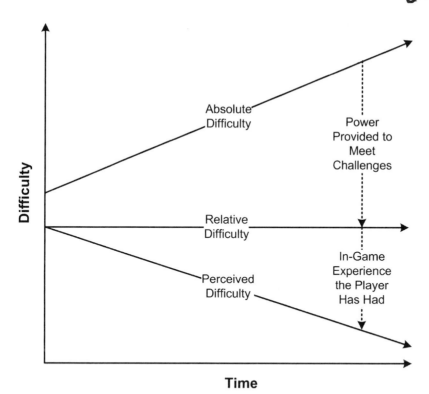

FIGURE 11.4 If relative difficulty is flat, perceived difficulty goes down as the player gains experience.

of the game. But relative difficulty should not be a flat line because when you factor in the player's increasing in-game experience, the perceived difficulty actually goes down—the game gets easier. Aim to increase the absolute difficulty of the challenges somewhat faster than you increase the available power to meet them. The gap between absolute and relative difficulty widens only slowly.

KEY POINT

In a long game, relative difficulty *must* increase over time to counteract the player's growing in-game experience, or he will perceive the game as getting easier and easier.

FYI *When Perceived Difficulty Should Not Change*

As we explained earlier, the perceived difficulty throughout the game should either remain flat or should rise. In most games, it rises. For some players, however, it should remain flat or rise only very slowly. Young children and casual gamers have a lower tolerance for frustration than older and more hardcore players. Mobility-impaired players may not get as much benefit from increasing experience as fully able players in games with physical coordination challenges. For these groups, try to keep the perceived difficulty level nearly flat throughout the course of the game.

Even if the perceived difficulty of a game rises only slowly, we do want the player to feel he attains bigger and bigger accomplishments as he goes. To achieve this, you must take into account all the factors pertaining to difficulty that we've discussed. Use the following guidelines:

- Increase the absolute difficulty of challenges over time.

- Increase the power available to the player to meet those challenges at a somewhat lower rate. (See *Understanding Positive Feedback,* later in this chapter.)

- Be sure the player doesn't gain experience so fast that challenges start to feel as if they're getting easier rather than harder. Space challenges so that their relative difficulty increases slightly faster than the in-game experience increases.

- Play-test your game to look for any dramatic spikes or dips in the perceived difficulty of its challenges so you can iron them out. A sharp, unanticipated rise in the game's difficulty will discourage many players and may prevent them from finishing the game even if the difficulty quickly falls again.

- Start each game level at a perceived difficulty somewhat lower than that at which the preceding level ended, and increase the difficulty during the course of each level as well. Each game level should also take a little longer to play through and have a slightly steeper rate of difficulty growth than the one before. A graph explains this process best; see Figure 11.5 for an example illustrating a game with only five levels. (In a game with more levels, the rate of difficulty should not increase as steeply as that shown in Figure 11.5.) This sawtooth shape creates good

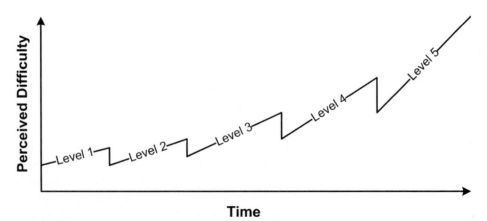

FIGURE 11.5 A sawtooth difficulty progression across multiple game levels.

pacing over the course of the game. We discuss pacing at greater length in Chapter 12, "General Principles of Level Design."

COMMANDMENT: Don't Jump Difficulty from Level to Level

Do *not* introduce sudden difficulty jumps between the end of one level and the beginning of the next. There is a good chance the player saved the game after completing the previous level and has not played it for some time, thus losing some of the benefit of her experience.

Establishing Difficulty Modes

In creating a single-player game, you should allow the player to choose how difficult the game will be, typically with three options labeled easy, normal, and hard, or similar terms. When players make this choice, we usually say they're playing in a *difficulty mode,* such as easy mode or normal mode. (Don't confuse these with gameplay modes.)

Multiplayer games don't always offer different difficulty modes because in many multiplayer games the player's skill determines how hard it is for others to beat her or for her to beat them. But in multiplayer games in which the environment itself sets challenges for the players, such as a road race, the players may want to choose the difficulty of the environment's challenges—to select easy, normal, or hard courses to race on, for example.

FYI   *Why Offer Difficulty Modes?*

Offering multiple difficulty modes allows the player to set the difficulty of the game in keeping with the two factors you cannot know or control: the player's previous experience of similar types of games and the player's native talent. Although nobody buys a game specifically because it offers multiple difficulty modes, a great many people *don't* buy games that they think might be too hard for them to play. Including multiple difficulty modes increases the market for your game by making it accessible to a broader range of players. In addition, difficulty modes give the player better value for the money at comparatively little development cost. Once players complete the game in an easy mode, they might enjoy playing it again in a harder mode. If it has only one mode, they're less likely to enjoy playing through it a second time.

11

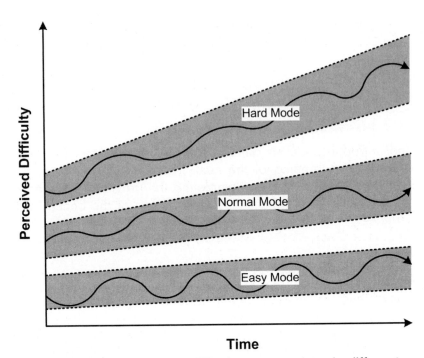

FIGURE 11.6 Perceived difficulty progressions in different difficulty modes.

When you create a game that offers the player a choice of multiple difficulty modes, in effect you promise that the perceived difficulty of the game will remain within a certain range throughout a game level. Figure 11.6 illustrates the idea for a single game level. In each mode, the perceived difficulty remains within the dotted lines that define it, but perceived difficulty still rises throughout the level. We've drawn the perceived difficulty lines as curves to reflect the variable pacing that you should build into a level.

How you adjust the difficulty of challenges for different modes will depend on the challenges and on the genre of your game. In action and action-adventure games, for example, designers normally give the enemies more health, allow them to do more damage, and make them more numerous. Designers also sometimes adjust the AI of enemies and artificial opponents, making them smarter or more aware of threats. We discuss how to adjust the absolute difficulty of different kinds of challenges in Chapter 9, "Gameplay."

In some cases, you may not be able to adjust the difficulty level of a challenge at all. With something like a static obstacle, such as a cliff the avatar must climb, the challenge is built into the shape of the cliff, and adjusting its difficulty would mean redesigning the landscape on the fly. Instead, give the player an alternative route that avoids the cliff climb in the easiest mode, but lock off the easy route in the harder modes.

IN THE TRENCHES: Adaptive Difficulty

Over the years, game designers have made a number of efforts to create games that detect the player's level of skill and adapt themselves to change the player's experience accordingly. Several approaches have been tried:

- First-person shooter *Max Payne* automatically adjusts the strength of enemies and the amount of aiming assistance provided to the player based on his performance. The changes work to keep the player's experience at an appropriate level of difficulty, but they are transparent to the user.

- The racing game *Burnout 2* automatically changes the performance of computer-controlled drivers so as to keep them near the player's car regardless of how well or poorly she does. No matter what the skill level of the player, this approach ensures a close race.

- *Crash Bandicoot*, an action game, offered the player extra shields against attack if he failed to get through a certain section too many times in a row. Players found this mechanism rather obvious. Furthermore, rather than being a global system like *Max Payne*'s, it had to be implemented separately for each region of the game where it offered extra shields.

- *Crimson Skies*, a combat flight simulation, gave the player the chance to skip a mission after failing at it three times. In this case, the game didn't adapt its difficulty; it simply offered the player a way around difficult sections. Some players complained that they found this rather patronizing; presumably others found it a relief.

Automated adaptive difficulty systems such as those used in *Max Payne* and *Burnout 2* are the subject of considerable debate within the game industry and for the moment remain experiments rather than standard industry techniques. Some designers feel that games should not include player-selectable difficulty modes at all but should rely entirely on adaptive systems to set the level of difficulty to the player's ability. Others believe that no automated system can accurately predict how hard a player *wants* his experience to be, so they should not even be tried.

Some adaptive difficulty systems do produce rather peculiar behavior, and smart players can learn how to trick them. By intentionally driving badly in the early parts of the race in *Burnout 2*, a player

11

▶▶ CONTINUED ON NEXT PAGE

▶▶ CONTINUED

can cause the system to reduce the performance of the AI-controlled drivers, allowing the player to race past them to victory in the final moments of the game. Also, a player who does extremely well finds that he stands no more chance of winning than one who does badly, which goes against some players' idea of fair play. Also, it's not always obvious what metric a game should use for determining how well a player performs in the first place, so as to know that the difficulty requires adjustment.

If you want to include an adaptive difficulty system in your game, we suggest the following:

- Don't use it as a substitute for ordinary difficulty levels that can be set. Players like to have the freedom to set these themselves.

- Make it optional, a feature the player can accept or reject.

- Use it to make the game harder but not easier. It is generally simpler to make a game more difficult than to make it easier. To make a game easier under computer control, the software has to determine the reason for the player's failure, which isn't always clear or measurable. Making a game harder doesn't depend as heavily on the computer's understanding of the reasons for the player's success.

So long as your adaptive-difficulty system remains an optional means of making the game extra challenging for the hardcore player, it will be less prone to the problems observed with such systems because the player cannot manipulate it to her advantage, and she can switch it off if it becomes a problem.

Understanding Positive Feedback

Positive feedback occurs when a player's achievement causes changes to the state of the game that make a subsequent achievement easier, which in turn makes further achievements easier still, and so on. The term does not refer to the effect of increasing experience but to a phenomenon of the core mechanics that occurs even if the player's performance does not improve with experience. The core mechanics often reward achievements with assets that the player can convert into power in order to make further achievements easier. See Figure 11.7 for a diagram.

Monopoly, as usual, provides a classic example. When a player achieves a monopoly by buying a group of related properties, the player may charge higher

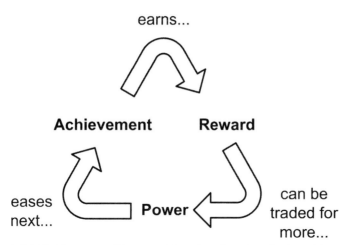

FIGURE 11.7 The positive feedback relationship among achievements, rewards, and power.

rents to any opponent who lands on these properties—the owner's reward for the achievement. The player may then use the money to purchase more property and collect more monopolies, thus producing a better chance of earning still more money.

Some games feature an even closer relationship between achievement and power in which the player's reward for achievement simply is power. The reward doesn't come in an intermediate form, such as money, that must be converted into power by buying a weapon or a spell. Whichever side loses a piece in a game of chess then plays with a depleted force, so the player who takes the piece obtains more power relative to his opponent than he had before taking it. In PvP games such as chess, achieving the lead often confers some advantage upon the leader that makes it easy for her to stay in the lead and difficult for the others to overtake her.

Not all games include positive feedback. If overcoming challenges does not produce a reward that the player can use to help him overcome further challenges, no feedback cycle exists. In a javelin competition, a good throw of the javelin does not produce additional power that influences subsequent throws.

Benefits of Positive Feedback

Positive feedback can benefit your game in two ways:

- **Positive feedback discourages stalemate.** As we said, a well-balanced PvP game should only rarely result in a stalemate, and PvE games should never end in stalemate. Positive feedback tends to bring games to an end because a player who takes a decided lead becomes unstoppable.

- **Positive feedback rewards success** and provides that reward in a useful form rather than a purely cosmetic form, such as a higher score. Even though the perceived difficulty of challenges may increase, thus requiring the player to work harder nearer the end of the game, she still feels rewarded by a sense of power and growth at being able to do things she could not do at the beginning of the game. Because avatar growth is one of the key goals in role-playing games, the positive feedback cycle serves as the central design feature of the internal economy of computer role-playing games.

Controlling Positive Feedback

Although positive feedback generally benefits by helping bring a game to an appropriately timed end, especially in PvP games that involve direct conflict between the players, you must not allow positive feedback to operate so quickly that the game ends too soon or a player who falls behind never has any chance to catch up. Part of balancing your game will consist of adjusting your positive feedback cycle to prevent these problems.

We propose six ways of controlling the rate of positive feedback, as follows:

- **Don't provide too much power as a reward for success.** In chess, taking one of the opponent's pieces gives the player an added measure of power. In shogi (Japanese chess), the player can then add that piece to his own side, acquiring even more power. Introducing the piece directly would give the player too great an advantage; instead, it comes in as a weaker piece, which somewhat reduces the size of the reward. Similarly, in many war games, such as *Warcraft,* a player can destroy enemy factories, but he cannot capture them and put them to use to produce weapons for his own side. If he could do that, he would become unstoppable too quickly. (In real wars, armies often destroy their own production facilities and materiel in order to prevent their falling into enemy hands for precisely this reason.)

- **Introduce negative feedback.** Negative feedback associates a cost with achievement to counteract the benefit—a negative reward, in other words. You may do this explicitly or allow it to happen automatically as a function of the gameplay. In *Dungeon Keeper,* the player could convert enemy creatures to fight for her own side, but once she had done so, she had to provide food, money, and living space for them—explicit costs associated with having added them to her army. In the pool game eight ball, the greater the lead a player has on his opponent, the more difficult it becomes to sink shots because he has fewer balls to target on the table, and his opponent has more balls left to get in the way. Pool doesn't include positive feedback to help the leader, so this negative feedback actually tends to keep games close.

- **Raise the absolute difficulty level of challenges as the player proceeds.** This approach applies primarily to PvE games such as role-playing games. As the player gains experience points and treasure through successful combat, he obtains more and more power through positive feedback. In order to continue to offer him meaningful challenges, increase the strength and numbers of the enemy. Defeating stronger enemies yields larger rewards, so the cycle continues. Near the end of the game, he fights enemies hundreds of times more difficult to beat—in absolute terms—than those that he fought at the beginning, and this gives him a great sense of accomplishment. But because you have matched the absolute difficulty of the challenges to the power you provide, the perceived difficulty remains under control.

- **Allow collusion against the leader.** In games with three or more players, you can write the rules in such a way that the other players can collaborate against the player in the lead. The collaborating forces may be sufficient to overcome the effects of positive feedback when the power of a single player might not be. *Diplomacy* encourages collusion—forming alliances is the main point of the game.

- **Define victory in terms unrelated to the feedback cycle.** If you define the victory condition of your game explicitly in terms of player rewards, power, or success at achievements that make up parts of the positive feedback cycle, then positive feedback will hasten victory. But you can also define victory in other terms. We pointed out that taking a piece in chess confers an advantage to whichever player took it, but the victory condition in chess requires the player to checkmate his opponent's king, not to take the most pieces. While a player may achieve the victory condition more easily with more pieces, it can also be useful to sacrifice a piece for strategic reasons.

- **Use the effects of chance to reduce the size of the player's rewards.** Role-playing games do this to some degree by randomly varying the amount of loot that enemies yield to the player when they are defeated. By occasionally giving players a lower reward for their achievements, you slow down positive feedback.

Positive Feedback in Action

The set of graphs in Figure 11.8 illustrates the effects of positive feedback, or its absence, in a variety of circumstances. Each graph shows the state of a hypothetical game between two players, A and B, over time. When the curve passes above the center line and into A's area, A leads; when it goes below the center, B leads. When the curve reaches the dotted line on one side or the other, the game ends and the player indicated wins.

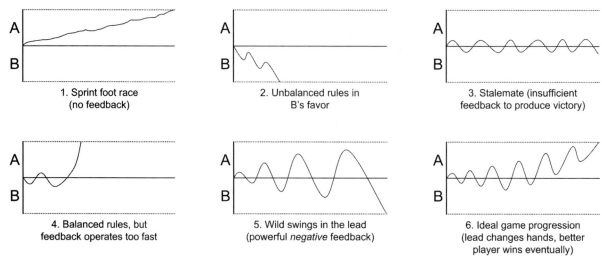

FIGURE 11.8 Graphs showing the effects of different adjustments to positive feedback.

Consider the following observations about these graphs:

- Graph 1 represents a game, such as a sprint foot race, in which no feedback loop exists to augment player power. A, the faster runner, wins.

- In graph 2, the game lasts only a short time. B takes the lead and wins almost immediately. A's few efforts to catch up allow A to gain ground temporarily but ultimately fail. This graph describes an unfair game, badly balanced in favor of B.

- Graph 3 depicts a stalemate, with neither side ever getting far enough ahead for positive feedback to take hold and lead to victory. The game probably involves little positive feedback (or possibly none) and closely matched competitors.

- Graph 4 shows a game with fairly balanced rules but one in which positive feedback operates too quickly. B goes ahead, then A, then B again, and then A goes ahead just enough for a dramatic positive feedback cycle to make A unstoppable.

- Graph 5 indicates a game with a feedback cycle such that being in the lead becomes a profound disadvantage, the effect of powerful negative feedback. A and B gain substantial leads and then alternately fall substantially behind so that the graph shows wild swings. *Mario Kart* and other multiplayer local games not intended to be taken too seriously sometimes use this mechanism.

- Graph 6 shows an ideal game progression: The lead changes hands and both players have a good chance of winning the game for a while, but eventually A's superior play places her in a leading position that she never yields. The action of positive feedback ensures that B, the less-skilled player, cannot catch up, although B has a pretty good chance for about two-thirds of the game and perhaps could have won if A's attention had wavered; that is, the outcome wasn't a foregone conclusion.

Other Balance Considerations

Here we address two undesirable qualities of unbalanced games, stagnation and triviality, that you should seek to avoid.

Avoiding Stagnation

Stagnation occurs in a PvE game when the game leaves the player in a position in which he simply does not know what to do next; he believes that he is stuck. (Don't confuse this with a stalemate, a situation in which the players *cannot* go on no matter what.) Stagnation tends to be caused by a design that doesn't give the player enough information to proceed. First-person shooters that require a player to run all over the place trying to find the hidden switch that opens the level exit, *after* having killed all her opponents, stagnate. Once the player kills all the opponents, the level exit should be obvious.

Stagnation seldom occurs in PvP games because such games almost always put the competitors in direct conflict with one another and provide them with means to act against each other's forces. Stagnation occasionally happens when one player's forces are so reduced that there is little he can do. But because he usually loses the game soon afterward, this doesn't represent a serious problem. The most common complaint about stagnation in PvP games occurs in scenarios where the victory condition requires a player to destroy all enemy units, and one last enemy unit (often not even a combat unit) remains hidden in an obscure location. You can avoid this by setting a different victory condition, such as to destroy the enemy's headquarters instead of all his units.

Stagnation can be difficult to avoid in a sprawling action-adventure with so many different combinations and configurations that you can't reliably anticipate what the player may or may not try. However, you can still give the players information as they progress, as follows:

- Tackle stagnation passively by hiding in plain sight clues about how to proceed.

- Tackle stagnation actively by having the game detect when the player wanders around aimlessly; make the game provide a few gentle nudges to guide her in the right direction.

Never let the player feel bewildered. If he has to resort to outside assistance in order to proceed—whether by cheating, reading a strategy guide, or looking up the answers on the Web—your game contains a design flaw.

11

Avoiding Trivialities

Players don't want to be bogged down in minutiae when they can be directing the big decisions. Forcing the player to decide where to store the gold when she must try to build an army and plan a campaign strategy merely distracts the player with uninteresting details. It moves the player out of the flow state and into boredom. Likewise, any gameplay decision that has no real effect on the game world, or any decision that requires the player to pick from a slate of options that includes only one reasonable option, is trivial. Let the computer handle it. (This doesn't apply to non-gameplay decisions, such as self-expressive acts—choosing a team color may not affect the gameplay, but the player should still be allowed to do it.)

Sid Meier's Alpha Centauri handles this magnificently. In this game, the player can choose to handle every decision from overall control of the planet all the way down to production and direction of individual units or to let a computer-controlled manager control his bases and his units. This accommodates players who want to micromanage every aspect of the game as well as those interested only in grand strategy. We admire this design because it gives the player a choice. Other games force the player to do all the micromanagement, whether she wants to or not.

Triviality can add to the player's enjoyment when done well and not too often. Consider a cops and robbers game. The player's avatar, a police officer, patrols the city as usual, on the lookout for crime, when he spots a group of suspicious-looking characters on the corner. He stops the car, and they immediately run down an alleyway and vanish; the player won't meet these particular characters again, and they do not form part of the game's story. These characters provide local color rather than part of the gameplay. If you don't lead the player *too* far down the wrong path, you can use such trivial interaction to give the impression that there is more to the city than meets the eye.

Design to Make Tuning Easy

In the later stages of game development, you will spend a great deal of time tweaking and tuning your game to improve its balance and remove any dominant strategies or difficulty spikes that may have crept in. Here we offer a few suggestions to make this process easier.

As we explained in Chapter 10, "Core Mechanics," you should seek to generalize when you can, to create a set of mechanics that apply to a wide variety of entities rather than creating separate mechanics for each entity. So, for example, in any game that involves combat, try to create one set of mechanics that governs combat between units regardless of what types of units the combat involves. Not only does this simplify the programming—the developers can concentrate on implementing the core mechanics and then adding entities on top of those core rules, rather than coding each entity separately—it also simplifies tuning the design.

If each entity has its own mechanics, the mechanics for each entity must be tuned separately, which could potentially cause balance problems. If you use universal mechanics as described above, then once you get them into balance in general, any tweaking you need to do should not throw off the balance in unpredictable ways.

Although describing implementation techniques is beyond the scope of this book, we would be remiss if we didn't suggest that you separate code and data. This allows designers to tweak the game by trying different values for attributes without changing the code. Toward the end of the development cycle, you will spend a lot of time play-testing your game and refining its balance by changing the values of entities' attributes. You can store these data in a database—or even just a plain ASCII file—during development, moving them into a proprietary format for the final release.

Tweaking doesn't mean changing parameters randomly; that's a good way to waste time. The following suggestions should help you fine-tune your game efficiently:

- **Modify only one parameter at a time.** Although you may be tempted to tweak several parameters in order to force a result, unless you are extremely lucky, you won't get anything useful. Even if you do, you will have no idea which of the parameter tweaks got you there. Correct experimental method dictates that you adjust one parameter, then check the results, then adjust another parameter, and so on. While this may seem slower than changing multiple parameters simultaneously, it's actually more efficient because you *know* which change produced the desired result.

- **When modifying parameters, make big adjustments, not small ones.** Brian Reynolds of Big Huge Games suggests beginning by doubling or halving the value of a parameter and checking the effect. Small adjustments may produce such subtle changes that you can't even detect them. Make a large change, then iteratively reduce and test, reduce and test, moving toward the ideal value. Changing by such a large factor makes it easier to zero in on your optimum setting.

- **Keep records.** Good testers keep close track of what they do so they don't end up wasting effort by trying the same thing twice. They can thus see the effects of the changes they've made and learn from experience.

- **Be sure your programmers use pseudo-random numbers.** As we explained in Chapter 10, "Core Mechanics," pseudo-random numbers allow you to control the effects of chance and hold the mechanics steady while you change parameters and test the result.

11

Summary

In this chapter, you have learned how to design games that are fair, avoiding dominant strategies and making use of chance in such a way that your game rewards skillful play. You have also seen how to manage difficulty so that the player's abilities match his challenges and keep him in the *flow* state of peak enjoyment. Finally, you should now understand the role that positive feedback plays in games and how best to make use of it and control it. All these factors play a role in balancing a game and if you keep them in mind, you should be able to adjust the core mechanics of your game to produce a challenging yet enjoyable experience for your player.

Test Your Skills

MULTIPLE CHOICE QUESTIONS

1. In both PvP and PvE games, one of the chief characteristics of a well-balanced game is that

   A. the game's dominant strategy is clear.

   B. the player perceives the game to be fair.

   C. the game is symmetric.

   D. the relative difficulty is greater than the absolute difficulty.

2. In a pioneer adventure game, you offer the player a choice of horses, mules, or oxen to pull wagons. Mules are stronger than horses, and oxen are stronger than mules. If a transitive relationship exists among these entities, then

   A. horses are stronger than oxen.

   B. horses and mules can together equal the strength of oxen.

   C. oxen are stronger than horses.

   D. horses are one-third the strength of oxen.

3. The benefits of implementing a small number of actions in a game include all of the following *except* that

   A. you encourage players to experiment to find the right action to surmount each type of challenge.

   B. you reduce the likelihood of introducing a dominant strategy.

   C. you will be able to test all actions rigorously.

   D. you risk accidentally creating exploits that render the player unstoppable.

4. You can balance the effect of chance in a game by

   A. allowing the player to decide how much to risk.

   B. using chance as much as possible.

   C. using chance infrequently with large risks and rewards.

   D. making sure players do not know the odds that significant events will occur.

5. Which of the following is true of symmetric games?

   A. Dominant strategies most often occur in symmetric games.

   B. Players often disagree about whether symmetric games are fair.

   C. Symmetric games can be considered contrived and uninteresting.

   D. All of the above.

6. Which of the following is a common option for balancing an asymmetric game?

   A. Give players the same amount of resources and let them choose how to utilize the resources.

   B. Give players different amounts of resources and keep everything else symmetric.

   C. Make sure all players in the game are playing by the same rules, as in Fox and Geese.

   D. Make sure that the attributes to which a player can assign points are not orthogonally related.

7. Which of the following is *not* one of the qualities of a fair PvE game?

   A. The game's challenges should represent a consistent level of difficulty.

   B. Stalemates should not occur.

   C. Players shouldn't have to make critical decisions without adequate information.

   D. Players should be encouraged to "learn by dying."

8. Two factors you cannot know or control as you design a game are

   A. the player's in-game experience and native talent.

   B. the game's relative difficulty and perceived difficulty.

   C. the player's previous experience and native talent.

   D. the game's power provided and the player's previous experience.

11

9. In order to determine how a player perceives a challenge, you must take into account
    A. absolute difficulty and relative difficulty.
    B. absolute difficulty, power provided, and in-game experience.
    C. relative difficulty, native talent., and power provided.
    D. relative difficulty, previous experience, and in-game experience.

10. Why is it a good idea to offer difficulty modes in a game?
    A. Multiple difficulty modes give the player better value for the money.
    B. Multiple difficulty modes make the game accessible to a broad range of players.
    C. Many people will not buy a game if they believe it will be too hard.
    D. All of the above.

11. If relative difficulty remains the same throughout a game, when you factor in in-game experience, the player will perceive the game as
    A. getting harder and harder.
    B. becoming repetitive.
    C. getting easier and easier.
    D. becoming slowly harder.

12. One of the chief benefits of positive feedback is that it
    A. balances difficulty and fairness.
    B. helps to balance asymmetric games.
    C. prevents games from ending too quickly.
    D. discourages stalemates.

13. All of the following are ways to control the rate of positive feedback *except:*
    A. Provide as much power as possible as a reward for success.
    B. Introduce negative feedback.
    C. Allow collusion against a leader.
    D. Use the effects of chance to reduce the size of the player's rewards.

14. One way to design a game to avoid stagnation is to
    A. avoid action-adventure games that are prone to this problem.
    B. provide a subtle means to guide a player in the right direction.
    C. make it easy for a player to look up his next move on a Web strategy site.
    D. concentrate on PvP games in which stagnation is seldom a problem.

15. When you test parameters as you fine-tune a game, you are advised to

    A. modify several parameters at once to save tweaking time.

    B. use completely random numbers during the tweaking process.

    C. start with big adjustments to parameters rather than small ones.

    D. start with small adjustments to parameters rather than big ones.

EXERCISES

1. Devise a type of challenge that involves direct player control over one or more units, *other* than conflict or racing challenges. Your type of challenge should involve units trying to accomplish some familiar task from the real world. (Your instructor may assign you a challenge type instead.) For your challenge, create three types of units in a transitive relationship with one another, such that the attributes of the units determine that type A is better at the task than type B, and type B is better than type C. Document the challenge, the unit types, and the attributes that govern their suitability for the task. Then propose a shadow cost that balances the transitive relationship in a way that seems credible in the context of the challenge (such as our fuel-tank-size example in the racing game).

2. You have been given the task of designing a game in which robots construct simple buildings consisting of a floor, walls, and a roof, assuming that the foundations are already laid. (Don't worry about challenges or the victory condition for this exercise.) The construction tasks required include fetching different kinds of raw materials from stockpiles, transporting them to the building site, positioning them, and fastening them to the building. Decide for yourself what the raw materials will be; there must be at least four types. Devise names, attributes, and appropriate functions for at least six different kinds of robots that work together to perform these tasks; you may divide the robots' responsibilities any way you like, but do it in such a way that if any one type of robot is unavailable, the building cannot be completed. Include at least four attributes per type of robot. Document everything that you have created, and explain how you have differentiated the robots orthogonally (which attributes each type possesses uniquely) as well as what features and abilities they all have in common. *Extra credit:* Now adjust the robots' functions in such a way that some of their abilities overlap and if any one type of robot becomes unavailable, the others will still be able to complete the building, but no single robot can do it all.

3. Choose three different types of challenges from Chapter 9, "Gameplay," and describe five different versions of each type at different levels of absolute difficulty: very easy, easy, moderate, hard, and

11

very hard (fifteen in all). Explain how each type of challenge differs for each level of absolute difficulty and give examples.

4. Modify the rules of checkers (draughts) to make the game asymmetric. Play-test the result with a friend to see if the game is still fair. Write a short paper explaining your changes, including types and numbers of units, types of moves allowed, and changes to the victory conditions for one or both sides.

5. *Monopoly* contains one game-balance weakness: The point at which one player becomes invincible due to the action of positive feedback is typically about an hour before the last player goes bankrupt and the game actually ends. Write a short paper proposing changes to the rules that would speed up the action of positive feedback in the later stages of the game without giving the first player who gets into the lead too much of an advantage in the early stages. Your proposed change must be fair: You cannot flatly offer the player in the lead a special advantage. While applying to all players, your rule change should be of the greatest benefit to the player with the largest amount of money. Explain how your proposal would work. (Hint: Your change may require a means of detecting that the game is in its later stages in order to come into effect then or to have its greatest impact then. Think about what is different between the early and later stages of the game and how a rule change might take advantage of that difference.)

DESIGN QUESTIONS

1. Is your game a PvP game or a PvE game?

2. Are the relationships among the player's options in the game largely transitive, intransitive, or a mixture of both?

3. If the relationships are transitive, how will you balance them so that each choice remains viable? Direct costs or shadow costs? What will these costs be? How, if at all, will the player learn what they are? Or will the transitive options simply be upgrades from one another with no need to be balanced?

4. If your game includes intransitive relationships, what will you do to make them more interesting for the player and not too obvious?

5. Do you plan to give the player a choice of units to control or control over a variety of units? If so, how will you differentiate them? Will each unit have a unique role to play, with qualities it shares with no other, or will the qualities of some units overlap?

6. Does the game contain any elements that the player might perceive to be unfair?

7. If yours is a PvP game, are the capabilities of the forces symmetric or asymmetric? If they are asymmetric, in what ways do they differ and how will they be balanced? By adjusting costs? By changing rules or probabilities to compensate?

8. Do the game's challenges increase steadily in difficulty, or are there peaks and troughs, or spikes, in the difficulty level? If so, where are they?

9. How do you plan to change the absolute difficulty of your challenges? Do you plan to increase the power you provide to the player to meet the game's challenges? Will the player's perception of the game's difficulty go up with time, or will it remain relatively flat?

10. What mechanisms, if any, will there be for changing the game's difficulty level? Hints? Shortcuts? A difficulty setting? How will the difficulty setting change the nature of the challenges offered? Will it make the enemies tougher or weaker, smarter or more stupid? Will it add or remove challenges entirely?

11. Does the game include positive feedback? If so, how will you control it to avoid runaway victory for the first player who gets ahead? A time delay? Negative feedback? A random factor?

12. How will the player know what to do next? What features does the game include to prevent stagnation?

13. To what degree is the player required to micromanage the game? Is the player obliged to look after trivia? Are mechanisms available for the player to delegate some of these responsibilities to an automated process? If so, can the player be confident the automated process will make intelligent choices?

11

Chapter | 12

General Principles of Level Design

Chapter Objectives

After reading this chapter and completing the exercises, you will be able to do the following:

- Understand how level design can enhance or undermine a game's story and gameplay.
- Know the difference between universal and genre-specific level design principles.
- List the possible level layouts and understand when to use each and how to combine them.
- Understand the importance of atmosphere, pacing, and progression.
- Describe the key aspects of the level design process.
- Recognize some of the pitfalls of level design, such as inappropriate scope and conceptual non sequiturs.

Introduction

If you have ever found yourself admiring the environment of a game or enjoying the way the game's challenges keep you guessing, you are appreciating the work of that game's level designer. The level designer creates not only the space in which the game takes place—its furnishings and backgrounds—but also the emotional context of the game. Successful level designers draw on fundamental design principles that apply to any kind of game, such as ensuring the player always knows his short-term goals and the consequences of risks, as well as design principles specific to the type of game being designed. Level designers work closely with the game designer to make sure layouts are appropriate for the storyline and to achieve the atmosphere and pacing required to keep players engaged in the game world. Level design cannot be a quick and easy process if it is to be done right. We identify 11 steps that the level designer takes, from initial handoff to user testing. The final section details problems to avoid in the level design process, including the key directive to never lose sight of your audience.

What Is Level Design?

In Chapter 2, "Design Components and Processes," we described level design as the process of constructing the experience that will be offered directly to the player, using components provided by the game designer. Note that the terms *game designer* and *level designer* are not interchangeable but refer to separate roles that, in a commercial environment, are almost always played by different members of the development team. In the rest of this book, we reserve the word *you* to mean *the reader as game designer,* but in this chapter only, *you* indicates *the reader as level designer*.

Level designers create the following essential parts of the player's experience:

- **The space in which the game takes place.** If the game includes a simulated space, as most do, then level design includes creating that space using a 2D or 3D modeling tool. While game designers determine what *kinds* of things will be in the game world, level designers determine precisely *what features* will be in each level of the game world and where these features will be. Level designers take the game designer's general plans for levels and make them specific and concrete.

- **The initial conditions of the level,** including the state of various changeable features (Is the drawbridge initially up or down?), the number of artificial opponents the player faces, the amounts of any resources that the player controls at the beginning of the level, and where resources may be found in the landscape.

- **The set of challenges the player will face within the level.** Many games offer challenges in a linear sequence; if so, level designers determine what that sequence will be, construct a suitable space, and place the challenges within it. In other games, the challenges may be approached in a number of different possible sequences or any order at all; see *Layouts* and *Pacing* below for further discussion.

- **The termination conditions of the level,** ordinarily characterized in terms of victory and/or loss. In many games, levels can only be won but not lost, and in a few, such as the default mode in *SimCity,* levels can only be lost and never won.

12

- **The interplay between the gameplay and the game's story,** if any. The writer of the story must work closely with the level designer to interweave gameplay and narrative events.

- **The aesthetics and mood of the level.** Whereas the game designer and art director specify the overall tone of a level and artists create the specific models and textures, level designers take the general specifications and decide how to implement those plans. If the plan says "Level 13 will be a scary haunted house," the level designers decide what kind of a house and *how* to make it feel scary and haunted.

Level designers normally construct all these things using tools created specifically for the purpose. Some games, including *Warcraft III* and *Half-Life 2*, actually ship their level design tools along with the game, so players can expand and customize the game world; if you own one of these games, you can practice level design by using those tools.

Level design could easily be the subject of an entire book. Here, we concentrate on introducing the general principles and the process of level design.

Key Design Principles

Two types of design principles will help you to design a level: *universal level design principles* aimed at designing levels in any kind of game, and *genre-specific level design principles,* focused on design issues specific to the different genres. We address each of these in turn.

Universal Level Design Principles

Barbarossa: The [Pirate's] Code is more what you'd call "guidelines" than actual rules.

—Pirates of the Caribbean: The Curse of the Black Pearl

Level designers have for some time tried to define a set of principles to guide the level design process so that new games will avoid the errors of older ones. Considerable debate surrounds this issue, as not everyone agrees on which, if any, principle is truly universal. Examining the important principles constitutes a valuable exercise in any case, so we present a brief list here. Some apply as much to game design generally as they do specifically to level design, but because the level designer constructs the play environment and sets the challenges, she will be the one who puts these principles into practice.

- **Make the early levels of a game tutorial levels.** We devote an entire section, *Tutorial Levels,* to this extremely important topic later in this chapter.

- **Vary the pacing of the level.** This is also critically important. We address this in *Pacing* later.

- **When the player surmounts a challenge that consumes his resources, provide more resources.** This may seem obvious, but you might be surprised how many games fail to do it. We address this, too, in *Pacing*.

- **Avoid conceptual non sequiturs.** Unless your level is either intentionally surreal or meant to be funny, you shouldn't build things that make no sense, such as rooms accessible only via ventilation shafts. Even more important, don't put dangers or rewards in places in which no sane person could possibly expect to find them. See *Avoid Conceptual Non Sequiturs* later in the chapter.

- **Clearly inform the player of his short-term goals.** Unless your game offers only a sandbox in which the player simply plays around for the fun of it, at any given time he will be working to achieve a whole hierarchy of challenges, from the overall victory condition of the game down to the problem occupying his attention (How do I get across this chasm?) at the immediate moment. (We discuss the hierarchy of challenges at greater length in Chapter 9, "Gameplay.") While you do not always have to tell the player exactly what he needs to do to win (he may have to discover the long-term goal through exploration or observation), you should never leave him wondering what to do next; the current or next short-term goal should be obvious.

- **Be clear about risks, rewards, and the consequences of decisions.** When facing a challenge, the player should always have some idea of the benefits of success and the price of failure or, if the player has to make a decision, the likely consequences associated with his options. Old video games used to implement a *learn by dying* approach, which gave players no means of knowing what elements of the game world were dangerous and what weren't, so the avatars died repeatedly as the players learned. Industry professionals now consider this extremely bad design practice. While the player should not necessarily know every detail of what consequences his decisions will produce, he should be able to make a reasonable guess based on the context in which you present the decision. If you give him a doorknob, it should open the door. It may *also* release a giant killer robo-camel into the room, but it should open the door first.

- **Reward the player for skill, imagination, intelligence, and dedication.** These four qualities distinguish a good player, and good players deserve to be rewarded. You may create rewards in many forms: powerups and other resources, shortcuts through the level, secret levels, minigames, cut-scenes and other narrative material, or simple praise. Players like to be told when they've done a good job.

- **Reward in a large way, punish in a small way,** or to use an old adage, you catch more flies with honey than vinegar. The hope of success motivates players more than the fear of failure does. If a game repeatedly smacks them down hard, players will become discouraged and abandon the game with a feeling that they're being abused. Don't forget that the *duty to empathize* is one of the obligations of player-centric game design: Your primary objective is to give players an enjoyable experience. Build more rewards into your level than punishments.

- **The purpose of an artificial opponent is to put up a good fight and then lose.** Design your level so that the player will get better and better at overcoming the challenges until he succeeds at all of them. In a multi-player competitive game, the skill and luck of the players decide who wins, but in a single-player game, we always want the player to win eventually, and it's up to you to make sure that happens. An unbeatable level is a badly designed level.

- **Implement multiple difficulty settings.** Make your game accessible to a wider audience by allowing them to switch the difficulty of your game to easy, normal, or hard settings. In games with an internal economy, you should be able to tweak the numbers to adjust the difficulty to accommodate the player's preference; we address this in more detail in Chapter 11, "Game Balancing." And *easy* should mean *EASY.* Very easy. You gain nothing by restricting your game so that only highly skilled players can enjoy it.

FYI *The 400 Project*

In 2001, veteran game designers Hal Barwood and Noah Falstein began assembling a list of design rules for video games, hoping eventually to compile a list of as many as 400 of them. Having gathered more than 100 rules from fellow designers so far, Barwood and Falstein's *400 Project* represents the combined wisdom of many people. Rather than outright commandments, these are tools to guide your own creative work, as a ruler guides a pencil. Some of the rules conflict with others, and it will be up to you to decide when one rule is more important than another. We *strongly* encourage you to download the rules and take them to heart as you design your game and the levels within it. *The 400 Project* may be found at: **www.finitearts.com/400P/400project.htm.**

Genre-Specific Level Design Principles

Some principles of level design apply only to games within specific genres. Since we don't have room to present a comprehensive list of principles specific to each genre, this section offers *one* genre-specific principle for each genre covered in Part Two of this book—the one principle we consider to be the most important. For more details on each genre, see the relevant chapter in Part Two.

Action Games   *Vary the pace*. Action games put more stress on the player than any other genre does, so the universal principle *vary the pace* applies more strongly to action games than to other genres; that is why we include it as the most important genre-specific principle as well. Players must be able to rest, both physically and mentally, between bouts of high-speed action.

Strategy Games   *Reward planning*. Strategic thinking means planning—anticipating an opponent's moves and preparing a defense, as well as planning attacks and considering an opponent's possible defensive moves. Design levels that reward planning. Give players defensible locations to build in and advantageous positions to attack from, but let the players discover these places for themselves.

Role-Playing Games   *Offer opportunities for character growth and player self-expression*. Character growth is a major player goal in any RPG; some players consider it even more important than victory. Every level should provide opportunities to achieve character growth by whatever means the game rewards—combat, puzzle-solving, trade, and so on. RPGs also entertain by allowing players to express themselves; that is, to role play. Every level should include opportunities for the player to make decisions that reflect the persona he has assumed for the game.

Sports Games   *Verisimilitude is vital*. Sports games, while not ordinarily broken into levels in the usual sense, consist of individual matches played in different stadiums or courses with different teams or athletes, so you can think of each match played as a level. Level designers design the stadiums and sometimes the teams and athletes. More than in any other genre, players of sports games value a close relationship between the video game and the real world. The simulation of match play must be completely convincing; try to model each team and each stadium as closely as possible on the real thing—which includes not only appearances but the performance characteristics of the athletes and the coaching strategies of the teams.

Vehicle Simulations   *Reward skillful maneuvering*. All vehicle simulations offer steering a vehicle as the primary player activity and steering well, often in adverse circumstances, as the primary challenge. Construct levels that test the player's skill at maneuvering his vehicle and reward him for his prowess. Other challenges, such as shooting or exploring, should be secondary.

12

Construction and Management Simulations *Offer an interesting variety of initial conditions and goals.* Most construction and management simulations start the player with an empty space and let her build whatever she likes within the constraints of the game's internal economy. In such games, you won't need to do much level design. However, a CMS can also offer the player an existing or partial construction and let her continue working from there, often with a goal to achieve within a certain time limit. We term these *scenarios* rather than *levels,* the difference being that a scenario, unlike a level, consists of a self-contained situation unrelated to any of the other scenarios. Typically the game allows players to try the scenarios in any order, and the gameplay (though not the goal) tends to be identical in each. Because you cannot alter the gameplay, scenario design becomes a matter of offering an interesting variety of initial conditions and goals. *SimCity 3000 Unlimited* came with 13 scenarios, from reuniting East and West Berlin to preparing for a World Cup soccer match in Seoul.

Adventure Games *Construct challenges that harmonize with their locations and the story.* Adventure games offer much of their entertainment through exploration and puzzle-solving. Designers set different chapters of an adventure game in different locations or landscapes to add novelty and interest to the experience. (A chapter is the adventure game equivalent of a level.) Create challenges that harmonize with the current level and with the current events in the story. In a room full of machinery, the challenges should involve machines; on a farm, the challenges should involve farm animals or implements. This principle applies to some extent to any game, but because story is so important in adventure games, we consider the principle especially important for them.

Artificial Life Games *Create many interaction opportunities for the creatures in their environment.* Much of the enjoyment in playing an artificial life (A-life) game comes from watching the simulated creatures in the game and giving them things to do within their environment. The level designer for an A-life game, then, needs to create interaction opportunities. The game should also offer many opportunities for the player to interact with the creatures as well, but generally the game designer, not the level designer, specifies these.

Puzzle Games *Give the player time to think.* Puzzle-solving is problem-solving, and it knows no timetable. Few players enjoy being forced to solve puzzles under time pressure. (*Lemmings,* a famous exception, at least allowed the player to pause the game.) You may not be able to offer the player multiple difficulty levels due to the complexity of balancing puzzle games—for further discussion of this issue, see Chapter 20, "Artificial Life and Puzzle Games"—which is another reason that time to think becomes important. Either create puzzles that give the player complete freedom to think things through before acting or allow him to pause the game and study the screen for a while.

Layouts

For games that involve travel, especially avatar-based games, the layout of the space significantly affects the player's perception of the experience. Over the years, a few common patterns have emerged, which we introduce here. We outline these in simplified form; you should not hesitate to create any layout that your game needs.

Open Layouts

In an open layout, the player benefits from almost entirely unconstrained movement. An open layout corresponds to the outdoors, with an avatar in principle free to wander in any direction at any time. Even levels with open layouts, though, may include a few small regions that cannot be entered without difficulty or can be entered by only a single path (such as passing through a door into a building). War games make extensive use of open layouts, *Battlefield 1942* being a particularly successful example. Role-playing games offer open layouts while the player goes adventuring outdoors, but they typically switch to network or combination layouts (described later) when the party goes indoors or underground.

Linear Layouts

A linear layout requires the player to experience the game's spaces in a fixed sequence with no side corridors or branches. It does not mean that the spaces are actually arranged in a line (see Figure 12.1). A player following a linear path

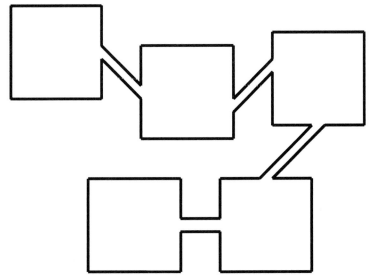

FIGURE 12.1 A level with a linear layout.

can move only to the next area or to the previous area and does not have to make any decisions about where to go next. A game in which all levels use linear layouts is often said to be *on rails* because, like a train on a track, the traveler goes wherever the predefined route takes her. Ordinarily, the player has no reason to go backward in a linear layout unless she forgot to pick up something that she needs. Linear layouts often require players to pass through one-way doors that actually prevent them from going back, so long as they have collected everything they need to go on. Be sure you don't lock a player out of a region that contains an item essential to her later progress—an elementary level design error.

Linear layouts naturally work well with linear stories; if your game features such a story, you might consider such a layout. See Chapter 7, "Storytelling and Narrative," for more on linear stories.

Traditional for side-scrolling action games and rail-shooters, the linear layout is otherwise uncommon nowadays. Today's designers tend to favor the parallel layout.

Parallel Layouts

A parallel layout—a more modern variant of the linear layout—resembles a railroad switchyard with lots of parallel tracks and the means for the player to switch from one track to another at intervals. The player passes through the level from one end to another but may take a variety of paths to get there. See Figure 12.2 for a much-simplified illustration.

Even though the parallel layout does not require players to pass through every available path, most players search them all anyway if the game will let them do so. One path may offer a greater risk and therefore a greater reward, while another path may give the player greater insights into the storyline. You can easily construct a parallel layout to reflect a foldback story structure. (See Chapter 7, "Storytelling and Narrative," for a discussion of story structures.)

You can also use parallel paths to provide shortcuts that let a player bypass particularly difficult challenges that lie on the more obvious path. If you do so, you may want to hide the entrance to the shortcut so only a particularly dedicated explorer will find it. When you create a hidden entrance, you must provide some clue, however subtle, that it is there. Otherwise, finding it becomes a trial-and-error challenge, a sign of bad design. The original *Wolfenstein 3D* contained hidden rooms accessible only through wall panels that looked exactly like the rest of the wall, which forced players to check every single wall panel in the entire level to see which might conceal a hidden room.

Ring Layouts

In a ring layout, the path returns to its starting point, although you may include shortcuts that cut off a portion of the journey (see Figure 12.3). Designers

FIGURE 12.2 A level with a parallel layout.

mainly use ring layouts for racing games, in which players pass through the same space a number of times, facing challenges from the environment and each other along the way. Shortcuts require less time but should be proportionately more difficult than the regular route; balancing this will be a big part of the level designer's job.

Rings do not necessarily look like circles. Oval tracks or twisting road-racing tracks qualify as rings.

Network Layouts

Spaces in a network layout connect to other spaces in a variety of ways. Figure 12.4 shows a simple example. A large network poses a considerable exploration challenge; just learning the way around made up a significant part of the gameplay in old text adventure games. Modern graphical games that implement three-dimensional spaces usually present architecturally appropriate and logical networks (going downstairs from the ground floor of a building leads to the basement, for instance) but still offer plenty of

12

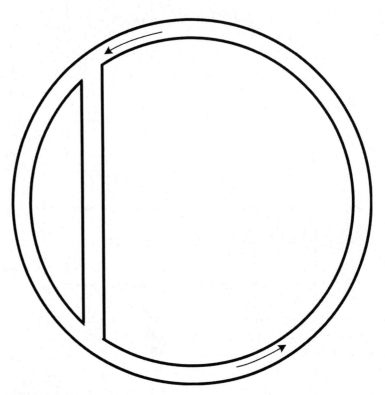

FIGURE 12.3 A level with a ring layout.

FIGURE 12.4 A level with a simple network layout.

opportunities to create enjoyable exploration challenges. See *Exploration Challenges* in Chapter 9, "Gameplay," for further discussion.

A network layout gives the player considerable freedom about what path to take, so you will find it difficult to tell a story that requires a particular sequence of events in a network layout. This doesn't mean that you can't tell stories, only that your stories have to tolerate the player experiencing events in any sequence. To enforce *some* sequence, use a combination layout, described in the section *Combinations of Layouts*, later in the chapter.

In a network with a small number of major spaces, every space may be connected to every other space for maximum freedom of movement. This arrangement poses little exploration challenge to the player but makes an ideal fighting ground for deathmatch contests in games such as *Quake*.

Hub-and-Spoke Layouts

In the hub-and-spoke layout, the player begins in a central hub that ordinarily doesn't present significant challenges or dangers. As such, it serves as a place of comfort or safety, a base to which to return. To explore the rest of the world, the player follows a linear path out from the hub and then returns back to the hub on the same path (see Figure 12.5). The return journey either should be quick—because the player covers old ground during the return—or should offer new opportunities for gameplay and new rewards as the player comes back. Normally you would also put a major challenge and a major reward at the outer end of the spoke.

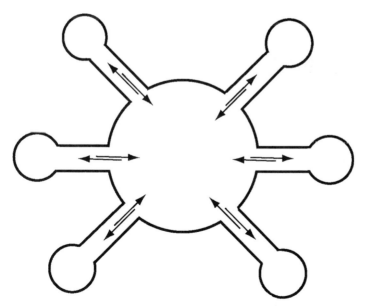

FIGURE 12.5 The hub-and-spoke layout.

12

This layout gives the player some choice about where he goes, which many players will appreciate. You need not offer the player access to all the spokes at the beginning of the level; in order to make sure that the player doesn't try the harder challenges too soon, you can lock off some areas until the player tries the easier challenges available in other spokes. Note that if you unlock the spokes only one at a time, you effectively change the hub-and-spoke layout into a linear layout.

The *Spyro the Dragon* games used a hub-and-spoke plan. The games included several hubs, called *homeworlds,* each of which was the center of its level. Various spokes led off from the hubs to areas with different themes.

Combinations of Layouts

Many layouts combine aspects of each type of layout, providing, for instance, networked spaces to accomplish tasks within a larger linear framework. The layout illustrated in Figure 12.6 corresponds to the story structure of many large RPGs, which tend to offer one major story arc and a large number of subplots or quests. Adventure games quite often use a combination structure too, letting players do considerable exploration in one area before moving on to another. Note the similarities with Figure 19.7 in Chapter 19, "Adventure Games."

Expanding on the Principles

Here we address a few particularly important issues that we raised in our list of universal design principles: atmosphere, pacing, and tutorial levels.

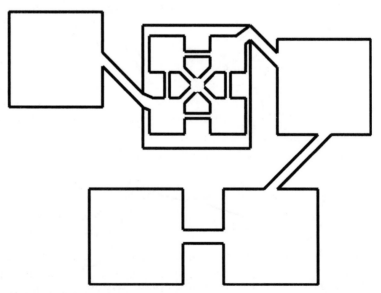

FIGURE 12.6 A combined linear and networked layout.

Atmosphere

The art director and lead game designer decide on the overall look of a game; the artists build the models; and the audio engineers create the sound effects. But it's up to the level designer to assemble all this material into a specific level in such a way that it's aesthetically coherent and creates the appropriate mood. A level designer does what in movies would be four or five jobs? set designer, lighting designer, special effects designer, Foley editor, and even cinematographer, because a level designer must look at the game world the way the player will see it, through the lens of the game's virtual camera.

As you work to establish the atmosphere of your game, you will use all of the following tools:

- **Lighting.** The placement and orientation of the lights in a level can create a sunny day, a moonlit night, or a dark alley. Soft morning light filtering in through a window creates a sense of warmth and well-being, whereas the odd glowing colored lights of a machine room evoke a sense of danger. The yellow of a sodium vapor street lamp or the harsh fluorescent lights of an office and any other lighting you choose must work with other aesthetic choices you make to set the mood of a level. What you choose *not* to light is just as important as what you choose *to* light.

- **Color palette.** Just as the color palette of the avatar's clothes reflects her character, the color palette of the level reflects its mood. The color palette of the level will emerge from a combination of the original colors of the objects you place in it (created by the artists under neutral lighting conditions) plus the lighting that you add. Notice how television commercials use color to telegraph an emotion, calm you down, get you excited, or keep you interested in watching. Do some research on color, and you will find many ways to create an effect in your level or elicit a particular response from the player.

- **Weather and atmospheric effects.** Fog, rain, snow, and wind all create distinct impressions. So many games take place in indoor spaces that we sometimes forget the importance of weather to our moods. Dark, tumbling skies presage a storm and make us instinctively react with "Find shelter!" even in a video game. Fog creates mystery, while strong winds suggest instability and disturbances to come.

- **Special visual effects.** When weapons recoil or screeching tires create smoke, when magic spells produce colored sparks or blood splashes across a wall, you're seeing visual effects. You can startle players, discomfit them, amuse them, or reward them, all with visual effects.

- **Music.** You won't write the music unless you're also a musician, but you may well choose the music of your level in conjunction with your game's audio director. The rhythm of the music helps to set the

12

pace, and its timbre and key help to set the mood. Generally, but not always, music remains consistent throughout the level, part of its overall tone.

- **Ambient audio.** Like music, ambient audio contributes to the overall mood of a level. Notice how golf games use the sounds of birds singing and crickets chirping to suggest the peaceful outdoor tranquility of a golf course. The ambient audio can also vary with place and time, which tells the player something about where he is and helps him to orient himself. Great steam engines churning create a feeling of power and danger; owls hooting and foxes crying tell us it's nighttime; the hubbub of talk and regular cries of vendors put us in a market square.

- **Special audio effects.** Audio effects naturally do for the ears what visual effects do for the eyes, and in some respects provide even more important information. From inside a car, you can't see the tires losing their grip on the road, but the squealing sound tells you you're on the edge of danger—you're pushing the vehicle to its limits.

Pacing

The *pacing* of a level refers to the frequency at which the player encounters individual challenges. A fast pace creates *stress,* offering challenges at a rapid rate while giving the player no opportunity to relax. (We define stress and discuss the relationship between *stress* and *difficulty* in Chapter 9, "Gameplay.") A slow pace offers challenges at a slow rate and permits the player to take his time about addressing them.

FYI *Classic Arcade Pacing*

In arcade games, especially old ones such as *Space Invaders*, the pace at which the player faced challenges became faster and faster as each level progressed. If the player succeeded in beating the level—destroying all the invading aliens—he got a few seconds of rest before the next level began. The next level offered identical challenges, but it started at a faster pace than the previous level started and ended at a faster pace than the previous level ended. The pace of *Space Invaders* increased both within each level and from level to level until it overwhelmed the player and he lost the game. He could not win, only hope to get a high score.

▶▶ CONTINUED ON NEXT PAGE

▶▶ CONTINUED

> This classic arcade pacing explains how arcade games used to make their money. It's now considered a bit old-fashioned and inappropriate for console and PC games because they don't need to make the player lose in order to force him to put more money in the machine. However, with the continuing popularity of retro gaming, classic arcade pacing remains common in simple Web-based games such as *Collapse!*

Pacing in Different Genres   The pace you choose for your level will depend to a considerable extent on the genre of the game you're creating; players expect a faster- or slower-paced game depending upon the genre. The fastest-paced games of all, the old 2D side-scrolling or top-scrolling shooters, required players to move the joystick and bang the fire button continuously just to survive. Multiplayer deathmatch shooters such as *Quake* and its kin represent the modern equivalent. (Shooting games such as the *Rainbow Six* series, which involve careful planning and stealthy movement, often move at a slow pace except for a brief wild flurry when the enemy comes into view.) Adventure games use the slowest pace because much of the activity consists of interactive dialog (generally a story action rather than an action taken to surmount a challenge), exploration without much effort, and puzzle-solving in which the players can take as long as they like. Play a variety of games and study their pacing for yourself.

Vary the Pacing   As a general principle, the pacing of a level in any game, especially a game with physical challenges, should alternate between fast and slow periods, just as the tempo of movements in a symphony or the levels of excitement in an action movie vary. Players need moments to rest, both physically and mentally, and on the whole, the faster the pace of the level, the more important rest becomes. A particularly stressful challenge should be followed by a brief period with no challenges at all and then by easier challenges that gradually ramp up to more stressful ones again. This also gives the player a chance to savor the pleasant emotions that accompany success.

12

Varying the pace not only gives the player a rest from physical challenges, it also produces a more balanced game. If overcoming a challenge requires spending a resource (ammunition or health or the like), then the more the player spends on a given challenge, the weaker and more vulnerable he will be afterward. In his weakened state, he should not face another demanding challenge immediately. You should also make fresh supplies available to him immediately after he surmounts a challenge that costs him a lot of resources, as we explain in Chapter 11, "Game Balancing." In shooter games, these traditionally take the form of boxes of ammunition and medical kits for restoring health, stored in an area immediately beyond a large group of enemies. In role-playing games, enemies drop valuable resources when killed, thus helping to replenish the player's supply.

FYI   *Pacing in* The Lord of the Rings

For a wonderful example of varied pacing from literature, read *The Lord of the Rings.* Almost every major adventure or threat the Fellowship experiences in the first two volumes is followed by a period of rest and refreshment to heal wounds and in particular to replenish food supplies. The hobbits flee the Black Riders and take refuge with Farmer Maggot. They are caught in the Old Forest and rescued by Tom Bombadil. After the attack at Weathertop, they find shelter in Rivendell. After losing Gandalf in the Mines of Moria, they find succor in Lórien, and so on. This change of pace not only creates emotional variety for the reader, allowing her to enjoy the beauty and warmth of the heroes' places of shelter after the terrors of their journey, but it also makes the story more credible. No one can carry six months' worth of food on his back, so the supplies had to come from somewhere.

The Da Vinci Code, notwithstanding its financial success, is less credible in this regard. Involved in almost nonstop action from start to finish; the heroes never seem to need any sleep.

You can vary the pacing in a variety of ways: by creating an area free of challenges in which the player can simply explore; by creating an area that contains only low-stress challenges; or by making the player's avatar temporarily invulnerable or particularly strong as a reward for successfully overcoming a demanding challenge. You can also deliver a bit of the story through narrative: Watching a cut-scene, for example, gives the player a moment to relax.

You will find it easiest to vary the pacing in games that involve avatar travel through a linear space, because you can control the sequence in which the player confronts challenges. Games that give the player freedom to explore at will give you less control. In genres that use multipresent interaction models rather than avatar- or party-based ones, you may have little control at all. For example, in a real-time strategy game, the pacing will depend to a large degree on the player's own style of play. Those who attack aggressively experience a faster pace than those who slowly build up huge armies before attacking.

Overall Pacing   Although the pacing of a level should vary from time to time (depending on the genre), the overall pacing of the level should either remain steady or become more difficult as the player nears the end. A longstanding tradition in action games, and many other genres as well, calls for the inclusion of a *boss* to defeat at the end of the level: a particularly difficult challenge. Victory, and the end of the level, reward the player for defeating the boss, and this sometimes includes a cache of resources or treasure as well. Bosses, although something of a cliché, fit neatly into games with a Hero's Journey story structure. We discuss bosses in greater detail in Chapter 13, "Action Games."

Levels should not, in general, get easier and easier as they go along. If the player does well, *positive feedback* may come into play to make the game easier, and you will need to design the level, or the core mechanics, to reduce that effect. We discuss positive feedback at length, including various means of limiting it, in Chapter 11, "Game Balancing."

Tutorial Levels

Years ago, video games shipped with large manuals that explained how to play the games. Designers had no other way to teach the player because the distribution media (cartridges and floppy disks) couldn't hold enough data to spare any room for tutorial levels. But no matter how much someone likes to read books, nobody wants to stop to read a book when he wants to play a game. Now, all games should be designed so that the player can start playing immediately. Games still use manuals, mostly in electronic form, but for detailed reference information rather than instructions.

Instead of instructions, games offer **tutorial levels**—early levels that teach the player how to play. Every commercial game except the simplest ones should include one or more tutorial levels. Although tutorial levels require more time and effort to build than a manual does to write, tutorial levels have the tremendous advantage that they let the player learn in a hands-on fashion. Players learn physical activities, such as how the control devices function in the game, far more quickly if they can try the actions for themselves.

A tutorial level is not simply an easy level or a short level. A tutorial level should be a scripted or partially scripted experience that explains the game's user interface, key challenges, and actions to the player. Use voiceover narration, text superimposed on the screen, or a special mentor character to explain things to the player.

As you design one or more tutorial levels for your game, consider these key principles:

12

- Introduce the game's features in an orderly sequence, starting with the most general and most often used features and proceeding to the more specialized and rarely used ones. Your tutorial should introduce each individual action that the game permits, but it need not discuss combinations of actions and what effects they may have. The players can work that out for themselves.

- Don't make all the game's features available at once. It will only confuse the player if he happens to select, by accident, a maneuver that you haven't yet introduced, which produces an effect on the screen that the player doesn't understand. Disable features until the tutorial introduces them.

- If the interface is complex, as interfaces tend to be in many war games and construction and management simulations, introduce the information over two or three tutorial levels.

- Highlight user interface elements that appear on the screen with an arrow pointing to them or a colored glow around them while your explanatory text or helpful guide character refers to them. Don't just say where these items appear on the screen and make the player look for them.

- Let the player go back and try things again as often as he wants, without any penalty for failure. All the costs of making a mistake that you might put into the ordinary game world should be switched off in the tutorial levels.

- Make the tutorial levels optional. Experienced players may not need them and will be irritated by being forced to go through them. (*America's Army* violated this rule, largely because of the game's function as a representation of the U.S. Army. The developers wanted to make the point that not just anybody would be allowed into the Army, so the tutorial levels symbolized Basic Training in the real army. *America's Army* was not a pure entertainment product, however.)

The Level Design Process

Having introduced the general *principles* of level design, we now turn to the *process*. Level design takes place during the elaboration stage of game design and, like the overall game design, is an iterative process. At points during the procedure, the level designers should show the work-in-progress to other members of the team for analysis and commentary. Early input from artists, programmers, and other designers prevents you from wasting time on overly complex levels, asking for features the programmers cannot implement, or making demands for artwork that the artists don't have time to meet.

At the 2004 Computer Game Technology Conference in Toronto, Canada, level designers Rick Knowles and Joseph Ganetakos of Pseudo Interactive presented an excellent lecture simply entitled, "Level Design" (Knowles, 2004). They described the 11-stage process by which their company builds levels, which we summarize here. In the following sections, we assume that the development teams consist of game designers, artists, programmers, and sound designers, as well as you: the level designer.

Throughout our discussion of this process, you will notice a strong emphasis on the relationship between the level designer and the art team, and less emphasis on the relationship between the level designer and the audio or programming teams. The reason for this is that level designers build prototype artwork that the art team then uses as a blueprint from which to build final artwork that will actually go into the game. This requires that the level designers hand off their prototype to the art team and receive the final artwork back from the art team at particular stages in the process. The relationship with the programmers and the audio team is less sharply defined. Level designers request special features from these groups, and the project manager will determine when and how that work gets done, but generally it doesn't involve handing off material *to* the audio or programming teams and receiving material back from them in the same way. Your relationship with the programmers and audio people is just as important as your relationship with the artists, but your interactions with them may be less formally scheduled.

A Note on Duties and Terminology

The nature of a level designer's job varies considerably depending on both the genre of the game and the technology that implements it. A few years ago, level designers were not expected to possess either art or programming skills. As the size and complexity of games has increased, so has the size and complexity of the level designer's job. In modern 3D games, level designers often use 3D modeling tools to construct temporary—and sometimes even final—artwork to go into a game. (The term *model* refers to a three-dimensional geometric structure that depicts a single thing, such as a human, vehicle, tree, or the underlying landscape of a level.) Also, games now often include *scripting engines* that allow level designers to write small programs, or *scripts,* that control some aspects of the behavior of the level during play. Scripting engines normally implement scripting languages less powerful than the programming language used by the programmers, but the scripting language will be sufficient for defining the behavior of automated traps, doors, and other special events that may occur in the level. We don't have room in this book to teach you the skills needed to use such tools, but you can find many resources for learning to use them on the Internet and at colleges and universities.

For simplicity's sake, in this section we assume that you are creating levels for a game that uses a 3D graphics engine to display a three-dimensional game world. If you are making a 2D game, where we refer to models, think in terms of their 2D equivalents: *sprites* (2D art and animation) for movable objects and the *background* (a 2D painting, often made up of interchangeable rectangular tiles) for the landscape.

12

Design to Level Design Handoff

In the first stage, the game designers will tell you in a general way what they want for the level: its setting, mood, key gameplay activities, and events. You should then generate a list of features you want to appear in the level:

- Events that can be triggered by player action
- Props (objects that will be present in the level)
- Nonplayer characters (NPCs)

At this point you also create a rough overview map of the level, showing how the landscape varies and what props and NPCs will be in which areas. See Figure 12.7 for an example from an unproduced driving game by Pseudo Interactive, set on islands inhabited by dinosaurs.

Planning Phase

Armed with the list and sketch created in the first stage, you now start to plan the level in detail. Use pencil and paper to work out the sequence of events: both what you expect the player(s) to do and how the game will respond. Begin

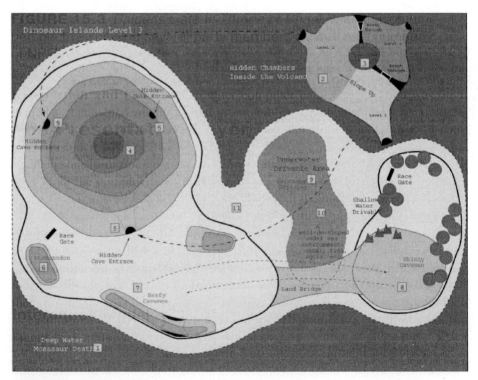

FIGURE 12.7 Rough level sketch for a driving game showing key features. Image courtesy Pseudo Interactive.

to document your decisions in the following key areas: gameplay, art, performance, and code requirements.

Gameplay   As you plan the gameplay for your level, you will need to consider all the following issues:

- **Layout** (discussed extensively in the *Layouts* section earlier). Where can the player-controlled characters (avatar, party, or units) go and where can they not go? What paths can they use to get there? Many parts of your level may be cosmetic: The player can see them but cannot reach them.

- **Areas devoted to major challenges.** Which areas carry strategic importance? Which will offer the biggest challenges? If the game involves combat, where would you like it to occur?

- **Termination conditions.** How does the player win or lose the level?

- **Resource placements.** Are depots of weapons, health points, powerups, or any other resources hidden in the environment? Where? What resources, and how much?

- **Player start and end points.** Do the player-controlled characters begin the level at one or more specific locations? Where? Do the characters end at one or more locations? Where?

- **NPC positions and spawn points.** If nonplayer characters—whether enemies, friends, or neutrals—appear in the level, where are they initially positioned? Can they suddenly appear in the level at a specific location or *spawn point* during play? Where?

- **Elevations.** How much vertical movement does the level permit, and how does that affect play? Higher elevations naturally allow the player to see farther in first- and third-person perspectives; will this cause problems or constitute a positive feature of your level?

- **Secret areas**. Do you plan to incorporate hidden areas or secret shortcuts? Where will they be, and what clues will be available to suggest they might be present?

- **Special event issues.** What special events, unique to this level, can occur? Where will they occur? What will set them off? How do the special events reflect the setting and tone of the level?

- **Landmarks.** How does the player find her way around? How can she tell where she is? Establishing major landmarks will help her out.

- **Destruction.** Can any part of the level be destroyed or its landscape radically altered? Where does this happen and what causes it? How does it affect the gameplay? Does it have the potential to introduce anomalies, such as enemies who wander off the edge of the world and never return?

12

- **Storytelling.** How does the sequence of events the player experiences integrate with the game's story? Which events are dramatically meaningful and which are not? Where and when do you want cut-scenes or other narrative events to occur?

- **Save points and checkpoints.** Does the level include save points or checkpoints? Where? In games in which the player fails frequently and has to reload, positioning the save points is a critically important part of balancing the game.

Art   In the art planning phase, you determine the *scope* of your level and decide how much artwork it will need. Scope refers to the magnitude and complexity of the level, both in terms of the number of objects and characters that it contains and the special events that it includes. You can make a serious error by choosing too large a scope; see *Get the Scope Right* near the end of this chapter.

You already have your sketch and a general idea of what the environment will be like, whether on the sea floor, in outer space, or inside an anthill. First decide on the scale of the level: How big will this level be in the game world's units of measure? This will help you to determine just how many other features the level needs. In almost every genre, if you've balanced the challenges correctly, the size of the level is directly proportional to the length of time that it takes the player to play through that level, so the scale you choose will, in a rough way, determine how much gameplay you can offer.

Next, start thinking about the kinds of objects that should be present in the level. Do research at the library or on the Internet for visual reference material to give you inspiration. Count the number of unique types of props that the level will require and plan in a general way where to put them. Certain generic items such as streetlights (or the infamous crates in first-person shooters) can simply be duplicated, but natural objects such as trees and boulders should come in several types, and the art team will need to know this. Try to avoid including too many identical objects in a level; it destroys realism.

Create a list of textures that the level will probably need. In an office, you may need tiles for the floor coverings, wood or metal for the desks, fabric for the chairs, and so on. Some offices may be streamlined, with severe geometric shapes, whereas others may be ornate, featuring a Louis XIV desk and antique chairs.

Decide on the visual appearance of any special effects that the artists will have to implement. It may take a while for the artists to come up with the visuals for a never-before-seen eruption of semisentient magma at zero gravity, so you need to plan ahead.

Performance   You normally think of performance as the programmers' problem, but it's up to the level designer not to build a world that bogs down the machine. You will need to sit down with the programmers and set some boundaries. How complex can the geometry be? How far into the distance will the graphics engine be able to render objects? How many autonomously moving units or creatures can the game support at one time? Know your machine's limitations as you plan your level.

Code   Finally, as part of the planning process, identify specific requests that you intend to make of the programmers for features unique to this level. These may take the form of special events that require coding, unique NPCs who appear only in this level but need their own behavior model and artificial intelligence, or special development tools you may require in order to build and test the level effectively. The more of these special coding problems you identify during planning and can discuss with the programmers in advance, the more likely that implementation will go smoothly.

Working through these steps results in an initial plan for the level. Don't expect the numbers and details in this plan to exactly match what you end up with in the finished level, but working out in advance as much as you can will ensure a smoother design process. Charging in without a plan and making it up as you go along creates more problems in the long run.

Prototyping

In this stage, you will build a prototype of the level. Much of this work will consist of using a 3D modeling tool to construct temporary models of the landscape and objects that can appear within it. The models you create will not end up in the game but will serve as blueprints from which the art team will create the final artwork.

The prototyping phase requires that at least part of the game engine be running so that you can load the model into it and test it. Your prototype should include such features as:

- The basic geometry (physical shape) of the game world created in a 3D modeling tool. If it's a 2D world, the prototype should show the layout of the 2D landscape.

- Temporary textures to place on the geometry to give it a surface. These will eventually be replaced by final textures created by the artists.

- Temporary models of props (trees, furniture, buildings, and so on) and NPCs that will appear in the level, so you can put them where they belong in the landscape.

- Paths planned for AI-driven NPCs—where they travel within the level.

- A lighting design for the level.

- The locations of trigger points for key events. Placing these triggers and documenting what sets them off is referred to as *rigging*.

In some cases, you may be able to use final audio effects in your prototype; that is, the sound effects that will actually end up in the game. If those are not yet

12

available from the audio team, use temporary sound effects and note that they will need to be replaced later.

Level Review

At this point, you have a working prototype of the level; if the programmers have the game engine running, you should be able to play your level in a rudimentary way. Hold a *level review,* inviting members of the design, art, programming, audio, and testing teams to get their feedback. Each should examine your prototype for potential problems that may come up in his own field when working on the real thing. The issues that the level review should address include:

- **Scale.** Is the level the right size? Will it take too much or too little time to play through?

- **Pacing.** Does the flow of events feel right?

- **Placement of objects and triggers.** Are things where they need to be to make the level play smoothly and produce the experience you want?

- **Performance issues.** Is the level too complicated for the machine's processor to handle? The programmers should be able to flag any potential problems.

- **Other code issues.** Does the level call for software that represents a problem for the programmers? For example, a unique NPC that appears only in this level still needs its own AI; will this be an issue?

- **Aesthetics.** Is the level attractive and enjoyable to inhabit? Because the prototype uses temporary geometry and textures, a certain amount of imagination will be called for here.

Level Refinement and Lock-Down

After the level review, take the feedback you've received and refine the prototype, correcting any problems and implementing any new decisions made in the course of the review. This can require any amount of work from tuning a few numbers to scrapping the entire design and starting over from scratch. When you think you've got it right, hold another review and make another refinement pass. Continue this process until everyone agrees (or the person in charge agrees) that the level is ready to go into full production.

At this point, lock the level design. Once a level is designated as *locked,* no additions or changes may be made except if grave problems are discovered. This corresponds to the lock-down that occurs in overall game design at the end of the concept stage. If you don't treat the level as locked, you could go on tuning and tweaking it forever, stretching out the development time and running up the budget.

Level Design to Art Handoff

With the level locked, it's time to hand off your prototype and all your design work to the artists who will use it as a blueprint to build the geometry, animations, and textures that will end up in the real game. The artists will need all your files, as well as a detailed list that explains each file. Your job includes making this list; you cannot simply give them a directory dump and leave them to figure it out. If they don't already know about your design from the level reviews, you should sit down with the artists and give them a thorough briefing not only on how everything looks in the level, but where everything should be and how everything works. From this information, the art director will create a task list to construct all the content the level requires: models, textures, animations, special visual effects, and so on.

If your prototype has been relying on placeholder audio, at this point you will also need to provide details to the audio team about what the level will need in the way of final audio. If any special code is required that has not yet been written, the programmers must be warned at this point so they can have it ready for the content integration stage. (*Content* refers to the nonsoftware part of the game: artwork, audio, movies, and text.)

First Art and Rigging Pass

The project now enters the first art and rigging pass, during which the art team builds the real artwork and rigging. You may be working on other levels at the same time, but you should also stay in close touch with them because they will undoubtedly have questions. It may also be your responsibility to incorporate the content they create into software, to make sure that it all works.

Art to Level Design Handoff and Review

When the art team finishes the final artwork, the artists hand all their work back to you, and you should conduct another review. This will highlight any problems or errors with the artwork that need correcting.

Content Integration

At this point, you will assemble all the assets into the completed (but not yet tested) level—artwork, new code required by the level, audio, and any remaining tweaks to the lighting. You'll also adjust any remaining issues with the rigging, by repositioning characters, effects, and triggers as necessary.

Bug Fixing

Test the level at this point, looking for bugs in the code and mistakes in the content. This will be another iterative process, working back and forth between the art, audio, and code teams and yourself. After finishing your own testing, you hand the level off to the quality assurance (QA) department for formal testing.

User Testing and Tuning

In the last stage, the quality assurance department will create a test plan for the level and begin formal testing, known as *alpha testing*. Their testing will ordinarily be more thorough and strict than the testing you've done; it will also find things that you missed because of your overfamiliarity with the material. As in your own testing, they'll work in an iterative process with the various teams involved, including reporting the bugs in the rigging and gameplay mechanics that you need to fix. When QA considers the level to be thoroughly tested, they may make it available for *beta testing* (testing by end-users).

Pitfalls of Level Design

We end this chapter with a discussion of some important mistakes to avoid—classic errors of level design that, unfortunately, some designers continue to make.

Get the Scope Right

The single most common error made by inexperienced level designers is to try to build something too big. (They almost never try to build something too small.) Everyone would love to make an epic such as a *Final Fantasy* game, but such games require huge production teams, giant budgets, and multiyear development cycles. And even among experienced professionals, epic projects often run late and go over budget.

You must design within the resources of your team, your budget, and the time you have available. Scope, you should remember, refers not only to the size and complexity of the landscape but to the number of props, NPCs, and special events in the level. In order not to undertake an unrealistically large level, you must make lists of these things during the planning stage before you actually start constructing the prototype. The process of making these lists may surprise you by showing you just how much work goes into making even a relatively small level.

Before you choose a scope for your level, determine how much time and staff you have available, taking into account any vacations and holidays that may be coming up. Then assume that half of your team will be out sick for a week at some point during the development process—it's entirely possible. *Now* think again about the scope. How many models can your team build in a day? How quickly can you detect an error, correct it, and test it again? Choose a level size that you and your team can manage. If you make a level too small, it's not easy to enlarge it, but at least you won't have the art team killing themselves to create all the content. If you make a level too big and find that there isn't time to complete everything, you'll have to either deliver a sparse, unfinished level or scramble to cut things out, which will almost certainly harm your level's balance and pacing.

Avoid Conceptual Non Sequiturs

At the beginning of the first level of *James Bond: Tomorrow Never Dies,* the player, in the persona of James Bond, sneaks into an enemy military outpost armed only with a pistol and faces numerous Russian guards; how many, he doesn't know. If he blows up some of the oil drums scattered somewhat randomly outside the outpost, he will find medical kits hidden inside, which he can use later to restore his health when wounded.

Hiding medical kits inside oil drums belongs to a class of design errors, usually made at the level design stage, called *conceptual non sequiturs*—game features that make no sense. No sane person would think of looking in an oil drum to see if a medical kit might be hidden within. Furthermore, any thinking player would reason that if he's trying to sneak into an enemy military installation armed only with a pistol, causing a loud explosion right outside is not a good idea; several dozen people will come running to see what made the noise. He would further assume that any medical kit that *was* inside an oil drum when it blew up wouldn't be good for much afterwards. Consequently, a reasonable player wouldn't blow up the oil drum and wouldn't get the benefit of the medical kit. In other words, the game punishes players for using their brains. It's simply poor design.

James Bond: Tomorrow Never Dies made the mistake of copying a 20-year-old cartoon-game mechanic—resources hidden in odd places—into a realistic game. A realistic game assumes that players can count on certain similarities between the real world and the game world (oil drums store oil, not medical kits; explosions destroy things rather than reveal things). No flight simulator bothers to explain about gravity, for the same reason. The player of a realistic game expects the assumptions he makes in the real world to be valid in the game world. By violating these expectations with a conceptual non sequitur, *James Bond: Tomorrow Never Dies* became considerably harder for all but an experienced gamer who already knew the conventions of cartoon-style video games.

In short, avoid conceptual non sequiturs in realistic games. They discourage new players and make your game unnecessarily hard without making it more fun. Remember the principle that level designers should reward players for using their intelligence, not punish them for it.

Make Atypical Levels Optional

Level designers naturally like to vary the content of their levels, and it is good design practice to make creative use of the game's features or to set your levels in different environments to provide the novelty that players like.

Still, you should *not* create wildly atypical levels and force the player to play them in order to get through the game. Level designers sometimes create a level filled with only one kind of challenge—an action game level consisting of nothing but platform jumps, say, with no enemies to fight or treasure to find.

Others like to take away some of the actions that a player uses routinely on other levels and force her to make do with a limited subset of actions for the duration. Some have created levels that borrow from a different genre entirely: a real-time strategy game level in which both sides control exactly one unit, thus turning the level into a strange sort of action game.

There are two reasons not to make these kinds of levels obligatory. First, it breaks the player's suspension of disbelief to be suddenly confronted with a situation that would never occur according to the rules of the game world as the player has already learned them. Second, it may actually make the game unwinnable for some players. If you create a level filled with only one kind of challenge, then a player who happens to be terrible at that kind of challenge—but who reasonably expected to make it through the game by being good at other kinds of challenges—might not be able to finish the game at all, stymied by one atypical level. And there may be many players who don't find that challenge as exciting as you do, who will find an entire level of it boring.

You shouldn't avoid making atypical levels at all; they can be a lot of fun. But make them optional—hidden levels the player can unlock through excellent play or side missions for extra points.

Don't Show the Player Everything at Once

As they say in theater, "Always leave them wanting more." This advice applies to the overall progression of the game, so both game designers and level designers need to be aware of it. If your players have faced every challenge, seen every environment, and used every action that you have to offer—all in a single level—then the rest of the game will be old hat for them. You have nothing further to offer but variations on a set of play mechanics and game worlds that they already know everything about. Let your game grow from level to level. Introduce new features gradually. Just as it all starts to seem a bit familiar, bring in a twist: a new vehicle, a new action, a new location, a new enemy, or a sharp change in the plot of the story.

Never Lose Sight of Your Audience

Level design, more than any other part of the game design and development process, brings with it the risk of building a game that your audience won't enjoy. *You* assemble all the components that the others provide, and when the player starts up the game, she finds herself in *your* environment. The game designers may decide on the types of challenges the game contains, but you decide when the player will face them, in what sequence, and in what combinations. Consequently, you, more than anyone else on the team, must apply the player-centric approach to every design decision you make. Go inside the mind of your player and try to imagine what it will be like to see it all for the first time.

Always remember that you are not the player. Your own personal circumstances have *nothing to do with the game*. You may be a 22-year-old male, but your player may well be a 10-year-old girl or a 50-year-old man. Understand the game's target audience and what that audience wants from the game; then make sure you give it to them—at all times!

Summary

In this chapter, you explored level design, a key stage in the development of any video game. The level designer is responsible for actually presenting the game experience to the player by designing elements such as the space in which the game takes place, deciding what challenges a player will face at each level of the game, creating the atmosphere of the game world, and planning the pacing of events for each level. Level design is governed by universal principles as well as principles specific to the game's genre. In a strategy game, for example, the level design should reward planning; in a vehicle simulation, the level designer creates levels that test a player's skill at maneuvering her vehicle. An important aspect of level design is the actual layout of the level. Different stories require different layouts, but every layout should be designed to enhance the playing experience.

The level design process requires interaction among the game's design team, including artists, programmers, and the audio team. Attention to detail and a methodical approach to the steps of level design can help to prevent the kind of level design pitfalls that will make your game infamous rather than famous.

Test Your Skills

MULTIPLE CHOICE QUESTIONS

1. The level designer's job includes
   A. choosing the look of the game.
   B. determining how the virtual camera will behave.
   C. deciding how to turn general specifications into specific plans.
   D. none of the above.

2. Which of these is a universal level design principle?
   A. Clearly inform the player of his short-term goals.
   B. Offer opportunities for character growth and player self-expression.
   C. Verisimilitude is vital.
   D. Create many interaction opportunities for creatures in their environments.

3. Which of these is a genre-specific level design principle?

    A. Make early levels of games tutorial levels.

    B. Be clear about risks, rewards, and the consequences of decisions.

    C. Give the player time to think.

    D. Implement multiple difficulty levels.

4. Which of these is a good design choice for a level layout?

    A. Using a parallel layout with hidden entrances that have no distinguishing marks or clues.

    B. Using an open layout for outdoor areas in role-playing games to allow the player to explore freely, then switching to a network layout when indoors.

    C. Using a ring layout with shortcuts that have identical challenges to the ring path itself.

    D. Using a hub-and-spoke layout whenever possible.

5. The network layout

    A. requires the story to tolerate the player's experiencing events in any sequence.

    B. is most often used with games that are races.

    C. is sometimes called a *homeworld*.

    D. creates a game that is said to be *on rails.*

6. Level designers use pencil and paper to work out the sequence of events to take place because

    A. most studios do not want to spend the money on expensive 2D rendering solutions.

    B. roughing things out on paper is fast and the design can be easily changed.

    C. designers have traditionally used pencil and paper.

    D. this initial artwork is often used to market the game to publishers.

7. When it comes to pacing, a good rule of thumb is

    A. vary the pacing, alternating between fast and slow periods.

    B. slow the level down; they tend to be too fast for most players to enjoy.

    C. all levels should start slow and get progressively faster like a ball rolling downhill.

    D. levels in action games should start fast and stay fast.

8. The music in a game is important because it

    A. helps the player orient himself within the game world.

    B. echoes the atmospheric effects.

    C. helps set the pace of the gameplay.

    D. responds to player actions.

9. Tutorial levels should be

    A. the same as normal levels but much easier.

    B. a required part of the game's sequence of levels.

    C. a scripted experience that teaches the player.

    D. all of the above.

10. One of the first things a level designer does once she has been given the handoff from the game designer is to

    A. start modeling everything the game designer has told her to model.

    B. generate a list of desired features to appear in the level, including events, objects, and NPCs.

    C. create thumbnails of textures she may need for the level.

    D. have a meeting with the programmers to discuss special coding requirements she will need.

11. As you plan the gameplay of your level, you will want to consider

    A. the layout and how it affects the gameplay.

    B. how the player can win or lose the level.

    C. landmarks, so that the player can find his way around.

    D. all of the above.

12. Once the level has gone through several reviews and refinements and is considered ready to go into full production, it is said to be "locked down," meaning no new additions may be added, because

    A. most art teams have difficulty following directions.

    B. most game designers feel the need to have complete control over the project.

    C. "locked down" is a military term used for first-person shooters.

    D. otherwise the level could be tweaked forever, stretching the development time and running up the budget.

12

13. Getting the scope of a level correct is important because
    A. the scope has a direct impact on the marketing budget.
    B. if the scope is too big you may not have the team or resources to complete the level on time or on budget.
    C. players don't like to play epic style games.
    D. it is hard to find good artists.

14. Conceptual non sequiturs are
    A. game features within a level design that do not make sense, even in the understood fantasy of a game world.
    B. bad coding that causes a game to crash.
    C. design features that enhance the gameplay by incorporating a sequence of new concepts.
    D. a product of poor dialog in role-playing games.

15. Showing the player everything at once is a pitfall to avoid because
    A. players hate to see everything at once.
    B. it puts too much of a burden on the art team.
    C. when the game begins to get a little too familiar you cannot introduce anything new to keep the player engaged.
    D. all of the above.

EXERCISES

1. Pick one of the layouts described in the chapter and, using pencil and paper, create a sketch of a level layout for a hypothetical first-person shooter. (Your instructor will tell you the required number of rooms or locations.) Mark in the layout all of the necessary objects for your level. Mark the starting positions of all the enemies and where the trigger will be or what action will trigger them. If you include such things as traps or doors, mark where they are and what triggers change their state. Mark where supplies such as medical kits and ammunition will be placed. Be sure to consider the path your player will take, remembering open spaces are good for outdoor exploration and parallel, linear, network, or combination layouts are good for indoor spaces. Now make one list of all the different kinds of objects that you think you will need and another list of all of your textures. (Do not forget floors, walls, furniture, decorations, weapons, and resources such as ammunition and medical kits.)

2. Choose a game genre that involves avatar travel through the game world and create the background details (not the layout or placement of objects) of a typical level in that genre. In four or five pages, describe what your

level looks like and what kinds of things happen in your level. Keep character backgrounds and backstory, if there is one, to minimal details. Instead, focus on the atmosphere, the look and the sounds, the actions the player will take, the events the player will experience, and the motivation(s) that keep the player engaged. Be sure to document what features will set the mood and pace.

3. In four or five pages, explain a tutorial level of an existing game that you have played. How does the player learn the character's moves and capabilities? Remember universal principles and keeping the player interested enough to actually want to play the game. Do the player's skills build on each other, or are they all separate actions? Does the player get to customize his avatar, and if so, how? What, if anything, did the game leave for the player to discover on his own?

4. Choose two levels from two different games, one that has a great level design and one that is, in your opinion, lacking. Take two or three pages for each level and describe the design features that made the great level great and the design pitfalls that detracted from the gameplay or undermined the story of the other level.

5. Go to: **www.finitearts.com/400P/400project.htm.** Read up on Hal Barwood's and Noah Falstein's 400 Project, the concept of design rules, and the reasons why they are worth breaking or keeping. Choose four or five design principles/rules listed and write a page each on why you think they should be used or broken. Can you come up with any design rules that are not listed? If so, explain why you feel they should be considered for the 400 Project.

DESIGN QUESTIONS

In designing a typical level in a game, consider the following questions:

1. Where is it? What is the time and place?

2. What are the initial conditions of the level? What resources does the player start with? Are there additional resources in the landscape, and if so, which ones, how much, and where?

3. What is the layout of the level? What freedom of movement does the player have within it? In what sequence will he experience challenges, and to what extent can he change that sequence?

4. How will you keep the player informed of his short-term goals? How does he know what to do next?

5. What challenges will the player face there? What actions can the player take?

12

6. What rewards and punishments are built into the level? How does the player win or lose the level?

7. How do you plan to control and vary the pacing?

8. What events in the level contribute to the story, if any? What narrative events might happen within the level?

9. What is the mood of the level? What is its aesthetic style? What will contribute to the player's experience of these things? Consider music, art, architecture, landscape, weather, ambient sounds and sound effects, and lighting.

Part Two

The Genres of Games

In this part of *Fundamentals of Game Design,* we look at how the principles we introduced in Part One can be applied when designing games in each of the classic game genres. In Chapters 13 through 20, we examine the game world, gameplay, core mechanics, user interface, and other elements of a video game as they apply to a specific genre, using famous games as examples. Our purpose is to identify the defining qualities that characterize a genre so that you can better understand how to design a game within that genre.

- **Chapter 13:** Action Games
- **Chapter 14:** Strategy Games
- **Chapter 15:** Role-Playing Games
- **Chapter 16:** Sports Games
- **Chapter 17:** Vehicle Simulations
- **Chapter 18:** Construction and Management Simulations
- **Chapter 19:** Adventure Games
- **Chapter 20:** Artificial Life and Puzzle Games

Chapter | 13

Action Games

Chapter Objectives

After reading this chapter and completing the exercises, you will be able to do the following:

- Identify the qualities that set action games apart from other genres.
- Recognize the distinct subgenres of action games and their particular features.
- Use the characteristic features of action games, such as levels, lives, and powerups, to design games of your own.
- Know the design limitations imposed by placing the player under time pressure.

Introduction

When most people hear the phrase *video game*, they tend to think of action games. The reason is historical: Almost all the earliest video games *were* action games, and some of those early games—*Asteroids, Pac-Man, Space Invaders*—have become iconic representatives of the genre. However, the genre is vast and covers just about any imaginable activity that can be characterized in terms of physical challenges. In *Paperboy*, even the task of delivering newspapers has been turned into an action game.

In this chapter, we examine the definition of an action game, then go on to discuss the many subgenres of action games. Following that, we look at the distinctive features of action games that set them apart from other genres.

What Are Action Games?

Action games require high reaction speed and good hand-eye coordination and are usually simpler than games from other genres because the player is often under time pressure. As a general rule, the faster an action game is, the harder it is to play. The fastest action games are sometimes called *twitch games,* implying that the action takes place at almost a reflex level. The player doesn't generally have time for complex strategy or planning.

> An **action game** is one in which the majority of challenges presented are tests of the player's physical skills. Puzzle-solving, tactical conflict, and exploration challenges are often present as well.

Most arcade games are action games, because arcade games make their money by quickly defeating unskillful players. Only highly skilled players can play them for a long time without losing. The simple core mechanics and gameplay of action games mean that those without too much audiovisual content are also well suited to less powerful machines such as handhelds and cell phones.

Action Game Subgenres

Action games fall into a number of subgenres based, like all game genre distinctions, on the kinds of gameplay that they offer. The most familiar and popular of these are shooting games of various sorts. We also look at platform games, fighting games, fast puzzle games, and a broad miscellany of other kinds. Bear in mind that there is no industry standard for these terms, and other authors may refer to these subgenres by other names.

Shooters

In *shooters,* the player takes action at a distance, using a ranged weapon of some kind. Shooting games therefore demand the key skill of aiming, particularly if the game provides only limited ammunition. In a shooting game, the player's attention must be focused in two places at once: the area around the avatar, and the target or targets that he is shooting at.

Shooting is almost always presented as a form of violence, and this discourages players who do not care for violence. However, shooting can be characterized in other ways, such as putting out a fire with a fire hose, painting a wall with a paint gun, filling up a space with objects, and so on.

We will consider two broad classes of shooting games: those that take place in a two-dimensional landscape (2D shooters) and those that take place in a three-dimensional landscape (3D shooters), of which by far the best-known are the first-person shooters. We discuss the differences between the first- and third-person perspectives in shooting games in the *Perspective* section, later in this chapter.

2D Shooters   The action in 2D shooters takes place in an environment viewed from either a top-down or side-view perspective. The avatar, which is often a vehicle, is under near-constant attack from enemies that shoot at him or approach him to attack at close quarters. For the most part, the player's goal is simply to shoot everything that moves or threatens him, as fast as possible. He is usually armed with one or more weapons, and some weapons may be better suited to particular enemies than others. It is rare for a 2D shooter to keep track of ammunition; instead, the player fires frenetically and indiscriminately. The weapons seldom damage anything except legitimate targets.

2D shooters don't bother with realistic physics. Projectiles move at a constant speed and in a straight line, unaffected by gravity; vehicles and characters change direction instantaneously, with no inertia. These are the conventions of the subgenre, and you change them at your peril.

Some of the older 2D games have endured and remained popular—even inspiring modern versions—because, despite their limited graphics, they have excellent gameplay. The original *Robotron: 2084,* released into arcades in 1982, became an instant classic of the genre (see Figure 13.1). The object of this game was to defend the last human family against wave upon wave of killing machines bent on their destruction. A second joystick gave players the ability to shoot independently of the avatar's direction of movement. The strength of the *Robotron* gameplay meant that, for many years, updates just weren't needed. In fact, you can still get pixel-perfect versions of *Robotron: 2084* for the PC, Gameboy Advance, and other consoles.

The first official update of this game, the 3D *Robotron X,* heralded the start of the retro-gaming fad. *Robotron X* offered the same gameplay as the original (apart from a few extra bonus levels), but the shift to 3D had a negative impact on playability. The advantage of the original *Robotron* was that all the

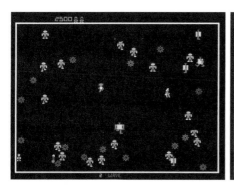
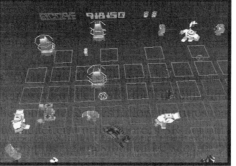

FIGURE 13.1 *Robotron: 2084* and *Robotron X.*

FIGURE 13.2 *Gauntlet II* and *Gauntlet: Seven Sorrows.*

action could be viewed onscreen at one time. The 3D update, with its swooping camera, often obscured parts of the playing area. This meant that occasionally the player's avatar would be killed by an enemy that suddenly appeared from an off-camera region—something that could not happen in the original game. This detracted from the playability because players rightly disliked being killed by enemies that weren't clearly displayed. In the original *Robotron,* if the player died, it was the player's fault—all the information was there to be interpreted, so he had no excuses if he failed to react to the situation quickly enough to avoid the danger.

Gauntlet, in its original arcade form, provided an option for cooperative multiplayer play, one of the first games to do so (see Figure 13.2). Each player could take on one of four avatars (Warrior, Wizard, Valkyrie, or Elf) and adventure together with the other members of the party through a seemingly endless series of dungeons, searching for treasure and food. This game introduced many of the common action game features we will be discussing later, such as the locked door and key, monster generators, team play, and dungeon exit.

There have been many updates for the classic *Gauntlet,* starting with the immediate sequel, *Gauntlet II.* Some have been more successful than others. The most recent of these updates, *Gauntlet: Seven Sorrows,* brings the graphics and environment up to date, adding a backstory and some extra features, but still manages to maintain the essential features of the original game.

3D Shooters Three-dimensional shooting games such as *Halo* and *Half-Life* have become so successful that to a great many gamers they are the epitome of the entire medium. Never mind that sports games are more popular than shooters on console machines, and strategy games are more popular on home computers (ESA, 2005); 3D shooters are at the cutting edge of what game hardware can do, and so they have the most dramatic graphics and get the most press. Figure 13.3 indicates just how far 3D shooters have come, from Atari's original first-person tank simulator, *Battlezone,* to the recently released *F.E.A.R.*

Three-dimensional shooters tend to be more realistic than 2D shooters, taking advantage of 3D hardware to present familiar, or at least recognizable, worlds. In first-person shooters, the physics of the game is much more like that

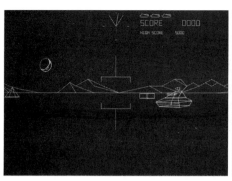

FIGURE 13.3 *Battlezone* and *F.E.A.R.*

of the real world. Gravity works correctly (for the most part), sound diminishes with distance, objects cast shadows, and collisions are modeled with a fair level of accuracy. Some of these games, such as Electronic Arts' *Black,* also implement deformable environments, in which the landscape actually changes shape in response to explosions and other events. The *survival horror* class of games, a subgenre of 3D shooters, makes use of the power of modern graphics hardware to display disturbingly realistic blood and gore.

This emphasis on realism carries over into other aspects of the gameplay: Avatars can carry only limited amounts of ammunition, which must be replenished at intervals. (Although they can often carry a surprising number of guns!) In some shooters, gunshots to the limbs, body, and head are detected individually and damage assessed accordingly.

Three-dimensional shooters can be further subdivided into those with a first-person perspective (the ***first-person shooter*** or ***FPS***), those with a third-person perspective, and a few that offer both. We address the implications of perspective later in this chapter.

Although not actually the earliest first-person shooter, *Doom* set the standard for all those that followed. Unlike its predecessors, it offered nonrectangular rooms, stairs, and other areas of different heights, as well as variable lighting conditions that strongly affected the emotional tone of the game. At the time, these groundbreaking features made *Doom* a worldwide classic.

Platform Games

Platform games, or ***platformers,*** are cartoonish games in which an avatar moves through a vertically exaggerated environment, jumping on and off platforms at different heights, while avoiding obstacles and battling enemies. The avatar has a supernatural jumping ability and can't be harmed by falling long distances (unless he falls onto something dangerous or into a bottomless chasm, both common features of platform games). Most of the player's actions consist of jumping, augmented by various flip-moves and by bouncy objects in the environment.

13

Platform games use highly unrealistic physics; the avatar can usually change directions in midair.

The vast majority of 2D side-scrolling games with a humanoid avatar are platform games; *Super Mario Bros.* is the classic example. The conflict in platform games is often mild and suitable for children. Both Mario and Sonic the Hedgehog attacked enemies simply by jumping on top of them. Stricken enemies disappeared without undue anguish.

Three-dimensional platform games, while popular, have never managed to achieve quite the same level of iconic status as 2D games. *Crash Bandicoot* was one of the more successful 3D platformers. Unfortunately, the addition of a third dimension makes control more complicated and difficult; we discuss this in more detail in the *Controls* section later in this chapter.

Fighting Games

Fighting games have little in common with other action games because they involve neither exploration, shooting, nor puzzle-solving. They're almost a genre in their own right, but we include them here because they do place great demands on a player's physical skills: reaction time and timing. Also sometimes called *beat-'em-ups,* these games simulate hand-to-hand combat, usually between pairs of fighters using highly exaggerated moves vaguely modeled on Asian martial arts techniques. (Serious boxing games belong more to the sports genre than to the action genre, as they try to model the techniques of boxing realistically.) Fighting games also make use of local effect weapons such as swords and shields, and a limited number of ranged weapons. Figure 13.4 shows screen shots from two fighting games, *Street Fighter* and *Dead or Alive 3*.

Apart from maneuvering the fighter around a restricted space, the player's actions are limited to attacking and defending moves of various sorts. Typically, certain defenses will block some attacks but not others, and players have to learn when and how they are effective through trial and error. Each successful attack takes energy away from the character hit, and the game continues until one

FIGURE 13.4 Fighting games.

fighter's energy drops to zero. The strategy of the game rather resembles rock-paper-scissors as players try to guess which move their opponent will use next.

A common feature of fighting games is the **combo move,** often simply shortened to *combo.* Because early console and arcade machines offered only a small number of buttons and a simple 8-way joystick or D-pad, there was no way to assign a separate button to each of the moves that the designers wanted to include. To compensate for this and create an extra challenge as well, they designed the game so that the player would execute an especially effective or spectacular attack if she could rapidly issue a particular sequence of buttons and joystick maneuvers. The effectiveness of the move is often related to its difficulty of execution—a period of time during which the avatar is open to attack. Thus, more difficult combos carry higher risk.

When the software detects that a combo move has been started, it sometimes displays a *combo meter* somewhere on the screen—a visual indicator of the player's progress through pressing the buttons. If the player stops or gets the sequence wrong, the meter resets to zero and she has to start over.

Fighting games tend to have rather similar interfaces, showing all the fighters onscreen at once from a side view. Even in a game that uses 3D technology to display the world and the fighters, the play is largely 2D in the plane of the video screen. The fighters move left and right and may jump up and down, but seldom move toward the player or away from him. Again, realistic boxing games are an exception because they try to model the ring and boxers' movements accurately—another reason why they're not usually classed with fighting games.

Most innovation in fighting games consists of developments in characters' actions and reactions. This includes their interactions with each other and their environment and their reactions to injury, as well as the methods used to control the fighters—especially when considering how to handle special moves and combos.

Fast Puzzle Games

Most computerized puzzle games, such as *Sokoban,* move slowly and allow the player to think about his next move for as long as he wants, so they're not action games. Fast puzzle games require the player to solve a problem as quickly as possible. These games are usually simple, visually abstract, have a limited control set, and so are easy to design and build. *Tetris* is the archetypal fast puzzle game. Other examples include *Collapse!, Columns,* and *Bejeweled* in its timed mode. Casual gamers like fast puzzle games because they are easy to learn and don't take a long time to play. They also don't make use of stereotypical content associated with many video games: no guns, no dragons, no scantily clad women. This subgenre is ideal for handheld devices and cell phones.

Action-Adventures

The action-adventure is a hybrid genre, combining features from both action games and adventure games. To play them well requires a fair amount of physical skill, but they also offer a storyline, numerous characters, an inventory system, dialog, and other features of adventure games. The later editions of the *Zelda* series for the Nintendo 64 and Nintendo GameCube are action-adventures, as is *Indiana Jones and the Infernal Machine*. The earlier, 2D isometric *Indiana Jones* games were pure adventure games.

We discuss action-adventures in more detail in Chapter 19, "Adventure Games."

Dance and Rhythm Games

Dance Dance Revolution, Parappa the Rapper, and similar games belong to a comparatively new subgenre of action games, those that challenge the player's sense of rhythm. They typically show an avatar on screen who dances in response to the player's button presses. In single-player mode, the player's avatar must dance better than a computer-controlled character; in multiplayer mode, two avatars compete head-to-head. The screen shows which dance step the player should perform next (by pressing the correct button on the controller or pad on a dance mat), and the game awards points for accuracy and for being on the beat.

Dance games are particularly popular with girls.

Other Action Games

A great many action games don't fit neatly into any of the preceding subgenres, and the variety among them is enormous. They are difficult to categorize except in negative terms: They *don't* involve shooting, hand-to-hand fighting, or abstract puzzle-solving. They do, however, frequently make use of representational puzzle-solving. Most of these action games demand skills such as maneuvering and path planning.

Frogger, shown in Figure 13.5, is a good example of an action game that belongs to no obvious subgenre. The player maneuvers the world's only nonswimming frog family across a busy road and a logging river infested with crocodiles. A highly successful arcade game launched in 1981, the *Frogger*

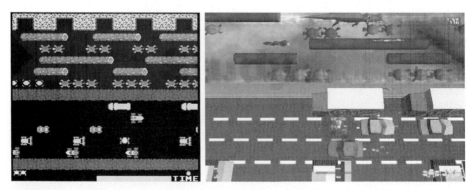

FIGURE 13.5 *Frogger* and *Frogger 3D.*

series eventually became one of the most successful of all time. Hasbro's 1997 remake, *Frogger 3D* (also shown in Figure 13.5) sold millions of copies, remaining on the software bestsellers charts for many months after release. The developers kept the gameplay virtually unchanged and just updated the presentation, increasing the variety of the levels available to the player. *Frogger 2: Swampy' Revenge,* a sequel to the remake released several years later, introduced a more structured game while still remaining faithful to the gameplay of the original.

Other notable action games that don't fit into other subgenres include *Pong, Marble Madness, Pac-Man, Q*Bert, Lemmings,* and *Katamari Damacy.* Both *Marble Madness* (1986) and *Katamari Damacy* (2004) make use of an excellent but seldom-seen challenge, controlling a rolling object that exhibits inertia. *Lemmings,* a brilliant game about trying to prevent a group of dim-witted creatures from killing themselves by falling off cliffs, involved selecting particular creatures and assigning tasks to them that influenced the way the others moved, all under time pressure.

Game Features

Action games provide a good field in which to study many features also found in other genres because the simplicity of action games means that the issues aren't obscured by other considerations. Action games tend to set simple, obvious goals and clear, direct ways to reach them (even though goals may be difficult to achieve).

We start our analysis of action game features with a discussion of how such games progress, that is, with features that help move the game along. We then turn to gameplay, that is, the challenges and actions most frequently found in action games. Following that, we consider core mechanics and victory conditions. Finally, we end with a discussion of the interaction model, perspective, and user interface design. Note that words in bold-faced type indicate references to other design elements discussed in this chapter.

Progression

The player's progress through an action game usually takes her through a series of levels that must be played in a linear sequence. Once the player completes all levels, she has won the whole game. (There are exceptions; in *Spyro the Dragon,* the player had a choice of levels at any given time, and completing some levels unlocked others that could not otherwise be chosen.) Within a level, progress may be linear (the player can go only forward or back) or nonlinear (the player has some freedom to choose her own path). Occasionally a linear level will include a hidden shortcut that, when discovered, allows the player to jump ahead, bypassing many obstacles and dangers.

Levels   In action games, designers often group levels by theme. All the levels in a themed set will have a similar appearance and a similar set of enemies or obstacles to be overcome. A set of themed levels usually ends with an encounter with a big *boss,* who must be defeated. In some cases, the player must acquire power-ups or gain skills while completing tasks in the levels in order to defeat that set's big boss and progress to the next set of levels.

Each level presents the player with a variety of challenges, and failure to surmount them will eventually cause the player to lose the game—whether it's dancing well in a dance game or shooting things in a shooter. However, in most such games, the sequence of the challenges in a given level remains the same from one play session to the next. Except for the occasional *wildcard enemy* (described later in this chapter), the player can be confident that if a given region contains certain challenges the first time it's played, the same region will contain exactly the same challenges the next time. Thus, players eventually finish action games by learning what tasks lie ahead and how to accomplish them through repeated attempts.

As a designer, you will find that levels are easier to balance when they contain fixed, rather than randomized, challenges. However, this approach makes the game repetitive, and that makes the game unattractive to two groups: those who don't like repetitive play and those who don't have a lot of leisure time. To avoid alienating those groups, include a save-and-reload feature so the player can restart the game in the middle whenever he loses. Alternatively, use *checkpoints,* as described in the next section.

Level design is discussed in more detail in Chapter 12, "General Principles of Level Design."

Checkpoints   Some action games allow the player to explicitly save and resume the game at any time, allowing recovery from failure, but many do not. Older games required the player to start again from the beginning of the current level or even the beginning of the entire game. In this case, a player must meet every challenge of the entire level perfectly in order to progress to the next level, making the game significantly more difficult and often frustrating the player; this is now considered poor design. In many modern games, the avatar's new incarnation appears in the same location at which it died, or if that is impossible (for example, if Mario falls into water), then the new avatar appears in the last safe location it occupied before it died (for example, the last platform that Mario occupied before he fell into the water). The state of the level remains unchanged—the avatar just appears, and play continues. Apart from the loss of a life and perhaps the loss of the avatar's possessions, the player is not punished for letting the avatar die.

Avatars may also reappear at a *checkpoint.* Checkpoints mark the positions on a level at which a player's avatar will appear in its next incarnation if it should die in that level. As the player progresses through a level, he passes through one or more checkpoints along the way, usually marked by some visual

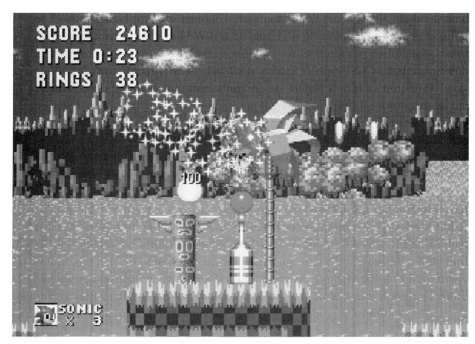

FIGURE 13.6 This lamppost checkpoint in *Sonic the Hedgehog* will turn red when he passes it.

indicator that changes to inform the player it has been passed. In *Sonic the Hedgehog,* for example, street lamps marked the checkpoints, turning from white to red when passed (see Figure 13.6). If the avatar dies, the level is reset to the condition it was in when the player last successfully passed a checkpoint, and the avatar reappears at the checkpoint location.

Level Exits, Level Warps, and Teleporters   Many action games that require the player to explore the layout of each level designate a particular location as the normal transition point to the next level—the ***level exit*** or ***dungeon exit.*** A level exit may be guarded by enemies, be well hidden, or both. Finding and passing through the level exit is usually the primary goal of the level.

Game designers often provide more than one exit from a level: the standard exit, which takes the player to the next level, and one or more special exits that jump the player ahead several levels or take the player to an otherwise secret level. These are known as ***level warps.*** Level warps are usually hidden or particularly difficult to reach, and the reward is proportional to the level of sacrifice required to get to them.

Games from *Stargate* to *Luigi's Mansion* and the *Super Mario* series use level warps. If you provide a hidden exit, you may want to give the player a subtle clue. For example, in *Super Mario World,* the world overview map shows levels with secret exits as flashing red dots, rather than flashing yellow dots.

13

A *teleporter* is a transition point that causes the player's avatar to jump someplace else within the *same* level. These points may be marked by a sign or object that tells the player he has found a teleporter, or they may be unmarked, giving the player no warning that he is about to be teleported or explanation for why he is suddenly somewhere else. Teleporters are often made available at the end of a long period of exploration, so the player can simply jump back to a previous location (such as a home base or camp) without having to walk all the way back.

Challenges

Action games have more different kinds of challenges than just about any other genre, although almost all of these challenges test physical skills—speed and reaction time, steering and shooting, timing and rhythm, and the ability to execute combo moves in fighting games. Other common types of challenges include pattern recognition (recognizing the attack and patrol behaviors of enemies) and exploration (learning your way around a space). A few action games, such as *Tetris* and *Lemmings,* include puzzle-solving elements. The puzzles cannot be too complex, however, because the player is usually under heavy time pressure.

In this section, we look at the way action games characteristically present and organize their challenges.

Obstacles and Dangers   In a game that requires navigation through a space, the player's avatar will typically be faced with three types of problems: passive obstacles, stationary dangers, and active dangers or enemies.

A passive obstacle impedes movement without actually threatening the avatar. To get past a wall or a chasm, the player climbs over or jumps across. Obstacles can also trap the avatar in a region with other dangers. Obstacles are usually, but not always, indestructible.

A stationary danger attacks the avatar when she gets close to it but does not move around the landscape. Examples of stationary dangers include electric fences, swinging blades on a pendulum, or plants that bite. Some stationary dangers must be attacked or destroyed to allow the avatar to pass by; others are indestructible and must be treated like obstacles, so the avatar has to avoid or surmount them.

Active dangers, or enemies, attack the avatar, moving around in the landscape. In old games, they often moved in a fixed pattern that the player could learn to avoid, but in modern games artificially intelligent enemies locate and pursue the avatar. See Chapter 6, "Character Development," for more information on designing enemy characters.

Waves   When enemies appear or attack in groups, usually groups of the same type or similar types of enemies, they are said to come in waves. Waves may arrive at scripted intervals or randomly.

Scripted waves of enemies have appeared in games ranging from the original *Space Invaders* to the recent *Max Payne* and many others. In these types of games, the emergence of enemies is a fixed part of the level design. When waves of enemies seem to arrive randomly rather than according to a script, their entrance is usually controlled by an algorithm designed to create enemies at propitious times in order to maintain a smooth progression of difficulty. The designer often creates a pool of enemy types and attack locations from which the apparently random waves are drawn.

In either case, a wave consists of a group of enemies arriving at the same time. The makeup of the group will vary, including a selection of enemies appropriate to the current level of the game. As the game progresses, the group will include stronger enemies. In some cases, the earlier weaker enemies will be phased out of the lineup, because they will no longer provide an effective challenge. Enemies increase in strength and number, reaching a peak at the end of the level.

The Big Boss   In many games, a large enemy, or big boss, significantly harder to fight than any of the previously encountered enemies, guards the end of a group of themed levels. Defeating the boss takes the player to a new set of themed levels. Boss characters often can't be hurt by normal methods; damaging them may require special weapons, a special attack method, or special timing. For example, the Piranha Plants in *Super Mario Sunshine* are invincible until they open their mouths.

The boss character's appearance and actions complement the theme of the set of levels it guards. The designers of the first set of levels in *Parasol Stars* chose a musical theme, and as you can see from the left side of Figure 13.7, the first big boss seems to be made of musical instruments.

The big boss is often a much bigger and stronger version of an enemy that the player encountered in the preceding levels. The right side of Figure 13.7 shows a classic example, taken from *Rainbow Islands*. Gardens provide the

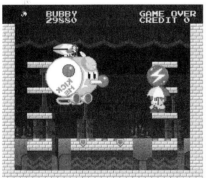

FIGURE 13.7 The first bosses in *Parasol Stars* and *Rainbow Islands*.

theme for the first set of levels, with the enemies being mainly insects and birds. The boss character is simply a much larger version of a spider the player already defeated. This enhances the gameplay by allowing the player to predict some of the boss's behavior and gives him a small advantage in knowing what to expect.

Games with a serious storyline aren't suited for such an unsubtle set of themed levels, but even so, the themed level and big boss are mainstays of action games. Virtually every level-based, action-based game today makes use of a succession of levels increasing in difficulty, culminating in a climactic defeat of a big boss. The game then starts again with a new set of levels on a different theme and begins at a slightly lower difficulty level. This is shown in Figure 13.8.

Wildcard Enemies   In order to break up the predictability of predefined waves of enemies, many games insert a randomly generated wildcard enemy to provide a fresh challenge. Wildcard enemies, unlike level bosses, normally attack at the same time as normal enemies and behave in unexpected ways.

The Atari game *Asteroids,* for instance, offers predictable waves of enemies (in this case drifting rocks; even they can be an enemy, because they are an active danger), but at random times during the waves, a UFO appears and follows an unpredictable path, shooting at the player. The game awards extra points for shooting the UFO, but trying to do this tends to distract the player and cause her to make mistakes: a perfect example of risk and reward in an action game.

Locked Door and Key   The player encounters a locked door that requires a key, although not necessarily a physical key, hidden somewhere in the level.

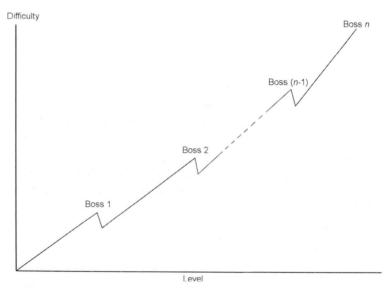

FIGURE 13.8 The general progression of an action game.

Designers commonly use such locked doors to partition levels and to control the player's progress in order to manage the pace of the gameplay. Some games use sequences of locked doors, such that a key used to open one door gives access to another key that in turn opens a different door, even a door the player encountered previously. *Doom* provides a particularly good example.

Locked doors and keys should be used with caution. Used too liberally or unimaginatively, locked doors may make the game feel clichéd, tedious, or old-fashioned. When implemented well, however, this strategy can be very effective. Remember that the door and key don't have to be traditional; come up with an original scenario. Doors and keys represent a challenge (acquiring the key) that, when met, allows the player to pass an obstacle (the door). In *The Secret of Monkey Island,* for example, at one point the avatar needs to figure out a way to shoot himself out of a cannon to get off a ship. Obtaining the items necessary to fire the cannon is the key to getting off the ship and onto Monkey Island.

Monster Generators and Spawn Points   Many action games include a feature that causes new enemies to suddenly appear in the game world to challenge the player. If the enemies appear from a visible object, the object is called a ***monster generator.*** If they appear seemingly out of thin air at a particular location in the world, that location is called a ***spawn point.*** The game *Doom* uses spawn points: Monsters suddenly appear, each in a flash of green light, and there is nothing a player can do to prevent it. In *Gauntlet,* on the other hand, monster generators are machines visible in the game world, and they can be attacked. If the player destroys a monster generator, no more monsters will come out of it. Hence, the player must choose between two strategies: fight the monsters or destroy the generator. The strategy with the lowest risk involves destroying the monster generators before they can spawn too many monsters, but players aiming for the highest score may delay destroying the monster generator until they boost their scores sufficiently by killing enough monsters. In this case, monster generators are not only an integral part of the gameplay; they offer multiple strategies as well.

Monster generators and spawn points may create an infinite number of monsters or merely a predetermined number. If monsters are produced indefinitely, you may want to consider using a monster generator that the player can destroy so that the game will end. A monster generator or spawn point may produce only one type of enemy, or it may offer a range of different foes. You can adjust the strength of the monsters that it generates based on the difficulty level of the game.

13

Player Actions

Action games routinely allow moving or maneuvering an avatar, aiming and shooting, selecting, collecting, manipulating or modifying objects, and various kinds of fighting moves—punching, kicking, defending, and so on. In addition, two specialty actions—*smart bombs* and *hyperspace escape*—are characteristic of action games and seldom found anywhere else. We discuss them next.

Smart Bombs   A smart bomb sounds like an object, but it's usually implemented as an action available to the player. Pressing the smart bomb button clears the area immediately surrounding the avatar, typically leaving it entirely free of enemies, although the range cleared varies from game to game. Because the smart bomb is so powerful, you should make it costly, generally by making it available only once or making its effect diminish every time it is used. The player will then be forced to save it for dire emergencies. If he doesn't know what lies ahead, he is always faced with the decision of whether to use it in a given situation or to try to make do without it in case he gets into even worse trouble later on.

    Defender introduced the smart bomb (see Figure 13.9).

Hyperspace Escape   Hyperspace escape is a button or other player-selectable option that instantly moves the player's avatar to another location in the game world, normally chosen at random. It's a means of getting out of trouble. However, unlike the smart bomb, a hyperspace escape is just as likely to land the avatar in an equally difficult situation as it is to transport it to safety. *Asteroids* (see Figure 13.10) provides an example of the early use of hyperspace.

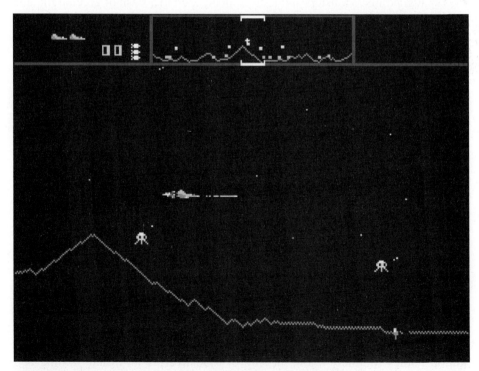

FIGURE 13.9 *Defender* required the player to defend humans on the ground from flying attackers.

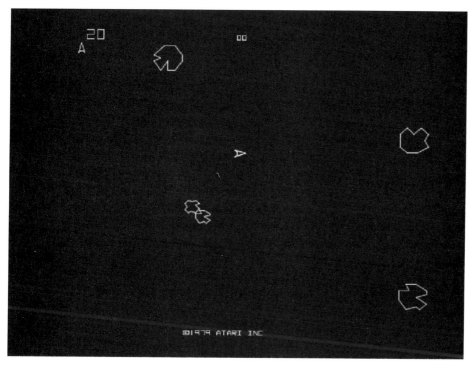

FIGURE 13.10 *Asteroids.*

Designers usually allow more frequent use of the hyperspace button than the smart bomb because the usefulness of the maneuver is balanced by the chance that the avatar could end up in an even worse situation than before. Ironically, the more likely the *Asteroids* player is to need it (usually because of the amount of debris on the playfield), the more risk there is to the player.

Core Mechanics Features

The core mechanics of action games should be simple and obvious. Action games have small numbers of resources, and the relationships among them are straightforward: Being hit by an enemy costs energy points; collecting gold stars increases the final score; and so on. The player in an action game is too busy to study a complex internal economy.

Lives   Designers usually allow the player's avatar a small number of reprieves from death. The number of lives provided usually ranges between three and five. Collision with an enemy or some other dangerous object costs the player a life. Players earn extra lives by picking up a powerup (a prize hidden in the level; some article which, if collected, gives the collector extra life) or reaching a certain score. The player's avatar is usually invulnerable for a few seconds when reappearing after losing a life, in order for the player to regain his bearings. When all lives are lost, the

13

player must either start over or return to the most recent checkpoint or saved game. The limited-life mechanic remains standard for arcade games, but is rapidly being replaced in console and computer games by designs that allow unlimited lives.

Energy   The player's avatar begins the game with a limited amount of energy, sometimes characterized as *hit points* or *health*. Dangerous encounters with enemies or other hazardous features of the game world deplete this energy; in some games time itself, just living in the game world, consumes energy.

This energy can often be partially or even fully replenished by the use of a *collectible* or a *powerup,* but when the avatar's energy is fully depleted, it dies. In a game in which avatars have multiple lives, when the avatar's energy is completely depleted, one of its lives is lost.

In some games, an avatar's energy is shared over a number of physical features—for example, energy can be a limited resource that is distributed between shields and fuel, requiring the player to carefully balance resources.

Powerups   As a reward for progress, the player may be given a powerup, that is, the opportunity to increase the strength of her avatar temporarily or even permanently. In the case of a shooter, this can come in the form of stronger weapons or shields.

A permanent powerup is one that remains with the avatar for an extended period—possibly the remainder of the game but at least the current life or level. *Space Tripper* (and many other shooters) uses this model, although *Space Tripper* is unusual in that when the avatar dies it loses only powerups gained on the most recent level.

Temporary powerups provide a powerful but short-lived advantage. These may be limited by time—for example, the avatar may move faster, but only for a short period, from a few seconds to a few minutes—or limited by the number of times the powerup can be used. For example, a shield may be used up after it has absorbed a certain number of hits. A general design rule is that the more powerful the advantage, the shorter the time the avatar should be allowed to make use of it. The Quad Damage powerup in *Quake III* provides a perfect example of the temporary powerup.

Some games vary the use of powerups by using power points. The player receives a certain number of points to spend on an upgrade and enjoys some latitude in deciding how she wants to upgrade her avatar. *Space Tripper* provides two main weapons; the currently selected weapon will be upgraded. Playing *Space Tripper* successfully requires that the player balance the upgrade points between both weapons.

Collectibles   *Collectibles* are bonus objects the player can pick up, not essential to the game, often used only to augment the player's score. The player is not penalized for failing to collect them, but if he can justify the risk, then the rewards are high.

Collectibles can also unlock secret levels or cause special bonus events to occur. In *Rainbow Islands,* the player could collapse rainbows onto his enemies, which in dying deposited crystals the player could collect to earn bonus points. Collecting the crystals in the right order (red, orange, yellow, green, blue, indigo, violet) opened a doorway to a secret level, which gave the player a huge score and a permanent secret powerup.

Time Limit   Many games employ a timer that counts down from some initial value to zero. When the timer reaches zero, some major game event occurs.

A level timer indicates how much time the player has to complete the level; if he fails to do so, the level and the level timer are reset, and the player has to start again. This is often accompanied by a life loss. If the player finishes the level with time remaining on the level timer, then this excess time may be multiplied by a constant as a score bonus, or the player may receive some other reward for completing the level early.

A timer may also be used as a countdown to a catastrophe. The player must achieve some task before the timer runs out, or the task will become much more difficult to achieve. *Sinistar* uses this form of time limit to good effect; when the timer runs out, the eponymous Sinistar has been built, and the player is in a lot of trouble.

Time limits may also govern the effectiveness of powerups. In this case, when the timer runs out, a temporary powerup stops being effective, and the player's avatar reverts to its normal state. *Pac-Man's* power pellets, which allow the Pac-Man to eat the ghosts for a limited time, are good examples of this use of time limits.

Score   Often in an action game, the score provides the only indication of progress. Points may be awarded for a variety of accomplishments: completing tasks, defeating enemies, collecting items, beating the clock, and so on. Players measure their success against others or against their personal best. Scores may be recorded in high-score tables to provide bragging rights for the best players.

Many games reward skillful play with bonus scores and multipliers. The classic example of the score multiplier can be found in *Pac-Man:* After getting the power pill, the first ghost eaten earns 200 points, the next earns 400 points, then 800, and then 1,600 respectively. Hence, higher and higher scores reward skillful play.

Victory Conditions

Not all action games have victory conditions because not all games can be won—in some games, the most the player can aspire to is a higher score. The object of *Space Invaders* was supposedly to save the Earth from the evil alien invaders, but as anyone who has played the game knows, after you've saved the Earth from one wave of evil invaders, another attacks. This continued, each wave faster and more aggressive, until the aliens overwhelmed the defender.

13

The game was unwinnable, which was characteristic of early action games because they didn't have enough memory to offer the player different settings or a variety of gameplay. All they could do was provide the same gameplay over and over, increasing difficulty until the player lost.

Unbeatable games are now considered outdated for any but arcade machines. Such designs are still prevalent there because arcade machines make their money by forcing the player to lose the game; if she can play indefinitely on a single token, the operator earns no money. On other types of machines, however, there is no reason to discourage the player from playing for as long as she wants, and indeed completing the game. In fact, for games sold at retail, it's better if the player *does* complete the game, because the publishers hope that she will then go buy another game. Thus the publisher's business model directly affects the design of victory conditions.

As processing power and storage capabilities increased, developers began incorporating structured stories into their games—and with stories come endings. Games such as *Golden Axe* (shown in Figure 13.11) had definite endings in which, after the defeat of the end-of-game boss, the players' avatars lived happily ever after (until the sequel came along, of course).

The victory conditions in simple action games tend to be either crystal clear and known to the player in advance—Banjo needs to rescue his sister in *Banjo-Kazooie*—or nonexistent, as in the case of *Space Invaders*. In action

FIGURE 13.11 *Golden Axe.*

games with a storyline, the designers often change the victory condition as the game goes on. In *Half-Life,* for example, the player's first goal is simply to get out of the Black Mesa research complex, but later on she discovers that there are more things she has to do before she can win the game.

IN THE TRENCHES: The Bug That Wins the Game

Sometimes a player *does* beat a game that has no victory condition, and it usually crashes the game. This happens when the game's developer fails to test the game completely from beginning to end, assuming no one could ever possibly get to the end. The most well-known example is probably *Pac-Man.*

For years, people tried to get a perfect score on *Pac-Man.* In July of 1999, Billy Mitchell of Fort Lauderdale, Florida, scored a perfect 3,333,360 points on a *Pac-Man* machine in Weirs Beach, New Hampshire. To achieve this score, he played for six hours, through 256 levels of *Pac-Man,* eating every pellet, power pill, blue ghost, and piece of fruit on every single level, without dying once. After the 256th level, the game freezes.

When he stepped away from the game after beating it, he said, "I never have to play that darn game again."

Interaction Model

The most commonly used interaction model for action games is the avatar, found in everything from the original *Space Invaders* to *Half-Life 2.* In games that involve exploration or defeating enemy attackers, it makes the most sense for the player to project his will into the game world at a single point, the location of the avatar. However, in subgenres in which the player neither fights nor explores, the avatar model makes less sense. *Tetris,* for example, uses a puzzle-manipulation model. *Lemmings* uses an omnipresent model; the player may click on any lemming at any time.

The nature of the actions you choose to include will tend to dictate your interaction model. Ask yourself what the player is going to do, and that will tell you how she should do it.

Perspective

Because the player must see and react to events so quickly in action games, the choice of perspective is critical. We look first at the distinction between 2D and 3D games and then at the choices available in 3D games.

13

2D Perspectives   Two-dimensional action games typically use one of two perspectives: a side view or a top-down view. *Tetris* uses a side view; *Robotron: 2084* uses a top view of the playfield, although the characters themselves are displayed side-on. If the side view can scroll long distances to the left and right, this is known as *side-scrolling* and is classic for avatar-based games from *Defender* to *Alien Hominid*. Top-down views sometimes scroll long distances from the top to the bottom of the screen as the avatar moves forward through an environment; this is known as *top-scrolling* and is best-known in flying games like *Xevious*. *Gauntlet* had a top-down view that scrolled in all four directions.

You may also design your game so that it scrolls continuously at a fixed rate from top to bottom or right to left; this is called *continuous scrolling.* It puts more pressure on the player because she cannot stop it; she can only deal with challenges as they come. *Variable scrolling* causes the landscape to scroll under, or behind, the avatar in direct response to the player's actions; if the avatar turns around and goes in the opposite direction, the view will duly scroll back again. In effect, it lets the player run away from enemies and perhaps even take a break.

Continuous scrolling and variable scrolling have a direct effect on the gameplay, because the latter allows the player to control the pace at which he faces enemies, whereas the former does not. You may also encounter another term, *parallax scrolling,* which is a cosmetic display technique with no actual effect on the gameplay. Parallax scrolling creates a slight illusion of three dimensions in a two-dimensional environment by having objects that are designated as being in the background scroll by more slowly than the ones in the foreground. This gives the impression that the background objects are farther away.

3D First Person   In games set in a 3D space, the perspective is most often, but not always, closely tied to an avatar: either a first-person or a third-person point of view. The first-person perspective is particularly successful for high-speed 3D shooting games such as the *Quake* series because it enables the player to see clearly what she is shooting at, without the avatar blocking part of the screen. Unfortunately, the first-person perspective does not let the player see the area around the avatar very clearly; she can only see ahead of the avatar, whatever faces the avatar, and so this point of view is unsuitable for fighting games (such as *Prince of Persia: The Sands of Time*) in which enemies attack the avatar from all sides.

Although the first-person perspective seems realistic in principle, in fact, on a conventional monitor with a 4:3 aspect ratio, the first-person view constrains the player's vision to about a 30-degree arc. The normal human enjoys an arc of vision of about 120 degrees horizontally, so the player's field of view is really only about one-fourth of normal size. Widescreen TVs will help with this in the future, and fortunately the mouse-based user interface of most first-person games enables the player to look left and right more quickly than she could in real life. In order to be fair to the player of a first-person single-player game, however, you must still make sure that most of her enemies approach her from the front.

The first-person perspective also allows nice touches such as zooming, giving the impression that the avatar is using binoculars or a rifle with a telescopic sight.

3D Third Person   Some 3D games, such as *Super Mario Sunshine, Max Payne,* and the *Tomb Raider* series, offer a third-person view. The player can see his avatar onscreen, usually from an over-the-shoulder view in which the camera is behind and somewhat above the avatar. Players can see some distance ahead of the avatar, though not as far as in the first-person view because the camera is tilted downward. In this case, you must not present the player with dangers at a very long range (for example, an enemy with a sniper rifle) because the player won't be able to see them until it's too late.

Players may also see a little of what is behind and to the side of the avatar. In these types of games, the camera must move to follow the avatar both predictably and unobtrusively. It must always allow the player to see what he wants to see, so, for example, opaque objects must never come between the camera and the avatar. A common solution to this problem is to render any object that comes between the camera and the avatar semitransparent.

Many third-person shooters allow the player to switch to a first-person perspective momentarily for more precise aiming. Some first-person shooters switch to third-person in particular situations. *Halo* switches from first to third whenever the avatar gets into a vehicle (at which time the vehicle itself temporarily becomes the avatar).

Gameplay Implications of 2D and 3D   In a 3D environment, it is difficult to tell the speed or distance of objects that come directly toward the player's point of view. (This is also true in the real world, while driving, for example.) By operating in only two dimensions, 2D games remove this problem and simplify the amount of visual processing that the player must do. She can directly see the distance between her avatar and other objects, clearly see the speed at which things are moving, and doesn't have to construct a mental 3D model of a space as she explores it. This means that 2D games can throw a lot more challenges at the player before overwhelming her—in short, they can simply be more frenetic than 3D games.

Three-dimensional games make greater use of the environment to present their challenges than 2D games do. The player must traverse a complex three-dimensional landscape, which requires him to remember how rooms join other rooms. This isn't so bad in environments with conventional architecture but can become nightmarish in unfamiliar spaces or those in which rooms or regions all look alike. *Descent* provided a particularly good example of this problem: The player's spaceship flew through a sort of zero-gravity 3D maze. Because the ship could rotate in any direction and the rooms had no clearly defined floors or ceilings, it was easy to become disoriented. The same room could look quite different from different camera angles.

13

In 3D combat games, enemies can hide behind doors and around corners in a way that is not possible in 2D games. They can also sneak up on the avatar from behind, although there is some debate about whether this is fair to the player. In 2D games, the player can always see what's coming. In practice, this means that 3D games have greater opportunities to startle and surprise the player, which has been used to great effect in survival horror games.

Context-Sensitive Perspective One other 3D perspective sometimes found in action games is the context-sensitive perspective. In this case, the camera moves around depending on the circumstances of the moment, controlled by AI. One of the best examples of this comes from *ICO,* shown in Figure 13.12. The camera, seeking to provide the best angle from which to show the action, changes its angle as the avatar moves from room to room. This works well for slower games, but in fast games, especially if the player is fighting for his life, it is a distraction. If the camera moves—especially if it jumps suddenly—the player will become disoriented and is likely to make mistakes. Context-sensitive perspectives are great for offering visual variety, but in high-speed action you should stick to more fixed and predictable points of view.

User Interface

The user interface for action games should be, as Einstein said of physics, "as simple as possible, but not simpler." Players must be able to quickly and accurately assess the play environment, and for that you need to keep distractions to a minimum. In this section, we look at some user interface features that you can use to meet this requirement.

Keep It Onscreen! All the information that the player needs should be immediately present onscreen. Most action games require only a limited amount of information, so this isn't difficult. For example, the HUD (head-up

FIGURE 13.12 The camera in *ICO* moves continuously to display the avatar from the best angle.

display) for *Quake III* shows the minimum amount of information: the player's current health, weapon, and amount of ammo.

Not only does the player have to contend with the frantic action in the game, he also has to pay attention to the graphics that indicate his status and that of his tools. He should be able to do this at a glance without having to work to interpret the data. Don't try to show too much information at one time. In the heat of the game, the player will be concentrating on the in-game action, not the status panel. If you need to draw the player's attention to something in the status panel, make it blink or flicker. On the periphery of our field of vision, the eye is attuned to detect *changes* in contrast or color, so the easiest way to draw the attention of the player is to use a flashing or flickering indicator.

Use Graphical Indicators Rather Than Numbers or Text   In an action game, players seldom need to know exact quantities. Recognizing and understanding the implication of numbers requires more mental processing than it takes to understand a simple gauge or power bar, and the player may not have time to think about it.

If you're dealing with large quantities, in the tens or hundreds or more, use a power bar or some other kind of linear indicator. If players need to know exact amounts of fairly small numbers, such as "lives remaining," put one icon on the screen for each item, and remove the icon as it's consumed. To further drive home the point, you can put a shadow in the space where an icon might go (or might have been) to indicate the possibility that there could be more of them there.

If you're really pushed for space, designate a small region that changes color from red to green or red to black, or whatever makes sense in your art style, as the resource it's tracking gets depleted. Relying solely on color as a differentiating indicator, however, excludes a portion of potential game players—those who are colorblind. See Colorblind Players in Appendix A, "Designing to Appeal to Particular Groups," on the Companion Website, for further discussion.

Companion Website

Maps and Mini-Maps   In some cases, the player needs more information than you can present comfortably in one small status panel. Avoid this whenever possible, but if you can't avoid it, you must choose a type of display that disrupts the game as little as possible. If the player loses out by having to switch to a secondary map or status screen, she won't enjoy the game. Many FPS games show the level map on a separate screen that obscures the main view; therefore, the player can't look at the map safely until there is a lull in the action. Some games display the map in a transparent overlay instead, which allows the player to clearly see both the current environment and the map. This is most effective if the map is not so complicated that it obscures the main view.

As action games became more complex, the play area began to be larger than would fit on the video screen. Although the player could see only one screen at a time, she still needed to be aware of what was going on elsewhere in the game world, so designers began to place small dynamically updated maps

13

called **mini-maps** (sometimes also called *radar displays*) on the screen. Over time, several common configurations have become standard for mini-maps. The earliest type of mini-map, used in *Defender*, showed the entire game world (see the upper part of Figure 13.9. Later games such as *Sinistar* displayed maps showing more of the area surrounding the player than could be shown on the screen but less than the full game world. Designers also sometimes augment the display with a text status line to notify the player of important events occurring outside of the mini-map range. See *Mini-Maps* in Chapter 8, "Creating the User Experience" for further discussion.

Although this is done more often in other genres than in action games, some maps show only those areas of the game world the player has explored, becoming more complete with more exploration. This process is known as *automapping* and is related to the *fog of war,* a concept discussed in Chapter 14, "Strategy Games."

Identifying Characters and Objects   In action games, the player's avatar must be extremely easy to pick out. FPS games, in which the avatar is not displayed on screen, don't present any problem in this regard, but in other action games, the avatar may show up in a clutter of other graphics. The avatar must be distinctive, with a unique shape, color, or position onscreen.

Color coding is the most effective way of ensuring that the player can easily pick out an avatar. Lara Croft wears a distinctive shirt in a teal blue used nowhere else in *Tomb Raider;* if the player can see a splash of that particular blue on the screen, then he is looking at Lara. Finding Lara onscreen does not require any conscious thought on the part of the player.

Two-dimensional scrolling games frequently use position to distinguish the avatar. In these games, the world moves around the avatar, which remains in the same absolute position, or at least on the same horizontal or vertical line, onscreen, giving players a fixed point of reference by which they can orient themselves.

Quickly identifying enemies is equally important. The majority of action games use color schemes that indicate enemies, extending the idea of the avatar's unique color such that enemies, too, follow a common scheme of color or appearance. Think of the old spaghetti westerns in which the good guys wore white and the bad guys wore black. In the film *Tron,* you can easily identify the bad guys because they're the ones in red; the good guys wear blue.

A similar scheme can help the player find collectible items. In fact, an often-used scheme casts the avatar in predominantly one color and all collectibles in another color, with the majority of the background yet another color. Anything else is an enemy. Older games used this arrangement due to hardware limitations (as in *Pac-Man*), but there is no reason not to design a game this way; after all, it works. Each level of *Space Tripper* uses a unique color scheme for enemies, collectibles, and avatar in colors chosen to give maximum contrast with the level's scenery, making analysis of the playing environment as easy as possible for the player.

Controls   Action games (with the exception of fighting games) require simple controls. Because of the fast pace of these games, the physical act of using the controls should, wherever possible, directly translate to avatar action—pushing left on the controls makes the avatar go left, pushing right makes the avatar go right, and so on. For 2D games, this is simple to design, but for first- or third-person 3D games, the third dimension complicates matters. Until recently, all our input devices—joysticks, mice, D-pads, and so on—have allowed input in only two dimensions, so movement in the third dimension had to be controlled by separate—usually binary—buttons, which is less convenient. Nintendo's Wii controller can input control data in three dimensions.

Some action games have attempted to implement more complex control schemes for 3D movement. The success of these games depended on the lengths to which players were prepared to go to learn the system. Games that succeed in this are usually the games that set the standards for new genres. For example, the *Doom* and *Quake* modes of interaction for FPS games are ubiquitous nowadays, but they're still by no means simple for a beginner. Learning to use a *Quake*-style interface is the biggest barrier to mass-market success for first-person 3D games. Similarly, the *Super Mario 64* control system has become the de facto standard control system for most console-based 3D platform games, but good as it is, it still isn't as easy to use as the controls of the old 2D *Super Mario Bros.* game.

As mentioned above, the user interface for fighting games presents more difficulty. Moves such as walking, kicking, and punching may be straightforward, but for the more complex and rewarding combo moves, the player must perform a long string of commands in the correct sequence. Because the commands bear no relation to the actual move executed, players find them harder to learn and remember.

At the other end of the spectrum, some games directly emulate the player's movements in the game world. Without considering virtual reality systems, a mass-market example of this is *Dance Dance Revolution*. The player dances on the controls, a set of footpads, attempting to match the flashing icons that appear on the screen. Consequently, the player's dancing directly controls the dancing of the player's avatar. The easy-to-learn moves undoubtedly account for part of *Dance Dance Revolution's* success.

Summary

Many of the examples in this chapter come from classic action games—some of them nearly twenty years old. The core gameplay of action games has remained essentially unchanged since the earliest days of the industry. We can learn lessons from old games such as *Pac-Man* or *Gauntlet* as effectively as from more recent action games such as *Half-Life 2,* even though gameplay may be more complex nowadays and the structure of the game has shifted more from continuous play (in which wave upon wave of enemies assail the player) to a more

13

story-oriented approach, with a well-defined beginning, middle, and end. The essence of the action game remains unchanged—fast and furious, emphasizing physical skill under time pressure.

In fact, the biggest change in action games as they've developed over two decades is in complexity of graphics. Only those designers who have understood the fundamental nature of action games have made the transition successfully, and they have done this in spite of—not because of—the more sophisticated graphical capabilities of the newer platforms.

Test Your Skills

MULTIPLE CHOICE QUESTIONS

1. Which of these is *not* a subgenre of action games?

   A. Fast puzzle games.

   B. Platform games.

   C. Real-time strategy games.

   D. Shooters.

2. Which of these is *not* a shooting game?

   A. The avatar is a star hunter who stands on the moon collecting different kinds of stars, each type with a particular point score, as they pass by, using a special star lasso that unreels from her hip belt.

   B. The avatar is a firefighter who must put out fires that pop up in apartment house windows one by one with a hose that spurts water 100 feet.

   C. In the world of the ancient Norse gods, the avatar must prevent imps, sprites, and demons from crossing the rainbow bridge to Asgard by sounding a horn which, if properly directed, can knock a demon from the bridge.

   D. They are all shooting games.

3. The best way to balance the advantage given to the player by a combo move is to do what?

   A. Take the move away when the player goes to the next level.

   B. Make the player vulnerable to enemies while pressing the necessary keys.

   C. Make the combo move limited, so that it can only be performed successfully one time.

   D. Design the level so it has no checkpoints.

4. Checkpoints should
   A. be invisible to the player.
   B. never be used in games for small children.
   C. only be used right before the avatar encounters the big boss.
   D. be visually distinguishable to colorblind players.

5. Which of the following would *not* be classed as a stationary danger?
   A. Bottomless pit that means instant death if the player fails to jump across it.
   B. A cliff that rolls stones onto the player's avatar unless attacked with blaster fire.
   C. Harry Potter's Whomping Willow—a tree that attacks intruders with its thrashing branches.
   D. An ocean beach that generates a tsunami wave if the avatar comes too close to the edge of the water.

6. A big boss character usually appears
   A. at the end of a set of themed levels.
   B. after the avatar learns a complex combo move.
   C. just before each checkpoint.
   D. after the player uses a smart bomb.

7. Which of these would be classed as a wildcard enemy?
   A. A big boss that is not designed as a more powerful version of an enemy encountered in the level.
   B. An enemy that appears randomly throughout the game to break up a pattern of enemies that come in waves.
   C. An enemy that shoots from an unseen position off-screen.
   D. A monster that guards the hidden exit to an undocumented level or room.

8. A monster generator is different from a spawn point because a monster generator
   A. requires power and, therefore, a supply line.
   B. is an object in the game world.
   C. can produce an unlimited number of enemies.
   D. produces fully grown enemies rather than merely monster-spawn.

13

9. A smart bomb is considered an action rather than an object because

   A. it is the most powerful object in the game world and so produces the most action.

   B. it is named for the first game that ever used such a bomb, *Smart Bombs*.

   C. it is usually implemented as an action and so no corresponding object appears in the game world.

   D. it is usually given to the player when he has amassed a high enough IQ score.

10. What would you call a hexagon that, when the avatar touches it, moves the avatar to another place in the same level?

    A. Spawn point.

    B. Locked door and key.

    C. Teleporter.

    D. Level exit.

11. The background of your game scrolls at a steady rate behind the player's avatar as it fights off attackers. Your game exhibits

    A. side-scrolling.

    B. continuous scrolling.

    C. variable scrolling.

    D. wave scrolling.

12. Which of the following is *not* a problem with a first-person 3D game?

    A. The player's field of vision is more restricted than the field of vision available to someone with normal vision in real life.

    B. Unseen enemies may pounce on the avatar from behind, and the avatar can't see them.

    C. It can be difficult to locate the avatar against the detailed graphics of the background.

    D. The player may have difficulty judging the speed or distance of objects coming right toward the player's point of view.

13. Which of these must you be aware of when considering using a context-sensitive perspective?

    A. The current state of AI sophistication doesn't allow this perspective; it is hoped we can use context-sensitive perspective in the future.

    B. This perspective can make players vulnerable because they have to take time to reorient themselves whenever the camera angle changes.

    C. This perspective carries a stigma because of its close association with survival horror games.

    D. Using this perspective limits you to using only 2D graphics.

14. Which of the following is true of the user interface for an action game?

    A. It should give as much information as can be given clearly, so the player doesn't have to look away from the game.

    B. It's good practice to use a flashing display to alert the player to important information.

    C. As much as possible, the player's action should translate directly into avatar action.

    D. All of the above.

15. We recommend using what to help the player identify her avatar quickly?

    A. Make the avatar larger than any enemy.

    B. Offer a special mini-map just for avatar location.

    C. Make items between the 3D camera's point of view and the avatar transparent.

    D. Designate a color to use for the avatar and for no other element of the display.

Case Study

Choose an action game that you believe, from your own experience of playing it, is an excellent example of the genre (or use one your instructor has assigned). Write a report documenting the features that place it into this genre as opposed to another one and explaining why you believe it is superior to others of its kind. Be sure to cover at least the following areas:

- **Gameplay modes and structure.** Describe each mode in a few sentences.

- **Gameplay in the primary gameplay mode, including both challenges and actions.** For each challenge that you document, indicate what class it belongs to: physical, logical, exploration, pattern recognition, etc.

- **User interface in the primary gameplay mode.** Describe the perspective and interaction model. Note important indicators that appear on the screen and discuss how they improve the playing experience.

- **Core mechanics.** Indicate resources, sources, conversions, and drains.

CONTINUED ON NEXT PAGE

13

> ▶▶ **CONTINUED**
>
> The design questions in the next section may help you to think about these issues. In your report, use screen shots to illustrate your points. End the case study with suggestions for improvement or, if you feel the game cannot be improved, suggestions for additional features that might be fun to have in the game.
>
> Alternatively, choose a game that you believe is particularly *bad*. Do the same case study, explaining what is wrong and how it could be improved.
>
> A case study is neither a review nor a design document; it is an analysis. You are not attempting to reverse-engineer the entire game but simply to explain how it works in a general way. Your instructor will tell you the desired scope of the assignment; we recommend from five to twenty pages.

DESIGN QUESTIONS

As you design an action game, consider the following questions:

1. Is this game a shooter or a nonshooter? If it is a nonshooter, what actions will the player take to defeat enemies?

2. Is the world (not the display mechanism) essentially 2D or 3D? If the world is 2D, should the display mechanism be 2D also, or would the gameplay benefit from 3D graphics?

3. If the world is 2D, will the whole world be visible on the screen, or will it scroll? If it scrolls, in which direction(s) does it scroll?

4. Does the player need a mini-map to see key off-screen elements of the world before they arrive onscreen? What about an automap for allowing him to record where he has been?

5. What physical challenges will the game incorporate and under what circumstances? Speed and reaction time? Accurate steering and aiming? Timing and rhythm? Combo moves?

6. Will enemies appear in waves? Will there be monster generators or wild-card enemies to break up the regular progression of the waves?

7. Will the game be broken into levels? What things will make one level different from another (landscape, enemies, speed, perspective, and so on)? What about the aesthetic style of things such as music and architecture? Will levels end with bosses?

8. How will the avatar's life be managed: as fixed numbers of lives, energy bars, or some combination? Can the player obtain more lives? If so, how?

9. What powerups will there be, if any? For each one you plan to incorporate, do the following: state what it does, what it looks like, what it sounds like when activated or how or where it is to be found or obtained, how common or rare it is, how long its effect lasts, and how the player will be able to identify it (by sight and the sound it makes).

10. Will the game give the player clues that allow him to anticipate challenges, or must the player depend entirely on trial-and-error to learn his way through?

11. Does the game involve exploring unknown territory? If so, how linear or nonlinear will it be? Traditional arcade and side-scrolling games gave little or no choice; games like *Spyro the Dragon* offer considerable freedom.

12. Is there a feature that prevents the player from having to start over from the beginning? What is it—saving and reloading, checkpoints, or something else?

13. Is the player going to collect anything, in either large or small numbers? Can collected items be exchanged for anything useful, or is the player awarded anything when particular thresholds are reached?

14. Is there a scoring mechanism? If so, how is it computed? Does it serve any function besides giving the player a record of achievement?

15. What locked doors will there be, and what keys will open them?

16. Will the game have, or need, a tutorial mode? If not, how steep do you want the learning curve to be?

17. Does the game have a victory condition other than simple survival? What is it?

13

Chapter 14

Strategy Games

Chapter Objectives

After reading this chapter and completing the exercises, you will be able to do the following:

- Know the definition of a strategy game and be familiar with the types of challenges that strategy games offer.
- Define the set of orders that a strategy player will be able to give in your game.
- Design a balanced set of units for use in a war game, including defining the attributes that govern their behavior.
- Compute the relative values of offensive and defensive units.
- Understand Lanchester's laws and how they affect the relative strengths of forces of different size.
- Create a technology tree of upgrades for the units that you have designed.
- Choose a system of logistics for your game and design the mechanism by which it works.
- Know the most common types of artificial opponents and their strengths and weaknesses.

Introduction

> *This is a war universe. War all the time. That is its nature. There may be other universes based on all sorts of other principles, but ours seems to be based on war and games.*
>
> —William Burroughs

Strategy games are among the oldest in the world. Tradition puts the invention of Go at around 2200 BC. The Royal Game of Ur, whose board and counters are on display in the British Museum in London, dates to around 2500 BC, although scholars do not know its rules—it might only have been a game of chance.

In this chapter, we discuss how the principles of game design apply to strategy games, concentrating on the most popular subgenre, war games. We begin with a formal definition of strategy games and then address in detail the features that characterize strategy games. We examine the types of challenges they typically offer and the actions that the players may take to meet those challenges. The bulk of the chapter, however, is devoted to the core mechanics of strategy games: designing the units themselves, special capabilities, upgrades and technology trees, issues with logistics, and some comments on the different kinds of game worlds that war games are frequently set in. We end with a brief discussion of the various ways that programmers can implement artificial opponents in strategy games. We don't expect you, as a designer, to do the programming, but you should be familiar with the techniques that are commonly used.

What Are Strategy Games?

Strategy games challenge the player to achieve victory through planning and specifically through planning a series of actions taken against one or more opponents. This definition distinguishes strategy games from puzzle games, which call for planning in the absence of conflict, and from competitive construction and management simulations, which require planning but not direct action against an opponent. Strategy games often include the reduction of enemy forces as a key goal, so most strategy games are war games in greater or lesser degrees of abstraction. Checkers (draughts), for example, is an abstract war game; *Risk* is slightly less abstract; and *Axis and Allies,* a board game about World War II, is fairly representational. However, not all strategy games focus on combat. The games *Cathedral* and Go are about surrounding and capturing territory; *Hex* and *Twixt* are about making a continuous line of pieces across a board; and of course tic-tac-toe (noughts and crosses) is about getting three symbols in a row.

> *A strategy game is one in which the majority of challenges presented are strategic conflict challenges and the player may choose from a large variety of potential actions or moves at most points in the game. Victory is attained by superior planning and taking the optimum actions; the element of chance must not play a large role. Other challenges, such as tactical, logistical, economic, and exploration challenges, may also be present. Physical coordination challenges play little or no part.*

Strategy games, with their long history of play with dice, cards, and boards, naturally developed into PC games. (Console efforts so far have been

14

few and far between.) The computer provides the power to impartially manage complex rule-sets, a task that would detract from the fun if the player had to do the work.

Strategy games are more symmetric than the games in other genres and so are somewhat easier to balance for difficulty. The resources and actions available to each side are, if not identical, generally similar. You can adjust the strengths and weaknesses of each side and study the probable outcomes of particular battles with statistical analysis even before any code is written. Contrast this with action games in which one avatar must fight a horde of enemies or adventure games in which the player must solve a number of puzzles of varying difficulty. In those genres, it is considerably harder to predict what the player will find difficult.

Game Features

Strategy games fall into two main subgenres: classical turn-based games and real-time strategy games. Pure strategy games (those that contain only conflict challenges) tend to be turn-based rather than operating in real time. In a turn-based game, players may mull over their moves, considering the benefits of one choice over another. In board games, this can result in frustrating "analysis paralysis" in which one player spends a large amount of time considering each move while the others have to wait. In single-player computer games, this doesn't matter—the computer doesn't mind waiting. Multiplayer turn-based computer games are often designed so that all the players choose their next move simultaneously, and the machine computes and displays the outcome of their actions. This cuts down substantially on the waiting time.

Real-time strategy (RTS) games developed after turn-based games. RTSs added time pressure to strategy games because everything happens at once and players do not have individual turns to ponder their moves. Though they're not as frenetic as action games, RTSs require the player to keep a sharp lookout and to think quickly.

Many books have been written about games such as chess and *Risk,* so we do not devote much time to abstract strategy games or those with simple rules. The vast majority of computerized strategy games are representational war games with complex core mechanics, so that is where we focus our attention.

Challenges

As we said in our definition, strategy games may include economic and exploration challenges, but strategic conflict generally dominates in strategy games. A game that includes only economic challenges without any fighting is more properly a construction and management simulation. For example, exploration and growth do feature in *StarCraft,* but only to enable the player to fight more effectively; players must explore the area to be conquered and set up resource-processing plants to allow resources to be converted into troops and vehicles.

Strategic Conflict   Conflict is most often characterized as combat between groups of individual combatants; by long tradition, these combatants are known as ***units.*** A unit can be anything from an ancient Egyptian warrior to a Napoleonic cavalryman to an imaginary spacecraft. Not all units fight; some can be used for transport, scouting, or other purposes. Units also need not be movable; a fixed gun emplacement is still a unit. In most modern war games, specialized units, often portrayed as buildings that must be constructed in the landscape, are used to produce new fighting units. These buildings generally don't move and don't fight, but they can be destroyed if attacked and perhaps be repaired by repair units. Although it is not an industry standard term, in this chapter we will refer to such buildings as ***factories.*** In general, when we refer to units we will mean fighting units, not factories.

The main characteristic that distinguishes units and factories from anything else on the battlefield is that they are under a player's control and provide some benefit to him, so if they die or are destroyed, that benefit is lost to the player. Units may be atomic, with no individually distinguishable parts (such as an infantry soldier with a rifle), or compound, with separate parts that can be added and removed and perhaps destroyed without completely destroying the whole unit (such as a large ship with many guns). Each unit behaves according to particular performance characteristics, such as how long it can survive when under attack, how rapidly it can fire a weapon, or how fast it can move. We discuss these attributes in more detail in the section on *Core Mechanics* later in the chapter.

In order to give the player interesting options, almost all war games offer the player a choice of different kinds of units. In chess, there are six kinds; in more representational games, there may be dozens. Checkers starts with only one kind of unit, but later in the game a new kind can appear, a king.

Most war games seek to reproduce the classic situations and tactics of military combat, whether at particular points in history or in imaginary conflicts. Depending on the degree of realism offered, tactics can include flanking maneuvers, sneak attacks, creating diversions, cutting off enemy supply lines, killing the superior officers to leave the troops without leadership, taking advantage of the effects of bad weather, and so on. In order for the player to use these tactics, the units and the rules of the game have to be designed in such a way as to support them. If you want your game to include sneak attacks, for instance, you will have to include a mechanism that hides the enemy's movements from the player. Obviously on some level the computer knows everything that is happening, but you can design the computer's AI to ignore the player's movements if the software determines that the player's units are not visible to the computer's troops.

14

Alternatives to Combat Conflict does not necessarily involve physical combat. Whereas RTS games and simpler strategy games tend to focus on combat, more advanced games include elements of diplomacy, crisis management, and espionage. For example, in *Civilization III,* the response of the enemy leaders to diplomatic overtures depends in large part on whether the player has the force to back up her tough words. Of course, diplomacy isn't all about threatening enemies—it also allows for the formation of alliances that can avert war and encourage trade.

Diplomacy and espionage suit a slower-paced strategy game, one designed to be played over a long period of time. The extra nuance and depth that diplomacy adds to an otherwise standard strategy game is well worth the extra time and effort spent designing and implementing a fully fledged system of diplomats and spies. Diplomacy gives the player an extra degree of freedom, which allows for the creation of more devious and interesting game plans than would be possible otherwise.

Strategy games nevertheless tend to reward aggressive measures more than they do peaceful ones because war is easier to model than diplomacy and is more exciting to watch. The consequences of war are presented as less dire than they are in the real world, and the goal of the game is often domination of the world, not peaceful coexistence. We would be interested in seeing a strategy game whose goal was to avert war and promote prosperity; the player's role would perhaps be the secretary-general of the United Nations.

IN THE TRENCHES: Balance of Power

Chris Crawford's *Balance of Power* ranks among the most brilliant games of diplomatic strategy ever created. The setting is the Cold War between the United States and the USSR. You take one side or the other and try to increase your own nation's geopolitical prestige and sphere of influence at the expense of your opponent by supporting the governments of friendly smaller countries and destabilizing or even overthrowing the governments of unfriendly ones. The actions you can take include giving economic aid to friendly countries, pressuring unfriendly ones through threats, signing defense and other treaties, and giving direct military support, including sending in troops. If a smaller country has an insurgency or a civil war going on, you can choose which side to support. If the government of a hostile country falls and is replaced by a government friendly to your side, you gain prestige. The victory condition is a net gain in prestige after ten years of play.

▶▶ CONTINUED ON NEXT PAGE

▶▶ CONTINUED

The real excitement, however, is not in manipulating smaller countries, but in what happens when the other side finds out about it—particularly if you interfere in a country that traditionally lies in the other side's sphere of influence. For each action that one superpower takes, the other superpower has a chance to object. Whoever initiated the action must then decide whether to insist or to back off. These events, called *crises*, raise the stakes enormously; tremendous prestige is lost when one side backs down in a crisis. However, if you push your opponents too far, the result is a nuclear war that instantly ends the game. The trick is to know when you are on firm ground and when you had better let the other side have its way. It's poker with nuclear weapons.

Each side has limited resources with which to undertake its activities. The game is asymmetric; the United States has more money, while the Soviets have more troops. More subtle tactics, such as signing treaties and diplomatic pressure, don't cost anything but aren't as effective. At the highest difficulty level, however, they are really the only way to win; sending arms and troops is too likely to provoke a holocaust.

Balance of Power simulated geopolitics with a depth and subtlety never before seen in a computer game and was so good that, for a brief time, the U.S. State Department used it to train diplomats. Crawford has written an excellent book called *Balance of Power: International Politics as the Ultimate Global Game* that describes the core mechanics of the game in detail, right down to the equations that govern particular behaviors. The book is out of print but is available from Internet booksellers specializing in used books.

Exploration Challenges   Exploration allows players to investigate unknown terrain in a game world. As a designer, you may give the player new worlds or make creative use of the familiar world. Consider *X-COM: UFO Defense,* which depicted the secretive invasion of Earth by aliens. Players were of course familiar with the map of the Earth, but the location of hidden alien bases and UFO landing sites was a mystery until the player sent out a squad of soldiers to investigate.

X-COM presented the player with a landscape shrouded in darkness, a darkness that dissipated only when the player's soldiers entered an area. This technique is used in most strategy games involving exploration to increase their difficulty. If the terrain is generally flat, you can decide that the area to be revealed is simply a circle of a certain diameter around a unit, but in hilly terrain you may wish to compute the actual lines of sight for the units so that enemy units behind hills or other obstructions remain hidden. The level design in a good many single-player war games makes heavy use of the player's ignorance of the landscape; in order to win a level, for instance, the player may have to explore enough to find some key feature, such as a bridge over an impassable river or a back way to sneak up on the computer player's headquarters.

Games often present territory that has been explored—but is not currently patrolled by the player's forces—as dim, with only landscape details and no information about the presence of enemy units. These two techniques—unexplored regions shown in black and explored but unpatrolled regions shown dimly—are collectively known as the *fog of war.* Figure 14.1 shows the bright area currently visible to the player, the dimmed area that has been explored but is not currently visible (due to lack of troops there to provide intelligence), and the black bulk of the land that remains unexplored.

The fog of war lends realism and excitement to the game. Because the player cannot see what is happening in areas where he has no troops, he could be attacked unexpectedly if he does not take appropriate defensive measures. These games reward those who set up guard units to warn of impending invasions and those who send out scouts to find out where the enemy is.

Hiding the unexplored landscape itself, however, is completely unrealistic in any game set after about the year 1500. Armies haven't had to fight wars without a map of the terrain for several centuries. Games continue to hide the landscape

FIGURE 14.1 The fog of war (from *Civilization III*).

from the player because the task of exploring makes the game more challenging. In a lot of games, if the player could see the landscape clearly he would be able to plan more effectively and therefore win more quickly. Many games also cheat, hiding the landscape from the player but allowing the computer's AI to see it. This gives the computer an advantage that the player does not have and helps to compensate if the AI isn't very good in the first place. It's a design solution to a programming problem: weak AI.

Economic Challenges

The sinews of war: a limitless supply of money.

—Cicero

Strategy games such as chess give the players a fixed number of units at the beginning of the game, and the players make do with what they've been given. Other games offer a mechanism for acquiring more units as the game goes on, which makes the campaign more a process of growth than of attrition. In *Risk,* for example, each player gets a number of new units at the beginning of his turn; the exact amount is based on a few easily calculated factors.

Computer strategy games allow for far more complex calculations than a human being playing *Risk* is willing or able to perform. Designers of computer strategy games frequently take advantage of this to include a richer internal economy for the player to manage. Rather than starting with a large number of units at the beginning of a level, the player has to obtain some resource—let's assume it's gold—that can be converted to units later on. This lets the player decide when to buy the units and what sorts of units to purchase and therefore offers her greater freedom to fight the battle in whatever way she prefers.

You can supply the players with a limited amount of gold at the beginning of a level and put more gold out in the landscape for them to discover. These locations, or mines, can produce either a limited or an unlimited amount of gold. If mines produce an unlimited amount, the game could, in principle, go on forever; if not, the game must eventually come to an end as the resource runs out.

More complicated games use several different resources; in fact, if the economy of a strategy game becomes complicated enough, the game really turns into a hybrid of strategy game and construction and management simulation. The *Age of Empires* and *Civilization* series are both really hybrids, not straight strategy games, though we'll use the economy within the former as an example here.

In *Age of Empires,* the player must obtain food, wood, stone, and gold, each from its source, worked by units designated for the purpose and brought back to a central storage area. The player spends resources to construct factories, and the factories in turn produce units (which also consumes resources). The factories effectively form the player's headquarters and must be defended, adding a new conflict challenge.

KEY POINT

Strategy games that hide gold in the landscape for the players to find often turn into rushes to grab the mines. Monopolizing production of resources then becomes a dominant strategy, and players avoid trying any other. To prevent this, make the map layout fairly symmetrical, with similar amounts of gold near each side's headquarters. If you put mines farther out in the landscape for the players to find, put comparatively little gold in them. That makes finding one a nice bonus but not a decisive advantage.

It is vitally important that the economic productivity of all sides be equally balanced, or economic advantages will rapidly outweigh strategic skill.

14

Player Actions

In a strategy game, the player's role is that of a commander, so most actions consist of giving orders to units. Each unit will respond to commands according to the AI programming for that unit or type of unit. Giving an order is usually a two-step process: First, the player selects the unit or units that will receive the order, generally by clicking on it with the mouse. Then the player issues the order, either by clicking somewhere in the landscape, on an enemy unit, or on a button or menu item. Here's a short list of actions and orders commonly found in strategy games (different games will use different names for them):

- **Move** to a given location in the terrain, optionally via a series of waypoints marked along the way. The unit uses *pathfinding* AI to find its way there, taking the quickest route while avoiding obstructions.

- **Attack** an enemy unit, which includes advancing until the enemy unit is in range, then opening fire, and pursuing if the enemy retreats.

- **Stop** moving; this order countermands both attack and movement orders. Because the AI for attacking will usually pursue an enemy unit to the ends of the earth (including right into an ambush), the player frequently needs to issue the stop order.

- **Hold** a particular position, meaning attack any enemy that comes into range, but do not pursue it if it retreats. The unit's AI may include an automatic tendency to attack certain enemies preferentially, or the player may have to manage this directly.

- Establish a **formation** that is tactically advantageous. Loose infantry formations give some protection against archery because a lot of arrows fall into empty space; tight formations are best against other infantry. Warships with guns along their sides can concentrate their firepower if several sail in a straight line, head to stern. Tanks with guns at the front can do the same if their formation is abreast. You may want to include a formation editor in your game that allows the player to design formations that he likes.

- **Produce** new units by consuming resources. This can be a command that is given by clicking a button in the user interface, but more often the command is given to a specific factory, whose function is to create mobile units.

You might want to consider variants of these common orders, such as **retreat,** a flight that leaves the unit more vulnerable but goes more quickly; **dash,** a rapid forward movement in which the unit does not attempt to attack enemies it encounters but tries to get to its destination as quickly as possible; and **patrol,** a cyclic movement between two or more designated points, allowing units to defend more territory than the hold command permits.

FIGURE 14.2 The *StarCraft* screen, with a menu of orders at the lower right.

Figure 14.2 is a screenshot from *StarCraft* showing, at the lower right of the screen, a menu of mouse-clickable icons that correspond to five of these commands. They are, from top to bottom and left to right, *dash, stop, attack, patrol,* and *hold.* The remaining visible icon invokes a special capability of the currently selected unit.

Specialized units will of course have their own special orders: building for construction units, repair for repair or medical units, picking up and dropping off troops or supplies for transport units, and so on. We discuss specialized units in the next section.

Core Mechanics

Strategy games with simple rules, such as chess, don't have an internal economy because they don't deal in numeric quantities; either a piece is on the board or it isn't. There is no flow of resources to manage, so their core mechanics are uncomplicated. (This does not, however, mean that their strategy is uncomplicated!) In war games, the internal economy centers on the production and consumption of resources such as units and factories and can be very complex indeed.

14

Designing Units

The units in war games almost always fall into types, such that all units of each type share a set of attributes, but some units or types of units will also have special capabilities that are unique to them and give them a special role. In this section, we discuss some design considerations for creating units.

The Rock-Paper-Scissors (RPS) Model   *The Ancient Art of War,* an early real-time strategy game, ran on a 4.77 MHz IBM PC. The machine did not have enough CPU power to cope with a complex model of real-time combat, so the game used only three types of fighting units and a simple rock-paper-scissors rule to resolve conflict among them. The unit types were knights, archers, and barbarians. (Spies, the fourth type of unit offered, could not fight.) Knights had an advantage over barbarians; barbarians had an advantage over archers, and archers had an advantage over knights. The player's challenge, as in rock-paper-scissors, was to try to anticipate which units his opponent would use and deploy the ones most likely to beat them. Units could be deployed in mixed groups, and the player could choose different formations for them to fight in, which made the game more interesting.

While RPS-style models are easy to implement and naturally balanced, they are suited only to simple games, and we do not recommend that you use these for a modern war game with large numbers of unit types. You can't balance a complex game by simply declaring that some units are vulnerable to others; there are too many pairwise matchups to consider. These models also don't take into account battlefield conditions. What if the knights sneak up on the archers from behind and engage them in close combat?

Instead, we recommend that you create numerical attributes that describe the combat strengths and weaknesses of unit types *independently* of whom they may fight. The relative combat effectiveness of different unit types against each other will then emerge from these attributes. This system, described in the next section, permits many more types of units and more interesting relationships among them.

Numeric Attributes   Modern war games assign numeric attributes to each type of unit that describe its abilities. Each unit of a given type begins with the values defined by its type, but these values change as the unit takes damage, consumes ammunition, and so on. The system is similar to that used to describe characters in role-playing games. However, RPGs tend to be about small numbers of quite diverse individuals, while strategy games tend be about large numbers of fairly similar units. Consequently, RPGs use more attributes than strategy games do.

The landscape in which the battles are fought also has attributes that vary from place to place and affect the activities of the units present. Forest terrain, for example, will slow down vehicles moving through it, and deep water is impassable to all units except boats.

The numerical attributes most commonly used in a war game include the following:

- **Health** is measured in health points (HP). These are reduced as a unit takes damage. When a unit's number of health points reaches zero, the unit is considered destroyed and therefore disappears from the game. An atomic unit does not have any pieces or parts that take damage individually, so it has only one health attribute and all damage is done to it as a whole. Compound units may have separate health attributes for each of the different pieces that make it up. (A cavalry unit, for example, might have one health attribute for the rider and another for the horse.) The maximum amount of health that a given type of unit may have is its **maximum health.** More robust units have a higher maximum health. Some units may also have **armor,** also measured in health points, which can absorb a certain amount of damage and protect the unit's health. Armor, too, will have a **maximum armor** value that varies with the unit. You can either let the armor absorb all damage until the armor is destroyed (in which case it's really just like extra health), or, more realistically, you can have the armor let more and more damage get through to harm the unit as the armor itself is degraded.

- Units may have zero or more weapons with which to attack enemy units. (Transport units typically have no weapons; tanks typically have three or four, though many games limit the number of weapons per unit to one, to make the game simpler.) Each weapon has attributes that describe its characteristics. When a weapon hits an enemy unit, it reduces that unit's health or armor by a certain number of health points. A weapon inflicts damage in individual instances called **shots;** the amount of damage it does per shot is its **shot power,** expressed in HP per shot. There must be a minimum period of time between shots; the number of shots per minute is the weapon's **rate of fire.** (We are using firearms terminology, but the same attributes also apply to swinging a sword; some swords do more damage than others, and some can be wielded more quickly than others.) If the game models ammunition consumption for a certain weapon, then that weapon also has a certain amount of **ammo;** each shot consumes one round, and the weapon ceases to operate when the number reaches zero.

- **Range** is the maximum distance at which a weapon can deliver damage. Some units will have only hand-to-hand combat weapons and can attack only adjacent units, so the range of their weapons is small. A few long-range weapons, such as longbows, are useless in hand-to-hand combat, and so may also need a **minimum range** rating below which they are not functional. Fixed units such as gun emplacements cannot always point in all directions; if that is the case, you will need to define

14

a **traverse arc** for the unit, two numbers that indicate the starting and ending bearings. All the bearings between these two constitute an arc through which the weapon may be traversed. A traverse arc of 0 to 90 degrees means the unit can fire in any direction between due north and due east.

■ Small projectiles such as bullets and arrows should hit only one enemy unit each, but if your game includes large, solid projectiles like cannonballs, you will have to define the **shot mass** and **shot velocity** of each. Their kinetic energy is great enough to let them completely destroy small units and continue onward. The amount of damage they can do is reduced in proportion to the mass of the units that they have already hit, until they finally stop. Explosive projectiles, on the other hand, require a **blast radius,** a measure of the distance from their landing point to the farthest point that the explosion can affect; any unit takes damage if it is within the blast radius. In principle, the amount of damage done to enemy units within the blast radius should be reduced by the inverse square law—that is, the shot power of the projectile is reduced in proportion to the square of the target unit's distance from the center of the blast; however, you may not wish to compute to that level of detail.

■ **Accuracy** is a measure of the chance that a given weapon will hit the point at which it is aimed, expressed as a real number between 0 (never hits) and 1 (always hits). Note that this is accuracy of aiming at a point, not hitting a unit; if a projectile is slow, the unit may not be there when the projectile arrives, even if the weapon is highly accurate. **Theoretical accuracy** is the average accuracy of a weapon under all conditions, but you may also add to or subtract from the theoretical accuracy to compute the **practical accuracy** based on the prevailing conditions when the weapon is used, such as the distance to the target, whether it's daytime or nighttime, and so on.

■ **Defensive dodging** is a unit's ability to successfully dodge an enemy shot; you may want to restrict its meaning to dodging solid projectiles such as bullets, not blast effects. Like accuracy, it should be expressed as a real number between 0 (never dodges) and 1 (always dodges). If your physics model is complex enough to include the velocity of shots, then defensive dodging should be less effective against faster-moving shots.

■ Units that move have a **speed** at which they are currently moving and a **maximum speed** that represents the fastest they can move over unrestricted terrain such as a road. Their actual speed at a given time is degraded by the **difficulty** of the terrain through which they are passing (a terrain attribute); difficulty is expressed as a real number between 0 (prohibits passage entirely) and 1 (allows maximum speed, like a road). Speed should also be degraded by moving uphill; the **altitude** of each point in the landscape is another terrain attribute, and the relative altitudes of two adjacent regions give the steepness of the slope between them. Slopes above a certain steepness should be impassable to ordinary ground units.

- The **turn rate** describes the rate at which a unit can turn to face a new direction; this applies both to moving and fixed units. The turn rate should not be so quick that the turn is instantaneous, or flanking maneuvers won't work.

- If you are making a highly realistic strategy game about vehicles such as tanks, you might also want to include the unit's **mass, acceleration,** and so on, but most strategy games don't bother. Without taking mass and acceleration into account, units don't speed up and slow down, they simply start to move at the maximum rate they can over the terrain, and they stop as soon as they receive a stop command.

- If your game includes the fog of war, you will need to include a number that describes a unit's **range of vision;** scouting units might have a larger number for this than other units. This value will naturally be modified by the altitude of the land relative to the region around it.

Note that accuracy and defensive dodging introduce an element of chance into the game. To determine if a weapon hits or misses the point it is aimed at, the software must choose a random number between 0 and 1; if the random number chosen is below the weapon's accuracy rating, it shoots accurately; if the random number is above it, it misses. Obviously if the weapon's accuracy rating is 1, it is completely accurate. You then have to determine whether a unit being shot at dodges the shot successfully (even if it is an accurate shot) by choosing another random number and comparing it to the target's defensive dodging ability.

Naturally, the preceding is not an exhaustive list of attributes, but it covers the basics. If we were to apply it to *The Ancient Art of War* mentioned earlier, we would design knights and barbarians to have only close-combat weapons while archers have only a long-range weapon; barbarians have high defensive dodging (making them less vulnerable to archers), whereas knights have low defensive dodging (making them more vulnerable to archers); and knights have more armor and more shot power than barbarians, making them superior to barbarians in hand-to-hand combat. In other words, numeric attributes can duplicate the artificial rock-paper-scissors relationships of *The Ancient Art of War,* but they can create much more complex and subtle relationships as well.

14

> ## COMMANDMENT: No Invincible Units!
>
> *Avoid designing any unit whose weapon range and maximum speed attributes are both greater than the range and speed of any enemy unit it may face. Such a unit has the speed to stay permanently out of range of its opponents and can shoot them with impunity. If it is sufficiently outnumbered, its opponents may be able to trap it; but such a maneuver often requires better AI than most strategy games can manage. A unit that is invincible in a one-on-one conflict with every type of enemy unit will unbalance your game.*

Special Capabilities   Many units in strategy games have special capabilities that strongly affect the tactics and strategy of play. Some special capabilities influence the attributes of a unit; others simply allow the unit to do things that other units cannot. We offer a short list of possibilities:

- **Stealth.** A stealth unit can become invisible to enemy units. This capacity is extremely valuable because it enables the unit to sneak past guards posted by the enemy and attack a vulnerable point. Designers traditionally require stealth units to reveal themselves when they use their weapons. Units able to attack while remaining invisible would be too powerful. Some designers reserve stealth capability for unarmed units, which serve as scouts.

- **Flying or sailing,** that is, traversing terrain inaccessible to ordinary land-based units. Aircraft and ships tend to be specialized and incapable of operating in any other medium, but there is no reason you cannot create amphibious craft if you want to.

- **Repair.** Units can be designed to repair themselves; you can also devise special units that repair others—essentially, medical units. This valuable feature rewards players who keep a sharp eye on the health of their units and set up systems to repair them efficiently. The repair feature is especially beneficial if new units cost resources to manufacture, but repairs cost nothing or at least, less than building a new unit.

- **Transport.** Transport units allow the rapid conveyance of a certain number of other units around the landscape. Destroying a transport unit destroys the units it carries as well. Because rapid transport is a valuable feature, designers often make transport units unarmed, to offset this strength by increasing the transport units' vulnerability. This requires the player to assign armed units to go with them in a convoy, which lends realism to the game.

- **Building construction** and **production of mobile units.** As we described in the section on strategic conflict challenges, most modern war games use a construction unit to build and repair factories, and the factory constructs other mobile units, often of a specific type.

- **Leadership.** Some games, especially those that represent ancient warfare, include special leader units that give a fighting bonus to other units near them or under their command. This bonus is lost if the leader is killed, thus simulating the loss of morale and organization that occurs in those circumstances.

For every special capability you create for one side in a battle, you *must* also create a capability of similar military value for the other side *or* a means of defeating the special capability. If you give one side stealth units, you should either give the other side something equally useful or give them special units that can detect stealth units. The special capabilities of either side need not be symmetric—Carthaginians use war elephants and Romans use catapults—but there must be a balance between them. Otherwise one side will exploit its advantage ruthlessly and the game will be no fun.

Computing the Relative Value of Units   If your game allows the purchase or construction of new units, you will have to decide on the relative cost of each type of unit, either in terms of the amount of time that the player will have to wait for it, the resources required to purchase it, or both. A unit's cost should be a function of its military value. Of course, the value of a unit depends a lot on the conditions in which it fights; snowmobiles are useless in the desert, and infantry can't do much against jet aircraft. However, you'll still need some kind of baseline for determining how much a unit is worth in absolute terms, regardless of circumstances or what it's up against, so that each side will pay roughly the same amount for the same amount of military effectiveness.

We propose two equations as a first approximation of the military effectiveness, and therefore the value, of a unit type. The first is for units designed primarily for attack; the second is for units designed for defense.

$$\textit{Attack Unit Value} = \textit{maximum health} \times \textit{shot power} \times \textit{rate of fire} \\ \times \textit{theoretical accuracy} \times \textit{range} \times \textit{maximum speed}$$

Very roughly, this equation reflects a unit's ability to accurately deliver damage from a distance, while surviving under fire itself. So, in comparing two types of attack units, if all the factors are equal except for maximum health, the one with the greater health will survive longer under fire and therefore do more damage to the enemy before it is destroyed. Likewise, if two units are identical except for their rate of fire, the one that fires faster will do more damage before it is destroyed. Speed is included because it is a measure of a unit's ability to get out of the range of another enemy's weapons. Any unit that is faster than an enemy can get in and out of harm's way quickly, allowing hit-and-run operations.

14

For defensive units such as fixed gun emplacements, the equation is slightly different:

$$\textit{Defense Unit Value} = \textit{maximum health} \times \textit{shot power} \times \textit{rate of fire}$$
$$\times \textit{theoretical accuracy} \times \frac{\textit{range}^2}{2}$$

Speed is left out because such units don't move much and don't generally need to; they're supposed to protect the place where they are. The range is squared because a longer range means more than being able to shoot farther away; it means being able to deliver fire on an *area* of terrain, and the area is proportional to the square of the range. We divided it by two because the vast majority of the time the enemy will be in front of the unit, not behind it; being able to cover the area behind the unit is less valuable.

Note: *These equations produce completely different ranges of values and cannot be used to compare the value of attacking units with defensive units.* They're only intended to compare attacking units to other attacking units and defensive units to other defensive units. As we said, the equations are only a first approximation, and you will almost certainly want to attach weights to the various factors they include. The equations also don't take into account special capabilities such as stealth or leadership. A unit with a special capability should cost more than a unit that is otherwise identical but lacks that capability, but there is no rule of thumb for determining just how much more it should cost. Only play-testing and tuning can produce a balanced set of units for all sides in the war. Be sure to read the section Avoiding Dominant Strategies in Chapter 11, "Game Balancing," before setting attributes for your units.

Production Rates, Unit Numbers, and Lanchester's Laws   Frederick William Lanchester founded the field of operations research, which studies subjects such as logistics and production efficiency. In the course of his work, he devised two laws regarding the relative strengths of enemy forces. One, Lanchester's Linear Law, states that in hand-to-hand combat the relative strengths of two armies are simply proportional to their numbers of troops. Since one fighter can only ever engage one other fighter at a time, the force relationship is a simple one.

His other law, Lanchester's Square Law, refers to the relative strengths of forces made up of units that can aim and shoot at one another from a distance and can concentrate their fire. In this case, the strength differential is not proportional to sizes of the forces but to the *square* of their sizes. Imagine two forces, Red and Blue, both made up of identical units. Blue has three times as many units as Red has. It seems as if Blue is three times as strong as Red. But in fact, it's *nine* times as strong. Here's why: Three Blue units are concentrating their firepower on each Red unit. But Red's firepower is also *diluted* over a force three times as big. Each Red unit is firing at only one Blue unit, and two other Blue units aren't being fired upon at all! The combined effect is that Blue is nine times as strong.

What this means in practice is that masses of concentrated firepower are not only effective, they're very, very effective. For strategy games, this means that if you give one side twice as many units as the other, you're actually giving it *four* times the advantage. You're unlikely to do this intentionally, but it might happen by accident if you don't set the production rates of units carefully. If one side can produce units faster than the other, its advantage is not the difference between the numbers of units but the square of the difference—assuming that we're talking about units with ranged weapons. Hand-to-hand units still follow Lanchester's Linear Law.

This also means that you can't balance the effect of one side's having twice as many units by giving the other side a twofold advantage in one of its units' attributes. Even if you double the smaller side's shot power, those shots are still being diluted over a larger force. You have to give the smaller side a *fourfold* advantage in shot power to compensate for the larger side's squared numerical advantage.

Lanchester's laws describe battle in abstract terms. They don't take into account battlefield conditions, maneuvering, reinforcements, and so on. Nevertheless, they serve as a valuable warning to game designers trying to balance strategy games: Numbers and production rates make a huge difference. It's critically important to balance your production economy well, or whichever player can turn out units faster—even if those units are relatively weak—can overwhelm the other by sheer numbers.

For a somewhat more thorough discussion of Lanchester's laws, see the "Designer's Notebook" column, "Kicking Butt by the Numbers," on the *Gamasutra* webzine (Adams, 2004).

Health, Morale, and Fighting Efficiency

As with almost all other genres, units in war games fight at full efficiency until their health points are gone even though that's obviously unrealistic. Making wounded or damaged units fight at reduced efficiency introduces too powerful an effect of positive feedback in favor of the dominant side. Once a unit's efficiency begins to suffer, it's more likely to take further damage and so lose yet more efficiency, resulting in a quick demise. Reducing the fighting efficiency of damaged units also produces situations in which each side has harmed the other to the point that neither is able to fight effectively. The result is a long stalemate or a boring war of attrition, so in general, we recommend that you avoid this approach.

The same is true of most mechanisms that try to implement the effects of morale. In such systems, morale is represented by a number that either increases or decreases an army's fighting effectiveness. If the number is positive, morale is high and the effectiveness goes up, perhaps by improving the weapons accuracy of all the units in the army. If the number is negative, morale is low and effectiveness is harmed. Morale goes up when the army is

14

doing well (that is, losing fewer units relative to the enemy) and down if it is doing badly (losing a lot of units).

Again, this tight loop produces too much positive feedback. If one side starts to lose units, morale is lowered, fighting effectiveness goes down, and so that side keeps on losing. Furthermore, the enemy's morale has gone *up* at the same time, making the problem even worse. It's better to avoid morale altogether or to give it only a small role in determining fighting effectiveness. The leadership bonus, mentioned in the *Special Capabilities* section earlier, is a better way to handle this; the value of the bonus is not based on how well the army is doing but on whether the leader is present, so there is no feedback loop.

In conflicts among small numbers of compound units, such as main battle tanks or capital ships, you may want to allow individual weapons or other systems aboard the unit to go out of commission as the unit takes damage. In a game about nineteenth century naval warfare, for example, you can allow the guns aboard a 74-gun ship to be destroyed one by one, thus incrementally reducing the fighting capacity of the whole. The guns on a ship are analogous to the soldiers in an army, and like a soldier, each gun should fight at full strength until its hit points are gone.

Upgrades and Technology Trees

In a game with a limited number of types of units, the players can sometimes exhaust the interesting battle combinations too quickly. For example, the knights, archers, and barbarians of *The Ancient Art of War* aren't enough to hold players' attention over many campaigns. You can make a game more interesting by adding more unit types, but if all the unit types are available at the beginning of a game, the player will undoubtedly concentrate on the most powerful ones and ignore the weaker ones.

To resolve this problem, you should look for a way to introduce new units or to upgrade the existing ones as the game progresses. These upgrades can improve the values of units' attributes or give the units entirely new capabilities. An upgrade might occur as a reward for some achievement. In checkers, for example, moving a piece to the opposite side of the board turns that piece from an ordinary unit that can only move forward into a king that can move both forward and backward. Because it takes a while to reach the opposite side of the board, kings don't appear until well into the game.

Researching Upgrades   Checkers is an abstract game with an arbitrary rule for upgrading units. In more representational games, the unit upgrade process is often characterized as a form of research that the player must initiate; it takes a certain amount of time and perhaps the expenditure of some resources. If your game offers several different upgrades, you may wish to organize them into a sequence, such that some upgrades become available only after others have been achieved. You may also offer the player a choice of upgrades to research at any given time, which gives her an interesting decision to make: Which is the most advantageous upgrade to choose given the units she has available and her preferred style of play? (A player who prefers a defensive style, for example, may wish to choose upgrades that enhance the defensive rather than the offensive capabilities of her units.)

Single-Unit, Unit Type, and Global Upgrades You may create a number of different types of upgrades: those that apply to a single unit (such as the conversion of a piece to a king, as in checkers); those that modify the capabilities of all units of a given type (such as the siege tank upgrade in *StarCraft,* which gives all tanks the ability to operate in siege-tank mode once the upgrade has been researched); and those that modify the core mechanics globally (such as the Hoover Dam invention in *Civilization,* which improves its entire society's productivity and reduces pollution). In role-playing games, skill upgrades naturally apply only to the individual character that has learned the skill, but in strategy games it is more common to apply a unit type upgrade to all the player's units of that type simultaneously. That makes the process of retrofitting the existing units unnecessary, so the player doesn't have to think about it. If you're making a highly representational war game, however, you may want to require the existing units to come back to headquarters to fit them with their new gun, engine, radio, or whatever other feature it is that the player has researched.

Permanent and Temporary Upgrades In turn-based games with long, complex campaigns (such as *Civilization* or *X-COM*), designers often spread the upgrades out over time, spanning several levels. Each time an upgrade is achieved, it lasts for the rest of the game. These ***permanent upgrades*** strongly support the player's sense of progression through an extended game. They typically occur only infrequently and represent a major achievement when accomplished. Permanent upgrades are ideal for game-time periods that span months or years.

In RTS games, however, you may want to have the research and upgrade process work fast enough to produce big changes in the gameplay within a single level but not fast enough to carry over to the next level. These are called ***temporary upgrades.*** This puts more pressure on the player, who has to decide quickly whether to expend resources on research or on building new units to help fight a battle taking place in real time. *Dungeon Keeper* was a good example of this kind of game: In each level, the player's creatures had to research a set of magic spells while still defending their dungeon against invaders. With temporary upgrades, the player loses the benefit of her research when she goes on to the next level; she has to research the technology over again. This seems a bit peculiar, but it works well if you don't think of the levels as part of a continuing story. It's more credible if you present each level as an independent scenario, unrelated to the others—as *Dungeon Keeper* in fact did.

14

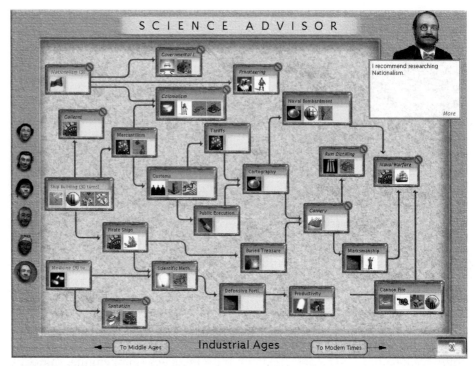

FIGURE 14.3 Part of the tech tree from *Civilization III*. Prerequisites are at the left; upgrades progress to the right.

Technology Trees   If your game has a large number of upgrades, you should organize them into a branching tree structure, in which achieving one upgrade makes available a choice of several others that are logically related to the preceding one. See Figure 14.3 for an example. Achieving the steam engine, for instance, could give the player the opportunity to research the railroad, steamships, or powered factories. Strategy games usually characterize these advancements as technological research, so such a structure is called a ***tech tree*** even though some of the upgrades may not actually be technological. In role-playing games, a similar mechanism applies to upgrading a character's individual skills; in that context it is called a *skill tree,* but the function is the same: It is a diagram of the available upgrade paths for a unit.

Once the player chooses to research an upgrade on a particular branch, you can force her to complete all the upgrades that are part of that branch before moving to another branch or even prevent her from *ever* researching upgrades on another branch. So, for example, choosing to research agriculture might force the player to stick with agricultural advancements, and others such as fishing or animal husbandry would be closed to her—either until the agricultural branch has been completed or perhaps even forever. This restriction encourages asymmetric play; if one player chooses agriculture and another chooses fishing, each will be committed to the approach he has chosen. However, it will make your game tricky to balance and will discourage some players. Many players, particularly women, dislike being forced to make irrevocable decisions whose consequences they do not know.

To design a tech tree, first think of all the upgrades that you would like to introduce in the course of the game. For each upgrade, note whether it applies to a particular unit, all units of a particular type, all units in the player's forces, or to the core mechanics generally. Also note what event will trigger the upgrade—the passage of a certain amount of time, the expenditure of resources, or some other achievement such as defeating a particular enemy unit or arriving at a certain place on the map. Once you have an idea of what upgrades you want to include, you can organize them into a logical sequence or tree; a simple diagram will show which upgrades lead to which others.

As a general rule, upgrades should strengthen the player's side and give the player new choices to make. Researching horse breeding, for example, might make cavalry units available for the first time and thus require the player to start thinking about how to use them. Don't worry too much about correctly setting the exact cost and length of time required by each upgrade. Pick some numbers that feel right; you will undoubtedly modify them during testing.

IN THE TRENCHES: Don't Disallow Upgrades Arbitrarily

In order to increase the difficulty of a particular level, some RTS games won't allow the player to research certain upgrades or use certain units in that level even though the player knows that those upgrades or units are available in other levels. Players find this frustrating because it feels arbitrary. We suggest some alternative methods.

Instead of disallowing upgrades that were accessible in previous levels, we recommend that you change the costs of the units you want to restrict on a level-by-level basis. That is, if the advanced cybermarine requires a large quantity of a certain resource, then make that resource extremely scarce on a level in which you really don't want the player using cybermarines. Or require that those resources be used in some other way to achieve victory on that level. Be clear about this—state it in the mission objectives. Then, if the player wastes all his resources on building cybermarines instead of achieving the mission, he will have only himself to blame. Another possibility is to make the restricted units costly by making sure the enemy is extremely proficient in destroying that kind of unit. If, say, you want to disallow flying units, arm the computer opponent with extremely effective antiaircraft weaponry.

▶▶ CONTINUED ON NEXT PAGE

14

▶▶ CONTINUED

Ensuring that the player knows it is not wise to deploy a certain kind of unit under certain circumstances makes for better gameplay than does simply preventing the player from deploying those units. The player then appreciates and accepts the restriction as a part of the game rather than resenting what seems to be an arbitrary decision by the game designer.

Logistics

Strategy decides where to act; logistics brings the troops to this point.

—General Antoine Henri Jomini

Logistics is the management of supply: the production, distribution, maintenance, and replacement of personnel and materials. In real life, it's an immensely complicated business. War games, on the other hand, tend to have simplified logistics. This is because real armies have huge general staffs to look after such things; in a war game, the player has to handle it all himself. Because the player is also busy with strategy and tactics, you should simplify the logistics. In the next few sections, we'll discuss different aspects of logistics and how to handle them.

Supplies and Consumable Items For the most part, computer war games ignore the soldiers' human needs. Soldiers don't eat and don't sleep, so the game doesn't track supplies such as food or sleeping bags. Similarly, vehicles don't require fuel or spare parts. Keeping track of these supplies is simply too much of a nuisance. The one major exception to this rule is ammunition; some games track it and some don't. In general, if ammunition is cheap, doesn't do much damage, and is quickly expended (such as arrows or bullets), you should give units an unlimited supply because it's not worth the player's time to look after it. If ammunition is particularly destructive, such as nuclear weapons, then you should make it rare and expensive and keep track of how much is around. To summarize it simply, "Don't sweat the small stuff."

Supply Lines A supply line is the route over which fresh troops and war materiel must be transported from their source to where they are needed, usually the battlefield. Cutting the enemy's supply line is a classic stratagem of war; it leaves the enemy troops without support and they often have to surrender when they run out of the things they need. Seizing bridges is a high priority in land warfare because a bridge is often a choke point through which troops and supplies must pass. Most computer war games model supply lines correctly for the troops themselves; fighting units *do* have to get from wherever they are produced (usually near their headquarters) to where the action is. Few games implement supply lines for items such as food and ammunition, however, for two reasons. First, supplying materiel is an additional task that players may not have the time (or inclination) to manage. Second, implementing supply lines realistically means creating transport units and modeling the supplies as individual objects. All this makes for a more complicated game engine and requires additional CPU time to execute.

Abstracting the Distribution Process   To reduce these problems—yet still require the players to create the resources that units need—you can make the production process concrete, but abstract the distribution process. For example, the troops in *Warcraft* eat food. The food is produced on farms (which may be destroyed by the enemy, thereby reducing production), but once the food is produced, it is magically available to all the player's troops everywhere. The existence of the troops causes the food to disappear from storage, but the food doesn't actually have to be transported to where the troops can eat it.

This decentralization of resources can permit unrealistic strategies if not carefully handled. In *Age of Empires,* for instance, a player can send a lone peasant into a remote area to build a barracks, which has the function of creating troops. Assuming that it is not spotted by the enemy, the barracks immediately starts producing troops right on the enemy doorstep with no regard for supply lines or resource distribution. Although this is an imaginative way of exploiting the decentralized-resources mechanic, it harms the players' suspension of disbelief because it's so unrealistic.

In his regular design column for U.K.-based *Develop* magazine, Dave Morris suggested another alternative that rewards a player for maintaining supply lines without actually requiring her to manage the transportation of materiel. His idea is slightly counterintuitive, but would meet those design objectives. Morris proposed that the software should compute whether there is an unobstructed route between a unit and its hypothetical source of supplies and, if so, allow that unit to heal or repair itself in the field. Units with no route back to a source of supplies don't have this ability. This rewards the player for keeping supply lines open but does not actually punish her for failing to do so. If you implement such a system, however, you will have to give the player some means of detecting when supply lines are obstructed so he knows *why* his troops can't repair themselves. He also will have to have some way of reestablishing the supply line and a way of knowing when it has been reestablished.

Road-Building   Another way to abstract the distribution of supplies while still requiring the player to pay some attention to them is to let the player build roads. Consider the territory map shown in Figure 14.4.

Town B has access to a forest—it has a road (supply line) leading directly to the forest, providing a ready source of lumber. This allows Town B to build wood-based units, such as catapults. Town A is linked to Town B via a road.

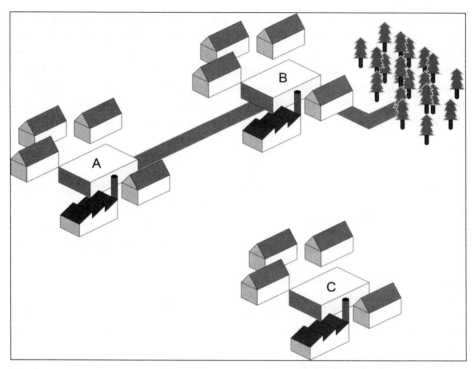

FIGURE 14.4 Resource distribution via a road network.

This road provides a readily available supply route between Town A and Town B. Hence, Town A has exactly the same production capabilities as Town B. Anything that is available to Town A is also available to Town B, and vice versa. Town C is a newly built town. No roads have been built to Town C, so it will not have access to the resources of Towns A and B until a linking road is built.

This is the approach taken by *Civilization III*. Of course, it's still not an entirely accurate solution—materials are assumed to travel instantaneously along the roads. (It's interesting to note, though, that previous iterations of the *Civilization* series *did* implement trade caravans, but *Civilization III* removed that feature to improve gameplay.)

Influence Maps   Another option is to assume that any unit within a certain distance from a supply depot can receive supplies from that depot even if no unobstructed route actually exists. This is a variation of the decentralized distribution of *Age of Empires*. Every supply depot magically transmits supplies to units within its circle of influence, but units that move beyond the range of any depot don't get them. Designers often call this influence of objects on the terrain around them an ***influence map*** because it is usually done by having the software track regions of influence on a map that it maintains internally. Most games that use influence maps include some means of displaying the areas of influence, either continuously or at the player's option.

Two out of the three races in *StarCraft* use an influence map to indicate where their influence has spread (although these maps are used only for determining where structures may be constructed and not for providing supplies to mobile units). For example, the Protoss power beacons, which provide power to the Protoss factories, have a limited radius of power distribution. When the player wants to construct a new factory, the game displays the influence map by color-shading the landscape, showing the areas where the factory may be built.

The Game World

The choice of setting for your strategy game is a vital consideration because different players prefer different fantasies. Dress up the underlying gameplay in a different setting and it can feel like a totally different game. You can transplant the core mechanics of a strategy game into many different settings; it's practically a universal game construction kit. Will your game be set in history? The contemporary world? The future (as you anticipate it)? Or a fantasy world of your imagination?

In spite of the ease with which strategy game mechanics can be reused in a new setting, you will need to keep some important distinctions in mind.

Historical Settings

Military strategy games, perennial favorites, tend to be set in the past—either an accurately portrayed past or one in the realms of mythology. People who play games about historical events tend to know a lot about the pertinent history, and the more representational your game claims to be, the more closely they will scrutinize it to see if it rings true. You can get away with a certain amount of simplification (as *Age of Empires* did) provided that you are honest about it.

The danger here is dipping too often from the same well. So many games have been set during World War II that the market has become oversaturated. Customers don't want to buy the same game again and again. However, there will always be room for original approaches so long as you can make them compelling. You should at least think about moving into less common territory; consider the Korean War, the wars of Shaka Zulu, the Warring States era in Chinese history, and so on. Humanity's long and bloody history offers plenty to borrow from.

Modern Settings

Choosing a present-day military conflict risks generating controversy and negative public opinion. Although this could gain your game some degree of notoriety, unless the game itself is a superlative addition to the gaming world

14

(like the *Grand Theft Auto* series, for example), the disadvantages of such exposure will greatly outweigh any advantages—especially when it comes to trying to get funding for your *next* game. If you want to make a game about a current conflict, you must be rigorously accurate and politically neutral.

With a modern setting, you will have to address the problem of battlefield scale. It takes foot infantry days to walk across a region that a jet fighter can fly over in a few seconds. You will therefore have to choose which scale your game is really designed for and perhaps exclude units that don't work well on that scale.

Future (Science Fiction) Settings

Science fiction settings remain popular and allow a lot of scope for invention, but unless you have a compelling world to present, you run the risk that your fantasy will not catch the public's imagination. It's easier to base them on a successful license (*Star Wars, Star Trek, Alien,* and so on) than to carve out a new universe for yourself. *StarCraft* managed it, but not everybody is so fortunate.

From a design standpoint, the danger with science fiction games is that it is easy to add fantastic components that magically solve problems—a consistent weakness of the *Star Trek* stories, in which the chief engineer is always reversing the phase inducers or inducing the phase reversers to get our heroes out of a jam. If you really want to make a self-consistent SF universe, you'll have to think hard about its technology. Alternatively, you can go for humor and make a game like *Strange Adventures in Infinite Space,* a combination strategy/spaceship simulator full of goofy weapons and odd features that aren't meant to be taken seriously.

Terminology also presents a problem in science fiction settings. Because the weapons and units don't really exist, the player doesn't have any idea what they can do. No one can tell from the names alone whether a *plasma rifle* is more or less powerful than a *photon blaster.* This was one of the very few weaknesses in *Sid Meier's Alpha Centauri*: The player either spent a lot of time looking things up in reference books or learned by trial-and-error. When players encounter an unfamiliar weapon for the first time, it's a good idea to indicate its power or value by some visual sign. In fact, this advice applies to just about any game world that you can't be sure the player knows much about.

Future settings have the same scale problems as modern battlefields. *StarCraft* handled this by simply stating that flying vehicles are only about five times as fast as foot infantry; if the foot soldiers walk at three miles an hour, the jet fighters fly at 15! It was grossly unrealistic, but it worked. The aircraft were still the fastest vehicles in the game, so their role as hit-and-run units remained consistent even though they were slower than they realistically should have been.

Fantasy Settings

The major distinction between science fiction worlds and fantasy worlds is that the former characterize their imaginary weapons as technological while the latter characterize them as magical. Fantasy worlds, often set in a quasi-medieval environment, also tend to place more emphasis on close-range and hand-to-hand combat (swords and arrows, not cruise missiles) and to eschew vehicles such as airplanes and tanks. Fantasy combat should not resemble modern combat too closely; that's not what the players want. The *Warcraft* series is by far the most successful group of strategy games set in a fantasy world, and we encourage you to study it. But we'd like to see a lot more games set in worlds *other* than northern European mythology. Skip the elves and trolls and look to the folk tales of India, Africa, the Americas, and Australasia for inspiration.

The Presentation Layer

Strategy games often have extremely complicated core mechanics. Consequently, the design of the presentation layer is critical, even more so if the game is in real time and the player is under time pressure. The interface must present complicated information in clear, well-organized ways so that the player can grasp it easily. If presentation is not handled well, the large amount of information available can make the game overwhelming, especially to inexperienced players.

Interaction Model

For strategy games, the interaction model tends to be on a large scale. Rarely will you find a strategy game with a single avatar, although the PC version of *Battlezone* (not to be confused with the original coin-op) is a notable exception. Generally, the player indirectly controls the units under his command while enjoying a godlike view of the game world. The true interaction model, in this instance, is related to the scale of the world. How many units does the player control? Is it a small squad, or is it a large army?

The feel of a small squad is much more personal and intimate than a large army. The personalities of the units can be explored more and the player tends to care more about the individual fates of his units. Also, with smaller groups, individual characters may improve their skills and abilities as the game goes along. The *X-COM* series of games was particularly strong in this area—the player controlled several small squads of about twenty soldiers each, small enough for the player to be able to keep a handle on each individual member. Incidentally, in these games, the player could also build up a team of noncombat units by recruiting one at a time the scientists that research the alien technology.

For larger-scale games, it would be too hard for the player to keep track of every single unit in the army, although some games do attempt this. *Civilization III*, for example, allows units to upgrade from Recruit to Veteran to Elite status, a simple progression that players can easily understand. Others, such as *Warcraft III*,

14

designate a small number of units as Heroes. A Hero has special abilities and requires personal attention from the player. The player can easily focus his attention on the small number of Heroes while treating the fighters in the other squads in the army as undifferentiated groups.

Perspective

For many years, computer strategy games displayed their game worlds in two dimensions as seen from above, effectively treating the video screen like a map or a tabletop game board. Later games adopted an isometric perspective in which buildings and units appeared to stand up above the surface of the landscape, although the underlying model of the world was still 2D. With the arrival of 3D display engines, strategy games began to include fully three-dimensional worlds with 3D modeled hills, valleys, and other landscape features, as well as 3D modeled units.

Regardless of the display technology, players of strategy games need to see the big picture, the overall view of the game world. The player cannot plan an effective strategy if forced to view only one avatar's perspective. Unless you're trying to model what warfare was like for a general of ancient times—back when generals fought alongside their troops—you should choose some form of aerial perspective. The player will also find it valuable if you allow her some control over the camera, so that she can zoom out to see the whole battlefield or zoom in on a particular fight, and move the camera around to different points of view. See *Rome: Total War* for a good example.

User Interface

The particular problem in designing the user interface of a strategy game is the requirement that the player control action at different scales; from that of the whole army to the individual fighter. Presenting such different kinds of information seamlessly without breaking the flow of the game can prove difficult.

Most strategy games present different kinds of data in separate windows in much the same manner as a windowed operating system. Most games do not offer all the window-management features of an operating system, however, nor do they use the operating system's visual style. No designer wants her game to look like just another business or productivity application. Assuming that you take a windowed approach, try to ensure that, within reason, the windows behave as the player would expect. Make buttons clear, concise, and recognizable. If a button is not appropriate for a given unit—a movement command for a building, for instance—leave it visible but dim it or apply a gray to indicate that it can't be used, or if possible remove the button from the window for units that can't use it.

Remember to cater to both experienced and inexperienced players. Inexperienced players need clear and easy ways to find commands, whereas more advanced players need quick access. You may also consider providing separate levels of command—a beginner mode and an advanced mode—so that the player can issue more complex commands as she becomes more experienced. For the advanced players, provide keyboard shortcuts for *every* command in the game.

Ensure that your game presents the user with sets of commands grouped by function. *SimCity 4,* though not a strategy game, provides an excellent example of a well-planned user interface in this regard. A nested sequence of menus ensures that related commands are displayed together. At the top level, the player can choose between *mayor mode* and *god mode.* Mayor mode provides standard commands for building the city grouped by functions such as those pertaining to roads, to water, or to civic buildings. God mode provides an unrelated set of commands that allow the player to unleash all sorts of fantastical and supernatural events upon her unsuspecting sims.

Artificial Opponents

Single-player strategy games often present the fiction that the player is opposed by another player like himself, making moves just the way the player does. In war games, it's fun to think of pitting one's wits against an enemy general. The old EA war game *Patton vs. Rommel* explicitly encouraged this fantasy; the player took the role of one general and the computer took the other. However, it *is* only a fantasy, of course; the opponent it provides is artificial, implemented by AI techniques. Here we include a brief introduction to some of the AI used to create artificial opponents in strategy games. As the designer, you won't have to write the software, but we want you to be aware of the strengths and weaknesses of several approaches.

Game Tree Search

In turn-based games such as checkers, chess, or Go, each player has a number of choices—possible moves that he can make—at each turn. You choose your move, then your opponent makes his move from the choices available to him, and then it's back to you with a new set of possible moves, and so on. If you draw a graph of this, showing how the options branch out at every turn, it looks like a tree, so the set of all possible future moves is called the ***game tree.***

With simple games, artificial opponents search through the game tree, looking for the moves that will produce the most advantageous result. The fewer choices there are, the easier this is. With tic-tac-toe, the problem is trivial; with checkers, it is comparatively easy; with chess, it is quite difficult; and with Go, it has proven nearly impossible to build a computer game that can play as well as a master human player. In Go, the board is large and the player can play nearly anywhere, so the number of possible future moves is simply astronomical.

14

As a designer, do not expect to use game-tree search in any but the simplest of games. The length of time it will take for the computer to compute a good move increases exponentially with the number of possible moves available.

Neural Nets

A neural net is a program that simulates, in a simplified form, the behavior of brain cells, or neurons. The details are too complex to discuss here, but put simply, a neural net mimics the brain's ability to recognize and correctly identify patterns of data. This is how we learn to tell an apple from an orange, for example: Our brains learn the visual patterns that apples and oranges fall into. Like the brain, a neural network has to be taught to recognize the pattern; after that, and with repeated exposure, the brain or the neural network identifies the pattern correctly.

Some efforts have been made to teach neural nets to learn to play strategy games by recognizing patterns of play that lead to success. While this technique is worthy of further research, you shouldn't count on it. Neural nets take a long time to learn, and the process doesn't work well for complex patterns of information, such as the dozens of possible choices available to a player in a modern war game. Furthermore, because of the way neural networks store data, there is no way to tell what the data actually mean. You can't teach the network a new pattern simply by tweaking the numbers stored inside it; you have to start over again from the beginning.

Hierarchical Finite State Machines

In the absence of orders, go find something and kill it.

—Erwin Rommel

Hierarchical finite state machines have proven to be the most successful mechanism for creating artificially intelligent opponents in war games because they can handle large numbers of units and produce seemingly intelligent, coordinated behavior.

What Is a Finite State Machine?   A finite state machine (FSM) is a conceptual machine rather than a real piece of mechanical engineering. Its rules establish a simple behavioral system for an individual automated character, such as a unit in a war game. The unit can inhabit a limited number of states (such as scouting, guarding, pursuing, and retreating), and it's only ever in one state at a time. As long as the unit is in a given state, it performs a particular activity. Certain events will cause it to make a *transition* to a new state, after which it starts performing a new activity. Here's an example from real life.

In 1960, researchers at Johns Hopkins University built a little robot called the Hopkins Beast. The only thing the robot did was wander around the computing laboratory. When its batteries got low, it would start to search for an electrical outlet with its photocell eye. (Electrical outlets were the only object that it could recognize.) If it found an outlet, it would plug itself in until its batteries recharged. Then it would set off wandering again. So the Hopkins Beast possessed only three possible states: wandering, searching, and recharging. Its initial state was always wandering. The only thing that would cause a transition to searching was a low battery. When it detected that its battery was low, it would transition to the searching state, the Beast would turn on its eye, and it would continue to move through the halls. Once it detected an outlet, it would transition to the recharging state and plug itself in. Once it detected that it was charged up, the Beast would transition back to the wandering state. It would unplug itself and start wandering again.

The Hopkins Beast was extremely simple, but you get the idea. You can use finite state machines to define the behavior of units. One state should be a default for that unit type—normally, holding its current position or patrolling (General Rommel's advice notwithstanding). For each state that you define, you must indicate how the unit behaves in that state and list all the things that will cause it to transition to a new state. FSMs have a weakness in that they can't walk and chew gum at the same time—that is, they can only be in one state at a time, so a single individual can't work on two things at once. However, the units in war games seldom need to do this anyway.

Hierarchical Finite State Machines in Games   A *hierarchical* finite state machine (hFSM) actually consists of several different FSMs, and the ones higher up in the hierarchy give orders to the ones lower down—that is, the controlling hierarchical FSMs send signals to those lower down in the hierarchy, ordering them to change states. An artificially intelligent opponent in such a system chooses a top-level goal, such as "take and hold this hill," and delegates the tasks required to achieve the overall goal to subordinate FSMs that further delegate down to the individual unit level.

This is the way commands move down through a real army. The captain decides that he needs to take a hill and so delegates different activities to different platoons under him: providing covering fire, creating a diversion, and so on. If done properly, the platoons will each have a different goal and won't get in each others' way. The sergeant in each platoon then commands his individual men what to do to achieve the platoon's goal in the same way that the captain commanded the sergeants. Each of the men then tries to achieve his own goal by executing the command he has been given. In a video game, each man has his own FSM that determines his behavior. The FSM reacts to changing conditions on the battlefield (for example, "The unit I was told to attack is dead, so I will look for another one to attack") and also to orders received from the superior FSM, that is, the sergeant's FSM that governs the platoon as a whole (for example, "Your mission is accomplished, so cease fire and guard your position").

14

The nice thing about hFSMs is that they produce emergent behavior—that is, they may cause units to behave in ways that are not explicitly programmed into the rules. hFSMs also allow you to design the AI from the top down, creating large-scale strategies that are made up of individual smaller-scale strategies. Hierarchical FSMs are not restricted to combat, either: You can also use them to try to achieve economic goals, directing worker units to produce different resources as needed and telling them to stop when they've stockpiled enough.

COMMANDMENT: Don't Ask AI to Micromanage Troops

You may be tempted to try to create large-scale AI systems that coordinate the movements of individual units right from the top—a sort of micromanagement. Don't do this; the result will be as unwieldy in your game as it would be in real life if a general tried to tell each individual soldier what to do. Create intelligent behaviors for each level of the hierarchy, and intelligent results will emerge.

A Final Note on Artificial Opponents

Don't expect to be able to create an artificial opponent that can routinely beat a human fair and square unless your game is a simple one—so simple that it can use game-tree search. hFSMs are very useful, but they're seldom good enough to beat a skilled player in an equal contest. Most strategy games make use of two additional features to provide a challenge to their players: hidden information that the player must find by exploring and unfair advantages for the computer's side, such as stronger units or more efficient production. But don't concentrate too hard on making an unbeatable AI anyway. You do want the player to eventually win the game. The function of game AI is to put up a good fight but lose in the end.

Summary

Covering all aspects of the whole genre of strategy games in a single chapter is an impossible task. Here we have focused on the key challenges of most modern war games: conflict, exploration, and economic management. We have showed you how to design units, choosing attributes and capabilities that will give them the qualities that you want. You should also be able to create an upgrade path or technology tree that allows for a sense of advancement, introducing new units and decisions in the game.

We also addressed the importance of establishing a balanced economic model for unit production so that all sides in a game have an equal chance of building up their forces. We looked at several ways of handling the question of supply lines, from literal transportation of supplies to abstract distribution systems.

You should be aware of some of the considerations for designing games set in different worlds, and you should now know the best ways of presenting those worlds to the player: with an aerial perspective and a multipresent interaction model. Finally, we gave you a look at a few different ways of designing artificial opponents.

If you plan to design a strategy game, a good way to start is to examine the mechanics of a good board game such as *The Settlers of Catan*. Board games are simple enough for a single person to grasp the entire rule-set and, consequently, lend themselves well to analysis.

Test Your Skills

MULTIPLE CHOICE QUESTIONS

1. Which of the following cannot properly be classed as a *unit* in a strategy game?

    A. An unarmed repair droid that can fix stranded robo-camels to get the supply caravan moving again.

    B. A genetically engineered hyperhero carrying a different type of weapon in each of its five hands.

    C. A monastery in which the unison chanting of the religious brotherhood mystically produces mana when enough members gather.

    D. All of the above are units.

2. Unexplored territory may be displayed to the user as dimmer than explored areas, or the landscape may be displayed although enemy units in unexplored areas will not be shown. This is called

    A. the black out.

    B. the fog of war.

    C. no man's land.

    D. ground zero.

3. If the player commands a unit to move to a specific position and doesn't specify any waypoints to determine the route, the game program's AI will choose the route using a process called

    A. pathfinding.

    B. GPS.

    C. mapmaking.

    D. scouting.

14

4. Which one of these common strategy game commands is wrongly defined?

    A. Retreat—reverse movement that is fast but leaves the unit more vulnerable.

    B. Hold—attack an enemy that comes into range but do not pursue if it retreats.

    C. Attack—advance to the enemy, open fire, pursue if the enemy retreats.

    D. Dash—similar to retreat, but with covering fire.

5. HP per shot is a way of calculating

    A. the number of health points a unit starts with.

    B. the shot power of a weapon.

    C. the minimum range of a projectile weapon.

    D. the blast radius of an explosive.

6. A weapon with an accuracy of zero is

    A. a weapon that can never hit its target.

    B. a weapon for which you need to go back and calculate a practical accuracy.

    C. never going to occur because zero is only a theoretical accuracy.

    D. a projectile rather than an explosive weapon because it has no blast radius.

7. The military effectiveness of an attack unit can be calculated as a function of several attributes, including

    A. how many units there are on each side.

    B. the unit's own rate of fire.

    C. the unit's size relative to enemy units.

    D. the area that the unit can defend.

8. Why does the calculation of the value of a defensive unit involve the square of the range?

    A. Ranged weapons are more effective than hand-to-hand combat weapons.

    B. An explosive weapon affects an area defined by the blast radius.

    C. Because most of the enemy will be in front of a defensive unit.

    D. Longer range means it not only shoots farther but also covers a two-dimensional area of terrain.

9. According to Lanchester's law, if you give one group of artillery twice as many units as another made up of identical units, you increase the first side's relative power by a factor of

A. 2.   B. 3.   C. 4.   D. 10.

10. The effect of positive feedback on unbalancing the game is a good reason not to

A. reduce the fighting efficiency of units that are partially damaged.

B. give stealth capability to both sides.

C. use the rock-paper-scissors method of balancing simple games.

D. compare the fighting efficiency of attack units and defense units using the equations provided.

11. Kings don't appear until well into a game of checkers. This is an example of

A. researching an upgrade.

B. giving upgrades as rewards for achievement.

C. a global upgrade.

D. upgrading using a tech tree.

12. Which is *not* a good way to limit use of a unit or upgrade in one particular level in order to balance that level?

A. Limit use of submarines in the level by giving the computer opponent accurate and deadly torpedoes.

B. Limit use of Ultra-megadeth rays in the level by making Ultra-megadeth ray guns run on Facetioum, an extremely rare element in the game world.

C. Limit use of flying dragons in the level by telling the player that the atmosphere has changed composition and won't support flight.

D. Limit use of a killer virus in the level by making the production of the virus use huge amounts of an expensive fungus, which is the only food in the game world that your crack clone squad can eat.

13. You will probably want to model supply lines

A. for ammunition realistically because it is cheap and small and so easily transported.

B. accurately so the player gets the full experience of the conflict, including making sure each soldier is supplied with appropriate shoes, clothing, and food.

C. correctly for getting the troops themselves from where they are produced to where they are needed.

D. perfectly to be sure that every soldier has first-aid supplies at all times.

14

14. An influence map is most likely to show the region in the game world where

    A. the terrain is inaccessible.

    B. the supplies from a factory can be assumed to be available to troops.

    C. the player's troops have already explored the game world.

    D. the effects of the units' weapons will be calculated using accurate mass and acceleration data.

15. A highly complex strategy game is most likely to have

    A. combat resolution based on a rock-paper-scissors model because it is inherently well balanced.

    B. a game world in a science fiction setting.

    C. a computer-generated opponent based on AI that searches a game tree because only that method allows weighing of all possibilities to determine the best next move.

    D. a newbie-friendly user interface with shortcut keys so that experienced players aren't held up by the user interface.

▶▶ Case Study

Choose a strategy game that you believe, from your own experience of playing it, is an excellent example of the genre (or use one your instructor has assigned). Write a report documenting the features that place it in this genre as opposed to another one and explaining why you believe it is superior to others of its kind. Be sure to cover at least the following areas:

- Describe unit types and their attributes, including any special abilities. If you feel that the different forces in the game are well balanced or unbalanced, explain this with reference to the units and their attributes.

- If you feel the game implements or allows for any classic military stratagems, document them. Consider flanking maneuvers, diversionary tactics, infiltration and sneak attacks, cutting enemy supply lines, the use of reserve troops, and any other stratagem that you

▶▶ CONTINUED ON NEXT PAGE

▶▶ CONTINUED

feel the game does well. Show how the way the units are designed enables these features. (For example, a stealth capability makes sneak attacks possible.)

- Discuss the role of logistics in the game, if any. What resources do the troops and factories consume? Explain how supply lines and/or influence are implemented.

- Explore the user interface in the primary gameplay mode. Briefly document the mechanism for giving orders to units. Note important indicators that appear on the screen and discuss how they improve the playing experience.

- Detail the core mechanics. Indicate resources, sources, conversions, and drains. Be sure in particular to describe the behavior of factories: how long it takes them to produce a unit and how many resources they consume to do so. If differential production rates influence the balance of the game, document this.

The design questions in the next section may help you to think about these issues. In your report, use screen shots to illustrate your points. End the case study with suggestions for improvement or, if you feel the game cannot be improved, suggestions for additional features that might be fun to have in the game.

Alternatively, choose a game that you believe is particularly *bad*. Do the same case study, explaining what is wrong and how it could be improved.

A case study is neither a review nor a design document; it is an analysis. You are not attempting to reverse-engineer the entire game but simply to explain how it works in a general way. Your instructor will tell you the desired scope of the assignment; we recommend from five to twenty pages.

DESIGN QUESTIONS

When beginning the design of a strategy game, consider the following questions:

1. Is the game turn-based or real-time? The answer to this question will have tremendous consequences for the nature and feel of the gameplay.

2. Is the game world 2D (as in checkers), 2.5D (as in *StarCraft*), or fully 3D (as in *Populous: The Beginning*)? Will the game offer a perspective other than the usual aerial one?

14

3. Will the game include challenges other than conflict, such as exploration or economic management? How will they work with the conflict challenges?

4. Some games, such as Go, are about control of territory rather than destruction of units per se. If this is true of your game, how is territory seized and how is it retained (or retaken)? What methods are used to indicate to the player who owns a particular region?

5. If the game involves units in combat, what are the units and what are their key characteristics (health, speed, range, rate of fire, etc.) and limitations?

6. Is the player given a fixed number of units at the beginning, as with most strategy board games such as chess, or is there a production mechanism? If there is a production mechanism, what are the production times and costs of each unit, and what (if anything) is consumed by production? If something is consumed by production, where does it come from in the first place?

7. Real-time strategy games are prone to certain dominant strategies such as the race for resources hidden in the landscape. These blunt approaches tend to overwhelm more subtle strategic details. Can you devise means of predicting and avoiding them?

8. Does the game include upgrades or a technology tree? If so, what are the upgrades and how are they obtained? What does it add to the player's experience of the game?

9. Does the game include logistics (maintenance of supply lines)? What supplies must be provided, and what happens if supply lines are broken? Does the supply mechanism include any abstractions to simplify it?

10. What is the game's setting, if any? If the units are unfamiliar to the player, what visual cues or other cues will you use to indicate the difference between, for example, a dragoon, a cuirassier, and a grenadier?

11. Is the game a large-scale one with hundreds or thousands of units or a small-scale one with tens of units? How will this affect the player's perception of them? What user interface features will be needed to manage them?

12. How much can the player see? Does the terrain have to be explored? Will the game include the fog of war?

13. If you can get hold of a copy, take a look at the level editor supplied with *Warcraft III*. Which of the level-building features (triggers, timed events, and so on) would you like to include in your game?

14. Strategy games require particularly powerful AI, especially if the game is supposed to play in general circumstances and not just prebuilt and prebalanced levels. Given the rules of the game, what goals should the AI work toward, and how should they choose the actions to achieve those goals?

Chapter **15**

Role-Playing Games

Chapter Objectives

After reading this chapter and completing the exercises, you will be able to do the following:

- Know the definition of role-playing games and the game mechanics common to them.
- Understand the history and evolution of role-playing games from tabletop to computer.
- Design character attributes for a role-playing game.
- Define a world and setting suitable for a role-playing game.
- Understand the use of experience points and character level for this genre.
- Know the different gameplay modes within this genre.

Introduction

R ole-playing games allow players to experience something impossible in the real world: a sense of growing from an ordinary person into a superhero with amazing powers. Many games offer players such powers immediately, but in a role-playing game, the player earns them through experience and gets to choose which particular abilities he wants to cultivate. This chapter will first define the role-playing genre and then describe the unique gameplay features, modes, and mechanics of this type of game. The chapter will focus on single-player role-playing games that use both avatar-based and party-based interaction models. (Online multiplayer games, including role-playing ones, are discussed in Chapter 21, "Online Games," located on the Companion Website.)

Companion Website

   In addition, we will discuss the world, story, and settings common to role-playing games and delve into the attributes of the avatars and other characters involved in the game. The various game modes will also be discussed, and the chapter ends with a discussion of some special issues for designing the user interface of a role-playing game.

Unfortunately, we don't have room for more than a general overview of role-playing games. They include more different types of gameplay than most other genres and have the second most complicated user interfaces. (Construction and management simulations have the dubious honor of the most complicated user interfaces of all.) For a more detailed discussion of the subject, we encourage you to read Neal and Jana Hallford's *Swords and Circuitry* (Hallford and Hallford, 2001).

What Are Role-Playing Games?

Computerized role-playing games are an outgrowth of the original noncomputerized, pencil-and-paper role-playing games, of which *Dungeons & Dragons* is by far the most famous example. (For simplicity's sake, we will call computerized role-playing games **CRPGs** and the noncomputerized kind *tabletop RPGs* to distinguish them from each other.) The object of both kinds of games, computerized and otherwise, is to experience a series of adventures in an imaginary world, through an avatar character or a small group of characters whose skills and powers grow as time goes on. A group of characters who go on these adventures together in an RPG is universally called a *party.*

In the tabletop games, the adventures, usually characterized as quests to achieve some goal, are devised and staged by one player acting in a special role as the *game master* or *dungeon master* (we will use the term *game master* or *GM*). The tabletop games' rules are complex by comparison to other noncomputerized games. Almost all the game activity takes place in the players' imaginations; only a few props or visual materials are used to depict the game world. Consequently, the players may propose to take almost any action that they can think of, and the GM must decide whether the action is permitted within the rules and determine its consequences. In general, tabletop RPGs are permissive rather than restrictive, and any reasonable action is allowed—with the definition of *reasonable* being the privilege of the GM. The process involves a certain amount of ad-hoc rule-making.

In CRPGs, the computer implements the rules, performs the activities of the game master, and presents the game world on the screen. Because the computer can offer the players only a fixed set of actions to take and can't invent new rules on the fly, CRPGs aren't as flexible as the tabletop games. However, because the players do not have to implement the rules and the graphics are often stunningly beautiful, CRPGs are somewhat more accessible and attractive to the novice player than tabletop RPGs.

Multiplayer online RPGs also include human game masters (GMs) who work within the confines of the computer-controlled rules. The GM acts similarly to a GM for a board game, modifying situations and keeping the game fresh.

Multiplayer online RPGs are covered in Chapter 21, "Online Games," available on the Companion Website.

A key aspect of tabletop RPGs is, as the name suggests, role-playing—that is, improvisational drama in which each player plays the role of his avatar character and the GM plays the roles of any nonplayer characters (NPCs). Emotional relationships can arise and change among the characters as the players play their respective roles. A good role-playing experience depends on the imaginations and acting skills of the players. For the most part, however, CRPGs have only borrowed the general themes and core mechanics from the tabletop games and not the role-playing activity itself. Single-player CRPGs don't yet have the power to simulate nonplayer characters with the acting skill of a human GM. Role-playing in single-player RPGs is therefore limited to holding conversations with NPCs by means of a *dialog tree,* a technique that we discuss in Chapter 7, "Storytelling and Narrative."

In contrast, multiplayer online RPGs do allow real role-playing between characters because the players can type messages to each other on the computer's keyboard and sometimes even talk to each other via a microphone and speakers.

The essential parts of a computer role-playing game, then, are the quest or story of the game and character growth. The quests usually require combat, and the rules of the game are designed to support it. The rules also define how character growth occurs. Creating a successful CRPG depends on providing a captivating story and a rewarding character growth path.

> A **role-playing game** is one in which the player controls one or more characters, typically designed by the player, and guides them through a series of quests managed by the computer. Victory consists of completing these quests. Character growth in power and abilities is a key feature of the genre. Typical challenges include tactical combat, logistics, economic growth, exploration, and puzzle-solving. Physical coordination challenges are rare except in RPG-action hybrids.

CRPGs have elements in common with many other genres; it is the way in which they implement them, and the combinations in which they occur, that set them apart. Because CRPGs include so many types of challenges, it's not unusual for people to make hybrids.

War Games

CRPGs and war games both include combat and a set of rules for determining how it takes place. However, CRPGs differ from war games in that CRPGs are about a small group of heterogeneous characters, almost always implemented as living humanoids, rather than a large group of often identical units such as tanks or airplanes. Unlike CRPGs, war games seldom keep track of the growth of individual units, and role-playing games don't normally have factories that can produce more units.

15

The *Heroes of Might and Magic* series crosses the CRPG and war game genres. The games include both individual heroes and troops who have to be managed in large battles.

Action Games

Action games frequently test the player's physical skills; CRPGs seldom do. The combat in CRPGs is usually implemented as a tactical challenge but not a physical one. Also, CRPGs include a lot of non–action-related activities such as buying and selling, as well as conversations with other characters in which the player has a choice of dialog. These activities are rare in action games.

Castlevania: Symphony of the Night (1997) was an action/CRPG hybrid. It was mostly a side-scrolling platform game, but it included an inventory system and character growth as well. The *Elder Scrolls* games, *Morrowind* and *Oblivion,* are both hybrids. They feature a single avatar and a user interface much simplified from the traditional party-based model.

Adventure Games

Like adventure games, CRPGs often have rich storylines with highly detailed characters. Both types of games also involve a lot of exploration. However, in modern adventure games the player's avatar is a highly specific character provided by the game, whereas most CRPGs allow the player to define his own avatar or party of characters. Adventure games also tend to concentrate on one character, not a party of them. Adventure games traditionally offer puzzles rather than combat challenges, and their characters are seldom defined by numeric attributes as in CRPGs. If any character growth occurs in adventure games, it is of a personal or psychological nature rather than in numerically measured abilities such as strength, speed, and dexterity. CRPGs have a complex internal economy, and much of the growth that takes place consists of increasing these numbers.

The *Final Fantasy* games could be considered hybrids of CRPG and adventure. Battles are turn-based, requiring no action skills, and they have some of the most vivid stories and most beloved characters of any games made.

Game Features

In order for the story to progress and the characters to develop, the characters have to have something to do; therefore, exploring and combat make up a big part of most CRPGs. In most such games, the stories and challenges are pre-scripted, so the player will experience the same things each time he plays. In a few cases, individual levels are randomized on each play, which makes the

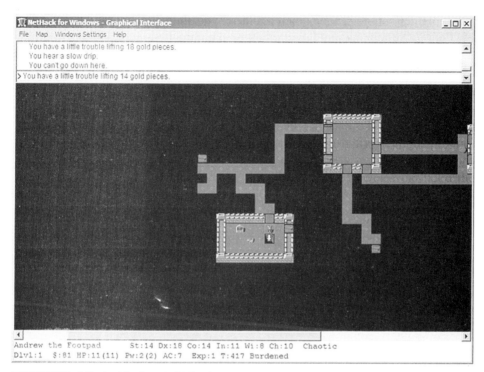

FIGURE 15.1 *Nethack* (Windows user interface shown).

games more replayable—well-known examples include the *Diablo* series and a rather extraordinary game called *Nethack* (see Figure 15.1).

Nethack is very small, so it contains almost no story. However, the character development, adventuring, exploration, and combat elements of the game are remarkable for its size. *Nethack* can offer so much variety because it doesn't have to display events with graphics; it simply describes them with text. (The earliest versions were entirely text-based.) Later designers successfully applied its basic game mechanic to other products. The original *Diablo* from Blizzard owed more than a little of its success to that design, though because it displays events with graphics, it couldn't support the extraordinary variety of *Nethack*.

In the distant future, we may expect to see dynamic story generation by an artificially intelligent game master.

Themes

CRPGs generally allow the player to experience a pivotal role in solving some hugely important problem. The premise of most role-playing games can be summed up in the statement: "Only YOU can save the world!"—or the tribe or city or whatever level of society is threatened. However, saving the world is a cliché, an adolescent power fantasy that has been terribly overused in this genre.

15

We encourage you to consider some alternative quests that *could* have a secondary consequence of saving the world but need not:

- Find and punish the person responsible for a loved one's murder.
- Learn the secret behind your hidden parentage.
- Rescue the kidnapped princess/prince.
- Find and reassemble the long-lost pieces of the magic object.
- Destroy the dangerous object.
- Find the evidence that will exonerate you from a false accusation.
- Transport the valuable thingy past the people trying to seize it.
- Try to get home after having been abducted.

While these are all very familiar themes, at least they're not specifically about saving the world.

FYI *Planescape: Torment*

We strongly encourage you to take a look at *Planescape: Torment* (if you can't find a copy, at least read the reviews and commentary available online). The premise of this unusual game had nothing to do with the typical quest to solve some enormous problem; rather, it was to discover something about the avatar's past—initially, just his name, which at the beginning of the story, the player does not know. The game was actually about the psychological growth of an individual rather than saving the world, but even so, there was plenty of combat, exploration, trading, and all the other traditional RPG challenges along the way.

Progression

RPGs almost always tell a story, characterized as a long quest in pursuit of some important goal. The quest will be broken down into a number of episodes that progress in a linear sequence, each with its own subquest and major challenge at the end. These end-of-episode challenges (almost always combat with a powerful enemy) are analogous to the boss characters at the ends of levels in action games. The story is mapped onto exploration—a journey, in other words—and each episode takes the player to a new location. Unlike in linear games such as rail-shooters or side-scrollers, it's often possible to go back to a previously visited location, though there may no longer be anything worthwhile to do there. A few games take the party back to a previously visited location for a new

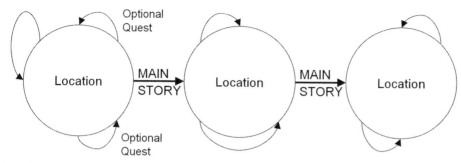

FIGURE 15.2 Typical CRPG progression.

episode; when they do this, it's often markedly different in order to give the player new things to do. In *Planescape: Torment,* the town of Curst is destroyed while the party is away.

In order to progress from one episode to the next, the player's party has to have enough strength to overcome whatever major challenge lies at the end of the current episode. This won't be possible right away (even if the player knows where the challenge is), so the activities during the chapter help the characters to grow strong enough.

Because the story of the game is intimately bound up with the game world itself, we address it in *The Game World and Story* later in this chapter.

In addition to the quests that lie along the main storyline, there will also be optional *side quests* that are unrelated to the main ones. These are not thrust upon the player but must be sought out. Visible or audible cues inform the player that one of the NPCs in the game has a problem the party can help to solve; if the party goes up and talks to her, the player will learn of the side quest and can choose to accept or reject it. Normally there's no penalty for refusing one apart from the missed opportunity to have another adventure and earn some more experience. Players can usually abandon a side quest without penalty as well.

Side quests seldom carry over from episode to episode. (If a quest does so, it's usually related to the main story rather than being a side quest.) The general progression of a CRPG is illustrated in Figure 15.2.

Gameplay Modes

Because CRPGs try to duplicate (within limits) the flexibility of tabletop role-playing games, CRPGs offer more kinds of activities than any other genre. Among these activities are exploration, tactical combat, stealthy operations, conversation, buying and selling, and inventory management.

CRPGs typically make use of four major gameplay modes and a variable number of less frequently used ones. The major modes are exploration and combat, conversation, trade, and inventory management. The minor modes are character creation (only used at the beginning of the game), character upgrade screens, and skill tree management. We'll describe the major modes briefly.

15

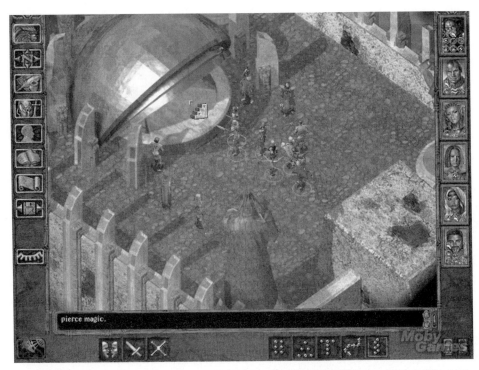

FIGURE 15.3 *Baldur's Gate II: Throne of Bhaal*, with an isometric perspective showing several party members as well as a number of NPCs.

Exploration and Combat In older computer games, exploration was often treated as a gameplay mode separate from combat, and the two modes had different perspectives. Modern games have combined them into a single mode, usually with an isometric perspective so the player can see the whole party. Figure 15.3 is a screen shot from *Baldur's Gate II: Throne of Bhaal,* which illustrates this well.

Note the complexity of the user interface, with buttons along three sides of the screen as well as a scrolling text window at the bottom.

If the game has only one character, first- or third-person perspectives are common; see *Perspective* later in this chapter.

The actions available in the exploration and combat mode include selecting one or more characters in the party, setting a formation in which they will move together, designating a location for them to walk or run to, designating NPCs for them to attack or to talk to, picking up objects, and exercising special skills such as casting magic spells or searching for traps. The buttons to the lower right in Figure 15.3 are for setting a formation.

Conversation Conversation modes often use the same perspective on the game world as the exploration and combat mode but replace the exploration- and combat-related user interface features with a dialog-display mechanism.

Occasionally, they switch the perspective to a close-up view of the character being talked to or display the character in a pop-up window.

Conversations are almost always managed via the dialog tree mechanism described in Chapter 7, "Storytelling and Narrative." The player selects a nonplayer character in the game world to speak to. A window opens on the screen, presenting a list of things that the avatar can say to the NPC. The player chooses one, and depending on what her choice is, the NPC replies, sometimes in text but often with an audio recording as well. Sometimes a scrolling window records the content of the conversation, so the player can go back and see what was said for as long as the conversation continues, or it may be recorded in a log or journal the player can bring up later. Asking the right questions or saying the right things elicits useful information from the NPC and sometimes gains experience points for the player as well.

Figure 15.4 shows the conversation mode in *Arcanum: Of Steamworks and Magick Obscura.* A portrait of the person being spoken to is shown in a window at the bottom, along with some information about how he is reacting to the situation. Immediately above the window, superimposed on the game world, are two lines of text, different lines of dialog from which the player may choose. Above them, displayed adjacent to the character, is his most recent speech.

FIGURE 15.4 *Arcanum: Of Steamworks and Magick Obscura* conversation.

15

Conversations almost always take place between the avatar character and just one other person. Conversations with more than one person become complicated because the dialog window must indicate to whom each statement was addressed.

Trade   Any purchasing or selling of items in the game takes place in a specialized trading mode. Most games in this genre have towns or settlements where friendly NPCs can be found. Within these settlements are usually shops, guilds, or other places where items or services may be bought and sold, and appropriate service personnel to go with them—blacksmiths, healers, and so on. The interface is similar to the conversation mode interface, with a view of the shop, sometimes an image of the person the avatar bargains with, and often a list or image of all the available items. The player can choose to buy an item or sell an item he already owns to get more money and can often bargain with the shopkeeper. Items purchased go directly into the avatar's inventory.

Inventory   The inventory mode lets the player manage the objects that a given character is carrying around. Because CRPGs tend to include large numbers of objects, players need a system for keeping track of them and trading them among characters.

It's not realistic to simulate the actual packing of items into a backpack, and in any case most games allow characters to carry more than would be credible if they were real people. Instead, a typical solution is to divide the character's carrying capacity into an array of boxes. Each box can carry one type of item. Large items take up several adjacent boxes. If an item is small enough, several of them may be stored in a single box, up to some maximum limit. Money, usually characterized as gold coins, can usually be stored with so many hundred coins per box. Figure 15.5 shows the inventory mode for *Dungeon Siege II,* which appears as a pop-up window over the main game world.

Item weight may be a secondary constraint. No matter how many boxes the player has free, his character can carry only so many lead weights around. The Bioware games assess a penalty on a character's speed if he is carrying more than a certain weight, and above another threshold the character cannot move at all. Money is often exempt from the weight limit because of the annoyance of having to store it whenever the player finds a big treasure hoard.

The player usually spends a disproportionate amount of time micromanaging the contents of the inventory, so inventory management becomes disproportionately important. Often, this task breaks a cardinal rule of human-computer interaction: Don't force the player to perform a menial task best handled by the computer. A simpler solution would be to display a simple table of the items in the inventory, without requiring the player to organize them in space. A pair of indicators, one for the total weight of the inventory and one for the total volume, could tell the player how much room he has left and how much more weight he could carry.

FIGURE 15.5 The inventory mode in *Dungeon Siege II*.

IN THE TRENCHES: The Rectangular Inventory Problem

Consider the situation in Figure 15.6. The player has found a staff but cannot put it in his inventory because he doesn't have enough free boxes in the right configuration. The staff takes up 4 boxes in a 1×4 configuration, and the longest space he has available is 1×3. If he moves the apple in the top space, however, he will have a space of 1×4 and will be able to store the staff. The question to ask should be: Is this activity fun for the player? Probably not; therefore, the computer should handle it automatically. Note that an adequate 4×1 horizontal space is available. Why can't the staff simply rotate 90 degrees and fit into the 4×1 gap at the bottom? Most CRPGs that we have played cannot handle that simple situation. What will happen if the player finds a staff that requires a 1×5 space, when the storage space available consists of a 4×4 grid of boxes? In the real world, we could

>> CONTINUED ON NEXT PAGE

15

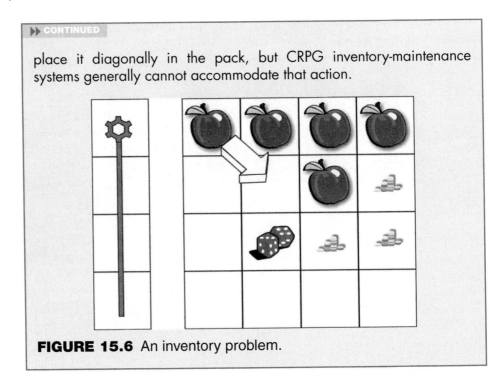

▶▶ CONTINUED

place it diagonally in the pack, but CRPG inventory-maintenance systems generally cannot accommodate that action.

FIGURE 15.6 An inventory problem.

Core Mechanics

During play, most of the actions in an RPG consist of the player's designating a character to attempt some particular activity. The player must then roll dice (in video games, the computer simulates this) to determine whether the attempt was successful or not. The rules governing success and failure for a particular activity describe how the die roll is to be tested against one or more of the character attributes. For example, consider the following situation: Jonny Rock, the warrior, wants to smash down a door. He has a strength of 17, and rules state that he must roll three six-sided dice and add their values. If he rolls higher than his strength, he fails to break the door. If he rolls lower than or equal to his strength, then the door splinters to pieces.

This play mechanic forms the basis of all the combat and most other activities in the game as well. As the character's attributes go up, the probability that a character will be successful at a given activity improves. Because character growth is a key element of all RPGs, their core mechanics are designed around the character attributes.

Rolling Dice

If you haven't already done so, please read the section *Random Numbers and the Gaussian Curve* in Chapter 10, "Core Mechanics." Adding dice together is a pretty good way of generating random numbers in role-playing games. It means that most of the time a player will get a middling die-roll, and only rarely will she get an extremely good die roll or an extremely bad one. However, as a designer you must understand the probability distributions of the possible die-rolls when you're assigning difficulty levels to tasks in the game because those chances are not evenly distributed. As we explained in Chapter 10, the chances of rolling an 18 with three six-sided dice are less than one-half of 1 percent. If you specify that a task requires a die roll of 18, it will almost never happen. On the other hand, if you specify that it requires a die roll of *less* than 18, it will almost certainly happen—over 99.5 percent of the time. Know your probabilities!

Character Attributes

We don't have space in this book to give any more than a general introduction to implementing characters in CRPGs. If you haven't played any kind of role-playing game before, we encourage you to examine the *Dungeons & Dragons Player's Handbook* (Tweet et al., 2003) for an introduction to how characters are described and designed in one particular game system. Although the attributes used do vary from game to game, many games borrow from, and sometimes expand upon, those defined in *Dungeons & Dragons* because they are the oldest and most familiar system.

Remember that, in Chapter 5, "Creative and Expressive Play," in the section *Self-Defining Play*, we divided attributes into *functional attributes* and *cosmetic attributes* and further subdivided the functional attributes into *characterization attributes* and *status attributes*. We look into these next.

Characterization Attributes   Characterization attributes determine the general abilities and qualities of a character and change only infrequently; status attributes describe the current state of a character and may change often. Choose attributes for your game based on the actions that you want characters to be able to take. The attributes will determine whether the character can in fact perform those actions and if so, how well, how quickly, how powerfully, and with what probability of success at a given task. For instance, in the *Dungeons & Dragons* system, the *dexterity* attribute determines how likely it is that a character will be able to pick someone's pocket without being detected.

Here is a brief overview of some particular types of characterization attributes that you may wish to consider:

- **Race,** an unfortunate misnomer, as most games (rightly) do not distinguish among the conventional human racial classifications (Caucasian, Native American, South Asian, etc.) except as a cosmetic attribute. In RPGs, race refers to groups of real and fantasy humanoids such as humans, dwarves, elves, giants, and so on. A better term

15

would be *species,* but we will bow to convention and continue to use *race.* Attributes connected with race usually govern the general body type and appearance of a character; they may also imply limits on the upper bounds of his strength or other physical attributes. Some games limit particular races' ability to perform certain types of activities.

- **Sex.** This naturally determines a character's body type and may determine with whom the character may form romantic relationships, if the game includes them. (Many games assume that all their characters are heterosexual; *The Sims* is an unusual departure in this regard.) Otherwise sex is almost always a cosmetic attribute rather than a functional one.

COMMANDMENT: No Sex Discrimination!

Do not place restrictions on a character's abilities on the basis of his or her sex, such as limiting the strength of female characters simply because such limits are commonly accepted ideas in the real world. If a player wants to play a six-foot-six woman with the strength of Arnold Schwarzenegger, she should be allowed to. See the FYI in Chapter 5, "Creative and Expressive Play," for more discussion.

- **Character class,** a form of specialization that permits the character to perform certain actions (for instance, the Spellcaster class may perform magic spells), gain particular skills, and improve certain attributes while limiting the growth of others. The object is to encourage, or even require, the player to create specialized rather than generalized characters. This in turn compels the player to set up a balanced party containing a mixture of character classes, which is an additional challenge. Effectively, a character's class determines his role in the party. Typical classes include fighters, spellcasters, thieves (with special stealth abilities), and clerics (with special healing abilities). You can undoubtedly think of others.

  While character class is a traditional feature of tabletop RPGs, we don't feel that it's essential, and it sometimes produces absurdities, such as a wizard whose class restrictions prevent him from using a kitchen knife. Not all games make use of character classes. If you want to implement classes, we suggest that you define them in terms of limits on a character's ability to *improve* certain skills rather than absolute prohibitions on certain activities.

■ **Physical attributes** such as height, weight, strength, dexterity, endurance, maximum speed, maximum health, and so on determine the performance of the character in movement, carrying weight and in combat. *Armor class* is a commonly used physical attribute that contributes to the formula that determines whether a character will be hit by an enemy attack; it is roughly equivalent to *defensive dodging* in war games.

■ **Mental attributes** such as intelligence and sanity affect the character's ability to learn or reason and to withstand disturbing or horrifying situations. Because a player may be more (or less!) intelligent than his character is, it's difficult to enforce intelligence except by fiat. Some game systems use intelligence levels to place limits on the ability to cast certain kinds of magic spells.

■ **Moral attributes** determine the character's attitudes toward justice and exploiting others; in simple terms, the extent to which he is good or evil. We encourage you to design a more subtle system of morality, however. Some people who think nothing of stealing wouldn't dream of abusing an animal—and vice versa.

■ **Social attributes** determine a character's social attitudes and ability to get along with others. Examples might be charisma, nurturing, or leadership abilities. You might also use social attributes to describe such things as a character's degree of xenophobia or conversational skill. When a character engages in conversations, the dialog engine may not give an inarticulate character as many things to say as a more articulate character would get.

Some games—for example, in the case of the *Fallout* series—allow the player to establish the values of a primary set of characterization attributes, then calculate the values of a second set based on those in the primary set. In *Fallout 2,* the primary set of attributes included strength, perception, endurance, charisma, agility, intelligence, and luck. The secondary set of attributes included hit points (that is, maximum possible health, calculated from strength and endurance), armor class (based on agility), and so on. *Fallout* has particularly well-designed core mechanics.

Status Attributes, Experience, and Character Levels   In CRPGs, a character's status attributes typically identify the character's location, health, state of needs (like a need for food or rest), relationships with other characters, inventory of items owned or carried, and any other value that may change from moment to moment.

15

> ## COMMANDMENT: Don't Penalize Low Health
>
> Do not reduce the fighting ability of a character because she has low health. We recommended against this in strategy games; for RPGs, we make it a commandment, because the number of characters is smaller and the consequences are more damaging. If you penalize wounded characters, whoever gets in the first solid blow in a fight has a big advantage. See the section *Health, Morale, and Fighting Efficiency* in Chapter 14, "Strategy Games," for further discussion.

Among the most commonly implemented status attributes are two related ones that effectively measure the character's growth: ***experience points,*** often abbreviated XP, and ***character level.*** Experience points are earned by successfully defeating enemies in combat and by other activities that the designer feels represent important achievements in the context of the game's story. Usually these consist of completing quests or conducting successful negotiations with NPCs via dialog. In a tabletop RPG, XP are awarded by the game master; in a CRPG, they are awarded by the computer when it detects that a particular event has occurred.

Typically, experience points have no intrinsic value and cannot be traded for anything else; they are simply a measure of progress, almost like a score. However, when a character achieves a certain level of XP, the character's level goes up a notch. The thresholds are sometimes determined by the character's class. Achieving a new character level (called ***leveling up***) usually gives the player an opportunity to raise one or more of his characterization attributes. In many games, the player is given a certain number of points, often two or three, that he can add to whichever characterization attributes he is most interested in improving.

If you implement character classes with different thresholds for leveling up, you should make this clear to the player before he has to commit himself to a given class.

> ## FYI *Why Do We Have Character Levels?*
>
> The notion of character levels is so ingrained in the culture of role-playing that most players take it for granted. However, there's no intrinsic mathematical reason why we should implement character levels. We already have experience points as a measure of character growth; why have levels as well? Levels are convenient in tabletop RPGs because they reduce the amount of bookkeeping required by the player and the GM: A character's characterization attributes
>
> CONTINUED ON NEXT PAGE

▶▶ CONTINUED

change only when the character levels up, except in rare circumstances. Now that we have computers to do the bookkeeping for us, however, simplification is not a sufficient reason to use them. It's perfectly possible for the computer to gradually give the player additional powers on a continuing basis every time he earns some more experience. By using a system based on fractional values rather than integers, characters could experience steady continuous growth rather than big "stairstep" jumps in power.

The big jumps caused by leveling up also harm the player's immersion; they're artificial and don't correctly model the increases in strength that a real person would experience in a training regimen, for example. We would be interested to see a level-less role-playing game in which the player became aware of his gradually increasing strength without knowing what the actual numbers were. Such a game might appeal to an audience who prefer an immersive storylike experience over knowing their character's precise numeric state; a hybrid of adventure game and RPG, perhaps.

However, there are good entertainment reasons for including character levels in an RPG. First, the levels give players a quick method of comparing the relative strengths of different characters, especially enemies. This is unrealistic but useful when trying to decide whether to include a particular character in the adventuring part or whether to attack an enemy character. Because most games don't display a character's strength visually, the player needs some other way of judging it, and the level provides that. Second, character levels provide players with a goal to work toward and a sense of achievement when it has been attained. Being granted points that they may add to their attributes feels like being given a reward, too. Finally, the leveling-up process lets the players decide where they want to distribute their new points, allowing them to upgrade their character as they see fit. If the system was continuously increasing their attributes, they wouldn't have as much control, nor would they notice the difference so much.

In short, character levels reduce the realism of a game but offer a number of useful compensations.

Cosmetic Attributes   Because part of the appeal of role-playing is the ability to play as a character of one's own design, CRPGs often have a great many cosmetic attributes. They add variety but don't influence the gameplay. Cosmetic attributes include such things as hair, skin, and eye color; facial features and body shapes within a particular race; clothing and jewelry that doesn't function as armor or have magic powers; tattoos, piercings, and other body modifications; and talismans,

15

pets, or other distinctive objects that a person might keep nearby, such as Indiana Jones's hat. In online role-playing games, rare examples of such objects are highly sought after and command high prices within the game economy, even if they serve no function in the game's combat challenges. Cosmetic attributes add richness to the play experience; the more of them that you can afford, the better—although they are not a substitute for good gameplay.

Magic and Its Equivalents

Magic is such a distinctive aspect of role-playing games that we have chosen to treat it in a separate section. Note that for *magic* you can substitute *psychic powers, spiritual power, mental energy,* or any other concept that allows characters to influence the world, themselves, or other characters, by means not available to us in real life. Science fiction games often posit advanced technology that is, as Arthur C. Clarke observed, indistinguishable from magic.

The use of magic is commonly restricted to a particular class of characters, often called *mages, magic-users,* or *spellcasters.* The purpose of this arrangement is to establish complementary classes of characters, one that is good at conventional physical combat and one that is good at magical combat, which encourages the players to create mixed parties containing members of both classes.

In tabletop RPGs, where it's up to the game master to decide what is and isn't possible, players can think up all kinds of interesting things to do with magic. In CRPGs, we are unfortunately limited by the fact that the software has to know how to implement any spell—and of course players expect a visible manifestation of the spell as well, which means creating animation and sound to go with it. Magic is most often used as a weapon or a shield and as a means of temporarily improving the values of the party characters' attributes and harming the attributes of enemies.

Because magic doesn't exist in the real world, you can't assume that your player will know how it works in your world. If you include magic in your game, you must define what kinds of things magic does and how it is invoked. You must also create a way to limit the amount of magic available, just as characters must have limited strength and health. Typically, when a spellcaster uses magic, he does so in a particular instance called casting a spell, the effects of which are usually immediate. (Few spells in games take time to begin working.) Some spells are over and done with right away, more or less corresponding to a *shot* in a strategy game; others may have a lasting effect that ends after a certain amount of time. The effects of magic spells are almost never permanent in games. Permanent changes are too significant to be allowed to happen frequently, so any permanent change is normally made by the ***leveling*** process.

Dungeons & Dragons uses a rather awkward system for placing limits on magic, requiring a character to "memorize" spells which, once cast, disappear from the character's "memory" rather as ammunition is consumed in a gun. The character must have time to rest and rememorize the spells before they can be used again. We don't find this metaphor compelling and prefer another system in which each spell consumes a certain amount of magical power, or *mana,* when it is cast. A character's definition includes a status attribute for the amount of mana the character has at the moment and a characterization attribute for the maximum amount that he may have. Mana is restored by drinking magic potions or simply by the passage of time. This system permits the character to cast any combination of spells that he knows, as often as he likes, until his mana is gone.

Skills and Special Capabilities

In addition to the basic human-like characteristics—strength, intelligence, beauty, and so on—most RPGs allow characters to use, and to improve, special skills and capabilities. CRPGs allow the player's character to learn new skills over time, a rarity in other genres. The best-designed games allow the player to attempt to learn as many skills as she wants, restricted only by the time available, though her character's aptitude in that skill will be based on previously assigned characterization attributes. You may want to allow characters to specialize, especially if the character practices a set of interrelated skills, while unpracticed skills gradually decline. For example, learning one skill, basic mechanics, could provide a solid basis for developing another, such as picking locks, whereas learning basic gardening would not.

Obtaining New Skills   Skills are somewhat analogous to the unit upgrades of strategy games; like unit upgrades, they allow a character to do something that he could not do before or to do it more effectively. The unit upgrade process in a strategy game is typically called research, whereas in a CRPG, acquisition of a skill is called learning. Sometimes a new skill (or the right to choose a new skill) is simply granted as a reward for having achieved a certain amount of experience. However, you can also require the player to seek out a mentor NPC who will teach the new skill to the character in exchange for money—similar to the cost of research in strategy games.

The analogy between skills in CRPGs and unit upgrades in strategy games is not exact, however, for the following reasons:

- In CRPGs, a skill earned by a character is *permanent* and stays with that character as long as he lives (and usually survives reincarnation as well). In strategy games, a unit upgrade ordinarily lasts only for the duration of the current mission or level.

- In a strategy game, an upgrade normally applies to all units of a given type, or sometimes to the player's entire army and economic system. In a CRPG, a new skill applies to exactly one character, the one who learned the skill. It's the difference between an industrial and a personal advance. CRPG skills are individual, like the ability to play

15

music, rather than industrial, like an improved engine. Each character will have to have his own record of skills learned to date.

- Finally, CRPG skill upgrades usually happen instantly, whereas research in a strategy game normally takes time. Although instant learning is completely unrealistic for something like archery or playing music, nobody wants to sit and watch while her character practices. Strategy game research doesn't have this problem because research happens in parallel with other activities.

Skill Trees Skills are usually organized into a *skill tree,* a growth path analogous to the *tech tree* discussed in Chapter 14, "Strategy Games." As with tech trees, learning a particular skill in the tree makes subsequent, more advanced skills available. Other than that and the differences mentioned above, they're really quite similar. See the discussion of tech trees in Chapter 14 for some other ideas on things you can do with skill trees.

Figure 15.7 illustrates the idea as implemented in *Diablo II*. The right side of the screen shows a skill tree, one of three different trees for a single character, an Amazon. The tree currently shown is labeled "Passive and Magic Skills." (The other two available for this character are labeled "Javelin and Spear Skills"

FIGURE 15.7 One of the skill trees for the Amazon character in *Diablo II* (right side).

and "Bow and Crossbow Skills," respectively.) Each icon represents a skill that may be learned, with the ones that are required first at the top (this tree is upside down). The arrows leading from icon to icon show the progression allowed. An unlearned skill appears in dark grey, such as the horned helmet at the lower left of the tree. Skills that have been learned are shown in white.

Skills in *Diablo II* are learned by assigning them skill points, which are earned through experience. The box marked "Skill Choices Remaining" indicates that the player has two skill points available to assign either to learn a new skill or to improve an existing one. The small boxes next to each icon hold the number of skill points assigned to that skill so far; each additional point strengthens the effect of the skill when it is used in play.

Character Design

Tabletop RPGs are specifically designed to allow the player to create her own avatar character before the game begins. Most CRPGs follow this model, particularly multiplayer online RPGs. Single-player CRPGs sometimes allow the player to create not only an avatar character but all the members of the party. Others let the player create only the avatar, then add further, predefined characters to the party as the player encounters them in the game world.

FYI   *Advantages and Disadvantages of Predefined Characters*

A small number of single-player games come with predefined avatar characters that the player may initially customize in only a limited number of ways. This system constrains the player to use the characters given, which players who want complete freedom may not like. However, it has the great advantage that it enables the designer to tell a story in which the avatar already has a past and relationships with other characters when the game begins. Because the game already knows something about the avatar, it can build those details into the quests that the player will face. If the game knows nothing about the avatar (because he doesn't exist until the player creates him), all the quests and other interactions in the game have to be generic and work for any kind of character.

Players are typically allowed to set their cosmetic attributes any way they like: name, gender, hair color, clothing, and so on. They can also choose their character's race, class, and moral attributes if the game implements such features. For other characterization attributes, the usual mechanism is to allow the players to roll simulated dice to generate a number of points and then allow them to distribute the

15

points among their attributes however they see fit. This lets them concentrate their points in whichever attribute they're most interested in developing. Players are sometimes allowed to ask for a new die roll if the first one is too low.

The Game World and Story

Once you know what the player is going to do, you'll need to think about where he's going to do it. We suggest you design the setting before the story. Although this advice is the opposite of that normally given to writers, the setting of a role-playing game is essentially a vast playground to adventure in. Decide what kind of environment is suitable for the sorts of activities you have in mind.

Settings

CRPG game worlds have tended to be set in fantasy and science fiction universes because both offer players opportunities to do things that they can't do in real life: use magic in the former case and use advanced technology in the latter. They also make possible a huge variety of enemies, aliens, and monsters that don't exist in the real world. Finally, such settings make the unrealistic rate of growth that game characters experience more plausible. If you were to set a role-playing game in the present day with ordinary humans as characters, it would be difficult to believe that within a few weeks of game time they could become dozens of times stronger or more resistant to injury than they were at the beginning. Even if you're the strongest man on Earth, you can still be killed by a single bullet and everyone knows it. Fantasy and science fiction settings help players to suspend their disbelief about these things.

This is not to say that you must choose only a science fiction or fantasy setting for your CRPG. You could, for example, create a role-playing game about a police officer or a spy whose character grows by acquiring new skills such as forensic examination or using bugging devices rather than weapons and magic. In such a game, you could easily set your story in the present day or the near future.

No matter what setting you choose, however, you must spend a lot of time and effort making it appealing to explore. This is more true of CRPGs than any other genre except adventure games and action-adventure hybrids. In an action game, the player is often moving too fast to appreciate the landscape much; and in a strategy game, he's often too busy commanding his armies and building his defenses. A CRPG is a slower-paced game, so players have time to look around. Novel and dramatic scenery are an important part of how these games entertain.

A recent trend with CRPGs, evidenced by *Neverwinter Nights, Elder Scrolls III: Morrowind,* and *Arcanum: Of Steamworks and Magick Obscura,* is the provision of an editor within the game to allow the more involved players to create their own scripted adventures in the game world.

This is a trend to be encouraged because it extends the sales life of the game, which in turn increases sales. *Neverwinter Nights* takes this to the extreme, allowing players to edit an adventure in real-time as other players journey through it.

Chapter 4, "Game Worlds," discusses the creative work you will need to do in designing your setting.

Story

Once you have a setting, you need to decide what will happen there—the story of the game. A CRPG story is seldom simply a straightforward quest in the style of *Lord of the Rings* style; it's also a mystery. It's a problem to be solved but also a riddle to be unraveled. The objective *bring back the really valuable treasure* is not sufficient to sustain player interest for long.

The story of an RPG is far longer than a movie or short story; it's more like a novel, and a pretty big novel at that. Consequently, much of the advice about length and pacing of screenplays and stories that is offered to beginning writers doesn't apply to CRPGs. Furthermore, the player will have the option to take (or to ignore!) numerous side quests, something that never happens in a movie.

We suggest that you first decide on the game's overall quest—that is, its ending. The player need not know exactly what this quest is until late in the game; usually the quest that he believes he's pursuing at the beginning is not the real quest. (To use an example from literature, *The Maltese Falcon* begins with Brigid O'Shaughnessy walking into detective Sam Spade's office and asking him for help in finding her sister. Later he discovers that there is no sister and she really wants him to help her find the Maltese Falcon.) You may want to have more than one possible ending to the overall quest (success, failure, or varying outcomes in between), but they should all be related.

Once you know the overall quest, then you have to decide how to get the player from wherever he starts to the end. As we said earlier, stories in CRPGs are typically presented as a journey through a landscape, with each episode of the story taking place in a different region. Work out the details of this journey, episode by episode, and all the new things and people that the player will discover along the way. There should be a number of twists and turns in the story—complicating factors that give the player more things to think about and to do. Common plot elements include long-lost relatives appearing unexpectedly; enemies who turn out to be friends, and vice versa; clues that lead to dead ends (or to unexpected changes); lost treasures coming to light in unexpected places; hidden heirs to a kingdom; and so on. Most of these will seem like clichés if not carefully handled, so if you use them, look for ways to make them fresh and new. Or create situations that are the opposite of what someone would ordinarily expect—the heir to a kingdom seeking not to obtain his crown but running away to avoid the onerous duties of monarchy, for example.

Once you have an overall story, complete with locations, adventures, and plot twists, then you can start adding side quests to give the player more experience.

15

These should be shorter adventures that the player can accept, reject, or abandon without affecting the main storyline. However, they should still feel as if they're in keeping with the player's overall goals. One of the weaknesses of many CRPGs is that they start the player off on some vast life-or-death quest, then perpetually offer him opportunities to abandon it and just be a mercenary, treasure-hunter, or errand boy. Try to make your side quests feel as if they are helping the player achieve his overall goals, even if only indirectly. For instance, suppose the player needs a specific valuable object in order to get past the challenge at the end of an episode and the only way to get it is to buy it. If he then accepts a number of side quests to earn the money, the side quests are helping him to pursue his main goal even though their own content is unrelated.

You will probably need to do some noninteractive exposition to set the stage—either an opening movie, voiceover narrative, or scrolling text story. As we mentioned earlier, if the avatar character is partially predefined, you can include some of her history in the opening exposition; if the avatar is defined entirely by the player, then the opening exposition cannot make reference to the avatar except in very general terms. You may want to have the opening exposition concentrate on the game world or the reason for the major quest in the game instead of the avatar.

You'll need to write the opening carefully to be mysterious yet enticing. The balance between what you reveal and what you withhold has to be just right in order to induce the player to probe further. If you're too mysterious, the player will have no reason to investigate the game world because he won't know what he's supposed to be doing, or why. If you tell too much, however, the player will be irritated because he wants to get started playing.

See Chapter 7, "Storytelling and Narrative," for more information on game stories.

IN THE TRENCHES: Opening Stories

Let's look at two examples of opening stories in CRPGs and mine them for the balance of what is told and what is withheld.

Planescape: Torment

You awaken, frigid and confused, and realize you're lying on a stone table. Scanning the room, you see only stone tables like yours and a sign that reads "The Mortuary." You aren't dead, so why are you here and, more important, who are you? Your thoughts are interrupted by the approach of a floating skull that starts talking! It informs you that you just died again. What does it mean, *again*?

This opening is a particularly good example of minimizing exposition and maximizing mystery. *Planescape: Torment* is unusual in that

▶▶ CONTINUED ON NEXT PAGE

the opening of the game presents only a mystery and not a quest. From the opening, the player can surmise that his avatar once had a normal life and that something strange has happened to cause him to become a cursed immortal. This is an interesting theme because of the inherent human fascination with mortality. *Planescape* poses the question: Who wouldn't want to be an immortal, no matter what the price? During play, the player discovers that sometimes the price of immortality is too high; the overall goal of the game is to undo the damage that caused the character to become immortal. The game also has several different endings based on decisions the player makes near the end, among which is to—intentionally—die.

Fallout

> The setting: A subterranean fallout shelter houses a thousand people after a nuclear holocaust. It's been nearly 80 years, and you still don't have any idea what's out there. Sure you've sent out volunteer scouts, but none of them returned.
>
> Now your water recycler has failed. Rationing has begun, but someone needs to leave the vault to get a replacement microchip for the water recycler and look for other survivors.
>
> And you drew the short straw.

At the beginning of this game, the player finds his character locked outside of his vault, Vault 13. The immediate priority is survival. It's dangerous outside the vault, and there is no hope (or reason) to attempt to return without the water chip. Fortunately for the player, it looks like the water chip will be easy to obtain. Vault 15 is only a day or two away, and provided that he can survive that long, it should be a reasonably easy matter to obtain a new chip.

Fallout's story begins with a seemingly simple quest, but no apparent mystery. As the game goes on, complications arise: The water chip cannot be obtained from Vault 15. Vault 15 stands in ruins and the control room lies under tons of rock. This false ending approach is used more than once in *Fallout*. When the character does finally get another water chip and returns to Vault 13, he realizes that Vault 15 was attacked—and that his actions have now revealed the location of his home vault to the same attackers. The adventure continues with the player now compelled to destroy the forces that threaten his home vault.

The opening uses the popular theme of returning home to good effect. The ironic twist at the end of the game, that his experiences in the outside world have changed the character so much that he cannot return to his home vault, is an excellent example of storytelling in a role-playing game.

15

The Presentation Layer

Like strategy games, CRPGs have complicated core mechanics, and the player needs access to a large amount of information. In addition to the game world, the player will need to see critical information about the health (and possibly mana status) of each member of the party. Spellcasting characters require a menu of the spells that they currently have available.

Interaction Model

The interaction model for most single-player CRPGs is party-based, with the player controlling the activities of a small group of people who generally stay close together. In a few cases, most notably the *Diablo* games, the player controls a single avatar. In multiplayer online games, the interaction model is always avatar-based, though the player may have a *familiar*—a pet or companion who is also under the player's control.

Perspective

The interaction model you choose to implement will determine what perspectives will work for you. With an avatar-based model, either first- or third-person perspective is possible in 3D games, and many of them offer both. The first-person perspective is useful for conversations with other characters and moving fast through terrain; the third-person is more useful for combat, in which the player will want to see her avatar fighting, casting spells, and so on. *Elder Scrolls III: Morrowind* is a good example of a game that provides both (see Figure 15.8).

With a party-based model, you will probably want an aerial perspective so the player can see all the members of the party at once and position them as he wishes in combat. The aerial perspective also lets the player see more of the surrounding terrain, which aids exploration and allows one character to scout a little way ahead for danger while still leaving the others visible on the screen. While CRPGs used to use top-down aerial perspectives, the isometric aerial perspective is now the de facto standard for party-based play. See Figure 15.3 for an example.

User Interface

CRPGs usually permit a much greater range of possible actions for the player than games of other genres. Consequently, there is a corresponding increase in the complexity of the interface. Most PC titles offer an interface in which the player uses the mouse to click on icons—though some still offer a keyboard-only interface—while console titles tend to duplicate the functionality of a mouse using analog controllers.

FIGURE 15.8 *Elder Scrolls III: Morrowind,* in the third-person perspective.

Figure 15.9, from *Knights of the Old Republic II: The Sith Lords,* illustrates some of the complexities of CRPG interfaces. Contrast it with Figure 13.7 (right side) for a traditional action game, and with Figure 14.2 for a strategy game. Figure 15.9 includes all of the following elements: a mini-map (upper left); details about the current health and status of an enemy (left center); combat options during battle (lower left and center); party portraits (lower right); and buttons for switching to other gameplay modes such as character and inventory management (upper right).

See Chapter 8, "Creating the User Experience," for more information on user interface design. Much of the advice in that chapter is directly applicable to CRPGs.

Visible Versus Hidden Mechanics   When the first computerized games based on the *Dungeons & Dragons* system were made, TSR (the company that owned the *D&D* system) insisted that the computer games follow the rules that they had created for the tabletop game to the letter. Furthermore, TSR not only wanted the rules to be identical in the computer games but to be *seen* to be identical, so they required that the games display references to the die rolls on

15

FIGURE 15.9 *Knights of the Old Republic II: The Sith Lords,* during a combat sequence.

the screen. TSR wanted to make sure that the players had no reason to complain that the computer games weren't following the real *D&D* rules.

That was nearly 20 years ago, however, and the need for it has long since ended. Unfortunately, many games have continued to follow this practice. *Baldur's Gate,* for example, flashed the words *Saving Roll* onscreen when a character had a lucky escape—irrelevant information with an adverse effect on immersion. The player does not need to be reminded that she is playing a computer game based on *D&D* rules. Of course, the player should have access to the basic information such as attributes and skills, but exposing the inner mechanics of the game system in this way is unnecessary and counterproductive. One of the great benefits of computer gaming is that the player does *not* need to know how the rules are implemented.

Finally, in tabletop games the rules had to be simple enough for a human game master to understand and apply, and this set limits on the complexity of the core mechanics. On a computer, those rules can be much more sophisticated. For example, there's no longer any reason to simulate die rolling or to restrict the mathematical operations to addition and subtraction. The *Fallout* series uses a percentage-based system and does a good job of keeping the mechanics out of the player's way.

Some players who are primarily focused on character advancement want to see all the numeric data, as opposed to the story-chasers who find that all the numeric data spoils the fantasy. Both types of player like CRPGs, but for different reasons, and it's tricky to serve both groups. It might be possible to create a game that could be played both ways—one mode that showed the arithmetical inner workings of the game and one that reduced the numbers to a minimum, converting them to power bars or other display mechanisms. However, such a game would still have to have fairly simple rules, or it would end up looking like a spreadsheet.

Repetitive Tasks   Another legacy of CRPGs' roots in tabletop RPGs arises from the turn-based nature of the original games. Consider a character that has a 10 percent chance of picking a lock; the player may repeatedly click on the Pick Lock button until he succeeds. This is dull and unnecessary, especially on a computer.

A better method would be to display a progress bar. The speed with which the task progresses depends on the character's skill in that area—that is, it progresses quickly for a character with a high skill level, slowly for one with a low skill level, or not at all if the task is beyond the character's ability entirely.

This approach also allows the player to interrupt the task if it is taking too long. The progress bar could flash red if there is a chance of being interrupted, for example, if an enemy is within range of the player's character and stands a chance of detecting the activity. Give the character a small amount of time—based on her dexterity and intelligence—to stop before being caught, or no chance of avoiding capture if the character's combined dexterity and intelligence is too low. This approach aids immersion and heightens the tension and immediacy of the game.

Summary

Role-playing games, either on tabletop or on computers, allow players to immerse themselves in complex worlds with manifold gameplay options. With several gameplay modes, including communication, exploration, combat, and inventory, CRPGs can be enormous undertakings requiring intense design and a lot of content. But the satisfaction of playing an avatar with wonderful powers makes it very rewarding to make. The designer needs to be concerned with creating a memorable world with a wondrous environment and giving the avatars the challenges to allow them to increase experience points and level up—if your design includes that—while unraveling the story by journeying through the world.

15

Test Your Skills

MULTIPLE CHOICE QUESTIONS

1. A computer role-playing game (CRPG) is best described as which of the following?

   A. A permissive game with undefined rules where a game master establishes the story and game mechanisms.

   B. A well-defined set of rules wherein a player controls an avatar, has the ability to increase skills, can collect and carry unlimited items, and has physical challenges that require adept use of the interface.

   C. A combination exploration and conversation or combat game where the player can increase his skills by overcoming challenges, collect and carry items in an inventory, and must solve a quest in order to achieve victory.

   D. A strategic game wherein the player tries to use her inventory in the most efficient way possible in order to complete assigned quests.

2. What are the essential parts of making a successful CRPG?

   A. Captivating story, series of quests, rewarding character growth path.

   B. Good experience points and leveling up algorithms.

   C. Well-rounded NPCs, well developed dialog, good inventory interface design.

   D. Solid story and quest with critical emphasis on inventory management and team organization.

3. To make the most realistic dialog within a CRPG, the designer should use

   A. state machines.

   B. dialog trees.

   C. a combination of state machines and dialog trees.

   D. an interface where the player can directly type in his dialog.

4. How are CRPGs similar to war games?

   A. Both require you to control large groups of characters to achieve your goals.

   B. Both involve inventory management.

   C. Both keep track of the growth of each character in the game.

   D. Both include combat and established rules for combat outcomes.

5. A CRPG is expected to offer

    A. factories for making more units.

    B. exploration, combat, and conversation.

    C. inventory management, resource management, and team management.

    D. exploration, physical challenges, and buying and selling.

6. Side quests are usually

    A. tied directly into the main storyline.

    B. solved before the player can progress in the game.

    C. thrust upon the player.

    D. unrelated to the main quest and are optional.

7. Stealthy operations within a CRPG are useful for

    A. gaining experience points.

    B. increasing magic skills or mana.

    C. avoiding capture.

    D. inventory management.

8. Which of the following actions is *not* available in the exploration and combat mode of a CRPG?

    A. Selecting characters for the party.

    B. Selling items to a trader.

    C. Designating a location for the party to walk to.

    D. Casting magic spells.

9. Which of the following is *not* an important issue when designing an inventory management system?

    A. The physical size and weight of inventory items.

    B. Access to the inventory items while in combat.

    C. The images used to represent the items in inventory.

    D. The ease of equipping the avatars throughout all gameplay situations.

10. What are the chances of rolling 3 with three six-sided dice?

    A. 10 percent.

    B. less than 1 percent.

    C. 15 percent.

    D. 5 percent.

15

11. Characterization attributes include
    A. social, moral, character class, mental and physical attributes.
    B. race, sex, magic skill, physical attributes, location.
    C. magic skill, weapons dexterity, skill tree, height.
    D. height, state of gambling addiction, gender, character class.

12. Experience points are most often earned by
    A. leveling up.
    B. purchasing weapons.
    C. memorizing.
    D. defeating enemies in combat.

13. "Learning" in a CRPG is the ability of a character to
    A. level up.
    B. gain experience points.
    C. achieve a higher level of skill at some action or task.
    D. buy more powerful weapons.

14. Character level is a quality that
    A. refers to a character's ability to use a game object.
    B. defines a character's height.
    C. reflects a character's overall experience.
    D. is proportional to the number of monsters killed.

15. Magic is best treated within a game as
    A. another weapon class.
    B. a skill to be earned through use.
    C. only useful to those with enough character class skill to use it.
    D. a skill that, once used, needs to be relearned throughout the game.

▶▶ **Case Study**

Choose a CRPG that you believe, from your own experience of playing it, is an excellent example of the genre (or use one your instructor has assigned). It should be a single player CRPG for the purposes of this exercise. You are free to select one with a single avatar or one in

▶▶ CONTINUED ON NEXT PAGE

which you control a party. Write a report documenting the features that place it in this genre as opposed to another one and explaining why you believe it is superior to others of its kind. Be sure to cover at least the following areas:

- Consider how much time you spent before the start of the game selecting, creating, or modifying your avatar(s). Was that time well spent? Was the system easy to follow and to use? Once in the game, did you feel that you had made good choices? If not, what information could the developer have provided you to make character selection easier?

- Describe how well the game maintains your immersion within the gameplay. Are there any interface interruptions that remind you of the computer? Are there any game mechanics that should be hidden but are not?

- Describe how well the game maintains your sense of immersion and emotional attachment through the character development of your avatar. Are the dialog choices fitting for your character and do they reflect the personality of your character? Do NPCs respond appropriately to the behavior, actions, or dialog choices you make? Does your play in the world impact the story?

- Review the interface for the inventory. Does it make it simple for you to store or use items? Are there limitations to the inventory system that impact your ability to play or that require you to spend an inordinate amount of time manipulating objects?

- Address the experience points and leveling up of your character(s). Does it make sense? Were you able to clearly understand how the leveling up worked when you selected your avatar(s)? Do you feel that the XP and leveling is well balanced and enhances or hinders the game play experience?

The design questions in the next section may help you to think about these issues. In your report, use screen shots to illustrate your points. End the case study with suggestions for improvement or, if you feel the game cannot be improved, suggestions for additional features that might be fun to have in the game.

▶▶ CONTINUED ON NEXT PAGE

15

> ▶▶ CONTINUED
>
> Alternatively, choose a game that you believe is particularly *bad*. Do the same case study, explaining what is wrong and how it could be improved.
>
> A case study is neither a review nor a design document; it is an analysis. You are not attempting to reverse-engineer the entire game but simply to explain how it works in a general way. Your instructor will tell you the desired scope of the assignment; we recommend from five to twenty pages.

DESIGN QUESTIONS

When beginning the design of a CRPG, consider the following questions:

1. Which type of game are you going to create? Is it going to be heavy on story (as in the *Final Fantasy* games), or will character advancement and combat be the main thrust (as in *Nethack*)?

2. If it is story-based, how will you structure the quests? One big overarching quest with side quests or a more free-form approach? This will have an impact on the difficulty of production and the feel of the game.

3. What is the setting for your game? Are you going for the standard science fiction/fantasy fare, or are you using something else? Are you using a licensed work? Are you convinced that your setting is different yet recognizable enough to be compelling?

4. How will your world function? What are the underlying rules for the way the world works? Are they self-consistent and logical? Are they based on a preexisting system (as in *Baldur's Gate*)?

5. Is the player going to be given a group of avatars, or will he be responsible for a single character? Will his character be configurable (as in *Arcanum*), or will he be forced to take a predefined role (as in *Anachronox*)?

6. What will be the primary focus of your game? Will it be uncovering the story, improving the player's character, or combat and exploration? The majority of games attempt to cover all these bases equally, but some exceptional ones have focused more on one aspect, such as *Anachronox* and *Diablo II*. This affects the pace of your game.

7. What will be the perspective used in your game? Will you use standard isometric 3D (as in *Fallout*) or will you use a fully 3D engine (as in *Elder Scrolls III: Morrowind*)? Will you use something else entirely?

8. Is your game going to include a magic system? How is this magic system going to be constructed? Will it be based on preexisting concepts, familiar regimes (such as law/chaos/good/evil) or something completely new? Will it be internally self-consistent or not? How will it be balanced with nonmagic forces within the game?

9. How will you handle inventory management within the game?

10. And finally, will your player's character end up saving the world? Are you sure you want to do that? Can you think of anything slightly more original (as in *Vampire: The Masquerade—Bloodlines,* for example)?

Chapter | 16

Sports Games

Chapter Objectives

After reading this chapter and completing the exercises, you will be able to do the following:

- Know the definition of athletic sports games and be familiar with the types of challenges that these types of sports games offer.

- Understand the challenges of meeting players' expectations about a real-world game in a video game implementation.

- Know the basics of adapting a physical sports game mechanic to a virtual world.

- Understand the design complexities for physics, AI, and player skill ratings required for a sports game.

- Use flowcharting to help define AI states within a sports game.

- Know the issues involved in licensing sports organizations, teams, and players, including the use of names and images.

- Understand mapping known physical game play mechanics to computer-human interface devices.

Introduction

Sports games are a special challenge for the game designer. So many people play or watch sports that they come to the game with a great many expecations about what the gameplay and visual design of the game will be like, and a designer must learn to meet those expectations. However, sports games remain one of the most popular genres in all of video gaming, and a well-tuned game can turn into a highly enjoyable, and profitable, product line.

In this chapter, we discuss how the principles of game design apply to sports games. We begin with a formal definition of sports games and then address in detail the features that characterize them. We examine the types of challenges provided to the player within the game. Also discussed are the legal issues inherent in making a video version of a professionally franchised game, including trademarks, personal publicity rights, and licenses. Most of the chapter is dedicated to the structure of sports games: the types of gameplay, the issues required for mapping to user input devices, the various game states, camera and other mechanics, and the design of athlete AIs for a rewarding experience. For a designer, sports games offer the unique challenge of simulating well-known game mechanics while at the same time modifying those mechanics to the video game system used.

What Are Sports Games?

Two things only the people anxiously desire: bread and the circus games.

—Juvenal

Unlike most other games, which take place in a world the player knows little about, sports games simulate a world the player knows a lot about: sporting events as they are in real life. No one has ever really led an army of elves into combat, and only a small number of people know how it feels to fly an F-16 fighter jet, but a great many people know what professional football looks like and how the game is played. Sports games encourage direct comparison with the real world.

Not all sports games are ultrarealistic, of course. Some, such as Electronic Arts' old Sega Genesis game *Mutant League Football*, are fantasy games even though they are based on real sports. Others, such as Midway's arcade game *NFL Blitz*, simplified a sport and deliberately made it more extreme for dramatic purposes. Most of these kinds of games are designed to appeal to kids, who might not know much about the real sport. But for aficionados, the game must be a reasonably accurate depiction of the real thing, and they will see any deviation as a flaw.

> *A sports game simulates some aspect of a real or imaginary athletic sport, whether it is playing in matches, managing a team or career, or both. Match play makes use of physical and strategic challenges; the management challenges are chiefly economic.*

This chapter discusses athletic sports, as opposed to sports such as motor racing. Although racing games are often sold in the sports category, from a design standpoint, they really belong in Chapter 17, "Vehicle Simulations."

> ## FYI *A Note on Terminology*
>
> Because sports games simulate other games, as opposed to a war, a race, or an economic competition of some kind, the words *player* and *game* are ambiguous. Does *player* refer to the person playing the computer game or to one of the athletes playing the game on the field? In this chapter, we use the following convention: *Player* refers to the person playing the computer game, as it does throughout the rest of the book. We call the people *in* the game *athletes. Game* refers to the computer game. When we refer to one particular contest, we call it a *match*. The type of match that the athletes are playing (basketball or soccer, for example) is called the *sport*.
>
> A great many sports involve a playing area with a goal at either end and athletes trying to manipulate some object into the goal. Basketball, ice hockey, water polo, and soccer are all examples. We refer to these collectively as *soccerlike* games.

Game Features

Most sports games concentrate on simulating actual matches, but many also include a number of management functions as well—the challenges of managing a team or an athlete's career. A few sports games implement *only* this aspect of the sport and don't allow the player to control individual athletes in matches. Occasionally called *manager games,* these are particularly popular in Europe.

Game Structure

The main gameplay mode in a sports game is match play, simulating the sport itself as it is played. Players can usually pause the game, which normally brings up a menu permitting them to substitute athletes, change the camera view, perform other sorts of coaching tasks, and sometimes adjust the AI. Players can also save the game for later or abandon it.

Outside of match play, most of the game's modes relate to other aspects of the sport: studying the athletes' ratings and performance statistics, hiring and trading them, deciding who the starting athletes will be, and following the sport's match or tournament schedule on a calendar. The screen layouts tend to reflect the bookkeeping nature of these activities, often resembling tables or graphs.

Player Roles

The player's role is most commonly that of an athlete, but in a team sport, that doesn't mean just one particular athlete; in that case, the player's focus of control

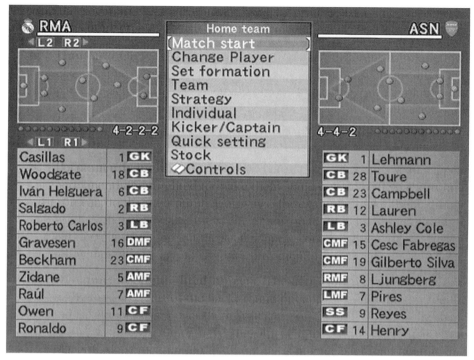

Figure contents:

RMA ◄L2 R2►   4-2-2-2   ◄L1 R1►

Casillas	1	GK
Woodgate	18	CB
Iván Helguera	6	CB
Salgado	2	RB
Roberto Carlos	3	LB
Gravesen	16	DMF
Beckham	23	CMF
Zidane	5	AMF
Raúl	7	AMF
Owen	11	CF
Ronaldo	9	CF

Home team
[Match start]
Change Player
Set formation
Team
Strategy
Individual
Kicker/Captain
Quick setting
Stock
◇Controls

ASN   4-4-2

GK	1	Lehmann
CB	28	Toure
CB	23	Campbell
RB	12	Lauren
LB	3	Ashley Cole
CMF	15	Cesc Fabregas
CMF	19	Gilberto Silva
RMF	8	Ljungberg
LMF	7	Pires
SS	9	Reyes
CF	14	Henry

FIGURE 16.1 *Pro Evolution Soccer 5's* strategy setup screen, a coaching function.

usually follows the action rather than being tied to a single individual. Thus, the player's role shifts rapidly, especially if some athletes play specialized positions such as catcher or goalie.

The player may sometimes elect to play the coach, again a role found chiefly in team sports. The coach selects the starting athletes for the team, sets offensive and defensive strategies, and makes athlete substitutions during the match. See Figure 16.1 for an example. The player usually switches to the coach role during timeouts or other pauses in the action.

Finally, there's the role of general manager of the team. The general manager hires and fires athletes, trying to recruit the best athletes within the limitations of the budget. In a game that allows it, the manager also tries to build up the team over a period of years, improving its standing in the league.

Gameplay and Rules

The challenges and actions of a sports game are those of the actual sport but with the actions of the athletes' bodies mapped onto the control devices of the game machine. Whatever the athletes try to achieve in the match, the player tries to achieve. In the coaching role, the challenges are to choose the most appropriate strategy for the moment from among those offered by the game and to manage the athletes so that they don't become overtired or injured (assuming the game implements those concepts).

The rules of a sports game are, for the most part, the rules of the sport that is being simulated. You might find that you need to relax these rules in some areas, particularly with respect to faults, fouls, or judgment errors that the player might make. Because the player is using a handheld device to manipulate an athlete onscreen instead of playing on the field himself, it's much more difficult to judge when his avatar is about to bump into someone, cross into a forbidden zone, and so on. A few games allow the player to set the level of computerized refereeing to forgiving or strict, depending on which way he likes to play.

You'll also have to decide if you want to simulate athlete mistakes that are outside the player's control. For example, in American football, a certain number of penalties are called each match for "holding," grabbing hold of another athlete instead of merely pushing him. This is an aspect of the sport that a computerized version could avoid entirely: It could simply make it impossible for one athlete to hold another, but a match in which no holding penalties ever occurred would feel unrealistic. On the other hand, a match in which holding penalties occurred at random might be frustrating for the player. This problem can be solved by allowing the player to adjust the strictness of the refereeing, as described in the previous paragraph.

Competition Modes

Sports games, unlike most other games, allow all possible modes of competition. Depending on the sport and on how many input devices your platform supports, you can offer single-player, competitive, cooperative, team, and league modes; people love to play sports games competitively. Sports games sell far more copies for console machines than they do for PCs primarily because console machines allow many people to play at once in the same room. In addition, console versions allow the use of a TV (usually with a 19-inch screen or better) instead of a monitor, so all the players have a better view of the action. Because many real sports are played by teams of people, these sports naturally offer opportunities for multiplayer action.

One other competition mode you should consider including is one with no players at all: the computer versus itself. Few other games besides chess games ever implement this mode; after all, people play computer games to interact, not to watch. However, with sports games, people do occasionally like to let the game play itself and watch the results, just as if they were watching a real match on TV. This also allows the computer to play simulated matches that the player doesn't want to play; see *Simulating Matches Automatically* later in this chapter.

Victory and Loss Conditions

The victory and loss conditions for a match are the same as in the real sport. However, many games that simulate team or league sports offer players a variety

16

of ways of playing the game, usually referred to simply as modes. (Note that these are not the same as competition modes or gameplay modes.)

- **Season mode.** The player selects a single team (or athlete, for individual sports such as skiing) from all those available and plays a series of matches throughout a season, trying to make it into the championships. The schedule of play for the season and the rules for moving into and up the championship bracket are adopted from the real sport. Some season modes allow a player to play not just one team's matches but every single match played throughout an entire season.

- **Exhibition mode.** In this mode, the players play one single match, but it has no long-term consequences, just like exhibition matches played by real teams. Whoever wins the match wins the game.

- **Sudden death.** As a variant of exhibition mode, players play a match only until the first score is made. Whoever makes the first score wins the game. This is handy for very quick games, although it means that luck plays a much greater role in determining the outcome.

- **Round robin.** Players in a group each take a team and play each other's team a fixed number of times, sometimes just once. Whoever has won the most matches at the end is the winner.

- **Tournament mode.** In a single-elimination tournament, any player who loses any match is dropped, and the winner goes on to play the winner of another match. This requires that the number of players be a power of two. You may organize tournaments in other ways as well.

- **Franchise mode,** also called dynasty mode. The player controls a team over the course of several seasons, trying to build its strength through the years. This mode is often found in games that include mechanisms for hiring athletes and trading them among teams. For games such as tennis, in which most athletes play alone, the equivalent mode is called **career mode**—that is, the player controls the athlete over the course of several years of his or her career.

Opportunities for Creative Play

As sports games are essentially simulations, they offer fewer opportunities for creative play than other genres. However, several do exist:

- **Team creation.** You may give the players the opportunity to create teams of their own, either by choosing athletes from the existing database or by entering new athletes with all their attributes. This will allow players to create dream teams or famous teams from the past. If you want to prevent them from creating unbeatable teams, you can require that the sum of all the attributes of all the athletes on the team must not go over a certain limit. (Strange though it sounds, once players know they can create unbeatable teams or unbeatable play strategies, they lose some respect for the game.)

- **Strategy design.** Players greatly enjoy setting up their own strategies, adjusting how the athletes will behave and what roles they will play in a team sport. You will have to work closely with the programmers, who implement the game's strategy and AI, in order to determine what parameters the user may be allowed to change. One risk of allowing the players to design their own strategy is that they may hit upon some combination that the game AI is completely unable to beat, regardless of the circumstances. Allowing the players to design their own strategies will require the development team to do a lot more testing in order to prevent this.

- **Playing field design.** Most sports rigidly define the shape of the field. However, in a few cases (baseball, cricket), the boundaries of the field may be variable. You can allow the player to edit the shape of the playing field or import new playing fields made in other tools.

Other Features of Sports Games

In this section, we address a few other features of sports games not generally found in other genres.

Invented Sports   From time to time, someone tries to create a sports video game of a completely invented sport as opposed to a simulation of an existing one. Experience shows, however, that this is a risky enterprise. Hardcore sports gamers seldom take an interest in completely new sports; they'd rather play a game that simulates a sport they're already familiar with. Other types of gamers aren't particularly interested in sports games anyway and so aren't very likely to want to play a one-off sports game unless it appeals to them for some other reason. If you're thinking of inventing a new sport, we advise you to design it primarily as a video game rather than designing it as an athletic sport for humans to play and then converting it to a video game. This is how Empire Interactive designed *Speedball;* although theoretically a sport, *Speedball* included powerups and other arcade-game elements to make it more interesting to people who didn't normally like sports games.

One of the trickiest aspects of sports game design is mapping real-world activities to a limited input device. Players are willing to tolerate some awkwardness in the user interface when it's a real sport because they understand the problems, but with an invented sport, they're unlikely to be so generous. When designing a completely new sport, you might consider working backward from the controller to the sport itself, designing around the limitations of your hardware.

Weather   Many sports have special rules regarding weather conditions: Rain stops play in baseball but not in football, and so on. The weather can definitely affect the play. Rain and snow make traction difficult, reducing the athletes' ability to accelerate and lowering the top speed that they can reach. Equipment becomes slippery and more difficult to control when it's wet. Hot, humid days cause athletes to tire out more easily.

Instant Replay   Instant replay is now an essential part of watching sports on television, so naturally video game players want it as well. An instant reply feature is not difficult to design, although it might be difficult to implement, because your game will need to keep track of the exact position and animation step of every athlete and other key objects on the field in each game frame or be able to reliably recreate them. When the player requests an instant replay, the game can play back what the player previously saw. Of course, the amount of data storage available will limit how much information you can keep around in case the player wants to see it again, and natural boundaries tend to suggest themselves: in baseball, the time since the most recent pitch; in American football, the time since the snap. In continuously flowing games such as basketball, you might need to establish an artificial time limit.

A good many games now show an instant replay automatically after important events, to better recreate the experience of watching the sport on television. Some players find this annoying, however, because it breaks up the flow of the game. All sports games should include instant replay, but players should be able to switch the automatic replay off and only bring it up manually if they want it.

The best instant-replay mechanisms allow all the following features for maximum flexibility:

- Play, stop, fast-forward, rewind, and single-frame advance and reverse operations, to allow the player to see exactly what happened at every instant.

- The ability to move the camera in all three dimensions to a different position above the field or court.

- The ability to pitch the camera up and down and to pan (turn it) left and right.

- The ability to lock the camera to a given athlete or to the ball in order to follow that athlete or ball wherever it goes. This is usually done by showing a symbol on the ground that represents the camera's focus of attention. If the symbol is directly under an athlete's feet when the player stops moving the camera, the camera locks onto that athlete.

Instant replay lets the players see the action from perspectives that they can't use when actually playing the game. For the game's publisher and developer, this kind of instant replay is an invaluable tool for grabbing dramatic screen shots or gameplay footage for sales and demonstrations. You should consider it an essential feature of any sports game that you design.

IN THE TRENCHES: Madden NFL Football

Madden NFL Football is one of the longest-established and best-selling game franchises in the history of our industry. From its earliest beginnings on the Apple II, it has grown into a financial powerhouse that produces a new edition on several different platforms every year and makes millions of dollars for its publisher, Electronic Arts. Versions of *Madden* have appeared for personal computers and every major console machine ever produced.

Madden is not redesigned every year, nor is its code rewritten. Electronic Arts updates its artwork and video sequences and adds new features each year, but undertakes a complete overhaul only every four or five years—often when a new generation of game console appears. The majority of the design work each year consists of tuning and improving the gameplay and adding more features. These features expand the football experience to include aspects of the sport that go beyond playing a single match against another team, including:

- Ability to hire and trade athletes among teams, subject to the limitations of the salary cap established by the NFL.
- Participation in the NFL draft.
- Detailed performance statistics on athletes.
- Season, tournament, and practice modes.
- Franchise mode, letting players take a team through several seasons in an effort to build a dynasty.
- A play editor, allowing players to customize their playbooks.
- Madden University, which includes detailed tutorials about offensive and defensive strategies, commentaries on the strengths and weaknesses of each team, and historical background.
- Adjustable AI, enabling players to set the coaching stances of computer-controlled teams to aggressive, neutral, or conservative.
- Arcade mode, a simplified and exaggerated form of the game.

As you can see, even though the sport itself changes little from year to year, new features and details can always be added to a sports game.

▶▶ CONTINUED ON NEXT PAGE

▶▶ CONTINUED

By far the largest single design task in developing *Madden* every year is research: rating the skills of the real athletes who appear in the game, keeping track of which team they're playing for, finding photographs of them, and so on. In addition to researching the athletes, the production team must research the coaches—trying to find out what kinds of plays they like to run, whether they're aggressive or conservative, and so on. The team's playbooks must be updated every year to reflect changes in coaching practice, and the new plays must be tested to make sure that they're effective but not unstoppable.

In short, *Madden* is a highly successful sports game that offers its players a wide range of playing styles, from the quick and easy arcade game to the detailed minutiae of designing plays and adjusting rosters. As a game that tries to do it all, it's well worth studying.

Core Mechanics

Football is brutal only from a distance. In the middle of it there's a calm, a tranquility. . . When the systems interlock, there's a satisfaction to the game that can't be duplicated. There's a harmony.

—Don DeLillo, *End Zone*

Sports games present a number of design issues that designers of other kinds of games rarely encounter. This section treats issues raised by the physics, AI, athlete skill ratings, and other aspects peculiar to sports games.

Physics for Sports Games

During play, your game will be running a physics engine that determines the behavior of moving bodies in the match. The physical behavior of an inanimate object such as a baseball is comparatively easy to implement. The physical behavior of humans, however, is much more complicated. Early sports games tended to treat a running athlete rather like a rocket: She had a velocity vector that gave the speed and direction of her movement and an acceleration vector that gave the force and direction with which she pushed. Modern sports games have much richer simulations with a great many variables, taking into account such things as the friction coefficient of the playing surface—for example, rain and snow make fields slippery and reduce traction.

Designing the physics simulation for a sports game is a highly technical problem and is beyond the scope of this book. However, we offer one caveat: Because a sports game is a simulation of the real world, it is a common error to think that the physics in a sports game should be as realistic as possible. It shouldn't be, for two reasons:

- First, the player is not actually running around on the playing field herself; he is sitting in a chair, watching a screen, and controlling an athlete through a handheld controller. He has neither the immediate experience of being on the field nor the precise control over his movements that a real athlete does.

- Second, the player is not a professional athlete. There is a good reason why only a small number of people can hit a baseball pitched at 95 miles per hour. The length of time that the ball is within reach of the bat is about 0.04 seconds. It's simply not realistic to expect that an ordinary person looking at a video screen without the benefit of depth perception could react quickly enough to "hit" a ball thrown at this speed.

For both of these reasons, it's necessary to adjust the physics to make the game playable. We slow the pitch so as to give the batter a reasonable chance of hitting the ball, and we artificially adjust the position of the bat so that it intersects the path of the ball. Whether the physics perfectly copies that of the real world doesn't matter as much as whether the game seems to be producing a reasonable simulation of the sport as it is played by professionals. Even in a highly realistic game, your objective is to provide an enjoyable experience, not a mathematical simulation of nature.

Rating the Athletes

One of the biggest tasks you take on in designing a sports game is developing a rating system for the skills and athletic abilities of all the athletes in the game. The rating system provides the raw data that the physics engine needs to accurately simulate the behavior of the athletes. As your programming team develops the physics engine and game AI, you should work with them to determine what ratings are needed. Researching the athletes' performances and setting the ratings for them can take many months, and the lead designer will probably want to delegate it to junior designers or assistant producers.

In most team games, all athletes share one set of ratings, plus specialized ratings that apply only to athletes playing a particular position.

Common Ratings   These are examples of the kinds of ratings that might be common to all the athletes in a game:

- **Speed.** The athlete's maximum moving (running or skating or swimming) speed under ideal conditions.

- **Agility.** A measure of the athlete's ability to change directions while moving.

- **Weight.** The athlete's weight, which affects the force he transmits in a collision and the inertia he has when struck by someone else.

- **Acceleration.** The rate at which the athlete can reach top speed.

- **Jumping.** The height to which the athlete can jump.

- **Endurance.** The rate at which the athlete gets tired during the course of the game.

- **Injury resistance.** The probability that an athlete will be injured.

Specialized Ratings   Some ratings apply to a specific position—for this example, we'll use the quarterback in American football:

- **Passing strength.** The distance that the quarterback can throw the ball.

- **Passing accuracy.** The precision with which the quarterback can throw the ball.

- **Dexterity.** The quarterback's general dexterity in handling the ball. This affects his chances of dropping the snap or fumbling a handoff.

- **Awareness.** The quarterback's ability to sense that he's about to be tackled and to try to get out of the way.

Athlete AI Design

In action games and first-person shooters, the player's AI-driven opponents typically exhibit a small number of behaviors each triggered by a specific event (appearance of the player on the scene, being shot at, and so on). When together in a group, the AI seldom assigns special roles to particular individuals or instructs them to help each other. It's every monster for itself.

These kinds of actions aren't acceptable in a sports game. People don't mind if a monster in a first-person shooter wanders aimlessly around, but the athletes in a sports game must behave like humans, and that means deliberate, intelligent action. Particularly in team games, each athlete works with the others on the team to accomplish particular goals. The position the athlete plays dictates behavior to some extent, but within those boundaries, the athlete still must respond intelligently to a number of possible events. In a relatively simple simulation such as tennis, there might not be many of these events, but a highly complex simulation such as American football, with 22 players on the field at a time, presents hundreds of them.

Defining the State Space   The play in a sports match can be broken down into *states* that are defined primarily by the rules and secondarily by the tactics and strategy of the game. For example, the period of time before a tennis player serves the ball is one state, and the rules dictate where she may stand and what

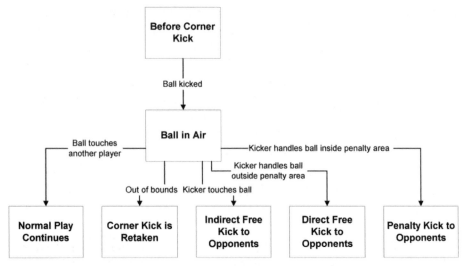

FIGURE 16.2 A flowchart detailing part of the corner kick situation in soccer.

actions she may take (and likewise for her opponent). The moment she serves the ball, the game enters a new state. The moment the ball passes over the net, it enters another one, and so on. The best way to design sports-game AI is to map out a game's states as a giant flowchart. There could be far more states than you realize at first. Corner kick in soccer is not just one state but several: the period before the ball is kicked, after the kick but before the ball touches another athlete, after it has been touched by another athlete, and so on. See Figure 16.2 for a partial example.

Consult the official rules of the sport as you construct the flowchart; they often describe states in detail, with special rules applying to each. However, the rules alone are not enough—rules describe game states for the purposes of listing legal and illegal actions, but not for purposes of tactics or strategy. Whenever something changes that requires the athletes to adopt a different tactic, the game has moved into a different state.

Setting Collective and Individual Goals   After you define the game states, you can start thinking about what the team should do in each state—where each athlete should be trying to go and what he should be trying to do to support the team's collective goal at that moment. In some cases, these activities are defined with reference to a specific individual on the opposing team, for example, trying to prevent an opposing player from doing his job. The software must have a way of matching up athletes with their opponents, just as the real athletes do.

After you define what the team should be trying to accomplish in a particular state and have assigned each athlete a role, you then must define exactly how the athlete is to perform that role: what direction he moves, what other movements he makes, which animations should be displayed, and so on.

An athlete with nothing to do shouldn't just stand still. Most sports games include *fidgets*, short animations in which the athlete shifts his weight, stretches his arms, or makes some other neutral action every few seconds. If play is under way, an athlete not closely involved—the third baseman on a fly ball to right field, for instance—should turn and watch the action.

Like war games, team sports games are good candidates for using hierarchical finite state machines to produce the artificially intelligent behavior required. Two-player sports can use simple finite state machines, one for each player. See the discussion on finite state machines at the end of Chapter 14, "Strategy Games."

Injuries

I wouldn't ever set out to hurt anybody deliberately unless it was, you know, important—like a league game or something.

—Dick Butkus, NFL linebacker

Injuries are a sad but common side effect of sports, and serious simulations take them into account. Because injuries occur somewhat randomly, they're outside the player's control and can be frustrating. Most sports games allow the players to turn off injuries if they don't like the effect that injuries have on the game.

Although it's possible for an athlete to injure herself simply by running or jumping, this doesn't provide the player with any visible explanation for why the injury occurred. A lot of sports games therefore limit injuries to cases of some kind of collision, ordinarily between two athletes. To determine whether an injury occurs, you should include such factors as the relative speed of the two athletes, their weights, their respective susceptibilities to injury, and a random probability just to introduce some uncertainty into the situation. The heavier an athlete is, the more force she imparts in a collision, and it is the force that does the damage to the other athlete.

The stress of playing some positions, such as pitching in baseball, can injure an athlete without a collision, with injuries becoming more likely the longer the pitcher stays in the game. You can compute the probability of an injury on every pitch and raise the probability slightly with each ball thrown.

You can also decide which part of the body sustains the injury and the length of time for which it will disable the athlete. Study reports of injuries and recovery times for the sport you are simulating. If your game tracks athletes over a period of time, you should consider the cumulative effect of injury and recovery time on their careers.

Arcade Mode Versus Simulation Mode

Switching into arcade mode skews the play toward lots of action and relatively few slow-paced game states, such as strikeouts or walks. Arcade mode makes the game more exciting at the expense of realism; simulation mode makes it a more accurate simulation of the real sport at some expense in fun. In baseball, for example, an athlete does well to achieve a .333 batting average—that is, gets a hit only once for every three at bats. Some players may find that a little dull. Switching the game to arcade mode could let the player get a hit 50 percent of the time or even more. In American football, you could artificially increase the number of completed passes by improving the quarterback's throwing accuracy and the receiver's catching skills. If you allow the player to switch between arcade mode and simulation mode, he can adjust the behavior of the game to suit his tastes.

To implement arcade mode, you'll have to decide what sort of changes to the real game would make it more exciting. If you want your game to have both arcade and simulation modes, we recommend that you start with the serious simulation first and then create the adjustments that make it arcadelike. Serious simulations are much more difficult to tune, and it's important to get them right first. If you start with an arcadelike design and then try to make it serious, you might never get it right.

Simulating Matches Automatically

Sports games that simulate an entire season for a whole league of teams often provide a means of simulating matches automatically without the player's having to play them. Each team in professional baseball plays 162 matches in a season; with 30 teams and 2 teams in each match, this totals 2,430 matches—only the most rabid fan would want to play each match personally. To generate results for matches that the player doesn't play, you need a way of simulating a match. Of course, you'll want the resulting scores to accurately reflect the relative strengths of the teams: A bad team should be able to beat a good team occasionally but not often.

Computer Versus Computer   The simplest way to simulate matches automatically is to let the computer play out the match in computer versus computer mode (as described in *Competition Modes*, earlier in this chapter) and record the results. A game with a good simulation model should produce scores that reflect the real abilities of the competitors.

However, if the player wants to generate results for a match that she doesn't want to play herself, she probably wants it done quickly. You can speed up the process by turning off the graphics. Because displaying the graphics often takes up the majority of the computer's time, an entire match can be simulated invisibly in a few seconds, and the computer can report only the result. Electronic Arts' *Earl Weaver Baseball* game did this successfully. It makes the programming more complicated, however, because throughout the whole program, there have to be repeated checks to see if the game is in simulation mode or whether display is required. When you implement a nondisplayed mode like this, test the game to be sure that the results without graphics are the same as those with graphics.

Faking It   The alternative many games adopt is to fake it—in effect, to roll dice to generate game scores. The dice are loaded somewhat so that good teams get high scores and bad teams get low ones, and whichever team rolls the highest score wins the match.

You will need to devise a suitable algorithm for generating point values; in games such as American football and rugby, in which different kinds of scores produce different numbers of points (touchdown, field goal, and so on), certain score values are much more common than others. It's extremely rare, for example, for a team to end an American football game with a score of 2. You'll also need to make sure that your algorithm creates reasonable scores and a reasonably random distribution of scores. No professional soccer game should ever end with a winning score over about 15, and even that will be rare; your algorithm should produce many more games with winning scores of 4 or less.

Unfortunately, the dice-rolling technique doesn't generate any statistics other than the scores themselves. In a particularly statistics-rich sport such as baseball, if you don't generate performance data for each individual athlete, some fans will consider your game to be a lightweight simulation rather than a serious one. It's up to you to decide just how important that market is to you and how much effort you're prepared to exert to meet their expectations.

Home-Field Advantage   Considerable debate has raged over the years about whether to build a home-field advantage into sports games. Although the home-field advantage is statistically significant in a number of sports, we recommend against it. Players like to feel that they are playing a fair game, and if they know that the odds are artificially stacked against them whenever they play an away game, they will resent it. It's also unclear exactly how the home-field advantage should be implemented. Fans normally observe the home-field advantage from win-loss statistics, but of course, the computer can't simply turn a loss into a win. You could shave off a percentage of goal-scoring attempts, but even this slight intervention is likely to generate odd side effects. If a scoring attempt that clearly should have succeeded fails for no visible reason, the players are bound to notice it.

The Game World

The setting of your game will be the normal venue for the sport, usually a stadium or an arena. It adds a great deal of verisimilitude to present these as accurate copies of real places. Players enjoy being able to recognize the architectural details of their favorite stadiums. Some sports, such as basketball or American football, require a playing area of a fixed shape and size, but others do not—different baseball fields famously have different effects on gameplay. Some sports, such as skiing and bobsledding, take place in venues that vary enormously and require a great deal of practice to learn.

Weather significantly affects games played outdoors. Rain hampers traction on a grass field or turns a racetrack to mud, and snow makes everything worse—even skiers have to adapt their technique if there's fresh powder on the giant slalom. Players run more slowly and carefully. Wind affects the flight of balls, javelins, or arrows, testing the athlete's accuracy. These factors all add enjoyable variety to a game.

The crowd also contributes significantly to the setting. Although you won't want to devote a lot of graphical resources to spectators, the sounds of a crowd add greatly to the atmosphere. Increase the volume at tense moments. Let the players hear chants if it's the kind of match at which spectators chant; add cheering after a score by the home team and a sudden silence after a score by the visitors. Horns, whistles, and vendors calling out, "Ice-cold beer here!" are all part of the experience.

Licenses, Trademarks, and Publicity Rights

Many years ago, small developers could make and sell computer games using names such as *NFL* and get away with it because the National Football League never knew about it. You can't do this now. Interactive entertainment is big business, and you have to be scrupulously careful to avoid violating trademarks or personal publicity rights.

Team and League Trademarks   The exact details vary from league to league and country to country, but generally in America the league holds the license to use the names, logos, uniform designs, and other indicia of all the teams in a league, plus the name and logo of the league itself. You or your publisher will have to negotiate an agreement with the league to use these symbols in your game. Before Electronic Arts signed an agreement with the NFL, early versions of *John Madden Football* referred to teams only by their town names (such as San Francisco or Chicago) rather than by their team names (the 49ers and the Bears) and did not show any logos, displaying the uniforms in colors similar to, but not exactly the same as, those used by the teams. You can pull this trick, too, if you dare, but you're risking a lawsuit if you use the exact color combination of a real team.

A variety of governing bodies in different countries around the world manage individual sports such as gymnastics or figure skating. The names and indicia of particular events, such as the Kentucky Derby, belong to the organizations that produce them—in this case, the Churchill Downs racetrack. In recent years, these groups have begun to exploit their intellectual property rights in a variety of ways, so they tend to come down hard on anything that seems to be an infringement. Don't assume that just because an event has been around for decades you can freely use its name.

Personal Publicity Rights   You cannot use the name or photograph of a real athlete without permission. An athlete's name and likeness make up part of his personal publicity rights, and of course, famous athletes sell the rights to use their names for millions of dollars when they endorse a particular product as an individual. You might need to negotiate with an organization that licenses the rights to use all the athletes' names collectively. This might be the league in some cases; in others, however, including the NFL and Major League Baseball, you have to contact the athletes' unions. Unless you have the endorsement of a specific athlete, you must make sure that your game displays all athletes in approximately the same way, or endorsement could be implied. You can't make it look as if an athlete has endorsed your game when that's not the case.

Photographs present further difficulties. You must obtain a license from the person *in* the photograph and also the photograph's copyright holder (usually the person who *took* the photograph). Again, some governing bodies use special clearinghouses for these kinds of things: NFL Photos, a special department of the NFL, licenses still photos for all the photographers who are accredited to take pictures at NFL matches. The license from the copyright holder, however, does not grant you the personal publicity rights of the athlete in the picture; you have to obtain those separately. You can also license photos from the trading card companies, as well as from journalistic bodies such as the Associated Press, and from private photo libraries.

In short, the whole issue of rights in sports games is a legal minefield. Nowadays, even the stadiums might claim special rights, and many stadium owners auction the name of the stadium to the highest bidder, as with 3Com Park in San Francisco. As a designer, you probably won't have to deal with obtaining all these licenses yourself, but you should know that it's not safe to specify simply that a game will use all the team and athlete names and photos. Obtaining them and the right to use them is a very costly and time-consuming business. It's best to design the game in such a way that it doesn't depend on having these things unless you're certain that they will be available.

Audio Commentary

Most sports games try to reproduce the experience of watching the sport on television. An important part of that experience is hearing the announcers' commentary, or play-by-play. Most TV and radio sports broadcasts include at least two people, the play-by-play announcer and the color commentator. The play-by-play announcer describes the action on a moment-by-moment basis. The color commentator, usually a retired coach or player, offers insights into strategy and tactics, as well as background material on the teams or individual athletes. To make the player feel she's right there in the stands, you might include a third voice, that of the stadium announcer over the public address system. His remarks tend to be quite formulaic, although they do occasionally include requests to move badly parked cars, retrieve found children, and so on.

To study what kinds of things your audio commentary will need to do, record a TV broadcast of a real match and then transcribe everything that is said and who said it. Do this for two or three matches, and you will begin to notice patterns in the play-by-play: The announcers tend to read out the score at particular times, they use certain repetitive language, and so on. As you watch the match on videotape, take note of the different kinds of events that occur and the different remarks these events elicit from the commentators. The events that provoke a reaction from the color commentator aren't necessarily the same events that trigger a response from the play-by-play announcer. The color commentator speaks at more dramatic moments or when an athlete has done something particularly spectacular (or particularly bad). For example, in tennis, you might have a color comment such as, "She's having a terrible time with those double faults" when an athlete commits four double faults in a single game. Remember, a commentator would use this line only once, not after every subsequent double fault.

When you need to create commentary for a set of match events, sit down with the programmers and discuss the events to make sure the software can detect them. Some, such as a strikeout in baseball, will be uncomplicated, but many events will be judgment calls. A dropped pass in football that the athlete really *should* have caught, for instance, is not so easily detectable; you can detect the dropped pass, but what determines whether the receiver should have caught it? The probability of the receiver's catching the pass must be calculated from such things as the receiver's dexterity rating and the accuracy with which the quarterback threw the pass in the first place—provided that the ball wasn't tipped away by a defender. It's always best to err on the side of caution in these cases: Don't design judgment calls that the player is likely to disagree with, or he'll think you've delivered a stupid game. As the saying goes, "It's better to remain silent and be thought a fool than open one's mouth and remove all doubt."

Don't forget the introductory and wrap-up material at the beginning and end of the match—commentary such as, "Welcome to Invesco Field for today's game between the New England Patriots and the Denver Broncos. It's a cold and windy day."

For more detailed information on writing commentary scripts, including the many tricky issues associated with assembling commentary out of speech fragments, we suggest you read Chapter 13, "Interchangeable Dialogue Content" of *Game Writing: Narrative Skills for Videogames,* edited by Chris Bateman (Bateman, 2006).

The Presentation Layer

Sports games offer some of the most beautifully realistic graphics and audio of any genre, and their presentation features borrow heavily from those seen on television. TV sports presentations have their own particular look and feel, which change from time to time, and many game art directors take their cue from them.

Interaction Model

The interaction model in sports games varies considerably depending on the sport, but in most cases, the player controls an avatar who is an athlete in the match. In one-on-one sports such as tennis, this is straightforward, but in team sports, the player's control typically switches automatically from one athlete to another as the focus of play changes. In basketball games, for example, control switches to the athlete who has the ball. If the player's team is on defense, most games allow the player to choose which athlete to control and allow him to switch quickly from one athlete to another as conditions change. This often requires significant changes to the user interface as play progresses; the functions of the buttons have to change if the player assumes control of an athlete with a specialized function—for example, switching from the thrower to a sweeper in curling after the rock has been delivered.

Perspective

In one-on-one sports games, the perspective is seldom difficult to manage. Choose a spot where you have a clear view of the athletes and where their movements and activities will map neatly onto the machine's input devices. As a general rule, you shouldn't do sports games in the first person. A lot of the fun of watching a sport is in seeing the athletes exercise their skills. In first person, you can't see your avatar doing that. For example, you could make a tennis game in the first person, but you wouldn't get to see your athlete playing tennis, and you might not even get to see your racket hit the ball. An overhead perspective, with your tennis player at the bottom of the screen and your opponent at the top, presents a much more natural view and lets you see both athletes running, jumping, serving, and so on.

Managing the perspective for a team game is trickier, particularly when the focus of attention moves from place to place. With most soccerlike games, an end view or a side view, from a somewhat elevated position, works best. American football, however, is almost unplayable from a side view because too many athletes block the player's view of other athletes, and you can't see gaps in the line.

Sports in which actions take place at widely separated locations pose a special challenge in choosing a perspective. In most sports, the action takes place around one focal point: the leader of a race, the ball in most ballgames, the skier on the slope. Sports such as baseball and cricket, however, offer two focal points: on the ball and on the runners. In baseball, the two focal points can be separated by as much as 400 feet. You can't show both the runners and the ball without zooming out to a blimp view so high that it's difficult to see anything clearly.

Most baseball video games implement a picture-in-picture solution: The camera follows the ball, but a small diagram of the baseball diamond in one corner of the screen shows the positions of the runners, often indicated by colored dots (see Figure 16.3). When a runner reaches a base, his dot changes color to indicate that he is safe. The player controlling the fielders watches the main

FIGURE 16.3 *MVP Baseball 2004.* Note the inset showing the baserunner's position as a circle on the diamond and a small window showing the runner himself.

screen, and the one controlling the runners watches the diagram (keeping one eye on the main screen to see if the ball is coming). Because cricket uses only two stumps instead of four bases, this arrangement works even better.

User Interface Design

In most other genres, the controls work the same way in most situations, and if their functions change, they do so only in response to explicit actions by the player. Sports games are unusual in this regard; the user interface changes on a second-by-second basis, depending on conditions in the match itself. American football is a particularly complex example. On each play, the player on offense selects the formation and play to be run; calls signals and makes adjustments at the line of scrimmage; and then takes the snap and either hands off the ball, passes it, or runs with it himself. If he passes it, control switches to the receiver and a whole series of new options for running, jumping, diving, and dodging defenders comes into play. Each of these different states requires that certain moves or choices be assigned to buttons on the controller, and these assignments change rapidly as play progresses.

The hardest thing about sports game user interface design is that you have to map athletic activities—complex motions of the whole human body—onto a game machine's input device, typically a handheld controller with binary buttons. Think about what kinds of things the player will want to do at each stage of the game and how best to make them available. Whenever possible, make sure that similar actions in different modes use the same buttons; for example, if the athlete can jump in both offensive and defensive modes, assign *jump* to the same button in both cases.

In team games, the player normally controls one athlete at a time. The game generally displays a circle or star under the feet of the athlete currently being controlled. A good many games also draw symbols on the field to help the player overcome the lack of depth perception—the spot where a flying ball is due to land, for example.

When the player's team is on the defensive, include a button to automatically change control to the most appropriate defending athlete (in soccerlike games, this is usually the one nearest to the ball). Another useful pair of buttons allows the player to cycle control forward and backward through all the athletes on the team.

Most sports games avoid pull-down menus and anything else that resembles the user interface for a computer's desktop so as not to interfere with the fantasy. Pop-up windows and semitransparent overlays make more sense, particularly if you can design them to look like the graphics seen on TV. Styles vary from year to year; we suggest that you watch matches on TV for examples of how to handle overlay graphics.

Unless you're simulating archery or bowling (the athlete aims and lets go), a sports game is essentially an action game. No matter how complex the sport is, the user interface must be as smooth and intuitive as you can make it.

Summary

A good sports game design requires compromises. We do not yet have the computing power to simulate a real sport in all of its complexity and detail on a home computer or video game console—and even if we did, we still don't have input and output devices that allow a player to feel as if he's really down on the field. Someday, when we perfect virtual reality and make home computers as powerful as today's supercomputers, we might be able to do this. In the meantime, it's the job of the sports game designer to fit the sport to the machine. Sports game design doesn't require nearly as much raw creativity as designing an adventure game or a role-playing game. It's a more subtle process that entails endless tuning and tweaking to find the right balance between realism and playability. When you get it right, you have a product that can sell for years and years.

Test Your Skills

MULTIPLE CHOICE QUESTIONS

1. A manager game is

    A. a game that allows the player to play as a team manager in addition to his role as an athlete on the pitch.

    B. a business simulation that doesn't belong in the sports genre at all.

    C. a game in which the player serves as a team manager, but all matches are simulated automatically by the computer.

    D. a game in which the player's opponent is managed by the computer, instead of another human player.

2. You might have to relax the real-world rules of the sport you are simulating because

    A. video game players can't be expected to know the rules of the sport.

    B. there are games in which the action happens simultaneously in far-flung areas of the field, making display a problem.

    C. you may not want to penalize the player for things that aren't his fault, such as holding penalties in football.

    D. if you want to implement a single-player mode you can't provide a league-play experience.

3. Above the level of the individual match, sports games may offer modes. This chapter discussed several of these modes, but *not*

    A. sudden death.

    B. franchise.

    C. round robin.

    D. exhaustive.

4. Inventing a new sport for a video game is seldom a recipe for success for several reasons, one of which is

    A. there's no way of implementing a home field advantage when you've invented the sport.

    B. they're usually designed for the educational market to try to make learning fun.

    C. sports fans won't be interested in a made-up sport, and video gamers who aren't sports fans would probably prefer another genre.

    D. it's not clear what the interaction model should be when working with an invented sport.

16

5. Instant replays

    A. should allow the players to see the action from perspectives they can't use when playing the game.

    B. must never be implemented so that the play seems to go backwards.

    C. are cluttered by other audio so should include only color commentary and play-by-play.

    D. must allow the player to replay any game in the match at any time.

6. Why is it okay to relax the physics of the real world when you are trying to accurately simulate an existing sport?

    A. Players don't have precise control over the movements of their athletes.

    B. Most players can't handle real-world sports physics, such as baseballs pitched at 95 mph.

    C. Watching the game on the screen deprives the player of some of the input needed to accurately play in real-world conditions, such as depth perception.

    D. All of the above.

7. Which of the following common ways of rating an athlete is *not* correctly paired with a game world action that is affected by that rating?

    A. Agility—probability that a tennis player who is moving to the right can return a shot hit to her left.

    B. Injury resistance—probability that a football player will be hurt in a tackle.

    C. Dexterity—probability that a basketball player can steal the ball from the other team.

    D. Weight—probability that the manager will drop the player from the team.

8. Which of the following is *not* a reason that AI for team games is more complicated than AI for action games?

    A. Enemies in an action game do not have to help each other out, but athletes on a team must act cooperatively.

    B. In action games, monsters can idly walk around when not occupied by game events, but in a sports simulation, athletes not involved in the action still have to be controlled so as to behave normally.

    C. Each individual athlete must have a goal for each game state, whereas monsters or aliens or other foes in action games generally have no individual goals.

    D. Athletes have free will and can disobey the coach, while monsters must obey the commands of the big boss of the level in which they appear.

9. Why might you decide to include an arcade mode for your sports simulation?

   A. Having the players put money in the machine is extra profit.

   B. To cater to players who want a game with more action and less realism.

   C. Arcade mode includes all the sounds of the stands, even hot dog vendors.

   D. You can knock together an arcade game quickly and fine tune the real simulation later.

10. Why might you want to have the computer simulate a match?

    A. To get around user interface problems in mapping real-world action to buttons.

    B. It's a way for you to balance the game by allowing a bad team to beat a good team occasionally.

    C. It's the only way to simulate league play when you have fewer players than teams.

    D. So the player doesn't have to play all possible matches to get to the championship.

11. If the player doesn't want to play all the matches in a tournament himself, which is the best method for generating scores and performance statistics for unplayed matches?

    A. Fake it by using a good algorithm to generate reasonable scores.

    B. Let the computer play itself and the numbers will fall out naturally.

    C. Download fake data from a website.

    D. Use a random number generator to create all the data.

12. Which of the following can be used without violating trademarks or personal publicity rights?

    A. Names of towns the teams come from, such as San Francisco or Chicago.

    B. Uniforms in team colors, if you don't use the team's name.

    C. Names of deceased players, such as Mickey Mantle or Knut Rockne.

    D. Pictures of Olympic athletes who are amateurs.

16

13. Which is true of perspective in one-on-one sports games such as tennis?

   A. The most natural way of presenting one-on-one sports is a first-person view.

   B. All you need is a spot with a clear view of the athletes, in which their activities map neatly onto the input devices.

   C. Players want the experience of being at the match, so you should shift perspective from one athlete to the other, alternating quickly back and forth to follow the ball.

   D. Don't bother with a blimp's eye view; the players will not want to see the court from overhead because that will spoil the illusion that the player is really there.

14. The main problem in designing the user interface for a sports game is that

   A. the controls—buttons, joysticks, mouse—do not always map conveniently to the actions required of an athlete.

   B. you have to convince players to overcome habits they formed when playing other games with the same control devices.

   C. the time it takes between when the button is pressed and when the computer responds is too slow for the fast-changing game states you get in sports.

   D. players want one button for every athlete in the match, and with team sports this overwhelms the input devices.

15. The cutting edge of user interface design for sports games includes

   A. displays that look like ordinary PC browser windows because that's what the player is comfortable with already.

   B. a unique color for the athlete that is the player's avatar (or in team sports, the athlete currently controlling the ball) so the player can always find it quickly.

   C. semitransparent overlays designed to look like the graphics you see when watching sports on TV.

   D. pie charts for quick lookup of each athlete's career statistics.

▶▶ Case Study

Choose a sports game that you believe, from your own experience of playing it, is an excellent example of the genre (or use one your instructor has assigned). It should be a team sport rather than an individual

▶▶ CONTINUED ON NEXT PAGE

>> CONTINUED

sport, and a real one rather than an invented one. Write a report documenting the features that place it in this genre as opposed to another one and explaining why you believe it is superior to others of its kind. Be sure to cover at least the following areas:

- Document the athlete attributes that the game implements, including any special abilities that are associated with a particular position or role.
- How well do you feel that the game simulates the strategy and tactics of the real sport? Are there any particular strengths or weaknesses? If so, point them out.
- Discuss the extent to which the game correctly implements the rules of the sport. Are there any rules that it does not enforce? How does it handle infractions that are not necessarily under the control of the player?
- Explore the user interface in the primary gameplay mode. Briefly document the mechanism mapping the athlete's body onto the control device. Note important indicators that appear on the screen and discuss how they improve the playing experience.
- Address the management features that the game offers. Can the player manage a team over the course of an entire season or several seasons? What challenges and actions are available for doing so? What kinds of things does the player have to think about *off* the field that he doesn't have to think about *on* the field? If the player's decisions during a match can affect the gameplay between matches, indicate how.

The design questions in the next section may help you to think about these issues. In your report, use screen shots to illustrate your points. End the case study with suggestions for improvement or, if you feel the game cannot be improved, suggestions for additional features that might be fun to have in the game.

Alternatively, choose a game that you believe is particularly *bad*. Do the same case study, explaining what is wrong and how it could be improved.

A case study is neither a review nor a design document; it is an analysis. You are not attempting to reverse-engineer the entire game but simply to explain how it works in a general way. Your instructor will tell you the desired scope of the assignment; we recommend from five to twenty pages.

DESIGN QUESTIONS

In designing a sports game, consider the following questions as a starting point:

1. What sport are you simulating? Is it a real sport or a made-up one? If it's real, do you want to get a license from a governing body?

2. What are the rules of the sport? If it's a real sport, can you really implement them all, or will the game be limited to a subset?

3. What competition modes will be offered—single-player, competitive, cooperative, teams? Which ones make sense for the sport and which don't?

4. In addition to playing a single match, what other game modes will be offered? Season, tournament, franchise, career?

5. What is the best perspective for playing the sport? Directly overhead, from the sidelines, from some other angle? What intelligence needs to be built into the camera to make the game easy to play? How will you handle displaying actions at widely separated points?

6. How do you map the actions of an athlete or an entire team of athletes to the controls available to the player? Will the functions of the buttons need to change during the course of play? When and why? What additional markings should be drawn on the field of play to compensate for the player's lack of depth perception? What pop-up windows over the play will the player need, and how do you prevent those from obscuring the action? When play is not in progress, how does the rest of the user interface look and work?

7. What roles will the player play in the sport? Athlete, coach, general manager? When does the player switch from one to another and why?

8. What's the general structure of the game? What screens are needed, and how do they lead from one to another? Can the player trade athletes among teams in the middle of the season, for example?

9. What changes must be made to the physics of the sport to make it playable by ordinary mortals?

10. What characteristics describe an athlete's abilities? How will they affect the way her behavior looks on the screen? Will some athletes have ratings peculiar to the positions they play?

11. What states can the game be in, even in times between active play? How does an athlete behave in each state? What are her goals in each state, and in team play, what is the collective goal of the team in each state?

How does the individual athlete's behavior contribute to meeting the team's goal?

12. Are you going to offer automatic simulation of matches? How will that be done?

13. What will the audio commentary be like? What events will it cover?

14. How does instant replay work?

Chapter 17

Vehicle Simulations

Chapter Objectives

After reading this chapter and completing the exercises, you will be able to do the following:

- Know the different types of vehicle simulation games.
- Know how the design of the game world influences the player's perception of speed.
- Know some ways to design artificial opponents for the game.
- Understand the distinctions between civilian and military flight simulations.
- Be familiar with the various views often used in vehicle simulation interfaces.

Introduction

Vehicle simulations create the feeling of driving or flying a vehicle, real or imaginary. In simulations of real vehicles, one of the chief goals is verisimilitude, an (apparently!) close relationship to reality. You can expect your players to know a lot about these machines and to want an experience that is at least visually similar to that of really controlling one. The machine's gross performance characteristics (speed and maneuverability) should also be similar to reality, although its finer details probably can't be, for reasons we'll discuss in this chapter.

If you're designing an imaginary vehicle, you're free to create any kind of driving experience that you like without being restricted by such things as gravity, G-forces, fuel capacity, and so on. Your game really needs to just create the feeling of movement; you can place whatever limitations you like on that movement.

In this chapter, we cover the definition of vehicle simulations and then explore the core mechanics of each. We focus the chapter primarily on driving and flying simulations, spending a lot of time discussing the creation of military simulations. The game environment requirements, the look and camera angles best suited for these simulations, and the behaviors of artificial opponents are also reviewed in depth.

What Are Vehicle Simulations?

Vehicle simulations cover several environments and game mechanics. They can be in the air, on the ground, on water, or in space. They can be races against other players or artificially intelligent opponents, or they can involve exploration or simply the experience of using the vehicle. The most common element is the sense of verisimilitude: Players are looking for an experience that feels the way it would truly feel to drive, fly, or otherwise control a vehicle. Because most of us have driven cars, we have an expectation of how that feels. But most of us don't know what it feels like to drive a car at 200 miles per hour or to drive a car that has various weapons installed. Most of us have not experienced flying a plane ourselves, but we know what being in a plane feels like.

Simulations vary from realistically representing the way the vehicle handles on the road or in the air to adding game mechanics such as combat, racing, special challenges like skids or slaloms, and so on. While space and water vehicle simulations also exist, they tend to follow the same fundamental features as the flying and driving simulations. Not only do the same physics generally apply, but the additional game mechanics and features are often the same.

Game Features

Flight simulators fall into two general categories: civilian and military. Civilian flight sims don't include aerial combat; they're mostly about the way the aircraft look and perform and so are often quite realistic. Military flight sims have to be simplified for reasons we discuss later in this chapter, but they offer exciting physical and tactical challenges.

Driving simulators also tend to fall into two categories: *organized racing* and *imaginary racing*. Organized racing simulators try to reproduce the experience of driving a racing car or motorcycle in an existing racing class, such as IndyCar NASCAR, or Formula 1. To use the official name and indicia of any of these racing organizations, you will need to get a license (see *Intellectual Property Rights* later). Imaginary racing games are just that: games about racing in imaginary situations, driving madly through cities or the countryside or even fantasy environments.

The players themselves also fall into two categories. The purists demand highly accurate simulations of real vehicles with all their quirks and limitations; if a purist forgets to retract the flaps after takeoff, he wants those flaps to be damaged by excessive airspeed and to be stuck in the down position with appropriate consequences for the plane's handling characteristics. On the other hand, casual players don't care about the details as long as they can fly or drive around, preferably fast, and maybe even shoot at things.

The Player's Role

The player's role in a flight simulator seems quite straightforward: It's that of a pilot. In single-seat aircraft, that's all that is required. However, if you're going to simulate larger aircraft such as bombers or two-seat fighters, you'll have to decide how you want to handle the varying roles available. In LucasArts' excellent World War II simulator *Their Finest Hour,* the player could play any of the waist and tail gun positions of the Junkers JU-88 bomber while leaving the plane on autopilot, or he could set the guns to fire automatically at any target that came into view. To drop the bombs, however, he had to take over the bombardier's position personally. Three-Sixty Pacific's game *Megafortress* required the player to manage no fewer than five different stations: pilot, copilot, navigator, electronic warfare specialist, and offensive weapons officer. Each station had its own instrument panel and responsibilities, and the player had to move constantly from one to another to check on conditions and respond to emergencies. At times when the player was away from the pilot's seat, the plane flew on autopilot toward the next waypoint.

In racing-oriented driving games, the player's role is that of a racing driver most of the time, but the more serious simulations, such as *IndyCar Racing,* also allow the player to be a mechanic, modifying the angle of the airfoils, changing tires to compensate for weather conditions, and so on.

Competition Modes

A few vehicle simulations aren't really games because they don't offer the player a goal, apart from learning to control the vehicle. They don't have any rules other than the laws of physics. Most vehicle simulations, however, offer driving or flying within a competitive context, either a race or a battle of some kind.

The competition modes of military flight simulators resemble those of first-person shooters: single-player modes against artificial opponents, multiplayer death matches (every player for himself), and team-based play. Civilian flight simulators usually offer only a single-player mode, although they sometimes also allow races and follow-my-lead competitions. Driving simulators are generally single-player games or multiplayer races and are seldom team-based.

Both military flight simulators and organized race-driving simulators often include a career mode, in which the player creates a pilot or driver and follows his career (trying not to get him killed, of course), racking up victories and collecting performance statistics.

These games also include campaign modes. In a driving game's campaign mode, the player, as a race driver, tries to win in a real racing circuit, collecting points according to the official rules of the circuit.

In military flight simulators, the campaign mode can work in a variety of ways. In one type of campaign mode, the game offers a series of missions, one at a time, in which the player must achieve a specified victory condition before going on to the next mission; completing all the missions constitutes winning the campaign. In another type of campaign mode, the player can play all the missions in order, whether she meets the mission objectives or not. However, if she plays through all of them without achieving enough mission objectives, she loses the campaign. The better she fights on any given occasion, the more chance she has of winning the war in the long run, but she can still afford to lose the occasional battle. This more closely approximates what happens in a real war, but as the designer, you must provide clear feedback to the player about how she's doing as she goes along.

Gameplay and Victory Conditions

The primary challenge in playing any vehicle simulator is in controlling the vehicle: learning to speed it up, slow it down, and steer it without crashing it into something. Without being able to feel the G-forces on his body, the player has to depend on other cues to determine how fast he is going and how hard he is braking.

In the case of flight simulators, you can make this challenge simple, requiring the player to know almost nothing about aerodynamics, or extremely difficult, accurately modeling the behavior of an airplane. Unlike a car, airplanes respond rather slowly to their controls, often beginning to execute a maneuver a few seconds after the player has first moved the yoke or joystick. Players used to driving a car will tend to overcontrol the plane; finding that it doesn't respond immediately when they turn in one direction, they'll push the stick farther; then, when the plane finally reacts and goes into a much sharper turn than they intended, they'll overcompensate by turning wildly in the opposite direction. If you want to present a realistic challenge, you can model this problem accurately; to keep the game easy, treat the plane more like a car.

Military Flight Sims   In military flight simulators, the player must not only fly the aircraft but also achieve the mission's objectives, usually attacking enemy aircraft and ground installations. Modern air-to-air combat, conducted with long-range guided missiles and often directed by Airborne Warning and Control System (AWACS) planes, is something of a chess game—a rather cerebral exercise. Hence the continuing popularity of World War I and II flight simulators and fictional battles such as those in *Crimson Skies* (see Figure 17.1). These let the players dogfight, twisting and turning through the sky, hiding behind clouds, diving out of the sun, and blasting away with bullets at short range. It's a much more action-packed experience.

The role of the aircraft being simulated defines the gameplay for military flight simulators. Fighter planes are designed primarily to attack enemy aircraft and to protect friendly aircraft and ground units from air attacks; attack planes are designed to attack moving ground targets; bombers are designed to attack stationary ones. Most military flight simulators offer a series of missions, often with primary and secondary objectives such that achieving either or both of them constitutes victory. Being killed or having the player's plane shot down

17

FIGURE 17.1 A pilot's view in *Crimson Skies*. Note the very simple instrument panel.

constitutes a loss. However, you don't have to establish binary victory conditions; you can allow for partial success by rating the accomplishments of a mission according to the number of objectives achieved, the length of time it took, and the amount of damage sustained by the aircraft, for instance. You can also assign bonus points for a swift and safe return.

Civilian Flight Sims   Civilian flight simulators such as the excellent *Microsoft Flight Simulator* (see Figure 17.2) seldom include any victory conditions unless they implement racing or tests of flying ability. Many of them simply let the player fly and try different things with the aircraft rather than present him with a specific mission to accomplish. However, civilian flight sims can present a wide variety of challenges: flying at night; flying in rain, fog, or strong winds; and using visual flight rules or instrument flight rules. Landing smoothly and safely, particularly in adverse weather conditions, is always the most dangerous moment in a flight and usually represents the toughest challenge that a civilian flight simulator offers. Most provide an auto-land function that simply returns the plane to the ground without the player's having to perform the landing.

Driving Sims   Organized racing simulations, like sports games, take their gameplay from the real thing. The challenge is primarily to win races without crashing.

FIGURE 17.2 An instrument panel in *Microsoft Flight Simulator 2002.* This is a game for people who take piloting seriously.

This may be just as complicated as real racing, including such details as fuel and tire management and compensating for the weather. Some games also include an economic element: The player wins prize money for doing well in a race, and the prize money enables her to buy better equipment. This produces positive feedback that must be counteracted to balance the game; as the player improves, her artificial opponents must also improve to offer her a worthy challenge.

In more arcadelike driving games, the games often include other challenges such as running other drivers off the road, gathering up collectibles or power-ups, threading through hoops or cones, shooting at enemies or dropping devices to delay them, and so on.

Core Mechanics

Designing a vehicle simulation is primarily a matter of research and compromise. Unless your game is a just-for-fun simulation such as *Super Mario Kart* or *Beetle Adventure Racing,* vehicle simulation is the most technologically oriented of games, so the core mechanics of the game are almost entirely about physics. Much of the entertainment value of accurate simulation games comes from the feeling of controlling a real machine instead of meeting strategic challenges or taking part in a story. To provide that value, you will need to research your vehicles thoroughly. If you're designing a military vehicle, you can probably find much of what you need from the Jane's Information Group, publishers of such volumes as *Jane's All the World's Aircraft,* and of course, from the vehicle's manufacturer. For automobiles, the various enthusiast magazines offer all the data you could want.

The compromises occur when you start trying to control a simulated vehicle with a computer or console machine's I/O devices, especially a large, complicated vehicle such as a B-52 bomber. The kinds of compromises you make and the places they take you will depend mostly on whether your target audience is the purist or the casual player.

Designing Opponents

The easiest way to design a variety of opponents in a vehicle simulation is simply to provide different drivers' vehicles with different performance characteristics. One plane climbs slightly faster than another; one can turn more sharply. The player will experience different challenges in dealing with each opponent based on its design parameters. However, once the player figures it out, the opponent is easily beaten. As soon as the player discovers that a Supermarine Spitfire can consistently outrun a Messerschmitt Bf 109 in level flight, the situation offers an obvious strategy for Spitfire pilots: *boom and zoom* (hitting and running away).

To create further variety, modify the behavior of individual opponent drivers (or pilots, etc.). The AI for those opponents should be designed by starting with perfect performance and then creating variations from perfection. For example, it's possible to create a "perfect" AI driver in a racing simulation, one that always follows the most efficient line around the track, always shifts gears at precisely the correct moment, and knows the ideal speed at which to take each corner without spinning out. If such a driver has a better car than the player's, he will be unbeatable. The trick, then, is to modify the AI driver's judgment so that it isn't perfect— so that he doesn't always shift at exactly the right time or follow the most efficient line. This combination of factors, both vehicle characteristics and variable driver skill, provides the variety among opponents in vehicle simulators.

As you research flying or driving, you will discover other tricks to incorporate in the AI: drafting behind other cars, for example, and diving out of the sun to surprise the enemy in a dogfight.

Damage

You'll need to decide what to do about damage. Comical or arcadelike racing sims may not simulate damage at all; if the car hits something, it simply bounces off, although doing so usually slows the car down. This allows the driver to be much more careless, and it is a good solution for children's games. They can afford to hit a few things and still win the race—at least in the earlier, easier stages of the game. Other games model damage as a single variable, like unit health points in a war game. When damage reaches a certain level, the vehicle simply stops running (which, in the case of an airplane, means that it crashes or explodes). If your target machine doesn't have much CPU power (as in a cell phone, for example), these approaches mean you don't have to model the physics very accurately.

Accurate modeling of damage requires dividing the vehicle into areas, determining which area has been damaged by a collision (or, in a military simulator, by enemy fire), and deciding how that damage affects the performance of the vehicle. For instance, a race car with minor damage to the airfoils or body can continue, although with a performance penalty, but a blown tire will force it to halt. With airplanes, the consequences can be dramatically different depending on what part of the aircraft sustains damage. A plane can still fly without its tail, but it will be unstable and extremely difficult to handle. These approaches give great verisimilitude but require sophisticated physics models to accomplish.

The Game World

The landscape that a simulated vehicle moves through is an important part of the game's entertainment—even if it's a relatively static landscape as in a racing game—because the landscape is connected with the function of the vehicle itself

The settings of flight simulators consist of the plane itself and the ground that it flies above. With a few exceptions, such as *Microsoft Combat Flight Simulator,* most flight sims don't offer interesting terrain. If your flight simulator has a historical setting, you can do a lot with the ancillary screens to set the mood. Electronic Arts' World War II flight simulator, *Jane's WWII Fighters,* shows a hanger full of period aircraft and other gear and even plays Glenn Miller tunes in the background. Unfortunately, in the pursuit of historical accuracy, Electronic Arts set all its combat missions above the Ardennes Mountains in the wintertime: a bleak, snowy landscape covered with leafless trees. The technical quality of the graphics was superb; it's too bad they weren't depicting something more interesting. Its competitor, *Microsoft Combat Flight Simulator,* was less historically accurate but arguably more fun to fly because you could buzz the Eiffel Tower or London's Houses of Parliament.

Driving simulators are set on either racetracks or roads except for a few off-road simulators that offer the fun of bouncing all over interesting terrain without having to steer carefully. Narrow, twisting mountain roads are a popular choice for road-based games because they offer both an interesting challenge and pretty scenery.

Weather is a critical factor to consider when designing the settings of both flight and driving simulators. Can the player drive or fly at night? In rain? In fog? Rain plays an important strategic role in automobile racing because each driver needs to make a pit stop to switch to rain tires, which hold the road better. The pit stop takes time, but drivers who don't take the time run an increased risk of crashing.

Because flight and driving simulators rarely show other people, their worlds can seem eerily devoid of life. Cities are depicted as collections of buildings with no pedestrians (and in flight simulators, no vehicles). Each airport has only one plane, the player's, and no ground staff. Simulator designers often feel that, because these things aren't critical to the gameplay, it is a waste of time to implement them. Still, they add considerably to the player's immersion. A World War II airfield should have other planes, pilots, and ground staff moving around; a track-based racing sim should certainly have a crowd in the grandstand.

Other Vehicles

Flight and driving simulators are by far the most popular kinds, but there are other sorts of vehicle simulators as well, usually for niche markets. The last few years have seen the arrival of large numbers of new vehicles from the hang glider in *Far Cry* to the magic broomsticks in the *Harry Potter* games. We address a few of the more common types here.

Boats and Ships

Most boat simulations are of powerboats or jet skis, offering the same kinds of speed thrills that driving simulators do (see Figure 17.3). The handling

FIGURE 17.3 *Jetboat Superchamps* in a third-person perspective. Note the map overlay.

characteristics of powerboats differ from those of cars; because boats move in a fluid medium, they don't hold the road the way a car's tires do, so they can't turn as sharply as a car can. Powerboat simulations usually offer racing over a twisting course marked off by buoys. Jet ski or fantasy water vehicle simulations often have outrageous jumps and other challenges as well.

There have been a few simulators of warships over the years, often fairly small craft with high speed and maneuverability, such as the PT boat of World War II fame. Larger vessels such as battleships and aircraft carriers move more slowly and deliberately and, therefore, tend to be simulated not as individual vehicles but as part of naval warfare simulations involving whole fleets, such as *Harpoon* or *Dangerous Waters.*

Submarine simulations such as *Silent Hunter III* are fairly popular because of the specialized nature of their situation and because they can move in three dimensions. They normally concentrate on rather old-fashioned submarine activities, such as looking through the periscope and firing torpedoes at surface ships. We associate these sorts of things with submarines from watching old war movies, and of course, they're the most visually dramatic. Relatively few games simulate the modern role of submarines, hunting and hiding from one another in total darkness, because it's too cerebral an activity.

Sailing simulations are comparatively rare, but they do exist; see *Virtual Skipper 4* on the left of Figure 17.4. Although sailing a boat is a complex and interesting challenge, such games appeal only to a specialized market. Most people prefer simulations in which you can point the vehicle in the direction you want to go and push the gas pedal to get you there.

Few ship simulations model the ocean in all its complexity, with shoals and currents, tides and storms. Rather, they tend to treat the water the way driving simulations treat the ground: simply as an area over which ships move. Pirate games such as *Sea Dogs II* (Figure 17.4, right side) and *Sid Meier's Pirates!* are usually arcade or role-playing games rather than sailing simulations.

FIGURE 17.4 *Virtual Skipper 4* and *Sea Dogs II.*

Tanks and Mechs

Tank simulations seldom implement the complexity of tank battles as they really happened in World War II, the Arab-Israeli wars, or the Gulf War. Real tanks have a top speed of about 50 MPH, have limited visibility, and carry only a few types of weapons, so they don't appeal much to the casual gamer. Like military flight simulators, tank simulators are typically about a lone tank operating against other tanks and a variety of other enemies.

From a gameplay standpoint, the most interesting characteristic of a tank is its rotating turret, which enables it to shoot in directions other than the one in which it is facing. (Notice the example in Figure 17.5.) It can be difficult to design a good user interface for this. You will need to provide a mechanism for rotating the turret that is separate from the mechanism that steers the tank and a separate view window for aiming and firing the gun. Real tanks have a commander and a gun crew as well as a driver, but as with bombers and other multi-seat aircraft, you will have to find a way to let a single player control everything.

A popular alternative is the *mech,* a science-fiction cousin to the tank that is usually depicted as a large armed and armored walking machine (see Figure 17.6). Because mechs aren't restricted by reality, they can carry all sorts of imaginary weapons and hardware, and they can be optimized for single-player play.

FIGURE 17.5 A tank in *Panzer Elite.* The turret is facing in a different direction from the tracks.

FIGURE 17.6 *MechWarrior 4: Mercenaries.*

Spacecraft

There are almost no simulations of real spacecraft—except for quasi-educational ones about the space shuttles—because real spacecraft respond far too slowly and move too deliberately to make for an interesting game. The majority of spacecraft simulations, therefore, are science fiction, and they typically consist of either fighter planes in space, such as the *Wing Commander* series, or capital ship (large warship) simulations, such as the many *Star Trek* games. The fighter types are simple action games with only a few variables to manage: fuel, ammunition, damage, shields, and rarely anything else. Capital ship simulations are more strategic, giving the player control of a wide range of weapons and other equipment.

Intellectual Property Rights

As a general rule, you can depict and simulate military equipment without obtaining permission from their manufacturers. Because such machines are not sold to the general public or generally exploited in the marketplace in any other way, you may safely make use of their images in your games without worrying about who owns the rights.

Automobiles are another story, however. If you are going to simulate an existing car and use its real name and logo, you must have a license from the manufacturer. The manufacturer might not be willing to let you show the car crumpled and burning by the side of the road either. This accounts for the large number of vehicle simulations in which the cars can flip over in an accident but never get damaged—they flip back upright a second or two later, as in *Beetle Adventure Racing*. Or, you can do as *Interstate '76* did and use cars that look rather like existing vehicles and have similar names but don't actually show the manufacturer's indicia.

17

The Presentation Layer

The presentation layer of a vehicle simulator is chiefly concerned with creating the visual and auditory appearance of being in the vehicle itself, so management activities are kept to a minimum. When there are different gameplay modes at all, they're usually established to offer the player a new perspective rather than a different set of challenges.

Interaction Model

The interaction model in a flight simulator is quite straightforward: The player's plane is his avatar. The plane's controls are mapped onto the computer's input devices, and the player's view is normally that of the pilot, forward through the cockpit windows.

Perspective

As with sports games, flight and driving simulations frequently offer a variety of camera perspectives. Although the game cannot be played from all of these angles, the unplayable angles can be used for taking dramatic screenshots or for viewing instant replays of the action.

Views Common to Driving and Flight Simulators   Both driving and flight simulators implement certain standard views:

- **Pilot's/driver's view.** This is the normal view that most simulators offer by default. The player sees what the pilot would see from the cockpit or what the driver would see from the driver's seat. The vehicle's instruments take up the lower half of the screen, and the upper half shows the view out of the windshield, often partially obscured by parts of the hood or the nose of the plane. Most sims offer separate look-left, look-right, and look-backward views, as well as a mode in which the player can swivel the view smoothly in all directions to see what's overhead and down to see instruments located below the pilot's normal line of sight.

- **Cockpit-removed view.** This unrealistic, but dramatic perspective uses the full screen to show the pilot or driver's view out of the front of the vehicle, unobscured by the cockpit controls. Semitransparent overlays in the corners of the screen allow the player to see instrument readings without much interference with the view. Even these overlays can be removed, providing an unobscured view of the world outside with no visible indication that the player is in a vehicle at all.

- **Chase view.** This is an exterior view of the player's vehicle, as if from another one following closely behind and mimicking its movements. In flight simulators, the plane always seems to be level when in chase view and the world turns around it. For example, if the player banks her plane, the horizon tilts while the player's plane appears to be level in the middle of the screen. In driving simulators, the point of view when in chase mode/view is usually somewhat elevated so the player's car does not obscure the view of the road in front.

- **Rear, side, and front views.** These are exterior views of the player's vehicle from all four sides. If the player's plane banks, the view does not bank; the ground remains below.

- **Free-roaming camera.** Generally used only in an instant-replay mode, this enables the camera to be moved anywhere in the world and tilted or rotated to look in any direction. This view is useful for players trying to analyze exactly what happened in a particular encounter.

Views Unique to Military Flight Simulators   The following views are found only in flight simulators—and military ones, at that:

- **Ground target view.** This is a view of the target on the ground that is currently selected for attack. The camera is positioned at a nearby ground location, facing the target, and does not move. This view lets the player watch incoming missiles or bombs arrive to see whether they accurately hit the target.

- **Bomb or missile view.** This is the point of view from a recently released bomb or missile, as if it had a camera in its nose (as many modern weapons do). This allows a particularly dramatic perspective as the weapon approaches its target. This view disappears after the weapon detonates, and the perspective returns to the default view.

Views Unique to Driving Simulators   The following views occur only in driving simulators. Obviously, the cars are not drivable from these perspectives, but they are great for instant replays.

- **Track-side view.** Many real racetracks locate cameras at fixed points around the track, and a good many games emulate this. The game's

FIGURE 17.7 A typical track-side view in *GT Legends.*

point of view can be either locked to a specific location or made to track the player's car as it moves past. It's also common to have a routine that automatically makes the display switch from one track-side camera to another to follow the leaders as they go around. This gives a good simulation of watching televised coverage of a race (see Figure 17.7).

- **Grandstand view.** This is the traditional spectator's view of the finish line.

- **Blimp view.** This is a high aerial view looking straight down onto the racetrack or course, letting you see all the cars at once.

User Interface Design

The biggest challenge in designing the user interface of a vehicle simulator is in mapping the vehicle's real controls to those available on the target machine. For serious simulations, analog controls are essential; the binary D-pads of older handheld controllers don't allow the kind of precision needed for accurate steering. At one time, console machines simply couldn't support serious simulations, but now that most console machines offer analog joysticks, mapping the controls of a race car to those of a home console machine presents less of a problem.

> ## FYI *Don't Rely on Fancy Controllers*
>
> Force-feedback joysticks, throttles, control yokes, steering wheels, and pedals (rudder for planes, and gas and brake for cars) all help immensely, and serious players will have them. You can greatly improve the quality of the simulation experience for such players by supporting them. However, don't design—and, more important, don't tune—your game with a presumption that your players will have this kind of hardware. Your game should be an enjoyable experience even with only a standard console controller or a mouse and keyboard. If it's not, you've severely limited your audience, and reviewers are bound to slam it.

Simplifications   Military flight simulators always require some simplification from the real thing; you will have to decide how much. Real military pilots require months or years of training, much of it spent sitting in classrooms. Because you want your players to be able to fly the planes within a few minutes of installing the software, you have to make considerable compromises in the realism of the games. You will almost certainly want to reduce the number of instruments in the cockpit and the number of functions that some of them perform.

Flight simulators commonly simplify navigation as well. Modern planes have global positioning systems, but World War I and II pilots still needed celestial navigation skills, plotting their courses by the stars at night and by landmarks or dead reckoning during the daytime. Because this isn't the most exciting thing about flying, it's acceptable to just give the player a map.

> ## IN THE TRENCHES: An Extreme Case
>
> The takeoff sequence in the game *Megafortress* is possibly the longest for any consumer-level flight simulator ever made. The game simulated a hypothetical stealth-modified B-52 bomber. To get the plane off the ground (fortunately, it was already lined up on the runway), you had to:
>
> 1. Switch on battery power.
> 2. Switch on interior lights.
> 3. Switch on power to all eight engines.
> 4. Fire starter cartridges for all eight engines.
> 5. Switch off battery power after the engines were running.
> 6. Switch on navigation lights.
>
> ▶▶ CONTINUED ON NEXT PAGE

> **▶▶ CONTINUED**
>
> 7. Switch on landing lights.
> 8. Pressurize the plane to noncombat levels.
> 9. Tune radio to correct frequency (this also served as the game's copy protection).
> 10. Lower flaps.
> 11. Release brakes.
> 12. Throttle up all eight engines (fortunately, this could be done simultaneously).
> 13. Pull back on stick (plane takes off).
> 14. Raise landing gear.
> 15. Raise flaps.
>
> This sequence involved moving back and forth from the pilot's seat to the copilot's seat a couple of times, too. Soon after you got into the air, you had to switch all the lights back off to avoid detection by enemy aircraft. If you forgot to pressurize the plane, the crew would complain of being cold. When you entered into combat, you were supposed to lower the air pressure to avoid a violent decompression if the plane was hit.
>
> *Megafortress* was a techno-geek's dream. It was not, however, a big financial success as flight simulators go.

Coordinated Flight   Another common simplification that almost all flight simulators make is to produce automatically coordinated flight. Ordinarily, the pilot of an airplane must coordinate the movements of the ailerons and rudder when turning to prevent the plane from skidding sideways in the air, in the same way that a car skids sideways on wet pavement if it takes a turn too fast. Because the plane has no tires gripping pavement to control the direction it is facing, this can happen even more easily in the air. However, most players have only one control mechanism, the joystick. To simplify flight, the left-right motion of the joystick controls both the rudder and the ailerons simultaneously, producing automatically coordinated flight.

Creating the Sense of Speed   In a flight simulation, simply going fast is rarely the point. Most players either are trying to fly accurately and aerobatically or are engaging in aerial combat. Although speed is an important factor in the game, conveying that sense to the player isn't critical to the experience.

In driving simulations, however, the sense of speed is all-important. Here are some ways to create it:

■ **Give the player a speedometer.** This is the most obvious way to inform a player of his speed, but it creates a purely logical awareness, not a visceral one. It might also help to give him a tachometer so he can see that the engine is near its maximum potential.

- **Vary the driving surface.** Don't present a smooth ribbon of black, but make the road a series of continuously changing dark grays. (Look back at Figure 17.7, *GT Legends,* to see this done well.) The rate at which these color gradations move toward the car will help to create the feeling of speed. Don't just use a set of random dots, though, or at high speed the player will just see a static, flickering surface. It's better to implement these cues as a series of narrow strips parallel to the road's edges. Also, on roads (as opposed to racetracks), be sure to implement the dotted white line down the center. The sight of the lines flicking by gives a continuous visual cue to the speed, as well as a good way to tell when the vehicle is speeding up or slowing down. (In a flight simulator, the equivalent is to be sure the ground is as detailed as possible.)

- **Include roadside objects.** A continuous fence, guardrail, or strip of grass doesn't do much to give the player a feeling of motion. Make sure there are lots of trees, road signs, and bridges. Anything that rises vertically beside the road or that passes over or under the car will help to create the impression.

- **Use sounds.** The sound of the engine is the most obvious auditory cue, but you could also include road noise (the sound the tires make on the pavement), wind noise, and tires squealing as the vehicle rounds corners. Another excellent cue is a Doppler shift as the car passes, or is passed by, some noise-making object.

G-Forces The driver of any vehicle feels a variety of forces affecting her body: acceleration, deceleration, and centrifugal force. She can feel these forces as pressure pushing her body in one direction or another, usually into the seat or against the belts holding her in. The forces give a lot of valuable feedback about the behavior of the vehicle. Unfortunately, in a home-based simulator, you can't provide any of those physical feelings, so you have to substitute other indicators. With driving simulators, it isn't as important because automobiles seldom generate significant G-forces, and the player will receive plenty of other visual cues, as described in the previous section.

Military aircraft can generate powerful G-forces, but because the player spends most of her time looking at the sky, there's no visual indication of them, even though the engines of modern fighter planes are powerful enough to tear the plane apart if it is mishandled. If you're doing a realistic simulation, you might want to include this deadly little detail. If so, or if you just want to give the pilot a sense of the G-forces involved, you should include a G-force meter showing the amount of stress being applied to the plane (and pilot). Most aircraft are designed to sustain strong downward G-forces, but not upward ones. In addition, pilots undergoing

strong downward G-forces can black out momentarily as all the blood drains out of their heads. They can also suffer an experience called *redout* if they encounter a strong upward G-force, because too much blood flows into their heads. Many games simulate these conditions by fading the screen to black or to red, which, in addition to preventing the player from seeing anything, gives a clear indication that something is wrong.

Summary

Vehicle simulations require a designer to knowledgeably represent a known physical world in a realistic manner to the player. You should spend time learning about the characteristics of the vehicles you wish to simulate within the game, work to adapt the core mechanics to the limitations of the user interface, and devise and create compelling opponents and courses for the player to use.

You should determine whether the audience of your game will be purists or casual players and design core game mechanics to satisfy that market. For the purist, the simulation needs to be the most accurate representation of the vehicle possible, whereas for the casual player, the simulation can more easily trade play mechanisms for realism.

The most critical things for you to consider after the choice of audience are the vehicle characteristics, the opponent behaviors, and finally the design of the courses or tracks within the game.

Vehicle simulations can be highly technical and challenging, and a dedicated designer must be prepared to undertake a lot of research.

Test Your Skills

MULTIPLE CHOICE QUESTIONS

1. Which of the following is true?
   A. A game about an alien spaceship could never be classed as a simulation because the ship isn't real.
   B. You can't do a tank simulation unless you design a multiplayer game so that one person can drive and another can shoot.
   C. Players may want to damage their planes if they make a mistake like leaving the flaps of their plane down on liftoff because that's what would happen in real life.
   D. You can easily switch your car racing game into a powerboat racing game because the handling of the vehicles is so similar.

2. What is a death match?

    A. A competition mode derived from monster truck arena shows.

    B. A solo mode for a military flight simulator against a computer-enhanced enemy.

    C. A multiplayer competition in which every player is pitted against every other player.

    D. A cooperative play mode in which if any team member dies, all the players die.

3. The competition mode in a driving game in which the player tries to win in a real racing circuit would be called a

    A. death match.

    B. campaign mode.

    C. NASCAR mode.

    D. career mode.

4. If a player finds that the plane in his new flight sim doesn't respond to commands as quickly as the cars in his old car sim, so he's always over-steering and recovering, it's probably because

    A. his hardware isn't up to the job; he needs an up-to-date processor to play the latest games.

    B. the UI design of the flight sim is faulty; the actions are mapped to the wrong controller buttons.

    C. the designer should have built in more cues so that the player can detect the G-force the pilot would feel.

    D. he doesn't yet know how a plane handles; he needs to learn to fly.

5. A civilian flight sim might be expected to offer

    A. no adverse weather conditions.

    B. an auto-land function.

    C. a button to lower air pressure to avoid violent decompression.

    D. a cabin crew to serve snacks.

6. The *best* way to design opponents for a civilian flight sim with a racing mode is to

    A. model the opponents on famous pilots of the past, using their strengths and weaknesses (but don't use their names, or you'll have to buy the rights to do so).

    B. not make any of them too aggressive because it's not a combat situation.

    C. make all the other pilots use the same AI, but vary the performance characteristics of the models of the planes they fly.

    D. design the AI for perfect opponent, and then vary the AI pilots' judgments so they all differ a bit from perfection.

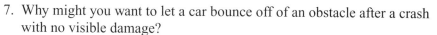

7. Why might you want to let a car bounce off of an obstacle after a crash with no visible damage?

   A. The carmaker might require it as part of the licensing agreement to use its car's look and logo.

   B. Your target machine doesn't have enough CPU power to model real damage.

   C. In a children's game or an arcadelike game, you might not want to focus the game on the crashes.

   D. All of the above.

17

8. Which of the following can you use in your game only if you have negotiated permission to use intellectual property belonging to someone else?

   A. A Bradley fighting vehicle in a Gulf War scenario.

   B. A PT boat in the Pacific theater of operations in WWII.

   C. A Ford Fairlane in a racing game.

   D. A twin-humped robo-camel from the selenium deserts of the planet Sirocco.

9. Why might you want to provide an unplayable camera angle for a vehicle simulation?

   A. You should never display the game from an unplayable perspective.

   B. Unplayable perspectives can make for good instant replays.

   C. It's where vehicle sims are going because these perspectives show off more creativity than a straight driving/flying perspective.

   D. A player who's bought special controllers wants some action on every button to get her money's worth.

10. What is a chase view?

    A. The external view of the player's aircraft in which the player sees all the plane's maneuvers against a static ground.

    B. The view used in follow-my-lead civilian driving sims when the player's vehicle is the chase vehicle.

    C. A rear view in a military flight sim showing a chasing enemy in a dogfight.

    D. An exterior view of the player's vehicle as if from a vehicle following behind it.

11. Which view in a military flight sim uses a stationary camera focused on a target so the player can see whether his missile has hit the target?

    A. Ground target view.

    B. Bomb view.

    C. Missile view.

    D. Ground bomb view.

12. You'll sell more games if your racing simulation
    A. doesn't clutter the cityscapes or landscapes with people as you drive through.
    B. can be enjoyed when run on standard hardware and doesn't require extra controllers such as gas and brake pedals.
    C. provides the quiet ride of a luxury car rather than a lot of distracting engine noise.
    D. requires the player to master a sophisticated UI and so takes a long time to learn to drive successfully.

13. Because the player doesn't have years to spend training to fly a military aircraft but wants to just sit down and play right away, you should plan your design to
    A. turn your design documents into extremely detailed printed manuals for players to consult.
    B. reduce the number of instruments shown in the cockpit and the number of functions some of them perform.
    C. reduce complicated graphics that slow run-time when the player flies in training mode.
    D. always provide a multiplayer mode so that flying tasks can be divided between team members.

14. Most flight simulators move the ailerons and rudder together for the player because the designer can only count on the player to have one analog input device, presumably a joystick. This simplification of the task of flying is called
    A. synchronized rudder flight.
    B. automatically coordinated flight.
    C. mechanically matched flight.
    D. pseudo automatic flight.

15. All of the following can make your driving sim seem more real to the player, but which one won't help her get a sense of whether the car is accelerating or decelerating?
    A. A continuous guardrail.
    B. A bridge.
    C. Streetlights.
    D. The dotted white center line.

Case Study

17

Choose a vehicle simulator that you believe, from your own experience of playing it, is an excellent example of the genre (or use one your instructor has assigned). It should be a serious simulator of a real vehicle rather than an arcadelike game about a fictional vehicle. Write a report documenting why you believe it is superior to others of its kind. Be sure to cover at least the following areas:

- Describe the challenges that the game offers and any rewards that it gives for achieving them.

- Compare the physics of the behavior of the real vehicle to that of the simulated vehicle. Try to find the performance characteristics of the real vehicle online, and see if you think the simulated vehicle accurately duplicates them or exaggerates them. If it diverges sharply from the real thing, explain why you think the designers made that decision and what it does for the game.

- Discuss the effects of weather and damage on the vehicle.

- Briefly document the steering mechanism that the game implements. Note important indicators that appear on the screen and explain how they improve the playing experience.

- Address the game's progression. Does it include a growth path such as a career mode or campaign mode? If so, describe it. What challenges and actions are available when the player is not actually driving the vehicle? If the player's decisions when *not* driving can affect the driving experience, indicate how.

The design questions in the next section may help you to think about these issues. In your report, use screen shots to illustrate your points. End the case study with suggestions for improvement or, if you feel the game cannot be improved, suggestions for additional features that might be fun to have in the game.

Alternatively, choose a game that you believe is particularly *bad*. Do the same case study, explaining what is wrong and how it could be improved.

A case study is neither a review nor a design document; it is an analysis. You are not attempting to reverse-engineer the entire game but simply to explain how it works in a general way. Your instructor will tell you the desired scope of the assignment; we recommend from five to twenty pages.

DESIGN QUESTIONS

When beginning the design of a vehicle simulation, consider the following questions:

1. What vehicle are you going to simulate? Is it an existing car, plane, boat, tank, and so on, or is it a fantasy vehicle?

2. If it is an existing vehicle, are you aiming for the purist player who knows all its technical specifications or for the casual player who simply wants to enjoy using it? How detailed is the physics model going to be?

3. How will the game handle damage to the vehicle? Can it be visually shown to be damaged? (Licenses for real vehicles sometimes forbid this.) Will damage be treated globally, like hit-points, or locally for individual parts of the machine?

4. What are the competition modes and victory conditions in the game? If this is a military vehicle, what sorts of missions are available for it? If it is a civilian one, what kinds of things can it do besides simply racing (if anything)?

5. What settings are available for the vehicle to travel through? Even a flight simulator needs ground to look at below.

6. What camera views are appropriate for this vehicle? If it is a military vehicle, are there special camera views that assist in fighting? Can the player record and even edit instant replays so as to relive and show off his triumphs?

7. How will you map the many controls of a plane or even a car onto the input devices available to the player? What aspects of the vehicle's controls will need to be simplified? Which can afford to have simple on-off buttons and which require analog controls?

8. If a vehicle is capable of steering in a direction different from that in which it shoots, how can the player control both at once conveniently?

9. What navigational facilities is the player going to need in order to know where he is (radar screen, overlay map, separate map mode that pauses the game, and so on)?

10. What artificial intelligence is needed to create suitable opponents in the game's competitive modes? What sorts of things will the artificial opponents need to manage? Will they be smart enough to take advantage of superior speed, acceleration, cornering ability, braking ability?

11. Do you want to create a sense of speed for the player? If so, how will you create it? (Remember, you can use both visual and audible cues.)

Chapter | 18

Construction and Management Simulations

Chapter Objectives

After reading this chapter and completing the exercises, you will be able to do the following:

- Know the definition of a construction and management simulation.
- Know the differences between plan-and-build and purchase-and-place gameplay mechanics.
- Know the basic gameplay modes and artificial behaviors common to this genre.
- Understand the issues facing a designer for user interface for this genre.
- Understand the core mechanics of economies, construction, and management.

Introction

Construction and management simulations offer players the chance to build things, such as anthills or cities, while operating within economic constraints. In this chapter we look first at the gameplay of construction and management, and consider the unique actions and challenges these games provide. We'll also explore designing user interfaces and the user interface for these games. As an example, we will spend time discussing *SimCity,* which was the first successful CMS.

Although they do not involve construction, we also discuss pure business simulations, games that focus on managing economic processes. The section on hybrid games examines titles such as *Age of Empires;* hybrid games blend certain qualities of CMSs and war games. Although we address war games in Chapter 14, "Strategy Games," some hybrid games include interesting economic elements as well; we'll refer to them throughout this chapter where appropriate.

What Are Construction and Management Simulations?

Construction and management simulations (CMSs) are games about processes. The player's goal is not to defeat an enemy but to build something within the context of an ongoing process. The better the player understands and controls the process, the more success she will have at building. CMSs typically include both a free-form construction mode, in which the player can build things any way she likes, and prebuilt scenarios for her to manage.

> *A construction and management simulation is a game in which the majority of challenges are economic, concerned with growth. Construction activity is an essential element of any CMS. Pattern recognition and exploration challenges may also be present. CMSs avoid physical coordination challenges and conflict challenges, unless they are hybrids with another genre.*

The first really successful computerized construction and management simulation was *SimCity,* which proved that computer games don't need high-speed action or violence to succeed. *SimCity* succeeded in part because it did not have those properties and, therefore, appealed to a broad audience. We'll examine *SimCity* in some detail later in the chapter.

Game Features

CMSs let the player construct and manage some organized system that can be built up from constituent parts—a city, a building, an anthill, or whatever the game permits him to design. Most CMSs offer two sets of tools: one set for building and one set for managing. Building is generally considered easy, but managing can be tricky indeed.

The Player's Role

When designing any game, the first question you have to ask yourself is: What is the player going to do? The answer to this question usually takes the form of a clear statement of the player's role in the game: pilot, general, adventurer, irradiated hedgehog, and so on. In a CMS, however, it's not as easy to define the player's role because that role seldom corresponds to an actual activity in real life. The mayor of a city doesn't really lay out its streets or make zoning decisions personally.

A CMS appeals to the player because he gets to make something of his own. Working carefully, tending and tweaking, he can build a tiny settlement on the banks of the Tiber into the glorious city that was Rome. Not the original

Rome or the game designer's Rome but *the player's* Rome—Rome as it would have been if the player had been in command. The desire to create is in the heart of all CMS players. To design a good construction and management simulation, understand that desire.

Progression

Unlike most other genres, CMSs usually don't include progression from level to level or a story of any kind. They may offer a set of scenarios for the player to play in, with varying degrees of difficulty, but one scenario doesn't necessarily have any relationship to the previous or next one.

Because many CMSs don't impose a victory condition, there's little sense of progress toward an end. In fact, many CMSs don't necessarily end at all. As long as the player avoids the loss condition (typically bankruptcy), the game can go on forever.

IN THE TRENCHES: *SimCity*

Although it isn't the oldest CMS, *SimCity* inspired every CMS that came after it. Published by Maxis (now a part of Electronic Arts) originally for the Commodore 64, *SimCity* achieved its greatest success on the IBM PC, and players can now try the first version of the game free on the Web. (Visit **http://simcity.ea.com/play/simcity_classic.php** if you're interested.) A host of other games in the same mold followed— *SimAnt, SimTower, SimFarm,* and so on—which met with varying degrees of success.

The object of *SimCity* is to build a city and attract people (called *sims*) to live and work there. The basic economic unit is money, which the player can spend in various ways to improve the city. The player's primary task is to zone tracts of land into one of three types: residential, commercial, or industrial. As people move into the city, their occupation of these areas begins to produce tax revenue, thereby replenishing the city's coffers. This produces a straightforward positive feedback loop: Zoning costs money, but occupied zones produce more money, thereby enabling the player to do more zoning.

The positive feedback is kept in check by other demands on the city's purse. Sims will not move into a region simply because it has been zoned; it needs other amenities as well. Foremost among these is electricity, so the player has to buy power plants and electrical lines to provide it. The sims also need a way to travel from the residential zones to the industrial zones to work and to the commercial zones to shop. This

CONTINUED ON NEXT PAGE

▶▶ CONTINUED

requires road and rail networks, which also cost money. If the roads are inadequate to meet the traffic or if the sims have to travel too far to work, they will begin to move out of the city, resulting in a loss of tax revenue. Finally, when the city reaches certain population thresholds, the sims begin to demand expensive amenities: a sports stadium, an airport, and so on. Again, if these are not provided, the sims begin to leave.

In addition to the electricity, roads, and civic amenities, the player pays for other common services, such as fire protection and police. Fires break out from time to time; left unchecked, they destroy the buildings and leave the land unzoned. To combat this, the player builds and maintains fire stations. Crime breaks out in industrial areas, depressing property values and reducing tax revenues. Building police stations, at yet more cost, suppresses crime. Industrial areas and roads also cause air pollution, which further depresses the value of nearby residential property. The player cannot reduce air pollution; he simply has to keep industrial and residential areas separate.

The game's algorithm mathematically determines the value of each area. A zoned area with fire and police protection will have lower value than a similar area with nearby recreational facilities and higher value than a similar area with polluted air. The more valuable a zone is, the more sims move in and the more tax revenues the zone produces. The player can build parks and situate residential zones near woods and rivers to increase their attractiveness.

SimCity, though now an old game, serves as an excellent model to study (see Figure 18.1). Being designed for low-performance machines, it couldn't be too complex, so its internal economy is easy to understand.

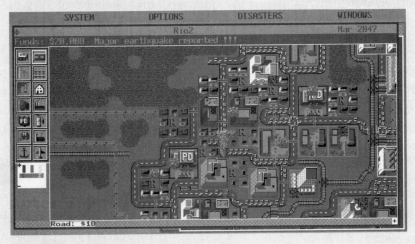

FIGURE 18.1 The original *SimCity*.

Gameplay

As we said in the formal definition, the challenges in a CMS are largely economic. The player must understand how the internal economy of the game works and how to manipulate it to produce economic growth. Growth provides the resources required for the construction that is usually the overall goal of the game.

Indirect Control   A war game is a game of direct control. The players tell their troops exactly where to go and what to do, and the troops do it. The simulated soldiers demonstrate little or no autonomous behavior. If told to stand and wait someplace, they'll wait there forever. The majority of CMSs, on the other hand, are games of indirect control. The game simulates a process that the player can alter only in limited ways. The process must be manipulated indirectly, and the player learns by trial and error how the changes that he makes affect the functioning of the process. The game may offer simulated people (see *Simulating Individuals* later in this chapter), but they are usually autonomous. Their behavior model governs what they do, and while they respond to stimuli, they can't be given direct orders.

However, the dividing line between direct and indirect control is a fuzzy one. Certain player activities, such as choosing the location of new construction, constitute direct control of the game. Others, such as trying to boost sales by reducing prices, are classed as indirect control. Reducing prices is a direct action with respect to the prices themselves, but not with respect to sales; the (hoped for) consequent rise in sales is the result of the player's indirect control of the game.

Construction   In most CMSs, the actual act of construction isn't a challenge: The player clicks the mouse on a location, and something appears there. The challenge is in obtaining the resources needed for the construction. Construction lets the player exercise her imagination and create something unique and personal. Accordingly, you, as the designer, need to find a way to make the user interface for construction easy and enjoyable to use.

Construction mechanisms in CMSs tend to be of two types: ***purchase-and-place*** or ***plan-and-build.*** Games in which construction is the primary activity tend to use the purchase-and-place mechanism; games in which the player alternates between construction and management modes are more likely to use the plan-and-build mechanism.

In the purchase-and-place construction mechanism, when the player buys an object (a segment of wall, say), the game deducts the resources to build that object from stockpiles, and the object immediately appears in a designated location. This lets the player build rapidly, adding pieces like using LEGO blocks. You should use this mechanism if construction is the primary activity in your game. The activity needs to be easy and continuous, not something the player has to wait for. This is how *SimCity* worked: Zoning property and constructing civic amenities such as police stations and airports happened instantly because zoning and constructing were the primary activities in the game.

The plan-and-build mechanism is more often seen in games in which the player does a little construction, then some management, then more construction, and so on. In plan-and-build, the player marks out an area in which new construction will appear. The game sometimes displays the new building in a ghostly, semitransparent form to indicate that it is under construction. However, construction takes time. If the game includes simulated people, you might be able to see them at work on the building; if those people stop work, the building might be left in a partially completed state. Plan-and-build is often found in strategy/CMS hybrids, in which the player may be under threat of invasion and time is of the essence.

In plan-and-build, you don't have to remove all the required resources from storage at once because the construction takes place over time. In *The Settlers,* wood and stone had to be transported a little at a time from stockpiles to the construction site. This puts an extra burden on the player to manage his resource flow but also gives him more control. In contrast, *Age of Empires* used plan-and-build but deducted the resources necessary for construction immediately when it was planned. Resources drained out of the game rather than being transported to the site. Although this was unrealistic, it meant that the player could build something only after he definitely had enough resources for it, and he didn't have to worry about moving resources from point to point.

Dungeon Keeper, another hybrid, makes a particularly interesting example because construction was actually excavation; it took place underground, and the player couldn't see the area under excavation. Excavations often encountered immovable rock or led to previously unknown caves, underground rivers, or pools of lava. Excavation was also irreversible; the game offered no way to close an excavated area. This encouraged players to be cautious. Suddenly digging an opening into an area full of enemy creatures was a major hazard of the game.

Demolition   In addition to letting your players construct things, you might need to give them a way to demolish things. A big part of the fun the player gets from a CMS is building the city, theme park, or other entity the way *she* wants to build it. If construction decisions are irreversible, then whatever the player builds can only get bigger— never smaller—and the player cannot change her mind or react to new circumstances. This might be okay for strategy games (many war games, for example, allow you to build factories and defenses but not to demolish them), but in CMSs, forbidding demolition prevents the player from exercising her full creative freedom.

You should consider whether you want demolition to cost something, cost nothing, or actually earn money. If it costs money to demolish something, you are, in effect, penalizing the player for changing his mind and perhaps encouraging him to plan more carefully in the future. He loses not only his initial construction cost for the item but the demolition costs as well. If demolition costs nothing, the player loses only his construction costs. If he actually gets something back, it's usually called selling the item or structure rather than demolishing it, an arrangement that further reduces the price the player pays for changing his mind. If he can sell a structure back for exactly as much as he paid, there is no net cost at all for building a thing and destroying it later. CMSs rarely work this way because to do so removes some of the challenge of managing their resources. Players can build madly, secure in the knowledge that they can always get their money back by selling.

FYI   *Functional Construction Challenges*

As we said, construction and demolition is easy in most games: point, click, and it happens, so long as the resources required are available. If you want to make the process more of a challenge, you can impose constraints on *how* things may be constructed and test to see whether the construction meets some required standard. The game *Bridge It*, for instance, requires its player to use certain predefined bridge elements—towers, beams, cables, and a roadway—to construct a bridge across a body of water. It also requires that the bridge actually support a load moving across it (see Figure 18.2). For further discussion of this idea, see the section *Constrained Creative Play* in Chapter 5, "Creative and Expressive Play."

Image courtesy Chronic Logic and Auran.

FIGURE 18.2 *Bridge It* challenges the player to build a functional bridge. This one was a failure.

Victory and Loss Conditions

A good many CMSs do not provide any victory condition; the player simply builds whatever she likes as effectively as she can within the constraints of the system. These games might well provide a loss condition, however. For example, total depletion of resources (or, in monetary terms, bankruptcy) is the loss condition in *Monopoly*. Victory in *Monopoly* consists simply of bankrupting all the other players; that is, forcing all the other players to meet the loss condition so that the last one left is declared the victor.

If you do want to define a victory condition, it's best to do it in the context of a predefined scenario that you have created for the player rather than a free-form construction mode. Give the player a partially constructed city (or whatever) and a set of initial conditions, and then define the victory condition as achieving some other condition. It could be as simple as "To win, your enterprise must be worth $5 billion," or it can be as complex as you like. You can also start the player in rapidly deteriorating conditions and challenge her to turn them around or simply to survive for a certain length of time.

Competition Modes

CMSs are almost always single-player games. It's possible to make them into multi-player competitions, but competition discourages the kind of creative experimentation that CMSs are designed to support. If the players are sharing a game world and competing for the same resources, such as land or minerals hidden in the environment, the game becomes a race to see who can grab the most, ignoring the other aspects of play. If the players are operating in separated game worlds and have symmetric starting and victory conditions, the game tends to be about optimizing efficiency. If the conditions are asymmetric, the game will be difficult to balance.

CMSs let the player be playful, to build and experiment in the world you've given him. That's seldom consistent with competition. One major exception is in hybrid games, those that have a military element as well as construction and management elements. They're discussed in *Hybrid Games* later in this chapter.

Simulating Individuals

Many CMSs simulate the behavior of a group of people (or in the case of *SimAnt,* ants) within an environment managed by the player. Games such as the original *SimCity,* which handle a large number of people, model behavior statistically rather than keeping separate values for each person. However, you might want to simulate the actions of particular individuals that the player can see moving around, as the modern versions of *SimCity* do. This will make your game a good deal more entertaining because the player can take an interest in the actions and progress of specific people. It appeals to a voyeuristic impulse and makes the consequences of the player's decisions seem more personal. It's particularly effective when the player can actually see unhappy people packing up and leaving.

Modeling particular individuals rather than statistical aggregates adds considerably to your design job. You will need to create a behavioral model and determine what aspects of the individual's condition the player will be trying to optimize. For example, many such games include a single-valued variable that tracks a character's degree of happiness or unhappiness and a set of needs that the simulated character desires to fulfill. Fulfillment may come as the result of the character's autonomous action (driving from home to work fulfills the need to get to work) or from action taken by the player (building a school fulfills the characters' need for educational opportunity). If a need goes unfulfilled, either through a problem that arises within the simulation (traffic jams prevent the person from getting to work) or the player's failing to act (no school has been built), there should be a negative consequence of some kind (the simulated person becomes unhappy).

Modeling individuals relieves you of the job of creating a statistical model because the behavior of the individuals collectively provides the statistics, but balancing such a game will be a more intricate task. You will probably discover emergent behaviors; that is, unanticipated consequences of design decisions. Some of these will be fascinating and almost seem like intelligence, but others will clearly be degenerate: simulated people locked in a tight behavioral loop, for example, only ever doing one or two things because your needs mechanism isn't balanced properly.

Behavioral modeling is too big a subject for us to address comprehensively here. We suggest that you consult the references on the Companion Website for further reading.

Companion
Website

Mind Reading

If your game allows the player to select a simulated character—usually done by clicking with the mouse—you can offer another useful analytical tool: mind reading. To let the player know what's on that individual's mind, pop up an icon or even a whole dialog box showing his internal state: current goal, degree of happiness, or whatever data might be useful to the player. This lets the player get a quick, rough sense of how the people feel without having to turn to a chart or a graph.

Advisors

Another tool commonly found in CMSs is the advisor: a game character who pops up from time to time and gives the player advice (see Figure 18.3). Because problems are often local to one area of the map, the player might be looking at another area when trouble occurs and not see it until it grows severe. By creating an advisor, you can warn the player of problem conditions wherever they occur. You might also consider including a screen button or menu item that moves the camera to the location of the most recently reported problem.

FIGURE 18.3 *Theme Park World.* Note the advisor in the lower right corner.

In addition to warning of emergencies, an advisor can give the player information about the general state of the game: "The people need more food," or "Prices are too high." This lets the player know of global problems without requiring her to consult the analytical tools.

To design an advisor, define both the local and the global problems that you think are important to let the player know about and then set the threshold levels at which the advisor will pop up. If the advisor will interrupt the player or say something aloud, don't set these thresholds too low, or the constant interruptions will become irritating. You should also make it possible for the player to turn off the advisor or to consult it only when wanted. Playing without the advisor adds an extra challenge to the game.

You can also create an advisor that consists only of an indicator that remains constantly on the screen, displaying the most urgent global need at all times.

Pure Business Simulations

Pure business simulations allow players to construct only financial fortunes, not visible worlds. A game like *Theme Park World* is a business simulation because it's about attracting customers and making profits, but because the player builds structures that exist in the virtual world, it is not a pure business simulation. Compare that with the game *Hollywood Mogul,* for example, which is a pure

FIGURE 18.4 *Mr. Bigshot* is a pure business simulation without a construction aspect.

business simulation about the business of making movies. It consists only of a series of menu screens about hiring stars and making deals. The player never sees a set or a camera. *Mr. Bigshot,* shown in Figure 18.4, is a fairly simple stock-market simulation and is even more abstract than *Hollywood Mogul.*

Most of the challenges of designing a pure business simulation are the same as for any other management simulation: You must devise an economy and mechanisms for manipulating it. The real trick is to find some way of making the subject visually interesting. Spreadsheets and pie charts have limited appeal, so if you're going to do a management simulation without a construction element, try to give it some kind of a setting or to find a visual representation of the process that will make it attractive and compelling. *Mr. Bigshot* accomplishes this with lots of animation, voiceover narration, music, and cartoon characters representing the player's opponents; the player feels rather like a contestant on a TV game show.

Capitalism II (see Figure 18.5), a huge, sprawling business simulation covering all kinds of products and industries, developed in a different direction. In addition to showing pictures of the products and all the raw materials that go into them, the game allows players to construct or purchase buildings in cities, so there's an attractive *SimCity*-like view as well.

Pure business simulations will never have the pulse-pounding excitement of a first-person shooter, but fans find them highly enjoyable games. As the

FIGURE 18.5 *Capitalism II.*

designer, you'll need to work closely with the art director to make the essentially numeric nature of the gameplay as lively as possible.

COMMANDMENT: Avoid Runaway Profits!

Never let a player buy low and sell high as often as she wants without further expenditure or the passage of time. She'll use it to rack up runaway profits. See Chapter 10, "Core Mechanics," for further discussion.

Hybrid Games

Civilization, Dungeon Keeper, and *The Settlers* are all hybrid games, each one a cross between a CMS and a war game. In addition to their economic challenges, all feature exploration and conflict challenges. The military aspect of *The Settlers* is quite simple, as it must be, because the economic aspect is exceedingly complex. *Dungeon Keeper* begins each scenario with construction and management of a dungeon complete with semi-autonomous denizens. In the later stages of the scenario, the player takes his army of creatures into battle, and the construction activities are finished. Control in *Dungeon Keeper* is a curious hybrid of direct and indirect in that creatures have a distinct behavior model but will obey orders as long as they're happy. (Unhappy creatures disobey or even desert.) However, *Dungeon Keeper* retains its economic challenges throughout: It's one of the very few games in which the troops have to be paid, fed, and given a place to sleep.

If you're going to design a hybrid game, it's a good idea to design the economic simulation first (unless it's really simple) and then add the other elements afterward. Because the other aspects of the game usually depend on the underlying economy, a mistake in the economic design can easily ruin the rest of the game. For example, a war game that includes an economy for weapons production might lose all its strategic challenge if the player can produce weapons too quickly. The player will exploit his economic strength and overwhelm the opposition with sheer numbers rather than strategic skill.

Core Mechanics

In Chapter 10, "Core Mechanics," we introduced the concepts of resources, sources, drains, and converters. Much of that material applied specifically to CMSs, which make more use of more kinds of resources than any other genre.

Resources

In many CMSs, the primary resource is money. Money is usually treated as an intangible resource; it is seldom seen in physical form. (*Dungeon Keeper* was an exception: Gold had to be mined and transported back to a treasury, and the player had to expand the treasury when it got full.)

People are the other major resource in most CMSs. They are above all a source of tax money or labor. Most CMSs simulate people only as workers; children and the elderly don't contribute to the economy of the game and so are not simulated. What sets people apart from other kinds of resources is that they have feelings: In many games, they have to be kept happy, or they will either leave or fail to act as desired. Consequently, managing their happiness becomes a big part of the gameplay, as discussed earlier in the section *Simulating Individuals.*

Building materials are generally treated as tangible entities for games that implement the plan-and-build construction mechanic, described earlier. Those that implement the purchase-and-place mechanic don't need to treat building materials as tangible, and some don't make building materials a resource at all, going directly from money to constructed objects.

One game that treats all resources as tangible, including money, is *The Settlers* from Blue Byte Software. In *The Settlers,* every kind of resource (and there are many) must be transported from where it is produced, either to storage areas or directly to places where it is consumed. Grain, for instance, must be carried from the grain farm to the windmill for grinding; the flour must be csarried from the windmill to the bakery; and the bread must be carried from the bakery to the mines, where the miners eat it.

TABLE 18.1 Common resources and their sources and drains

Resource	Source	Drain
Money	Taxation on people or gold mines in the environment	Purchases and construction
People	Immigration and reproduction	Emigration and death
Food	Farms	People eating
Labor	People	Construction activities
Land	Part of the environment; claimed as it is explored	No drain, but only a limited amount is available
Construction materials, e.g., wood	Found in raw form in the environment, e.g., trees	Converted into buildings by construction activities
Buildings	Constructed from money, materials, and labor	Destroyed by demolition or disasters

Table 18.1 lists some resources commonly found in construction and management simulations and how their sources and drains appear to the player.

The Construction Converter

Construction is a conversion activity that changes labor, money, and materials into buildings (or whatever the CMS constructs). Construction happens only when the player wants it to, so she controls the spending, and she can usually defer construction until such time as she can afford it. Although it drains money, the player can see immediately what she gets in return, and in any case it's an investment because the constructed object does something useful in the economy.

Drains and Maintenance

A drain is a feature that takes a resource out of the game for good. *Decay* is the usual drain in construction and management simulations: Buildings or other entities wear out and have to be replaced, which costs money. In *SimCity*, for instance, the roads wear out and have to be repaved. If the player doesn't repave them, the sims will start to emigrate because they can't get to work.

The player has to manage the repaving in *SimCity* personally, but in many games, these *maintenance* tasks are automated so the player only has to pay for them without actually performing them. Maintenance annoys some players, who would rather buy something once and never have to worry about it again. However, maintenance is an important game balancing tool; it drains resources and prevents the player from building profits endlessly. If you characterize maintenance as an ongoing cost rather than a purchase of assets, it makes more sense.

Paying employees is a maintenance cost. You can't own employees, but you have to pay their wages on a continuing basis; if you stop paying them, they stop working.

You may want to give the player the power to turn off or adjust the level of automatically managed maintenance (and suffer the attendant consequences), so he can make use of the money for something else that he needs in a hurry. *Stronghold 2,* a game about managing a medieval castle and its inhabitants, allows the player to set his peasants' food rations to one of five levels: none, half, normal, extra, and double. With these settings, he can manage the peasants' food consumption, which is one of the drains in the game.

Disasters

Decay is a continuous drain that the player may or may not have to act upon, depending on whether you allow automatic maintenance. For a more dramatic effect that forces the player to act, you can include disasters. *SimCity* puts more pressure on the player by having fires, tornadoes, and monster invasions crop up periodically, doing considerable damage. If the player does not take action to repair the damage (which costs money), the city dies, not just through the destruction of buildings, but also through the loss of needed infrastructure such as roads and electricity lines. Disasters need not be natural ones, of course. In a good many games, the disaster is invasion by hostile armies.

IN THE TRENCHES: *Theme Park,* a Disgusting Example of Positive Feedback

Bullfrog Productions' CMS *Theme Park* let the player build a single theme park, ride by ride, into an empire of theme parks around the world. In addition to buying the rides, which attracted visitors, the player built shops and restaurants to extract money from them and hired maintenance and cleaning staff to keep the rides working and the park clean.

Each visitor to the park had a number of attributes: how much money he had, how hungry or thirsty he was, and so on. One of these attributes was his current degree of nausea. If a visitor became nauseated enough, he would vomit, leaving a mess on the ground that had to be cleaned up. Nausea could be caused by three things: riding a particularly violent ride, being near an unclean bathroom, and—you guessed it—being near someone else's vomit. In a crowded park, if the player hadn't hired enough cleaning staff to deal with bathrooms and vomit, visitors created a chain-reaction of vomiting. This did nothing for the reputation of the park and tended to hurt future ticket sales but did inject a degree of juvenile comic relief into an otherwise straightforward business simulation.

The Game World

It's easy enough to say that CMSs focus on processes, but the processes must be meaningfully displayed on a computer screen and must fire the player's imagination. To do either, you must have an attractive setting. CMSs take place in a simulated physical space, usually an outdoor world viewed from an aerial perspective in which the players can construct buildings or other objects. In *Caesar,* the player builds an ancient Roman town, so the setting is a landscape near a river. In *Civilization,* the player explores a world while at the same time advancing a civilization both culturally and technologically, so its setting is an entire continent or several of them.

CMSs are often set in 2D or 2.5D worlds, even if they're actually implemented with a 3D engine. Using a 2D world simplifies things for the player. Just as strategy games remove the logistics so that the player can concentrate on strategy (because he doesn't have a staff to help him), so do CMSs remove the third dimension so that the player can concentrate on planning without worrying about the exact details (again because he doesn't have a staff to help him). When a player lays down a water pipe from a reservoir to a neighborhood, he doesn't want to have to worry about whether the pipe goes *over* or *under* the subway system. He just wants it to get where it needs to go.

A few pure business simulations don't take place in a physical setting. The interaction model of *Mr. Bigshot,* discussed earlier, is contestant-based and doesn't use a location.

The Presentation Layer

The emotional tone of a CMS game world—as evoked through sounds, art, and animation—should befit its theme of creativity and growth. We've never seen a pure CMS set in a grim, decaying world and don't imagine one would be very popular. (As in several other areas we've mentioned, *Dungeon Keeper* is an exception, but it is also a hybrid, not a pure CMS.) The player will also want a clear, unobstructed view of things; fog, darkness, and shadows won't help. The artwork of CMSs is often reminiscent of the *ligne claire* style pioneered by the Belgian author Hergé for his Tintin books: clean, strong lines, flat-shading, and even lighting.

Interaction Model

The player is almost always multipresent in a CMS because she needs to see what is happening all over the game world. It's difficult to control a large-scale process from the inside, where you can't see everything that's going on. Most CMSs don't give the player any kind of avatar. However, players do like to see what the worlds they're building look like from the inside, so games sometimes implement a *walkthrough mode* that lets players walk around the world in a first-person perspective. In *Dungeon Keeper,* which is ordinarily played in a multipresent mode, it is possible for the player to take temporary control of a creature in her dungeon, walk it around, and view the game world through the creature's eyes (see Figures 2.4 and 2.5 in Chapter 2). This feature, while occasionally useful in the military aspects of *Dungeon Keeper,* is not at all helpful in the management aspects. In short, we think the walkthrough mode is entertaining and the player will enjoy it, but the primary interaction model in a CMS needs to be multipresent.

18

Perspective

The user's perspective in a CMS naturally depends on what's being simulated. Most CMSs simulate a process taking place over a land area—whether it's a city, a farm, or an entire planet. As a result, these games tend to use an isometric perspective. The early games were all tile-based, and some still are, but for the most part, modern CMSs now use 3D environments. This has the advantage that players can zoom in and out and move the camera freely, which lets them see a broad overview most of the time, then focus on a local problem when one arises.

If your game simulates a process taking place in a three-dimensional space, you might find it useful to divide the space into layers to make it easier for the player to navigate around the game world. It's also helpful to provide a button that returns the camera instantly to a default perspective so that the player can reorient himself if he gets lost.

User Interface

Because CMSs aren't trying to create an illusion of reality in the way that first-person shooters or flight simulators do, their user interfaces can be more computerlike, using pull-down menus and rows of buttons along the edges of the screen. CMS games emphasize convenience over verisimilitude.

In a CMS, the player tries to understand and control a mathematical model—although that's not the way you will present it to her. She needs convenient access to key variables within the model. You should display the most important **scalar variables** (*single-value* variables)—for example, the amount of money she has to work with at the moment—on the screen at all times. The display can show digits if that's most appropriate or a bar graph or some other kind of graphic device, depending on the nature of the simulation.

Often the player needs to know not only the current value of a variable, but also how that variable has changed over time. This lets her track and respond to trends before trouble occurs. In *Theme Park,* a business simulation about building and managing (surprise!) theme parks, visitors came into the park, spent time, and left again. The player could see them wandering around but had difficulty getting a sense of the park's popularity just by counting heads. The player could bring up a graph in order to see how the population had changed over the past 1, 3, or 12 game years.

With **vector variables** (*multivalued* variables), you'll need a different approach. In *Caesar,* for example, every area of the Roman town that the player built needed a water supply of some sort, whether a well, pipe, or fountain. The amount of water available was, therefore, a vector, having a separate value for each square on the town grid. The game's default perspective showed all of the buildings and all of the water wells and fountains and so on but made it difficult for the player to visualize exactly how far each water supply could provide services. To get a clearer picture, the player could bring up a different view of the game world that hid most of the buildings and instead showed only structures supplying water, while displaying the amount of water available in each area as a shade of blue, from light blue indicating little water to dark blue indicating plenty.

Such analytical tools are essential to give the player an understanding of what's going on inside the simulation. *SimCity* supplied several: fire danger, crime, pollution, and so on. They allow the player to quickly locate trouble spots and to respond. These kinds of map overlays should not be snapshots that freeze a moment in time but should be continuously updated by the simulation, so that the player can watch them for a while and tell whether particular situations are getting better or worse—and most important, whether her actions are having the desired effects.

Summary

Construction and management games are about process. The player is challenged by a requirement to make the individuals in the game happy and thereby reap financial or other rewards. As a designer of these games, you need to consider the player's control of the process and the player's understanding of the current situation through the presentation layer and user interface. CMSs fulfill a desire to create and manage an entire world (or part thereof) on our own, and you should make sure to give the player plenty of tools to do it with. Economics plays a primary role in the game mechanics, and the designer who spends time making a solid economic system will find the remainder of the game easier to create.

Test Your Skills

MULTIPLE CHOICE QUESTIONS

1. What is the goal of the player in a construction and management simulation (CMS)?

   A. To defeat an enemy.

   B. To collect the most resources.

   C. To build within the context of an ongoing process.

   D. To change the process to fit a new situation.

2. Within the CMS genre, the majority of challenges are structured around
   A. combat.
   B. economics.
   C. puzzle-solving.
   D. controlling human beings.

3. The two major groups of tools that a CMS normally provides to the player are used for
   A. construction and demolition.
   B. economic and mechanical.
   C. exterior and interior.
   D. building and managing.

18

4. In the purchase-and-place construction mechanism, the player
   A. can build rapidly, using predefined elements.
   B. has the amount of the building deducted as the building is completed, which takes time.
   C. must recruit enough builders to actually make the building.
   D. gets used to waiting for one building to finish before starting another.

5. If the player chooses a place for a new building and construction happens over time rather than immediately, the gameplay mechanic is called
   A. place-and-build.
   B. plan-and-build.
   C. buy-and-sell.
   D. purchase-and-place.

6. What is a common victory condition imposed in many CMS games?
   A. Defeat the enemy.
   B. Earn a predefined amount of money.
   C. Recruit a predefined number of people.
   D. There usually isn't any victory condition.

7. What is a primary consideration when designing a multiplayer CMS?
   A. Keeping the game from becoming a race for resources.
   B. Designing the combat system.
   C. Creating artificial opponents.
   D. Keeping the robo-camels fed and watered.

8. What benefits does simulating individual people have over modeling them as a statistical aggregate?

   A. Individuals make it easier to determine overall happiness of the populace.

   B. Simulating individuals makes the player's actions more immediate and personal.

   C. Watching people voyeuristically is a primary control mechanism of the CMS genre.

   D. It requires less design work.

9. What is the relationship between needs and happiness in a CMS?

   A. Happiness and needs are both represented as scalar values.

   B. None—happiness is unrelated to needs.

   C. Unmet needs positively impact happiness.

   D. Fulfillment of a need directly affects the degree of happiness of an individual in the game.

10. What is the primary difference between a business simulation and a CMS?

    A. Business simulations never use graphics.

    B. Advisors in business simulations give financial advice.

    C. Business simulations are primarily about meeting financial goals.

    D. CMS games do not need an economic system.

11. What is the first thing you should consider designing if you're building a CMS–war game hybrid?

    A. Design the economic simulation first.

    B. Design the combat system first.

    C. Balance the unit strengths with resource placement.

    D. Design strategic goals first.

12. While some form of money is the fundamental resource for most CMS games, what other resource is commonly found in the CMS genre?

    A. Gold.

    B. Groceries.

    C. Health points.

    D. People.

13. How is the resource from the preceding question developed as one of the core gameplay mechanics?

    A. Managing their happiness becomes a big part of the gameplay.

    B. Managing their food and transportation is the most important mechanic.

    C. Harvesting gold is a primary monetary goal.

    D. Growing more food is a big gameplay mechanic.

14. How is maintenance an important mechanic in a CMS?

    A. It's an easy way for a designer to make the levels last longer.

    B. It always forces players to be active.

    C. It is a useful balancing tool to keep players from reaping endless profits.

    D. It is a source of money.

15. How do "disasters" differ from "decay" in a CMS?

    A. Disasters can be caused by the player; decay is caused by the player's lack of attention.

    B. Disasters cause the player to start the game over; decay causes her to lose more slowly.

    C. Disasters are dramatic unexpected events that force the player to act; decay is a predictable and continuous drain.

    D. There's no difference between them except the name.

Case Study

Choose a CMS that you believe, from your own experience of playing it, is an excellent example of the genre (or use one your instructor has assigned). It can be a pure CMS, a hybrid, or a pure business simulation. Write a report documenting the features that place it in this genre as opposed to another one and explaining why you believe it is superior to others of its kind. Be sure to cover at least the following areas:

- Determine if this is a purchase-and-place or plan-and-build CMS. Describe any game mechanics that are unique to this game.

CONTINUED ON NEXT PAGE

▶▶ CONTINUED

- Make a table that documents the resources, sources, and drains available to the player at the start of the game.
- Estimate what percentage of your game-playing time you must spend in maintenance. What percentage must you spend repairing damage from disasters? Does this change as the game progresses or remain the same?
- How well does the presentation layer represent the activities of the player and of the inhabitants (if there are any) of the CMS world? Can you easily see if the people are happy? Can you quickly and easily determine, through visuals, if you need to work on maintenance? If not, what method does the game use and does it work well for the player?
- Explore the user interface in all the game play modes. Is it easy to understand? Is it clear to the players what they can or cannot do, i.e., the cost or consequence of an action? For example, consider the interface for building as compared to the interface for increasing taxes in *SimCity*. How are they different? How could they be changed for the better?
- Address the economy of the CMS world. During play, is it clear how your action will impact that economy? Is there an immediate reaction or is it delayed? How does this cause the player to modify her management behavior?

The design questions in the next section may help you to think about these issues. In your report, use screen shots to illustrate your points. End the case study with suggestions for improvement or, if you feel the game cannot be improved, suggestions for additional features that might be fun to have in the game.

Alternatively, choose a game that you believe is particularly *bad*. Do the same case study, explaining what is wrong and how it could be improved.

A case study is neither a review nor a design document; it is an analysis. You are not attempting to reverse-engineer the entire game but simply to explain how it works in a general way. Your instructor will tell you the desired scope of the assignment; we recommend from five to twenty pages.

DESIGN QUESTIONS

When beginning the design of a construction and management simulation, consider the following questions:

1. What process is the player going to manage? What actions will the player take in managing that process?

2. What resources exist in this process? For each resource, how is it produced, consumed, stored, transported, and converted into other resources? Is it tangible, intangible, or a hybrid? Is it limited or unlimited? What determines its production and consumption rates?

3. Which resources can the player manipulate and which can she not?

4. Will the process settle into a balanced state or will it run down if not tended by the player? Will disasters affect it?

5. What will the player be constructing, and what function does the constructed item have? Will objects be purchased whole or planned and built over time? What does each item that the player can construct cost and how long does it take to build?

6. Can the player demolish or sell things that she builds? Does demolition cost or earn resources for the player?

7. Will the game have scenarios with victory conditions? What are they like?

8. What is the player's perspective and interaction model with the game? Is there a way to get inside the things she builds?

9. What analytical tools are provided to help her understand the workings of the simulation?

10. Is the simulated population modeled as individuals or as a statistical aggregate? If they are individuals, what is their behavior model? Are there multiple types of individuals? Can the player read their minds?

11. Will the game have advisors? What will they advise about?

12. Is this game a pure business simulation? Accounting and finance are often considered rather dull, so what makes this compelling? Does the game have a setting? If not, how can it be made visually interesting?

13. Is the game a hybrid with other sorts of games? What other elements in the game make it a hybrid (strategic problems, action challenges, puzzles, and so on)? How do they affect the way the game is controlled?

Chapter | 19

Adventure Games

Chapter Objectives

After reading this chapter and completing the exercises, you will be able to do the following:

- Know the definition of an adventure game and the common game features of the genre.
- Understand the importance of character and story in the genre.
- Describe the different interaction models and perspectives common to adventure games.
- Understand how to use puzzles and inventory in designing an adventure game.

Introduction

Adventure games are seldom a technological challenge to build, but what they lack in technological challenges they make up for in creative ones. As the designer of an adventure game, it's your job to bring not just a story but a world to life—a world in which a story is taking place. Your talents at creating places, characters, plots, dialog, and puzzles will be tested as in no other genre. Because the adventure game is not bound to flying or shooting or commanding troops in battle—indeed, it isn't bound to any particular mode of interaction—it has the greatest potential for creativity of any genre.

This chapter defines adventure games and covers the history and evolution of these games from text-based to today's hybrids. The features common to adventure games and the game play mechanics that define the genre are explored in depth. Puzzle structure, game flow, dialog, and language, all of which form integral parts of the adventure game, are covered. The chapter finishes with a discussion of the art and user interface that is unique to this genre.

What Are Adventure Games?

The thirst for adventure is the vent which Destiny offers; a war, a crusade, a gold mine, a new country, speak to the imagination and offer swing and play to the confined powers.

—Ralph Waldo Emerson, "Boston," in *Natural History of the Intellect,* 1893

The term *adventure game* is a bit misleading because a lot of games about being adventurous aren't adventure games—and a lot of adventure games aren't about adventures, at least in the fairy-tale sense of going forth to seek one's fortune. The reason for the term is historical. *Adventure game* is really short for *Adventure-type game,* meaning a game similar to the one named *Adventure* (sometimes referred to as *Colossal Cave*). All adventure games are conceptual descendants of the original *Adventure,* although nowadays they include many features that *Adventure* lacked.

Adventure games are rather different from most other games on the market. An adventure game isn't a competition or a simulation. An adventure game doesn't offer a process to be managed or an opponent to be defeated through strategy and tactics. Instead, an adventure game is an interactive story about a character who is controlled by the player. This character is the player's avatar, but he's more than merely a representative of the player. He is a fictional person in his own right, a protagonist, the hero of the story. A few adventure games have been made (most recently, *Dreamfall*), in which the player switches from one avatar to another at different points in the game, but they are not the norm.

> An **adventure game** is an interactive story about a protagonist character who is played by the player. Storytelling and exploration are essential elements of the game. Puzzle-solving and conceptual challenges make up the majority of the gameplay. Combat, economic management, and action challenges are reduced or nonexistent.

This definition doesn't mean that there is no conflict in adventure games (although many adventure games have none)—only that combat is not a primary activity. Adventure games seldom have an internal economy. All the relationships within the game are symbolic rather than numeric. Manipulating or optimizing an economic system forms no part of the adventure game experience; this (among other things) sets them apart from role-playing games.

The Original *Adventure*

Adventure was a text-only game. It offered simple but—at the time that it was written—completely novel gameplay. The player, as an explorer, wandered around in an enormous cave filled with treasures and dangers. A variety of obstacles prevented her from getting into the deeper parts of the cave, but by cleverly using the things that she found, the player could overcome the obstacles and continue exploring. The object of the game was to gather all the treasures and bring them out of the cave.

Adventure was the first computer game to give the player a credible illusion of freedom, which remains an important quality of adventure games today. Before *Adventure,* computer games, all of which were text-based at the time, tended to ask specific questions and expect specific, often numeric, answers ("How many seconds should the lunar lander fire its engine?") or to present players with a fixed list of options and ask them to choose one. The player could type anything she wanted in *Adventure,* and the game would try to respond appropriately. Of course, the game understood only a limited number of words, but because it didn't explicitly tell her the list of allowed commands, she always felt as if she might discover something else that it could do.

Adventure also brought personality to computer gaming. Most of the games written at the time spoke to the player in a kind of programmerese. Games gave prompts such as "Enter horsepower" and printed error messages such as "Value too high, re-enter (5–500)." *Adventure* spoke to players as if it were a person rather than a machine, saying "I don't know how to do that" rather than "Invalid command." It could become sarcastic if the player tried to do something ridiculous or impossible, or even be funny occasionally, another rarity among games of its day. Comedy remains a major element of many adventure games because it discourages the player from taking the game too seriously. Breaches in suspension of disbelief don't bother the player as much in a comic setting as they do in a dramatic one because the player is less immersed in the story in the first place.

The Growth of Adventure Games

Adventure games were highly popular in the early days of personal computers. Having no graphics made text adventures inexpensive to develop and allowed great scope for both the designer's and the player's imaginations. A group of researchers at the MIT Artificial Intelligence Lab, inspired by the original *Adventure,* wrote a much larger adventure game named *Zork* on the mainframe there. Soon afterward, they converted it to run on personal computers and founded a company, Infocom, devoted to developing text adventures. Infocom published games about all kinds of things: fantasy magic, *film noir* detective stories, exploration of an ancient Egyptian pyramid, and so on.

The original *Adventure* didn't have any plot; it just offered a space to explore and puzzles to solve. With minor exceptions, its world did not change as time passed. But it wasn't long before games began to explore the notion of *interactive storytelling,* which we discuss in detail in Chapter 7, "Storytelling and Narrative."

As soon as personal computers began to develop graphics capability (the very earliest were text-only), developers started to add graphics to adventure games, and the games really took off. LucasArts and Sierra On-Line dominated the genre and for a while produced the best-looking, highest-class games on the market: funny, scary, mysterious, and fascinating. Adventure games provided challenges and explored areas that other genres didn't touch. *Myst,* a point-and-click graphic adventure, was for many years the best-selling personal computer game of all time. (It has recently been supplanted by *The Sims.*)

Adventure Games Today

In the past few years, the market for adventure games has grown less steadily than the market for other genres. Adventure games depend less on display technology than fast-paced action games do; as a result, they get less attention from the gaming press, contributing to a misconception that the adventure game genre is dead. In fact, adventure games are alive and well; they're just not as highly publicized as their high-adrenaline cousins.

The invention of 3D hardware accelerators actually gave adventure games a new lease on life. Players usually think of dynamic three-dimensional worlds in the contexts in which they first appeared—vehicle simulations and first-person shooters—but 3D hardware offers a lot to adventure games as well. The first graphical adventure games came with gorgeously painted but static backdrops for every scene that looked much like theatrical stage sets. Players could see a lot of things but could touch only a few of them. But when graphics technology renders every object in three dimensions and it's possible to move freely among them, the world becomes much more immediate and alive. Many adventure games now display a 3D world.

The static-backdrop adventure game is still around, but nowadays it may use scenes created with 3D-rendering software and ray tracing rather than pixel painting. *Myst,* the first commercial game to use 3D-rendered backgrounds, owes some of its success to its sophisticated graphics.

At the same time, other genres have begun to adopt the puzzle and storytelling features that were once unique to the adventure genre.

Action-Adventures   The arrival of 3D hardware also gave rise to a new sort of game, a hybrid of action game and adventure game called, unsurprisingly, an *action-adventure.* The action-adventure is faster paced than a pure adventure game and includes physical as well as conceptual challenges. *Indiana Jones and the Infernal Machine* provides a good example of the type. The modern *Zelda* games might be considered another, although with their levels and bosses, they are closer to being pure action games. Exactly when a game stops being an adventure game and becomes an action game is a matter of interpretation. Some might consider the *Tomb Raider* games to be action-adventures because they include puzzles, but the puzzles are quite simple, and the games rely so heavily on physical challenges that we would classify them as an action game.

Many adventure game purists don't care for action-adventures; generally, they dislike any sort of physical challenge or time pressure. If you plan to make your game an action-adventure, you should be aware that, although your design might appeal to some action gamers who might not otherwise buy your game, you might also discourage some adventure gamers who would. Without doubt, however, action-adventure hybrids are now more popular than traditional adventure games.

The Replayability Question   At first glance, the lack of replayability seems the greatest disadvantage of adventure games. Most adventure games consist of a sequence of puzzles, each of which has a single solution; when you know the solution, there's not much challenge in playing it again. An adventure game that requires 40 hours to finish the first time might take only 4 hours the second time.

A good designer should consider making puzzle sequences or challenges that allow the player a choice of solutions. The consequences of the choices can affect not only the game being played but also the story being told. The player who chooses to blow up the gate blocking her way might accidentally hurt someone in the process and be chased out of town. The player who needs a specific key might have to steal it and have someone chasing her as a thief. Offering alternate solutions adds to the replayability of the game. Adventure game puzzle design and challenges are discussed later in this chapter.

In practice, however, replayability isn't much of a problem. Research shows that a great many players never finish these games at all; even if the game offers 30 or 40 hours of gameplay, many players play for only 15 or 20. This suggests that if they can't replay a 40-hour game for another 40 hours, it's unlikely to affect their purchasing decision. Provided that the game gives good value for the money the first time around, it doesn't necessarily need to be replayable.

Game Features

In adventure games, the player's avatar visits an explorable area containing a variety of puzzles or problems to be solved. Solving these problems opens new areas for exploration or advances the storyline, giving the player new information and new problems to solve. Exploring the environment and manipulating items in it are essential elements of an adventure game. It's possible to develop a game that consists entirely of conversations with nonplayer characters (NPCs), but that wouldn't be considered an adventure game.

Adventure games typically offer only a few gameplay modes. Unlike sports games, with all of the associated team-management functions, or war games, with associated battle-planning modes, adventure games don't need a lot of specialized screens. Apart from the need to look at a map or the avatar's inventory or to examine objects closely, the player always sees and interacts with the world in the same way, and that doesn't change from one end of the game to the other.

Setting and Emotional Tone

In some kinds of games, such as chess and *Quake,* the setting is almost irrelevant. Serious players ignore the idea that chess is a medieval war game or that *Quake* involves space marines on an alien planet. They concentrate on the bare essentials of the gameplay: strategy in the former case and blazing action in the latter. If the setting intrudes, it is only a distraction.

Adventure games reverse this situation. The setting contributes more to the entertainment value of an adventure game than settings in any other genre. Whether it's grim and depressing, fantastic and outlandish, or funny and cheerful, the setting creates the world the player explores and lives in. For many players, the setting is the reason for playing adventure games in the first place.

The majority of computer games offer little emotional subtlety. Games of pure strategy have no emotional content at all; action games and war games have little more. Nor do most single-player games inspire complex emotions in the player. "Yippee!" and "Damn!" are about the limit of it—exhilaration and frustration, respectively. Role-playing games (RPGs), with their deeper stories, offer greater opportunities for emotional expression, but even when their designers take advantage of this depth, the emotion tends to get lost in a morass of bookkeeping. Multiplayer games are an exception; their social context allows for richer interactions because they take place among real people.

Adventure games are always single-player games, so they can't rely on social interactions to create richness. They don't have intricate strategy, high-speed action, or management details to occupy the player's attention. The games move more slowly, which gives designers the chance to create a world with a distinct emotional tone. Good examples from the past and present are *Phantasmagoria,* one of the first graphical horror games; the *Myst* series, with its surreal buildings and empty spaces; and *Shadow of the Colossus's* vast and beautiful landscapes, which made it distinctly more than an ordinary action-adventure.

Interaction Model

Adventure games always use an avatar-based interaction model because the designer wants to put the player inside a story. However, the nature of the avatar in adventure games has changed over the years. The early games *Adventure* and *Myst* used nonspecific avatars, an idea that we discussed in Chapter 6, "Character Development." In effect, the games pretended that the player *was* the avatar.

Eventually, however, game designers abandoned this model so that they could develop games in which the avatar possessed a personality of his own, someone who belonged in the game world rather than being a visitor there. Sierra On-Line's *Leisure Suit Larry* series and Revolution's *Broken Sword* games are good examples. In these games, the player could see his avatar walking around, interacting with the world.

Perspective

The preferred camera perspective of graphical adventure games is changing. The context-sensitive approach is traditional, but third- and first-person games are becoming increasingly common. Here we examine the advantages and disadvantages of these approaches.

Context-Sensitive Perspective Using the context-sensitive perspective, the game depicts the avatar from whatever camera angle is most appropriate for her current location in the game world. If the avatar moves to a new location that is significantly different from the previous one, the camera behavior takes this into account. For example, going from indoors to outdoors, the camera might move farther away from the avatar to show more of the environment.

In the early days of graphic adventure games, the camera angles tended to be quite dull, as in Figure 19.1, from *Leisure Suit Larry in the Land of the Lounge Lizards*. As display hardware improved, game development required more artists and the quality of the artwork improved considerably. The game's art director chose a camera position designed to show off each location to best effect. Compare Figure 19.1 with Figure 19.2 from *Grim Fandango*.

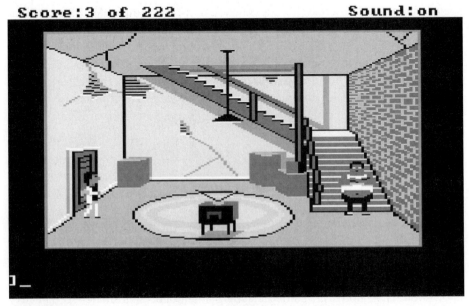

FIGURE 19.1 A scene in the original *Leisure Suit Larry.*

FIGURE 19.2 A scene in *Grim Fandango.* Note the camera position.

A context-sensitive perspective lets the designer (or art director) play cinematographer, using camera angles, composition, and lighting to enhance the story. Use these techniques with discretion, however. A light touch is best. If you watch movies closely, you'll notice that the majority of shots use a pretty straightforward camera angle. Movie directors don't use unexpected angles just for the fun of it; they do so to make a deliberate point.

First-Person Perspective   One of the most famous graphic adventure games of all, *Myst,* used a first-person perspective. You may be familiar with the look of contemporary first-person games, but unlike these, *Myst* did not render a three-dimensional game world in real time even though it used a first-person perspective. The *Myst* world consisted of a large number of prerendered still frames that appeared one at a time as the avatar walked around. Prerendering made finely detailed and highly atmospheric images possible. On the other hand, *Myst* couldn't depict continuously moving objects or changes in the sunlight as time passed, and the number of angles from which the player could look at things was limited. The world was rich but static.

A real-time 3D first-person perspective gives the player the best sense of being in the world but doesn't let the player see his avatar unless he happens upon some functioning reflective surface in the game world. This perspective also tends to encourage a more action-oriented approach to playing the game, running around without paying much attention to the surroundings. Because much of the entertainment of an adventure game comes from seeing the avatar explore the world and interact with other characters, the first-person perspective doesn't offer as many opportunities for visual drama as other perspectives do.

Third-Person Perspective   The third-person perspective keeps the player's avatar constantly in view, as in *Indiana Jones and the Emperor's Tomb,* an action-adventure hybrid. This perspective is common for action-adventures in which the player might need to react quickly (see Figure 19.3).

If the camera in the third-person perspective always remains behind the avatar's back, however, the view can become rather dull and doesn't let the player appreciate the environment. And unlike pure action games in which the avatar's actions and motivations are simple, adventure games sometimes need camera perspectives that allow for more subtle situations. In Figure 19.4, from *Gabriel Knight 3,* Gabriel hides to see when the maid leaves the room.

The later *Gabriel Knight* games also allowed the player to move the camera around somewhat (see Figure 19.5)—as do some of the better action games, such as *Spyro the Dragon* and *Toy Story 2: Buzz Lightyear to the Rescue!* This mimics how a real person can turn his head to look in a given direction without moving his whole body.

FIGURE 19.3 *Indiana Jones and the Emperor's Tomb.* This is the typical action-adventure perspective.

FIGURE 19.4 *Gabriel Knight 3* in a context-sensitive camera angle.

FIGURE 19.5 *Gabriel Knight* as seen from a player-adjusted camera position. The Volkswagen bus would not be visible if the camera were behind him.

IN THE TRENCHES: *The Secret of Monkey Island*

The Secret of Monkey Island, now more than sixteen years old, remains worth studying because it spawned a highly successful franchise. Although ostensibly set on a Caribbean island in the 1700s and concerning a young man who wanted to be a pirate, the game featured anachronistic touches and was played for laughs. In that respect, it seemed a lot like certain Disney animated films—*The Jungle Book*, for example—although slightly edgier.

When Ron Gilbert, the designer of *The Secret of Monkey Island*, started work on the game, he had already created an adventure game engine called SCUMM, an acronym for Script Creation Utility for *Maniac Mansion* (an earlier LucasArts adventure game). SCUMM represented an important innovation for graphic adventure games: It put the possible actions on the screen so players no longer had to guess what their options were, and it did away with typing. More important for the developers, SCUMM enabled them to create new adventure games easily without programming them from scratch each time. Three of the five *Monkey Island* games used the SCUMM utility in addition to *Maniac Mansion* itself and several other LucasArts games.

The Secret of Monkey Island included a number of other innovations as well, most notably an insult-driven sword fight between the avatar, Guybrush Threepwood, and a master swordswoman. Rather than making the fight a physical challenge, which would have required a lot of additional programming and would have turned off some players, Gilbert chose to make use of (and make fun of) the way adversaries always insulted one another in old swashbuckling movies. When his adversary insults Guybrush, the player must choose an appropriate comeback quip. Choosing a good comeback gives Guybrush advantage in the fight; choosing the wrong one forces Guybrush to retreat. For Guybrush to win the fight, he must choose enough correct quips. The insults themselves contain clues as to which reply is correct, so players don't have to find out by trial and error.

It's this kind of lateral thinking about the design that separates great adventure games from merely good ones. The *Monkey Island* series belongs among the greats.

Player Roles

In most computer games, the player's role is largely defined by the challenges offered, whether as an athlete in a sports game, a pilot in a flight simulator, or a martial arts expert in a fighting game. But adventure games can be filled with all kinds of puzzles and problems unrelated to the player's stated role. Indiana Jones is supposedly an archaeologist, but we don't see him digging very much. The role of the player in an adventure game arises not out of the challenges (unless you specifically want it to), but out of the story. The player can still be a pilot, if that's what the story requires, but that doesn't necessarily guarantee that she'll get to fly a plane. And she might be anything else or nothing in particular—just an ordinary person living in an extraordinary situation.

A good many adventure games do connect the player's role with the game's activities, however. Almost all adventure games treat the story as a journey (see the section *The Story as a Journey* in Chapter 7, "Storytelling and Narrative"), mapping the plot of the story onto physical travel through the game world, so the player's role often involves travel or investigation: explorer, detective, hunter, conquistador, and so on.

Be sure that the player's role is suitable for the genre, however, or it could be frustrating for the player. *Heart of China,* an otherwise straightforward adventure game, included a poorly implemented 3D tank simulator. To get beyond a specific point required the player to use the tank simulator success-fully. This created a real problem; adventure game enthusiasts seldom play vehicle simulations, and many could not get past that point. The obligatory action element spoiled the game for them.

Structure

Because adventure games map a story onto a space, they establish a relationship between different locations in the world and different parts of the story. Over the years, the nature of this relationship has evolved. The earliest adventure games, including the original *Adventure,* emphasized exploration at the expense of story. The game provided few cues that could give the player a sense of time passing—that is, of making progress through a story toward an ending. The game simply gave her a large space and told her to wander around. Structurally, the game looked rather like the drawing in Figure 19.6.

As adventure games became larger and began to include a more detailed story, designers started to break them into chapters (see Figure 19.7). The player could wander around all he liked in the area devoted to a given chapter, but when he moved on to the next, the story advanced and there was no way back. This had the effect of making the story more linear, which was both easier to write for and easier to program. If the player needed to take a particular object from one chapter to the next, the story would not let him progress until that object was in his inventory. This arrangement is functionally identical to the foldback story structure described in Chapter 7, "Storytelling and Narrative." In a foldback story, the player has some dramatic freedom, but his options eventually narrow to a single inevitable event before branching out again. In adventure games, this inevitable event is normally the transition to the next chapter.

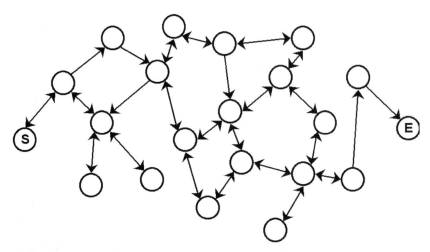

FIGURE 19.6 The structure of early adventure games. Each circle represents a room. S is the starting room, and E is the end.

With the arrival of 3D graphics and the action-adventure, the stories became more linear still. Areas occasionally offered simple side branches but few complex spaces to explore. The space in an action-adventure is structured more like that of a first-person shooter (see Figure 19.8), because action-adventures emphasize conflict challenges (often shooting and fighting) over exploration. A good many action-adventures have a lot more action than they do adventuring.

Storytelling

We discuss storytelling at length in Chapter 7, "Storytelling and Narrative." In this section, we reiterate a few of the key points and talk about their significance in adventure games, because adventure games rely on storytelling more than any other genre.

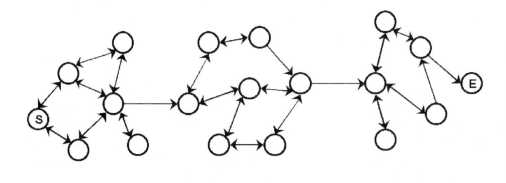

Chapter 1   Chapter 2   Chapter 3

FIGURE 19.7 The structure of story-driven adventure games.

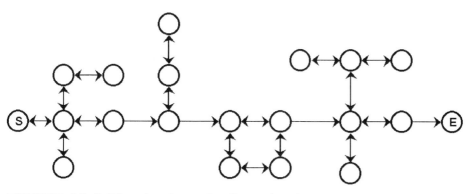

FIGURE 19.8 The structure of action-adventure games.

19

Dramatic Tension   Dramatic tension, which arises from an unresolved situation or problem, is what holds the reader's attention and keeps her around to see how the story comes out.

To create dramatic tension, start by presenting the problem. In adventure games, this often happens in a cut-scene right at the beginning of the game. The meaning of the scene doesn't have to be immediately clear; mystery and uncertainty may help set the mood for your story. For example, *The Longest Journey* begins when April Ryan, the player's avatar and heroine of the game, has been having increasingly vivid nightmares whose meaning she does not understand. At the beginning of the game, she has no goal other than to find out why she's having nightmares. Later, dramatic tension increases as we learn the source of those nightmares and new problems emerge.

The resolution of dramatic tension occurs at a moment called the dramatic climax, usually near the end of the story. Shorter stories frequently have only one source of dramatic tension and one dramatic climax; longer stories can have several, of progressively increasing importance. An extremely long story can have several major dramatic climaxes at intervals, tied together by a common theme, setting, or characters. Richard Wagner's cycle of four operas, *The Ring of the Nibelungs*, is one such extended work. Each opera is a self-contained story with its own dramatic climax, although some characters carry over from one opera to the next, and all of the operas concern the fate of the same magic ring.

Because adventure games are usually much longer than movies or short stories, you will probably want to create several different dramatic climaxes as well—each one resolving a current or immediate problem until the last climax, which should resolve the overall problem of the whole story. In the adventure game, dramatic tension is created through the combination of dramatic storytelling and interactive puzzles. Impending doom that can only be stopped by the player's intervention can provide a dramatic point to the story, as long as the player doesn't feel as though the tension is contrived.

As an adventure game designer, you can use puzzles to create a minor form of dramatic tension. However, puzzles of the types designers usually employ (as described later in the section *Challenges*) alone are not enough to keep the player actively interested in the story for the length of the game. Puzzles present small, individual problems. Your story will need a larger problem that underpins the whole story, something that, even if it isn't revealed to the player at the beginning of the game, is the reason that there is a story.

The Heroic Quest   The majority of adventure games fall into the category of heroic quests, each one a mission by a single individual to accomplish some great (or, in the case of *Leisure Suit Larry,* not-so-great) feat. You can imagine adventure games structured along other lines but will find few on the market that don't adhere to the heroic quest scenario. Although it's possible to write an adventure game based on a detailed character study, no one has done so as a commercial product.

The heroic quest traditionally involves a movement from the familiar to the unfamiliar and from a time of low danger to a time of great danger. The biggest, most dramatic climax you offer the player should be the last major climax in the game because anything that follows is likely to seem irrelevant. Remember that the boss enemies appear at the ends of levels in action games; if you defeat the Lord of Terror, it feels anticlimactic and rather unfair to have to fight his second-in-command afterward.

Occasionally exceptions to this structure arise, such as in stories in which the hero is abducted at the beginning, escapes, and must return to his home. However, in these stories, the protagonist's struggles don't get easier and easier until he just strolls in happily. He often returns home to find that things have changed for the worse and must be corrected or that he must leave again to hunt down his abductor.

None of this means that there can't ever be periods of quiet; in fact, there should be. In both of J. R. R. Tolkien's most famous books, *The Hobbit* and *The Lord of the Rings,* periods of great danger alternate with periods of safety and rest for the heroes, during which they regain their strength. A long story that consists of nothing but action will feel unrealistic and silly after a while.

The works of Joseph Campbell and Christopher Vogler discuss the heroic quest at length, and we encourage you to read them for inspiration (see the references for details).

The Problem of Death   For many years, game designers have debated the question of whether adventure games should allow the avatar to make a fatal mistake. Some adventure games proudly advertise on their boxes that the player can't ever die; the manuals of other games warn that the player might encounter mortal danger. In some respects, this seems like a strange thing to worry about. After all, avatars routinely die in action games and in flight simulator crashes, so why shouldn't they be able to die in adventure games?

The nature of the gameplay makes the question controversial. In a first-person shooter or a military flight simulator, it's obvious that the avatar is in mortal peril all the time. In fact, in games of most genres, it's win or lose, kill or be killed by clearly marked enemies, all the time. Adventure games differ because they seldom provide an explicitly declared enemy; instead, the game encourages the player to go everywhere and touch everything. If you tell the player to explore the world and then you fill it with deathtraps, he's in for a frustrating time. Nowadays, most adventure games adopt a *fair warning* approach, making it clear when an object or action threatens danger and (usually) offering a way of neutralizing or circumventing that danger. If you put a dragon in a cave, it's a nice touch to litter the entrance with the bones of earlier adventurers. That ought to get the point across.

Most adventure games supply a save-game feature, so death isn't necessarily catastrophic; on the other hand, stopping to save the game does tend to hurt the player's feeling of immersion. Adventure games shouldn't be so dangerous that the player needs to save all the time. If you are going to let the player's avatar be killed in your game, using an autosave feature to save the game at intervals allows the player to restore it later, even if he hasn't explicitly saved it. The player doesn't have to know that the game is being saved for him; telling him only harms the suspension of disbelief.

Challenges

The majority of challenges in an adventure game are conceptual: puzzles that can only be solved by lateral thinking. The following list of a few popular puzzles—of the many types available—will help get you started:

- **Finding keys to locked doors.** By *doors* and *keys,* we mean any obstruction that prevents progress and any object that removes the obstruction. Because this type of puzzle is so common, the challenge for you as a designer is to give players enough variety that the door-and-key puzzles don't all seem the same.

- **Figuring out mysterious machines.** This is, in effect, a combination lock instead of a lock with a key. The player manipulates a variety of knobs to make a variety of indicators show the correct reading. Try to make the presence of these knobs reasonably plausible—too many adventure games include mysterious machines that clearly function only as puzzles, not as realistic parts of the game world.

- **Obtaining inaccessible objects.** In this kind of puzzle, the player can see but not reach an object, which may be a treasure or a key to open some door elsewhere in the game world (remember that this doesn't need to be an actual key). The player must find a clever way of reaching the object, perhaps by building some device that will give access.

- **Manipulating people.** Sometimes an obstruction is not a physical object but a person, and the trick is to find out what will make the person go away or let the player pass. If it's a simple question of giving the obstructor something he wants, then the problem is really just a lock-and-key puzzle. For a more creative approach, create a puzzle in which the person must be either defeated or distracted. The player should have to talk to him to learn his weaknesses.

- **Navigating mazes.** Use mazes—confusing areas that make it difficult for the player to know where he is or where to go—sparingly. Making a bad maze is easy; making an interesting maze is difficult. A maze should always contain clues that an observant player can notice and use to help her learn her way around.

- **Decoding cryptic messages.** Many players enjoy decoding messages, as long as you give sufficient clues to help out.

- **Solving memorization puzzles.** These puzzles require the player to remember where something is—a variant of the game Concentration. She can usually defeat these by taking notes, but that's reasonable enough; it's how we remember things anyway. The real challenge for you as the designer is to create a realistic reason for a memorization puzzle to be in the game.

- **Collecting things.** The player must find all the pieces of the magic whatchamacallit. Finding, rescuing, or retrieving the individual pieces will involve puzzle solving; collecting itself is not a puzzle.

- **Doing detective work.** Instead of solving a puzzle per se, the player figures out a sequence of events from clues and interviews with witnesses. The situation doesn't necessarily have to involve a crime; you could use any unknown event. Detective work forms the basis for many police-procedure games.

- **Understanding social problems.** No, we don't mean inflation or unemployment. The challenges of understanding and perhaps influencing the relationships between people make up a little-explored aspect of adventure game design. Most adventure games limit characters to very simple, mechanical states of mind. If we devote a little more effort, people, rather than objects, could become the primary subject of adventure games, and this would make the games much more interesting.

When designing puzzles, try to allow for lateral thinking of the players. If there's more than one way to solve a puzzle, don't arbitrarily restrict the player to *your* preferred method. Obviously, you can't build in multiple solutions to every puzzle, but if the player tries something entirely logical and there's no good reason why it doesn't work, she's going to be frustrated. Only play-testing can tell you whether a puzzle is too hard or too easy, and you can't adjust an adventure game's difficulty by tweaking some numbers the way you can adjust the difficulty of games in some other genres.

Conversations with Nonplayer Characters (NPCs)

From the original *Adventure* onward, adventure game designers have faced the problem of how to create realistic nonplayer characters (NPCs). Computer role-playing game (CRPG) designers must address this problem, too, but in most CRPGs, an NPC's conversation is defined by the character's role: blacksmith, healer, tavern keeper, and so on. The player doesn't expect to be able to discuss arms and armor with a tavern keeper (although the games might be more interesting and certainly less formulaic if he could). But because adventure games are interactive stories, players expect the characters in them to be more like humans and less mechanical.

A good many games try to sidestep the problem entirely by setting the game in underpopulated worlds with extremely few, if any, people. This certainly creates a mysterious atmosphere, but suits only a limited range of stories. Imagine how Rick's bar in *Casablanca* would feel if it weren't full of people drinking and gambling. A world with no people seems artificial and sterile.

A few early text-based games tried to implement parsers that could understand limited English sentences as typed by the player, but these seldom succeeded. NPCs either said "I don't understand that" or gave answers not quite to the point when the player asked a perfectly reasonable question giving the impression that the NPCs were drugged or mentally ill.

In the end, most adventure game designers gave up on trying to create the impression that the player could talk to anyone about anything and devised the *scripted conversation,* a mechanism that became the de facto standard for both adventure games and CRPGs. Scripted conversations are discussed in detail in Chapter 7, "Storytelling and Narrative."

Mapping

In the old days, when playing text adventures, players usually needed to make maps for themselves as they went along. Because such games didn't display the rooms graphically but only described them, players found it difficult to remember how the rooms related to one another. A lot of text adventure designers made worlds illogical on purpose, so the player found it doubly important to keep a map showing the relationships between different areas.

With the arrival of graphical adventures, mapping became less critical because the graphics provided cues to the player's current location and how that location related to other areas in the world. However, we still think it's a good idea to give the player a map. A few games deliberately deny the player a map to make the game more difficult, but this—like any obstacle that slows down the play without providing any entertainment value—usually indicates poor design. There's not a lot of fun in being lost. If you force the player to make his own map, he has to constantly look away from the screen to a sketch pad at his side; that's a tedious business that rapidly destroys suspension of disbelief.

The map that you give the player doesn't have to be complete at the beginning of the game; it can start out empty and be filled in as the player moves around, a process called *automapping*. The player should be able to refer to this map conveniently at any time. It's also a good idea to give the player a compass to tell him which direction he's facing. You can also include the map as an item to be found in the game, along the lines of a treasure map. This provides the player with a way to find his way around and keeps the map within the game world as well.

Automapping destroys the challenge imposed by mazes, but we think mazes are one of the most overused and least-enjoyed features of adventure games. Unless you have a strong reason for including a maze (such as recreating the adventures of Theseus in the Minotaur's labyrinth) *and* can construct one that's really clever and fun to be in, don't do it. If you strongly feel the need for a maze, consider making it an optional mini-game.

Journal Keeping

Another common feature of adventure games—one that is conceptually similar to automapping—is automatic journal keeping. The game fills in a journal with text as the player goes along, recording important events or information she uncovers. If the game includes a convoluted plot or large numbers of characters, the journal can be an invaluable reference tool for the player. Let her call it up and look at it at any reasonable time (though not, perhaps, while hanging over the edge of a cliff or being interrogated by a villain). As with conversations with NPCs, the journal gives you an opportunity to define the avatar's character through his use of language. Journals are ideal for games in which the player must collect informational clues, such as mysteries in the Nancy Drew series.

A Few Things to Avoid

As adventure games evolved, designers created many different kinds of puzzles and experiences for the player. Some of these are extremely clever, such as the insult-driven sword fight in *The Secret of Monkey Island*. A good many others, however, proved to be only tiresome time wasters, obstacles that add no entertainment value to the game.

Puzzles Solvable Only by Trial and Error   If you give the player a puzzle that has a fixed number of possible solutions of equal probability (in effect, a combination lock), but no hints about which solution is right, then the player simply has to try them all. The Infocom text adventure *Infidel* included a puzzle like this: The player had to line up four statues of Egyptian goddesses in the correct order, but there were no clues about what the correct order might be. The player could do nothing but try all 24 possible combinations and keep track of the ones she had already tried. There's not much fun in that. Instead, find clever ways to provide the clues.

Conceptual Non Sequiturs   This is a variant of the trial-and-error puzzle, a problem whose solution requires thinking so lateral that it's completely irrational. The term describes something along the lines of "put the sombrero on the bulldozer" or "sharpen the headphones with the banana." A few games try to get away with this by claiming that it's surrealism, but true surrealism is informed by some kind of underlying point; it's not just random weirdness. We discuss conceptual non sequiturs at greater length in Chapter 12, "General Principles of Level Design."

A variant of this is the opposite-reaction puzzle, one whose solution turns out to be the exact opposite of what you'd expect. You could give the player a rubber dagger and then have it turn out to be a deadly weapon after all. In the original *Adventure,* the player could drive away a menacing snake by releasing a little bird from its cage. Fortunately, at that point in *Adventure,* the player didn't have many options, so he usually found the solution quickly. But unless you design an entire game on this principle, players may see it as just an annoying gimmick.

Illogical Spaces   Illogical spaces were a classic challenge in text adventures. If you went north from room A, you got to room B, but if you went south from room B, you didn't necessarily go back to room A. Modern games use teleporters to give a similar effect; the player may step out of a teleporter with no idea where it has taken her. In such a space, the player simply has to wander around taking notes until she can figure out the relationships among the various locations. Unless you offer some clues, this is another puzzle that can be solved only by trial and error.

Puzzles Requiring Outside Knowledge   Many adventure games include references to things outside the game world for comic effect, but those references shouldn't be part of a puzzle. A game that requires the player to know information from a source other than itself is unfair. For example, *Haunt* offered puzzles that could be solved only by players familiar with the 1960s-era cartoon series *Beany and Cecil* and with the movie *Monty Python and the Holy Grail.* It didn't really matter because *Haunt* was free and was mostly a joke anyway, but in a commercial game, such puzzles would be unreasonable unless you explicitly made it clear that the game required a knowledge of trivia. If you want to make humorous references to popular TV shows, movies, and so on, do them in narrative or in an NPC's conversation rather than as solutions to puzzles. Beware, though: Cultural references age quickly and will make the game seem dated after a few years.

You have to be even more careful when developing games for foreign markets because other countries don't always have the same idioms. For instance, the action "Wear the lampshade on my head" could cause other characters in the game to assume that the player's avatar is drunk, which might be desirable in the context of the story. However, wearing a lampshade as a sign of drunkenness is an American cultural idiom that might not be understood in, say, Japan. Again, it's okay to make cultural references in your game; just be careful about requiring the user to understand them in order to win.

Click-the-Right-Pixel Puzzles   A few adventure games with point-and-click user interfaces require the player to click on a tiny and inconspicuous area of the screen to advance the story for no particular reason except that that particular pixel is difficult to find. This is lazy design—a cheap way of creating an obstacle for the player without any entertainment value. *Indiana Jones and the Holy Grail*, for example, required the player to click exactly on one pixel during the end game in order to duck under a swinging blade. For most players, this was a tedious and irritating solution to a well-known movie sequence.

Too Many Backward Puzzles   A *backward puzzle* is one in which the player finds the solution before finding the puzzle itself. She finds a key but doesn't yet know of any locked doors. However, she picks it up and carries it around with her all the time, just in case. When she does eventually find a locked door, she immediately has the solution, which means it's not much of a puzzle. By including a large number of backward puzzles, you force the player to carry around a big inventory of stuff that she has no idea why she's carrying. It encourages players to pick up everything they see whether they need it or not, which is now considered an outdated mechanic and harmful to the game's immersion. A few backward puzzles are okay; a world full is poor design.

You may run across situations where you didn't intend to insert a backward puzzle in your game, but the player finds the solution before finding the puzzle because it's difficult to predict in what order the player will traverse the terrain of the game. It's not always possible to prevent the player from finding the solution first because the solution has to be available, but it can be inconspicuous—a poster on a wall full of posters or an object in a trash can. Be aware, however, that *inconspicuous* is not the same as *obscure* or *nonsensical*. If the key to a puzzle involves finding a live monkey, the monkey shouldn't turn out to be locked in a freezer.

Too Many FedEx Puzzles   A *FedEx puzzle* is one that you solve by picking up an object from one place and taking it to a different place, as if you were a courier. Of course, carrying objects around until you find a place to use them is a common feature of adventure games, but some games consist of little else. This gets dull after a while, especially if the solution to a puzzle consists only of fetching and carrying without any lateral thinking or other activity. Liven up the game with a variety of puzzles and tasks. Create objects that have a variety of different uses, such as Indy's bullwhip in *Indiana Jones and the Infernal Machine* or objects that are left over from one puzzle but have a part to play in another.

The Presentation Layer

Adventure games, more than most other genres, try to hide the fact that the player is using a computer. By comparison to vehicle simulators, sports games, or RPGs, adventure games offer very simple user interfaces. The player needs to move through the world, talk to NPCs, and manipulate or collect objects using intuitive commands or actions that do not interfere with his sense of immersion in the story.

Avatar Movement

The movement interface that you design depends considerably on the perspective you choose. When playing from a first-person or third-person perspective, the player needs a way of steering her avatar around the world, as in an action game. We suggest that you look at Chapter 13, "Action Games," for a discussion of avatar movement in games featuring first- and third-person perspectives.

Games featuring context-sensitive perspective commonly use one of two user interfaces: *point-and-click* or *direct control.*

Point-and-Click Interfaces   In this user interface, the player clicks with a mouse cursor somewhere on the screen. If the corresponding location in the game is accessible, the avatar walks to it. If the player clicks an active object, the avatar walks to that object and picks it up or manipulates it in an appropriate way. We discuss object management more extensively in *Manipulating Objects* later in this chapter. The disadvantage of a point-and-click UI is that the player can easily point to areas that aren't accessible to the avatar (halfway up a cliff for example). Sometimes an area that looks as if it should be perfectly accessible is actually inaccessible, which can be frustrating for the player.

The point-and-click interface is an indirect control mechanism and was for many years the de facto standard for adventure games. It makes the player feel as if the avatar is a person separate from himself rather than a puppet whose every movement is directly controlled, and this contributes to the depth of the character. First the player clicks, then the avatar walks—if she can; if she can't, she will usually say so aloud. It works well in traditional adventure games with no action challenges. However, because traditional adventures are increasingly rare and action-adventure hybrids have become more common, the point-and-click interface is gradually being replaced by direct control interfaces.

Direct Control Interfaces   In a direct control user interface, the player steers the avatar around the game world, rather like driving a car. On a console controller, the joystick or D-pad normally manages this; on a personal computer, the mouse or keyboard steers the avatar as in an action game. This is now the standard for action-adventure games, whether in third-person or context-sensitive perspectives. A few more traditional adventure games have started to adopt a direct-control interface also. *Grim Fandango* from LucasArts was one such that used a context-sensitive perspective, which was rather unusual. See the section *Screen-Oriented Steering* and *Avatar-Oriented Steering* in Chapter 8, "Creating the User Experience."

Movement Speed   No matter what perspective or user interface you choose, we strongly suggest that you implement both walk and run movement modes so the player can move slowly through unfamiliar spaces and quickly through familiar ones. If the game requires the player to move repeatedly through areas he already knows well, the player may find watching the avatar walk deliberately from place to place boring. On the other hand, if you offer a rich, detailed world and your game expects the player to examine everything closely for clues, the user interface must make slow and accurate movement possible.

Manipulating Objects

Determining how the player should manipulate objects presents one of the greatest challenges of designing an adventure game. The player typically must figure out what to do with particular objects to solve puzzles and advance the game. In text adventures, this amounted to guessing the correct verb. Play often produced interchanges that looked like this:

```
> OPEN DOOR
The door is locked, but it looks pretty flimsy.

> BREAK DOOR
I don't know how to do that.

> SMASH DOOR
I don't know how to do that.

> HIT DOOR
I don't know how to do that.

> KICK DOOR
The door flies open.
```

Sometimes this was fun; a lot of the time it wasn't. In graphic adventure games in which the player uses a mouse or a handheld controller, designers no longer face that sort of problem but still have to decide how to allow the player to manipulate objects. We outline some approaches in the following sections.

Identifying Active Objects   With the advent of 3D-modeled worlds and powerful physics engines, just about every object that's not part of the scenery could, theoretically, be manipulated or picked up by the avatar. However, most objects in a scene don't actually play a role in the story; they're just part of the set decoration. The player needs a way of recognizing the active objects in a particular location. Text adventures used to print a list of active objects. Graphic adventures typically use one of four mechanisms:

- **Hunt and click.** Active objects don't look any different from anything else; the player simply has to click everything in the scene to see which parts are active. This makes the scene look realistic, but the player may find it annoying, especially if some active objects are small or partially hidden. Designers have generally abandoned this method in favor of the following ones.

- **Permanently highlighted objects.** The active objects in a scene appear permanently highlighted to make them stand out from the background. You can do this in a number of ways; for example, make them slightly brighter than the rest of the scene or surround them by a line of light or dark pixels. The moment the scene appears on the screen, the player can tell which objects are active. It's convenient, if artificial.

- **Dynamically highlighted objects.** The active objects in a scene normally look like part of the background but appear highlighted when the mouse cursor passes over them. You can, for example, change the shape of the mouse cursor or have the object light up. It still requires the player to do some hunting, but hunting is much easier than hunting and clicking; a quick wave of the cursor tells the player if there's an active object nearby.

- **Focus-of-attention highlighting.** This mechanism is typically used with handheld controllers when the player doesn't have a cursor. As the avatar moves around, the focus of his attention changes depending on the direction he is looking. Whatever active object lies directly in front of him commands the focus of his attention and appears highlighted. When he turns away, this highlighting disappears. If two active objects are close together, however, the player may find it tricky to point the avatar in exactly the right direction to put the focus of attention on the desired object

One-Button Actions   In a graphic adventure game played with a handheld controller, designers often assign one button of the controller to a generic *use* or *manipulate* function. The player moves the avatar near the object and presses the use button for obvious functions such as opening a door or throwing a switch; the player can always count on the button to do the right thing with an object, whatever that might be. Some mouse-based games use a similar mechanism, such that clicking an object causes the appropriate action. Players find such games easy to play because there's no guessing about what can be done. However, because there can be only one action per object, this method doesn't allow the designer to do as much to challenge the player's lateral thinking.

Open   Walk to   Use   hunk of meat
Close   Pick up   Look at   stewed fish
Push   Talk to   Turn on   pot
Pull   Give   Turn off   chicken

FIGURE 19.9 The action menu in *The Secret of Monkey Island.*

Menu-Driven Actions   A number of games use a menu to allow the player to select which action to take and which objcct to manipulate (see Figure 19.9). This gives the player a clear picture of available choices, but the presence of the menu makes the game feel more like a software tool and less like a fantasy adventure.

In another variant, right-clicking an object makes a pop-up menu appear, showing a series of icons that represent the actions *take, use, examine,* and possibly others (see Figure 19.10). The player left-clicks one of the icons to perform the desired action. This mechanism in effect shows the player all the available verbs that can be used with that particular object and lets him pick one.

Managing Inventory   Adventure games have always required the player to pick things up and carry them around until they're needed later. Most games implement a limit on the amount of baggage the player can carry. (However, a few did not, for humorous effect. In *Haunt,* a noncommercial text adventure, the player could walk through a haunted house wearing a wetsuit and carrying a stereo, an antique chair, an oil painting, and a bone from the Missing Link along with an unlimited number of other items.) With the arrival of graphics, games began presenting the player with a visible inventory mechanism—usually a box that pops up on the screen and shows everything that the avatar is currently carrying. A box with a fixed size on the screen creates a natural limit on the amount a player can carry. When the box is full, she can't put anything else in it unless she takes something out first. It may help to give the avatar a natural container in which things can be carried—a backpack, saddlebags, or the like—so that the inventory mechanism is a close-up view of the container and its contents.

FIGURE 19.10 The pop-up menu in *The Longest Journey* (at right, under tent). Note that the icons are an eye, a mouth, and a hand, meaning *look at, talk to,* and *manipulate.*

The player will need to stop frequently for inventory management tasks, so you should make adding, removing, and viewing inventory items as easy as possible. You could choose to devote a part of the screen to the inventory all the time. Players find this easy to work with, although it tends to remind the player that he's using a computer, and unless you sacrifice a lot of screen area or implement a scrollbar, the inventory area can't be very big.

Most designers choose to give the player an inventory mechanism that she can open and close on demand. She should be able to do this with a single keystroke or button click. The mechanism should not obscure the whole screen—that feels like a major mode change and tends to compromise suspension of disbelief. The game should allow the player to drag objects into and out of the inventory bag or box quickly and efficiently. *The Longest Journey* included convenient shortcut keys that allowed players to change the object currently being held in the avatar's hand without opening the inventory box. Allowing the player to manage the inventory with such shortcut keys also means that you won't have to create animations of the avatar picking up and dropping every possible item in the game. *Asheron's Call,* an online CRPG, includes *pick up* and *drop* animations but doesn't actually show the object in the avatar's hand.

FIGURE 19.11 *Loom.* Note the musical distaff at the bottom of the screen, used for all actions other than movement.

Most adventure games feature inventories, but not all. The LucasArts adventure *Loom,* designed to be especially accessible to people who were not already familiar with adventure games, didn't require the player to keep an inventory. Instead, the player performed all actions in the game by spinning musical spells on a distaff, which was the only object he carried (see Figure 19.11). Although short and considered by die-hard adventurers to be too easy, *Loom* remains one of the most imaginative and beautifully executed adventure games ever created. (Note, too, the clever pun: The game combines the idea of a walking staff, a distaff, and a musical staff in a single object.)

Summary

Adventure games are best-known for their storytelling, but they are much deeper than that. Though they are the most story-driven genre of game currently available and often provide the most cinematic experience in gaming, adventure games also offer deeply challenging puzzles. To design an adventure game, your most important task is to create compelling characters and an interesting story and then combine them *seamlessly* with puzzle challenges to give the player a rewarding gameplay experience. Your puzzles should heighten dramatic tension when the player encounters them and help move the story forward when she solves them. The future of adventure games is tied closely to action and role-playing games, and designers should look to ways to combine and create new hybrids while staying true to the story and puzzle heritage of the original genre.

Test Your Skills

MULTIPLE CHOICE QUESTIONS

1. Essential elements of adventure games include
   A. exploration and action.
   B. exploration and object manipulation.
   C. dialog trees and quests.
   D. team management and puzzles.

2. How does the setting contribute to an adventure game?
   A. Setting is unimportant.
   B. Setting creates the puzzles.
   C. Setting establishes the emotional tone.
   D. Setting defines the actions the avatar may take.

3. The avatar in *Myst* was a nonspecific avatar because
   A. the player could imagine herself in the game.
   B. the player controlled a puppet-like character.
   C. the player directed a character with personality.
   D. the avatar was always visible.

4. What type of interaction model is most common in adventure games?
   A. Unit-based.
   B. Story-based.
   C. Puzzle-based.
   D. Avatar-based.

5. Which of the following perspectives offers the most opportunities to display dramatic camera angles?
   A. First-person.
   B. Third-person.
   C. Context-dependent.
   D. Isometric.

6. Player actions suitable for adventure games include
   A. puzzle solving, exploration, collection.
   B. exploration, inventory management, team management.
   C. collection, target shooting, engaging in dialog.
   D. vehicle control, data manipulation, exploration.

7. Adventure games are best known for their storytelling. What gameplay mechanism can take advantage of this?

   A. Use puzzles to heighten dramatic tension.

   B. Use scripted conversations to tell the narrative to the player.

   C. Use puzzles to separate story elements.

   D. Allow the avatar to level up, indicating character growth.

8. Adventure games generally address the problem of death by

   A. not allowing the avatar to die at all.

   B. giving the player fair warning about dangerous situations.

   C. supplying a save-game feature so a player can restore to an earlier point.

   D. All of the above are reasonable approaches.

9. If you design a game in which the player must talk with various characters to gain information and then use the information to help convince a jailer to unlock a door, this is an example of

   A. lock-and-key.

   B. maze navigation.

   C. obtaining inaccessible objects.

   D. manipulating people.

10. In *The Secret of Monkey Island,* the avatar could only get off a ship and onto land by figuring out how to shoot himself out of a cannon. This is an example of

   A. a locked door and key puzzle.

   B. doing detective work.

   C. obtaining inaccessible objects.

   D. manipulating people.

11. How do most adventure games today implement conversations with nonplayer characters in the game?

   A. State machines.

   B. Parsers.

   C. Scripted conversations.

   D. Dialog boxes.

12. As originally used in adventure games, a parser allowed a player to

    A. type one of a known set of commands.

    B. try any command to see if it would work.

    C. explore the environment at will.

    D. more easily identify actions that could be taken.

13. To assist a player through a complicated world, you can supply

    A. a journal that automatically updates.

    B. NPCs that offer advice.

    C. a map that fills itself in as the avatar explores.

    D. a complete map of the environment.

14. The best way to control an avatar

    A. is direct control.

    B. is point-and-click.

    C. depends on the current game state.

    D. depends on the current perspective.

15. What interface issues does the designer of an adventure game need to consider?

    A. Some device for carrying inventory.

    B. How to equip the character for combat.

    C. Integrating the menu into the game art.

    D. Displaying a skill tree when the character levels up.

19

Case Study

Choose an adventure game that you believe, from your own experience of playing it, is an excellent example of the genre (or use one your instructor has assigned). It can be a classic graphic adventure game or a hybrid action-adventure game but should not be a text adventure. Write a report documenting why you believe it is superior to others of its kind. Be sure to cover at least the following areas:

- Describe the challenges that the game offers and any rewards that it gives for achieving them.

▶▶ CONTINUED ON NEXT PAGE

▶▶ CONTINUED

- Discuss the design of the puzzles. Was the reward for solving the puzzles balanced with the difficulty of the puzzle? Did any of them require you to be familiar with the culture of the designer/developer/publisher?
- How does the designer get the personality of the lead characters across to the player? Is visual style, language, or behavior more important?
- Briefly document the interface for the game. Does the player interact with the world in a direct or indirect manner? How well does the interface allow the player to interact, or does the interface inhibit or limit interaction?
- Address the game's progression. Does it include a growth path for the avatar? Is the story linear, branching, or foldback (see Chapter 7, "Storytelling and Narrative")? Support your answer with a diagram documenting some of the locations available in the game and the way they are connected to each other.

The design questions in the next section may help you to think about these issues. In your report, use screen shots to illustrate your points. End the case study with suggestions for improvement or, if you feel the game cannot be improved, suggestions for additional features that might be fun to have in the game.

Alternatively, choose a game that you believe is particularly *bad*. Do the same case study, explaining what is wrong and how it could be improved.

A case study is neither a review nor a design document; it is an analysis. You are not attempting to reverse-engineer the entire game but simply to explain how it works in a general way. Your instructor will tell you the desired scope of the assignment; we recommend from five to twenty pages.

DESIGN QUESTIONS

When beginning the design of an adventure game, consider the following questions:

1. Who is the central character in the game—the player's avatar? What is the avatar's sex? (For the purposes of these design questions, we'll assume that the player is male and the avatar is female.) What does she look and sound like? What are her personal qualities: strengths, weaknesses, interests, likes, and dislikes? What sort of vocabulary and

grammar does she use? What are her ethnic, social, religious, political, and educational backgrounds? What is her personal history? What is her family like?

2. What is the story of the game? What is the avatar's ultimate goal? What will occur at the dramatic climax? What things must she collect, learn, or achieve for the dramatic climax to take place?

3. Where does the game take place? What sort of a world is this? Is the player free to move around these areas continuously throughout the story, or do one-way elements prevent him from returning to earlier areas?

4. What other characters inhabit the game world? What functions do they serve? How do they look and act? How do they respond to the avatar? Can she affect their moods and attitudes?

5. How is conversation implemented? What consequences can arise from conversations? Can the player choose a variety of attitudes in which to speak?

6. What kinds of puzzles does the game offer? What obstacles will the player encounter, and what actions will he be able to take to overcome them? Is this a pure adventure game or an action-adventure? If it's an action-adventure, what are the action elements like?

7. What graphics technology will be used to display the world? Two-dimensional backgrounds? Real-time 3D? How will this affect the look and richness of the world?

8. What perspective will the player have on the game setting? Context sensitive? First-person? Third-person?

9. What is the user interface for moving the avatar around the game world? Will it be point-and-click, direct control, or some other mechanism?

10. How does the player recognize active objects in the world? How does he command the game to manipulate them? What verbs are available for each object?

11. Is there an inventory, and if so, how is it displayed and used? How does the player pick things up and put them down again? Can objects be combined or used together? How is this handled?

12. Does the player need a map? If so, will it be static or maintained automatically?

13. Should the game keep a journal to help the player remember things?

19

Chapter | 20

Artificial Life and Puzzle Games

Chapter Objectives

After reading this chapter and completing the exercises, you will be able to do the following:

- Know the different forms of artificial life games and simulations.
- Design basic artificial life systems.
- Know the steps to designing puzzle games.
- Understand the player's needs for puzzle games.

Introduction

In this chapter, we discuss two game genres that aren't currently as fashionable as the ones we've already covered: artificial life and puzzle games. That doesn't mean there's anything wrong with them; some extremely successful games belong to these genres. In fact, because there are fewer games in these categories, the market isn't crowded with look-alike products. Working in one of these genres, you may have a better chance of creating something distinctly new. However, you might have trouble persuading a conservative producer that a really good puzzle game is a better bet than another first-person shooter.

Because we're covering two genres in this chapter, we don't have room to explore the elements of each one; instead, we'll just hit the highlights. We summarize artificial life games by using *The Sims* as an example and then offer an overview about genetic life generators. We also explore the subgenre of god games. The chapter continues with puzzle games, defining them and summarizing how to create and simplify them for the computer. *The Incredible Machine* is described as an example.

Artificial Life Games

Artificial life is a branch of computer science research, just as artificial intelligence is. Artificial life, or *A-life* as it is sometimes called, involves modeling biological processes, often to simulate the life cycles of living things. A-life researchers hope to discover new ways of using computers by using biological mechanisms—mutation and natural selection, for example—rather than algorithmic ones. In particular, A-life is the study of *emergent properties*, unanticipated qualities or behaviors that arise out of the interactions of complex systems. Life itself is considered an emergent property of the planet Earth.

20

Because they're intended for entertainment rather than research, commercial A-life games implement only a subset of what A-life research investigates. There aren't any commercial A-life games about observing thousands of generations of one-celled animals evolving in an environment. Typically, A-life games focus on maintaining and growing a manageable population of organisms, each of which is unique.

Artificial Pets

Artificial pets make up one subcategory of artificial life games. These simulated animals live on your computer (or mobile device), either in an environment of their own or on your desktop. They can be simulations of real animals, as in the *Nintendogs* game for the Nintendo DS, or fantasy ones like the Tamagotchi, which inhabit a tiny and very simple electronic game built into a keychain.

Artificial pets are almost always cute. The gameplay concentrates on training, maintenance, and watching the creatures do endearing things. They seldom reproduce or die (though there are exceptions, and sometimes they run away if ignored or mistreated), and the player usually wants to interact with only one or two at once. (We discuss games about whole populations of organisms, in which individuals do reproduce and die, in *Genetic A-Life Games,* later in this chapter.)

If the player is going to spend much time looking at an artificial pet, then the pet needs to have quite a lot of AI: a variety of things that stimulate it and behaviors that it exhibits. An artificial pet should have a number of emotions or moods that manifest themselves through the pet's behavior. The player should be able to tell, by observation, how the pet is feeling and to influence its feelings by interacting with it in different ways. The animal also needs to interact meaningfully with others of its own kind: teasing, playing, grooming, fighting, and so on. Above all, it needs to be able to learn, so there must be a way for the player to show it how to do things. The learning process must not be too long (or the player will get frustrated and think his pet is stupid) or too short (or the player will run through everything he can teach it very quickly). Tamagotchi are exceptions to this principle, as they were very inexpensive and not really intended to provide as much gameplay as interaction.

This quality of rich artificial intelligence distinguishes artificial pets from other kinds of A-life, in which individuals have simple rules but the population as a whole develops emergent properties. Artificial pets, on the other hand, can have properties that appear only after they have been around for a while, but typically these are preprogrammed and are not truly emergent.

Because an artificial pet doesn't have much of a challenge or a victory condition (apart from training it to do something specific), we class it as a *software toy* rather than a game. (*Software toy* is a term coined by Will Wright, designer of the original *SimCity,* for entertainment software that you just play around with, without trying to defeat an opponent or achieve victory.) The entertainment of an artificial pet comes from watching it do things and interacting with it. In *Nintendogs,* shown in Figure 20.1, you can see two puppies, both eating from the same bowl. The game takes advantage of the Nintendo DS's two screens, one of which is touch-sensitive so that you can "pet" your dog. An artificial pet exhibits a large number of behaviors that the player sees repeatedly and others that occur more rarely. Part of balancing such a game—making sure that the player doesn't get bored with it—is making sure that these

FIGURE 20.1 *Nintendogs* from Nintendo.

rare behaviors occur often enough that the player does get to see them but doesn't take them for granted.

The Sims

The Sims (and its sequels and many modules) is almost the only game of its kind. There was one game a bit like it, *Little Computer People,* many years ago on the Commodore 64, but it was a much simpler game. *The Sims* is a virtual dollhouse: It simulates a family in a suburban home. You can make the people— each of which is called a *sim*—move around, cause them to complete certain tasks, tell them when to go to bed and when to get up, and so on. You can indirectly influence their relationships by making them talk to each other, but you can't decide what they will say, and you can't guarantee that they will like each other. Each simulated person comes with his or her own personality, likes, and dislikes.

One of the selling points of *The Sims* is that there are multiple ways to play with it. It can be thought of as a cross between an artificial pet and a construction and management simulation. Like a CMS, there is an economy: Sims need money to build additions to the house and to buy new furniture for it. At least one member of a Sim family earns that money by having a job. Players can spend quite a lot of time in the buying-and-building mode, if they can afford it, which has nothing at all to do with artificial life. Some players, the particularly goal-oriented ones, really concentrate on this aspect, working hard to construct a mansion and fill it with luxuries. Others are more interested in the interactions and relationships among the sims and spend a lot of the time giving them things to do and watching their reactions.

Needs   The main challenge of *The Sims* is to manage this group of slightly incompetent people and to improve their career prospects by teaching them things that will help them get better jobs. Each sim has eight needs that she must meet on an ongoing basis: hunger, comfort, hygiene, bladder, energy level, fun, social interaction, and room (which, in effect, means uncrowded, attractive surroundings). These needs drive her behavior. When a sim feels a need, she takes actions to meet it. If the need goes unmet for too long, the sim becomes unhappy and can even die (in the case of an unmet hunger need). Each sim always has a queue of things to do to meet her current needs, unless they're all met at the moment. The player can also give the sim orders, in effect inserting a behavior at the front of the queue. This need-based AI is at the heart of most simple behavior simulations.

Skills   Unlike artificial pets, sims don't need to be taught by repeatedly showing them what the player wants them to learn. Instead, the trick is finding the time for them to improve their skills, which they can do by a variety of means. The sims have six skills: cooking, repair, charisma, body (physical strength and dexterity), logic, and creativity. These skills influence the jobs that they can take and, consequently, the amount of money that they can earn. Unfortunately, the sims stay so busy and do everything so slowly that often they don't get enough leisure time to study or work out. The game is very much an exercise in time management.

Personalities   Unlike almost every other computer game, *The Sims* tries to simulate relationships among individual people. These relationships are not terribly sophisticated, but they do include such emotions as jealousy, anger, and love. Five key variables define each sim's personality: neat, outgoing, active, playful, and nice. These determine how sims react to one another and whether they're likely to get along. *The Sims* also encourages the player to develop friendships among his sims because career advancement depends upon having a certain number of friends.

The Success of _The Sims_   _The Sims_ likely owes its huge success to two things: the unprecedented scope for creativity it offers and its emphasis on interpersonal relationships.

First, it enables the player to exercise his creativity in a familiar sphere: the ordinary suburban home. In addition to building and furnishing a house, players can design their own _skins_ for the sims, creating people who look like themselves (or anyone else). The game actually offers more creative play than _SimCity_ or _SimTower,_ for example, because _The Sims_ offers more different kinds of things to do. Players can also take photographs of their sims' houses and store them in albums, along with written commentary that the player supplies, effectively creating illustrated stories. And they can share all of these things over the Internet. The game offers more scope for personal creativity on the part of the player than just about any other video game or software toy on the market.

The second reason for the success of _The Sims_ is its focus on human relationships. The player's immediate objective in playing _The Sims_ is to make sure his sims' physical needs are met; but his secondary, longer-term objective is to meet the sims' mental or emotional needs: fun, social interaction, and quality living space. The sims' need for social interaction is considerably more complex because it involves building relationships with other people rather than simply interacting with objects, and those social interactions can produce emergent properties. Players enjoy watching and influencing these interactions. In fact, the player's imagination plays a very large role in the game, just as it does in playing with dolls. The sims are not terribly complex simulations, but players give them names and personalities and ascribe many more characteristics to them than they actually possess. The fact that the game is about human relationships rather than abstract challenges contributes strongly to its success, especially among female players.

God Games

The term _god game_ refers to games in which the player takes on the role of a god, but one with limited powers like the gods of ancient Greece, rather than an all-powerful god from monotheistic traditions. In a god game, the player's power derives from a population of simulated worshippers—artificial characters that the player, in his capacity as their deity, must nurture and care for. The population is usually depicted as a tribal people rather than a civilization.

God games make use of an omnipresent (of course!) interaction model and an aerial perspective. They often share qualities with both construction and management simulations and with real-time strategy games. (Sometimes games in these genres are described as god games, but if a game doesn't specifically refer to the player's role as that of a god, we don't consider the term to be appropriate. The *Civilization* games are not god games.) As in a CMS like *SimCity*, the player of a god game exercises only indirect control over the population. He can't tell specific individuals what to do, as he can in a strategy game. On the other hand, as in an RTS, he competes directly against an enemy—in this case, a rival god—who has his own population of supporters. And unlike either RTS or CMS games, god games offer the player godlike powers: controlling the weather, reshaping the landscape, and the ability to bestow various blessings (such as fertility) on his own population and various curses upon the population of his enemy. We include god games as a subgenre of artificial life games because so much of the player's role involves tending to a population of simulated people whom he controls only indirectly.

The Economy of God Games   In a god game, the player's power, usually called *mana,* grows along with the number and prosperity of his worshippers. The size of the population typically influences two critical values: the maximum amount of mana the player may have and the rate at which mana is restored when it is below maximum. Using godly powers consumes mana, and the player spends much of his time using his godly powers for his people's benefit—flattening hills to make good farmland, reclaiming land from the sea, blessing their crops, and so on. Mana often grows in exponential proportion to population size, so as the population increases the player acquires vastly greater powers—a progression that god games share with spellcaster characters in role-playing games. However, if his population declines, the maximum amount of mana that he may expend declines also, reducing his ability to help them.

The close connection between population size and available mana could easily create runaway positive feedback: The more mana the player gets, the more he can do for his people, and the more their population grows, the more mana he gets. Positive feedback is usually limited by several factors, however. First, his people do not reproduce instantaneously, so in spite of the player's increasing power, he cannot force rapid population growth. Furthermore, they often need land in which to expand, and creating suitable land consumes mana. Second, the mana cost of using his higher-level powers also increases exponentially, so mana growth is balanced by increased spending as he exercises his powers. Finally, many of his higher powers cannot be used to help his own population, but only to do damage to his rival's people. We discuss that next.

Gameplay in God Games   The primary challenge in a god game is to produce population growth, but the player cannot defeat the rival god simply by helping his own population. He must also do damage to the other god's worshippers, while repairing the damage that the rival god does to the player's people. This damage usually takes the form of harming his opponent's population by bringing down natural disasters upon them: spectacular events such as floods, volcanoes, earthquakes, lightning strikes, tornadoes, plagues, rivers of blood, and so on. Because it's more fun to watch natural disasters than it is to watch crops growing bountifully, god games tend to offer more destructive powers for use on the player's enemies than they do constructive ones for the benefit of his own people. The mana cost of these events rises rapidly in proportion to their destructiveness. A god game could almost be called a *destruction* and management simulation.

To design a god game, begin, as always, with the question, *What is the player going to do?*—in this case, as a god. What kinds of powers would you like her to have? And what will differentiate your god game from those that have gone before? Also ask a lot of questions about the culture of the simulated people. What do they do? How do they spend their time? What circumstances are needed for their population to grow? How do they react when their world is damaged by a hostile god? A god game needs a lot of interesting animations for the people; it is an artificial life game, after all. Some of the entertainment of a god game comes (perhaps a little cruelly) from watching the people run around and scream in terror in response to the player's wreaking destruction upon them.

20

Genetic A-Life Games

Some A-life games involve managing a population of creatures over time. Rather than concentrating so much on individuals, the player tries to achieve certain goals with the population as a whole. By far the most successful of these was the *Creatures* series from Creature Labs, in which the player managed a small group of beings called Norns, creatures who could learn things through repetition. Norns also had distinct genetic characteristics that were reflected in their appearance and behavior. Unlike the people in *The Sims,* Norns had a limited life span, so the game focused on breeding generation after generation of Norns and exploring and manipulating their world indirectly through them.

Designing a Genome   To create a game in which you crossbreed creatures and get new, unique individuals, you need to devise a *genome:* a set of descriptors (genes) that define all the important characteristics of the creature. These characteristics should include everything about the creature that can vary from individual to individual: shape, size, coloration, and so on. You can leave out details common to all creatures. For instance, if all your creatures will have two eyes and that will never change, there's no need to store a gene called "number of eyes."

When two individuals reproduce, they mix their genes, and you will need to define how this mixing takes place. It's a common mistake to think that you should average the values from the two parents; but if you do this, within a very few generations, all your creatures will be the same height or very nearly. Human genetics works differently. Humans have not one value for each characteristic, but two, one inherited from the mother and one from the father. These two values are called *alleles.* If a person's two alleles for the same trait don't match, one of them dominates the other according to a rule. The allele for brown eyes dominates the recessive allele for blue, so people with one brown allele and one blue allele will have brown eyes. When a human reproduces, one of the two alleles is chosen at random to go on to the next generation. This means that it's possible for a brown-eyed person to still pass on the allele for blue eyes. Otherwise, the allele for blue eyes would disappear from the population almost immediately.

Mutation   *Mutation* is a change to a gene that occurs as a result of some environmental factor. Radiation famously causes mutations; so do some chemicals. Bear in mind that a mutation will not have a lasting effect on the population unless it occurs in reproductive cells, and even then the results appear only in the offspring of the individual whose cells mutate. Such mutations may benefit the population by introducing random new values into the gene pool but may just as easily be detrimental or even lethal to the individuals that inherit them. For the purposes of your game, you probably don't want to allow lethal mutations—those that produce miscarriages or stillborn offspring. If your creatures' gestation period is long, allowing lethal mutations wastes the player's time and doesn't add anything of value to the gene pool—or the game.

Life Span, Maturity, and Natural Selection   Each of your creatures needs a natural life span, or your population will explode. (In *Creatures,* the life span of a Norn was about 30 real-time minutes.) If you want your population to evolve through natural selection—that is, to become better adapted to its environment—then your creatures also need a period of immaturity, when they are not fertile, followed by a period of maturity, when they are. Natural selection works only if it kills off creatures with maladaptive genes before they mature enough to reproduce. If creatures could reproduce immediately after birth, maladaptive genes would never leave the gene pool.

If there's one thing we know about random mutation and natural selection, it's that the effects of these processes appear slowly. The life span of the Norns in *Creatures* was really too long for the player to breed hundreds of generations. If you want evolution to be a part of your game, you'll need to find ways of making it work nonrandomly or keep the life span of your creatures very short. Of course, the shorter the life span, the less chance you give each creature to exhibit an interesting behavior, so there's a balance to be struck.

What Does the Player Do?   A genetic A-life game might not seem to have much for the player to do except wind it up and watch it go. A closer look shows a fair number of ways the player can interact with the creatures. She can create completely new individuals and add them to the population to observe how their genes influence the population. She can add and remove environmental hazards that would tend to weed out certain genes. She can play with the rate and nature of mutation by adding or modifying mutagenic objects or areas of the environment. She can also mate particular individuals to select for particular characteristics (with animals, this is considered useful and is called *breeding;* with people, it is considered evil and is called *eugenics*).

Puzzle Games

Puzzles appear in games in several genres: Many single-player computer games contain puzzles; in action games, the player often has to figure out the boss opponent's weakness; adventure games are full of puzzles, frequently about obtaining inaccessible objects or getting information from other people; even first-person shooters offer the occasional puzzle, figuring out how to get past locked doors and other obstacles. Puzzle design is an essential element of game design, and it's harder than you might think.

In puzzle games, puzzle solving is the primary activity, though puzzles may occur within a storyline or lead up to some larger goal. That doesn't mean that you can offer a random collection of puzzles and call it a game; puzzle games usually provide related challenges, variations on a theme. The types of puzzles offered include pattern recognition, logic, or understanding a process. In all cases, the puzzles give the player clues that have to be somehow unraveled or solved to meet the victory condition. We classify fast puzzle solving—as in *Tetris*—as an action game rather than a puzzle game. *Tetris* and the many games similar to it depend more on physical coordination challenges than they do on logic problems.

To be a commercial success, a puzzle game needs to be challenging (but not too hard), visually attractive, and above all, enjoyable. It also needs to be fresh and to offer enough gameplay to justify the purchase price. Although solitaire card games such as *FreeCell* belong in the class of puzzle games, unless you sell a lot of them together as a collection, people are unlikely to want to pay for them.

Scott Kim's Eight Steps

Scott Kim is a designer who creates puzzles for the print media, Web sites, and computer games. Having worked in the field for many years, he has identified eight steps in puzzle game design. The first four steps comprise the process of specifying the rules, while the last four comprise the process of building the puzzles and the game itself:

1. **Find inspiration.** This can come from a variety of sources, including other games. *Tetris,* for example, was inspired by a noncomputer game called *Pentominoes.* You can be inspired by a piece of art (the drawings of M. C. Escher have a very puzzlelike feel), a story, or some particular subject matter. Another source of inspiration is a play dynamic of some kind: flipping switches, turning knobs, sliding objects around, or picking them up and putting them down. Or there are more complex dynamics among objects: balancing, reflection, connection, and transmission.

2. **Simplify.** Suppose you have an idea for a puzzle: efficiently parking vehicles of different sizes in a crowded parking lot so that when someone

asks you to retrieve his car, you have to move as few other cars as possible. Part of making this task fun is simplifying it to its essentials. First, identify the essential tricky core skill (in this case, space planning on the fly) and concentrate on that. Second, eliminate any irrelevant details. Don't make your player worry about crashing the cars, for example. Third, make the pieces uniform. Instead of having cars with infinitely variable shapes and sizes, it's better to have several standard types that conform to a square grid. Finally, simplify the controls. Figure out what the essential moves are and devise controls that implement them with a minimum of fiddling.

3. **Create a construction set.** The only way to be sure that a puzzle concept works is to play it, but obviously you don't want to code up the whole game before you know whether it's fun. You can build a paper prototype or a simple version in something like Macromedia Flash to see if it works. The rule designer can play with the prototype to tweak the rules, and later the level designer can use it to build levels. You can also code a construction set into the final game so that players can build puzzles for each other.

4. **Define the rules.** This is the key part of puzzle design. Most puzzles are characterized in terms of four things: the *board* (Is it a grid? A network? Is it irregular? Or is there no board at all?), the *pieces* (How are they shaped? What pictures are on them? What other attributes do they have? Where do they come from?), the *moves* (What is allowed and what is not? Are they sequential or simultaneous? What side effects do they have?), and the *goal* or victory condition (Does it have to be an exact match, or will a partial one do?).

5. **Construct the puzzles.** A puzzle challenges the player to get from a problem to a solution, but of course, the path isn't simple. Every puzzle requires that the player make choices, some of which lead to dead ends. In an adventure game, each puzzle appears in a larger context (the story) that gives it meaning, and solving it advances the plot somehow. Some puzzle games also offer an overall plot of sorts or won't let you try the next puzzle until you've completed the current one. Good puzzles require insight from the player, the "Aha!" moment that occurs when the player realizes how the puzzle works and how to solve it. But you mustn't require an insight that's too obscure, or it will feel unfair. If you tell the player that he's in a maze, it's unfair for the only solution to be to knock down the walls unless you indicate somehow that this is possible.

6. **Test.** Testing tells you several things. It tells you whether the puzzle is too easy or too hard (this can be difficult to predict in advance), and it also tells you whether it's fun in the first place. It helps you find out if there are alternate solutions that you didn't think of, and it helps you

discover errors in the rules. And, of course, it lets people try out the user interface. Because puzzle actions tend to be repetitive, it's important that the interface be smooth and not frustrating.

7. **Devise a sequence.** Now it's time to order all your puzzles into a sequence. The most obvious arrangement is a linear or accelerating sequence going from easy to difficult, but in practice, that becomes tiring and discouraging. A better arrangement is a sawtooth shape, which gets difficult for a while, then goes back to an easy puzzle, and so on, over and over. And, of course, you can give the player the freedom to play the puzzles out of order or let her earn that right. You also need to think about transitions between puzzles, something that will keep her moving on to the next one. War games and role-playing games often do this with a storyline. Or, the player can be working on a *metapuzzle* (a single large puzzle, parts of which the player solves in between the regular puzzles), which motivates her to complete the whole game.

8. **Pay attention to presentation.** Finally, of course, there are all the other details of game design: sound, graphical style, animation, user interface elements, storyline (if any), and so on. If you're used to designing other kinds of games, it might be tempting to move this to an earlier point in the process, but with puzzle games, the puzzles are 90 percent of the battle. Get them right first, and the rest won't be nearly as hard.

What Computers Bring to Puzzles

Computers enable us to make a lot of puzzles that would be impossible or expensive to create in the real world—consider the logistics of supplying all the parts in *The Incredible Machine* in physical form, including the mandrills, cats, and goldfish that appear in the game. Even if a puzzle is physically possible, the computer can add a number of useful features to make the gameplay easier and more enjoyable.

- **Enable nonphysical or awkward moves.** The computer can let players do things that don't correspond to physical actions in the real world—for example, changing the color of something. You can also let the player control several things at once with just one key, something that would be awkward to do in a physical implementation.

- **Include computation features.** You can use the computing power available to automatically generate new puzzles, find solutions to the current puzzle, or generate hints about what the player should do next.

- **Enforce the rules.** In a lot of physical puzzles, it's up to the player to enforce the rules. Sometimes players make mistakes and break the rules accidentally. A computer game can make sure that never happens.

- **Undo and record moves.** This very useful feature for games involves moving objects around in a sequence, as in Solitaire.

- **Structure the experience.** The computer allows you to present the experience in a particular order, if necessary, passing automatically from one phase to another. In the real world, the player would be looking at the instructions and saying, "Let's see, what am I supposed to do next?"

- **Teach.** You can include tutorial modes and step-by-step instructions to help your player get into the game.

- **Use bells and whistles.** Obviously, with sound and animation, you can make a puzzle much more aesthetically interesting on the computer than it would be as a physical object.

- **Enable online play.** The computer lets players compete against one another, compare solutions, and be part of a puzzle-solving community.

Checking the Victory Condition

Bear in mind that players don't always find the solution to a puzzle the way that you envisioned when you invented it. There might be more than one path to the goal. When your game checks to see whether the player solved the puzzle, you should test only to see whether the player met the victory condition you gave her, *not* that she has done it in the way you expected. Otherwise, you've cheated her, and she'll be justifiably frustrated. She's managed to get to the correct solution state, but your game refuses to recognize it.

This problem appeared in the game *Interstate '76,* which, while not a puzzle game, did offer a level containing a puzzle of sorts. The player drove an armed and armored car in an area enclosed by a concrete wall, and the victory condition for winning the level stated that (among other things) the vehicle must escape the enclosed area. The game's designers put in a hidden ramp, which they wanted players to find and use to drive out of the area. However, players discovered another way to get out: If a player dropped a land mine near the wall and then drove toward it at full speed, the force of the explosion lifted the car high enough to clear the wall, and the car would fly over it and out. Unfortunately, the software didn't test for the solution state that the player was given: Is the car outside the wall? Instead, it tested to see if the player used the ramp. If a player escaped without using the ramp, the game didn't know that the player had completed the level, even though the victory condition had been met.

Of course, sometimes games contain bugs that allow a player to cheat and reach a solution by a means that's completely outside the rules. In *Interstate '76,* however, the trick with the land mine wasn't a bug but an innovative solution that the designers didn't consider. When the software checks the victory condition, be sure it checks the solution state that you told the player to achieve, not the way in which he achieved it.

IN THE TRENCHES: *The Incredible Machine*

The Incredible Machine furnishes an excellent example of an imaginative and clever puzzle game that sold well. In fact, it's not just a game but a whole game franchise with five editions so far. The current version, *Return of the Incredible Machine: Contraptions,* is published by Sierra Entertainment (formerly Sierra On-Line).

The game consists of a series of puzzles, each of which involves building a Rube Goldberg–like machine to accomplish a certain task. The player constructs each machine in a two-dimensional space upon which a variety of mechanical devices can be placed. (Some of these devices are actually animals, which can be frightened by noises or lured by food.) Each puzzle starts with a few objects in given positions, and the victory condition states what the player must accomplish (for example, pop the balloon) using a limited number of additional devices. The player must place these devices and hook them together in such a way that the resulting machine, when set in motion, achieves the goal. Playing the game consists of adding elements to the machine, trying them out, adjusting them, trying again, and so on. Figure 20.2 shows one of the scenarios in *The Incredible Machine*. The goal is given at the left. Available parts are in the area beneath the main workspace.

Scott Kim identifies three key design decisions that he feels made *The Incredible Machine* the prototypical construction puzzle game.

1. **Allow the player to build things.** This makes *The Incredible Machine* a construction game and differentiates it from, say, *Tetris* (an action puzzle game) or *Marble Drop* (a logic game in which the player decides where and when to drop marbles into a mechanism). The player is exercising his creativity.

2. **Include no real-time decision making.** Constructing the machine and running it take place in separate modes. The player can take as long as he wants to think about what he's doing. This is in contrast with *Lemmings,* an excellent game but one that requires the player to solve its puzzles on the fly. Often if the player doesn't solve the puzzle in time, he has to start over.

3. **Allow players to design their own puzzles.** Any time players can build their own elements, it adds value to the game and helps create a community of devoted fans. Players can

>> CONTINUED ON NEXT PAGE

20

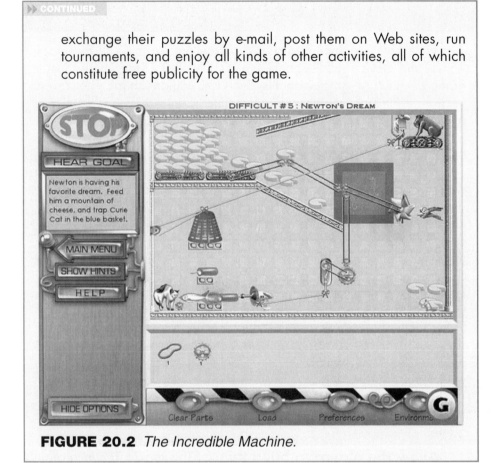

>> CONTINUED

exchange their puzzles by e-mail, post them on Web sites, run tournaments, and enjoy all kinds of other activities, all of which constitute free publicity for the game.

FIGURE 20.2 *The Incredible Machine.*

Summary

Although artificial life might not seem very much like a game, simulations about people, pets, and even entire species can be entertaining and have been made into successful and fun products. An A-life game could be about individuals and relationships, or it could be a simulation of an ecosystem. The designer of this type of game needs to consider how the simulation will run and the interactions of the player. Puzzle games, on the other hand, provide the player with hours of strategy and problem solving. The designer needs to provide a game that combines high-quality presentation with well-thought-out game mechanics and interaction. Players can be very opinionated about puzzle games, but the individuals who enjoy puzzle games are often also very loyal.

Test Your Skills

MULTIPLE CHOICE QUESTIONS

1. What type of gameplay is common for artificial pets?
   A. Grooming and training.
   B. Breeding.
   C. Watching them grow.
   D. Training and maintenance.

2. What helps distinguish artificial pets from other forms of A-life?
   A. Individual rules.
   B. Population control.
   C. Deep artificial intelligence.
   D. A wide variety of stimuli.

3. In A-life games about large populations
   A. the rules are simple for the individual and complex for the population.
   B. the rules are complex for the individual and simple for the population.
   C. the rules are simple for the individual and the population displays emergent behaviors.
   D. the AI is complex for the individual and the population requires complex rules.

4. Most behavior simulations have at the heart of them
   A. a need-based AI.
   B. a logical set of rules.
   C. conditions for reproduction and death.
   D. puzzles and strategies.

5. A big part of the success of *The Sims* can be attributed to
   A. its highly complex personality simulation.
   B. the quality of its graphics.
   C. the unprecedented scope for player creativity that it offers.
   D. the mechanism of teaching the sims by repeatedly showing them what to do.

6. In a god game, the player obtains mana in proportion to
   A. the amount of power he has.
   B. the fertility of his population's crops.
   C. the size of his population.
   D. the size of his enemy's population.

20

7. In a god game, the player spends a lot of time
   A. planting crops.
   B. commanding units to fight.
   C. constructing production facilities.
   D. damaging the enemy population.

8. In an A-life simulation that allows reproduction, rules need to be established for
   A. mixing the parent creatures' genes.
   B. gene splicing.
   C. starvation and mutation.
   D. gender bias.

9. A genome is a set of
   A. mutated genes.
   B. characteristics defined by the player.
   C. genes that define a creature's life cycle.
   D. descriptors that define important characteristics.

10. A period of immaturity when creatures cannot reproduce weeds out
    A. maladapted genomes.
    B. maladaptive genes.
    C. shorter life cycles.
    D. maladapted emergent properties.

11. To design a puzzle game, you should start out by
    A. finding inspiration and simplifying the gameplay.
    B. creating a construction set and defining the art style.
    C. focusing on the target market and the user interface.
    D. creating a series of puzzles that can be loosely connected with story.

12. Which of these is part of the process of simplifying an idea for a puzzle game?
    A. Simplify the controls.
    B. Identify the essential tricky skill.
    C. Eliminate irrelevant details.
    D. All of the above.

13. Which of the following is *not* an added advantage that computers bring to puzzles?

    A. The ability to undo and record moves.

    B. The ability to offer visually attractive puzzles.

    C. The ability to enforce the rules.

    D. The ability to play online.

14. When your software checks to see if the victory condition of a puzzle has been met, it should always

    A. test to see if the player achieved it in a way that you did not intend.

    B. test the exact condition that you told the player was the victory condition.

    C. test to see if the player has cheated.

    D. none of the above.

15. What types of other genres do not usually include puzzles?

    A. First-person shooters.

    B. Action.

    C. Adventure.

    D. A-life.

Case Studies

For this chapter, there are two case studies. The instructor may ask you to work on a single study or both.

   Choose an A-life game that you believe, from your own experience of playing it, is an excellent example of the genre (or use one your instructor has assigned). It can be a commercial simulation with humans or pets or a research simulation of life. High-level graphics are not a requirement. Write a report documenting this simulation. Be sure to cover at least the following areas:

- Describe the game mechanics and the player's role. Discuss what makes the product a "game," or if it is not a game, discuss why not.

- If the product involved the life cycle and reproduction of a life form, compare the evolution and genetics in the game to those of real life. Did the life cycle make sense? Was it balanced so

CONTINUED ON NEXT PAGE

▶▶ CONTINUED

that the artificial life could succeed and remain a viable life form for more than just a few generations, or did the life form die out without your intervention?

- What forms of interaction did the player have in the simulation? Did you perceive the player interactions as fun? If not, why not?

- If the product did not involve the life cycle of a life form, what forms of interaction did the player have in the simulation? Did you perceive the player interactions as fun? If not, why not?

- Briefly document the interface for the game. How does the player interact with the world, in a direct or indirect manner? How well does the interface allow the player to interact, or does the interface inhibit or limit interaction?

- Address the game progression: Did the game change over time? How did the player interactions affect the life form(s)?

Choose a puzzle game that you believe, from your own experience of playing it, is an excellent example of the genre (or use one your instructor has assigned). It should be a solitaire (single-player) game where puzzle solving is the primary activity. Write a report documenting this simulation. Be sure to cover at least the following areas:

- Describe the gameplay and game mechanics. Describe the presentation of the game and interaction of the player.

- If the game has a physical representation in the real world (solitaire card games, for example), what does the computer bring to the video game version? What rules or designs were changed for the new medium?

- Does the game have levels or increased difficulty? Is it clear to the player how the game progression works? In your opinion, does the game ramp up too quickly or not quickly enough?

- Address the combination of puzzles: Is there more than one type of puzzle in the game? Is the mechanism that is used to combine the puzzles into a single game clear to the player and does it make sense?

- Discuss whether the victory condition for any level or the overall game is clear to the player.

In your report, use screen shots to illustrate your points. End the case study with suggestions for improvement or, if you feel the game

▶▶ CONTINUED ON NEXT PAGE

▶▶ CONTINUED

cannot be improved, suggestions for additional features that might be fun to have in the game.

Alternatively, choose an A-life or puzzle game that you believe is particularly *bad*. Do the same case study, explaining what is wrong and how it could be improved.

A case study is neither a review nor a design document; it is an analysis. You are not attempting to reverse-engineer the entire game but simply to explain how it works in a general way. Your instructor will tell you the desired scope of the assignment; we recommend from five to twenty pages.

20

Glossary

A

absolute difficulty The difficulty of a challenge, taking into account both the *intrinsic skill required* and the *stress* on the player, as compared to the trivial case of a similar challenge. See also *relative difficulty* and *perceived difficulty*.

abstract (adjective) A quality of a game that indicates it bears little relationship to the real world, and the player may not rely on his understanding of the real world in playing the game; its rules are arbitrary. Abstract is one end of the *realism* scale; the other end is *representational*.

abstract (verb) To remove a complex mechanism from a simulation (often a mechanism intended to simulate a real-world phenomenon) and replace it with a simpler mechanism or none at all.

action game A game whose gameplay consists primarily of physical coordination challenges.

action-adventure A hybrid genre of *action game* and *adventure game*. The action-adventure is now more popular than either of its two constituents.

actions Player behaviors permitted by the *rules*. Many game actions are intended to overcome *challenges*, but others serve to add to the player's enjoyment in other ways.

adventure game An interactive story in which the player takes the role of the protagonist. Puzzle-solving and conceptual reasoning challenges form the majority of the gameplay; physical coordination challenges are few or nonexistent.

art-driven game A game whose design is primarily driven by the goal of showing off the game's artwork.

artificial intelligence A suite of programming techniques that allow a computer to mimic human behavior in certain domains. Video games use AI to provide artificial opponents for players to play against, among other functions.

asymmetric game A game in which the players do not start with identical conditions, do not play by the same rules, or do not seek to achieve the same victory condition.

atomic challenge A challenge that the player faces immediately during play. One of the lowest-level challenges in the *hierarchy of challenges*. A challenge that is not composed of other subchallenges.

attract loop A continuously cycling noninteractive demonstration on an arcade game designed to attract the attention of passersby.

attributes Data values that describe one or more qualities of a character or unit. These may be symbolic, numeric, or collections of data. See *characterization attributes, status attributes, functional attributes,* and *cosmetic attributes* for the different kinds of attributes.

augmented reality A form of computerized interaction in which computer-presented data and input mechanisms are combined with real-world events. The computer is said to augment the player's experience of the real world.

avatar A fictional character in a game with whom the player identifies as the personification of herself within the game world. The character need not be human; it may even be a vehicle.

avatar-based interaction model An *interaction model* in which the player is represented by a single character, vehicle, or other entity in the game world, the key point of which is that the player may influence the game world only through the avatar and, therefore, only those regions of the game world where the avatar is present.

B

backgrounder   A document that describes the personality, attitudes, and other characteristics of a game character.

balance   In a player-versus-player game, the design task of making the game fair to all players. In a player-versus-environment game, the design task of managing the difficulty level of the game.

boss   A large and particularly difficult challenge that must be overcome, typically the last one required in order to complete a *level* of a game.

bot   An artificially intelligent opponent, usually in a first-person shooter, that players may implement as a modification to the game.

branching story   An interactive story whose plot is pre-planned by the designer, but may take alternative paths as a result of actions the player takes.

C

challenge   A nontrivial task the player seeks to perform in order to move toward the game's goals.

character level   A numeric *status attribute* that roughly describes a character's power to perform certain activities. In role-playing games, characters rise from level to level with experience.

characterization attributes   Attributes that describe something fundamental about a character or unit and change only slowly by small amounts or not at all. Maximum speed might be a characterization attribute for a vehicle. See *attributes.*

checkpoints   Points in a game level at which the game may be saved or at which the avatar will be reincarnated if he dies.

collectible   A game world object that is in the player's interest to find and collect.

combinatorial explosion   An undesirable property of branching stories such that the number of plot lines grows to unmanageable numbers as each line offers more and more branch points.

combo move   A rapid sequence of joystick movements and button presses that must be performed perfectly to produce an avatar action. Usually found in fighting games.

competition mode   One of a variety of different forms of competitive or cooperative play, such as team play or multiplayer cooperative play. Many video games allow players to choose a competition mode.

compound entity   An entity made up of more than one datum. An entity describing the wind that included both speed and direction would be a compound entity consisting of two *attributes,* one for wind speed and one for direction.

concept   See *game concept.*

concept art   Sketches drawn during the early stages of game design to give developers and publishers an idea of how game world features and characters may look in the game. Concept art is not incorporated into the final product.

concept stage   The first major stage of game design, in which the designer works to turn an idea for a game into a *game concept.*

conflict challenge   A challenge requiring the direct opposition of forces under the player's control. Not to be confused with *conflict of interest.*

conflict of interest   The defining quality of a game in formal *game theory:* a situation in which the players seek mutually incompatible outcomes.

constrained creative play   Creative play artificially constrained by rules. The rules may impose physical, aesthetic, or economic limitations on what the player may create. Contrast with *freeform creative play.*

contestant-based interaction model   An *interaction model* in which the player acts like a contestant in a TV game show. Interactions consist of answering questions, choosing correct answers, and making simple strategic decisions.

context-sensitive perspective   A *perspective* in which the camera moves in response to the events and circumstances of the game rather than being fixed with respect to the game world or the avatar.

continuous scrolling   A characteristic of scrolling 2D *perspectives* such that the landscape scrolls continuously in one direction; the player is unable to change it but has to deal with whatever appears.

converter   A mechanic, sometimes automated, that converts one or more resources into one or more other resources.

cooperation   A form of play in which the players act together to achieve the same goals.

core mechanics   A symbolic and mathematical model of the game's rules that can be implemented algorithmically.

cosmetic attributes   Attributes of a character, vehicle, or other object that affect only its appearance, not its interaction with the core mechanics of the game. The paint color of a car is a cosmetic attribute. Contrast with *functional attributes.*

crane   To move the game's virtual camera up or down in space.

CRPG   Acronym for computer role-playing game, used to distinguish it from noncomputerized table-top role-playing games.

cut-scenes   Short noninteractive visual sequences that momentarily interrupt play.

D

deadlock   A condition of the game's *internal economy* in which either (a) a *production mechanism* cannot begin to operate because it requires a *resource* that is not available and no means exists to produce the needed resource or (b) a production mechanism ceases to operate because it has run out of some needed input resource and no means exist to produce the needed resource. Deadlocks are caused by the presence of a *feedback loop* or a *mutual dependency* in the flow of resources.

deathmatch   A multiplayer competitive competition mode.

degree of freedom   The number of possible dimensions that an input device can move through.

designer-driven game   A game whose designer retains all creative control. Such games usually reflect the designer's own personal desires rather than a wish to entertain others.

desktop model   An *interaction model* that mimics a computer or a real desktop.

dialog tree   A structure documenting player dialog choices and nonplayer character responses to those choices in a *scripted conversation,* which can be drawn on paper in a diagram that looks rather like a tree. Each player option produces a new branch in the tree.

difficulty   One of several measures that determines how hard a game is to play. See *absolute difficulty, relative difficulty,* and *perceived difficulty.*

dimensions   Collections of related properties that define how the player experiences the *game world,* e.g., the physical dimension, emotional dimension, ethical dimension, etc.

dolly   To move the game's virtual camera forward or backward along a line in the same direction that it is facing.

dominant strategy   A *strategy* so effective that the player has no reason to use any other strategy. A game containing a dominant strategy is said to be poorly *balanced.*

drain   A mechanic that permanently removes *resources* from the game world without introducing anything in exchange.

dramatic action   An action the player takes that changes the direction of the plot and, thus, future events in the story as the player will experience it. Many player actions contribute to a story but are not dramatic actions; they do not change the future.

dramatic freedom   The player's freedom to take *dramatic action,* that is, to change the direction of the plot in a story.

dramatic tension   An audience's sense that an important problem or situation in a story is not yet resolved, leaving the audience wondering how it will come out. Do not confuse with *gameplay tension.*

dungeon exit   See *level exit.*

E

elaboration stage   The second and longest stage of game design, during which the designers elaborate on the game concept they built during the *concept stage.*

embedded narrative   Narrative material that is written by the designer and built into the game software (embedded) during development. See *narrative* and *narrative events.*

emergent narrative   Events that are produced by the core mechanics as part of an interactive story, rather than being written by the designer in advance.

Should really be called *emergent storytelling,* because *narrative* refers to narrated material.

entity   A datum or collection of data that describes some object, character, quantity, or state of affairs in the game. See *simple entity* and *compound entity.*

exclusionary material   Content or features that tend to drive players away from a game they might otherwise like, e.g., racist or sexist content.

experience points   A resource earned by the player through combat and other activities in a *role-playing game.*

explicit challenge   A challenge the player is explicitly told about by the game. Typically the explicit challenges are the *victory condition* and the *atomic challenges.*

F

factories   Entities, usually characterized as buildings, under player control that convert or produce resources of use to the player.

fair   (1) In a player-versus-player game, a perception on the part of the players that they all have an equal chance of winning the game when it begins and that the rules do not create advantages for one player over another other than by the operation of chance. (2) In a player-versus-environment game, a set of player expectations about the nature of the game experience.

feedback   (1) Information provided to the player to let him know the effects of his actions upon the game world and other data he may need to evaluate his status and plan future actions. Used in the context of user interfaces. See *feedback element.* (2) A phenomenon occurring in automated internal economies; see *feedback loop* for further information. (3) A common phenomenon occurring in the *balance* of a game such that the player's successful efforts make the game easier or harder. See *positive feedback* and *negative feedback.*

feedback element   An audible or visible part of the user interface that informs the player about the effects of his actions upon the game world and other data he may need to evaluate his status and plan future actions. Sound effects and visible *indicators* are feedback elements.

feedback loop   In an *internal economy,* a situation in which some of the resource produced by a production mechanism must either (a) be used to initiate the production mechanism in the first place or (b) be fed back into the production mechanism to keep it operating. Feedback loops run the risk of creating a *deadlock.*

first playable level   The first level created by the level design team that actually includes gameplay, as opposed to being a prototype or mockup. It should be a typical example of a level, not the first level that the player will play.

first-person perspective   A *perspective* always used with *avatar-based interaction models* in which the *virtual camera* displays the *game world* from the point of view of the avatar's own eyes.

first-person shooter (FPS)   A *shooter* game in which the game world is displayed from the *first-person perspective.* Also sometimes called a POV (point of view) shooter and, in Europe, an egoshooter.

fog of war   (1) The technique of hiding unexplored regions of a terrain from the player using an aerial perspective by showing them as featureless, usually black. (2) The technique of hiding regions or some aspects of terrain, even if previously explored, from a player using an aerial perspective, if the player has no *units* in the region to see what is going on there. Typically used in war games to prevent the player from observing enemy troop movements unless he has units nearby to see them.

foldback stories   A variant of a *branching story* in which the branching plot lines eventually return to an inevitable event that the player will experience regardless of his choices before branching out again.

freeform creative play   Creative play constrained only by the options that the game offers and the technological limitations of the machine but not by rules. Contrast with *constrained creative play.*

free-roaming camera   A *perspective* used in 3D *game worlds,* normally with *multipresent interaction models,* in which the *virtual camera* may move anywhere around the world often under player control.

functional attributes   Attributes of an avatar or other character that influence gameplay through their effect on the core mechanics. Contrast with *cosmetic attributes.*

G

game   A type of *play* activity conducted in the context of a pretended reality in which the participant(s) try to achieve at least one arbitrary, nontrivial *goal* by acting in accordance with *rules.*

game concept   A statement of a group of design choices sufficient to convey, among other things, what a game will be like to play, for what audience it is intended, and on what machine it will run.

game engine   That part of the game's software that implements the *core mechanics.*

game theory   A branch of mathematics aimed at discovering optimal solutions in situations where the parties to the situation have a *conflict of interest.*

game tree   A hypothetical specification of all possible future events in a game, which can be drawn on paper in a diagram that looks like a tree, as future choices branch out. Normally used only for two-player turn-based games.

game world   An imaginary universe in which the events of the game take place. Most computer game worlds are simulated two- and three-dimensional spaces containing characters and objects.

gameplay   The challenges presented to a player and the actions the player is permitted to take to overcome those challenges.

gameplay mode   The subset of its *gameplay* that a game offers at any particular time, along with the *perspective* from which it displays the *game world* and the *interaction model* with which the player acts upon the world. Whenever any of these changes significantly, the game has entered a new gameplay mode.

gameplay tension   The player's uncertainty about whether he will overcome the challenges he faces and, in a player-versus-player game, what his opponent will do next. Do not confuse with *dramatic tension.*

global mechanic   A mechanic that operates throughout the game regardless of which gameplay mode the game may be in.

goals   Desired results or conditions that the player seeks to achieve. The goals of a game need not be achievable, so long as players can work toward them. Games usually have many goals, defined by the *hierarchy of challenges.* The *victory condition,* if the game has one, is always one of these goals.

granularity   The frequency with which the game presents *narrative* elements to the player.

group play   A form of social play in which a group of people take turns at playing a single-player game while the others watch. Also called hot seat play.

H

handicap   An adjustment to the rules of the game (often of the *victory condition*) intended to balance differential skill among the players and give the less skilled an equal chance of winning with the others.

harmony   An aesthetic quality of a game such that it feels as if all its elements—visual, auditory, gameplay, and others—belong together and complement each other.

hierarchy of challenges   A theoretical hierarchy of goals the player tries to achieve at any given moment, consisting (from the top down) of completing the entire game, winning the current level, complcting a sub-mission within the level, if any, and so on down to the challenge immediately facing him at the moment, an *atomic challenge.*

high concept   A very short description, no more than two or three sentences long, that conveys the most important aspects of an idea for a game.

hypersexualized   Quality of a character whose sexual attributes have been exaggerated to an extreme extent.

I

immersion   The feeling of being submerged in a form of entertainment and unaware that you are experiencing an artificial world. Players become immersed in several ways: tactically, strategically, and narratively.

immutable rules   Rules that may not change during play.

implicit challenge   A challenge the player is not told about directly but must infer from the rules, observation of the game, trial-and-error, or by knowing what the *explicit challenges* are.

indicator   Any visual user interface element that shows the status of some important value in the game and changes continually as the value changes. Digits, power bars, lights, gauges, *small multiples,* and many other design elements are used as indicators.

influence map A map maintained internally by the game software that records how a building in the game world landscape influences the area around it. Used to simplify logistics by having units in the neighborhood of the building receive support automatically.

in-game events Events performed by the core mechanics of a game as part of an *interactive story.*

in-game experience Experience the player has gained from confronting a particular type of challenge during the course of a game. A factor in computing the *perceived difficulty* of a challenge at a given point in the game.

interaction model The means by which the player projects her will into the game world, which is facilitated by the user interface. Common interaction models include *avatar-based, party-based, multipresent, contestant-based,* and desktop.

interactive fiction Text-only adventure games, played by typing on a keyboard.

interactive story A story that a player interacts with by contributing *player events* and possibly by changing its plot through *dramatic actions.*

internal economy That subset of the *core mechanics* that deals with the numeric relationships among entities in the game and the way those relationships change over time and in response to events in the game.

intrinsic skill required The amount of skill a player must have to meet a challenge independently of time pressure, as compared to the trivial case of the same challenge. One component of *absolute difficulty.*

L

LAN parties Multiplayer networked play in which all the players are in the same location but each has her own machine networked to the others over a local-area network (LAN).

level Ordinarily refers to a portion of a video game, usually with its own victory condition, that must be completed before moving on to the next portion. Levels are often, but not always, completed in a prescribed sequence. In storytelling terms, levels may be thought of as chapters; in war games, they are missions; in fighting games, they are individual bouts; in simulations, they are scenarios. Used with a qualifier, however, the word may take on a different meaning. See *character level.*

level exit In a game that involves exploration, the standard transition point from the current *level* to the next.

level warp In a game that involves exploration, a transition point other than the standard level exit that enables the player to jump to the next level (or even several levels ahead) without completing the current level.

leveling up or **leveling** In a game that implements *character levels,* the attainment of some accomplishment (usually arriving at a threshold number of *experience points*) that causes the character to gain a level and with it an increase in *characterization attributes.*

license A contract between the owner of an intellectual property such as a character, movie, book, or sports league, and a game developer or publisher to use that property in a game. The term *license* is often used to refer to the property itself, as in "Electronic Arts has the Harry Potter license."

linear stories Stories whose plots do not change in response to player actions.

localization The process of modifying game content to make the game suitable for sale in a country other than the one it was originally developed for.

loss condition An unambiguous true-or-false condition that determines when a player has lost a game. Not all games have a loss condition. Many games may not be lost; they simply remain unfinished.

M

magic circle A theoretical concept related to the act of *pretending* that occurs when we choose to play a game. When we begin to *play* and agree to abide by the *rules,* we enter the magic circle. Within the magic circle, actions that would be meaningless in the real world take on meaning in the context of the game.

mana An expendable resource of magical power consumed by casting magic spells. The word is of Polynesian origin, although in that context its meaning is considerably more complex.

market-driven game A game whose features are included simply because they are known to appeal to a given market, whether or not those features are consistent with the game's real premise.

mini-map A small, dynamically updated map of a *game world,* usually displayed in the corner of the screen in the *primary gameplay mode,* for quick reference. Also sometimes called a radar screen.

mixed reality See *augmented reality.*

model sheet A sheet of paper containing a large number of drawings of a single character showing a number of different poses and facial expressions.

mods Player-created modifications to a game that provide new content and sometimes new ways to play the game.

monster generator A device visible in the environment that serves as a *source* for enemies entering the game world.

moveset A list of animations that shows how a character can move, both voluntarily and involuntarily.

multiplayer distributed gaming Playing games among multiple players at distributed locations (i.e., over a network), which enables each to have her own video screen and individual view of the game world. Contrast with *multiplayer local gaming.*

multiplayer local gaming Playing games in the same room with other people, all looking at the same video screen. This approach makes it impossible to provide individual players with secret information.

multipresent interaction model An *interaction model* in which the player may influence many areas of the game world at one time.

mutable rules Rules that can be changed during a game according to other rules that define how the changes may take place.

mutual dependency A condition of an *internal economy* in which two processes each require the output of the other as an input in order to function. If one of the input supplies is diverted elsewhere and no more becomes available, a *deadlock* will occur.

N

narrative Noninteractive story material that is presented by the game to the player, consisting of *narrative events*. It differs from *in-game events* in that narrative is written as part of the design process rather than produced by the core mechanics.

narrative events Events that are shown to the player through narration rather than through the action of the player or the core mechanics. Equivalent to *embedded narrative.*

native talent The inherent ability that a player brings to a game.

natural language Ordinary language as spoken or written by human beings.

negative feedback A phenomenon of the game's *balance* such that successful player action makes subsequent challenges more difficult.

networked play Play among characters on computers connected together by a network. See *multiplayer distributed gaming.*

nonlinear stories Stories whose plot can change in response to *dramatic actions* on the part of the player.

O

object (of a game) See *goals.*

P

pace The rate at which the player is obliged to interact with the game; the speed at which the game presents challenges.

pan To turn the game's virtual camera about its vertical axis.

parallax scrolling A display technique in which background objects in 2D environments scroll by more slowly than foreground objects, creating the impression that they are farther away. Normally used in the *side-scrolling perspective* to create an illusion of depth.

party A group of characters, normally under the control of one or more players, who act cooperatively in a game, most commonly a role-playing game.

party-based interaction model An *interaction model* in which the player influences the *game* *world* through a *party* of characters who generally stay together in one area but may sometimes separate briefly. The player controls most or all the members of the party.

pathfinding An artificial intelligence technique for finding the most efficient route from one point in a landscape to another while avoiding obstacles along the way.

perceived difficulty The player's actual perception of how hard a challenge is to overcome. It takes into account four factors: *intrinsic skill required, stress, power provided* by the game, and the player's *in-game experience* at surmounting similar challenges.

perfect information A quality of a game such that each player has full knowledge of his own status and the other players' status including all previous actions taken; no information is hidden, and there is no element of chance.

permanent upgrade An upgrade to the capabilities of the player's avatar or units that lasts for the remainder of the game.

persistent world A large online game with no definite beginning or ending that allows players to join, play, and depart at any time. Most frequently implemented as a server-based computer role-playing game played over the Internet.

perspective The point of view ordinarily adopted by the game's *virtual camera* when displaying the *game world,* along with instructions about how the camera should behave during play. The perspective is one component of a *gameplay mode.*

plan-and-build A construction play mechanic in which the player plans a new object at a location in the environment and the resources necessary to construct it are consumed over time as the object is built. See *purchase-and-place.*

platformers Action or action-adventure games in which a common avatar action involves jumping on and off platforms in the game world.

play Nonessential, recreational human activities. One of the four key elements of a game.

player events Actions performed by the player as part of an interactive story.

player-centric An approach to game design that requires the designer to empathize with the player and concentrate on entertaining that player.

positive feedback A phenomenon of the game's *balance* such that successful player action makes subsequent challenges easier.

power provided The resources, actions, capabilities, and other game features under the player's control that enable him to meet challenges.

powerup An object in the game world that, when found by a character (usually the avatar), gives that character added powers.

presentation layer Another term for the *user interface.*

pretending The mental ability to establish a notional reality that the pretender knows is different from the real world. One of the four key elements of a game.

previous experience The amount of time the player has spent playing games similar to the one under development. This factor influences the *perceived difficulty* of the game but lies outside the designer's knowledge or control.

primary gameplay mode The *gameplay mode* in which the player spends the largest part of her time in the game. In a few games, the player divides her time equally between two or more gameplay modes, but these are rare.

production mechanism A mechanic that either is a source of a resource or converts an unusable resource (such as buried gold) into a usable one.

purchase-and-place A construction play mechanic in which the player purchases a new object by expending some resource and immediately places it in the game world. See *plan-and-build.*

puzzle A mental challenge with at least one correct solution state that the player must find.

PvE Short for player-versus-environment. A type of game in which the player seeks to overcome challenges provided by the game's environment but does not directly compete with or oppose other players. Most single-player nonnetworked games are PvE games.

PvP Short for player-versus-player. A type of game in which multiple players compete to see who will be the winner or, in a *persistent world,* who will prevail in a particular conflict between players. In a single-player PvP game, the sole human player plays against an artificial opponent simulated by the computer.

R

realism   A continuous scale upon which the game's relationship to the real world is measured. One end of the scale is *abstract* (little or no relationship); the other end is *representational* (very close relationship). Different aspects of the game may have their own levels of realism (such as the graphics and the physics), which combine to form the game's overall level of realism.

relative difficulty   A measure of the difficulty of a challenge relative to the *power provided* by the game to meet the challenge. Relative difficulty is computed from the *absolute difficulty* of the challenge and the power provided.

representational   A quality of a game such that it represents ideas and relationships familiar from the real world, such as gravity, money, death, parenthood, or fear, and presents its game world in a photorealistic way. Representational games expect players to apply some of their understanding of the real world to the game world. The opposite end of the *realism* scale from *abstract*.

resources   Entities in the game world that may be created, destroyed, gained, lost, transferred from place to place or from player to player, or converted into other entities. Resources must be measured in numeric quantities. An entity in a game that never changes and cannot be traded, such as a hill in a war game, is not a resource.

rigging   The process part of level design that involves deciding where key events will take place in that level and what will trigger their occurrence.

role-playing game   A game in which the player controls one or more characters, typically designed by the player, and guides them through a series of quests. Character growth in power and abilities is a key feature of the genre.

roll   To rotate the game's virtual camera about a line through the lens, so that the horizon is no longer level.

rules   Instructions that dictate to the player how to play. Rules normally include lists of required, permitted, and prohibited actions; the sequence of play; the challenges and actions that make up the gameplay; the goals of the game; the termination conditions of the game; definitions of the meanings of symbols in the game (its semiotics); and any metarules if some of the rules are changeable.

S

sandbox mode   A *gameplay mode* in which the player is not presented with a victory condition. This mode has few restrictions on what he may do and offers no guidance on what he *should* do.

scalar variable   A variable quantity consisting of exactly one value, such as the amount of money in a bank account. The value changes, but there's only one value at any given time. Contrast with *vector variable*.

scripted conversation   A technique that allows a player to have a conversation with a nonplayer character in a game by selecting a line of dialog from a menu of options. His avatar says the line, the NPC responds, and the player receives a new menu of lines to choose from. Scripted conversations may be documented with a *dialog tree*.

self-defining play   Game activities that allow the player to choose, customize, or construct an avatar thus defining the player's imaginary self in the game.

shadow costs   Secondary or hidden costs that lie behind the apparent costs of goods or services.

shell menu   A menu of options implemented by game software outside of the game world. Chiefly used for loading and saving games and customizing the user interface.

shooter   A subgenre of action games whose primary challenge is shooting.

side quest   A quest or mission, usually found in a role-playing game, that the player is free to accept or reject without his decision affecting the progress of the main storyline.

side-scrolling perspective   A *perspective* normally used with *avatar-based interaction models* in which the game's *virtual camera* follows the *avatar* through a 2D *game world* presented in a side view.

simple entity   An entity containing a single datum, such as a number or a symbolic value. The number of points a player has scored is a simple entity.

simulation   A mathematic or symbolic model of a real-world situation.

skill tree   A diagram showing the sequence by which a player may add new skills to his avatar or the characters in his party in a role-playing game.

small multiple   A visual *indicator* used to show an amount by displaying multiple copies of a small image on the screen. The number of lives remaining in an action game is often shown as a small multiple of pictures of the avatar; as the player gains or loses lives, pictures are added or removed.

source   A mechanic that introduces resources into the game world without requiring anything in exchange.

spawn point   A location in the game world where enemies appear (which means it is also a *source*). Sometimes also used to refer to locations where the avatar reappears after dying, typically in multiplayer first-person shooter games.

status attributes   Attributes that describe the current state of a character or unit and may change frequently. Current speed and current health are examples. See *attributes.*

story   A credible and coherent account of dramatically meaningful events, whether true or fictitious.

strategy   A plan or approach for playing and winning a game.

stress   The time pressure placed on a player while she tries to complete a challenge. Stress is one element of the challenge's *absolute difficulty.*

structure of a game   The relationships among a game's *gameplay modes,* including a specification of the circumstances in which the game switches from one mode to another.

survival horror   A subgenre of action or action-adventure game that makes use of some of the qualities of horror movies: lone protagonists, disturbing images, and startling attacks.

suspension of disbelief   Term originally coined by Samuel Taylor Coleridge to refer to a reader's willing choice to believe in the fantasies of romantic poetry despite their incredibility. Subsequently adopted by the game industry and other fictional media and significantly redefined. See *immersion,* which is now used synonymously, for the game industry's definition.

symmetric game   A game in which all the players begin with the same initial conditions (resources, starting positions, and so on), are trying to achieve the same goals, and play by the same rules. Such a game is usually considered to be *fair* and is generally easier to *balance* than an *asymmetric game.*

T

tech tree   Short for *technology tree.*

technology tree   A diagram that represents the available sequences in which a player may upgrade his units in a strategy game by means of research. The diagram is tree-shaped because at intervals it branches, allowing the player to choose one particular sequence or another.

technology-driven game   A game designed to show off a particular technological achievement.

teleporter   A mechanic, often implemented in the game world as a visible object, that instantaneously transports a character from one place in the world to another.

temporary upgrade   An upgrade in the capabilities of a player's avatar or units that lasts for less time than the remainder of the game—either until the end of the current level, until a fixed number of real-time seconds have elapsed, or until some resource has been consumed.

termination condition   An unambiguous true-or-false condition that determines when a game has ended. Not always identical to a victory or loss condition; a race ends not after one runner wins but after the final runner crosses the finish line.

third-person perspective   A *perspective* intended for use with *avatar-based interaction models* in which the *virtual camera* follows the *avatar* as he moves around the *game world.*

tilt   To cause the game's virtual camera to look up or down.

top-down perspective   A *perspective* in which the *virtual camera* displays the 2D *game world* from directly overhead. Its 3D equivalent is the *free-roaming camera* perspective.

top-scrolling perspective   A *perspective* in which the *virtual camera* displays the 2D *game world* from directly overhead and the world scrolls by from the top to the bottom of the screen at a constant rate; most often used in *avatar-based gameplay modes* involving vehicles.

toy A physical object that a person can play with, typically in an unstructured fashion and without any formal rules (though the player may invent rules of his own if he wishes).

trader An on-demand mechanic, often implemented as an NPC, that exchanges resources with the players and NPCs for other resources.

treatment A document, typically about 20 pages long, intended to describe a game in enough detail to allow a funding agency to decide whether or not to fund development of the game.

truck To move the game's virtual camera laterally, perpendicular to the direction that it is facing.

tuning stage The final stage of game design in which designers refine the core mechanics and other aspects of the design without adding any new features.

tutorial level A *level* whose purpose is to teach the player about the *user interface* and the game's *atomic challenges* and its actions.

twitch game A game whose primary challenges are physical, concentrating chiefly on reaction-time tests.

U

unique entity An entity describing an object, character, or datum of which there is only one example in the game world.

unique selling points Unique characteristics of a game that will make it stand out in the marketplace.

unit In a strategy game, a combatant or support entity (such as a transport vehicle) under the control of one of the players.

upgrade A change to gameplay that gives the player an advantage or capability he did not formerly possess. It usually occurs in one of two forms: as an improvement in the performance of his avatar or units or as a new action that was not previously available. The term is typically used in RPGs and strategy games; in action games it is more commonly called a *powerup*. See *permanent upgrade* and *temporary upgrade*.

user interface The collection of presentation elements and control elements that mediate between the player in the real world and the game world, translating player actions performed on the machine's input devices into game-world actions, and game-world events and other data into images and sounds produced by the machine's output devices.

V

variable scrolling A characteristic of 2D scrolling perspectives in which the landscape scrolls under, or behind, the avatar in response to his movements. Contrast with *continuous scrolling*.

vector variable A set of related numbers that collectively describe something. In physics, a vector normally describes how to get from one point in space to another (on a 2D plane, this requires two numbers, an angle and a distance). In games, any collection of related data can be considered a vector. Data describing the amount of water available at each point on a map would be considered a vector.

victory condition An unambiguous true-or-false condition that determines when a player has won the game or the current *level*. The highest challenge in the *hierarchy of challenges*. Not all games have a victory condition. Many construction and management simulations can be lost (through running out of resources) but not won.

video game A game mediated by a computer.

virtual camera An imaginary camera that displays the *game world* in the main view. Decisions about how the virtual camera behaves set the *perspective* of the current *gameplay mode*.

W

walkthrough mode A mode of play that allows the player to walk through an environment that he has constructed to see what it looks like from the inside; mostly used by construction and management simulations.

wildcard enemy In an action game, an enemy that attacks the player at unpredictable times, outside the ordinary waves of enemies.

Index

References

Introduction

Poole, Steven. 2004. *Trigger Happy: Videogames and the Entertainment Revolution.* Reprint edition. New York: Arcade Publishing.

Chapter 1

Dini, Dino. 2004. Gameplay Cinderella. *Develop* 41 (July).

Gee, James Paul. 2004. *What Video Games Have to Teach Us About Learning and Literacy.* New York: Palgrave Macmillan.

Gee, James Paul. 2005. *Why Video Games Are Good for Your Soul.* Altona, Victoria, Australia: Common Ground.

Huizinga, Johan. 1971. *Homo Ludens: A Study of the Play Element in Culture.* Boston: Beacon Press.

Koster, Raph. 2004. *A Theory of Fun for Game Design.* Scottsdale, AZ: Paraglyph Press.

Moriarty, Brian. 1997. Listen: The Potential of Shared Hallucinations. Lecture delivered at the Game Developers' Conference, Santa Clara, California, 1997. At **http://ludix.com/moriarty/listen.html** (referenced June 9, 2006).

Rollings, Andrew, and Dave Morris. 2003. *Game Architecture and Design: A New Edition.* Indianapolis: New Riders Games.

Salen, Katie, and Eric Zimmerman. 2003. *Rules of Play: Game Design Fundamentals.* Cambridge: MIT Press.

Samuels, Arthur. 1959. Some Studies in Machine Learning Using the Game of Checkers. *IBM Journal of Research & Development* 3:211–229.

Chapter 2

Bateman, Chris, and Richard Boon. 2006. *21st Century Game Design.* Hingham, MA: Charles River Media.

Elling, Kaye. 2006. Inclusive Games Design. Lecture delivered at the Animex International Festival of Animation and Computer Games, University of Teesside, February 2006.

Ray, Sheri Graner. 2003. *Gender Inclusive Game Design: Expanding the Market.* Hingham, MA: Charles River Media.

Rollings, Andrew, and Dave Morris. 2003. *Game Architecture and Design: A New Edition.* Indianapolis: New Riders Games.

Chapter 3

Costikyan, Greg. 2005. Imagining New Game Styles. Lecture delivered the Future-play Conference, 2005. At **www.costik.com/presentations/Imagining%20 New%20Game%20Styles.ppt** (referenced May 6, 2006).

Chapter 4

Jones, Gerard. 2002. *Killing Monsters: Why Children Need Fantasy, Super Heroes, and Make-Believe Violence.* New York: Basic Books.

Chapter 5

Rouse, Richard. 2000. Designing Design Tools. *Gamasutra* webzine, March 23, 2000, at **www.gamasutra.com/features/20000323/rouse_01.htm** (referenced May 19, 2006).

Chapter 6

Campbell, Joseph. 1972. *The Hero with a Thousand Faces.* Princeton, NJ: Princeton University Press, Bollingen reprint edition.

Meretzky, Steve. 2001. Building Character: An Analysis of Character Creation. *Gamasutra* webzine, November 20, 2001, at **www.gamasutra.com/ resource_guide/20011119/meretzky_01.htm** (referenced June 14, 2006).

Poole, Steven. 2001. Lara's Story. *The Guardian.* June 15, 2001.

Vogler, Christopher. 1998. *The Writer's Journey: Mythic Structure for Writers.* Second edition. Studio City, CA: Michael Wiese Productions.

Chapter 7

Adams, Ernest. 2004. How Many Endings Does a Game Need? Designer's Notebook column in *Gamasutra* webzine at **www.gamasutra.com/features/ 20041222/adams_01.shtml** (referenced May 2, 2006).

Bateman, Chris, ed. 2006. *Game Writing: Narrative Skills for Videogames.* Hingham, MA: Charles River Media.

Campbell, Joseph. 1972. *The Hero with a Thousand Faces.* Princeton, NJ: Princeton University Press, Bollingen reprint edition.

LeBlanc, Marc. 2000. Formal Design Tools: Emergent Complexity, Emergent Narrative. Lecture delivered at the Game Developers' Conference, San Jose, California, March 2000. Slides available in PowerPoint format at **http://algorithmancy.8kindsoffun.com/gdc2000.ppt** (referenced June 14, 2006).

Vogler, Christopher. 1998. *The Writer's Journey: Mythic Structure for Writers.* Second edition. Studio City, CA: Michael Wiese Productions.

Chapter 8

Bateman, Chris, ed. 2006. *Game Writing: Narrative Skills for Videogames.* Hingham, MA: Charles River Media.

Brandon, Alexander. 2004. *Audio for Games: Planning, Process, and Production.* Indianapolis: New Riders Games.

Garrett, Jesse James. 2003. *The Elements of User Experience.* Indianapolis: New Riders Publishing.

Sanger, George. 2003. *The Fat Man on Game Audio: Tasty Morsels of Sonic Goodness.* Indianapolis: New Riders Games.

Tufte, Edward. 2001. *The Visual Display of Quantitative Information.* Second edition. Cheshire, CT: Graphics Press.

Chapter 9

Cousins, Ben. 2004. Elementary Game Design. *Develop* 44 (October).

Chapter 10

Crawford, Chris. 1986. *Balance of Power: International Politics as the Ultimate Global Game.* Redmond, WA: Microsoft Press.

Chapter 11

Csikszentmihalyi, Mihalyi. 1991. *Flow: The Psychology of Optimal Experience.* New York: Harper Perennial reprint edition.

Sirlin, David. 2000. Rock, Paper, and Scissors in Strategy Games. At **www.sirlin.net/archive/rock-paper-scissors** (referenced June 2, 2006).

Chapter 12

Barwood, Hal, and Noah Falstein. The 400 Project. At **www.finitearts.com/400P/400project.htm.** (referenced April 20, 2006).

Knowles, Rick, and Joseph Ganetakos. 2004. Level Design. Lecture delivered at the Computer Game Technology Conference, Toronto, Ontario, April 2004. Slides available at **www.cgt.auc.ca/ppt/ld_pi.zip** (referenced June 14, 2006).

Chapter 13

Entertainment Software Association. 2005. 2005 Essential Facts About the Computer and Video Game Industry. At **www.theesa.com.**

Chapter 14

Adams, Ernest. 2004. Kicking Butt by the Numbers. Designer's Notebook column in the *Gamasutra* webzine at **www.gamasutra.com/features/20040806/adams_01.shtml** (referenced May 13, 2006).

Crawford, Chris. 1986. *Balance of Power: International Politics as the Ultimate Global Game.* Redmond, WA: Microsoft Press.

Chapter 15

Hallford, Neal, and Jana Hallford. 2001. *Swords & Circuitry: A Designer's Guide to Computer Role-Playing Games.* Roseville, CA: Prima Publishing.

Tweet, Jonathan, Monte Cook, and Skip Williams. 2003. *Dungeons and Dragons Player's Handbook.* Renton, WA: Wizards of the Coast.

Chapter 16

Bateman, Chris, ed. 2006. *Game Writing: Narrative Skills for Videogames.* Hingham, MA: Charles River Media.

Chapter 19

Campbell, Joseph. 1972. *The Hero with a Thousand Faces.* Princeton, NJ: Princeton University Press, Bollingen reprint edition.

Vogler, Christopher. 1998. *The Writer's Journey: Mythic Structure for Writers.* Second edition. Studio City, CA: Michael Wiese Productions.